# Virginia Wine

# Virginia Wine:
# Four Centuries of Change

ANDREW A. PAINTER

**George Mason
University Press**
Fairfax, Virginia

Virginia Wine: Four Centuries of Change
By Andrew A. Painter

George Mason University Press
Fairfax, Virginia

Copyright © 2018 by George Mason University Press

ISBN:    978-1-942695-06-6       (paper)
ISBN:    978-1-942695-07-3       (ebook)

Second printing

Library of Congress Cataloging-in-Publication Data:
Painter, Andrew A., author.
Virginia Wine : Four Centuries of Change / Andrew A. Painter.
First edition. Fairfax, Virginia : George Mason University Press, [2018]
Includes bibliographical references and index.
LCCN 2017057429| ISBN 9781942695066 (pbk. : alk. paper) |
ISBN 9781942695073 (ebook)
Wine industry—Virginia—History. | Wine and wine
making—Virginia—History.
LCC HD9377.V8 P35 2018 | DDC 338.4/7663209755--dc23

Printed in the United States of America

Book design by Emily L. Cole
Cover illustration: "Mountain Vineyard" by Christopher Mize;
Used with permission.

*For MARY ANNE*

# Table of Contents

## —Foreword & Introduction—

## —Chapter 1—

## —Chapter 2—

# —Chapter 3—

# —Chapter 4—

# Foreword

By the Honorable Gerald L. Baliles, Felicia Warburg Rogan, Gabriele Rausse, Lucie T. Morton, and Hudson Cattell.

## —The Honorable Gerald L. Baliles—

WINE EVOKES MANY images; in its purest sense, it represents balance, moderation, civility, culture and beauty. It is poetry in a bottle. It speaks a universal language, easing conversation while enhancing food, and representing preservation as well as profitability. Such images are the inheritances of pioneer efforts over millennia to cultivate, nurture, harvest, and produce the "liquid elixir" over many seasons of trial and error, of triumph and tragedy.

Wines in Virginia have been the inspiration for this type of determined individuality, from the early days of English settlement at Jamestown in 1607, to Thomas Jefferson's efforts to produce wines at Monticello, to the beginning of today's modern wine industry in the 1970s and 1980s. Andrew Painter's portrait of the commonwealth's wine industry captures it all. His is an important work about the landscape of wine in Virginia—historical, financial, political and meteorological. It is an elegant account of the vision and perseverance of a "growing tradition" in Virginia—a tradition that, I am pleased to have played a role in promoting.

As Virginia's sixty-fifth governor, I frequently proclaimed that winemaking in Virginia was a "growing tradition," and I did so for several reasons. Not only does winemaking create and enhance attractive destinations for visitors to the state, where tourism is one of our most important industries, but it contributes to agricultural diversity, as we seek to broaden the base for farming and produce crops for which there are identified markets. Of chief importance to my administration, wine production also equated to economic development, as winegrowing became an impressive and growing business for Virginia's rural and open lands.

Of course, as we well understand, the principal responsibility for the success of the Virginia wine industry rests with the industry itself. Providing the initial capital, ensuring the quality of the product, and organizing the distribution—these are for the owners and investors to handle. What was clear to me then—and remains even more so today—is that winemaking offers Virginians the potential of harnessing one's resources and having the foresight to invest in their development. It requires perspiration and commitment, as a successful vineyard involves capital, time, and a willingness to endure the difficulties and setbacks. Painter's book catalogues these stories and introduces the reader to several of the determined and unyielding personalities that made them possible.

As governor, however, I recognized that there was an important, if not critical role for Virginia's state government to play. We saw, in particular, that we could harness the power of our sometimes disconnected administrative agencies and secretariats in marketing wine as a distinctive Virginia agricultural product.

In 1988, for example, my administration issued the first "Virginia Wine Month," along with the first Governor's Cup ceremony at Sully Plantation in Northern Virginia. That same year, we also approved plans to place the first "grape clusters" icons on highway signs and roadmaps, all to indicate the locations of the commonwealth's vineyards and wineries as a way of increasing public awareness of Virginia wines. We also charged the Virginia Winegrowers Advisory Board to produce Virginia's first structured wine marketing initiative; one that included a national and international market study and an annual plan for broader domestic sales and exporting of Virginia wines.

Promotion of wines did not end at home. My administration touted Virginia wines on various trade missions through Europe and Asia throughout the late 1980s. Indeed, Japan's second largest air carrier, ANA, was persuaded to carry Virginia wines from Washington Dulles International Airport in Northern Virginia to Tokyo. Lufthansa agreed to offer Virginia wines on its flights from Dulles to European cities.

Since the late 1980s, succeeding governors and members of the legislature have joined in to support Virginia's vineyards and wineries. State agencies, boards, and commissions have all shown a strong interest in the wine industry's continued success. Of particular note, the Virginia Wine Board has worked hard—and successfully—to support viticultural and oenological research, education, and marketing. That is the Virginia way—building upon the accomplishments of others over time, advancing goals and objectives in a civil and bipartisan way.

Today, perhaps more than ever before, it can be said with confidence that Virginia wines are as old as the commonwealth, yet as new as their future. I admire what Virginia's modern wine industry has accomplished in a relatively short period of time—a few decades, really. The number of vineyards has grown impressively, from 17 vineyards in the 1970s to 40-some in the 1980s, and today, more than 25 years later, 370 vineyards and wineries exist in the Commonwealth, with more than 230 open for touring and tasting. That's what I call a "growing tradition!"

At the same time, there has been a concurrent rise in the quality of Virginia wines. Our vintages have received widespread notice, and the character of wine-making operations has become more sophisticated. The two highly rated wine magazines of the world, *Decanter* and *Wine Spectator*, have given glowing reviews to the world-class wines produced in the Commonwealth.

But why should that surprise us? After all, here is an American industry—winegrowing—that began in Virginia centuries ago, and it is an industry that continues to be distinctive in that it not only produces a product to sell, but it also attracts visitors to watch production. It is agriculture and tourism com-bined—a trend that is good for the wine industry, good for the agricultural community, and good for Virginia.

Painter's impressive work celebrates the collective and individual achieve-ments of the Commonwealth's wine industry. I heartily commend it to the reader with interest—and curiosity—to know more about the history, the ele-gance and the poetry of Virginia wines.

Of course, in the world of wines, consumer choices are many. Painter's one omission is the absence of advice on how to choose among myriad Vir-ginia wines. Personally, I would demur to the Greek philosopher Diogenes, who was once asked whose wine he liked best. He answered, "Someone else's." If Diogenes were here to read Painter's book and traverse the Commonwealth's vineyards, he would still be hard-pressed to answer the question any differently.

*Gerald L. Baliles served as the 65th Governor of Virginia from 1986–1990.*

## —Felicia Warburg Rogan—

I HAVE BEEN fortunate to have received many accolades in my role in helping establish a modern wine industry in Central Virginia. The late 1970s and early 1980s was a time of transition for me, having been recently married to my now late husband, John B. Rogan. I had left New York City, where I had lived for half a century, to savor the bucolic life on his beautiful Oakencroft Farm outside of Charlottesville, Virginia. Vineyards and wineries were far from my mind at that point, but having been a so-called "doer" in New York, as well as a writer and member of charitable boards, I had always led a very active life and was used to challenges.

John, for his part, was a stalwart and vibrant member of the Charlottesville community and his Boar's Head Inn, which he founded and would later bequeath to the University of Virginia, kept him busy and in touch with myriad friends. It was one of those friends, Coralee Burson "Coco" Davis, now in her 90s and still with vivid memories of her notable life, who wanted us to meet Lucie T. Morton.

Lucie's mother was a great friend of Coco's, and Lucie was in charge of her family's vineyard on Morland Estate in King George County along the Northern Neck. She had recently translated Pierre Galet's *A Practical Ampelography* from French to English, and the wine world was taking notice of this accomplishment. We were particularly proud of Lucie's work in Virginia, where stirrings of vineyard plantings were beginning to actually take root.

In 1979, during harvest time at Morland, John, Coco, and I were invited to help pick the grapes. At Lucie's urging and under her tutelage, we brought home some grapes and embarked on setting up a grape press, carboys, and equipment for amateur winemaking in our Oakencroft garage. We were proud to produce wine with homemade labels, but any resemblance to serious wines was totally accidental.

Fast forward a few years and, once more with Lucie's enthusiasm, we planted an experimental vineyard in our garden at Oakencroft. John built our winery building from an old cow shed, while I searched for old refrigerated milk tanks from Shenandoah Valley farmers. I also set up Oakencroft Vineyard and Winery Corporation and, for twenty-five years, we enjoyed great success, being the closest winery to Charlottesville. It was great fun: we hosted weddings, monthly musical acts, and wine instruction seminars. Friends were inspired by our amateur efforts and began planting vineyards and establishing small wineries around us in Albemarle County. Before too long, a nascent Central Virginia winery renaissance had begun.

As we became more knowledgeable about wine making techniques, we were privileged to have Jacques Recht, a veteran Belgian oenologist then working for Ingleside Vineyards, tutor our gardener, Deborah Welch, who later became our first winemaker. Philip Ponton, who with Lucie's advice became our vineyard manager, supervised our 16-acres of vineyard plantings. Philip is still at Oakencroft, though with new owners is now making artisanal and sparking grape juice.

As the 1980s progressed, it became clear there were no women in leadership positions in our emerging Monticello area wineries. Being fearless of character, my husband and I sought to do what we could to establish a Central Virginia viticultural area and support its wineries. I co-founded The Jeffersonian Wine Grape Growers Society and served as its president for 23 years. John lent a hand by allowing the Society to host an annual Albemarle Harvest Wine Festival on the grounds of the Boar's Head Inn and hold an annual "Bacchanalian Feast" in its banquet room. The festival featured local Virginia wines, costumed entertainers, a grape stomping contest, and Greek music and dancing. It was great a attraction and sold out every year.

The memories from that period of my life are too numerous and fun to count. We helped create what I continue to believe is the finest concentration of wineries in Virginia. When asked many years ago what I might predict for the future of the Virginia wine industry, I responded then as I do now that, with the recognized success and quality of our state wines, we will rival the Napa Valley region in wine touring activities and achieve critical acclaim for our vintages.

Indeed, it has come to pass that Virginia wines are being exported all over the world and garnering national and international medals. Both academic and recreational interests in Virginia's wine industry have exploded in recent years. Wineries have sprung up in all regions of the commonwealth and prosper in places heretofore unimagined. The industry has received increased attention in books, periodicals, journals, and even film.

Andrew Painter's book has thus sought to provide readers with a detailed, yet readable history that addresses an unmet need for a written record similar to those already available for the world's more established wine regions. Virginia viticulture and winemaking have come of age, and deserve no less.

*Felicia Warburg Rogan was a vintner and co-founder of Oakencroft Vineyard & Winery in Charlottesville.*

## —Gabriele Rausse—

I FELL IN love during my childhood in Italy with everything that had to do with agriculture. I quickly learned that wine grapes were the only agricultural crop which did not have to be supported by the Italian government. My father owned two farms, on which he processed grapes to make wine for family use. He sold the rest to a cooperative. When I was 15, the Italian government imposed a prohibition on the use of American and hybrid grapes in the winemaking process. I remember acres and acres of vineyards being removed and land sitting idle.

Following my graduation from the University of Milano in 1971 with a degree in agricultural sciences, I worked on farms. I learned to tend grapes, harvest them, and make wine from them. Such an appreciation for the art of viticulture and winemaking was absent when I arrived in Virginia in April 1976. I had come to assist Italian winemaker and businessman Gianni Zonin in his quest to build a world-class winery at Barboursville. There, I encountered an intimidating landscape: native and hybrid grapes were the only wine grapes grown in Virginia at the time, the infrastructure for planting, harvesting, and promoting vitis vinifera was non-existent, and we encountered resistance from many governmental and agricultural officials.

For those of us interested in quality winemaking at the time, we had to create an industry from scratch. At Barboursville, we were not successful in our first year, but after six years, we had proven quality vinifera wine could be made in the Old Dominion. I moved on to Simeon (later Jefferson) Vineyards, later founded my own winery, and eventually landed at Monticello, where I have spent much of my professional career tending to the estate's plants and vineyard. It has been a pleasure working at Monticello, and I have been particularly intrigued and enchanted with the estate's builder, Thomas Jefferson. This is especially true on the subject of viticulture.

Jefferson could not imagine a Virginia without wine. From the eve of the American Revolution, the author of the Declaration of Independence and the third president of the United States believed that both the cultivation of the vine and the consumption of wine would come to play a crucial role in the Old Dominion's transformation from British colony to an independent American state. Despite the fact that Jefferson likely never succeeded in making his own wine at his plantation at Monticello, his belief in the centrality of wine to the development of Virginia's taste, culture, and economy could not have been more prescient.

During his years as U.S. trade minister and ambassador in Paris, Jefferson developed a keen palate for exceptional European wines. In selecting only what he deemed to be the highest quality French or German wines for export back to America, Jefferson demonstrated that only superior vintages could move beyond regional or national borders and attract international attention. Today, the commonwealth's wines are just beginning to make an impact on the world because of their quality and unique character. This commitment to excellence is what will increase Virginia's sphere of influence across the world in the years to come.

While traveling through the wine country of Europe, Jefferson offered detailed descriptions of the process of cultivating grapes, should Virginia ever turn to the "culture of the vine." But he also declared viticulture to be a "species of gambling," because of the extensive and skilled labor needed to grow grapes, and because vineyards inevitably lay at the mercy of Mother Nature.[1] Still, Jefferson almost always equated the quality of the wines he tasted with the care taken with the vines. Two hundred years later, the same rule stands—the more man hours spent in the vineyards, the better the wine. Mechanized harvesting and increased fruit yields per acre have not improved the quality of Virginia wine—the best wine, however, and the wine that will make a name for Virginia in the wine world, is still tended by hand.

With the end of the American Revolution, Virginians no longer had a guaranteed British market for their tobacco. Although Jefferson and other planters switched to wheat and rye in order to satisfy the European demand for grain in the late 1700s, these crops were less profitable than tobacco. Which crop might replace tobacco and survive in Virginia's marginal soils while also turning a profit has been an open question since Jefferson's era. Jefferson had suggested that the "vine is good, because it is something in the place of nothing." Today, grapes are proving to be that "something" as a profitable agricultural product in Virginia, contributing hundreds of millions of dollars to the commonwealth's economy.

At Monticello, Jefferson's vineyards were experimental gardens. In 1807, for example, he planted 287 rooted vines and the cuttings of 24 grape varieties, of which 22 were European. Although few, if any, of Jefferson's trials yielded successes, he remained unfazed by failure. His emphasis was always on the process, rather than on the final product. What mattered to Jefferson was the experience and knowledge gained from his experiments in grape growing. This emphasis on experimentation is still relevant for Virginia now. In order to compete in a global market, Virginia wine growers must "try all things," as Jefferson did, and experiment with different grape varieties in order to determine which ones might grow best in Virginia.

Every day, I am thrilled to see how far our Virginia wine industry has come. Most of us in the industry are thrilled to have played a part in Virginia's wine story. This book sheds light on many of the struggles and victories and help explain how it happened. But I continually return to Jefferson, whose belief in the beneficial influence of wine on Virginia society resonates in our culture today. Like Jefferson, today's wineries in Virginia aim to do much more than provide drinkable wines—they seek to revolutionize taste in Virginia and to educate and enlighten its citizens.

*Gabriele Rausse is the former winemaker at Barboursville Vineyards in Orange County and is the vintner and founder of Gabriele Rausse Winery in Charlottesville.*

1 TJ to William Drayton, July 30, 1787.

## —*Lucie T. Morton*—

WHEN ANDREW PAINTER asked me to review some of the material for this book, I was reluctant as one often can be when requested to critique an over-ly-familiar and oft-told tale (including one written by me in my 1985 book, *Wine-growing in Eastern America*). My history major notwithstanding, I rather quickly found—circa 1972—that my interest in Virginia wine lay not with the politics and industry of it all, but rather with grapevines viewed from the seat of a trac-tor or undergoing strategic surgery with pruning shears. Indeed, the four chap-ter titles in Andrew's book reflect quite well my own journey into international viticulture from a home base that had always been in Virginia.

The first Chapter, "On Distant Shores," is largely devoted to the Common-wealth's colonial period. The title, though, reminds me of the period in my own life where I informed my parents that I would find some perspective as to what it might mean to plant a vineyard on the family farm on the banks of the Poto-mac. It was in France and not California, or even New York, where the interplay of Vitis vinifera and a host of native American Vitis species had already been field tested and vinified on a large scale for almost a century.

The two pioneering lights of Eastern American viticulture, Marylanders Philip Wagner and Hamilton Mowbray, were both avid Francophiles. They knew that I stood the best chance of rising above the politics of grapevine classism of the time by studying at Montpellier, then affectionately known as the "Univer-sity of Phylloxera," where professor Pierre Galet taught every botanical detail of Vitis riparia, Seyval blanc, and Cabernet Sauvignon.

As a Virginian studying in Europe, my status in a viticultural context was complicated by those notoriously deleterious trans-Atlantic exports—downy mildew, powdery mildew, black rot, and phylloxera. If being an American viti-culture student meant smiling when introduced as "This is Mlle. Morton who is here to study how to make Coca-Cola out of Vitis labrusca" then so be it. (After all, Coca-Cola would soon merge with the largest wine concern in the East, the Taylor Wine Company).

Andrew's second chapter, "Contrast, Conflict, and Change," describes a growing, but struggling industry in the face of disease, depression, war, and national Prohibition. "Moribund" is accurate as to the state of Virginia viti-culture when I returned home from studying abroad to the young three acres of wine grapes in King George County. Farm wineries were non- existent in the Old Dominion at the time, leading me to create a customer base of home winemakers for the fruit from our vintages of 1975. This lasted until several of my students founded their own farm wineries, notably Felicia and John Rogan at Oakencroft and Carl Flemer at Ingleside Plantation, who bought our grapes by the ton, not the pound.

In total contrast with France and its sophisticated appellation system based on centuries of experience, Virginia was a vinicultural terra incognita. Highly educated and culturally sophisticated men and women from other fields were ranked beginners when it came to grape growing. They were pioneers with a destination in their minds, but without a map of how to get there. Their aspirations also differed, as some were looking for a sustainable new crop for their family farms while others were hoping to leap to national prominence with world class wines.

In the 1970s and 1980s, our wine grape choices were unnecessarily politicized, which sometimes created rancorous tension over whether to plant Chardonnay or Vidal blanc, Chambourcin or Cabernet. In reality, though, there was no reason not to embrace them all. Pioneers like the Hortons and Jennifer McCloud ignored divisive thinking and set the stage for genetic diversity among varietals by planting Petit Manseng and Viognier together with Norton, the historic native Virginia grape that is prohibited in Europe.

The third chapter, "Revolution," recounts that America is the land of the free; free, that is, until one transformed fruit into wine. Without political change in Virginia in the 1970s and 1980s, there would have been no hope for even the noblest of grapes. Simply producing wine thrust one into the same federal regulatory category, not with other farmers, but with purveyors of smoke and firearms. Revolutions are propelled by deep economic imperatives and, as is shown in the following treatise, Virginia's grapevines in the post-Prohibition era had no economic status until pioneer vineyardists became rebels armed with lawyers and lobbyists. This book brings to light in a well-structured manner the unnecessary obstacles that can be thrown in the way of successful winegrowing. Given that history has a way of repeating itself, it is important to draw lessons here.

On a personal note, when I see the names of Virginia's early viticultural pioneers, my thoughts recall their important on-the-job research into viticultural training systems. There are, for example, a plethora of multiplex trellises holding up large cordoned vines with names like Casara, lyre, ballerina, Geneva double curtain. These have all been successful under some circumstances and not others, but it took time to learn this. Wine vine training today is trending to smaller vines, planted closer together, with a simple vertical plane of canopy. With a single fruiting zone, the precious fruit is more easily protected with netting, and lends itself to labor saving mechanization that is important for future sustainability.

The original title of Andrew's last chapter, "The Industry Matures" can be a loaded term, as the next step logically after mature could be moribund. The current heading, "End of the Beginning" is more apt. When we say something has matured, we mean that with time and experiences both pleasant and painful, it has reached a state of balance; it has grown into what it is meant to be. Certainly, the Virginia wine industry has matured, perhaps to the human equivalent of 21 years. There remains so much more promise here.

I am often asked my opinion as to the "best" Virginia wine. In my experience, value judgments can lead quickly into a battle of divisive versus inclusive attitudes on all manner of subjective criteria. Of course, I take pride when vineyards I have worked with receive critical acclaim. However, the real satisfaction comes when a family business is established on a family farm where no other agricultural endeavor would have made that possible, and when historic properties have new means of economic support.

There is one criterion that stands above all others: while Virginia wineries can legitimately make and sell wines from other places, Virginia wine can only be made from Virginia fruit. We now know that those whose intentions and diligence to produce estate-grown Virginia wine can be successful and lauded from afar.

I am grateful Andrew persisted in showing me his work in its formative stages, because he has brought a youthful enthusiasm and journalistic punchiness to a story I have lived. His concern for historical accuracy is refreshing in the pile of old chestnuts about Virginia wine history found on back labels and other venues for public relations and marketing. This is indeed an important reference to which I will be happy to refer when I need reminding of the human dynamics behind what we hope will be an expanding, evolving, and sustainable wine grape industry here in the Commonwealth.

*Lucie T. Morton is a Charlottesville-based viticulteralist and author of* Winegrowing in Eastern America, *published in 1985.*

## —Hudson Cattell—

WHEN ANDREW PAINTER asked me to contribute photographs for his book on the history of Virginia wine, I had never heard of him nor was I aware that a new state history of wine was being written. He invited me to look at his manuscript and I was surprised to see how extensive his project was.

Andrew Painter had chosen 1967 as the year when the modern era in Virginia wine got its start. It was then that Charles Raney planted 110 French hybrid vines at Flint Hill. Raney went on to open Farfelu Vineyard, Virginia's first farm winery, in 1976.

As a wine journalist, I covered the Virginia wine scene for more than three decades beginning in 1977. Reading the chapter in Andrew's book on the emergence of Virginia wine brought back strong memories. I was once again surprised at how faithfully he was able to record what was going on at that time. I had known and interviewed many of the dominant personalities of that era including Robert de Treville Lawrence, Sr., Elizabeth Furness, and Archie Smith, Jr., and his family, but I was glad to see space devoted to a less prominent individual, S. Mason Carbaugh, Virginia's Commissioner of Agriculture and Consumer Services, who took a personal as well as governmental interest in what was happening in Virginia wine.

The wine history of eastern North America includes more than three centuries of failure to grow grapes that would make European-style table wines. Not until after World War II did advances in viticultural knowledge and the development of modern pesticides and fungicides make it possible for the vinifera and the French hybrids to be grown in the eastern United States. Virginia was no exception in having to rely on native American varieties as the basis for its wine industry.

The East had an impressive wine history prior to the modern era, and Virginia's contributions have been notable. Virginia had a wine president, Thomas Jefferson, who has become an icon for wine throughout the nation. Paul Garrett built a wine empire using muscadine grapes, Scuppernong in particular, and his Virginia Dare wine became the bestselling wine in the United States. A native grape variety, Norton, was developed in the middle of the 19th century and is having a significant comeback today not only in Virginia but in other states as well. These stories are well told in the first two chapters of Andrew's book.

The chapters on the industry in the early centuries rely exclusively on secondary sources. For the last chapter on the industry after 1990, Andrew was able to visit wineries and conduct interviews with winemakers, governors and others who have shaped the maturing of today's industry. As in other states, the growth of the industry has not been even. The decision of the Supreme Court on the direct shipment of wine in 2005 caused problems in many states, but affected Virginia harder than other states. Together with zoning problems, pitting neighbors against wineries, the difficulties have been outweighed by the accomplishments that have made Virginia a preeminent wine state in the nation

As a wine historian, I am grateful for the voluminous notes included in this book. They testify to Andrew's six years of research – and, I might add, to his occupation as an attorney. An obvious purpose of the notes is to identify the sources of information in the main part of the book, but there is a great deal of text included in them that should not be overlooked. Anyone researching Virginia wine history in the future will be thankful to have these notes as a starting point.

Andrew offers his own hope for the future of the industry. The best way to move forward, he says, is to remember the lessons and experiences of the past while freeing them from their grasp. I couldn't agree more.

It is only in the past decade that a number of wine histories of individual states in the East have been written. Andrew's is not the first, but it is certainly one of the most comprehensive and should be a model for others to follow. If history is the bedrock on which the future lies, it is well served in Virginia by Andrew Painter's detailed exploration of the past.

*Hudson Cattell co-founded and edited* Wine East *for more than 25 years and is the author of several publications, the most recent being* The Wines of Eastern North America, *published in 2014.*

# Introduction & Acknowledgments

UPON GRADUATING FROM the University of Virginia with a master's degree in urban planning in May 2004, several of my classmates and I celebrated by crowding into a van and heading west to the small Albemarle County hamlet of Crozet. Most of our merry band had studied the greater Charlottesville area academically for two years; we had conducted countless team exercises and collaborated on multiple visions for rural preservation from within the hallowed classrooms of Mr. Jefferson's University. To be in the countryside for pure amusement, though, was something quite different and most pleasant. There are few more beautiful places in America. One this trip we visited King Family Vineyards and over the course of several hours, we took in the scenery and managed to down several bottles of excellent wine. It was my first visit to a winery, and, from what I can recall from our Bacchanalian befuddlement, I enjoyed it immensely.

Although a newcomer to the Virginia wine industry, I had known about Virginia wine for many years; my parents were frequent attendees at early Virginia wine festivals in the 1980s and 1990s, and posters promoting the Commonwealth's wines adorned the walls of our home. I also possessed what I thought to be a basic understanding of rural Virginia, having spent several seasons as a farmhand in Fairfax County—yes Fairfax County—spending time with my grandparents in bucolic Amelia County, and sneaking off in my parent's car to roam the countryside at every opportunity.

After I entered the University of Richmond to study law, I celebrated my inaugural winery visit several times over and to no particular schedule. Excited at the proposition of acclimating others to a new and most pleasant experience, I marshaled my friends and colleagues from the hermetically sealed world of academia on what could best be described as all-day winery jaunts. A few years later, newly established as a zoning attorney in Leesburg, I found myself in the heart of Virginia's fastest growing wine region. It was only appropriate, then, that the winery outings should continue and expand, each time with new friends and more wineries.

I began searching for a way to marry my growing interest in Virginia wine with my love of research and writing. And so it was, in December 2008, that I set about trying to put together a book. Originally conceived as a conventional winery tour guide, its focus shifted dramatically when I learned that no one had yet undertaken a comprehensive historical account of the development of the industry from the earliest days of the Commonwealth to the present. Perhaps every industry is a promising subject for an historical account of its foundations, major events, and key personalities—in short, its own biography—but wine is different. It is intimately interwoven with society, history, and culture as few man-made things have been. One wonders how many great books, and great conflicts, have been born over a glass of good wine. Given the widespread interest in both the business and consumption of wine, and its increasing importance to Virginia commerce, the challenge proved irresistible.

What I did not know at the time—nor could any rational person have predicted it—was that this project would consume more than one-fifth of my life. In the years since I began, I have married, become a father, purchased my first home, and become a partner at my law firm. I have spent countless hours at numberless libraries, visited more than 200 of Virginia's wineries, and met several of the industry's pioneers and present leaders. My viticultural lexicon has increased, as has my personal collection of wine-related books and memorabilia, not to mention wine itself.

The result is a work that, I hope, provides both an accurate historical chronicle and a fair portrait of the industry, from the earliest Spanish accounts in 1570 through its rebirth and extraordinary growth in the modern era. It seeks to chronicle the dynamic personalities, diverse places, and engrossing personal and political struggles that have played a role in establishing the Old Dominion as one of the nation's preeminent wine producers. Although its focus is on Virginia, I have found the story to be quintessentially American. It represents the marriage of individual inspiration and determination, persistent experimentation, and remarkable ingenuity, with long reluctant and then steadfast and critical, public sector support.

I offer a word about the order of the book and the topics and personalities discussed. The piece is divided into four substantive chapters, each covering a different era of Virginia's wine history. The length of each and the topics covered vary between periods, as can be expected in a history of an industry that, despite its present healthy state, was essentially unsustainable until the present day. To the extent possible, each chapter is chronologically arranged except where discussions of general industry trends or personalities do not permit such organization.

The book does not limit itself to select regions of the Commonwealth, particular personalities or wineries, or to a single period. Rudimentary "tourist" information commonly found in existing books on the subject—such things as directions to wineries, hours of operation, the types of varietals produced at each, etc.—is not included. My purpose, to the extent that I have achieved it, is different.

In preparing the work I found that Virginia's wine story is difficult to tell for more than a few reasons. The source material is widely scattered and some difficult to find, all of which needed to be collected and synthesized. I also found it difficult to relay a singular narrative in strict chronological order, largely because of the interplay of disparate ideas and practices that have woven in an out and back and forth through time, and over widely separated parts of Virginia. It is difficult to arrive at a set of common facts, or common recollections of specific events and dates among the witnesses or even the records. Perhaps this truth is one uncovered by all historians, who must cull the narrative from the detritus of lives lived and work done without a particular eye toward history.

I was thus especially reliant upon the hundreds of wine books that now sit on my shelves, the most important of which are Thomas Pinney's *A History of Wine in America*, Leon Adams' *The Wines of America*, and Hilda and Allan Lee's trilogy of *Virginia Wine Country* books. Added to these were articles in *The Washington Post*, the *Richmond Times-Dispatch*, the Fredericksburg *Free Lance–Star*, the Charlottesville *Daily Progress*, and the *Fauquier Times-Democrat*, among others. It became clear during this process that newspapers, alongside their very capable reporters, had been chronicling the story of Virginia wine for decades, albeit not in book form. It is truly said that journalism is the first draft of history, and their work, often unsigned and the reporters thus unknown, was vital.

I also struggled with whom to include. While I have attempted to incorporate by name as many of the industry's personalities as possible, and to weave in the contribution of each winery, not all could be included. Given the large increase in numbers of wineries and the people behind them, any attempt to incorporate everyone would have been at once incomplete, immediately dated, and profoundly tedious. This is not to diminish the efforts and impact of those not mentioned. It is perhaps enough that the central developments of the industry have been captured. I have sought to document my work and sources, and I welcome the reader to contact me directly with suggested edits or corrections.

Throughout this process, several individuals generously offered their time and advice. I am greatly indebted to Felicia Warburg Rogan; I consider her the matriarch of the Central Virginia wine industry. Her counsel and opinions were invaluable and, although her Oakencroft Vineyard and Winery closed in 2008, she continues to be a force. I am also thankful for the friendship of veteran winemaker Gabriele Rausse who, as he has done with countless individuals who have come under his influence and tutelage, generously gave of his thoughts, good cooking, and friendship. Viticultural consultant Lucie Morton helped me cut down the final product by at least half—all while chastising me for not making more of an effort to focus on grapes and viticulture, and giving me unadulterated versions of stories (that I thought it best not to include). Husband-and-wife duo Gordon and Anita Murchie, longtime advocates of all things Virginia wine, provided spectacular expertise on the work and made me proud to be a fellow Northern Virginian.

Special gratitude is accorded to my friend and mentor John Foote. John is the finest writer I know. Whether in the office, on weekends, or on vacations, John offered meticulous editing of each chapter and each more of the ephemeral documents that went into this enterprise. Similarly, my firm administrative assistant Jacqualine Allison generously lent her time to edit each page and footnote for grammar and detail. I dare say that between John and Jackie, half the book is theirs. I am also appreciative of our managing partner of my firm's Leesburg Office, J. Randall Minchew, for hiring me in the first place, of Terri Motley for scanning in photographs, and of the entire Leesburg Office staff for putting up with me during this process. To them and everyone at Walsh, Colucci, Lubeley & Walsh, P.C., I cannot say how much of a pleasure it is to work at such a congenial firm, with so many skilled practitioners and administrative staff. Thank you for helping me pursue what can best be described in the legal world as a non-billable extracurricular dream.

I am also indebted to those who lent their time to review and comment on all or portions of the manuscript, respond to multiple inquiries, and provide assistance. These include former Virginia Governor Gerald R. Baliles, who initially made contact with George Mason University Press on my behalf. Thanks also to former Director of Marketing at Meredyth Vineyards Susan M. Smith, former Virginia Secretary of Agriculture S. Mason Carbaugh, colonial historian Edward Ayers at the Jamestown-Yorktown Foundation, Virginia Wine Board Marketing Office Director Annette R. Boyd, Rose Marie Owen formerly of the University of Virginia's Miller Center, Philip C. Poling of the Williamsburg Investment Group, Ltd., Virginia Tech Professor Emeritus Bruce Zoecklein, Virginia Tech Professor of Viticulture Tony Wolf, longtime Virginia Secretary of Agriculture Todd P. Haymore, Wine Institute Counsel Terri Cofer Beirne, Jamestown-Yorktown Foundation curator and former student Katherine Egner Gruber, Monticello Historian Christa Dierksheide, former Gunston Hall Deputy Director Mark J. Whatford, and Hampden-Sydney professor emeritus, author, and Virginia historian Dr. Ronald Heinemann, and Hampden-Sydney Professor Emeritus and former Rose Bower proprietor Tom O'Grady, Mary

Washington Professor Emeritus William B. Crawley, Mary Washington Professor Stephen J. Farnsworth, Southside Regional Library Executive Director Leigh Lambert, Dr. Angelita Reyes of Arizona State University, W. Curtis Coleburn of the Virginia Department of Alcoholic Beverage Control, Mecklenberg County historian and author Susan Bracey Sheppard, and Susan Payne of Payne, Ross & Associates Advertising, Inc. in Charlottesville, King Family Vineyards Founder David King, Mountain Cove Vineyards founder Al Weed, Willowcroft Winery owner Lew Parker, Linden Vineyards founder Jim Law, Claire and Pat Reeder and Burnley Vineyards, Patrick Duffeler and Diane Race at The Williamsburg Winery, Hartwood Winery founder Jim Livingston, Barrel Oak Winery founder Brian Roeder and his Director of Events, Adale A. Henderson, Viticultural experimenter Dennis Horton and his wife, Sharon, Chris Pearmund of Pearmund Cellars and Vint Hill Craft Winery, Barboursville winemaker Luca Paschina, Shenandoah Vineyards founder Emma Randel, Benjamin Rose at Bowman Consulting, two former students of mine, Katherine Gruber of the Jamestown-Yorktown Foundation and Drew Gruber of Civil War Trails, and John P. Barden, Paul Garrett's great grandson.

I have appreciated the assistance of my book publishing team, especially John Warren and Emily Cole at George Mason University Press. After several fits and starts, John made publication of this book possible. Alongside the Press, critical thanks go to Richmond publisher Wayne Dementi, who greatly helped focus my energies in the early stages of this process, and introduced me to the practical realities of publishing. Wayne has long used his publishing house to make aspiring authors' dreams come true. This has certainly been the case with me, though he may have doubted my commitment at those times my other life responsibilities tugged away. I was introduced to Wayne by sheer coincidence through Leeanne Ladin, of late herself a most capable author who served as Virginia's first wine marketing director.

I relied heavily on the extraordinary editorial talent of three associates of the Library of Virginia, including indexer and former copy editor Emily J. Salmon, her husband and former archivist John S. Salmon, and editor Ann E. Henderson. I was introduced to Emily and her team through the Library of Virginia's Director of Public Services and Outreach Gregg Kimball, who provided sound guidance at the outset of the project. I also appreciated the quality review of Claire Gould, a budding editor-writer with a bright future, at the Colonial Williamsburg Foundation. I would also like to thank my sister, Hannah Moser, for toiling away her last semester at Mary Washington in service of this cause. A very dear friend, Mark Helms, also provided sage editorial comments and assistance with citations free of charge. Their encouragement and attention to detail put the book in good order and allowed me to publish the type of history I had long envisioned.

Additional appreciation go to those teachers, professors, friends, and mentors who taught me to appreciate the importance of conveying and preserving history. I would also like to thank my parents, Mark and Jill Moser. Whether they grasped it or not at the time, the two Virginia wine posters which hung in our home (and now can be found in mine) provided my first introduction to the very subject contained within these pages.

To that end, my last and most important expression of gratitude goes to my wife and best friend, Mary Anne. She has allowed me to work on this book the entire time we have been together. Without her love and encouragement, this book would have never come to fruition. She selflessly took care of our beautiful children, Eve, Walter, and Barron, over countless weekends and nights while I burned the midnight oil. Of course, there were times when she lost patience with me but, to her credit, she took comfort in knowing the only thing more arduous than writing a book about the Virginia wine industry was actually starting a Virginia winery.

To all of them, and my readers, I hope this book provides solace for those who still revere the Old Dominion as a slower, more relaxed place—one of grandeur, symbolism, and passion. I, therefore, offer this work in the spirit of genuine academic and historical enterprise, and, perhaps with that of the Greek playwright Aristophanes: "Quickly, bring me a beaker of wine, so that I may wet my mind and say something clever."

Now on to the next project.

*Andrew A. Painter*
*Falls Church, Virginia*

# 1

## On Distant Shores: The Beginnings of Virginia Viticulture, 1572–1800

RAIN BATTERED THE windswept beaches of North America's Atlantic coast before dawn on April 26, 1607, as a perilous storm of high waves and gale force winds drove a tiny flotilla of three unassuming wooden ships steadily toward the shore.

Setting off from England five months earlier at the behest of the Virginia Company of London, the *Godspeed*, *Susan Constant*, and *Discovery* ferried some 144 adventuresome souls under the command of the able Captain Christopher Newport. The boats were buffeted every stretch of the way, but despite the company's occasional thoughts of returning to England, the winds carried the ships ever onward.

The passengers found themselves at the entrance of a great bay at dawn's first light. As the clouds cleared and the sun rose, they made landfall on the southernmost of two peninsulas, which they named Cape Henry in honor of the Prince of Wales. Against a sandy tableau of pounding waves and thick, salty air, the exhausted men and women raised a large cross and thanked the Lord for a calm end to a perilous and grueling journey.

The tranquility of the day did not last; the group was attacked almost immediately by a band of Native Americans, forcing a speedy retreat to the ships. Sailing upstream and facing more uncertainty, on May 14th, the boats eventually came across a small wooded peninsula that seemed to offer protection and essential resources. This the colonists named in honor of their sovereign, King James, who had chartered the Virginia Company a year earlier in the expectation of establishing a new English colony in North America. The party unloaded its supplies and began constructing a small village that they also named for the king: thus was born Jamestown.

Settlement at Jamestown commenced more than four centuries of permanent settlement in the New World—a history that found its genesis in the vast and unexplored realm named in honor of the Virgin Queen. The English, of course, colonized the New World for a host of reasons, including pursuing gold and silver, claiming land ahead of French exploration, and finding a passageway to Asia. But it was the cultivation of the grape—whether for agriculture, horticultural curiosity, or the production of wine—that, perhaps next only to tobacco, came to absorb the ambition of countless Virginians.

While the colony was replete with naturally occurring fruits, and although the settlers managed to cultivate practically every other European plant that they brought with them, they could not grow delicate European grapes, known as *Vitis vinifera*. Roughly translated to mean "the wine bearer" in old Latin, vinifera had been grown by man over the course of thousands of years in Europe to make superior wine. The most notable of the group included Chardonnay, Cabernet Sauvignon, Cabernet Franc, Merlot, Riesling, and Pinot Noir.[1]

What was not known then—but is known today—was that vinifera varieties were unfortunately susceptible to North America's harsher climate, to fungus and bacterial infections, and to destructive pests. Vinifera was particularly vulnerable to *Phylloxera vastatrix*, a microscopic and deadly root louse native to eastern America that ravaged vines and killed them after but one or two years. Without chemical sprays or fungicides—the first development of which lay more than a century and a half away—vinifera could neither withstand the colony's humidity, nor overcome its pests and diseases.

To make matters worse, the thick, juicy, plump native grapes settlers found flourishing in the meadows and forests surrounding Jamestown—and that appeared at first glance to be perfectly suited for winemaking—produced absolutely dreadful wine.[2]

The irony of discovering native grapes that could grow, but produced no wine, along with the inability to grow exotic grapes that would, was at the heart of what would become Virginia's distressingly erratic viticultural narrative. It is an account that marries individual inspiration, determination, and experimentation, with reluctant, then steadfast and critical, public sector support. Similar stories would later play out in other American colonies during the seventeenth and eighteenth centuries.[3]

Virginia's Colonial-era disappointments, including the efforts of committed oenophile Thomas Jefferson, would be followed by adventurous, but ultimately doomed, antebellum and post–Civil War wine industries. Moreover, by the late 1960s, Virginia winemaking was again moribund, thanks largely to the disastrous and lingering effects of national Prohibition.

Beginning in the early 1970s, however, Virginia wines and wineries commenced an exceptional rise in prominence and reputation that would have exceeded the wildest dreams of the state's earliest vintners. One by struggling one, pioneering and enterprising men and women across the commonwealth proved willing to gamble on the cultivation of the state's first significant commercial vinifera vineyards.

But even through the terrible early years, the dream of establishing a New World wine industry persisted. The lure of cultivating quality wine grapes for commercial production was simply too great, and the potential reward too enticing, to disregard. Indeed, no state can claim a longer history of experimentation and promotion of—nor boast a more spectacular record of initial failure followed by ultimate success—than can Virginia.

This is an attempt to tell that story.

## — The First Accounts —

While reports of grape cultivation in the New World are as old as European exploration of the Americas, the first accounts of viticulture in Virginia come not from the English settlement at Jamestown, but rather some 37 years earlier from another colonial empire, Spain. While Spanish priests likely planted the first European varietals at their missions throughout the American Southwest, Spain's empire under King Phillip II extended European civilization to North America's eastern shores as well.[4]

On September 10, 1570, a band of seven Jesuits led by Father Juan Bautista Segura established a small mission near present-day Jamestown, along the peninsula between the York and James Rivers. They hoped to spread Christianity in an area of the mid-Atlantic that the Spanish referred to as the "Bahía de Santa María" (meaning "Saint Mary's Bay," today known as the Chesapeake Bay). They were accompanied by an interpreter, Don Luis de Velasco, a former Indian chief who had converted to Catholicism after being captured and imprisoned in Mexico.[5]

Five days after landing, de Velasco abandoned his Spanish colleagues and fled into the woods with other Native Americans. Several months later, in February 1571, de Velasco led an Indian attack that resulted in the deaths of six of the missionaries. Only a young boy, Alonso Olmos, was spared and taken captive by the Indians. When a Spanish resupply vessel arrived in August 1572, Alonso returned to the Spanish.[6]

In one account of the resupply ship's travels to the Virginia mission, a Spanish friar, Father Juan de la Carrera, recorded his observations of another indigenous settlement:

> We made landfall in the Bay of the Mother of God, and in this port we found a very beautiful vineyard, as well laid out and ordered as the vineyards of Spain. It was located on sandy soil and the vines were laden with fair white grapes, large and ripe. These the Lord had prepared there for us and we gave Him many thanks.[7]

While no other records exist to verify the accuracy of de la Carrera's description, an early historian of the Jamestown colony, William Strachey, later described the village as comprising nearly 1,000 Native Americans, 300 homes, and

> viniards of two or three thousand acres; and where, beside, we find many fruit trees, a kind of gooseberry, cherries, and other plombs, the maricock aple, and prettie copsiesor boskes (as it weere) of mulberye trees.[8]

Historians have posited that the village described by de la Carrera was likely that of the Algonquian community of Kecoughtan, located near the present-day location of Buckroe Beach in the City of Hampton. Some have also thought that the descriptions of well-ordered vineyards in Native American settlements rivaling those of Europe were exaggerated: "No doubt he saw grapes growing, and perhaps the vineyards of sixteenth-century Spain were somewhat unkempt," wrote wine historian Thomas Pinney, "but much imagination would still be required to make pre-European Virginia exactly resemble long-settled Spain."[9]

The Jesuits retreated to Mexico and, because of priorities further south, never returned to their Chesapeake Bay mission, but they were the first Europeans to document the possibility of grape cultivation in an area of what would become Virginia. Along with France, the Spanish explored the planting of vineyards in their other American colonies. Both empires, however, quickly grew fearful that colonial viticulture might someday supplant the wine industries of their mother countries. Consequently, both imposed heavy restrictions on the planting of new vineyards in their American colonies. Such economic protectionism inadvertently provided encouragement to Spain and France's chief colonial rival, England, which was indeed eager to unleash a vast and profitable wine industry in the New World.[10]

As with other European nations, England pursued colonization in the New World for a host of economic and military aims. While it hoped to establish a band of English-speaking settlements and to discover the Northern Passage to Asia and the South Pacific, the economic imperative to shift the nation's trade imbalances from hostile foreign countries served as England's primary motivation for colonizing the Americas. The country sought to strengthen its defenses through the creation of new colonies, increase its production of raw materials such as gold and silver, and produce high-demand luxury goods, such as silk and wine.[11]

Wine, particularly of the dry French variety, gained gradual popularity in late-1500s Elizabethan England. England's demand for wine soared, with its price nearly quadrupling during Queen Elizabeth's storied reign between 1558 and 1603, led by a sovereign who appreciated the drink. England's thirst for fine wine was, however, entirely beholden to competing foreign nations—particularly France, Spain, and Portugal—that dominated Europe's wine industry and were often antagonistic to England's interests.

The geopolitical realities of the day prevented England from exercising much control over the international wine trade and, accordingly, it worked to encourage internal cultivation of wine grapes in the British Isles beginning in the 1580s. Given climatic difficulties and soil challenges, these efforts never advanced beyond minimal wine production or the ornamental uses of grapes. The need to secure a sustainable national wine supply endured, however, and gradually, England looked beyond its shores in the hopes of taking advantage of Virginia's abundant natural resources.[12]

That the English might seek to foster a New World wine industry in Virginia to rival hostile competitors came as no surprise to Jamestown's settlers. By the time they landed on Jamestown Island in 1607, the colonists had long been captivated by earlier Italian, Dutch, Spanish, and French reports that bountifully described Virginia as a new El Dorado—a terrestrial paradise replete with abundant plants, animals, fertile soil, and fishing grounds. The colonists were also encouraged by viticultural descriptions from famed explorers Verrazano, Cartier, and Ribault, each of whom exalted the prospect of abundant vines growing wild along America's Atlantic coast.[13]

To the Jamestown settlers, it was not a foregone conclusion that they could grow grapes and make wine in Virginia with ease. Among the Jamestown colonists' first tasks was to inventory the local vegetation, fruit, and natural resources. While gold and silver eluded the settlers, the native *rotundifolia* and *labrusca* grapes were found everywhere. Indeed, North America boasted about half of the world's known native wild grape species, and settlers noted

5

the prevalence of wild grapes growing in the forests such that the grape itself was described as emblematic of the potential fertility of the New World, and Virginia in particular.[14]

One letter from explorer Ralph Lane, for example, reported that Virginia's native grapes were larger than those found in France, Spain, or Italy. Another settler described Virginia as "so full of grapes as the very beating and surge of the sea overflowed them, of which we found such plenty...that I think in all the world the like abundance is not to be found."

William Strachey, the early historian of the colony, recounted his impressions of the colony's bountiful grapevines:

> It would easilie raise a well-stayed judgement into wonder...to behold the goodly vines burthening every neighbour bush, and clymbing the toppes of highest trees, and those full of clusters of grapes in their kind, however dreeped and shadowed soever from the sun, and though never prined or manuered.[15]

These descriptions of America's abundant vines were sufficiently voluminous that one historian has suggested the impossibility of sorting them all. While such overly optimistic accounts rightly symbolized native grapes as a free good, they also led Virginia's colonists into the mistaken belief that the difficult, tedious process of producing wine would be as easy as catching fish or growing wheat. The writings further emboldened Virginia's settlers with a great, but unfounded, hope that "where wild vines grew so profusely, cultivation would produce veritable rivers of wine."[16]

The colonists were sadly mistaken. They could not claim to be experts in viticulture, and they certainly did not possess the skills needed to make wine or distinguish the viticultural potential and biological complexities of native grapes from those of Europe. As bountiful as Virginia's viticultural condition appeared at first glance, in short order the Colonists' aspirations proved illusory.[17]

Of course, it was not preordained that the Jamestown colony would survive at all. It might have easily suffered the fate of the Roanoke Colony, abandoned under mysterious circumstances. Food was scarce and necessities such as potable water were in short supply. Jamestown's water, which was often brackish and of mixed quality, contributed to dysentery and typhoid. "Our drinke," wrote colonist and later colonial governor, George Percy in 1607, was "cold water taken out of the river, which was at a flood very salt[y], at a low tide full of slime and filth; which was the destruction of many of our men."

Alcohol, on the other hand, was an ample vessel for water delivery to the human body. Doctors recommended its consumption during hot days or while engaged in physical labor. It was reportedly used as a cleaning agent and served at religious events, holidays, in court, social gatherings, and before bed. Ale, beer, distilled spirits, and especially wine, were all viewed correctly as healthier alternatives to salty, bacteria-laden water. This made the quest for wine as much pragmatic as it was pleasurable.[18]

The Jamestown settlers thus jumped headfirst into winemaking. Encouraged by what they saw in the surrounding woods, some tried to produce wine almost immediately from native grapes taken directly from the forest; others attempted first to cultivate wild varieties in the hopes of extracting higher-quality juice. Celebrated explorer and author Captain John Smith—the first to map the Chesapeake Bay region—recorded his impressions of grapes and winemaking across the colony in his *Generall Historie of Virginia, New-England, and the Summer Isles*:

> [There are] vines in great abundance in many parts that climbe the toppes of the highest trees.... Except by the rivers and savage [Native American] habitations, where they are not overshadowed by the sunne, they are covered with fruit.[19]

Smith's observation of the condition of grapes in the vicinity of the colony's rivers and Indian settlements suggest that he and his contemporaries considered the cultivation of grapes as early as settlement in 1607:

> Of those hedge grapes, we made neere twentie gallons of wine, which was like our French and Brittish wine, but certainely they would prove good were they well manured. There is another sort of grape neere as great as a Cherry, this they [Indians] call *Messamins*, they be fatte, and the juyce thicke. Neither doth the taste so well please when they are made into wine.[20]

Smith may have been among the first European winemakers in Virginia, and his early denunciation of "Messamins"—likely *Vitis riparia* grapes—certainly confers on him the title of the colony's first wine critic. His condemnation of wine produced from native grapes is unsurprising, considering that there then existed no native New World grapes that could, without refinement, produce wines of the quality of European vinifera varieties.

Virginia's native grapes were certainly beautiful, hardy, and thick-skinned and in all likelihood shared a common ancestor with vinifera varieties. But, unlike their Old World counterparts, Virginia's wild grapes had grown organically, without benefit of human cultivation, for thousands of years. They were not the product of selective breeding or domestication as vinifera had been, and natural selection had failed to eliminate their more undesirable traits for winemaking. Consequently, native grapes often lacked sugar, were high in acidic content, and produced wines with strange and unappealing flavors.[21]

Herein lay the limited ability and supreme irony of native American wild grapes—while they were abundant and appeared perfectly suited to winemaking, the wine they produced was most assuredly musky and "foxy." Without attention to proper cultivation and selective guidance by men, there was no hope of producing high-quality wine from Virginia's native grapes.[22]

Life in the young colony was replete with hardship, and as 1609 turned to 1610, conditions worsened. That winter proved particularly brutal, and colonists witnessed both Indian attacks during the First Anglo-Powhatan War and a near disastrous shortage of food. The lack of clean water and adequate supplies made conditions in the colony nothing short of desperate. The "Starving Time," as the winter of 1609–1610 became known, saw the deaths of more than three-quarters of Jamestown's 500 colonists—most of whom died from Indian attacks, starvation, and starvation-related diseases.[23]

The Virginia Company appointed Thomas West, the Lord De La Warr, as the colony's first resident governor-in-chief. The Company hoped thereby to save its colony and quell dissenters who questioned the whole enterprise. De La Warr arrived with 150 men in June 1610 and with a reputation for stern discipline. He immediately appointed new colonial officers and encouraged Virginia's inhabitants to persevere.

De La Warr also looked for ways to shore up the colony's precarious financial situation. He shared the Company's belief that the production of wine could serve both as a pacifier and as an important export. Even before he departed London, De La Warr drafted a list of potential commodities he expected the colony to produce for shipment to England, including grapes and a sample "hoggeshead or two" of wine—even if the wine proved sour.

De La Warr's hopes for a Virginia wine industry undoubtedly derived from the same unrealistic and superficial viticultural impressions of Jamestown's first settlers. De La Warr's enthusiasm only increased—as it had for the original colonists—once he arrived in the colony and saw firsthand the abundant natural vines covering trees and meadows. Writing to the Company in July 1610, De La Warr requested subsidies for grape-growing and proclaimed that a wine industry might yet prove a source of revenue for the new colony:

> In every boske and common hedge, and not farr from our pallisado gates, we have thousands of goodly vines running along and leaning to every tree, which yeald a plentifull grape in their kind. Let me appeale then, to knowledge if these naturall vines were planted, dressed, and

ordered by skilfull vinearoones, whether we might not make a perfect grape and fruitfull vintage in short time?[24]

De La Warr hoped to jump-start grape production, and ordered Jamestown's settlers to clear trees. He also charged several Frenchmen who had arrived with him to "plant Vines which grew naturally in great plenty." These Frenchman were true "vignerons," those who cultivate vineyards for winemaking. Their presence in Virginia came in response to several requests that the Company introduce foreign winemaking expertise to the Jamestown colony. With no particular history of winemaking of their own, the English had long been compelled to rely on secondhand French gardening books for wine advice—nearly all of which proved ill suited to Virginia's climate and terrain. "So the thing we crave," Captain Christopher Newport pleaded, "is some skillfull man to husband, sett, plant, and dresse vynes."

Once in Virginia, the French vignerons announced the same confidence in the potential for Virginia winemaking as had Jamestown's first settlers. Everyone, it seemed, was captivated by the profusion of abundant native vines, and the French told De La Warr that they could produce a "plentifull Vintage" within two years' time.[25]

De La Warr's orders of 1610 to "plant Vines which grew naturally in great plenty" constituted the first in a series of deliberate directives issued by the colony's government for the promotion of wine for commodity diversification and profitability. Emblematic of the troubles most such attempts would face over the next four centuries, however, this first public winemaking effort was to be short-lived. After arriving in Virginia, De La Warr quickly became ill and left the colony for England in March 1611. It is unclear what became of the French vignerons' efforts.[26]

Accompanying De La Warr home was his doctor, Lawrence Bohune, who had arrived with the governor and French vignerons the previous year. The first physician-general to be appointed by the Company for service in the colony, Bohune possessed knowledge of medical botany and was perhaps the colony's first medical researcher.

Before departing Virginia, Bohune sought to address Virginia's deteriorating health conditions and critical shortage of medicines by establishing the New World's first botanical garden. There he experimented with native plants, trees, and soils, as well as with European trees, seeds, and shrubs. According to historian William Strachey, this work also led Bohune to investigate grape-growing and winemaking:

> We have eaten there, as full an lushious a grape as in the vilages betweene Paris and Amiens [France], and I have drunck often the rathe [young, early] wine, which Dr. Bohune and other of our people have made full as good, as your French British wyne. Twenty gallons at a tyme have bene sometimes made witout any other helpe then by crushing the grape with the hand, which letting to settle five or six daies, hath, in the drawing forth, proved strong and heddy. Unto what perfection might not these be brought by the art and industry of manie skilfull *vineroones*, being thus naturally good? And how materiall and principall a commoditie this maie prove, either for the benefitt of such who shall inhabit there.[27]

While Bohune evidently succeeded in making wine, his efforts ended when he left Virginia in March 1611. Records suggest Bohune was reappointed physician-general in December 1621 and set sail for Virginia early in 1622. En route, however, he was killed on the high seas during a battle with a Spanish fleet. At least one historian has noted that Bohune's death was perhaps "an omen, of the ill-luck that [Virginia's] winemaking enterprise was destined to encounter."[28]

Following De La Warr's and Bohune's departure, the colony's Secretary, Captain Ralph Hamor, wrote of an additional effort to spur colonial commercial grape-growing in his book, *A True Discourse of the Present State of Virginia*. Serving as Secretary between 1611 and 1614, Hamor noted that the colony boasted "wilde grapes in abundance all the woods [over], there juce sweete and pleasant in taste."[29]

He also noted that a three- or four-acre wild grape vineyard had been established near a settlement known as "Henrico," where vines were "plentifully laden" and speculated "to what perfection they will come."[30]

Hamor's description is believed to be of the vineyard of Sir Thomas Dale, who had arrived at Jamestown in May 1611 to serve as acting governor after Lord De La Warr's departure two months earlier. After his arrival, Dale not only abolished the settlement's failed communal gardening system, but explored the upper James River in the hopes of finding an alternative site for a new, less mosquito-laden permanent settlement.[31]

While sailing up the James, Dale founded the Henrico settlement along the south side of the river in modern-day Chesterfield County. He believed that the area's drier climate and sandy soils would provide a much-welcome reprieve from Jamestown's swampy and deleterious conditions. He also hoped it would offer suitable grounds for testing whether native grapes could be substituted for European varieties in winemaking.[32]

Mirroring the swift departure of the governor and his doctor, however, whatever grape-growing Dale attempted was momentary. The Henrico settlement was destroyed by an Indian attack in 1622. Nothing more is known of Dale's vineyard.[33]

## —The First Major Public Efforts—

Though the colony's first efforts to establish a commercial wine industry did not last, the importance of cultivating grapes remained critical to the colony—so critical, in fact, that in 1612 a decree was issued protecting vineyards and imposing a particularly harsh penalty for their disturbance:

> What man or woman soever, shall... robbe any vineyard, or gather up the grapes..., whether in the ground belonging to the same fort or towne where he dwelleth, or in any other, shall be punished with death.[34]

The decree, issued by Acting-Governor Sir Thomas Gates, was the first written colonial action addressing viticulture. It implied that the colony faced a pressing need to produce wine, and it would be followed by several more measures in the coming decades as the colony's government grew increasingly desperate for results.

In 1619, the Company undertook a more ambitious, comprehensive approach to the encouragement of winemaking. In July of that year, Virginia's new legislative body, the House of Burgesses, met for the first time at Jamestown and, alongside a new "Governor's Council," (which together would be referred to as the "General Assembly") passed a law. This was commonly referred to as "Act 12," making the planting of vines compulsory for every household. Articulating the importance of grapevines to the young colony, Act 12 also compelled every household to maintain the vines:

> Moreover be it enacted by this present Assembly, that every householder doe yearly plante and maintaine ten vines untill they have attained to the art and experience of dressing a Vineyard either by their owne industry or by the Instruction of some Vigneron.[35]

Act 12 rewarded those who planted vines and sought to penalize those who did not. While it did not enumerate penalties, it placed responsibility for enforcement with the governor and the governor's council as they deemed fit.[36]

Act 12's passage was followed late in 1619 by the Virginia Company's importation of eight "divers and skillfull [French] vignerons" to Virginia as well as

11

10,000 European vines "of the best sort." This effort represented the first large-scale transplantation of European vinifera vines to eastern North America. It also reflected a more formal attempt to attract viticultural experts and favor the cultivation of European grapes over that of the colony's wild native varietals.[37]

The French vignerons who made the journey in 1619 had been hand-selected by King James's royal silk master, John Bonoeil, from the southern French provinces of Saintonge, Languedoc, and Gironde. Each signed contracts with the Company for transportation to America and wages in return for their "planting of Vynes and ordering of Silkeworms." The Company hoped these foreign experts would give the colony its best chance to re-create France's great silk and wine industries. It is not known when they arrived in Virginia, but by 1620, all were settled along the Chesapeake Bay near the Buckroe area in the present-day city of Hampton.

Like their hopeful but misguided fellow Frenchmen who had toiled unsuccessfully before them in 1610, these new vignerons were seized by the colony's winegrowing potential. Just as their predecessors, they assured the colony's treasurer that "no Countrie in the World is more proper for Vines... than Virginie." The new vignerons planted whatever European vines they had at their disposal sometime about October 1, 1620 and—though hardly believable—reports indicate the vines allegedly produced grapes the following spring.[38]

At first, this new comprehensive winemaking scheme proceeded according to plan. Initial accounts by the Frenchmen indicated that their efforts successfully spurred vine growing across the colony and, in some instances, the grapes produced were of such "unusual bigness" that they were not believed to be grapes at first inspection. The Company, too, appeared to take seriously its desire to cultivate a wine industry. It spent money to import a hefty number of grapevines (lest any should fail), paid for the services of new winemaking experts, and, through Act 12, sought to force each colonist to join in the fun.[39]

Despite initial optimism, the outlook for the Company's 1619 endeavor came to a tragic halt two years later, on March 22, 1622. That day, the colony suffered a brutal attack at the hands of Powhatan Confederacy Indians that resulted in the deaths of some 400 colonists—nearly one-third of the colony's population—including some of the French vignerons. Records do not say how much damage the slaughter levied on Virginia's fledgling wine industry, but it must have been significant. In the wake of carnage, farms and outlying settlements were abandoned. Nevertheless, reports indicate that the surviving Frenchmen who escaped with their lives continued to teach their skills to English planters.

While the colony had sent samples of wine to London before the Indian attack, none were sent to London in 1623 or the following year, suggesting that Virginia's budding wine industry was decimated. One Company report from 1623 noted the colony's winemaking hardships following the attack:

> Careful order hath been taken for the setting [up] of that [wine] Comodotie, which wee doubt not in short time will shewe [itself] in great plenty. And had not the business been interrupted by ye Massacre, [believe] this the effect had been seen, there beinge divers Vyneyears planted in the Country wherof some conteyned Tenn thousand Plantes.[40]

As destructive as the Indian attack was to the Company's viticultural efforts, it is probable the measures undertaken in that regard would in time have fallen prey to other obstacles. No number of imported vinifera vines, for example, could withstand the colony's humidity or overcome its pests and diseases without chemical sprays and fungicides—the development of which lay years into the future. Equally important, by 1623, interest in viticulture had waned as Virginia's colonists increasingly devoted their efforts to the crop that had come to dominate Virginia's economy: tobacco.[41]

It has been widely thought that no resource has played a more significant role in the history of a state or nation than did tobacco in young Virginia. Though the Company had initially hoped Virginia's earliest settlers would profit from Virginia's natural resources, John Rolfe's 1612 cultivation of a new strain of tobacco provided the colony with a guaranteed income stream.[42]

Rolfe, perhaps most often remembered as the man who wed Pocahontas, came to the idea of widespread Virginia tobacco plantings as a means to undercut Spanish tobacco imports. While Native Americans had planted wild varieties of the leaf well before the arrival of the English, Rolfe's experiments produced a milder strain that grew well in the colony and earned the praise of London buyers.[43]

The popularity of Rolfe's tobacco, coupled with the relative ease with which it could be grown, led to an increase in its production that grew nearly tenfold between 1615 and 1619, and again threefold between 1619 and 1622. With higher yields and lower shipping rates per acre than other products, tobacco was soon planted in practically every available field, clearing, and street, and was even used as a form of credit.[44]

While the Company adopted a land policy in 1618 that encouraged tobacco production to ensure the financial stability of the colony, and though it gladly accepted the substantial revenues derived from the leaf, early on it feared soil depletion and the occasional collapse in tobacco prices. Accordingly, the Company encouraged colonists to pursue other products for purposes of economic diversification. Such calls, however, were rarely heard or responded to as Virginians planted tobacco to the detriment of practically every other staple.[45]

As one might expect from a product that required a high level of expertise and much labor, wine production figured poorly in this equation. It could not demonstrate sufficient economic advantage to the colonial government or Virginia's settlers, and such investment as there was in winemaking came only as a result of short-term anticipation of fast returns that never materialized. Viticulture found itself relegated to a position far behind more profitable products such as wheat, hemp, corn, flax, and silk. The prospects for establishing a New World wine industry looked particularly bleak after the 1622 Indian attack, and it simply could not compete with tobacco.[46]

Three months after the Indian attack, none other than King James himself attempted to use his influence to discourage the planting of tobacco and to promote winemaking. Known to possess a rather disagreeable temper and fond of making tyrannical demands on his subjects, James had a well-known distaste for tobacco. As early as 1604, he had published a rambling treatise disparaging the golden leaf, not so subtly entitled *A Counter-blaste to Tobacco*. In it, the monarch condemned tobacco as a "common herbe" that contributed to England's ruination. He also claimed, rather presciently, that the plant polluted the "inward parts of men fouling and infecting them with an unctuous and oily kind of soote." The king pushed the colony to develop other products he thought were of greater consequence, including wine, believing that Virginia could no long prosper solely on tobacco.[47]

In 1620, two years before the Indian attack, James turned to John Bonoeil, his silkworm breeder, to prepare a manual that could provide instruction to colonists on raising silkworms, growing grapes, and making wine. Bonoeil was equal to the task, having handpicked the Virginia Company's eight French vignerons only a year earlier.[48]

Once completed in July 1622, Bonoeil's pamphlet featured some fourteen pages of "instructions how to plant and dress vines, and to make wine." It also argued that the colony's economic strength lay in international trade and, to that end, that the manufacturing of silk and wine were to be considered of global economic importance.[49]

Despite the authority with which he wrote, Bonoeil had never visited Virginia. This, of course, did not stop him from applying his silk and viticultural expertise toward what he imagined to be Virginia's conditions. For example, he advocated the use of native vines for fast results, including the native "fox grape" that had long since been found unsuitable by locals for making wine.

Bonoeil also issued a set of absurd instructions for planting that recommended that grapes be planted in well-drained soil, on south-facing slopes, and that they be planted in trenches one-and-one-half-feet deep. He also recommended that, in the first year, vines be pruned in the first quarter of the season, while fast-growing vines be pruned as "the Moone wayneth."[50]

To make claret (a dark rosé wine), Bonoeil instructed colonists to pick red and white grapes when they were ripe, crush them "with bare legs and feet," and ferment the resulting juice for five or six days before draining the liquid into barrels. Greener grapes, he asserted, could also be pressed to make a "small wine for the household" while a "prettie small wine for the servants" could thereafter be made by adding water and re-pressing the remains of the grapes. "I have oftentimes seen such wine made reasonable good for the household," Bonoeil wrote, "and by this means every man may presently have wine in Virginia to drink."[51]

Bonoeil's pamphlet was the first viticultural manual drafted for American winemakers. King James, of course, enthusiastically endorsed it, noting in the preface that he expected Virginians to produce results posthaste:

> And forasmuch as our servant, John Bonoe[i]l, hath taken pains in setting down the true use of the silkworm, together with the art of silk-making and of planting vines... we do hereby likewise require you to cause his directions both for the said silk works and vineyards to be carefully put in practice throughout our plantations there, so the work may go on cheerfully and receive no more interruptions nor delays.[52]

The king forwarded the pamphlet to the Virginia Company in July 1622 and directed it to "command a speedy course… for the setting up of Silkworks and the planting of Vineyards throughout the whole Colony." Bonoeil's treatise was subsequently sent to Virginia's governor along with direct orders from Henry Wriothesley, the Earl of Southampton, who ordered that a copy of the pamphlet be distributed to every Virginia family.

Wriothesley admonished the colony for failing to heed the Virginia Company's previously issued instructions to produce wine. He also suggested that the time for winemaking excuses had come to an end: "herein there can be no Plea, either of difficulty or impossibility" in bringing about a wine and silk industry, he wrote, nor any "excuses will be admitted, nor any other pretences [serve], whereby the businesse be at all delayed." Wriothesley sternly concluded that if any Virginian should fail—either through negligence or willful conduct—to plant vines and mulberry trees, "we desire they may by severe censures and punishment, be compelled thereunto."

As James and Wriothesley would discover, however, even the most ardent directives from London could not compel the colonists to do the impossible, nor persuade the colonists to devote the time necessary to perfect wine made from native varieties.[53]

The Company forwarded Bonoeil's manual to each household in the colony as instructed, and declared that it was met with enthusiasm by the settlers. It also proclaimed that Virginia had quickly recovered from the 1622 Indian attack. Anecdotal evidence, however, suggests otherwise.[54]

Writing in April 1623 following a visit to the Jamestown colony, the governor of Bermuda, Captain Nathaniel Butler, expressed his disappointment with the conditions he found in Virginia, including the lack of a wine industry. "Expecting according to [the Company's] printed books a great forwardnes of divers and sundry Comodities at myne aryvall," Butler wrote of Virginia's would-be wine industry, "I found not any one of them." Concerning Bonoeil's instructions, Butler wrote that the pamphlet was "laughted to scorne" by the colonists and that "[t]obacco onely was ye business."[55]

Butler's remarks prompted the Virginia Company to issue a stern written defense addressing his allegations point-by-point. At the Company's behest, a group of planters stressed the demoralizing effects of the 1622 Indian attack and hinted that Butler—who was eager to populate Bermuda—possessed an ulterior motive for discrediting Virginia.

Such "emulous and envious reports," the planters argued, were those "of ill willers whose priyate ends by time will be discovered and by God recompenced." Specifically concerning the colonists' failure to foster a wine industry and their scorn of Bonoeil's treatise, the planters countered:

> As for Vines likewise ther were diverse Vineyards planted in sundry places butt all of them putt back by ye Massacre, butt for the peoples [deriding] of these Comodoties or the books sent by ye Company: wee have never heard of any such scoffinge or derisions butt as the Governor and Counsell there are very desirous and have sett forth Proclamations to cause all men to sett both Vines and Mulberry Trees, so ye people generally are very [desireous] & forward to rayse those former Comodties of Wine and Silke.[56]

One month after Butler issued his damning account, another disparaging letter went public—this one from an internal group of discontented Virginia Company members led by Alderman Robert Johnson and Sir Thomas Smith. The Johnson-Smith letter directly refuted official Company reports and alleged that it was the Company's mismanagement of a host of matters, not the least of which was the mistreatment of the French vignerons and the doubtful future of winemaking in the colony.

The Johnson-Smith letter highlighted that the colony had failed to send wine to London in 1623 and that no stable wine industry had yet developed in the colony. "The vignerons that have beene sent are some of them dead," the letter noted, "soe can Wee hope for little of that Commodity from Virginia." Calling attention to a Company claim that a large commercial vineyard had been planted with some 1,000 European vines, the Johnson-Smith letter countered that whatever vineyard existed amounted to little more than a small garden plot consisting of a mere acre of native vines.

The Johnson-Smith letter also claimed that while the Company had procured thousands of "Choice plants of the best kinde of Christendome" in 1619, it neither cared for them in London nor bothered to forward them to Virginia for cultivation. The result of all of this mismanagement, the letter concluded, was to deny Virginians the "speedy raisinge of that soe much desired [wine] commodity; for the Advancement were of wee have received expresse directions from his most Sacred Majesty."[57]

The April 1623 account by Governor Butler and issuance of the Johnson-Smith letter the following month were indicative of growing discontent over the lack of progress and financial mismanagement in the colony. Whatever may be said in the Company's defense of its failed winemaking efforts, the publication of constant diatribes against the Company showed the lack of a strong and financially sound colonial administration. They also warned of a colony on the brink of financial ruin and, as would be seen shortly, rang the death knell for Company-led self-government in Virginia.[58]

Amid growing disenchantment with the Company, and increased frustration over the colony's failure to diversify from tobacco, a new colonial treasurer arrived. George Sandys was the politically connected and educated brother of one of the Company's founders, Sir Edwin Sandys. He arrived in Virginia late in 1621 just prior to the 1622 Indian attack. Ostensibly sent to improve the colony's financial records, he is perhaps better remembered as a poet, having translated to English the Roman poet Ovid's fifteen-book narrative *Metamorphoses*.[59]

On the subject of viticulture, Sandys reported in March 1623 that many vines had been planted the prior year, but that the effort amounted to little thanks to the Indian attack, the lack of viticultural skill, the poor quality of vine cuttings, and sheer neglect. Sandys also wrote, however, that a special order had been issued requiring every plantation to fence one quarter of an acre of land for vines, employ two persons to cultivate the plot for seven years, and thereafter enlarge the plot by two acres as labor permitted. Rather than apologize for

17

the Company given his familial ties, he remarked of the new measures, "By this meanes, I hope this worke will goe really forwarde, & the better if good store of Spanish or French vines, may be sent us."[60]

It is perhaps owing to such circumstances, with an increased emphasis on the planting and preservation of mulberry trees, that the General Assembly enacted a new law, "Act 18," in March 1624. Act 18 mandated the planting of twenty vines by every freeman above the age of twenty years in the colony:

> That every freeman shall fence in a quarter of an acre of ground… to make a garden for planting of vines, herbs, roots, &c. subpoena ten pounds of tobacco a man, but that no man for his own family shall be tyed to fence above an acre of land and that whosoever hath fenced a garden and of the land shall be paid for it by the owner of the soyle; they shall also plant Mulberry trees.[61]

While Act 18 did not specify the number of vines required to be planted, or how much of each garden was to be devoted to grape cultivation, it was supplemented by a proclamation issued the same year:

> It is ordered that A Proclarnatione shall be presently sent for the impaling of gardens Accordinge to the Act of the general Assembly for the planting of 4 mulberry trees and 20 vynies for every male head about 20 yeers of age between this and the last of february next coming straightly Charging all Commanders of every Plantation to see them not only planted but Carefully tended & looked to at their p'ill, And to give information of all such as shall be delinquelit therein.[62]

Sandys himself appears to have honored the 1624 law and proclamation, and census records show that by the following year, he boasted a two-acre vineyard at his estate in modern-day Surry County. A 1625 survey of his property identified at least one full-time Frenchman employed to manufacture wine and silk. Sandys likely left the colony in 1625 or 1626 and, with his exodus, it is possible to surmise that his viticultural experimentation concluded.[63]

By 1624, few results were evident from the Virginia Company's measures to stimulate a wine industry in the colony. This was caused, in part, by the Company's unsettling habit of calling for commodity diversification in one breath, while at the same time eager to collect increased tobacco revenues. It was also because of a lack of reliable, sustainable winemaking investments and expertise, the terrible 1622 Indian attack, and the prevalence of something as simple as Virginia's natural pests.

Even when the colony managed to yield enough wine to send to London—as it had in June 1622—tasters in London found it to be "rather of scandall than creditt" to the Company, as it was spoiled by a "long carrying," the inevitable process of oxidation, and a "[m]ustie caske wherein it was putt."[64]

The Company grew increasingly desperate for revenues and wine, for it needed to repay investors and demonstrate progress. But things worsened during the early 1620s when a new phenomenon—a reduced supply of alcoholic beverages in the colony—led to price hikes in "strong waters, and other such Drunke." The pain was particularly felt among the "common sort of people" who would pay almost any price rather than go without alcohol. These higher prices led to increased crime and caused Virginia Governor Sir Francis Wyatt to institute price controls on several imported wines in August 1623.[65]

Feeling pressure from detractors inside and outside the colony, in April 1622 the Company sought reimbursement from anyone who had received instruction in the "art" of planting vines and "mystery" of making wine from the Company's eight French vignerons. This levy no doubt came as a surprise to the colonists, who could not have foreseen that they would be retroactively charged for what they most assuredly believed was free winemaking advice. The following summer, the Company went further by issuing a stern but apprehensive plea to Governor Wyatt reinforcing its expectations for winemaking:

> We hope you have got a good entrance into Silk and Vines, and we expect some returns—or it will be a discredit to us and to you and give room to the maligners of the [colony]. Encourage the Frenchmen to stay, if not forever, at least 'till they have taught our people their skill in silk and vines.[66]

The Company was so desperate that it was receptive to any idea—no matter how harebrained—that might finally provide the miraculous, long-searched-for means of stimulating Virginia viticulture. Two years earlier, for example, it fielded an untraditional proposal by an English chemist and alchemist, William Russell, who suggested that the Company institute a low-cost, low-labor method of manufacturing wine by boiling sassafras and licorice in water. Russell asserted the concoction—even in the hot Virginia climate—would neither decay nor sour, and "shall be as harty, holsome pleasinge and comfortable for the body as any beere or wyne whatsoever." Because Russell admitted his non-alcoholic brew would "make noe man drunk," it is unlikely the proposal found a receptive audience.[67]

As might have been expected, Virginia's wine shortage only worsened. By January 1624, Governor Wyatt complained to the Company that the colony's alcoholic beverage situation had deteriorated to the point that Virginians were forced to rely on the importation of expensive "rotten Wynes which destroy our bodies and empty our purses."[68]

Outwardly, of course, the Company sought to present a reassuring face to its investors and the government that the colony was on solid footing. Even if true, it came too late. Longtime financial mismanagement caused the Company to run an annual debt and fail to pay dividends. Moreover, the 1622 Indian attack had sullied the Company's reputation for the maintenance of public safety and neighborly relations. On May 24, 1624, King James revoked the Company's charter, dissolved the Company, and converted Virginia into a Crown colony. The king's decision vested direct oversight of affairs in the Crown and, until the American Revolution, Virginia would be overseen by a royal governor appointed by, and directly accountable to, the king.[69]

Governor Wyatt, previously appointed by the Company and a proponent of economic diversification, agreed to stay on as Virginia's first royal governor. Believing himself freed from the relentless demands of the former Company, Wyatt wrote in May 1626 that other commodities, including wine, would be given his full attention "since all neither can nor must bee suffered to tend Tobacco."

Despite Wyatt's hopes, the administrative change from Company to Crown did little to ease Virginia's viticultural troubles. The colony's new overseers soon exhibited as much exasperation as their predecessors, as they simply could not fathom why wine could not be produced. The government then searched for a scapegoat that could be held responsible for the colony's viticultural shortcomings. In this sad effort, Virginians pinpointed the one group of colonists whose sole charge had been to produce wine, but who had failed: the French.[70]

For years, the French had struggled with Virginia viticulture alongside their English-speaking brethren. Like other settlers, their efforts had been checked repeatedly by a host of man-made obstacles, and the natural ones of untreatable vine diseases and pestilence. Over time, many turned to tobacco and other crops that offered some promise of profitability. To the English Crown, though, such behavior was suspect.

A March 1628 report to the King—jointly issued by Acting-Governor Francis West, thirty-one members of the House of Burgesses, and five members of the governor's Council—placed the colony's winemaking failures squarely on the French, alleging perfidious behavior:

> They conceive that the planting of vines will prove a commodity, both beneficial and profitable, but none of them are skilful therein. The

vinerons sent over spent their time to small purpose and either purposefully neglected or concealed their skill.[71]

In 1632, the General Assembly retaliated against the woe-begotten French by enacting a discriminatory statute, known as "Act 16," that forbade French vignerons and their families from planting tobacco. Imprisonment and exile were available penalties:

> Upon a [protest] preferr'd to the assembly, complayninge that the ffrenchmen who were, about ten yeares since, transported into this country for the plantinge and dressinge of vynes, and to instruct others in the same, have willinglie concealed the skill, and not only neglected to plant nay vynes themselves, but have also spoyled and ruinated that vyniard, which was, with great cost, planted by the charge of the late company and theire officers here; and yet notwithstandinge have received all favour and encouragement thereunto, which hath dishartened all the inhabitants here, It is therefore ordered that the sayd ffrenchmen, togeather with their families, be restrayned and prohibited from plantinge tobacco, uppon penaltie to forfeit theire leases, and imprisonment until they will depart out of this colony.[72]

The government's prohibition of French tobacco farming, which forced them to make a livelihood from a commodity that had little chance of success, represented the nadir of Virginia's public attempts to encourage winemaking. Act 16's genesis ignored reality, and many found both the blame misplaced and the law unjust. British writer Edward Williams posited in his 1650 treatise, *Virginia… Richly and Truly Valued*, that it was the colonial government—rather than the French immigrants—that was most responsible for Virginia's lack of a wine industry. Writing of the poor treatment of the French since their arrival in the colony, he asserted that discrimination by the colonial government had contributed to their failure to produce wine:

> Those contracted with as hired servants for that imployment, by what miscariage I know not, having promise broken with them, and compelled to labour in the quality of Slaves, could not but express their resentment of it, and had a good colour of justice to conceale their knowledge, in recompence of the hard measure offered them.[73]

Had the French been better treated, Williams argued, the colony could have realized a wine industry much earlier "to an absolute perfection."[74]

It remains unclear how long Act 16 was in force or whether it was enforced, but the General Assembly passed two other wine-related laws in 1632. One required the recipients of patents for 100 acres or more to "establish a garden and orchard, carefully protected by a fence, ditch, or hedge." Another, "Act 17," required corn and tobacco growers to plant five grapevines in March of the first year, and 20 vines by March 25th the second year. Act 17 also imposed a penalty of one barrel of corn for every grower in default, with half of the barrel to be distributed to the informer and the other half going to public purposes.[75]

By late in the 1630s, the General Assembly had given up mandating wine-making by legislative fiat, instead opting for a new approach—rewarding successful wine producers. Act 17, for example, was reenacted in 1639 as "Act 25," and provided a premium payment to those who succeeded in growing grapes and penalties for those who refused:

> It is provided and ordered, That all workers upon corne and tobacco shall this ensuing springe before the first day of March next... plant, or cause to be planted 20 vyne plants per pol uppon penaltie to forfeite one barrell of corne for every one that shall make default one halfe to be to him which shall make information thereof and the other halfe to publique uses. And the commissioners for the mounthlie cort shall have full power to heare and determine this matter and to see that the sayd vynes bee weeded, tended, and well preserved.[76]

In 1658, the General Assembly passed yet another law encouraging the "makeing of staple comodities" and granting individuals who made two tons of wine from their own vineyards an award of 10,000 pounds of Virginia tobacco. Even with this substantial public encouragement, however, records do not show whether anyone won the prize.[77]

Despite the General Assembly's limited success in first attempting to force and then to encourage Virginians to try viticulture, at least some quantity of wine was, in fact, being made across the colony by the mid-seventeenth century. In 1648, one Captain William Brocas planted a vineyard along the Rappahannock River in Lancaster County and "hath most excellent Wine made...as proper for Vines as any in Chrissendome." One 1686 inventory of the cellar of Rappahannock County magistrate William Fauntleroy listed rum, lime juice, and twenty dozen bottles of local wine. Such records were commonplace in household inventories across the colony during this period.[78]

Yet another account, this from English physician Thomas Glover who lived briefly in the Chesapeake Bay region, made special mention of Virginia wine in his 1676 *An Account of Virginia*, noting:

> In the Woods there are abundance of *Vines,* which twine about the
> Oaks and Poplars, and run up to the top of them; these bear a kind of
> *Claret-grapes,* of which some few of the Planters do make Wine, whereof
> I have tasted; it is somewhat smaller than *French* Claret.

Like many of his predecessors, Glover said,

> I suppose, if some of these Wines were planted in convenient vine-
> yards, where the Sun might have a more kindly influence on them, and
> kept with diligence and seasonable pruning, they might afford as good
> grapes as the Claret-Grapes of France are.[79]

Even where wine was not made, many foreign writers continued to express optimism in the face of years of failure. To be sure, most of these observers were
ill-informed, and many had never visited the colony. Like the original Jamestown settlers, though, virtually all persisted in a belief that the colony remained
thoroughly capable of producing fine wine, whether it be from European or
native grapes.[80]

British writer Edward Williams, for example, included a thirty-page treatise
on silk and wine manufacturing in the colony as part of the second edition of
his 1650 book, *Virginia Richly and Truly Valued.* Williams had earlier criticized
the General Assembly for its 1632 anti-French law, and suggested instead that
the future of Virginia grape-growing lay in grape varieties from those areas
in Europe that existed on the same latitude as Virginia—namely grapes from
Greece. Growing Cyprian, Canadian, or Calabrian grapes, in particular, would
produce

> a Staple which would enrich this Countrey to the envy of France and
> Spaine, and furnish the Northern parts of Europe, and China it selfe…
> with the Noblest Wine in the World, and at no excessive prices.[81]

Williams also suggested the importation of new Greek vinedressers and the
dissemination of Greek viticultural advice to planters in Virginia. Such efforts,
he predicted, would allow the typical Virginia planter "who usually spends all
the profits of his labour in forraigne Wines [to bury] all the memory and sense
of his past labours in a cheerfull rejoycing by his owne harth with the issue of
his owne vineyard."[82]

Despite Williams's suggestions, by the late 1600s, most Virginians had long
since stopped planting vines. The colony's government had also abandoned its
dream of a New World wine industry and, beginning in 1685, Virginia's governors were no longer instructed by the Crown to encourage wine production.

From a social perspective, beer, hard cider, and distilled spirits had also emerged as the beverages of preference for Virginians, as wine and vineyards faded into the past.[83]

If there was to be any hope for resuscitating Virginia's dashed plans for a wine industry, such prospects would have to come from outside of the colony and, indeed, from beyond England. What was needed was new blood, innovative ideas, and a fresh start. Unsurprisingly, the Old Dominion turned once more to immigrants, beginning, ironically, with the French—the very people who had been maligned for all of the colony's past viticultural failures.

## — The Emergence of Viticultural Settlements —

Despite the colonial government's aversion to French vignerons, by the late 1600s social and political changes in Europe increased foreign immigration to America and renewed the colony's hopes of fostering a wine industry. The French, in particular, again came to play a pivotal role in a minor viticultural revival during the second period of French immigration between 1680 and 1732. Much of this immigration, consisting largely of French Protestants known as "Huguenots," came as a direct result of Louis XIV's October 1685 Revocation of the Edict of Nantes.

The original Edict of Nantes, promulgated in 1598 by Louis's grandfather, Henry IV, ratified Catholicism as France's official religion, but afforded protection to French Protestants. Louis XIV revoked the Edict and imposed harsh penalties on the Huguenots. During what became known as *le Refuge,* between 1680 and 1710 hundreds of thousands were forced into exile. Most fled to England, Holland, and southwestern Germany, but many looked across the Atlantic for a chance to rebuild their lives.[84]

Louis's government, nervous about the potential for a British wine industry that could challenge its own dominance, imposed restrictions on the emigration of Huguenot vinedressers. With support from both England's William III, and a Huguenot-friendly resettlement organization known as the "Protestant Relief Committee," however, waves of Huguenots emigrated from London to Virginia between 1688 and 1700. The group included winemakers and vinedressers, many of whom brought with them European grapevines for planting.[85]

This second wave of French arrivals to Virginia—among the colony's first, large-scale non-English immigrations—sparked Virginia's second major public sector attempt to encourage a colonial wine industry, the first since the Virginia Company's failed 1619 winemaking effort. It gave rise to the creation of a chain of frontier communities primarily inhabited by foreigners that could serve as a buffer for the rest of the colony.[86]

The idea for creating these small colonies of non-English colonial settlers was nothing new; as early as 1621, the Virginia Company had considered a proposal to establish French winemaking settlements across the countryside. The concept was ultimately tabled thanks to poor relations between England and France at the time; it was followed, however, by another in June 1629 when two French Protestant nobles—Antoine De Ridouet and Benjamin de Rohan—requested permission to establish a French Protestant colony in Virginia to make silk, salt, and wine. This second request was approved and French settlers reached the southern shores of the James River in what is today the City of Suffolk. There is no evidence, however, that the French colony survived.[87]

Huguenots had experimented with wine near present-day Jacksonville, Florida, between 1562 and 1563, but by the late 1600s French immigration to Virginia appeared more sustainable. Virginia's colonial government, alongside individual landowners and the Protestant Relief Committee, published advertisements and promotional tracts in England extolling the virtues of resettlement in Virginia. These pamphlets pronounced the supposed fertility of the colony's soil and climate, the abundance of natural grapes, and the potential for vineyards and winemaking.

One such account, *A Huguenot Exile in Virginia*, was written by a French Huguenot nobleman, Durand du Dauphiné, who exalted the virtues of America, calling it "the most beautiful, the most pleasant, and the most fertile land in all the West Indies."[88]

After crossing the Atlantic on a nineteen-week journey, du Dauphiné survived a shipwreck off the coast of Gloucester County, Virginia in September 1686. From then until March 1687, he traveled the colony, observing its people and economy. While visiting one prominent Middlesex County planter, Ralph Wormeley, du Dauphiné noted that the picturesque rolling banks of Wormeley's land along the Rappahannock River featured wild vines that would "undoubtedly... make good wine."[89]

Du Dauphiné also wrote of his December 1686 visit with Colonel William Fitzhugh, a prominent Northern Virginia lawyer, merchant, and planter. Fitzhugh owned approximately 24,000 acres of land—which his son later named Ravensworth—lying generally between present-day northern Stafford, Arlington, and Fairfax Counties. A believer in the virtues of exploiting the benefits of Louis's Revocation to Virginia's benefit, Fitzhugh wrote to a London merchant in May 1686 offering portions of his property for sale or lease by French Huguenots. Fitzhugh advertised his land as being "principal good land

and is proper for Frenchmen, because more naturally inclined to vines, than yours or any about our neighborhood."[90]

Encouraged by the fertility and viticultural prospects of Fitzhugh's property, du Dauphiné wrote that it boasted "six times" more native grapevines than practically anywhere else." Although du Dauphiné's account was published in Europe in 1687, Fitzhugh was unsuccessful in attracting Huguenots to Ravensworth. He did, however, attract small French settlements along Accotink Creek basin in Fairfax County prior to his death in 1701.[91]

With French Huguenot immigration to Virginia in full swing by 1700, the General Assembly passed a law liberalizing Virginia's system of land grants, out of a desire to populate the colonists' largely uninhabited Piedmont region. The law granted public trust lands to new property owners and resulted in fierce competition between landowners to attract settlers to their lands as quickly as possible.

French Huguenots suddenly found themselves in demand, and two prominent Virginia landowners—Dr. Daniel Coxe, the court physician to England's Queen Anne, and William Byrd II of Richmond—vied for the honor of being the first to settle the newcomers on their properties. Ultimately, Byrd's property won out and a small portion of his property became the French community of Manakin Town.[92]

Named in honor of the Monacan tribe that inhabited an area just east of the settlement, Manakin Town was located on some 10,000 remote acres along the south side of the James River approximately twenty miles west of present-day Richmond. The site's isolation and lack of amenities came as unwelcome news to the approximately 400 Huguenots who settled there in the fall and winter of 1700. Many were of the merchant class and possessed little experience or knowledge of agriculture or "roughing it." Most had hoped to settle in Virginia's more populous eastern region where they could engage in business as they had before fleeing France.[93]

Despite Manakin Town's lack of navigable access along the James River or significant communication with the balance of the colony, the Huguenots quickly adapted to the frontier. By the spring of 1701, the settlers had managed to clear fields, cultivate crops, and construct a small village patterned after a French provincial town, with several community buildings. Four years later, the settlers were seen raising cattle and buffalo, manufacturing their own linen and threads, cultivating hemp and flax (for rope and cloth), and producing their own clothing.

The Manakin French also proved particularly adept at winemaking. Given the handsome prices paid by England's government for wine, the settlers viewed the cultivation of the grape as an industry that might best deliver the urban commercial life they had left behind in France. As early as 1702, Manakin Town evidently boasted a young and vibrant grape industry largely centered on native American grapes. Virginia's most prominent early colonial historian, Robert Beverley, wrote that the Huguenots had crafted from wild vines in the vicinity of the settlement a curiously-flavored "noble strong-bodied Claret, of good flavor" that received "great Commendation" from at least one respected judge.[94] A Swiss geologist, Francis Louis Michel, visited Manakin Town in 1702 to investigate the condition of the French settlement in the hopes of fostering a similar settlement for Swiss expatriates. Michel was particularly impressed by the settlement's hopes for viticulture:

> I have seen the most awful wild grapevines, whose thickness and height are incredible. There are several kinds of grapes, the best are as large as a small nut. They make fairly good wine, a beginning has been made to graft them, the prospects are fine.[95]

While Manakin Town's experiment with viticulture showed great promise, the settlement as a whole never proved a sustainable commercial venture. The community experienced a rapid decline and, by 1705, fewer than 150 people inhabited the town. By 1708, some of the settlers had decamped into uninhabited areas farther west while others relocated to North Carolina. By 1750, the town was all but deserted.[96]

Historians note that, even with greater wealth and skill, failure in viticulture at Manakin Town—despite using native grapes—would have been inevitable given the difficulties of viticulture in the Virginia wilderness. Most of the Manakin French had turned their attention to other pursuits by 1715 and, like their French predecessors nearly a century before, those who remained switched to that far more profitable agricultural endeavor, tobacco.[97]

News of Manakin Town's early success, however, spread across the Atlantic to residents along Germany's Rhine River who, like their Huguenot counterparts, had suffered religious persecution, taxes, and war. In April 1714, two years following Governor Alexander Spotswood's discovery of iron deposits north of the falls of the Rappahannock River, some forty-two immigrants from the Nassau-Siegen area of northeastern Germany landed in Virginia. The settlers—the first organized group of Germans to arrive in the colony—came at the invitation of Governor Spotswood's friend, Christoph von Graffenried, Baron de Graffenried, with the understanding that they would be relied on for both frontier defense and the development of iron ore.[98]

Governor Spotswood settled the Germans on property he owned along the south bank of the Rapidan River in present-day Orange County, some twelve miles upstream from its confluence with the Rappahannock. There he constructed a small fort and, by 1715, had outfitted the post with a stockade, two cannons, and ammunition. The fort was named "Germanna" to honor both the colonist's homeland and England's recently deceased Queen Anne.[99]

Though Spotswood equipped the Germanna fort with provisions, and although the legislature enacted a law exempting the German settlers from taxation, conditions at the settlement were poor. One visiting French Huguenot writer wrote that "the Germans live very miserably." Despite these rough frontier conditions, the German colony evidently managed to produce both red and white wines.[100]

Writing in his 1724 work *The Present State of Virginia*, the Reverend Hugh Jones found that, thanks to the efforts of the late Colonel Robert Beverley, Germanna's inhabitants were "encouraged to make Wines" and that Germanna's winemaking

> was done easily and in large Quantities in those Parts; not only from the Cultivation of the wild Grapes, which grow plentifully and naturally in all the good Lands thereabouts, and in the other Parts of the Country; but also from the Spanish, French, Italian, and German Wines, which have been found to thrive there to Admiration.[101]

Germanna's first recorded vintage may have been sampled as early as September 1716 when Spotswood, along with an expedition party known as the "Knights of the Golden Horseshoe," visited the site on their way to the Shenandoah Valley. One traveler with the party, John Fontaine, noted that Spotswood's "Knights" celebrated their crossing of the Blue Ridge Mountains with a toast of Virginia wine:

> We had a good dinner. After dinner we got the men all together and loaded all their arms and we drunk the King's health in Champagne, and fired a volley; the Prince's health in Burgundy [wine], and fired a volley; and all the rest of the Royal family in Claret, and a volley. We drunk the Governor's health and fired another volley.[102]

During the fête, Fontaine noted the party tasted a variety of strong drinks that day, including "Virginia Red Wine" and "White Wine." Both were likely made by the Germans at Germanna, and historians have noted that this celebration may, in fact, have been the first comparative wine tasting of New World wines.[103]

Like Manakin Town, the German colony enjoyed no sustained presence and its vineyards ultimately succumbed to pests, vine diseases, and mildew fungi. By 1719, twelve of the remaining families moved to what is now the Germantown area of nearby Fauquier County. Though a second wave of German settlers arrived in the area in 1717, they moved to the Robinson River valley of Madison County. No records indicate whether they made wine; it is suspected, however, that they brought vinifera vines with them to the New World.

## — An Era of Private Experimentation (1640–1750) —

Despite the promising, but abbreviated, experience of the French at Manakin Town and the Germans at Germanna, Virginia's government by the 1720s had once more halted all public initiatives for winemaking. Largely discouraged by the physical labor and capital required to make wine, most Virginians gave up on viticulture and continued planting tobacco.

In the absence of public support, the future of Virginia wine was left to the colony's more idealistic and optimistic men of means. The notion of reserving viticulture to the colony's wealthy elites had been documented as early as 1649 by an anonymous writer—likely a man by the name of John Ferrar—who wrote in *A Perfect Description of Virginia*,

> Vines in abundance and variety, do grow naturally over all the land, but… the Commodity of Wine is not a contemptible Merchandize; but some men of worth and estate must give in these things example to the inferiour inhabitants and ordinary sort of men, to shew them the gain and Commodity by it, which they will not believe but by experience before their faces.[104]

Ferrar's suggestion carried some truth. Without the financial support of the government, lower- and middle-class Virginians living in the countryside could not be counted on to produce wine; they were content with planting tobacco, drinking beer, and obtaining wild grapes from nearby forests. Those living in settlements and cities, such as Williamsburg, were equally unreliable since they could import liquor and wine from merchants or purchase it in local taverns.[105]

Indeed, if Virginia were to witness any scientific advancement in grape-growing, it would take the efforts of men who had the necessary money, land, education, time, and labor to bring viticulture to fruition. To their credit, many of Virginia's landed gentry—some of whose names are often famously associated with the colony's early years—rose to the challenge, signaling the beginning of a new era of private sector innovation.

Calls to create a wine industry and diversify the colony's economy came from many quarters; none were louder than those of Sir William Berkeley. A leading political and social figure in seventeenth-century Virginia, the British-born Berkeley arrived at Jamestown in 1641 and became the colony's longest-serving governor from 1642 to 1652 and again from 1660 to 1677.[106]

By the time of Berkeley's second administration, the overplanting of tobacco had not only resulted in glutted English markets and depressed prices, but had also physically depleted the land and effectively ruined many of the colony's planters. Like others before him, Berkeley disdained Virginia's economic addiction to what he termed the "vicious, ruinous plant of Tobacco" and, throughout the 1660s, worked to restrict its production. He promoted policies that favored other valuable commodities—including wine—which, he believed, as had many before him, would develop the colony's abundant natural resources and lead to the diversification of Virginia's economy.[107]

Berkeley's estate, Green Spring, was constructed in the 1640s and consisted of a 2,090-acre farm in James City County, just outside of Williamsburg. Berkeley turned Green Spring into a veritable horticultural testing station and experimented with silk, hemp, flax, the fermentation of fruits into wine, and pottery. He did so hoping to serve as an example to fellow Virginians that diversification in commodities could succeed and be profitable: "I am incessant and unwearied in my prosecution of [alternative commodities]," Berkeley noted of his efforts, adding, "the Country by my example, and my mens teaching them are all intent upon it."[108]

Green Spring's well-stocked gardens eventually boasted an orchard, and a vineyard from which Berkeley obtained grapes and raisins. The garden and nursery were so large and well maintained that the property became widely known on both sides of the Atlantic as a popular source for plants and trees.[109]

Believing Virginia's soils ripe for viticulture, Berkeley experimented in grape cultivation and winemaking with mixed results. Virginia historian Robert Beverley remarked that Berkeley unwisely attempted to grow grapes in unsuitable lowland areas and, to save labor, planted trees to serve as espaliers for the vines. Noting that the governor was constantly "full of projects," Beverley wrote that Berkeley's winemaking efforts suffered from his other pressing commitments, "so [he] never minded to bring them to Perfection."[110]

Despite his other obligations, however, reports suggest that Berkeley did, in fact, make wine. In 1663, Berkeley wrote to his friend, English statesman Edward Hyde, that it was his hope to send a hogshead (sixty-three gallons) of wine to Britain the following year. Berkeley noted to Hyde that "the last year I drank as good of my own planting as ever came out of Italy."[111]

Another account of Berkeley's winemaking success comes from the Reverend John Clayton, a traveler and amateur scientist who arrived in Virginia in 1684. Before returning to England in 1686, Clayton provided detailed accounts of Virginia's soils, flora and fauna, climate, and inhabitants. Clayton wrote that he had been assured that Berkeley had made many "noble experiments," including those of wine, so that "others might reap the Advantage."[112]

While Clayton asserted that Berkeley's attempts at cultivating grapes ultimately failed because of his lack of time and attention and "haveing many irons in the fire," he wrote that Berkeley "cultivated & made the wild sour grapes become pleasant, & large, & thereof made good wine." Most fittingly, Clayton characterized the late governor as "a man whose memory I honour mch, tho he was dead before I came into those parts, but a man of a generous ingenious Soul, & who would have done the Country good had they but been capable thereof."[113]

Such a portrayal was particularly apt. While the governor's second administration ultimately met its demise as a consequence of Nathaniel Bacon's 1676 rebellion, few Virginians proved more industrious or forward-thinking as to the need for economic diversification or more accustomed to the role of "gentlemen farmer" than Sir William Berkeley.[114]

One of the more revealing portraits of Virginia's early-eighteenth-century viticultural progress comes from Robert Beverley's *History and Present State of Virginia*, originally published in London in 1705 and revised in 1722. The colony's foremost pre-Revolutionary historian, Beverley was a scholar, traveler, and cataloger of the colony's documents. Unlike those in London and elsewhere who wrote of Virginia but had never visited the New World, Beverley proved uniquely positioned to write his *History* as an account of his home colony—the first ever authored by a native son of Virginia.[115]

He devoted a complete chapter of his *History* to the colony's "wild fruits," which detailed the profusion of indigenous cherries, persimmons, plums, and more. On the subject of grapes, he asserted that few Virginians cultivated European vinifera grapes due to the abundance of native varieties found in the woods and forests near settlements. Indeed, Beverley remarked that the colony's native grapes were so plentiful that

> when a single Tree happens in clearing the Ground, to be left standing with a Vine upon it, open to the Sun and Air; that Vine generally

produces as much as 4 or five others.... I have seen in this case, more Grapes upon one single Vine, than wou'd load a London Cart.[116]

Beverley argued that the primary obstacles to Virginia grape cultivation flowed from flawed decisions to plant vines along lowland areas near eastern Virginia's coastal waterways. "The experiments that have been made of Vineyards," he wrote, "have not only been near the malignant Influence of the Salt-Water, but also upon the low Lands, that are naturally subject to the Pine." He suggested that grape growers should instead cultivate grapes on hillsides and gravelly areas near freshwater streams away from the acidic presence of the Tidewater area's pine and fir trees.[117]

Beverley also wrote of his personal viticultural travails at his estate, Beverley Park. The plantation was located along the Mattaponi River and spread across portions of King and Queen County as well as Caroline County. There, in 1704, Beverley planted white native grapevines, a majority of which bore fruit the same year. "I remember I had seven full [b]unches from one of them," he later wrote.[118]

By 1709, Beverley's viticultural success caught the attention of the colony's government in Williamsburg and even merited mention in a report written by Joshua de Kocherthal to the Lords of Trade in London. "Of all the experiments which hitherto have been tryed," de Kocherthal wrote, "that of Mr. Robert Beverley upon the highlands in Virginia is the last and most remarkable, whose vineyards and wine all persons are talking of in Virginia."[119]

Such thoughts were echoed by John Fontaine, the writer who had also visited the Germanna colony. Fontaine called on Beverley twice, first in June 1715 on his way to observe the German settlement, and again one evening in September 1716 while returning from Governor Alexander Spotswood's "Knights of the Golden Horseshoe" expedition.

During his first visit, Fontaine wrote that Beverley had cultivated a three-acre vineyard along a hillside with several native varieties and, perhaps, several French vines. He also wrote that Beverley Park boasted multiple wine storage caves and a wine press from which Beverley made 400 gallons of wine. Fontaine found, though, that Beverley "hath not the right method" for producing wine "according to the method they use in Spain," nor was Beverley's vineyard "rightly managed." Beverley entertained Fontaine with "wine of his own making," but Fontaine found that "by the taste of the wine... [Beverley] did not understand how to make it." Nevertheless, during the visit, the two "were merry and drank prosperity to the vineyard."[120]

Fontaine wrote that Beverley's initial impetus for grape-growing came in response to a wager with a "gentlemen of the country who thought it impossible to bring a vineyard to any perfection." Under the terms of the bet, the unnamed gentlemen would give ten guineas for every guinea Beverley wagered if Beverley managed to cultivate successfully a vineyard that yielded 700 gallons of wine in one vintage. Whether Beverley ever made good on the wager is not certain, although the Reverend Hugh Jones, a traveler living in Williamsburg in 1717, wrote that Beverley indeed won the wager, and used his earnings to enlarge his vineyard and produce wine for his family and slaves.[121]

One of the more flamboyant figures in Virginia wine history, William Byrd II, also experimented with winemaking. The patron of the Huguenot settlement at Manakin Town, and the scion of an English immigrant who enjoyed high standing in Tidewater society, Byrd exuded all of the social and intellectual trappings of a well-bred young gentleman of his day. A prolific writer, historian, and playboy, Byrd was schooled in England and read Latin, Hebrew, and Greek daily—all of which enabled him to harness the power of the word to become a brilliant conversationalist and entertaining host.[122]

Byrd became captivated with the British lifestyle while abroad; he visited some of England's finest gardens and country estates and developed a taste for the sophisticated English model of landscaped gardens. After resigning himself to the fact that he could not afford to reside permanently in England, Byrd returned to his elegant mansion along the James River, Westover, and set about re-creating British-inspired formal gardens around his home.

Over the course of several years, Byrd turned Westover into one of the finest plantations of the day. It featured terraced formal gardens that stretched to the James River, and included a variety of hedges, cedar trees, fruit trees, plants, gravel walks, and even a bowling green. Such gardening and landscaping at once combined Byrd's own intellectual curiosity with his desire to emulate the sophisticated lifestyle he had reluctantly left behind in England.[123]

Infused into this passion for British-style gardening was Byrd's desire to find profitable alternatives to Virginia's tobacco addiction. Westover eventually boasted a small vineyard with some twenty varieties, for Byrd thought wine to be the "cheerer of Gods & Men." Like Sir William Berkeley, Byrd hoped his experimentation with several grape species would help him identify a few that would prove the financial feasibility of viticulture to his fellow colonists. "I have lately," Byrd wrote, "planted a small vine[yard] to show my indolent country-folks that we may employ our industry upon other things besides tobacco."[124]

Byrd consulted with experts for advice and sources of vines, including Irish physician Sir Hans Sloane and English botanist Peter Collinson. Ever the

Anglophile, Byrd wrote to an expert British gardener, John Warner, for advice on how to emulate Warner's celebrated gardens at Rotherithe, which were particularly well-known for their vineyards.[125]

Byrd concurred with Robert Beverley's assertion that grapes grew best along hillsides. He was also among the first to recognize the promise that lay in grafting European vinifera grapes to the roots of native grapes to produce hybrid varieties: "I have now, above 20 sorts of vines growing," Byrd wrote in 1729, "but am told... that the way to succeed, in a vineyard, is to graft choice [European] vines, on stocks of our wild ones, to naturalize them better to our soyl & Clymate." Such forward thinking would prove vital to the rescue of French vineyards in the late nineteenth century as well as to the emergence of a Virginia wine industry in the twentieth century.[126]

By 1736, Byrd was noting the difficulties in winemaking presented by Virginia's notoriously unpredictable late spring frosts. Writing to a friend, he admitted his failures, yet underscored his determination:

> Most of my Grapes were demolished again by the frost, in the latter end of April, & what was left are discoulour'd, and drop off. This you will say is discouraging to a new beginner, yet not sufficient to shake my Perseverance.[127]

Despite his setbacks, Byrd sounded an optimistic note in a 1737 letter to English naturalist Mark Catesby:

> I cannot be of your opinion, that wine may not be made in this country. All the parts of the earth of our latitude produce good wine—and tho' it may be more difficult in one place than another, yet those difficulties may be overcome by good management, as they were at the Cape of Good Hope, where many years pass'd before they could bring it to bear.[128]

Byrd's optimism as to Virginia's viticultural promise was perhaps best described in his *Histories of the Dividing Line*, a romantic account he wrote in 1728 while surveying the boundary between Virginia and North Carolina. Largely intended for a British audience in an effort to attract settlers to his vast landholdings, Byrd wrote that he had become enamored with the idea of cultivating grapes "while surveying the boundary and seeing that vines grow very thick in these woods, twining lovingly round the trees almost everywhere, especially to the saplings. This makes it evident how natural both the soil and climate of this country are to vines, though I believe most to our own vines. The grapes we commonly met with were black, though there be two or three kinds of white grapes that grow wild."[129]

Byrd also reported the profusion of wild black and white grapes growing abundantly in the woods he surveyed: "We were so cruelly intangled with Bushes and Grape-Vines all day," he wrote. "This makes it evident how Natural both the Soil and Climate of this Country are to Vines, tho' I believe most to our own Vines."

Although arguing that it would take skilled people to properly cultivate Virginia's wild vines, Byrd wrote, "I have Drunk tolerably good Wine prest from them, tho' made without Skill. There is then good Reason to believe that it might Admit of great Improvement, if rightly managed."[130]

In May 1737, Byrd announced that he was embarking on a plan to settle Swiss immigrants on land he owned near the present-day city of Danville for the purpose of making wine. Much like the failed Manakin Town settlement some three decades earlier, Byrd hoped that a more substantial colony of 1,000 foreign families in the area would, with the help of what he termed "Moderate Industry," thrive. "Besides grazing and Tillage, which would abundantly compensate their Labour," Byrd wrote, Swiss settlers "might plant Vineyards upon the Hills, in which Situation the richest Wines are always produced."[131]

As with earlier Virginia settlement schemes, Byrd primarily promoted his southern Virginia properties through writings published abroad. Chief among these was a 1731 book he authored in German, *William Byrd's Natural History of Virginia; or, The Newly Discovered Eden*. The book was distributed throughout Europe and sought to induce German-speaking Swiss immigration to Virginia by exclaiming the virtues of the colony's favorable soil, climate characteristics, and grape varieties. Byrd even went so far as to bestow on himself a German-sounding name, "Wilhelm Vogel," which, translated literally in English, is "William Bird."[132]

While Byrd's publication of his *Natural History* had some success in attracting Swiss settlers, many of the Swiss were severely injured during foul weather while traveling through Lynnhaven Bay in the Hampton Roads area. "I was so unlucky," he lamented to his friend Peter Collinson in July 1736, "as to be disappointed of my Swiss Colony." In an attempt to hedge his bets, Byrd noted of the Swiss, "In case they should fail me a second time, I will endeavor to supply there places with Scots-Irish from Pensylvania, who flock over thither in such numbers, that there is not elbow room for them."[133]

· Byrd's subsequent colonies of Swiss or Scots-Irish immigrants regrettably failed to materialize and he never realized his "Switzer" settlement before his death in 1744. His attempt to encourage a Virginia wine industry was, however, emblematic of the seriousness with which many of the Virginia elite pursued winemaking, and his work remains one of the bright spots of wine cultivation in eighteenth-century Virginia.

## — *Resurgence of Public Interest* —

In 1753, nine years following Byrd's death, William Hunter, publisher of the *Virginia Gazette* in Williamsburg, sought to rouse Virginians to viticultural action by writing an article on the subject in his *Virginia Almanack*. The piece, written for "poor Planters," was intended to remind readers of the pecuniary advantages of making wine. Hunter provided a detailed description of grape cultivation, information on the washing and storage of grapes, and instructions on the fermentation and aging of wine.[134]

Hunter's article proved to be a harbinger of things to come. A few years following its publication, calls to diversify Virginia's economy away from tobacco, along with political pressure from some of the colony's largest landowners, sparked renewed public sector interest in viticulture. It began in 1759, when Virginia's government set aside moneys to encourage agricultural diversification and winemaking. Then, over an eight-year period beginning in 1769, public sector support reached its high-water mark when the General Assembly appropriated funds to hire a public winemaker, buy land for a public vineyard, and directly engage in winegrowing experimentation.

As might have been expected in the tortured trajectory of Virginia viticulture, these substantial public investments proved momentary. By March 1777, with the shifting of public priorities toward independence from Great Britain, Virginia's government once more diverted its energies from winemaking toward waging war. Public financial support for Virginia viticulture would not appear again for more than a century.

In 1759, at the urging of several of the colony's private landowners, Virginia's government established a prize for agricultural innovation. Such an undertaking largely resulted from the efforts of Charles Carter, the third of five sons of the politically influential and land-wealthy Robert "King" Carter. Born in Virginia and educated in England, Charles Carter served in a variety of public capacities throughout his life. He inherited sizable property holdings from his father in 1732, including a King George County estate, Cleve, which featured an imposing Georgian manor overlooking the Rappahannock River.[135]

At Cleve, Charles Carter devoted substantial efforts toward agriculture. He shared in his contemporaries' belief that Virginia's large plantations should simultaneously produce high profits and move away from their historic dependence on tobacco. In attempting to make his estate a "showplace for the profitability of commodity diversification," Carter subscribed to various mining, milling, distilling, and shipping ventures, and attempted to produce wheat and flour.[136]

Like his late father, Charles Carter invested in labor-intensive schemes, including the making of wine. It seems his curiosity for winemaking was first piqued by his 1742 marriage to Anne Byrd, daughter of former wine industry hopeful William Byrd II. By 1760, Charles claimed to have made two types of wines: one, a "light pleasant white Wine" from Portuguese summer grapes; the other a wine from a winter grape "so nauseous till a Frost that Fowls of the Air will not touch it."[137]

Charles Carter recorded his rather tedious method for propagating grapes that involved placing cuttings

> about two Foot and a half long in Rows in a Trench with the lower Butt twisted, either with or without a small horse Bean put in the Split, at any Time between the last of October and the last of February, there to remain till November following, in which Time they will have formed many Roots, then they are to be taken up and put as thick as possible in Tubs with Holes in their Bottoms, or Baskets, and some of the Earth that they werent in, made into a thin pappy Consistance, so as to fill up the Interstices between the Roots and Stems.[138]

By 1762, Cleve's vineyard reportedly boasted 1,800 vines. Despite such a large planting, Carter was apparently unable to make more than one hogshead of wine thanks to a severe summer drought.[139]

Not only did Carter promote commodity diversification at his estate, but he advocated for it in the public arena as well. In 1759, it was he who sponsored legislation in the House of Burgesses that established a nineteen-member committee for the encouragement of agricultural and industrial diversification. The committee was charged with overseeing the disbursement of £1,000 in promotional grants to anyone who produced inventions or useful discoveries that would "be of singular advantage to this colony in its present distressed situation." The legislation also permitted the committee to correspond with "all such persons as they shall judge may give them any useful insight or intelligence in any art or manufacture."[140]

Three years later, in 1762, the legislature modified the 1759 statute to provide particular enhancements to encourage the production of wine. The amended legislation was proposed by several "publick-spirited gentlemen," of whom Carter was one, and who had previously formed a private club to promote Virginia's viticultural development. The club was modeled on a well-established British organization known as the "Premium Society," which dispensed privately raised prizes to individuals who discovered new techniques or inventions useful to mankind.[141]

Sensing that the legislature's incentives were too small to spur winemaking and shift planters away from tobacco, Carter's private club requested additional public support for viticulture from the General Assembly:

> It has been long lamented that this colony should pay annually a considerable sum of money for foreign wines, often mean in quality, and at an extravagant price, when we have the greatest reason to believe our climate capable of producing as fine wines as any in the world, were the cultivation of the vineyard properly attended to.... The experiments of wine and silk are attended with little expense; and should either of them fail, the damage cannot be very great. Small premiums have been already offered by [the Premium Society] in England, and the committee of arts and manufactures in this colony; but such is the force of habit that we have little reason to expect any benefit from these. The prospect of future distant advantage is not strong enough to engage our attention: And we shall find the [tobacco] planter continue, without deviation, in the beaten tract, until he is roused by some great and certain profit.[142]

In response, the legislature ordered that a new £500 award be given each October 30th "to the person who shall in any one year from that date make the best wine, in quantity not less than ten hogsheads." A second-place prize of £100 was also authorized, and funding for the prizes was to be raised by Carter's organization, which would choose the winners.[143]

Charles Carter, selected as chairman of the new committee, initiated correspondence with Peter Wyche, chairman of the London Premium Society's Committee of Agriculture. The two exchanged several letters between 1761 and 1763 covering a broad range of topics, from winemaking to Virginia's economic outlook to ideas for diversifying the colony's agricultural sector.

Carter's first letter, written in early May 1761, provided Wyche with an introduction to Virginia's economy and bemoaned the colony's unhealthy dependence on tobacco. Hoping to emulate the Premium Society's practices and quality, Carter proposed to Wyche a variety of potential alternative commodities that might be appropriate for Virginia, including the establishment of a wine industry. To this end, Carter put forward the cultivation of French, Spanish, Portuguese, Madeira, Fayal, Tenerife, and Canary Island grape varieties. He also suggested that the foreign grapes should be discreetly procured so as not to give off the impression that Virginia sought to rival any of the great world wine powers.[144]

Wyche responded late in May 1761, but was cool to the idea of a Virginia wine industry. Though he had never visited Virginia, Wyche confidently asserted that Virginia's topography was too flat and its soil too rich to cultivate wine grapes properly. Moreover, because Virginia was geographically situated some ten latitudinal degrees south of France, the colony's excessive heat would make grape-growing difficult. If Carter was intent on starting a wine industry, Wyche wrote, he might compensate for Virginia's shortcomings by trellising wine grapes on the understories of trees—particularly orange or lime trees—that offered canopies to protect the grapes in times of heavy rains and droughts.[145]

Wyche's suggestions echoed those of British actor and writer Aaron Hill, whose "Directions for Cultivating Vines in America" was published in a 1759 reference book, the *Annual Register*. Like Wyche, Hill had never visited America and yet felt himself an authority on the subject. Virginia, Hill wrote, was "too rich and too oily," and the climate too hot, all of which "excit[ed] a rapid and strong fermentation" and contributed to "clammy" grapes that produced a "turbid must" and a coarse pulp that "floats up and down in the liquor." Hill also admonished Virginians for looking to "Frenchmen as the only men proper to instruct them" in winemaking and instead suggested that Spaniards, with their similar latitude, would perform far better.[146]

Hoping to prove Wyche—and perhaps Aaron Hill—wrong, Charles Carter dispatched a sample of his late-harvest White Lisbon and winter grape wines to the Premium Society in May 1762. Surprisingly, Wyche responded that while members of the Premium Society had never heard of the native American winter grape, they nevertheless judged Carter's wines "good" and thought them pleasing and sweet. Wyche even asserted that Carter's wines were good enough to compete with sweet German wines, then in vogue.[147]

In recognition of Charles Carter's efforts, Wyche's Premium Society awarded him a gold medal in 1763 "as the first who had made a spirited attempt toward the accomplishment of [the Premium Society's] views respecting wine in America." Acknowledging Carter's efforts, Wyche crowned him the "Heroe" of the Virginia committee's efforts—a citation that engendered a certain level of jealousy among Carter's fellow committeemen.[148]

While Charles Carter's correspondence with the Premium Society undoubtedly expanded inter-hemispheric knowledge about winemaking and other potential colonial industries, one historian noted that "none of the projects discussed ever developed into a major crop or dominant industry of the colony." Records do, however, indicate that the Carter-Wyche exchanges may have led to the exportation of 135 gallons of Virginia wine to England in 1768.[149]

Whatever the effect of Virginia's 1759 and 1762 legislation, at the close of his life Charles Carter believed he had sufficiently diversified his agricultural enterprises at Cleve, and he reveled in his establishment of a new system of land cultivation. By 1763, one year before his death, a certified statement attested to by Virginia governor Francis Fauquier noted that Carter's vineyard boasted 1,500 mature vines and 1,200 young vines of red and white Portuguese grapes, and that the vineyard was well-tended.[150]

Charles Carter prepared a directional manuscript for his heirs that was to govern Cleve following his passing, entitled *A new system of Virginia Husbandry, or the Little farm improved wherein the business of making Tobo., farming, improving lands and making Wine. are largely treated of and earnestly recommended.* As one might imagine from the length of the title alone, his son, Charles Carter, Jr., found his father's orders difficult to comprehend and costly to implement.[151]

Charles Carter's commitment to agricultural diversification at Cleve was, however, shared by his brother, Colonel Landon Carter. Like Charles Carter, Landon Carter had inherited significant property holdings from his father, including land on the Northern Neck in Richmond County. There, between 1738 and 1744, Landon Carter built Sabine Hall, a stately Georgian brick manor with architectural materials and features designed to convey a sense of familial perpetuity and social rank.[152]

Following in the footsteps of William Byrd II, Landon Carter kept a detailed journal of his plantings and agricultural pursuits. Further emulating Byrd and his brother Charles Carter, Landon Carter appears to have been driven to impress others with his agricultural skill and spent nearly five decades focusing attention on Sabine Hall's fields, orchards, and gardens.[153]

Landon Carter made his first batch of wine as early as 1763 which, after sampling the following year, he found to be lacking. Between 1763 and 1766, his diary reflected his dismay that three consecutive wet springs and summers had all but destroyed his grape crop. In an effort to protect the vines from heavy precipitation, Carter planted peach trees around the vines, which he later cut down believing that they retained too much moisture.[154]

In October 1777, Landon Carter made some fifty gallons of "pleasant wine." To ensure its drinkability, he used a tedious and unconventional winemaking process. After spending three days of gathering grapes, for example, he engaged in a cumbersome procedure to hasten their ripening without bruising the fruit, and then boiled the grapes to obtain a reddish color. He then added honey for a sweetener and brandy to "give it strength" and prevent acidity. He allowed the wine to ferment for four days before placing it in a cask. Hoping to obtain a "pleasant liquor," he bottled the beverage and stored it in dry sand.[155]

As noted, Virginia's establishment of a winemaking prize in 1762 was followed in 1769 by an even more substantial public viticultural attempt. This time, the government established its own vineyard and hired employees for grape experimentation at public expense.

The idea for a public vineyard came at the behest of André Estave, a Frenchman who had arrived in Virginia two years before. At the time, Estave worked in Williamsburg and was convinced that the colony's previously unsuccessful wine initiatives was owed to a lack of the vintner's skill. To be truly successful in producing "very fine wine," Estave argued that the colonial legislature must directly assist in its manufacture.[156]

Claiming to have conducted an in-depth study of Virginia's soils and believing that the colony's natural grapes would prove larger and "better tasted" than the wild grapes of France if properly cultivated, Estave requested that the General Assembly establish a public vineyard under his management. In return, he guaranteed the production of wine within four years.

The legislature—perhaps eager to assist once more in this latest attempt at economic diversification at the request of a Frenchman—approved an "Act for Encouraging the Making of Wine" in November 1769, noting that:

> the climate, soil, and natural productions of this colony, make it very probable that the most delicious wines might be made here, and [its] introduction... would bring great riches to the people, and give a very favourable turn to the commerce of the mother country [Great Britain].[157]

The General Assembly hoped that the venture would both "serve as an object lesson to planters" and spark a large wine industry that could compete with expensive foreign wines. To oversee the enterprise, the legislature appointed a board of trustees consisting of nine prominent planters and politicians from eastern Virginia. The trustees were given £450 to purchase 100 acres near Williamsburg that was "fit for the culture of vines," and construct a home for Mr. Estave. They were also directed to purchase three slaves and three other "poor boys" to serve as indentured apprentices.[158]

Acreage was purchased just east of Williamsburg, and Estave was granted six years to establish a vineyard and produce ten hogsheads (630 gallons) of "good merchantable wine" to the satisfaction of a majority of the trustees. Should he succeed, the trustees were directed to convey the land and slaves to Estave as compensation.[159]

By 1772—two years into the venture—all appeared to be going according to plan. Estave reported to the trustees that he was diligently attending to his vineyard and was "convinced of the Practicability of the Scheme." While he alleged that his vines—which reportedly consisted of both native and European varietals—were "thriving," Estave admitted that he had experienced some difficulties with his servants and was forced to fire one for being "unprofitable."[160]

Despite public claims of success, Estave's vineyard suffered from poor management. Estave, for example, was notorious for his cruel and inhuman treatment of his slaves. Between 1771 and 1776, no fewer than six slaves ran away. In the summer of 1775, one fifteen-year-old enslaved women ran away three times—she was each time captured and punished with forty lashes. During her fourth attempt to flee, the girl fled to the Governor's Palace in Williamsburg to seek sanctuary directly from Governor Dunmore. She was returned. Estave administered eighty lashes and poured fire embers on her back.[161]

In March 1773, three-and-a-half years into his winemaking endeavor, Estave replanted his vineyard exclusively with native grapes after failing to grow European vinifera successfully. Self-appointed as the colony's official viticulturist, Estave wrote in the *Virginia Gazette* that the reason Virginians had not yet succeeded in grape-growing was primarily due to their insistence on cultivating exotic, foreign grapes.

He argued that foreign varieties were ill-suited to Virginia's growing conditions as they were "exposed to too many and great Inconveniences," including worms and insects, heavy rains, and excessive heat. These factors, he concluded, resulted in an evaporation of the foreign grapes' "spirit" and forced them to ripen two months earlier than native grapes.[162]

Estave also asserted that only native grapes could be successfully grown in Virginia and that a properly cultivated vineyard would result in such grapes that were "infinitely richer," more "spirituous," and one-third larger than those left to grow in the wild. Mindful of growing public impatience for results, particularly in the face of two years of drought, Estave noted,

> The Vineyard which I planted has appeared, hitherto, to answer so little to the Expectations of People that many begin to despair of its Success, but I beseech them to suspend for a While their Judgment.... Yet I hope,

notwithstanding, with Heavens' Assistance, to fulfill my Obligation before the Expiration of the Time with which I have been indulged.[163]

In May 1774, nearly five years on, Estave's project suffered from a harsh late May frost. According to the *Virginia Gazette*, the unseasonable frost had affected the entire colony and "was the severest, at this Season of the Year, ever remembered." The *Gazette* noted that "The Fruit, of all Sorts, is destroyed every Where but upon the Rivers; Vines, of all Kinds, are killed."[164]

Estave was devastated and in desperate need of additional funds. Professing to need a cellar press, he again requested additional funding. Growing weary of Estave's excuses, however, the General Assembly had failed to act on his request by the close of the 1774 session and no records indicate money was allocated.

One year later, with no wine to show for nearly six years of efforts, Estave's vines were again damaged, this time by hail. By this point, Estave had apparently switched to raising silkworms instead of grapes, though he reported to the *Virginia Gazette* that he had a "prospect of making three or four hogsheads of wine" by the fall of 1775.[165]

By October 1776, still no wine appeared. The General Assembly finally gave up on Estave's project, and passed legislation to dispose of the vineyard, house, and slaves. Curiously, the legislature laid the blame squarely on the vineyard as being "unfit for that purpose," rather than Estave.

The legislation dissolving the venture noted that the slaves and the land under Estave's management had become "useless, and of no advantage to the publick." The property, equipment, and slaves were listed for sale in February 1777 and in June of that year, brought £560.50.[166]

Estave reportedly fled to Georgia after the Revolution, where he continued to exude confidence, telling at least one person of his ability to "cultivate the native vines of any country, preferably to exotics." Given that he had failed to produce "good merchantable wine" after six years in the Old Dominion, it is doubtful he was ever successful in the Peach State.[167]

Though Estave enjoyed the support of the General Assembly and several prominent planters during the operation of his public vineyard, his efforts were not met with universal acclaim. He met with criticism particularly from a young Buckingham County landowner, Colonel Robert Bolling, Jr. A purported descendant of Pocahontas and member of an aristocratic family, Bolling was educated in England and had studied law in Williamsburg before serving in a variety of public capacities, including service as a member of the House of Burgesses.[168]

During his short thirty-seven-year life, Bolling developed a reputation as a gifted linguist as well as a man of "strong principles" and an "irrepressible pen" who would become one of the most prolific poets of his era. Bolling's works were published in several British and American literary journals, and he left behind several volumes of poetry at his death. He frequently wrote in Latin, Italian, and French; indeed, he mastered the last so well as to write a history of the Virginia branch of the Bolling family entirely in that tongue.[169]

As with other prominent Virginia planters, Bolling enjoyed a taste for wine and became interested in mastering viticulture and winemaking. As early as 1767, he attempted to produce wine from native summer bunch grapes that grew wild in the woods surrounding his large tobacco plantation, Chellow. He found the wine to be highly acidic and attributed the repugnant taste to the wine's native grapes that he described as "too pulpy…whence a thin acid Liquor." After this single failure with native varieties, Bolling developed an unshakable opinion that quality wine could only be produced from European grape varieties.[170]

In 1773, after planting a four-acre European vinifera vineyard at Chellow, Bolling penned one of the earliest serious studies of viticulture written by an American for Americans. The treatise, written to "the increase of happiness, of numbers, of industry, of opulence," was divided into two volumes. The first, *Pieces Concerning Vineyards & Their Establishment in Virginia*, was published in the *Virginia Gazette* in 1773; the second, *A Sketch of Vine Culture for Pennsylvania, Maryland, Virginia and the Carolinas*, likely composed between 1774 and 1775, was never published in its entirety.[171]

Material for the two books was gleaned from Bolling's personal observations as well as from other writings by eminent European agricultural writers, including the Roman agricultural writer Columella, the Roman poet Virgil, French agronomist and winemaker Nicolas Bidet, and British agricultural writer John Mills. Bolling also drew heavily from Edward Antill's 1769 work, *An Essay on the Cultivation of the Vine, and the Making of Wine, Suited to the Different Climates in North America*," first published after Antill's death in 1771.[172]

Aside from using his writings to advance his view of the benefits of planting of European vinifera, Bolling's works described the organic parts of the vine, methods of cultivating grapes, pruning, and the effects of various soils. Much like William Byrd II, Bolling was among the first to advocate for, and predict the attraction to, the hybridization of native and foreign vines:

> Would it not be well for us to attempt the raising of some new varieties, by marrying our native with foreign vines? The plan is this; plant each kind, alternately, in the same row. Put up posts and lathes to tie them up

to; and, in trailing them on these, so interlock their branches that they shall be completely blended together. They will feed from the blossoms of each other, and when the fruit is ripe, if seeds are saved from it and sown in nurseries, suffering them to remain therein till they begin to bear, that we may the better judge of them, it is probable we may obtain varieties better adapted to our soils and climates, and better for wine or the table, than either of those kinds from whence they sprang.[173]

Bolling was a firm believer that a high-quality wine industry in Virginia would afford, among other things, substantial employment, easier purchase of expensive foreign wines, greater exports to England, the introduction of a glass-blowing industry in Virginia, and enhanced values for mountainous timber lands.

Though bullish on grape-growing generally, Bolling's appreciation for Virginia viticulture did not extend to Estave's efforts at the Williamsburg public vineyard. He not only believed that little would come of Estave's efforts, but given his own negative experiences with native grapes, he also countered Estave's contentions that Virginians should focus on the cultivation of native varieties at the expense of European vinifera. Bolling also disagreed with Estave's promotion of the Tidewater area of Virginia as the only suitable region for viticulture, instead believing that the hilly, well-drained soils of his native western Virginia were best matched to grape-growing.[174]

In February 1773, Bolling made his feelings on Estave's vineyard publicly known. He published his lengthy "Essay on the Utility of Vine Planting in Virginia" in the *Virginia Gazette*, criticizing the General Assembly's public expenditures for Estave's vineyard, the limitations of Estave's work, and Estave's focus on native varietals. Bolling's letter questioned the efficacy of Estave's efforts, particularly considering that no prior attempt at native grape production had yet delivered a wine industry in the colony. He advocated the cultivation of European varietals in Virginia much in the way those same varietals had been successfully grown elsewhere:

> Let us, with the utmost Expedition, provide Vineyards in various remote Counties, and in Places where it would be lost Labour to cultivate Tobacco. Let Orphan and spurious Children be bound to the Managers, and let us procure foreign Viners, and Vines from the same Countries whence we draw our Viners.[175]

Whatever his motivation—whether to discredit Estave or promote himself—Bolling's letter resulted in the House of Burgesses granting him a £50 annual stipend in March 1773, for a period of five years, for the purpose of cultivating grapes and making wine in Virginia's upper mountainous regions. A competition was now on: on one side, a self-professed French winemaking expert growing native vines in the lowland areas of Virginia; on the other, a well-heeled planter growing vinifera vines in the hilly, well-drained Piedmont region of the colony.

Estave was quick to respond to Bolling's broadside, writing in the *Virginia Gazette* the following month that he did not "[pretend] to place [him]self on the same parallel, or engage in any Competition with its respectable Author [Bolling]." Rather, Estave demurely asserted that the "little Experience" he had gathered in four years of cultivating vines at the Williamsburg public vineyard suggested to him that native vines grew better in the lower Tidewater areas of Virginia and were capable of making high-quality wine.

Whether out of actual humility, political expediency, or simply to put the issue to rest, Estave conceded that his knowledge was limited to the Tidewater areas of the colony and that the higher areas "being altogether unknown to [him], may justify perhaps the Opinion of Colonel Bolling, and be more favourable to the Cultivation of Foreign Vines."[176]

Nonetheless, Bolling fired another salvo at Estave in July 1773 by publishing an open letter "To the Friends To Vine-Planting" in the *Virginia Gazette*. He suggested that Virginians should plant only foreign grapes since the juice culled from native grapes was "not spirituous enough to furnish the Wine obtained from them with a sufficient Body." Bolling also alleged that the while the colony's government "has unhappily a great Partiality for native Vines," Virginia must "like the different People of Europe who make Wine, import foreign Vines, and expect Success from a judicious Choice."[177]

Estave responded in turn, defending the worth of his native grapes in a September 1773 edition of the *Virginia Gazette*. This time, Estave claimed that while it was still too early to judge the results, his public experiment at Williamsburg was the colony's only major effort to transplant, enclose, cultivate, and dress native vines in the European manner. But, he cautioned, it was still too early to criticize the results: "If all this has been done, and yet their Product has appeared not superior to that of the wild unmanaged Vine, I yield," Estave asserted. "But no one, I imagine," he continued, "has a Right to condemn it until the Experiment has been fairly made."[178]

The broadside feud between Bolling and Estave simmered during the cold winter of 1773–1774, but Bolling never issued a reply to Estave's September 1773 defense. His distaste for Estave was apparently strong enough, however, as to have extended to Bolling's private life. Bolling authored a series of unpublished poems strongly criticizing Estave:

Let Estave, to end the quarrel,
Let Estave produce a barrel!
Here's a goblet, here's a borer:
Drink to Bacchus peace-restorer.
Let us drink of our own pressing
Why postpone so great a blessing?...

Estave, if I must celebrate
The wonders of your art
My thirsty soul first recreate....
The purple juice impart.[179]

The dispute between the two was never resolved. In July 1775, while representing Buckingham County at the Third Virginia Revolutionary Convention in Richmond, Bolling died suddenly, at the age of 37. His death occurred before his vineyard at Chellow could mature. Two months later, in September 1775, however, an unsigned article appeared in the *Virginia Gazette* suggesting that Bolling's vision might yet still bear fruit:

> The vines planted by Mr. Bolling in the County of Buckingham, although managed according to the directions of the French writers of the 48th and 49th degrees of latitude, are in a condition to yield wine the ensuing year, if well attended to. The slips planted by that gentleman the last year, after the method of the vignerons of Europe inhabiting a climate similar to our own, have now the appearance of vines 3 or 4 years old. A slip planted by him in the spring of the present year has produced two bunches of grapes; a fact which would not be believed in the wine countries of the old world.[180]

Bolling's son Lenæus Bolling evidently continued his father's farming tradition, but he later wrote that his father's untimely passing, on the eve of the American Revolution, combined with the "confusion produced by the war," rendered Chellow's "promising and flourishing little vineyard...totally neglected and finally perished." Lenæus Bolling also noted that his father had endeavored to "afford his countrymen a practical demonstration of the facility and certainty with which grapes might be raised, and wine made, in Virginia."[181]

Bolling's was a worthwhile endeavor, yet despite the heated feud between Bolling and Estave, both failed. Moreover, Bolling's death in 1775 and the termination of Estave's public vineyard two years later left the great question of native versus vinifera grapes unresolved, and thus ended t he last of the public monetary subsidies for winemaking for two centuries.[182]

## —*Philip Mazzei*—

Philip Mazzei, a most colorful personality, deserves special mention in the history of Virginia wine, not only for the contributions he made to Virginia's viticultural heritage, but also for being one of only a handful of Italians to participate in the colony's struggle for independence from Great Britain. An intellectually curious farmer, raconteur, physician, philosopher, diplomat, and patriot, Mazzei had a charm that endeared him to many of Virginia's elite during the latter half of the eighteenth century, none more so than Thomas Jefferson.[183]

A native of Poggio a Caiano, a small village west of Florence, Italy, Mazzei was born in 1730 to a merchant family. He initially sought a surgical degree, but voluntarily withdrew at the request of hospital administrators: he was found drinking wine before taking communion one Holy Thursday. He subsequently relocated to the town of Leghorn (now Livorno) to practice medicine and later practiced in Smyrna (now Izmir), Turkey.

Mazzei immigrated to London in 1756 to serve as an agent of the Grand Duke of Tuscany. He sold Turkish goods, gave Italian lessons, and established a small importation firm for Italian products. In 1767, Mazzei met Benjamin Franklin and a Virginia businessman, Thomas Adams, both of whom were visiting London and were impressed by Mazzei's credentials and political convictions.

Mazzei was equally captivated by Franklin and Adams's democratic beliefs, and was later introduced to several other influential Virginians. At Adams's urging, and believing Virginia to be suitable for growing Mediterranean produce, Mazzei determined to form a company to manufacture and produce Mediterranean wine, oil, plants, and silk in Virginia.[184]

By 1771, Mazzei's plans called for the growing of Mediterranean commodities on approximately 4,000 acres "in the back part of Virginia where hills and risen ground favor the cultivation of the vine and olive trees," as well as the importation of thousands of olive and fruit trees. Some 10,000 grapevines were to be selected from Portugal, France, and Spain and shipped to Virginia. To assist, Mazzei proposed hiring some fifty farmers skilled in wine and silk production for a term of four years. Unable to finance his ambitious proposal, however, he scaled back his plans and instead planned to send 1,000 grapevines and ten skilled indentured vignerons to Virginia.[185]

By 1773, Mazzei had obtained permission from the Grand Duke and, in exchange, Mazzei was to ship Virginia grain, tobacco, and animals to Tuscany.

That September, Mazzei joined his crew, plantings, his wife-to-be and her daughter, as well as ten Italian vine dressers, and set sail for Virginia. He arrived in the colony late in November and stayed with Thomas Jefferson's brother-in-law, Francis Eppes, near Williamsburg. Mazzei was introduced to Virginia luminaries, including George Washington, Thomas Jefferson, and George Wythe.[186]

Thomas Adams, who had met Mazzei in London, arrived ahead of Mazzei and secured from the Virginia House of Burgesses a public grant of approximately 5,000 acres for Mazzei's import-export venture. Mazzei declined the offer on learning the grant was split into several tracts that would make managing his enterprise difficult. As an alternative, Mazzei agreed to consider land that adjoined Adams's property in Augusta County in the Shenandoah Valley.[187]

Mazzei and Adams headed west to view the property and stopped to visit Thomas Jefferson at Monticello late one night. Early the following morning, Mazzei accompanied Jefferson on a tour of Monticello, during which Jefferson showed Mazzei beautiful views of the surrounding valley. Jefferson was consistently interested in befriending sophisticated men who could help with his own personal horticultural pursuits, and offered Mazzei assistance in securing use of a fifty-acre property adjoining Monticello.[188]

Jefferson also suggested that a small cottage on the property would be suitable for Mazzei's ten workers and, as an added benefit, offered Mazzei an additional 2,000 acres adjoining the east side of Monticello along the southeastern face of the Green Mountains near Jefferson's birthplace at Shadwell. The property had "a southeast aspect and an abundance of lean and meagre spots of stony and red soil, without sand," Jefferson later wrote, "resembling extremely the Cote of Burgundy from Chambertin to Montrachet where the famous wines of Burgundy are made."[189]

Mazzei agreed to Jefferson's proposal, and the two returned to Monticello to inform Adams. Mazzei later recalled that Adams sensed immediately that Jefferson had persuaded Mazzei to stay: "By the time we returned home, everyone was up," Mazzei wrote. "Looking at Mr. Jefferson, Mr. Adams said: 'I see by your expression that you've taken him away from me. I knew you would do that.'" Jefferson shrugged off the comment, "Let's take breakfast, and later we'll arrange everything."[190]

Mazzei's vignerons arrived at Monticello several days later and, in the spirit of Virginia's prior French and German immigrant colonies, his property soon became a quasi-Italian settlement. The workers immediately began clearing additional land atop a small hill for Mazzei's house, which he named "Colle" ("hill" in Italian), while one of Mazzei's workers reportedly made Jefferson an

Italian hunting suit. The workers also planted Italian grapes, melons, nuts, and other vegetables.[191]

It was to wine, though, that Mazzei and his workers devoted their attention. Mazzei was immediately impressed with Colle's potential for viticulture, and soon found thirty-six native varietals on his property. He recalled that two of the vines were more than "a yard and a half in circumference." Based on these initial observations, Mazzei exclaimed that "especially in Virginia, nature seems to favor vineyards. I have never seen such perfect, varied, and abundant wild grapes." Such findings also undoubtedly led him to write to George Washington, "This country is better calculated than any other than I am acquainted with for growing wine."[192]

While it is likely that Mazzei's first vines were planted in the spring of 1774, they were struck that May by the same unusual late spring frost that killed Andrew Estave's grapes at the public vineyard in Williamsburg. Mazzei recounted the experience,

> On the night of May 4, 1774, a frost, caused by a northwest wind, ruined the corn and the wheat just above the ground, froze the small oak and other young trees, and caused all other trees to shed their leaves, which did not bud again until the following year. It was horrible to see the woods entirely stripped of leaves in summer, as if it had been mid-winter. The bunches of grapes were already quite large, but they froze with the new crop. The old part of the vine, from which the branches had sprung, suffered too. But the vines put out new shoots, which produced about half the amount of grapes of the preceding years, and ripened at the usual season in the woods and gardens.[193]

Despite the challenges of Virginia's weather, Mazzei brought an additional six Italian vignerons across the Atlantic later that summer. Accompanying the new vignerons were "sundry Seeds, Vine Cuttings, Plants, etc." along with some 1,500 Tuscan vinifera grapevines that were planted in June 1775. While only half of these were successfully rooted, Mazzei recalled that they "produced grapes with more flavor and substance than those grown in Italy." Mazzei also cultivated a shoot of the Lugliana e Lugliola dei Toscani grape that was evidently such a success that an Italian colleague remarked to him, "Master, don't write home about it, because nobody there would believe you and they would call you a liar."[194]

By the fall of 1774, Mazzei had developed yet another detailed proposal for a wine, silk, citrus fruit, and oil corporation. He raised some £2,000 to finance the effort from £50 subscriptions pledged by several of Virginia's social and political elite—many of whom had supported Virginia's past viticultural endeavors, including George Mason, George Washington, Governor Dunmore, and Thomas Jefferson (the latter of whom later purchased two subscriptions).[195]

Mazzei added another 2,000 native grape cuttings in the spring of 1776 from which he produced two barrels of wine. He recorded that the wine was comparable in quality to wines made in France and Italy and, after pulling the cork three months later, "it was like the sparkling wine of Champagne." Mazzei distributed all but one bottle to his men, who subsequently sold the bottles for one shilling each.[196]

As was the case with practically every other significant attempt at winemaking in the colony, Mazzei's role was but fleeting. He became a naturalized citizen on the eve of the American Revolution in 1774 and his desire to further the cause of American independence quickly came to dominate his priorities. He authored a series of patriotic writings published in the *Virginia Gazette* during 1774 and 1775 under the pseudonym "Furioso" in which he staunchly defended the American cause.[197]

Mazzei also spent an increasing amount of time in Williamsburg and, following the landing of British troops in nearby Hampton, joined Jefferson and other Albemarle County property owners in enlisting in the Albemarle Independent Company, a patriotic volunteer unit. His intense political interests and aspirations came at the expense of his viticultural endeavors at Colle. "I have not said much about my agriculture," he wrote, "for I did not attend to it as I should have, because the great public issue occupied almost all of my time." Despite his frequent absences from Colle, Mazzei wrote that "from time to time I went home to see how my orders were being carried out, and to issue new ones."[198]

With the Revolutionary War dragging on into its third year by late in 1778, Mazzei was persuaded by Patrick Henry, George Mason, and Thomas Jefferson to intervene with the Duke of Tuscany to secure war supplies and a loan for the Revolutionary cause. After he departed Virginia for Italy early in 1779, Mazzei's vineyard operations were disbanded and his remaining vine dressers either enlisted in the Continental army or were hired as gardeners by others.[199]

At Jefferson's urging, Mazzei rented Colle to Major General Friedrich Adolf Riedesel, a German prisoner of war captured after the Battle of Saratoga who was awaiting a prisoner exchange. Jefferson recalled several years later that the leasing of the property led to the vineyard's demise, for within a week of taking over the property, Riedesel's horses "destroyed the whole labor of three or four years, and thus ended an experiment which, from every appearance would in a year or two more have established the practicability of that branch of Culture in America." Another account, however, holds that the vineyard's destruction was caused by several British officers who stayed at Colle prior to Riedesel's arrival.[200]

Regardless of the cause, Mazzei returned in 1783 to find his home a victim of the Revolution. He also was saddened to find that his good friend Thomas Jefferson had left to serve as a minister to France. This, along with a reluctance to be separated from his wife, seems to have led Mazzei to return to Europe in July 1785. Before departing Virginia one last time, however, Mazzei joined James Madison, James Monroe, and Patrick Henry in organizing the "Constitution Society," formed in 1784 and dedicated to the maintenance of a constitutional democracy in America.[201]

After his return to Europe, Mazzei reunited with Jefferson in Paris and traveled extensively promoting American democracy. He also authored a four-volume historical defense of the United States, *Historical and Political Enquiries Concerning the United States of North America*, which was translated into French. The book, published in 1788, was intended as a "complete, impartial description" of the new United States as a defense against contemporary public attacks made by French writers. In a proud nod to his American citizenship, Mazzei signed the book "By a Citizen of Virginia."[202]

During his travels across Europe, Mazzei also became acquainted with Polish King Stanislaw II, who appointed him privy counselor and later a diplomat in Paris during the French Revolution. Following the overthrow of France's King Louis XVI in 1793, Mazzei fled to Warsaw where he remained until just prior to Stanislaw's abdication in 1795. Mazzei subsequently returned to his native Italy, where he continued to correspond with Jefferson, Madison, and others, before dying in Pisa in March 1816 at the age of eighty-five.[203]

Colle, the Albemarle County home where he planted his first vineyards in the shadow of Monticello, was razed in 1933, but portions were incorporated into additions to the historic Michie Tavern. Mazzei's vineyards have long since disappeared and were reclaimed by the forest that was once cleared by Mazzei's vignerons.

Despite the absence of lasting imprints on Virginia's landscape, Mazzei's time in Virginia had an enduring effect on the viticultural philosophy of the commonwealth. As with his predecessors, he was persistently optimistic as to the promise of Virginia wine, and believed in America's slow but certain path toward a role as a viticultural colossus: "In my opinion," he wrote July 1774 following the destructive May frost, "when the country is populated in proportion to its size, the best wine in the world will be made here."[204]

Mazzei also left a political impact on his adopted country. Aside from his service during the American Revolution, he secured the work of two Italian sculptors—Andrei and Giuseppe Franzoni—to assist architect Benjamin Latrobe in designing friezes and sculpture for the new United States Capitol.

His efforts earned Mazzei a United States postage stamp issued in his honor in 1982. Felicia Warburg Rogan, the founder of Albemarle County's Oakencroft Vineyards, wrote in commemoration of the stamp's issuance that, "had not the American Revolution taken place, the stamp might well have been issued anyway, honoring Mazzei not as a patriot but rather as the father of viticulture and wine-making in America."[205]

In the end, it was Mazzei's attachment to the United States that left him forever regretting his departure for Europe in 1785. Writing to James Madison just prior to leaving America for the last time that June, he wrote,

> America is my Jupiter, Virginia my Venus. When I consider what I felt on crossing the Potomac, I am ashamed of my weakness. I do not know what will happen as I lose sight of Sandy Hook. I am well awayre that no matter where or in what situation I may be, I shall never tire of exerting myself for the prosperity of my dear adoptive country.[206]

He never did.

## —The Father of American Wine—

Much has been written of the wine preferences, habits, and viticultural curiosity of the nation's third president. Thomas Jefferson was a committed oenophile throughout his life, but it must be acknowledged that he was neither the first Virginian to attempt to grow vinifera, nor the most successful. Yet, no history of wine in Virginia, or of the industry's growth in America, would be complete without a nod to this enigmatic and extraordinarily influential man.

Jefferson is, of course, known today for many things: the author of the Declaration of Independence and the Virginia Statute for Religious Freedom, the founder of the University of Virginia, a delegate of the Continental Congress, governor of Virginia, and ambassador to France. He was a scholar, architect, inventor, and lawyer. It was in the realm of viticulture, however, that his life's experiences transformed him into the eighteenth century's most-distinguished wine connoisseur and the nation's foremost advocate for the development of a domestic wine industry. Put simply, no figure had a more profound impact on and enduring legacy for the future of American viticulture.[207]

Born April 2, 1743, at Shadwell plantation east of Charlottesville, Jefferson delighted in the natural world. Tom spent his youth in the woods and open fields of rural Albemarle County, and he enjoyed reading about agriculture and horticulture. His formative experiences led to a lifelong interest in horticultural experimentation and a seemingly insatiable appetite for all manner of agricultural pursuits. As he confided to a friend during retirement,

> I have often thought, that if heaven had given me choice of my position and calling, it should have been on a rich spot of earth, well watered, and near a good market for the productions of the garden. No occupation is so delightful to me as the culture of the earth.[208]

Jefferson promoted farming as an occupation that offered both income potential, a satisfactory manner of living, and the best chance for America to become economically independent of Great Britain. He spent much of his life gathering agrarian information he believed to be useful to his fellow countrymen, and toyed with the development of fertilizer, farm machinery, crop rotation techniques, and animal husbandry.[209]

Jefferson's lifelong appetite for agricultural improvement was particularly robust in the realm of wine. He experimented with grapes, kept meticulous records of his wine purchases, and wrote more on the subject than any of his contemporaries. While he favored sweeter and fortified port, claret, and Madeira wines earlier in his life, he later grew so fond of drier, less-alcoholic Bordeaux and Burgundy wines that his passion often proved a financial liability.[210]

Simultaneously pragmatic and idealistic, Jefferson worked to imbue his fellow countrymen with an affection for sophisticated European wine styles. Familiarizing the populace with wine, he reasoned, would have a positive effect on the morals, manners, and customs of his fellow citizens. He believed good wine to be a necessity of life, and a beverage of temperance, one that possessed curative powers. Viticulture also provided an opportunity for agricultural diversification and a chance for agricultural independence from Europe; thus, he actively encouraged any new attempt at American winemaking.[211]

Jefferson announced his view that American viticulture would, in due course, rival Europe's most renowned winegrowing regions. "We could, in the United States," he wrote in 1808, "make as great a variety of wines as are made in Europe, not exactly of the same kinds, but doubtless as good." As time would prove, however, Jefferson's hopes for viticulture in America were as optimistic as his personal viticultural pursuits were experimental.[212]

In 1760, the seventeen-year-old Jefferson enrolled at the College of William and Mary, in the then-colonial capital at Williamsburg. He quickly developed a reputation for studiousness and, two years later, found himself studying law under America's first law professor, the great, if largely unsung, George Wythe.

It is probable that Jefferson's first introduction to wine came during this time, for he socialized in elevated circles and often dined with royal governor Sir Francis Fauquier and Wythe, the latter of whom, at least, had a decided penchant for wine.[213]

Following his father's death, and his inheritance of some 2,750 acres, Jefferson returned to Shadwell in 1764 and established a successful law practice in Albemarle and the Shenandoah Valley, from Staunton to Winchester. He was elected to the Virginia House of Burgesses in 1769. One year later, Jefferson moved to Monticello, his new home then under construction. Building began in 1768; it would take him another forty years to complete if, indeed, it can be truly said that it was ever finished.

Like his Italian friend Philip Mazzei, Jefferson was consumed by political events between 1775 and 1784. He was elected a delegate to the Second Continental Congress in March 1775, where he was again exposed to wine—most likely Madeira and port wines—in the company of America's revolutionary elite. He assumed Virginia's governorship in 1779 in the midst of the Revolution, and, while briefly residing once more in Williamsburg, he no doubt observed and enjoyed the extensive wine cellar at the Governor's Palace, perhaps especially as the royal governor was involuntarily absent.[214]

After two terms as governor, Jefferson returned to Monticello in 1781 to focus on his long-neglected domestic affairs. The next year, his wife Martha Jefferson died following the birth of her sixth child. Martha's premature death, at least in part, prompted Jefferson's return to public service, this time as a delegate to the Continental Congress in Annapolis. His time there was also short-lived; disappointed with the political infighting, Jefferson accepted an appointment to join John Adams and Benjamin Franklin as a special trade minister to France in 1784, at the age of 41.

Though he was sent to Paris to seek out new markets for American goods and to make commercial treaties with European nations, Jefferson's extended appointment to the court of Louis XVI between August 1784 and September 1789 caused a second revolution in his ideas and tastes. He promptly established himself in Paris and adopted a respectable and comfortable lifestyle commensurate with his prestigious post. He spent much of his first year organizing his home and staff, and dining with Adams and Franklin, both of whom were oenophiles with sizable wine collections. Jefferson collected art, ordered furniture, made notes about the types of wine served at various functions, and promptly ordered his own from Europe's finest wine houses. It was here that he developed a taste for drier, more flavorful, and less alcoholic fine French and Italian wines, and even experimented with grape-growing in his Paris garden.[215]

After Adams and Franklin returned to America in 1785, Jefferson was promoted Minister Plenipotentiary to France. He immersed himself in the intellectual and artistic milieu of Paris, and easily fit into the French social scene and its finest salons. Though he found much of the French aristocratic system archaic, and the social condition of French cities and many of its citizens repugnant, he came to speak excellent French, attended wine tastings, and studied wine hierarchies. Hoping to ensure respect, Jefferson developed an ample appreciation of the diplomatic importance of setting an inviting and proper table. Jefferson made certain that only the finest meals and wines were served to France's intellectual elite.[216]

One of the more transformative periods of Jefferson's life commenced February 28, 1787, when—at the age of 43—he left Paris for an eye-opening, three-and-a-half-month trip through southern France and northern Italy. The idea for the journey was initially conceived after he broke his wrist the previous autumn. His doctor recommended treatment in the warm and healing mineral springs at Aix-en-Provence. The doctor's prescription conveniently came as Jefferson was already looking for a change of scenery; he had grown bored with his diplomatic duties, and, so far as history permits us to ascertain, had recently concluded a brief romantic interlude with British-Italian artist Maria Cosway.

While he characterized at least part of his trip as therapeutic, Jefferson used the opportunity to research French agriculture, architecture, and engineering, and to collect observations about the morals and manners of France and northern Italy. Such observations, he hoped, could help inform America's agricultural and commercial policies and fulfill one of his diplomatic responsibilities. Jefferson later observed that the trip afforded him the opportunity for "instruction, amusement, and abstraction from business." He traveled alone as a private citizen in search of solitude, taking with him maps, personal notes, letters of introduction, and guidebooks. It was to be the longest such journey of his life.[217]

Armed with a corkscrew, Jefferson charted a nearly 1,200-mile out-of-the-way, circuitous route through the heart of some fifty of Europe's most celebrated wine regions. The journey took him south of Paris along the Seine River to the heart of Burgundy, through the Rhône Valley, across the Maritime Alps into northern Italy, and finally to Bordeaux. Along the way, he questioned experts, conversed with locals, and visited the homes of laborers. In hopes of procuring beneficial technical information he made nearly forty-five pages of concise notes on the geography, irrigation systems, soil conditions, engineering, foods, and lifestyles he encountered.[218]

While Jefferson's travel diary constituted a broad survey of European politics, economics, and social strata, the subject of viticulture was omnipresent.

He recorded observations on the regions' wine production and cultivation—indeed, they are the only known records concerning eighteenth-century viticulture in Europe—because he hoped to use this knowledge to encourage an American wine industry. Although he had become knowledgeable about French wines during his diplomatic mission, the trip also educated him as to the selection of the finest wines and how to order them, how to serve wine properly, and a mastery of viticultural terminologies, shipping methods, and grape varieties—things he later shared with his friends. He also established a list of contacts who would furnish him with wines after his return to the United States.[219]

At each stop, he recorded his observations as to the best reds and whites in each region. Jefferson spent more time in Burgundy than anywhere else during his tour, where he saw prized Pinot Noir and Chardonnay vineyards along the Côte d'Or. South along the Rhône, he visited the 11th-century Chateau du Clos de Vougeot, founded by Cistercian monks, and marveled at its ancient wine presses. He observed the Maison Carrée, an ancient Roman temple at Nîmes, which would later influence his design of the Virginia State Capitol at Richmond.

In Beaune, Jefferson met Étienne Parent, a master cooper and wine merchant who served as his guide through part of Burgundy. Parent offered Jefferson advice on the shipment and storage of wines, and warned him about the notorious dishonesty of French wine merchants. Parent's admonitions would cause Jefferson ever after to order wine directly from the producer. Parent's recommendations would also help shape Jefferson's wine collection in Paris, in Washington, and at Monticello.[220]

Heading farther south into the Rhône Valley, Jefferson is believed to have sampled wine made from an obscure vinifera grape then planted exclusively in Condrieu—the Viognier—a variety that would ultimately play a major role in the reemergence of Virginia's wine industry in the twentieth century. He also sampled the white wine of l'Hermitage, which he judged to be "the first wine in the world without a single exception."[221]

Jefferson rode into northern Italy on a rented mule, along a steep and twisty road, and visited Turin, Milan, and Genoa. He encountered his first rice fields, and recorded highly technical notes about husking machines, planting of vines, and even the making of Parmesan cheese. After smuggling a handful of short-grain Italian rice that he later sent to the South Carolina Society for Promoting Agriculture, Jefferson crossed back into southern France near Provence. He toured Bordeaux's Cabernet Sauvignon and Merlot vineyards, and provided what is believed to be the first hierarchical ranking of Bordeaux wines.[222]

Jefferson returned to Paris on June 10, 1787, having by now tasted the finest wines available in both France and Italy, and witnessing the art of winemaking firsthand. He wrote to a friend of the infinitely pleasurable journey, and said that he had "never passed three months and a half more delightfully." The experience and expertise Jefferson developed on the trip made him a self-trained authority on viticulture and wines.[223]

The journey also contributed greatly to his views on the development of an American wine industry. Jefferson's intimate observation of the winemaking process, including its susceptibility to weather and the poor conditions of the laborers, led him to question the sustainable profitability of the whole affair. "The culture of the vine," he warned a friend, "is a species of gambling, and of desperate gambling too, wherein whether you make much or nothing, you are equally this class of cultivators." He also noted the effects of viticulture on the men and women who tended the vines and made the wine. To his former law mentor George Wythe, Jefferson suggested corn and cotton were more profitable, and that the vine was "the parent of misery. Those who cultivate it are always poor."[224]

The trip even caused Jefferson to question America's ability to compete with Europe's established wine regions, particularly at a time when encouraging the production of agricultural commodities for non-British markets held a greater importance. He did, however, envision a day when America could challenge its counterparts:

> [Wine] may become a resource to use…when the increase of population shall increase our production beyond the demand for [basic crops] both at home and abroad. Instead of going on to make useless surplus of [basic crops] we may employ our supernumerary hands on the vine. But that period has not yet arrived.[225]

Jefferson returned to the United States in 1789 for what he expected to be a six-month leave of absence. After his arrival in Norfolk that November, however, he was surprised to learn that Congress had confirmed his nomination as George Washington's first Secretary of State—a position he reluctantly accepted. While Jefferson was happy to return to Virginia, he would always reflect fondly on his time in France for, as biographer Dumas Malone observed, "It seems that in France, Jefferson was better able to do the sort of things he wanted to do, and to be the sort of man he wanted to be."[226]

Reflecting on his experience abroad, Jefferson could only say of his time in Europe that,

> A more benevolent people, I have never known, nor greater warmth and devotedness in their select friendships. Their kindness and

accommodation to strangers is unparalleled, and the hospitality of Paris is beyond anything I had conceived…. So, ask the travelled inhabitant of any nation, on what country would you rather live?—Certainly my own, where are all my friends, my relations, and the earliest and sweetest affections and recollections of my life. Which would be your second choice? France.[227]

Though he so thoroughly enjoyed the hospitality and patriotic devotion of the French people, Jefferson would never return.[228]

Initially quartered in New York and later Philadelphia, the new Secretary of State found himself consumed with the affairs of the new nation, and wrote longingly for Monticello and his family. Not all was drudgery, however. Once in Philadelphia, he stocked his wine cellar with French and Madeira wines, and President Washington relied on his guidance in selecting presidential wines. This, unsurprisingly, was a task Jefferson took most seriously. He set about employing the experiences and contacts he had developed during his 1787 journey to meet Washington's needs; he ordered fine French wines directly from vineyard proprietors, and demanded that his wines be bottled at the chateau. The selection of each wine forced Jefferson to navigate issues of cost, the timing of shipping, the president's tastes, and the expectations of visiting dignitaries—all things of diplomatic importance for a young nation seeking international legitimacy.[229]

His unofficial role as George Washington's sommelier made him an influential wine advisor in the Early Republic—a role he later repeated with Presidents John Adams, James Madison, and James Monroe, not to mention himself. In advising each president on his wine selections, Jefferson hoped to use his influence to spark a cultural revolution in wine appreciation. Indeed, all but five lines of his lengthy congratulatory letter to James Monroe on his presidency dealt with those wines most suitable for public entertaining.[230]

Conflict with Jefferson's chief political rival, Alexander Hamilton, and President Washington's alignment with Hamilton, led him to resign from the Cabinet in late 1793. He would return to public life as vice president in 1797, and as the nation's third president four years later. When he moved into the unfinished President's House in the new capital of Washington, D.C., now-President Jefferson brought with him his strong views as to the image he wished to convey as the nation's first Republican chief executive. He took it on himself to entertain the fledgling city's social elite, as well as visiting dignitaries.

For all of his republican tastes, he did so lavishly with three or four dinners a week at the President's House, often regaling guests with stories of his travels, and his interests in architecture and gardening. Most important for our story, he served fine wines from France, Austria, Germany, and Italy, including sparking table wine—then a rarity at American dinner tables. He stocked the President's House wine cellar with no fewer than 20,000 bottles of wine during his two terms, and had a wine vault constructed below the west entrance of the ground floor that contained an eclectic mix of European and American wines.[231]

As with his other endeavors, Jefferson meticulously recorded his expenses and wine purchases throughout his administration. He apparently spent an astonishing ten percent (or more) of his $25,000 annual salary on wine. He spent some $3,200 per year on wine during his first term and eventually spent $16,500 on wine before leaving office. He rationalized such expenses as being in the public interest. Indeed, he hoped to elevate his countrymen's tastes and manners. But such a lifestyle came at a cost; at the end of his eight years in office, Jefferson found himself $10,000 in debt.

Jefferson dealt with the domestic and international matters of his presidency, from judicial appointments to the First Barbary War, from the Louisiana Purchase to his struggles with Chief Justice John Marshall. In the midst of national and global adventures, however, viticulture remained a vital part of his public policy initiatives. Among other things, he believed high taxes on wine encouraged many Americans to rely on more ardent spirits, with drunkenness the result. "No nation is drunken where wine is cheap," he later wrote the French Ambassador, "and none sober, where the dearness of wine substitutes ardent spirits as the common beverage."[232]

Jefferson directed Secretary of the Treasury Albert Gallatin to study the equalization of taxes on wine imports, and believed wine could serve as a beverage of temperance for rich and poor alike. As he wrote to a friend in 1818,

> I think it a great error to consider a heavy tax on wines, as a tax on luxury. On the contrary it is a tax on the health of our citizens. It is a legislative declaration that none but the richest of them shall be permitted to drink wine, and in effect a condemnation of all the middling & lower conditions of society to the poison of whiskey.... Whereas were the duties on the cheap wines proportioned to their first cost the whole middle class of this country could have the gratification of that milder stimulus.... I should therefore be for encouraging the use of wine by placing it among the articles of lightest duty.[233]

Reduced taxes on fine wine, and the encouragement of its widespread consumption over other alcoholic drinks, would be causes he would continue to promote until the end of his life.

After 35 years in the public eye, Jefferson happily retired to Monticello on the conclusion of his second term in March 1809. There, he found himself at last free to relax and to indulge in gardening, writing, and other pursuits. "Never did a prisoner," he wrote, "released from his chains, feel such relief as I shall on shaking off the shackles of power. Nature intended me for the tranquil pursuits of science, by rendering them my supreme delight."[234]

Though removed from office, Jefferson's affection for social gatherings led him to entertain hundreds of guests at Monticello throughout his seventeen-year retirement. Jefferson attempted to fashion a decidedly cosmopolitan, indeed French, atmosphere at Monticello, hoping to turn his estate into a center of thought in the Virginia countryside.

Food delighted him, and he had his French-trained slaves dazzle Monticello's guests with foreign delicacies including ice cream, pasta, waffles, and macaroni and cheese. Though he consumed Madeira wine, beer, and cider, Jefferson also gave way to his compulsion for fine wines. He always purchased more of the available moderately-priced vintages, but their lower prices were more than offset by the prodigious rate at which they were consumed. Indeed, between just 1822 and 1824, for example, Jefferson and his guests consumed no fewer than 1,203 bottles of wine.[235]

Most of Jefferson's wines were housed in Monticello's extensive 220-square-foot wine cellar directly below his dining room. The design of Monticello's cellar underscored its importance. The room featured brick floors protected by a fortified two-layer thick, iron-strapped, double-locked door with two locks requiring separate keys. Borrowing an idea he observed from the Café Mécanique in Paris, Jefferson even designed two weight-and-pulley dumbwaiters that were concealed in two locked cabinets by the fireplace. The dumbwaiters allowed four bottles at a time—two in each dumbwaiter—to be lifted from the wine cellar to the dining room.[236]

While he spent much time entertaining, it was in Monticello's garden that Jefferson employed his significant horticultural skills to become, among his other remarkable accomplishments, a distinguished gardener. Jefferson spent most of his adult life trying to transform Monticello into a model horticultural laboratory. Often giving written directions to his farm managers, he experimented with grapes and attempted intermittently to cultivate a vineyard between 1770 and 1826.[237]

Much of what is known of Jefferson's affinity for viticulture at Monticello comes from his *Garden Book*, a private horticulture diary he kept between 1766 and 1824. He recorded his earliest planting of five grape vines on March 28, 1771, followed by more substantial plantings on April 6, 1774. These succumbed to that devastating May frost. He attempted additional plantings in 1778 and 1802, and laid out a 9,000-square-foot northeastern vineyard below the vegetable garden and pavilion in 1778.[238]

Jefferson's most important vineyard planting came in 1807. This included 287 cuttings of 24 vinifera varieties he received from friends and a Washington, D.C., nursery. The grapes were planted in a reconstituted northeast vineyard and, that same year, Jefferson created a larger 16,000-square-foot southwest vineyard in which he planted other vinifera varieties.[239]

Though his plantings never fully succeeded, he yet engaged in other wine-related pursuits. To manufacture his own corks, for example, he sought to obtain cork trees to plant at Monticello. He also founded the Agricultural Society of Albemarle County in 1817, to encourage others to experiment with viticulture. He supported Philip Mazzei's various efforts and, by 1811 with the continuation of the Napoleonic Wars and the related impacts of the Embargo Act of 1807, Jefferson softened his position as to his nation's readiness to accommodate a domestic wine industry. Jefferson wrote to John Dortic his revised thoughts for American wine drawn from both his continued interest in producing wine and his trepidation over growing unrest in Europe,

> I am come over to your opinion that…we must endeavor to make everything we want within ourselves, and have as little intercourse as possible with Europe in its present demoralized state. Wine being among the earliest luxuries in which we indulge ourselves, it is desirable it should be made here and we have every soil, aspect, and climate of the best countries.[240]

Jefferson's perceptions as to the future of a domestic wine industry followed on the rapid development and widespread dissemination of native American grapes. He enthusiastically received cuttings of the native Alexander grape from Washington, D.C., grower John Adlum (discussed in Chapter 2), who also provided Jefferson with samples of wine he made from the native Catawba grape. John Hartwell Cocke sent wine to Jefferson produced from the native Scuppernong grape, which Jefferson proclaimed to be "distinguished on the best tables of Europe, for its fine aroma, and chrystalline transparence." Historians have posited that Jefferson's growing receptivity to native American grapes, after a lifetime of enjoying superior European wines, suggested pragmatism with respect to grape varieties that could be successfully cultivated in Virginia, strong patriotic fervor and, perhaps, a deterioration in his tastes caused by age.[241]

In the winter of his life, Jefferson ceded the planting of grapes to younger generations. His interest was momentarily rekindled in 1815, when he received a letter from Jean David, a young French viticulturist, who sought Jefferson's assistance. Despite Jefferson's protestations that he was too old to take up the vine once more, he purchased cuttings in anticipation of David's arrival. Sadly, David never traveled to Monticello, and the venture—as with all of Jefferson's other vineyard attempts—fizzled.[242]

Jefferson died on July 4, 1826, at the age of eight-three—fifty years to the day after the signing of the Declaration of Independence. There remained 300 bottles in his cellar, and he had firmly established himself as America's best-known advocate for popular democracy, human rights, and wine. Despite more than thirty years of viticultural experiments, however, none of Jefferson's grape-vines survived, having either perished in transit or having died once planted. Despite occasional trials, he never produced wine. A 1782 attempt to make wine from the native winter grape resulted in vinegar.

There were, of course, a multitude of reasons for Jefferson's viticultural failures. Perhaps the soil was inferior; perhaps Jefferson's orders of vine cuttings were weakened by improper packaging; or perhaps the climate was too hot, beset by too many diseases, or wet. Others have suggested that, as Sir William Berkeley before him, Jefferson's lack of winemaking success must be attributed to his extended absences from Monticello and his devotion to other priorities.[243]

Whatever the reason or result, Jefferson sought to democratize wine growing and wine consumption to the benefit of his new nation. Later viticulturists and winemakers would be inspired by Jefferson's ambition and invoke his name and legacy to promote their own endeavors for, as wine historian Thomas Pinney has noted, Jefferson "cared much that others should succeed, and, by virtue of his zeal and his eminence, can be called the greatest patron of wine and winegrowing that this country has yet had."[244]

Jefferson was perhaps a century-and-a-half ahead of his time, but he foresaw a day when America would develop a high-quality wine industry. He died before realizing his dream, but the "Sage of Monticello" did more to influence the scientific and viticultural knowledge of his countrymen than anyone else during the history of the Early Republic. His work led many later to label him America's first distinguished viticulturist, the father of American wine.[245]

## —Cultivating the Vine Across Virginia—

While Thomas Jefferson is, with good reason, cited as the most educated and devoted American president on the subject of wine, it is easy to overlook the accomplishments of the nation's first president. George Washington shared many of Jefferson's beliefs regarding the health benefits of wine and the notion that Virginia could one day support a vibrant wine industry.

Writing to Philip Mazzei in 1779, Washington observed, "I have long been of opinion, from the spontaneous growth of the vine, that the climate and soil in many parts of Virginia were well fitted for Vineyards and that Wine, sooner or later, would become a valuable article of produce."[246]

Though he is better known today as the only founding father to operate a whiskey distillery, Washington's preferred beverage was Portuguese Madeira. He not only enjoyed sipping the wine while entertaining guests after dinner, but he also occasionally ordered substantial quantities and frequently gave gifts of the wine to his friends. Washington also enjoyed clarets and offered guests French Champagne, which presumably helped lighten otherwise tense or awkward moments.[247]

Washington's thoughts on wine were rooted in his general view regarding the importance of agriculture to the young nation—another belief shared with Jefferson. "The life of a Husbandman of all others," he wrote, "is the most delectable. It is honorable. It is amusing, and, with judicious management, it is profitable." At Mount Vernon—Washington's stately mansion overlooking the Potomac River in Fairfax County—he welcomed every opportunity to harness his horticultural and agricultural skill and carve out gracious living as the quintessential "gentleman farmer."[248]

While perhaps not as ambitious as Jefferson in Monticello's landscape design, Mount Vernon's gardens were among the most artistically planned and comprehensive in colonial Virginia. Likely inspired by French and English landscape designs of the day, Mount Vernon's gardens included a four-acre "vineyard enclosure," which initially served as a place for both cultivating native and imported grapes and, later, witnessed other horticultural experiments.[249]

By 1763, Washington had planted some fifty cuttings of Madeira vines. He repeated his attempts with grapes of an unspecified origin (likely also a foreign variety) in 1768. These first attempts at foreign cultivation were, however, unsuccessful. Reflecting on his own disappointment, Washington wrote in 1787 that the failures of his contemporaries to make high-quality wine were "owing either to an improper kind, or the want of skill in the management." Washington's experiments also led him to conclude that Virginia's hot summers and warm autumns invariably hastened the ripening of foreign vinifera grapes that, in turn led to excess fermentation and highly acidic wine.[250]

Dissatisfied with European varieties, Washington next turned his attention to their native counterparts: "The spontaneous growth of the Vine in all parts of this country," Washington wrote, "the different qualities of them and periods for maturation, led me to conclude, that by a happy choice of the species I might succeed better than those who had attempted the foreign vine."[251]

Between November and December 1771, Washington planted twenty-nine rows of an estimated 2,000 cuttings of the native "winter grape" and five rows of the "summer grape" in the vineyard enclosure. Several of these 1771 cuttings grew along wooden rail espaliers as "living fences" to separate sections of the enclosure. Washington revived his interest in foreign grape-growing by 1784 when, after commanding the Continental army between 1776 and 1783, he requested that New York governor George Clinton forward to him several vines of "the most valuable eating grapes in France."[252]

Washington also demonstrated a renewed interest in planting European grapes and frequently ordered vinifera vine cuttings from the same French statesman and minister—Chrétien-Guillaume Lamoignon de Malesherbes—as did Jefferson. Writing to an acquaintance in 1787, Washington said,

> If, notwithstanding my former plans, Monsr. De Malesherbes will honor me with a few sets, or cuttings of any one kind (and the choise is left altogether to himself), I will cultivate them with the utmost care. I will always think of him when I go into my little Vineyard, and the first fruits of it shall be dedicated to him as the Author of it.[253]

Beginning in June 1787, Washington also made the first of several visits to the botanical garden of John Bartram, Jr., located along the west bank of the Schuylkill River southwest of Philadelphia. Bartram, whose father had been selected by King George III in 1765 as North America's Royal Botanist, was much interested in viticulture, and his garden featured both fruit trees and a vineyard. In March 1792, Washington ordered two large shipments of more than 200 trees and plants, including grape cuttings and grape seeds, to be sent to Mount Vernon.[254]

Washington's viticultural interests shifted once more in the 1790s, this time away from wine grapes and in favor of table grapes. By then, Mount Vernon's vineyard enclosure had given way to a larger experimental nursery, which boasted fruit trees, boxwoods, and a variety of vegetables. Washington described the area as his "Fruit Garden," and the space became Mount Vernon's most important orchard.[255]

As with so many of his contemporaries, Washington had other priorities— the American Revolution and his presidency—that prevented him from fully dedicating the necessary time and expertise toward the cultivation of grapes. These other responsibilities meant that he had to oversee Mount Vernon largely through correspondence. By one estimate, Washington spent half of his time away from Mount Vernon from when he moved there in 1759 until his death in 1799. "Had I remained at home," he later wrote, "I should…have perfected the [grape-growing] experiment which was all I had in view."[256]

No evidence exists that Washington ever attempted to make wine from Mount Vernon's grapes. Indeed, perhaps to allay fears that his cultivation of wine grapes would pose a threat to French wine interests, Washington assured a French acquaintance in 1783 that it was not his intent to grow wine grapes on a large scale. Some historians have speculated that Washington's grape plantings were intended to solely serve as feedstock for Washington's distillery which, by the 1790s, was already noted for its apple, peach, and persimmon brandies.[257]

Washington found other ways to support Virginia's viticulture prospects, often encouraging upstart winemakers or viticultural enterprises, including Philip Mazzei. He did so to the very end of his life. The first of thousands of posthumous drawings depicted a feeble Washington lying on his death bed with a bottle of wine on the table at his side.[258]

Twelve miles south of Mount Vernon, along the Potomac River peninsula that today bears his name, Mason Neck, statesman and "Father of the Bill of Rights" George Mason dabbled in viticultural experimentation at Gunston Hall. Mason twice attempted to cultivate French grapes on his plantation, but without success. He wrote of his struggles to his son in France in 1783, that his limited skill placed him "at a Loss to know the different kinds of Grapes, & which are the best worth cultivating."

Mason is also reported to have taken vine cuttings from Philip Mazzei's ubiquitous vineyard in Albemarle County. Mazzei evidently lent Mason encouragement and growing advice and, in exchange, Mason joined George Washington in subscribing to Mazzei's 1774 effort to establish a company to produce wine, silk, citrus fruit, and oil.[259]

Mason's hopes for a Virginia wine industry, however, extended beyond a personal hobby. As early as October 1759, he had solicited investors to underwrite a loan for a German winemaker, Maurice Pound, who had settled at Colchester, a small river port town near Mason's property along the Occoquan River. Pound had evidently arrived in Virginia three years earlier with a group of German Protestants who brought with them vine cuttings from vineyards along Germany's Rhine and Moselle Rivers.[260]

Pound planted his cuttings in a vineyard along Colchester's main thoroughfare, Essex Street, where he established a wine press and other winemaking facilities. Regrettably, the vines suffered during the hot, dry summers of 1758 and 1759, and Pound struggled to realize a profit from his grapes. In dire straits, he offered to mortgage his property to anyone willing to advance him £100.

In return, Pound offered to pay interest on the loan while "prosecut[ing] with Industry all measures possible to bring [the] Vineyard to perfection."[261]

Mason had frequented Pound's vineyard, and promoted Pound's prospects to other wealthy area landowners in the hopes of raising money to support Pound's efforts. Reporting that he had known Pound since he had first settled at Colchester, and desirous that his work might jump-start the colony's wine industry, Mason wrote that Pound's undertaking was "likely to be so usefull, & beneficial to this Colony" and that, "if our Soil & Climate is capable of producing good wine that [Pound] will, with proper Encouragement, bring it to perfection."[262]

Mason accordingly contributed £10 to Pound's efforts and, along with his neighbors, George Washington and George William Fairfax, ultimately raised £118. By 1772, however, nothing had come of the vineyard project; Pound apparently moved from Colchester to Augusta County while Washington— and most likely Pound's other subscribers—wrote off the whole affair as a bad loan.[263]

Elsewhere in Virginia, other, less well known, individuals attempted wine-making during the colonial period. It is unknown how many tried, but it is reasonable to think that experimentation occurred in all segments of the population. One Richmond County farmer, Rawleigh Downman, and his brother, William Downman, had an interest in making wine. William Downman appears to have had a vineyard enclosure with mature grapevines. A "Colonel Baker" of Smithfield collected native and foreign grapevines. Landon Carter's neighbor at Sabine Hall, the Reverend Isaac W. Giberne, apparently cultivated wine grapes by 1772, while James Pendleton, older brother of Virginia politician Edmund Pendleton, produced a recipe for making wine from American grapes by adding honey and cider.[264]

In Buckingham County, Continental army captain Anthony Winston grew a large garden with several hundred fruit trees at his home, Huntington. He also produced 100 gallons of wine as early as 1772, and noted in the July 13, 1775 issue of the *Virginia Gazette* that, "if it had not been for the [May 1774] frost I could have made five hundred or six hundred gallons, which quantity I expect to make this year."[265]

Fredericksburg lawyer and future American president James Monroe expressed an interest in winemaking, imported grapevines, and grew wine grapes at his Albemarle County home, now called Ash Lawn–Highland. Monroe's friend and neighbor, Thomas Jefferson, attempted to procure small cuttings of Monroe's vines for replanting at Monticello, and offered his advice on French and Italian wines while Monroe was in the White House. Jefferson's brother-in-law, Francis Eppes VI, frequently sent vine cuttings from his western Chesterfield County home, Eppington, to Colonel Robert Bolling at Chellow. None of these efforts resulted in the stable establishment of successful vineyards for the production of wine.[266]

## —End of an Era—

The enthusiasm with which Virginia's earliest settlers conceived the potential for grape cultivation did not result in a viable wine industry during the commonwealth's colonial period. Successive generations were undaunted, and attempted time and again to revive the endeavor, only to fall prey to the same difficulties and mistakes as their predecessors. Even where efforts showed promising signs of success, they eventually met with unsatisfactory results and were much too limited in scope to be considered part of a growing or thriving industry.[267]

Many explanations for the colony's viticultural shortcomings were offered. Some placed blame in a failure to pursue the proper type of European grapes. Others, including Robert Beverley and Robert Bolling, believed the problem lay in the mistaken citing of vineyards in the lowland Tidewater areas of Virginia.

Failed winemaker André Estave argued that a lack of skill among Virginia's viticulturists doomed the colony's efforts, while George Washington, Philip Mazzei, and Sir William Berkeley each had more pressing commitments that kept them from properly attending to their vineyards. During its short life, the Virginia Company had searched in vain for any excuse for its failures to produce wine, and frequently pointed to the 1622 Indian attack as the cause. Many more blamed Virginia's harsh winters, late frosts, damp springs, and humid summers. Practically everyone blamed the French. Tobacco, which offered great profits and relatively low production costs so long as the soil sufficed, was also an oft-indicted culprit, as high revenues overshadowed all public efforts to cultivate grapes.[268]

Missing from this, of course, was the role played by grapevine pests and diseases which led to the death and decay of European vinifera grapevines. The only other alternative—the colony's abundant native grapes—did not suffer from the same threats, but proved inadequate for quality wine production. Without adequate and continued public support, and the skilled labor required to improve the winemaking potential of native grapes, the colony's efforts were limited. The colonial era was thus paralyzed by a schizophrenic public policy whereby both the Company and Crown routinely demanded wine production and commodity diversification, yet were dependent upon, indeed addicted to, the great wealth generated by tobacco.[269]

Winemaking—and economic diversification generally—was subsidized and encouraged in Virginia only when it seemed to make financial sense for the colony, as when the price for tobacco fell precipitously. As colonial wine historian David J. Mishkin noted, a certain cycle developed with respect to the constantly changing role of wine in the economy of the colonists:

> At first, sources suggest that wine be a primary staple in the Virginia colony...[and then] Englishmen question the economic feasibility of commercial wine production. They examine capital and labor investments, noting the time factor between investment and return. Later sources continue to discuss commodity availability, but no longer consider wine an important commodity. Finally, Englishmen again advocate colonial wine production, stressing that a change in comparative costs and returns make it once more feasible and economically rewarding.

Unpredictable public policies did little to no good, and, with each spike in tobacco prices, by the close of each tobacco price glut, frenzied planting of the golden leaf began anew.[270]

The government's occasional attempts to compel the manufacturing of wine through ill-conceived legislation proved equally fruitless. Without the necessary recognition that winemaking required detailed knowledge of botany, chemistry, and biology, hastily-enacted colonial laws were largely ignored, seldom enforced, and were almost never accompanied by an adequate public educational or financial support system. To the colony's credit, the government did manage to bring in French vignerons in 1610 and 1619, provide premiums for wine production in 1759 and 1762, and even operate a publicly funded vineyard between 1769 and the Revolution. However, these intermittent public sector attempts were simply insufficient and failed to stir colonists' imaginations or tickle their pocketbooks.

The same could be said of the valiant private efforts of some of the colony's largest landowners—Sir William Berkeley, Robert Bolling, William Byrd II, Charles Carter, and others—each of whom sought in vain to demonstrate the benefits of wine production to their fellow citizens. Other occasional attempts to build on the expertise of foreigners in the colony met a similar fate.[271]

In the face of this depressing tale, it is easy to forget that wine, almost surely manufactured from native grapes, was nevertheless produced by the likes of Lawrence Bohune, Berkeley, Robert Beverley, the Carters, Robert Bolling, Philip Mazzei, the French at Manakin Town, the Germans at Germanna, and others. While most of this wine was likely of dubious quality, these growers had proved that wine could, in fact, be made from Virginia's natural grapes. In some cases, such as Charles Carter's May 1762 "winter grape" wine, some native wines were quite drinkable.[272]

The success of these growers suggests that, with proper public sector inducements and sustained encouragement, the colony might have seen the gradual improvement of native wines that might then have led to an industry focused around their cultivation. This, however, was not to be. The government's conservative and inconstant fiscal policies as well as colonial economic conditions ran counter to the need for prolonged and scientific efforts and investments in the vine—native or European. It was, in the end, Virginia's lukewarm and intermittent public support, rather than poor environmental conditions, which led directly to its colonial oenological failures.[273]

History has recorded what it can of the colony's early winemaking efforts. There are few remains from Virginia's colonial-era viticultural saga; aside from sporadic highway markers, the occasional archaeological exhibit, and disparate written accounts passed down through generations, these efforts left little physical trace.

One Irish writer, Isaac Weld, Jr., visited Monticello in May 1796 and observed that while "several attempts have been made in this neighbourhood to bring the manufacture of wine to perfection," none had "succeeded to the wish of the parties." These observations, of course, could be applied to Virginia's colonial winemaking narrative more universally. Weld, however, joined the chorus of those who sang a more-optimistic note, and believed that over time, the pioneering spirit and winemaking potential of Virginians would prevail:

> We must not, however, from hence conclude that good wine can never be manufactured upon these mountains…. It will require some time, therefore, and different experiments, to ascertain the particular kind of vine, and the mode of cultivating it, best adapted to the [soil]…. However, having been once ascertained, there is every reason to suppose that the grape may be cultivated to the greatest perfection.[274]

As Virginia greeted the nineteenth century as an American state, it left behind nearly two hundred years of failed winemaking attempts under colonial rule. What a time it had been—replete with trials and dashed hopes, minor successes and major failures. Yet, through it all, in their signature revolutionary ways, Virginians were undeterred in their struggle to produce a commercially viable wine industry. As citizens of a new nation, their story would continue; the Old Dominion would chase its viticultural dreams for another two centuries, until the remarkable successes that were to come.

1. Perceived as a veritable land of plenty, colonial settlers managed to cultivate nearly every European plant that they brought with them, but they could not grow delicate European grapes.

2. Philip Mazzei, an Italian entrepreneur, American patriot, and close friend of Thomas Jefferson, assisted Jefferson in planting grapes at Monticello in the mid-1770s.

3. Captain John Smith was among the first to record impressions of grapes and winemaking across the colony.

H.E.MAGRUDER, PREST.
R.T.W.DUKE, VICE-PREST.

M.KAUFMAN, SEC & TREAS.
ADOLPH RUSSOW, SUPT.

PARIS 1878.

NEW ORLEANS 1884-5

PARIS 1889

VIRGINIA 1888.

OFFICE OF THE Monticello Wine Co.

GROWERS & DEALERS IN

Pure Native Wines and Grape Brandy.

Charlottesville, Va. 5th Dect. 1896

4. Trade card of the Monticello Wine Company, Virginia's foremost winemaking enterprise in the late nineteenth century, highlighting some of the company's many international wine competition victories.

5. Though reports indicate he never manufactured wine, no figure had a more profound impact on and enduring legacy for the future of American viticulture than Thomas Jefferson.

6. Paul Garrett, "Dean of American Winemakers," established Garrett and Company in North Carolina in 1900 and, to escape North Carolina's prohibition laws, later moved the company's headquarters to Virginia in 1903. The company, which manufactured wine from scuppernong and other American varietals, grew into a national winemaking empire.

7. Labels symbolic of the style and quality of wine made in Virginia in the post-Prohibition era. For the most part, Virginia wines manufactured during this period were decidedly sweet and often fortified.

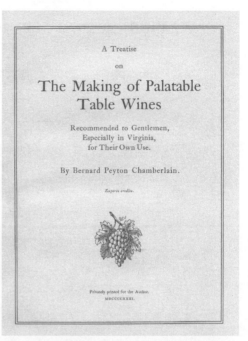

A Treatise

on

# The Making of Palatable Table Wines

Recommended to Gentlemen,
Especially in Virginia,
for Their Own Use.

By Bernard Peyton Chamberlain.

*Experto credite.*

Privately printed for the Author.
MDCCCCXXXI.

8. Cover page from Charlottesville attorney Bernard Peyton Chamberlain's self-published treatise, *The Making of Palatable Table Wines* (1931), which sought to redress the deficiency of quality wine in the commonwealth by providing helpful information to would-be Virginia winemakers.

9. Army veteran John June Lewis's Woburn Winery in Mecklenberg County. Founded in 1940, it was believed to have been the first winery owned by an African American in the United States.

10. Robert de Treville Lawrence tending to vines at his home, Highbury, in The Plains.

11. Meredyth Vineyards founder Archie Smith, Jr. (right) engages in dialogue with Governor Gerald L. Baliles (left) during the governor's three-day vineyard tour in 1988.

12. Meredyth Vineyards winemaker Archie Smith III, was the first Virginia winemaker to use the French technique of carbonic maceration, which fermented juice while inside the grapeskin.

13. Virginia Senator John Warner and Piedmont Vineyards' founder Elizabeth Furness pouring wine into the Vinifera Wine Growers Association's coveted Montieth Wine Bowl Trophy in 1981.

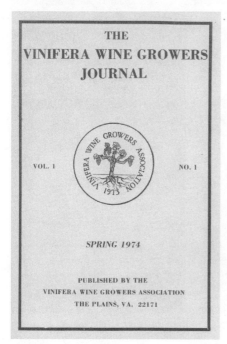

14. Cover from the first edition of "The Vinifera Wine Growers Journal."

15. Bob and Phoebe Harper's Naked Mountain Vineyards in the early 1990s.

16. From left, Shenandoah Vineyards owners Jim and Emma Randel and winemaker Alan Kinne.

17. Al and Emily Weed, daughter Julia, and son Tres at their Mountain Cove vineyard in Nelson County.

18. Viticulturist, author, and ampelographer Lucie T. Morton.

19. Ingleside winemaker Jacques Recht.

20. Dirgham Salahi at Oasis Winery in 1982.

21. Lee, Pat, and Claire Reeder at Burnley Vineyards.

22. Willowcroft Farm Vineyards founder Lew Parker.

23. Gordon Murchie (right) meeting celebrity chef Julia Child in 1997 as wife Anita (left) looks on.

24. Linden Vineyards' Jim Law tending to the vines.

25. Commissioner of Agriculture and Consumer Services, S. Mason Carbaugh, confers with wine writer Leon D. Adams in the early 1980s.

26. John and Felicia Rogan inspecting vines at their Oakencroft Winery in Albemarle County.

27. Archie Smith III and Annette Ringwood Boyd sitting atop Governor Gerald Baliles' limousine during the governor's three-day winery tour in June 1988.

28. State Enologist and Virginia Tech Professor Emeritus Bruce Zoecklein.

29. Virginia winemakers visit with Governor Charles S. Robb and Commissioner of Agriculture and Consumer Services S. Mason Carbaugh during the proclamation of Virginia Farm Winery week in 1983.

30. Old Dominion University professor Roy L. Williams at the school's Enological Research Facility.

31. Poet, author, and winemaker Tom O'Grady of The Rose Bower Vineyards in Prince Edward County.

32. Winemaker Jim Livingston inspecting his vines at Stafford County's Hartwood Winery.

33. Barboursville Vineyards owner Gianni Zonin and winemaker Gabriele Rausse inspect vines in the 1970s.

34. Winemaker Joachim C. Hollerith in front of the gates at Orange County's Rapidan Vineyards in the 1980s.

35. Labels from Shenandoah Vineyards in Virginia and California during the height of the California-Virginia labeling wars of the early 1980s.

36. Thomas Jefferson's viticultural aspirations realized: Barboursville Vineyards in Orange County.

37. Ingleside Plantation Vineyards on the Northern Neck.

38. The Boar's Head Inn hot air balloon during the first Albemarle Harvest Wine Festival in 1981.

39. Waiters racing to the finish line to win a case of Virginia wine at the 11th annual Vinifera Wine Growers Association Festival in August 1986.

40. Wine crushing at a wine festival at Morven Park in Leesburg in the mid-1990s.

41. Spectators at the 1979 Vinifera Wine Growers Association Festival on the grounds of Elizabeth Furness' Piedmont Vineyards in Middleburg.

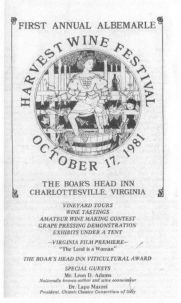

42. The Vinifera Wine Growers Association booth at its 1988 festival at Valley View Farm in Middleburg.

43. Advertisement for the first Albemarle Harvest Wine Festival in October 1981.

44. Dominion Wine Cellars in Culpeper.

45. Tony Wolf, Virginia Tech Professor of Viticulture, leads a class at the Alson H. Smith Jr. Agricultural Research and Extension Center near Winchester.

46. Sharon Livingston looks on as Governor Gerald Baliles proclaims Virginia Wine Month in 1988.

FOLLOW
THE GRAPE...

highway signs and see why Virginia's farm wineries are proud of their growing tradition.

For information on tours, ask for your 1987 Virginia wineries brochure here.

THE SPIRIT THAT BUILT AMERICA IS TAKING NEW ROOT.
VISIT VIRGINIA'S WINE COUNTRY.

47. A 1987 poster advertises the grape cluster directional signs installed that year within 10 miles of all Virginia wineries.

48. A state wine promotion poster in the 1980s highlights Virginia wine's colonial roots and its growth.

# 2

## Contrast, Conflict & Change, 1800–1967

LONG HOME TO several of America's Revolutionary firebrand political writers and orators, during the seventeenth and eighteenth centuries Virginia had also cemented a well-deserved reputation as the New World's most prominent viticultural laboratory. Regardless of the natural and man-made impediments that hindered the creation of a functioning wine industry, Virginians had proven themselves adept and optimistic, certain that the key to the New World's great viticultural promise lay but an experiment away.

After a prolonged hiatus that began in the middle years of the eighteenth century, a time that required the commonwealth's more prominent viticultural experimenters to focus their attention on winning a war against Great Britain, Virginians once more found themselves leading the new nation's viticultural discourse during the century-and-a-half that followed the American Revolution.

At the start of the nineteenth century, many viticulturists experimented with native and American hybrid varieties in the hope of finding suitable wine grapes for the commonwealth's climate and soils. Their work culminated in the development of Virginia's first truly successful wine industry by the close of the 1880s, and by the turn of the twentieth century, the Old Dominion served for a time as the headquarters for one of the nation's largest wine companies.

At much the same time, ironically, other Virginians worked to curtail the state's viticultural progress. Their work, perversely, proved as important to the fate of the state's wine industry as that of the vintners themselves, for the commonwealth led much of the nation in the restriction of alcohol manufacture and consumption—including that of wine. Following the end of Prohibition in 1933, many of those same people responded to repeal by working to create a new alcoholic beverage control system that hampered viticultural innovation for at least two generations. By late in the 1960s, the results of this continual tug-and-pull of competing visions were self-evident: Virginia had no significant wine industry, and what wine it produced was largely relegated to less reputable, highly alcoholic, low-grade "bum" wines.

The years from the wine industry's ascendancy to its decline, those from 1800 to 1967, were a time of economic expansion, scientific experimentation, civil war, and social conservatism, and often bitter debates regarding the permissible scope of personal liberty. Through it all, and despite differing tastes, loyalties, and beliefs, Virginians demonstrated leadership and optimism—whether it was for the cause of wine and commitment to a wine industry, or against it.

## —Post-Revolutionary Virginia—

Once their new nation had thrown off its European masters, America's nineteenth-century viticulturists sought to inject their profound patriotism directly into American wine. Unlike their colonial predecessors, who had spent vast sums in vain attempts to cultivate vinifera grapes and emulate European winemaking techniques, this new generation of post-Revolutionary grape growers focused its attention on creating and discovering new grape varieties of quintessentially American extraction capable of competing with its European counterparts.[1]

Many of these new varieties had evolved naturally through nearly 200 years of cross-pollination between English grapes and their native counterparts, and could be found in the woods and overgrown vineyards surrounding the homes of earlier planters whose efforts found unexpected success. The result was the creation of so-called "American hybrid" varieties that combined much of the fruit quality and flavor of European grapes with the hardiness and disease resistance of the New World's native grapes. Frequently named in honor of a locale or person most associated with their discovery, the most prominent American hybrid grapes carried names like "Alexander," "Catawba," "Delaware," "Niagara," "Isabella," "Concord," and "Norton."[2]

The excitement surrounding the discovery of these new grape varieties coincided with equally stirring developments in scientific experimentation. Using basic scientific methods and just plain luck, hobbyists, farmers, and gardeners found themselves in a race to discover the next best grape. In the mad dash for fame, they promoted new grape varieties almost as soon as they were discovered, each being advertised as more perfectly suited for wine than its predecessors.[3]

One of the first hybrids to receive widespread national attention, the "Bland" grape was allegedly discovered just prior to the American Revolution by a Virginia soldier and statesman, Colonel Theodorick Bland. At some point in the 1770s, Colonel Bland had visited the Eastern Shore of Virginia, where he reported discovering a grape he believed was a hybrid between vinifera and the native fox grape. Described as having large berries "about the size of the common white grape of Europe," and exhibiting a dark purple or red wine color when ripe, the Bland was reportedly well flavored and made good wine, despite its propensity to mildew and its intermittent failures to ripen.[4]

Records do not tell us whether Colonel Bland in fact discovered the grape, or whether it had been previously cultivated by others. Some suggested he created the variety from the seeds of raisins; others speculated it was a Madeira grape obtained from Kentucky or Indiana; still others speculated that it was a cross between native vinifera grapes introduced by either a Frenchman or by the redoubtable Philip Mazzei. Regardless of the grape's origins, the Bland was widely planted by the 1830s, particularly in southern states where it served as the heart of many vintages.[5]

Even more popular was the "Alexander" grape. It was discovered in 1740 in Philadelphia near the place James Alexander—late gardener to the son of Pennsylvania's patronymic William Penn—had first planted vinifera vines in 1683. As with so many American hybrid grapes, the biological origins of the Alexander are unknown, but were widely believed to be a cross-bred hybrid of James Alexander's 1683 vinifera variety and a wild *Vitis labrusca* grape that happened to grow wild in a nearby forest.[6]

Wine from the Alexander was made by many in its day, the most prominent being Major John Adlum, a Revolutionary War veteran who had settled on a 200-acre property in what is today Georgetown in Washington, D.C. At his farm, The Vineyard, Adlum produced an Alexander wine early in the 1800s, and gave a complimentary bottle to then-president Thomas Jefferson.[7] Jefferson was evidently pleased with the wine, noting in an October 1809 response that Adlum's wine resembled a Burgundy varietal and that the Alexander grape had finally provided America with a variety that "would give us a wine worthy of the best vineyards of France." Jefferson wrote to Adlum requesting cuttings of the grape for his personal cultivation, noting: "I think it would be well to push the culture of that grape without losing our time & efforts in search of foreign vines, which it will take centuries to adapt to our soil & climate."[8]

Though widely planted in Pennsylvania, Virginia, Maryland, and New Jersey, the Alexander's prominence quickly faded relative to still newer hybrid grapes as the 1800s progressed. No doubt Jefferson's endorsement, however, aided in the promotion of the Alexander as an American grape of great quality and propelled John Adlum's reputation as a winemaker. He would later be given the honorary title of "Father of American Viticulture" and came to be associated with another grape that featured prominently in the history of American wine, the "Catawba."[9]

The Catawba was believed to have originated in western North Carolina and South Carolina, and produced a white, foxy juice that could be easily converted into a dry white wine. Adlum first produced a 400-gallon stock of Catawba wine in 1821, and once again hoping to generate positive publicity, sent complimentary bottles to James Madison and Thomas Jefferson, in anticipation of rave reviews.[10]

This time, however, Jefferson's reaction was considerably cooler. He wrote that the Catawba produced wine "of no particular excellence." Despite Jefferson's lackluster reception of his effort, Adlum promoted the Catawba widely and even made use of Jefferson's letter, having it published in a popular agricultural journal, *American Farmer*. Adlum further promoted the reputation of the grape by extolling its virtues in a treatise he published in 1823, *Memoir on the Cultivation of the Vine in America, and the Best Mode of Making Wine*. The book was not only the first to be dedicated exclusively to American viticulture, but Adlum's praise also helped launch the Catawba as one of the most popular hybrid grape varieties in American history.[11]

Other new native and American hybrid grape varieties were widely planted as well, each promoted by their discoverers as the latest American hybrid variety to compete with Europe's noble grapes. Nearly three decades after Adlum's first Catawba vintage, George Campbell, the editor of a newspaper in Delaware, Ohio, discovered what he called the "Delaware" grape. Like so many hybrid varieties, the Delaware was widely cultivated by 1860. In 1849, Ephraim Wales Bull developed his "Concord" grape in Concord, Massachusetts, after reportedly evaluating more than 22,000 *Vitis labrusca* seedlings. Later, in 1868, C. L. Hoag and B. W. Clark cross-pollinated Concord grapes with another *Vitis labrusca* variety to produce their "Niagara" varietal.[12]

No American hybrid captured Virginia's imagination more than the Norton, a grape introduced in Richmond in the 1830s and that would soon prove central to Virginia's viticultural heritage. Described by wine historian Thomas Pinney as the "best of all native hybrids so far for the making of red wine," the Norton grape proved particularly well-suited to Virginia's climate and is considered among the most disease- and pest-resistant of any native American grape.[13]

Most evidence indicates that the variety originated with Dr. Daniel Norborne Norton of Richmond early in the 1800s.[14] A physician born to a politically-connected and wealthy Williamsburg shipping family, Norton settled in Richmond after attending medical school at the University of Pennsylvania. He married Elizabeth Call in 1818, after which Norton's father-in-law gave the newlyweds slaves, money, corporate stock, and the 29.5-acre Magnolia Farm outside of Richmond in what was then Henrico County. There he constructed what he termed a "quiet, pleasant home," and planted a garden containing twenty-seven varieties of native, French, and Italian grapes, as well as an assortment of fruits and trees.[15]

Alas, Norton's marriage was to be short-lived; his wife died in 1821, leaving him emotionally devastated. To cope with his grief, Norton poured himself into viticultural experimentation at Magnolia Farm. His experimentation perhaps addressed Norton's long-held wish to increase his status and social standing in Richmond: "I have all my life," Norton wrote to his brother in January 1824, "been as proud as Lucifer and as poor as a church mouse…. Amongst the gaudy crowd, [I have] been seen only when sought for." An inferiority complex, if it existed, led to Norton's need to entertain and to engage in a horticultural pursuit that proved, indeed, to be cherished by Richmond's social elites.[16]

Sometime in the 1820s, Norton is believed to have fertilized the "Bland" grape with pollen from another variety known as "Miller's Burgundy." Though the story is uncorroborated, Norton allegedly saved the seeds from the cross-pollinated clusters and planted them. One of these seedlings, which he named "Norton's Virginia," quickly garnered a citation in William Robert Prince's 1830 work *A Treatise on the Vine*, where the grape was given its Latin name, *Vitis nortoni*.[17]

The mention of the variety in Prince's *Treatise* propelled the variety to greater popularity and enhanced reputation. Widely believed to be the most reliable secondhand resource on the Norton grape's origins, Prince wrote that the grape "was raised from the seed of the Bland," with shoots that were "strong and vigorous," and that resisted "the cold of the most severe winters, never failing to produce fruit…almost equaling the Isabella." Having received both cuttings and a description of the grape's origin from Norton himself, Prince concluded his description with a statement (a self-serving quote from Norton describing his grape): "For the purpose of making wine, this is hardly to be excelled by any foreign variety."[18]

While Prince's account of the grape's origin has been the most widely accepted, there is a competing tale, which asserts that another Richmond physician, Dr. F. A. Lemosy, originally discovered the variety growing wild sometime between 1835 and 1836, on Cedar Island in the James River. Writing nearly two decades after Norton's death in 1861, Lemosy's son claimed that it was his late father who either provided the wild vine cuttings to Norton, or who told Norton of the grape's location. While Lemosy's account gained some acceptance, given that Norton was no longer around to dispute it, later observers discerned that the timeline of the Lemosy account appears at odds with the 1830 publication of Prince's *Treatise*, some five years before Lemosy's alleged discovery.[19]

Like the story of its discovery, the Norton's biological makeup is also unconfirmed. This is largely because of the grape's small berries and lack of "foxiness" (a quality that has traditionally accompanied wines produced from native American grapes). Norton evidently grew the variety in two different locations at Magnolia Farm, both of which were near his house, and in a vineyard alongside multiple varieties. While the Norton's foliage certainly resembles that of the Bland grape and shares the hairs, tendrils, and the flavor of other native grapes, Norton emphatically denied that the Bland was the cross-pollinator.[20]

Whatever the foundations of the Norton grape's Mendelevian genealogy, Dr. Norton must be credited with bringing the variety to the public's attention and promoting its qualities. As wine writer and vintner George Husmann wrote in 1866, the Norton grape "opened a new era in American grape culture, and every successive year but adds to its reputation," noting that the grape surpassed even the "best red wines of Europe." Norton's Virginia grape was made available commercially beginning in the 1830s, and its cultivation quickly spread across the mid-Atlantic and Midwestern states.[21]

On the eve of the Civil War in 1861, plantings of the Norton quite nearly surpassed the Catawba as the most widely cultivated wine grape in the United States. The fact that the grape was difficult to ripen in regions north of the Potomac River, however, practically guaranteed that Virginia would enjoy a monopoly in its cultivation; after the Civil War, the Norton grape served as the bulwark of the commonwealth's first significant wine industry.[22]

Norton died in 1842, leaving behind "a pleasant memory of dignity and sociability" of his life in Richmond as he achieved posthumously the social standing he had long sought. His viticultural work not only helped lead Virginia into the annals of American wine history, but also secured him a lasting place within the Richmond elite whose opinions he had so cherished. His obituary, printed in both the *Richmond Enquirer* and the *Richmond Whig & Public Advertiser,* described Norton as:

> a gentleman of an enlarged mind, of fine literary taste, and celebrated for his knowledge of the vine, and his skill in horticulture. His disposition was amiable; his society most agreeable. The scope of his observation had been extensive—various in his reading and original in his reflections. We bid him a last and most affectionate Adieu![23]

While Norton was perhaps the most successful grape grower in antebellum Virginia, he was certainly not alone. One impression of early-nineteenth-century grape growing in Virginia came in 1830, when a Constantinople-born polymath of French and German heritage, Constantine Rafinesque, published his short pamphlet, *American Manual of Grape Vines and the Method of Making Wine.*

A self-proclaimed botanist, Rafinesque highlighted several of the young nation's native grapes, and provided what is perhaps the earliest estimate of vineyard acreage in the United States. He wrote that in 1825, there existed only 60 vineyards nationwide; by 1830, he counted some 200 vineyards consisting of nearly 5,000 acres. Rafinesque included a list of known winegrowers in Virginia, including "Lockhart," "Zane," "R. Weir," "Noel, J.," "Browne, J." and "Duling"; he did not provide locations of most of their vineyards or information as to whether they produced wine.[24]

It is known, however, that one of the names Rafinesque mentioned, Josiah Lockhart, lived in the Back Creek Valley area of northwestern Frederick County, perhaps near the community of Gainesboro. There, Lockhart hired a Swiss vigneron to clear two acres on which he planted some 2,000 cuttings of Catawba vines in February and March 1825. The cold winter of 1825–1826 resulted in the flourishing of fewer than half of the Catawba cuttings, but by 1827, Lockhart's vigneron sold grapes and had made approximately fifty gallons of wine. By 1827, Lockhart had increased his vineyard to nearly six acres, and reported that his grapes prospered.[25]

Another notable viticultural contributor during the early 1800s—though not mentioned in Rafinesque's work—was John Patten Emmet, a Dublin-born Charlottesville resident who had been brought to the University of Virginia by his friend Thomas Jefferson in 1825. Hired as the University's first Professor of Natural History and Chemistry, Emmet became the commonwealth's first academic viticultural experimenter.[26]

In 1834, after several years of living on the Lawn at the University, Emmet moved with his wife and his growing family to a nearby house called Morea. There he engaged in horticultural experimentation, including the planting of flowers, fruit trees, and grapevines. Morea eventually boasted a six- to eight-acre vineyard, and Emmet hired experts to plant vinifera varietals and to graft them onto native rootstock. From these, he produced various fruit wines and brandies beginning in 1836.[27]

While Emmet's viticultural endeavors were time consuming and evidently interfered with his academic responsibilities, they served as a source of inspiration and enjoyment for the professor. "My farm is so close to the University," he wrote to his sister-in-law, "that without omitting the discharge of any professional duties I shall be enabled to ride my silk and wine hobbies to death even, should I choose to do so." Emmet died in 1842, and it is unclear whether those who survived him at the University continued his experiments.[28]

At the time of Emmet's passing, Virginia's agricultural industry—like that of the nation itself—was in a state of transition. Since the beginning of the 1800s, the United States had undergone massive changes in commerce and politics: a second, modestly successful, war with Great Britain; a grander war with Mexico; the Louisiana Purchase; the evolution of the justice system at the hands of the great Virginian, John Marshall; and more. The nation was growing rapidly and beginning its long march away from agriculture toward industrialization. For the first time, textiles were being mass produced, farming was becoming mechanized, and factories were emerging in big cities and small towns alike.

Advances in transportation accompanied industrialization, and waterways proved particularly useful as major highways of commerce. Canals, along with railroads and steamships, enabled the shipment of goods from orchards, fields, and gardens in the interior of the country to previously undreamed-of markets. By the 1850s, canals had sprung up in Alexandria, Fredericksburg, the Great Dismal Swamp, and Richmond, while a new berry fruit export industry flourished in the Hampton Roads area, centered on the commonwealth's extraordinary ports.[29]

While most of the state's fruits had previously been grown for personal or local consumption, things changed forever in 1854 when a steamer, the *Roanoke*, sailed from Norfolk laden with Virginia-grown strawberries and vegetables bound for hungry New York City consumers. To be sure, nearly numberless ships departed Norfolk daily, but this particular dispatch—the first to carry large quantities of fruit to a northeastern market—heralded the beginning of a commercial fruit production and distribution industry in the Mid-Atlantic, with Hampton Roads as its center.[30]

Shortly after the *Roanoke* sailed, Virginians made crucial improvements to an otherwise disjointed and incomplete railroad system. While there were only 384 miles of railroads in the commonwealth and no rail lines west of the Blue Ridge in 1850, railroads linked Hampton Roads with Richmond, Washington, D.C., Lynchburg, and Winchester by 1861. Alongside waterways, these new railroads offered unheard opportunities for fruit growing and distribution to areas that, heretofore, had been forced to rely solely on turnpikes or poorly maintained roads.[31]

Just prior to the Civil War, grapes therefore joined a handful of other widely planted fruit crops in Virginia, including pears, peaches, and apples. Virginia was suddenly among the largest wine producers in the nation, producing some

13,911 gallons annually by the 1840s. While most of the state's fruit growing had previously occurred in Tidewater thanks to its coastal climate and transportation access, by that time small commercial vineyards had been established in Albemarle and Warren Counties as well.[32]

By 1860, the commonwealth joined thirty-two other states and nine territories in producing an estimated 1,627,000 gallons of wine nationwide, with most now coming from Ohio and California. With ample transportation connections and a growing interest in producing American wine, the prospects for a steady, growing, Virginia wine industry centered on native and American hybrid grapes looked bright.[33]

## —An Industry Deferred:
### The American Civil War & Its Aftermath—

As with so many prior episodes in the tortured saga of Virginia's wine, just when all seemed to be going well the industry was once again set back by devastation; this time the American Civil War. From the war's first major battle in July 1861 at Manassas until Lee's surrender in April 1865 at Appomattox, armies crisscrossed Virginia and transformed the commonwealth, indeed the South, socially, economically, and politically. The war was the most physically devastating in Virginia's (or the nation's) history—a fate assured once Richmond was selected as the Confederate capital one month after the commonwealth seceded in April 1861. Virginia saw by far the greatest number of battles, and was left reeling and destitute after four years of unmitigated conflict. Among the casualties were Virginia's vineyards. Although no records exist to quantify their wartime destruction, given the physical scattering of vineyards and private winemaking enterprises across the commonwealth, it can be said with some certainty that many engagements were fought near, or over, the commonwealth's vineyards.

Reports of such events are scarce, but one such action occurred during the Second Battle of Fredericksburg in May 1863, when a Union general noted that he had formed "a line of battle" near the rear of the 500-acre Hopewell Nursery, a large commercial nursery located along the Plank Road outside of Fredericksburg that grew some 300,000 fruit and ornamental trees, including grape vines. A second vineyard clash occurred one month later during the June 1863 Battle of Upperville, located on the Fauquier-Loudoun County line. Indeed, much of the fighting occurred atop Vineyard Hill, so named for a thorny hedge-enclosed vineyard that offered a clear view of nearby roads and fields.

There, some 10,000 cavalry and infantrymen clashed in hand-to-hand combat. Confederate Major General J. E. B. Stuart employed the hill's strategic location to delay Union Major General Alfred E. Pleasonton from advancing west; the time granted Confederate commander Robert E. Lee the space needed to turn north and invade Pennsylvania.[34]

Wine, likely manufactured in Virginia, also played a role in halting a bungled Union raid on Richmond in March 1864. While marching east toward the capitol city that month, a 400-man column led by Union Colonel Ulric Dahlgren stopped at the home of the Confederate Secretary of War James A. Seddon. Though Seddon was in Richmond at the time, Dahlgren was received by Seddon's wife, Sarah Bruce Seddon, who invited the Northern officer to discuss their mutual acquaintances over a vintage 1844 bottle of blackberry wine. Mrs. Seddon's gesture was not as altruistic as it may have seemed. While the two exchanged pleasantries and drank to each other's families and health, Mrs. Seddon sent a servant to Richmond to warn the Confederate government of the nearby presence of Union troops. While other events forced Dahlgren to head north after leaving the Seddon plantation instead of proceeding east to Richmond, Mrs. Seddon has been fondly remembered as the woman who saved Richmond over a bottle of Virginia wine.[35]

The ruin of the war and the imprint left by soldiers and fleeing civilians—like the destruction caused to Philip Mazzei's Colle vineyards following the occupation of Hessian troops during the American Revolution—was significant. Vineyards were destroyed, workers became soldiers, slaves were conscripted, and theft occurred. Crops were ruined; grape markets, and the ability to transport goods, were all but destroyed. The Civil War all but halted wine production for years. Grapes, which had preoccupied so much of early American social and agricultural history, were of necessity an afterthought during a war to determine the future course of American life. As one Albemarle County writer summarized the importance of wine—or the lack thereof—during the conflict,

> Grapes and their product, wine, are reverently spoken of in the Bible as symbols of contentment, peace and social happiness. This unpleasantness between the sections of the union promoted neither of these triad conditions. Self-preservation, simple existence in barbaric aspect was the utmost of our efforts.[36]

In the aftermath of the fighting Virginia's wine production was understandably much reduced. Like the commonwealth's other agricultural commodities, the Civil War left vineyards without care, cultivation, or expertise. By 1865, fewer than 100 acres of grapes were reported under cultivation across the commonwealth.[37]

The devastation wrought on Virginia's vineyards mirrored that of Virginia's agricultural industry. Large plantations were divided into smaller tenant farms, and Virginia's surviving large farmers were compelled to seek innovative ways to diversify in the absence of their previous supply of labor—slaves. Throughout the ruin, Virginians maintained their optimism, working to restore their farms, fertilize the soil, and get on with their lives.[38]

Shortly after the end of hostilities in 1865, newspapers began suggesting that Virginians return to the production of fruits and wine grapes as a new source of income in a struggling economy. Those who signed on for the effort looked once more—as they had before the war—to native and hybrid grapes. Almost immediately, small experimental vineyards sprouted among the fertile fields of Virginia's Piedmont and Tidewater regions, focusing primarily on native varietals. These vineyards included plantings of Norton, Catawba, Delaware, Clinton, and Concord grapes.[39]

Albemarle, Norfolk, Warren, and Fairfax Counties quickly emerged as Virginia's most prominent grape areas, and observers—like those two centuries before—made note of the commonwealth's abundance of indigenous grapes, and their belief was renewed that Virginia was once again ripe for grape production. Virginians were caught in "grape fever" as cultivation spread yet farther across the state to the Blue Ridge Mountain region. By 1868, Virginia again boasted a large commercial grape growing business and, over the next three decades, during which national wine production would increase fiftyfold, the state's wine industry would rise to international recognition.[40]

One French citizen, listed only as "Monare," was apparently so impressed with the prospects of vineyards in Virginia's Tidewater region that he sought out other Frenchmen in the hopes of founding a French colony along the Potomac River in Prince William County. Much like the idealistic dreams of earlier such colonies, however, Monare died before his dreams came to fruition.[41]

Commercial fruit and tree nurseries were established or had reopened across Virginia by the late 1860s, most located in the soil-rich and mild climate eastern portions of the state. These nurseries propagated and grew plants to a usable size and then sold them to agricultural growers and horticultural hobbyists alike. For the first time, fruit and fruit tree species of all types—including grapevines—were made widely available to the general public, which helped to spread viticulture and the availability of grapes across the commonwealth.[42]

One of Virginia's largest and oldest commercial nurseries, Franklin Davis Nursery Company, was established by Franklin Davis early in the 1850s in

Rockbridge County. By 1858, the nursery had relocated to Staunton and, after seeing its fruit stock destroyed by the Civil War, moved again to Richmond. The company later opened a second branch in Baltimore and, by the mid-1880s, Franklin Davis boasted some 400 acres in nursery stock, becoming one of the largest nurseries in the eastern United States. The enterprise shipped fruit trees and vines throughout the East Coast, selling upwards of 500,000 fruit trees annually. The nursery's stocks also included forty or more grape varieties.[43]

Another large nursery, the Virginia Nursery & Wine Company, was founded in January 1868 in Richmond. It grew fruits and manufactured wines from Norfolk, Concord, Clinton, and Catawba grapes. A third nursery, the Cleveland Nursery Company, relocated from Ohio to the Richmond County community of Rio Vista in 1892, and propagated small fruits and grapes. Other nineteenth century Virginia nurseries included Richmond's Joseph Stinton Nursery, Thomas S. Pleasants's nursery in Petersburg, Hopewell Nurseries in Fredericksburg, Henry B. Jones Nurseries in Brownsburg and Staunton, Oliver Taylor's nursery in Loudoun County, Spring Hill Nurseries in Prince Edward County, and the A. F. Mosby Nursery in Staunton.[44]

The postwar expansion of Virginia's commercial nursery operations and fruit industry led materially to the establishment of a number of organizations that advocated on behalf of horticulture and fruit plantings in the Commonwealth. For example, the Virginia State Agricultural Society, the Norfolk Horticultural and Pomological Society, the Potomac Fruit Growers' Association, the Lynchburg Pomological Society, the Catoctin Farmers' Club, and the Amherst County Horticultural Society joined dozens more in providing local communities an opportunity to exchange advice and learn of the latest fruit-growing advancements and techniques.[45]

One of the more prominent advocacy groups was the Virginia Horticultural and Pomological Society, founded in Richmond in May 1867. The Society held monthly meetings and annual exhibitions that later evolved into the Virginia State Fair. In 1869, the Society partnered with the Norfolk Horticultural and Pomological Society to invite the American Pomological Society to a joint conference in September 1871. The conference, held in Richmond, attracted more than 100 fruit experts from across the United States. Given that the American Pomological Society was comprised almost entirely of pomologists from northern states, nearly everyone in attendance appreciated that the conference's location in the capital of the former Confederacy was a way not only to exchange ideas, but also to help mend wounds left by the war.[46]

In the South, the former Confederate states struggled to shake loose the yoke of Reconstruction and to restore their previous economic foundations.

Virginia saw its fair share of renewed prosperity; tobacco was once again king, but the state's fruit and equestrian industries also flourished. In Richmond, millionaire James Dooley built a 100-acre Victorian estate, Maymont, and Lewis Ginter constructed an expensive eponymous suburban subdivision. In Danville, textile and tobacco executives competed for architectural superiority along the city's "Millionaires Row."

With new commercial nurseries, a growing economy, expanding grape societies, and more, the social and economic environment was once again open to ingenuity, industrial mechanization, oil and steel conglomerates, the advent of high-rise buildings, and, for the first time in many years, actual growth. In the midst of it all, the commonwealth's first truly great wine industry emerged.

## —The First Virginia Wine Industry—

Virginia's fruit and grape industries thrived from the 1870s through the turn of the century, expanding rapidly to enjoy a relatively stable period of uninterrupted growth. New vineyards popped up across the commonwealth. Development was dramatic, prompting Virginia's Commissioner of Agriculture, Col. Randolph Harrison, to remark,

> Virginia, aye, the United States, can compare most favorably with the grape-growing countries of the Old World…. In the United States, and especially in Virginia, frosts of any great severity are rare in the month of May. Sunshine in summer in plenty can always be relied upon, and the autumns are generally dry, warm, and protected, and favorable to the thorough maturing of the grapes as well as the vines…. Let it be known everywhere that…we will see very soon each side of the railroads covered with fine orchards and vineyards.[47]

Perhaps the Colonel was overly optimistic; perhaps not. With the Civil War over, there emerged a growing optimism both within the state and beyond that the Old Dominion might at long last give birth to a stable and sustainable viticultural industry. From the devastation wrought by 1865, the commonwealth boasted some 3,000 acres of grape plantings and produced 26,283 gallons of wine annually by 1870. Just ten years later, Virginia's production had increased nearly tenfold. After yet another decade, by 1890, vineyards covered 4,100 acres and the state manufactured an astonishing 461,000 gallons of wine, ranking sixth nationally in terms of wine production.

"Virginia, the 'Mother of Presidents,'" wrote one observer "has as fine grape lands as has 'Sunny France' herself, and a sufficient acreage to make her one of the foremost states in the Union in wine production." Others hailed the Shenandoah Valley as "the greatest wine and fruit producing section of the United States," while one New York wine dealer confidently asserted that Virginia would "become the wine cellar of America."[48]

Such comments reflected the reality that by the 1870s Virginia had indeed managed to cobble together its first production wine industry. Chiefly founded on wines from native varieties, this fledgling industry experienced the heavy participation of German newcomers to the state, as well as the re-emergence of the Charlottesville–Albemarle County region as the industry's geographic center. The state's first major wine companies evolved during this period as well, and some produced wines that won national and international awards for their quality.

Wine was now produced in all corners of the state, though, relative to today's standards, the wine produced was likely of medium- to low- quality. But, for an emerging industry in a state that lacked a recent experience of wine consumption and had suffered relative failure in fomenting an industry, it can be assumed that the quality of wine produced for the unrefined palates that it touched was equal to the task.[49]

The Piedmont region of Virginia quickly emerged as a leader in the new industry, with growers focusing on Norton, Catawba, and Concord varieties. It offered abundant slopes, well-hydrated soils, more moderate climates, and what growers then thought to be the best conditions for the cultivation of the grape. Three Piedmont counties—Albemarle, Prince William, and Warren—all enjoyed phenomenal growth. In Loudoun County, William Giddings, the county's second school superintendent and a former Confederate colonel, grew some 10,000 Concord vines at his 1,000-acre estate, Melrose. In neighboring Fairfax County, some growers boasted 4,000 to 5,000 vines each, many of which produced table grapes to sell for a profit in Washington, D.C.[50]

One Falls Church judge, J. H. Gray, planted a vineyard in 1870 from which he produced grape juice and communion wine. Faced with diseases and destruction from the rose chafer beetle—a pest that attacked the foliage of his grapes—Gray planted and replanted his vineyards once every three years to avoid decimation. In Prince William County, one "Mr. Wagener" reportedly owned a large vineyard and cellar from which he manufactured and stored approximately 2,000 gallons of wine per year.[51]

In Virginia's capitol region, multiple growers had successfully cultivated Norton and Concord vineyards by the 1880s, and some observers believed that Richmond, and not Albemarle, with its transportation network, was on the cusp of becoming the center of the commonwealth's wine industry. Hanover County, for example, claimed some 100 acres of vineyards, while Henrico County counted twice as much land under cultivation.[52]

East of Richmond, a "Dr. Gilmer" operated a vineyard comprised of Norton, Concord, and Herbemont (a brown French grape) varieties, from which he produced wine and grape brandy. Some ten miles outside of the city, Richmond resident and hairdresser Raphael Ferrandini cultivated a thirty-five-acre vineyard, where he grew a variety of native wine and table grapes and produced wine. A few miles away, one French native constructed a wine cellar and manufactured a claret wine that won a prize at a Richmond competition. Other plantings occurred in Chesterfield and in Dinwiddie County, where Thomas F. Rives grew Concord and Catawba grapes.[53]

This nascent wine industry was alive in Hampton Roads as well. There, the scuppernong grape flourished on the regions' riverbanks and sandy soils. Scuppernong—the only grape of the Muscadine family deemed suitable for making wine—grew readily in the Southeast. The variety produced a semisweet wine that was preferred by early–twentieth-century American consumers (it was enjoyed by Thomas Jefferson, for example), and was perhaps perfect for the unrefined and long-neglected wine palates of Dixie.[54]

Surprisingly, many Tidewater area growers found that their region's coastal climate caused native grapes to ripen too early, and to produce insufficient sugar for winemaking. Area growers persisted nevertheless. In what was then Norfolk County (today the City of Chesapeake), English immigrant Albert Dodge grew some 10,000 pounds of Concord grapes and 1,000 pounds of Martha grapes annually on a mere one-and-a-half acres of flat, sandy loam soil. From these he made a few barrels of wine and sold the rest.[55] Another Norfolk County grower, J. E. Baker, cultivated Ives, Concord, Norton, and scuppernong grapes on 48 acres and was reportedly a significant regional producer of wine. At Norfolk County's Laurel Hill Vineyard, proprietor F. W. Lemosy planted approximately 500 acres in vines and was considered one of the commonwealth's pioneer pomologists. Elsewhere in the region, the Montrose Wine Company operated a small 4-acre vineyard and produced wine in Smithfield, while several King and Queen County residents made small amounts of wine from uncultivated native grapes that were deemed to be "quite palatable."[56]

Small vineyards could also be found outside of Virginia's major population centers, with a majority of their wines and grapes shipped to Richmond and Petersburg. Lunenburg County, better known (even today) for tobacco, developed "a very respectable wine interest" from its mere 20 to 30 acres of mostly

Concord grapes. Bedford County, filled with orchards and vineyards, manu-factured high-quality wine made from fruit and grapes grown along the south-ern slopes of the Blue Ridge Mountains.[57] In Buckingham County, a handful of dedicated growers cultivated table grapes. In Rockbridge County, William Weaver and his family tried to grow grapes and make wine at their Vineyard Hill estate, only to find the wine unpalatable. In the Lawrenceville area of Brunswick County, where few vineyards comprised more than an acre, Congressman and attorney Robert Turnbull successfully grew Norton and Concord grapes. Even in the southwestern corner of the state, Bland County produced wines made from cultivated and wild apples, peaches, pears, cherries, and plums. There, Brit-ish immigrant Glen Walker planted some 11,000 grape vines, and established a small wine cellar for his manufactured wine.[58]

While vineyards came to be spread throughout the state, the industry's prospects seemed most promising in the greater Charlottesville region. There, several growers envisioned the Rivanna River—which cuts through Albemarle County near Charlottesville—as the would-be "Rhine of America" and a new wine Eden. Albemarle County was also home to several large and small wine cellars.[59]

One such Albemarle County cellar belonged to J. W. Porter, who cultivated some 60 acres near Monticello. Experiencing firsthand the phenomenal growth in the region's grape industry, Porter speculated in 1876 that "the day will come when the culture of the apple and the grape will supplant that of tobacco and corn." Within a few years, Porter was more right than wrong, for by the 1880s some 100 vineyards dotted the county, covering more than 3,000 acres and pro-ducing one million pounds of grapes annually.[60] Most of these grapes were either manufactured into wine or transported to New York, Richmond, and to natural spring resorts across the state. Albemarle was soon lauded as the place "from which the famous Virginia Claret wines are made"; local residents proudly proclaimed Charlottesville as the "Capital of the Wine Belt of Vir-ginia." One 1888 promotional pamphlet for Albemarle County boastfully (if not so honestly) assessed the region's potential for winemaking thusly:

> A stranger approaching Charlottesville by rail, will perceive that he is getting into the land of the vine. Hill-side after hill-side covered with grape vines attest the extent the culture has attained here. The great wine cellars at Charlottesville are a revelation to many strangers, who have not dreamed of the extent to which this culture has been carried here. Virginia Claret has attained a reputation, with competent judges, which places it ahead of the adulterated imported article, and the demand for

it is constantly increasing. The Albemarle grapes are among the first to reach the Northern markets, and the early table grapes are sure to command remunerative prices…. The hills of Albemarle will become more and more vineclad, and be a source of renewable profits to our people.[61]

The steady rise of Albemarle's grape industry spawned a monthly publication, the *Monticello Farmer and Grape Grower*. Published between 1883 and 1887, the magazine featured contributions from area vineyard owners and winemakers, including frequent letters and updates from representatives of the Monticello Wine Company. The magazine's "Grape Department" offered topical and timely articles, as well as advice on grape cultivation, irrigation, soils, sugar content, plowing techniques, and grape varieties. Replete with promotional references to the superiority of Virginia's suitability to grape growing, the *Grape Grower* rarely hesitated to remind its readers of the history and benefits of winemaking in Albemarle County, including such reminders as that "Albemarle County contains many excellent people, for no better fruit grows in the world than in old Albemarle."[62]

Local advocacy groups and societies also formed, dedicated to furthering the advancement of the wine industry. In November 1884, after years during which Albemarle growers highlighted the need for a local grape and fruit association, the Monticello Grape and Fruit-Growers Association was established in Charlottesville. Its ninety-five initial members included prominent winemakers from central Virginia, including Adolph Russow, Henry Minor Magruder, and Oscar Reierson, and several professors from the University of Virginia. The Association organized numerous committees, including a "Committee on Theft" and a "Committee on Experiments," the latter of which, led by C. A. Uber of Falls Church, planted 150 varieties of grapes for testing and research.[63]

The Association's formation had been preceded in January 1878 by the creation of a statewide grape organization, the Virginia Wine Growers' Association. This Association, formed in Richmond by several Virginia grape growers, soon had branches in Albemarle, Norfolk, Warren, and Fairfax. Other Charlottesville-area organizations included the Piedmont Fruit Growers' Association, founded by thirty fruit and grape growers in 1886 in the Gordonsville area of Orange County, which advocated for better shipping facilities and lower shipping rates for Virginia fruit growers. The following year, the Grape Growers Association of Albemarle joined the fray.[64]

One large and prominent Albemarle family that undoubtedly benefited from the economic advantages of grape growing in Albemarle were the Minors. The owners of several properties spanning both sides of the Rivanna River north of Charlottesville, the Minor family shared equipment, collaborated on growing techniques, and oversaw a successful, if small, family grape-growing enterprise. Led by family patriarch William W. Minor, Jr., a former Confederate soldier and part-time attorney, the family's grape growing hobby began shortly after Minor's acquisition of a small circa-1770 house, known as Windie Knowe, from his father late in the 1880s. Nearby, on a large tract of land that featured rocky soils found to be perfect for grape growing, Minor planted a large vineyard. He hired Tom Flannagan and Isaac Ross—two of Minor's late father's former slaves and the family's most trusted "loyal hands"—to oversee the vineyard's operations. One relative noted of the family's grape growing hobby,

> In the late summer the grapes were gathered and though most of these were carelessly thrown in barrels and carried to town to the wine cellar, some fancy varieties were carefully packed for shipment to the northern markets. All of the family helped in this packing and it seemed like a protracted picnic to me, for the packing house was about a mile from our house and we often did not go home for dinner.[65]

Despite success in grape growing in Virginia, the white South experienced Reconstruction as a largely unmitigated disaster. Most white farming families were suddenly hampered by the lack of access to credit, while former slave-holders were forced to confront the fact that their labor force had employment options—as limited as they may have been. While farmers struggled to maintain their prewar agricultural practices, the plantation system no longer existed. Virginia's older mansions and vast tracts of cleared land were left fallow, in a state of disrepair, or simply abandoned altogether, as families were forced to move to urban areas.

Into this economic and social abyss stepped immigrants of German stock, many of whom proved particularly adept at grape cultivation and viticulture.[66] Largely eschewing the more profitable agricultural commodities of corn, tobacco, oats, and wheat, many of these German arrivals found their place in the production of wine. Their efforts not only helped develop the state's wine industry into a national player during the late nineteenth century, but they also played a prominent role in founding and administering Virginia's wine companies.[67]

One such industrious German immigrant, William L. Hotopp, established his Pen Park Vineyards along the Rivanna River just north of Charlottesville late in the 1860s. The first commercial producer of wine in Albemarle County, Hotopp was a native of the Celle region of Germany who had immigrated to the United States at eighteen. He worked as a manufacturer in New Jersey before settling in Virginia. He became a stockholder in the Monticello Wine Company, and was among the first to envision a large grape-growing industry in central Virginia.[68]

Hotopp bought his Albemarle County property in 1866, and almost immediately began planting Delaware, Norton, Ives, and Concord grapes. Believed to be the first large commercial vineyard in the commonwealth, Pen Park cultivated fourteen acres of native varietals by 1872 and sixty-one more by early in the 1890s. With a storage capacity of some 130,000 gallons by the mid-1880s, Pen Park produced nearly 100,000 pounds of grapes annually and manufactured more than 30,000 gallons of both red and white wines by 1871. Most of Pen Park's wines were sold in New York, Philadelphia, Baltimore, and Washington, D.C., with the balance shipped to Richmond, Alexandria, Lynchburg, and Charlottesville.[69]

In the Greenfield area of Nelson County, another German grape grower, Fritz Baier, produced some 6,000 gallons annually from wine made from grapes at his eighty-acre Castle Hill Vineyard. Perched on the southeastern slope of the Blue Ridge Mountains overlooking the Rockfish Valley, Castle Hill featured a wine press, fermenting room, and a cellar. Baier produced Catawba, Claret, Clinton, and Norton wines. While he attempted unsuccessfully to cultivate some 1,000 vinifera vines, Baier noted proudly that his vineyard "is certainly the finest... I have met with in this country, and certainly compares favorably with the best localities in Germany."[70]

Near Castle Hill, German immigrant Louis Ott made wine and evidently cultivated one of the largest vineyards in central Virginia. He served as a contributor to the *Monticello Farmer and Grape Grower* magazine, and frequently criticized Virginia's penchant for relying too heavily on native grapes. Elsewhere in Virginia, near Fredericksburg, John Van Opsdale produced between 6,000 and 8,000 gallons of wine from his large vineyard that were sold in New York. Van Opsdale's vineyard was planted in 1879 by Monticello Wine Company superintendent George Arnaud and consisted of Ives, Norton, Elvira, Martha, and Herbemont grapes, as well as French and German varieties.[71]

At the northern end of the state, Prince William County emerged as a major center for Prussian and German immigrants after the Civil War, particularly outside the sleepy village of Haymarket. The newcomers established fruit tree farms and vineyards with native varieties, and brought with them German viticultural techniques and winemaking traditions. One resident, William Heuser, wrote that several small Prince William County vineyards produced some 175,000 pounds of grapes and 12,000 gallons of wine annually, including Claret, Rhenish, and Hocks (German style wines).[72]

Prince William County's largest vineyard belonged to Robert Portner, a true beer baron from the Westphalia area of Germany, who experimented with grapes early in the 1890s. The owner of several of the South's largest breweries, Portner arrived in the United States at the age of sixteen and purchased 191 acres just north of Manassas where he built a large three-story stone summer house named Annaburg that featured a small winery and a 40-acre vineyard planted in Concord and other assorted varieties. Portner produced wines for his guests and family from an estimated annual production of 100,000 pounds of grapes, and stored the wines on the ground level of his manor house. While it is assumed that Portner's winemaking operations commenced more or less as a hobby, this changed following his introduction to another area German transplant, Christian Xander.[73]

Xander, a Washington, D.C. winemaker, arrived in the United States in 1853 and for several years served as winemaker in his family's liquor and wine business. Branching out on his own late in the 1860s, Xander opened a large beverage wholesale business in Alexandria and Washington, D.C., known as "Chr. Xander: Wholesale Wine Merchant." The operation distributed more than 130 different beverages to consumers in eight states, and manufactured its own lines of whiskies and "medicinal" beverages. The company also produced three wines made from Virginia grapes, including a port blend, a Norton Claret, and an Ives Claret. Each of Xander's wines was praised by observers for its "high efficiency in a medical sense," and were found to be "clean and full of taste, and...as soft and mellow as no other old wines."[74]

Beginning as early as 1883 Xander began producing wines from grapes taken from Robert Portner's Annaburg estate as well as from six other Virginia vineyards in Albemarle and Prince William County that were reportedly of the "highest class." Then, after nearly four years of aging, Xander's wines offered the "perfect adjustment of the elements of grape acids, tannin and iron oxide."[75]

Xander's winemaking was so successful that by 1893, demand for his wines exceeded output by nearly 20,000 gallons annually. He also received international recognition at the September 1900 Exposition Universelle in Paris, where he was awarded a bronze medal for his "Pride of Virginia Port" wine. As *The Washington Post* exclaimed of the victory,

> France is the land of wines; hence a medal for wines made from Virginia grapes, the merits of which Mr. Xander has discovered and developed, is, indeed, a high honor.... During sixteen vintages Mr. Xander

has made in his city winery, those delicious-tasting Virginia wines which have just received such high endorsement for quality and purity at the Paris Exposition. The general high opinion of Mr. Xander's wines and cordials has received the highest endorsement in the world by the medals just conferred.[76]

Following his 1900 Parisian success, Xander's Virginia Port grew in popularity and was manufactured as late as 1907. It is unclear when Xander ended his winemaking career, but today, Robert Portner's Annaburg estate is today the site of a nursing home, while the original Xander company buildings in Washington, D.C., have been demolished. In 1925, J. Harry Shannon, a contributor to the *Washington Star*, reminisced about Annaburg's vineyards, and Xander's award-winning Virginia Port,

and again by the way do you remember Xander's port…. Those grapes had the chivalrous, romantic and hospital[able] spirit of Virginia and Prince William County, and that fine old spirit lives in the port. Twenty years are gone since those grapes were plucked, and in their juice are harmony, the fragrance of rose, violet and mignonette, the radiance of May mornings, the light of the moon on Summer nights, the scent of all the gentle airs that blow across the Jurassic sandstone plains of Manassas.[77]

Elsewhere in Prince William County, one of the more successful wine businesses in late-nineteenth-century Virginia, the Mill Park Wine Company, was founded by German immigrants Franz Peters and Christian A. Heineken in 1869. Peters's foray into viticulture began following his purchase of a modest two-story frame house situated on 200 acres outside of Haymarket that he called Batavia. There he tended pastures, orchards, vegetable gardens, and vineyards, and made wines from Concord, Ives, and Martha grapes, which he later stored in his cellar.[78]

Peters struck up a friendship with Heineken, a descendant of the renowned Dutch and German Heineken beer-brewing family, who had arrived in the United States in 1846. Heineken had purchased his own two-story home, Mill Park, two miles north of Haymarket. There he began cultivating a ten-acre vineyard that featured Concord, Delaware, and Hartford grapes that were described by one observer as:

most luxuriant, fully demonstrating the fitness of the soil and climate for grape culture, and convincing even the most skeptical that there is almost absolute certainty of their doing remarkably well, and being a most profitable speculation. Those even who were loudest in their sneers at the absurdity of attempting to grow grapes in this locality would now like to have a few vines for their own use at least.[79]

Peters's and Heineken's success in viticulture encouraged the two to found the Mill Park Wine Company, which manufactured several red and white wines including the "Prince William" (a Norton wine), the "Rose of Virginia," two "Virginia Claret" wines, a "Virginia Sauternes" blend, a "Virginia Port," and a "Virginia Sherry," as well as Burgundy and Rhine wines. While the company produced by 1880 some 9,000 gallons of wine, by the 1890s the drought and diseases that ultimately slew Virginia's young and promising wine industry also beset the company's efforts. The company was forced to shutter its winemaking operations and, by the turn of the century, Heineken had turned to making brandy and fertilizer. [80]

Christian Heineken died in 1917; Peters followed him two years later, a victim of Spanish flu. Peters's Batavia eventually burned as part of a fire department training exercise, while Heineken's Mill Park property passed through different ownerships and is presently located in a large residential subdivision. Little else remains of the company, save a tribute song written by H. M. Clarkson, a friend of both Peters and Heineken in the Haymarket Agricultural Club, sung to the tune of "Auld Lang Syne":

> How oft we've met in days of yore,
> Around our festive board,
> And emptied bottles by the score,
> Till wine like water poured!
>
> And how we used to pledge our host
> In good old Mill Park wine,
> With gibe and jest,
> With het and boast,
> In days of Auld Lange Syne.[81]

## — The Monticello Wine Company —

German immigrants also oversaw Virginia's foremost corporate winemaking effort during the late nineteenth century, the Monticello Wine Company.

Formed in Charlottesville as the state's first farmer's cooperative in May 1873, the Company sought to produce affordable, high-quality table wines from native American grapes with a low alcohol content.[82]

The Company's subscribing members collaborated on a variety of vineyard projects and provided grape-growing expertise to one another, seeking to elevate the production and quality of Virginia wine while advocating for the type of temperate, moderate drinking habits Jefferson had recommended. To ensure a healthy, ready market especially for Albemarle County grapes, Company members pledged to purchase grapes from the Company at a price that was commensurate with juice quality.[83]

With some $40,000.00 in initial capital, the Company erected an impressive three-story brick winery, wine cellar, and storage facility on 2.6 acres near downtown Charlottesville. Grapes were obtained from multiple vineyards within a ten-mile radius of the cellar, whence they were transported to the winery building, conveyed into small flatcars, and pushed by hand to the top floor for processing.[84]

A rail spur to the winery enabled the Company to sell its wines throughout the eastern United States and helped it grow quickly. It produced some 5,000 gallons of wine during its first year in operation; 22,000 gallons by 1880; and 28,000 gallons by 1885. The Company advertised that it specialized in "pure native [*sic*] wines and grape brandy," including wines made from Delaware, Norton, Clinton, Catawba, and Ives grapes. The company also produced a Hock wine, a Norton Port, a Virginia Sherry, a grape brandy, and its most popular wine, an "Extra Virginia Norton Claret."[85]

In September 1881, the Company suffered a setback when its cellar was destroyed in a fire that destroyed valuable machinery, fixtures, supplies, and, most sadly, more than 18,000 gallons of wine and 469 gallons of brandy. The origins of the fire were never discovered, but speculation included everything from thieves to late-night employees failing to extinguish candles properly before leaving. One report summed up the blaze:

> As the fire burned, [*sic*] frequent explosions could be heard, and immense sluices of wine flowed out into the stream at the base of the hill on which the cellar was built. Some of it was caught up by adventurous spectators, but the greater portion was lost.[86]

The Company rebuilt a new four-story winery in 1882, larger than the first and featuring fireproof vaults with seventeen fermenting vats and a total storage capacity of 180,000 gallons. By the late 1880s, the Company's business was again booming but was once more derailed in 1887 by the onset of a widespread grapevine fungal disease known as "black rot." The disease, which decimated Albemarle County's vineyards, forced the Company to look beyond Virginia for its grapes. Indeed, its local grape sources grew so scarce that by the turn of the century, the Company offered free vines to anyone willing to plant them.[87]

Most of the Monticello Wine Company's success can be attributed to its leaders, especially Adolph Russow, Oscar Reierson, George Arnaud, William W. Minor Sr., and William L. Hotopp. Russow was born in 1851 in the Holstein region of northern Germany and immigrated to the United States in 1868. Serving as a New York City streetcar operator before arriving in Virginia, Russow later helped establish vineyards in Fauquier and Nelson Counties. His affiliation with the Company began in 1872, when he and his wife moved to a 307-acre property near Proffit Station in Albemarle County, where he established Bellevue Vineyards and sold grapes to the Company while serving as its new general manager.[88]

Joining Russow was the Company's secretary and treasurer, Oscar Reierson, a Dane who arrived in Virginia in 1858. After attending the University of Virginia, Reierson enlisted in the Confederate cavalry and, following the end of the war, established a law practice in Charlottesville.[89]

The Company's superintendent, the French-born George Arnaud, rejected the notion of planting vinifera varietals in Virginia, preferring instead to plant native grapes such as Norton, Ives, and Concord. As part of his duties, Arnaud made multiple visits to Fredericksburg, where he cultivated some twenty acres in vines and found Virginia's climate similar to France's Bordeaux and Burgundy regions. He was outspoken in his belief that Virginia was just as good, if not "much better" than France for grape cultivation:

> We have the climate, we have the soil. Let our grape-growers bear in mind that good and careful cultivation and proper training of the vines will bring perfect grapes, from which a perfect claret will be produced… as it is made in Bordeaux or Burgundy, and soon our claret will be acknowledged everywhere, as it is already in many places, as the best claret of America.[90]

Such declamations were not necessarily out of turn as the Company racked up an unprecedented number of state, national, and international awards. The first of its several accolades came in 1873 when its Extra Virginia Norton Claret received a gold medal at the Vienna World's Fair in Austria. Five years later, the Company shipped a case of twelve bottles of its Norton Claret to Paris's 1878

Exposition Universelle, where, despite a lack of representation or public promotion, the wine received the Exposition's silver medal for red wine. As Oscar Reierson cheerfully reported of the victory,

> Without any one being interested to bring this pitiful dozen, surrounded as it was by splendid pyramids of casks, cases, and bottles of other exhibitors, to the attention of any one, it has thus passed the crucial test under the most unfavorable circumstances. It certainly not only established itself, but drew attention to this section of country as one eminently fitted for grape culture.[91]

The Company again received a silver medal, and as well as a bronze, and a diploma for its Norton's Virginia wine, at Paris's 1889 Exposition Universelle. Two first class medals were awarded at Chicago's Worlds' Columbian Exposition in 1893, followed by another bronze medal and diploma at the 1900 Paris Exposition Universelle.[92]

The Company incorporated images of its medals on its wine labels. One enthusiastic customer proclaimed that the Company's wines were "so pure and excellent, medicinal, delicious, and grateful to the taste that... no vintage of any clime or country can or ever has excelled them." By 1899, the Company even gained the praise of future president Theodore Roosevelt, who praised the Company's wines as "superb."[93]

The Monticello Wine Company's achievements spurred Virginia wine sales and solidified its claims of high quality, which were heavily promoted—albeit with becoming modesty. As Oscar Reierson wrote in an 1888 advertisement,

> The company does not claim cheapness. It offers, at figures so reasonable as to be accessible to all, well-matured, pure fermented grape wines. Imported wine, of similar good quality, would cost double the price. It does not claim to produce the equals of the Grand Vins of Europe. Taking pride and character into consideration, it does claim a quality at half the price of that imported, when of similar character.[94]

The Company entered its golden years during the 1890s, producing some 68,000 gallons of wine annually. With the onset of the Charlottesville local option Prohibition law in 1907, the Company was compelled to look for ways to circumvent the law and attempted to purchase manufacturing licenses and offices in other states. Its efforts to outlast Virginia's Prohibitionist sentiment were ineffective, however; by 1915, with support for national Prohibition gaining ground, the Company failed. It sold its remaining stock of wine, liquidated its equipment, and sold the building to the Michie Company, a Charlottesville law book publisher. Michie used the building as a storage facility until 1937, when it, too, burned down.[95]

Today, the Monticello Wine Company—like much of Virginia's past wine industry—has been largely forgotten. There are, however, a few notable remnants worth highlighting. The names of two Charlottesville streets, Wine Street and Wine Cellar Circle, hark back to the Company. A historic marker commemorating the Company was erected in 2005 on Perry Drive in Charlottesville, near the site of the former winery building. The home of the winery's general manager, Adolph Russow, survives at 212 Wine Street, and an original bottle of Extra Virginia Norton Claret can be found in the Albemarle-Charlottesville Historical Society headquarters.[96]

## —Phylloxera—

Just as Virginia's wine industry appeared to be hitting its stride, Europe's great wine producing countries experienced a ruinous turn, caused by a small greenish-yellow winged aphid known as *Phylloxera vastatrix*. Phylloxera is believed to have been transplanted accidentally to the Rhone region of France in either 1858, 1862, or 1863. Phylloxera was, however, indigenous to eastern North America, and the insect fed on vinifera grape leaves and roots.

While how and when it was introduced to French wine country remains disputed, what is not in dispute is that Phylloxera caused one of the most catastrophic agricultural disasters in recorded history. Almost overnight, beginning in 1863, it began to feed on Europe's older grape roots and produced spawns— called "leaf galls"—which, in turn, fed on foliage and killed the vines.

The destruction caused by the pest was unparalleled; it feasted unchecked on vinifera in Great Britain, France, Spain, Austria, Germany, Italy, and Romania. Some estimates placed the destruction of European vineyards at between 60 and 90 percent. France, unsurprisingly, experienced the lion's share of Europe's damage. Its production levels were halved from 1.5 billion gallons to some 700,000,000 gallons almost overnight, and, by the late 1880s, the formerly famous wine-exporting country found itself a net importer of wines and winemaking supplies.[97]

Remarkably, America's native and American hybrid grapes had developed a partial resistance to Phylloxera. Their progeny had co-existed for thousands of years, and genetics had worked its magic. The pest had little effect on Virginia, whose wine industry consequently benefitted from Europe's troubles. Between 1870 and the turn of the century the "Great French Wine Blight" allowed the

United States to develop a healthy wine industry, particularly in California, New York, Ohio, Missouri, and Virginia.[98]

Government-sponsored research committees searched for answers as panic in Europe spread. Unsure as to the cause of the devastation, however, some European growers reluctantly replaced their infected vinifera vines with native American and American hybrid grapes. Others chose to burn their vinifera vineyards entirely. Many more devised fanciful remedies that used everything from walnut leaves to bovine urine to stop the insect.[99]

For nearly three decades, European grape growers pursued what proved to be dead ends; only a handful ventured to suspect that since the insect was native to the Americas, the solution to the problem might be found in the New World as well. It was not until 1879 that Charles V. Riley, a British-born entomologist living and working in America, discovered that by grafting European varieties onto the more resistant native American rootstocks, vinifera could indeed be made resistant to the pest. Riley's discovery brought an end to the destruction, and European wine flowed once again.[100]

His work also signaled the dawn of another era in wine grape growing, that of so-called "French hybrids" (also referred to as French-American hybrids). In their efforts to defeat Phylloxera, scientists of the era developed new, specialized grape varieties that exhibited the refined characteristics of vinifera while possessing the disease-resistant trades of American grapes. These French hybrid grapes proved easier to grow and maintain than vinifera, and their plantings proliferated across France.

While scientists eventually produced hundreds of thousands of French hybrid varieties, in the end only twelve or so proved suitable for commercial quality wine. Most showed little advantage over their pure vinifera cousins. Troubling, too, they had the distinct disadvantage of exhibiting the wild and foxy scent a year or more after bottling that had earlier been noted as a characteristic of some Virginia wines; unsurprising given their American grape lineage.[101] As a result, the mature wine regions of Europe quickly grew to disdain French hybrid varieties, eventually relegating them to the status of "vines of necessity." They are typically found today only in those areas where higher quality vinifera varietals simply are not suitable.[102]

French hybrids did, however, have important advantages over vinifera that resulted in positive effects on Virginia's modern-day wine industry. They proved not only easier to grow and hardier in colder and wetter climates, but they were also more disease resistant and by-and-large produced commercially-acceptable wines that were more refined than those produced from pure native or American hybrid varieties. In more recent times, French hybrid vines have earned a special place as part of Virginia's wine revolution that took place from the late 1960s to the 1990s, when they were used as a building block in the development of a wine industry later dominated by vinifera.[103]

With Virginia's first wine industry in full swing by the 1870s, and with the high demand for the state's rootstocks during the Phylloxera outbreak, the commonwealth's public officials came to express renewed optimism about the future of Virginia's wine industry. Thomas Pollard, Virginia's Commissioner of Agriculture in the late 1870s, said, "We can see no reason why Virginia should not became [*sic*] a great wine producing state and derive much revenue from it. Wherever in the state wine making has been attempted with any skill, it has succeeded." Pollard also argued that, with the devastation of French vineyards from the Phylloxera infestation, the resulting potential for new wine markets, and the need for Virginia farmers to realize additional sources of revenue following price declines in wheat, corn, and tobacco markets, "this is a favorable time to inaugurate the industry."[104]

Aside from speeches supporting industry expansion and innovation, Virginia's government did little to support its development financially. Unlike its colonial predecessor, which offered payment for experimentation and passed laws mandating the planting of grapes, Virginia's nineteenth-century government established neither strategic economic goals nor tax and other financial incentives to spur industry growth.

One exception, however, was found in academia. In what may have been the first postsecondary-controlled study of Virginia wine, students of Practical Chemistry in the University of Virginia's chemistry laboratory researched native grapes as early as October 1875 in the hopes of "furnishing some information which may be useful in the improvement of the manufacture" of wine. One enterprising student, R. M. Cooper, analyzed several wines produced by the Monticello Wine Company, Norfolk County's Laurel Hill Vineyards, and Front Royal's Belmont Vineyards. After testing the wines for alcohol levels, acidity, nitrogen, ash, potassium, and glucose content, Cooper found that each possessed high alcoholic and acidic content, and that greater care was thus required during the fermentation and bottling stages of the wines.[105]

Perhaps signaling a modern adage that the best wine is made in the best vineyards, Cooper also found that Virginia's winemakers were not paying "due attention… to the full ripening of the fruit and its careful selection in gathering." He argued that winemakers were including too many "unripe and partially decayed grapes" in the vat. Despite this, however, he concluded that the prospects for Virginia's wine industry offered much promise "for the future in reference to the production with adequate care of sound, wholesome, and palatable wines."[106]

## — *The Father of Modern Virginia Horticulture* —

The most important academic contribution to Virginia viticulture during the nineteenth century—and arguably through the present day—came in March 1886 when the General Assembly established the Virginia Agricultural Experiment Station at Blacksburg. Founded in anticipation of congressional passage of the 1887 Hatch Act, which provided federal funds to state land-grant colleges in order to create a series of agricultural experiment stations across the country, the Virginia Experiment Station followed the 1872 establishment of the Virginia Agricultural and Mechanical College (known after 1944 as Virginia Polytechnic Institute, or, simply, as Virginia Tech), a state-supported land-grant military institute using federal funds obtained under the federal Morrill Act of 1862.[107]

The need for the Experiment Station was clear: for years, funguses, viruses, diseases, and pests had ravaged the commonwealth's fruit crops. Lacking a central clearinghouse for agricultural information, the General Assembly charged the new facility with conducting scientific investigations and finding solutions to many of the problems that plagued Virginia farmers—particularly its fruit growers.[108]

The success of the Experiment Station and, to a large degree, that of all of Virginia Tech's early years, is owed to one particularly hard-working man, William Bradford Alwood. His appointment as Vice Director of the Experiment Station in 1888 coincided with the first formal academic studies of plant pathology and pest management in the commonwealth's history. These were conducted by Alwood himself, and not only commenced a major public effort to eradicate fruit pests and ensure the future of Virginia's grape industry, but paved the way for what would become Virginia Tech's present College of Agriculture and Life Sciences.[109]

Perhaps one of the least recognized of Virginia Tech's early faculty members, Alwood was a graduate of Ohio State University and The George Washington University. He also received training at both Germany's Royal Pomology School and France's Institut Pasteur. Serving as both Vice Director of the Experiment Station and head of horticulture, entomology, and mycology at the college, Alwood was for nearly sixteen years a one-man department and energy source, simultaneously developing the agricultural station and teaching courses in each of three disciplines.[110]

101

During his tenure at Virginia Tech between 1888 and 1904, Alwood criss-crossed the commonwealth—often at his own expense—to lecture and assist farmers, all the while planting more than 100 trees on the college's campus. He conducted extensive research and issued more than sixty bulletins and pamphlets on fruit and the biology of grapes, as well as grape disease control, wine-making, commercial wines, and fermentation. Alwood also spent considerable time demystifying the causes and solutions to grape diseases such as black rot, anthracnose, brown rot, and powdery mildew. He experimented widely with copper fungicide sprays and other early pesticides, and is credited for improving chemical-spray standards for Virginia's fruit growers.[111]

By August 1889, Alwood had introduced European spray technology to Virginia farmers when he published an article in the *Southern Planter* advocating for the use of a French-made sprayer, the "Japy Knapsack Sprayer," for control of black rot and mildew. Disappointed in the quality of similar American sprayers, Alwood stressed that the French sprayer was considerably cheaper and more effective than its American-made counterpart. He even imported and sold them at cost to Virginia's farmers.[112]

Alwood's experiments led him to conclude that plant and grapevine diseases could not be "cured," but could only be prevented, through the thorough and early spraying of fungicides and pesticides, as well as by the removal of rotten and decaying fruit and vines. Alwood also promoted the Norton grape variety as a source of high-quality wine that, if improved, could enable Virginia to compete favorably against European grapes. In 1891, Alwood asserted confidently the importance of his experiments:

> The work has been confined mostly to treatment of grapes and apples for the diseases now so seriously affecting them in this State and I am glad to report that the work has been quite successful. It can be confidently stated that the question of controlling the black rot…and the mildew… of grape[s] is now settled, and the statements which I have published during the past two years concerning the efficacy of the weaker preparations of Bordeaux mixture are fully substantiated.[113]

In September 1904, after sixteen years as Vice Director of the Experiment Station and fourteen years as the college's mycologist, Alwood's tenure in Blacksburg ended in the wake of an administrative reorganization. While Alwood had succeeded in establishing the college's Department of Horticulture in 1904, he had long been discouraged by the lack of financial support for the Experiment Station and from being passed over for an appointment as its director.[114]

Alwood and his family relocated to Charlottesville, where they purchased an estate named Stonehenge. Shortly after the move, the United States Department of Agriculture created a "Department of Enology" to study all aspects of wine-making, grape growing, and grape harvesting, and Alwood was tapped to serve as the new department's first director. He then rented Stonehenge to the USDA to establish a national enological laboratory.[115]

At the rechristened Stonehenge Laboratory, Alwood continued his experiments developing chemical analyses of wine and cider, and crafting industry standards to comply with the recently enacted 1906 Pure Food and Drug Act. Alwood also used Stonehenge's cellar for the storage of wines, and conducted a majority of his experiments in the estate's barn. He remained with the USDA until 1913, when the new "Bureau of Chemistry and Soils" was organized under the Internal Revenue Service and the Stonehenge Laboratory was relocated to Sandusky, Ohio.[116]

Alwood's work as an enologist ceased with Virginia's imposition of state-wide Prohibition in 1916. In the Jeffersonian tradition, however, Alwood long argued for the need for scientific study in the field of viticulture, even in the face of growing Prohibitionist sentiment. To advance his cause, he donated his personal library to Virginia Tech in 1927, an act that was met with an expression of hope by College President Julian Burrus that:

> the splendid service which Professor Alwood rendered this institution will ever be remembered and that some day his name will be honored in some permanent manner, which will remain here for all time to let those who come after us know of his part in the making of this institution.[117]

Between the 1920s and his death in 1946, Alwood lived between Stonehenge and a farm located in the Greenwood area of western Albemarle County. During his career he traveled extensively, serving as a juror at the 1904 Louisiana Purchase Exposition in St. Louis, as well as the Vice President of the International Congress of Viticulture in France in 1907. Also in 1907, Alwood was awarded the cross of "Officier" of the *Ordre National du Mérite Agricole* (National Order of Agricultural Merit) by the French government, for his contributions to agriculture. He was later named as a fellow of the American Association for the Advancement of Science, and the Royal Horticultural Society. These awards brought recognition not only to Alwood, but also to the commonwealth.[118]

Alwood died in April 1946 and he faded into relative obscurity as Virginia Tech grew and time marched on. In 2011, however, belatedly recognizing the significant contributions made by one of the commonwealth's most prolific and skillful viticultural researchers and writers, Virginia Tech unveiled a series of posthumous tributes in his honor. That year, the school's Board of Visitors awarded Alwood a posthumous special citation as the institution's "favorite son" for his extraordinary contributions, and they announced plans for the construction of a small memorial plaza on the site of the original Experiment Station. The institution also dedicated to Alwood a large, iconic bur oak tree he had first planted in 1895, a tree that today stands prominently on the campus drill field.[119]

Though he is now accorded many accolades such as "the father of Virginia horticulture" and "the savior of the Virginia fruit industry," Alwood was, fundamentally, a dedicated scientist whose work did much to support the early Virginia wine industry. Perhaps the most befitting tribute can be found in the form of a relatively obscure grape variety developed by Virginia Tech's grape-breeding program late in the 1960s, which today carries his name. The aptly identified "Alwood" Grape—a Concord derivative that was found to ripen earlier than its counterparts—exhibits qualities much like its namesake: hardy, bold, and incredibly productive. Alwood likely would have been pleased with the honor.[120]

Briefly assisting William Alwood during his early years at the Experiment Station was a notable personality, Henry Minor Magruder. An outspoken member of the Virginia Pomological Society, an Albemarle County farmer, and one-time chairman of that county's board of supervisors, Magruder understood the devastation that had befallen Virginia's grape growers from the plague of fungal diseases, and had long championed the idea of a state agricultural experiment station.

Magruder felt, however, that such a research facility should have been established in Charlottesville rather than in the distant, rural reaches of Blacksburg. He also felt that the station should be managed by farmers, rather than academics or other special interests. This led him to author a series of articles published in a regional agricultural journal, the *Southern Planter*, between 1889 and 1890, that roundly criticized the location and indeed the feasibility of the newly established Blacksburg Experiment Station.

The public relations pressure brought to bear by Magruder's writings may have led to his appointment as the Experiment Station's superintendent in December 1890. As superintendent, he traveled the state assisting farmers, making him perhaps the first of the commonwealth's agricultural extension agents. Magruder also championed legislation to assist troubled grape growers who had experienced crop decimation at the hands of grape diseases and pests. His work was described by the editor of the *Southern Planter*:

It appears to be the intention of the Board [overseeing the College] that Col. Magruder shall travel over the State for the purpose of meeting and consulting with farmers, addressing public meetings, and making a special study of the conditions and needs of agriculture in the several sections of the State…. These are certainly strides in the right direction. The farmers of Virginia desire that agriculture shall be taught by modern illustrative methods, in field and laboratory, rather than by day class lectures and textbook recitations.[121]

Magruder's position at the helm of the Experiment Station was to be short-lived, however. In June 1891, barely six months into his tenure, he died of a heart attack at the age of forty-seven.[122]

## —*Zenith and Decline*—

By 1890, Virginia's first wine industry had reached never-before achieved heights and, alas, not soon to be achieved again. With an estimated annual production value of 461,000 gallons, the commonwealth ranked fifth nationally in overall production and seventh in the nation in cultivation. Virginia's wine grape growers oversaw some 4,100 acres of table and wine grapes of predominantly native extraction, including the Norton, Delaware, and Etta varieties, and American hybrid varietals. Cultivating vinifera and French hybrid varieties had not yet been proved plausible, much less profitable.[123]

The state's relatively cheap vacant land boded well for a new generation of farmers looking for a fresh start in a budding industry. The Phylloxera outbreak in Europe, coupled with the Northeast's growing demand for table grapes, put Virginia root stock in high demand and the wine industry's prospects were bright.[124]

The industry's meteoric nineteenth-century rise is attributable predominantly to private enterprise. Smaller wine companies joined the state's more-established stalwarts. In Richmond, optimistic residents encouraged by the success of Charlottesville's Monticello Wine Company established a "Richmond Wine Company" to increase local grape acreage and address the limited production and storage capacity at local wineries and cellars. In Winchester, the wonderfully-named Virginia Seal Wild Cherry Wine Company was chartered in 1897 and manufactured, bought, and sold cherry wines, liquors, and extracts. The Roanoke Wine & Liquor Company, advertised as being the "Oldest and Largest Mail Order House" in Virginia, produced wines and liquors with distinctively regional names like "Moore's Creek," "Tinker Valley," and "Cream of Carolina."[125]

Matters appeared optimistic enough that one report suggested that the state's Blue Ridge region should be more aptly named the "fruit belt," and that it was poised to become the most notable wine and fruit-producing region in the eastern United States. Though the commonwealth's Department of Agriculture and Commerce acknowledged that the "superiority" of Virginia's wine quality was "slowly but surely being made known," Virginia's grapes had in fact proved themselves a staple crop, and knowledgeable observers believed they were assured a promising future.[126]

Such optimism was easy to understand, but it was unfortunately misplaced. Within a decade, the appearance of structural and physical impediments led to the industry's rapid decline and near collapse, resulting in the end of yet another chapter of Virginia's recurrent struggle with the grape.[127]

Part of the problem lay in economics. America experienced a long depression between 1873 and 1896 that resulted in the failure of thousands of businesses and brought about declines in manufacturing, construction, and agriculture. Moreover, completion of the first Transcontinental Railroad in 1869 changed the way fruit products were transported across the country and, for the first time, West Coast grapes could easily be shipped to consumers in the East on a large scale. This transformed California into a dominant agricultural force, and the focus of American viticulture shifted to the Golden State. In 1860, California represented just 15 percent of the nation's total production of wine, but by 1880 it produced more than 80 percent. There, grapes could be grown year-round and far more cheaply, without the East Coast's fungal diseases, frost, and rain. Moreover, vinifera varieties could be grown in the West, while the East Coast's winemakers were constrained to native grapes.[128]

Moreover, Virginia's wine industry was incredibly disorganized. This not only minimized the ability for wine marketers and distributors to promote Virginia wines, but it inhibited the commonwealth's ability to compete with larger wine markets. There existed no strategic plan, no champion in state government, and no large-scale advocacy organization that could organize industry participants and speak on their behalf. It was difficult to ensure consistent quantities and qualities of grapes and, given the large number of smaller vineyards across the state, little regard was paid to the need for Virginia's growers to focus on a small set of uniform varietals that could be identified for gradual improvement.[129]

Much of the problem was political. Though the Democratic-controlled state government enjoyed strong ties to alcohol interests, and had long resisted statewide Prohibition, the party was increasingly forced to yield to the Temperance Movement's growing political influence. This pressure ultimately forced the General Assembly to pass the Local Option Act in February 1886, which permitted Virginia's local governments to hold referendums to determine whether licenses should be issued to sell alcohol within their respective boundaries.[130]

Perhaps ironically, in the spring of 1886, Albemarle County—then home to the Monticello Wine Company—became the first Virginia jurisdiction to adopt local option Prohibition. Albemarle's action brought a sudden halt to the planting of additional grape acreage in the county, and, according to one industry observer, was "destined to chill the [wine] movement unless the law [was] repealed."

Such views were shared by one Commissioner of Agriculture, Randolph Harrison, who was an enthusiastic supporter of Virginia's wine industry and a staunch opponent of local option laws. "I have been urging our people, and shall continue to do so, to plant vineyards and make wine," Harrison noted to the Monticello Grape and Fruit-Growers Association in 1886. Local option laws, he argued, "acted as a damper upon the entire industry. There are men who hesitate to make investments in lands and to plant vines, as they were preparing to do because of uncertainty and dread of what wild legislation will come next." His words would soon prove prophetic, for in November 1916 Prohibition became statewide.[131]

Not even these political or economic sorrows, however, could match the havoc wreaked by the large-scale invasion of grapevine fungal diseases in the 1880s, particularly between 1886 and 1890. During that period, Virginia's grape growers sustained severe crop losses from a variety of biological afflictions, the most prominent being downy mildew and black rot disease. Both were the result of excessive summer rainfall, and both thrived in high humidity climates—which, of course, Virginia offered in abundance.[132]

In an 1883 edition of the *Monticello Farmer and Grape Grower*, it was noted that these fungal diseases ravaged Virginia's vineyards and contributed to drastically uneven quality in the state's wines:

> Very many appear to be discouraged at the outlook for the grape industry…the question comes home to every one who has suffered from the rotting of the fruit on the vines, as to how long we can stand such losses. We are all in the dark as to the cause.[133]

Virginia's grape farmers appealed to the federal government, the University of Virginia, and the newly established Virginia Agricultural Experiment Station for advice on how to combat what the Virginia Department of Agriculture termed "the enemies of vineyard culture." Over time, farmers learned to develop and apply new fungicides, including the so-called Bordeaux Mixture—a combination of copper, sulfate, and lime—originally developed in France early in the 1880s to treat Phylloxera and downy mildew, but at the outset were powerless to avoid the loss of their vineyards.[134]

Growers were also advised to experiment with different grape varieties and found that the native Ives, Delaware, Norton, and Etta grapes responded somewhat better to Virginia's climate and available fungicide treatments. Vinifera and French hybrid varieties, however, were commonly avoided as too susceptible to disease. One grower lamented the futility of planting European grapes: "I have seen no result to justify any effort in this direction [of planting vinifera], save only the localities of Florida and California, and there only on native, resistant stocks."[135]

The total extent of destruction from the diseases is not known, but it is generally accepted that they damaged or destroyed up to 75 percent of the state's grape crops by late in the 1880s.

Perhaps the only silver lining—if it could be viewed as such—was that the whole affair finally focused Virginia's public sector on the need for improvements to the wine industry. Henry L. Lyman, a Charlottesville resident and grape grower, noted that the diseases had aroused "an active interest amongst all the better class of vine-growers in the needs of the vine, which interest is leading up to a very commendable and desirable permanent establishment of the vine industry." Such attention, however, seemed to come too late, as Lyman later lamented that the diseases had all but "stopped the extension of vineyards [and had] caused indifferent vineyardists to abandon vines for other crops."[136]

By 1900, the damage wrought by myriad economic, political, and environmental forces had proved so severe that the commonwealth's status as a serious wine state fell below that of far less mature wine-producing states, including North Carolina, Arkansas, Iowa, and Indiana. Virginians gravitated toward the one fruit that came to dominate the commonwealth's agriculture in the years to come: apples. In what has been termed the "Winter Apple Period," the years from 1887 through the 1920s saw a vast expansion of apple planting, virtually converting Virginia into a "one-fruit state."[137]

For Virginia wine, all looked lost.

## *— The Fleeing Winemaker —*

At the very moment that Virginia's wine industry appeared to be on its last legs, one North Carolina winemaker held fast to the promise of producing Virginia wine from native grapes. Nicknamed "Captain" because of his inordinate confidence and an ability to sell great quantities of wine, Paul Garrett maintained steadfastly that vinifera varietals were ill-suited to the climate of eastern North America, and that native wines, if properly manufactured and promoted, could yet achieve great success.

Garrett's persistence not only helped him establish a Virginia-based national winemaking empire before Prohibition, but focused his efforts on the production of wildly popular wines from that oft-scorned southern grape, the scuppernong.

Garrett's impressive rise in the American wine industry began in 1877, when, as a very young boy, he went to work for Ringwood Wine Company, a small winemaking operation owned by his father and his uncle in Brinkleyville, North Carolina. Ringwood specialized in scuppernong wines, and Garrett was to promote the company's wines from a distribution office in Arkansas. As wine historian Thomas Pinney has noted, Garrett faced a daunting task:

> The scene in the South at the time Garrett set out to sell wine could hardly have been more unpropitious. The South, even twenty years after Appomattox, was still dirt poor. Outside of a few coastal cities— Charleston, Savannah, New Orleans—there was no tradition of wine drinking. Whiskey—bourbon or moonshine—was the drink of the rural South.[138]

Despite the South's disinclination toward wine, Garrett managed to sell Ringwood's wines well beyond the company's ability to produce it. Not content with simply promoting wine, Garrett also established a bottling plant and warehouse in Little Rock to speed distribution. He also obtained additional sources in California and New York. In 1890, Garrett founded his own North Carolina wine sales company, Garrett & Company, which initially focused on selling New York and North Carolina wines, but later transitioned to making scuppernong wines exclusively.[139]

Sensing a vast untapped market for wines in the South, Garrett became a proselytizer of the scuppernong. Writing to the Virginia Commissioner of Agriculture of the advantages of the grape in 1902, Garrett proclaimed,

The grape is indigenous to the soil of Southeastern Virginia and Eastern North Carolina. Its wonderful possibilities were mentioned by the first voyagers who landed on Roanoke Island…. The disregard of the wonderful possibilities of these grapes is best explained, perhaps, on the theory that men usually overlook the ordinary advantages supplied by nature. However this may be, with few slight exceptions, the wonderful possibilities of this grape have been overlooked for three hundred years. That it will produce a wine of exceptionally fine character has been demonstrated beyond any controversy.[140]

At a time when few wine manufacturers produced high-quality and moderately-priced wines from native varieties, Garrett promoted the scuppernong and other native varietals—including Norton and Ives—as being superior to foreign grapes. He took pride in marketing his wines as distinctly "American" and gave them names that evoked the nation's history, wrapped in patriotic imagery and phrases.[141]

Garrett's line of wines, for example, included "Minnehaha," a dry scuppernong blend named in honor of the Native American woman born in Henry Wadsworth Longfellow's epic poem "The Song of Hiawatha"; "Pocahontas," a red scuppernong wine named in honor of the Native American daughter of Powhatan; "F.F.V. Claret," a wine named in honor of the so-called First Families of Virginia; "Garret's American," a Norton-Ives claret; and "Paul Garrett's Special Champagne," which won the coveted grand prize for sparkling wines at the 1904 Louisiana Purchase Exposition in St. Louis. None of Garrett's beverages, however, experienced the immense popularity of his red-and-white "Virginia Dare" wine, a sweet scuppernong blended beverage that possessed a cheery fourteen-percent alcohol by volume. It was named in honor of Virginia Dare, born in 1587 and believed to have been the first child born to European settlers in the New World.

Garrett's Virginia Dare wine would prove unique in at least two ways. First, unlike most other American wines of the day that were manufactured in bulk, Garrett directly controlled the quality of Virginia Dare wine by bottling it prior to distribution. Second, never had any wine—and an American wine at that—been so innovatively and aggressively promoted by its proprietary name.[142]

Combining aggressive salesmanship with an historical namesake symbolizing purity and wholesomeness, Garrett promoted Virginia Dare through a variety of media, continually reinforcing the brand's name and its distinctly American origin wherever possible. Advertisements, posters, placards, and labels depicted a woman—clearly intending to represent the legendary Virginia

Dare herself—in period dress and cap. The image was accompanied by a tagline, "The First Lady of the Land."[143]

Garrett developed other slogans to describe Virginia Dare wine as well, including "the wine with song in it" and "America's Great Social Drink." As one Virginia Dare advertisement exclaimed,

> Every popular wine you can name belongs to the famous Garrett family. Every occasion has a Garrett Wine that gracefully becomes it. And for those times when it's easier to serve one wine, Virginia Dare fills the bill completely. It's a natural drink with appetizers...tempting with dinner... the preference of more and more people at parties. Order some today. You'll be surprised how little it costs now to entertain royally.[144]

Virginia Dare was also the first wine to be advertised on national radio, and Garrett relied on the Virginia Dare name to distance the wine from prejudices against the scuppernong.[145]

In what can only be termed a wildly successful attempt at corporate promotional revisionist history, Garrett even gave away copies of a book, *The White Doe: The Fate of Virginia Dare*. Each book—mostly false, even by the lax standards of the day—offered an "Indian legend" to explain why some grapes were red. Each also carried a stamp, "Compliments of Garrett & Co. pioneer American wine growers, Norfolk, VA, producers of the famous Virginia Dare brand of scuppernong wine."[146]

Invented histories of Virginia Dare could be found in other promotional pieces, too. One advertisement claimed of the scuppernong that "the grape she loved we offer you—only enriched and mellowed by three centuries of care and cultivation." Garrett even offered purchasers of two or more cases of Virginia Dare wine a lavish oil painting depicting a buxom, blonde, early-twenty-something Virginia Dare—a likeness, as he put it, "after the most trustworthy traditions." (Almost nothing is known of her actual fate or, indeed, whether she even survived past the age of three years.)[147]

Garrett's belief in heavy branding turned Virginia Dare into a national household name and a cherished American wine. It proved to be the nation's most popular pre-Prohibition wine with more than one million cases sold annually. The beverage was so popular, in fact, that its sales far exceeded Garrett's supply of scuppernong grapes and forced him to commit heresy: he mixed California grape juice into the concoction.[148]

But Garrett's success with Virginia Dare could not protect him from the political and social realities of the day. He had to act, so with increasing numbers of North Carolina counties prohibiting the sale or use of alcoholic beverages by 1903, and sensing the need to create a large central depot for his expanding line of wine products, Garrett moved his operation to the burgeoning industrial town of Berkeley, Virginia (incorporated in 1906 into the City of Norfolk). There, at the end of Liberty Street, near the confluence of two branches of the Elizabeth River, Garrett built an impressive, modern six-story winery. After its 1906 completion, the nearly 202,000-square-foot building had convenient rail access to two spurs and was the first fireproof Armored Concrete building in the southeast.[149]

The new winery imported grapes from southeastern Virginia and northeastern North Carolina, and boasted a mammoth storage capacity of approximately four million gallons as well as aisle upon aisle of resting racks for some two million gallons of champagne. The building was capped by a handsome tower that featured a two-story, four-sided clock with faces twenty-five feet in diameter. This industrial era trophy, promoted by Garrett as the "largest clock on earth," could be seen some fifteen miles away in Newport News. Adjacent to the winery, Garrett purchased a building that had served as the first marine hospital in the United States and renovated it as his family's residence.[150]

Despite his enviable geographic location and sizeable investment in Norfolk, Garrett's sojourn in the Old Dominion was brief. While Garrett had ostensibly chosen Norfolk as the closest urban center to his large North Carolina scuppernong vineyards, and though he had hoped Virginia's politics were less inclined to temperance, the commonwealth soon followed North Carolina into Prohibition. This forced Garrett once again to relocate his headquarters farther north—this time, in 1912, to Penn Yan, a small community in the Finger Lakes region of New York.[151]

The two relocations, while inconvenient, did little to stunt Garrett & Company's growth. The popularity of Garrett's wines fueled the company's rapid expansion, and Garrett acquired interests in vineyards in California, Ohio, New York, and Missouri—each of which helped diversify his grape varieties and sources, and corporate mobility should the need arise again to respond to increased restrictions on alcohol. By the time of national Prohibition in 1919, Garrett presided over an empire of vineyards and wineries with a storage capacity of 10 million gallons.[152]

Although catering his wines to his southern clientele, Garrett broke with the majority on the issue of Prohibition. As a leader of the Brewers, Wine, and Spirit Merchants of Virginia, Garrett actively lobbied against the enactment of statewide Prohibition. He was particularly adamant that wine was a great agricultural commodity and natural resource that could, in fact, provide the solution to the nation's vexing liquor problem rather than contributing to it. Like Jefferson, Garrett argued that wine was the "antitoxin of intemperance," and that "wine-growing countries are and always have been the most temperate and in many respects the most progressive."[153]

Optimistic that Prohibition would not long survive, Garrett diversified his business through the promotion of nonalcoholic products. He helped found Fruit Industries, Inc., which manufactured a variety of household foods including sauces, jellies, grape cola, tonics, and grape concentrate. Through a specially-developed "de-alcoholization" process, he managed to extract pure alcohol from his wines and to produce a non-alcoholic Virginia Dare. Much of the extracted alcohol was later used in other applications, including some twenty-one different flavors of double-strength flavoring extracts that were claimed to give desserts "a new and undreamed of deliciousness."[154]

As was the case with other alcohol producers, Garrett also sought ways around Prohibition-era laws. One of his more successful ventures was "Vine-Glo," a concentrated non-fermented grape mixture that could be easily re-fermented and turned into wine. Ever the wine lover, Garrett shipped his non-alcoholic grape concentrate to buyers—along with a yeast pill (to aid in the fermenting process) and a printed statement warning about the illegality of mixing the two.

Following Repeal, Garrett was one of only a handful of American vintners who controlled grape-processing facilities across the country, and he concentrated his efforts on reviving the nation's wine industry. His Virginia Dare wine was among the first to reemerge following the ratification of the Twenty-First Amendment in 1933. "The wine industry," Garrett told *Fortune* magazine in 1934, "ought to be—it can be—bigger than the automobile industry, bigger than the steel industry, if wine makers will seize the opportunity that lies before them."[155]

Garrett died a multimillionaire in March 1940. The wine enterprise he founded however, Garrett & Company, as with the industry generally, never recovered during his lifetime. After a series of mergers and divisions, Garrett's proud Virginia Dare name—the only American wine with national brand recognition—was sold to the Guild Winery in 1961 and, later, to Constellation Brands, Inc. The Virginia Dare brand was subsequently acquired by Francis Ford Coppola, who later began producing under this label again.

Garrett is remembered today as the "Dean of American Winemakers." His passionate advocacy for native varieties, combined with a belief in the viticultural promise of the American South and an unmatched gift for marketing, not only helped him fashion a wine empire but allowed Virginia to serve—if only for a brief moment—as the headquarters of one of America's most successful winemaking operations.[156]

## — The Noble Experiment —

By the turn of the twentieth century, few Virginia vineyards and wineries of any note remained operational. With the exception of Paul Garrett's successful scuppernong beverage empire in Norfolk, the market for Virginia wines had begun to shrink. Prices had declined, the commonwealth's vineyards were neglected or abandoned, and increased competition from California, New York, and Ohio made Virginia's wine industry an increasingly losing proposition. Added to this dispiriting state of affairs was a new foe that promised to halt Virginia wine production entirely and, presumably forever: Prohibition.[157]

While colonial Virginians viewed alcoholic beverages as a natural extension of agriculture and food, claims for alcoholic temperance were as old as the commonwealth itself. The General Assembly began regulating liquor distribution in 1619, but with the exception of laws against public drunkenness, legislation as to the limits of alcohol production or consumption was rarely deemed appropriate during the colonial period. Laws were modified—but only slightly—in antebellum Virginia, when the state imposed license fees and required certificates for sellers of alcoholic products.[158]

This began to change again in the early 1800s, when small and disorganized Christian temperance societies began forming across the state. By the 1850s, Virginia led the South in the number of such societies, the leading edge of what became the Temperance Movement, most of which sought to address the ill effects of excessive and uncontrolled alcohol consumption through prayer and voluntary abstention. As historians have noted, these early societies advocated the idea of temperance as a religious and physiological imperative drawn from the moral virtue of moderation in drink.[159]

Conscious of the limited success of voluntary temperance, however, these societies increasingly advocated for laws prohibiting the sale or use of liquor. Portland, Maine, passed the nation's first citywide ban on alcohol in 1843; the following year, the Oregon Territory banned its sale, and in 1851, Maine adopted the first statewide Prohibition law.

Wine was typically exempt from the temperance discussion. With a lower alcohol content than whiskey or beer, and with a production process more directly related to agriculture, wine had historically been promoted as a staple food and "temperance beverage"—that is, a drink that would provide drinkers a needed boost, but in moderation. Wine promoters acknowledged that wine had the potential to intoxicate, but they insisted that its lower alcohol content rarely encouraged its use as an intoxicant or the source of the oft-complained of "evils" of intoxication. As none other than Thomas Jefferson said,

> No nation is drunken where wine is cheap; and none sober, where the dearness of wine substitutes ardent spirits as the common beverage. It is, in truth, the only antidote to the bane of whiskey.[160]

Wine producers frequently cited France and Italy as exemplars—noting that both countries had high wine consumption per capita and that neither country experienced the social problems associated with drunkenness.[161]

The Civil War brought a temporary halt to the Temperance Movement, as its Christian founders shifted their focus to the absolution of the nation for the even greater sin of slavery. The movement was quickly revived when the war ended, and reached new heights by the turn of the century. The Virginia Women's Christian Temperance Union emerged as the foremost temperance society late in the nineteenth century. Founded in Richmond in September 1882 as a branch of the national WCTU, the Virginia Union quickly grew, preaching a political platform that cleverly blended calls for alcohol restrictions with female virtuousness and women's rights. The Union's activities were largely focused on educational campaigns, literature dissemination, and anti-alcohol education programs for schoolchildren.[162]

The Union recognized the difficulty of enacting statewide Prohibition, so it advocated for the adoption of so-called "local option" laws, whereby each locality could decide for itself whether to ban alcohol. In response to such calls, and perhaps hoping to blunt the whole issue, the General Assembly passed the Local Option Act in February 1886.[163]

In the spring of 1886, Albemarle County—then home to the Monticello Wine Company—became the first Virginia jurisdiction to institute countywide Prohibition. Other counties quickly followed suit, but even within dry counties local Prohibition rather swiftly proved porous. The laws, for example, did nothing to prevent residents in those counties from simply carrying or mail-ordering wine from wet counties. To the advocates of temperance, it was apparent that something more needed to be done, and after 1901 the drive toward statewide Prohibition gained momentum with the founding of the Virginia Anti-Saloon League.[164]

The League was established as the Virginia branch of the national Anti-Saloon League and became the commonwealth's leading organization advocating for statewide Prohibition. Its position was simply that an outright ban on alcohol was essential, not only for health and religious salvation, but also to ensure sober fathers and the protection of families, particularly of the weaker sex and children. Alcoholism was posited to be a male problem.

The organization's efforts were increasingly formalized after 1904, when a new director was appointed, a controversial and combative Methodist bishop, the Reverend James Cannon, Jr., from Blackstone, Virginia, in Nottoway County. Reverend Cannon established the League's headquarters in downtown Richmond and commenced his mission.[165]

Once described as "the most powerful cleric in America," Cannon had previously served as principal of the Blackstone Female Institute and editor of a Christian newspaper. He was known as an "outspoken, indefatigable, and extraordinarily able man," who was hard-working and popular in Virginia's temperance circles. Cannon preached vividly of families that were ashamed of their drunken fathers, of wild college students who were "dangerously drunk," and of the women battered and bruised from alcohol-induced violence.[166]

As the 1900s progressed, Cannon's "dry" organization matured, becoming increasingly organized and professional, and ever more influential in Virginia's politics. Bowing to League pressure as early as 1903, the General Assembly passed the "Mann Act," named for its patron, Nottoway County senator William Hodges Mann, which sought to eradicate alcohol from rural areas by imposing a complex network of laws and levies intended to discourage the sale of alcohol. The Mann Act effectively stopped alcohol sales in those areas without a police presence, placed heavy taxes on rural saloons, and required the judicial grant of liquor licenses.[167]

Five years later, in February 1908, the General Assembly strengthened the Mann Act through its "Mann-Byrd Law" which prohibited the issuance of alcohol licenses in all localities with a population less than 500, outlawed private membership clubs in dry jurisdictions, increased regulations on passenger trains and in drugstores, and made illegal the sale of any malt drink with an alcohol content greater than 2.25 percent.[168]

Though Virginia's local option laws and increasingly strict state regulations effectively approached statewide Prohibition, efforts at the total elimination of alcohol had for years been thwarted by the commonwealth's conservative Democratic machine. This machine, conservative that it was, held an outright aversion to any reform movement—including Temperance—that threatened to disturb the status quo. Thanks, too, to the Democrats' strong ties to liquor interests, Virginia trailed her southern sisters in enacting statewide Prohibition.[169]

By 1908, the political divide prompted Virginia's Temperance Movement to bifurcate its strategy. It would first seek to amend the state constitution, and then the United States Constitution, to ban the sale and use of alcohol. Virginia Prohibitionists received a boost in 1910, when a strong temperance advocate and author of Virginia's earlier local option laws, that same "Bone Dry" William Hodges Mann of Nottoway, was elected Governor (1910–1914). His election was followed swiftly by the Virginia Anti-Saloon League's establishment of a daily temperance broadside, the *Richmond Virginian*, which began circulating widely-read articles advocating for statewide Prohibition.[170]

The Temperance Movement proved remarkably effective in short order. In February 1914, the Democratic-controlled General Assembly bowed to its pressure and approved a referendum on statewide Prohibition. Mann's successor, a reluctant Governor Henry C. Stuart (1914–1918), signed a law that called for the referendum to take place in September 1914, but only if proponents could garner at least 18,000 signatures by June of that year.[171]

This yeoman's work fell to the politically adept Bishop Cannon, who wasted no time in organizing his League's members into "small armies" across the state. In each congressional district, county, and voting precinct, League representatives were given the task of disseminating propaganda and obtaining signatures. It was no easy task, however, to obtain signatures from voters in a state that had no history of participatory democracy. Virginia had long been run by a political oligarchy, and would be until well into the latter half of the century. In the face of it, Cannon managed to secure more than 71,000 signatures by the deadline.[172]

Governor Stuart ordered the referendum for September 22, 1914. If successful, the commonwealth would go dry two years later, on November 1, 1916. Temperance advocates began the race to secure votes. Across the state, League representatives distributed flyers, affiliated ministers preached Prohibitionist sentiments, and the Prohibitionist *Virginian* newspaper repeated the "dry" argument over and again.

The Prohibitionists were relentless in attributing virtually every societal problem to alcohol. They believed that if Virginia were to cleanse itself of the menace of alcohol, it would restore hope and create a new society.[173]

The Anti-Saloon League's positions resonated with many Virginians, who either identified personally with them or were moved by the many lurid tales of drunkenness, devastation to homes, and financially-ruined families, all kneeling before demon rum. The League also received strong support from labor unions, several of which opened their meetings with temperance songs. Baptist and Methodist ministers recited mortality statistics during their sermons, replete with anti-wet homilies, while dry proponents held parades in the commonwealth's urban centers, which frequently included children who marched singing, "Please Won't You Vote It Out?" and "We're Out for Prohibition," the latter being sung to the tune of "Dixie."[174]

For their part, the "wets" mounted a spirited defense, but they could see that the tide was against them. Many of the Anti-Saloon League's opponents organized themselves into the Virginia Association for Local Self-Government and, like the League itself, the Association leased headquarters space in downtown Richmond. Asserting that statewide Prohibition would merely force alcohol manufacturing and consumption underground, the Association argued that Prohibition would induce crime and would fail to bring about the great moral and social improvements promised by the Prohibitionists.[175]

The Association received help from none other than veteran Virginia winemaker Paul Garrett, who was then also serving as one of the leaders of the Brewers, Wine, and Spirit Merchants of Virginia. It was also aided by the formation of another wet group, the Personal Liberty Association, which argued for the less draconian preservation of the local option laws.[176]

As the date for the referendum drew near, the campaigns of both sides went into overdrive. Exchanges between wets and drys became heated and, as is the case with most other political movements, the rhetoric became more irresponsible. Both sides predicted victory. Virginia's newspapers unfailingly carried articles and letters on the subject, broken—and then only briefly—by news of the outbreak of World War I. The weekend before the vote, the Prohibitionists plastered walls with posters, hosted countless parades, and offered prayers in support of Prohibition.[177]

When the polls finally opened on September 22, 1914, after an exhausting season of political discourse on the evils of alcohol, the turnout was uncharacteristically large for a Virginia election. After the polls closed, thousands gathered in Richmond, both outside the *Times-Dispatch* building and the Anti-Saloon League headquarters, to await the result.

In the end, the electorate had spoken, with a resounding victory for the drys: 94,251 Virginians voted in favor of enacting statewide Prohibition; 63,886 were opposed. By more than 30,000, Virginia's voters had professed their desire to ban alcohol.[178]

Not only did Virginia's rural counties vote for Prohibition (two-thirds of which were already dry by the time of the referendum), but so too did seventeen of the Commonwealth's twenty cities, where anti-Prohibitionist sentiment had long been rumored to be strongest. The wets' "get out the vote" efforts were largely confined to the Richmond area and lacked the broader, rural and statewide appeal of its Prohibitionist counterparts. Addressing his followers that evening, a visibly-moved Reverend James Cannon shouted, "My friends, I feel like the fellow who had too much whiskey—too full for utterance."[179]

The General Assembly passed the Mapp Prohibition Act during its 1916 session, prohibiting the sale, use, and manufacture of "ardent spirits," including wine; the legislation took effect at midnight, November 1, 1916. The nation followed suit a little more than three years later, when the Eighteenth Amendment went into effect on January 16, 1920. By that time, thirty-three of the forty-eight states had already enacted statewide Prohibition measures similar to that in the Old Dominion.[180]

Congress presented the Eighteenth Amendment to the states in 1917, and on January 11, 1918, Virginia became the second state—three days after ratification by Mississippi—to approve it. By January of the following year, the necessary number of states had ratified, and Congress passed the National Prohibition Act (commonly known as the "Volstead Act") in October 1919.[181]

The Volstead Act prohibited the manufacturing and sale of any intoxicating beverage—including wine—containing more than one half percent alcohol by volume. While wine had never been the primary target of earlier calls to temperance, the Volstead Act's low alcohol content restrictions had the immediate effect of pouring it into the same barrel with liquor and beer. Despite objections from wine industry supporters that wine ought to have been exempted because of its moderating effects, Prohibitionists retorted, "The rich man ought not to have his wine if the poor man could not have his whiskey."[182]

A small percentage of the overall electorate thus affected the substantive liberties of millions of their fellow citizens. Though President Herbert Hoover declared as late as 1928 that national Prohibition was an "experiment noble in motive and far-reaching in purpose," and though it had been instituted with relative ease, enforcement of the Volstead Act during its fourteen-year life would prove immensely difficult. Quite contrary to the hopes of its proponents, the "noble experiment" in the end proved a colossal failure, and wrought devastation on the nation's wine industry.[183]

It is widely accepted that Prohibition—whether statewide or national—did little to curb the excesses of alcohol consumption. Both empirical and anecdotal evidence suggests that it gave rise to an era of unprecedented criminality: bootlegging, black market alcohol sales, underground consumption, criminal empires, and violence. During the seventeen years Prohibition was in effect in Virginia, the legal alcohol trade was ended but the commonwealth still struggled to remain dry. While criminals and racketeers may have had less impact on the state than in the nation's major cities, the Old Dominion still managed to defeat much of the government's efforts to enforce Prohibition laws.[184]

Not only did parts of Virginia enjoy a longstanding tradition of moonshining, but Virginia's coastline—with its tens of thousands of acres of rivers, salt marshes, tidal mudflats, bays, and open water—was virtually custom-built for smuggling. Moreover, Virginia's neighbor to the north, Maryland, did not enact a statewide ban before the Eighteenth Amendment, and its enforcement of federal Prohibition laws was halfhearted at best, facilitating the illegal importation of liquor across the Potomac.[185]

In truth, the government barely enforced the laws at all. Nationally, the total number of Prohibition agents never exceeded 3,000 at any one time, making federal prosecutions minimal at best. Virginia's own statewide attempts fared no better. The 1916 Mapp Prohibition Act established a new enforcement agency, the Virginia Prohibition Commission, to protect "the public health, peace and morals, and the prevention of the sale and use of ardent spirits." Lacking sufficient manpower and funding to control the flow of alcohol, the Commission's focus in its early years was on halting the illegal importation of alcohol. After the passage of the Eighteenth Amendment, however, the Commission added efforts to stop illegal production as well.[186]

In August 1922, the Commission's functions were absorbed by a new "Department of Prohibition" housed in Virginia's Office of the Attorney General. Field service in the Department was dangerous; between 1918 and 1930, five of the state's Prohibition Enforcement agents died in the line of duty, all from gunfire.[187]

Putting aside the purely criminal element in Prohibition, the Volstead Act and Virginia's own Mann Act forced the closure of hundreds of the state's saloons, distilleries, and wineries. Secondary industries, such as vineyards, bottle makers, and coopers, struggled or were outright destroyed. After the enactment of statewide Prohibition, but before the ratification of the Eighteenth Amendment, the commonwealth's six breweries were permitted to continue operating so long as their products were sold out of state. By 1918, however, even those breweries had all closed.[188]

Ironically, national wine consumption increased during Prohibition, and vineyard acreage almost doubled, thanks in no small measure to various loopholes in the Volstead Act. For example, commercial wineries were permitted to manufacture and sell wine for religious and medicinal purposes, while individuals could manufacture up to 200 gallons of wine per year for non-intoxicating home use. The government did not waste its enforcement time and money on wine, and it accounted for less than five percent of the government's Prohibition-era seizures.[189]

While these loopholes encouraged enterprising individuals to find new ways to increase wine production, such increases belied the reality that America's wine industry had been paralyzed by Prohibition. This paralysis stemmed not necessarily from enforcement of the law itself, but rather from the disastrous effects on American palates, and decimation of the craft of high-quality winemaking.

During Prohibition, the notion that wine was a refined, temperate, and healthful expression of agricultural art was lost in American's desire to obtain a quick, cheap, and readily-available, semi-legal, buzz. The strictures surrounding the production of alcoholic beverages during Prohibition encouraged underground winemakers to produce wines of abysmal quality, while America's remaining vintners—if they could be labeled such at the time—proved little more than "fumbling amateurs" using the most rudimentary equipment. Winemakers attempted a variety of novel tactics to satisfy the nation's craving for wine. They sold inferior grape juice and grape juice concentrate by the barrel, and sent inexperienced employees to buyers' homes to make wine in kitchens illicitly. They sold pressed hydrated grape bricks that fermented when water and yeast were added. Saloons sold cheap wine by the jug full and people clamored for medical prescriptions for alcohol.[190]

Winemaking during Prohibition also necessitated the secret transport of native grapes hundreds or thousands of miles by rail. Winemakers were compelled to order grapes of inferior quality and thicker-skins that could sustain the journey. While these cheaper grape varieties seemed capable of making high-quality wine, unlike the more delicate vinifera varieties most proved wholly unsuitable. Cheap grapes, including native table grapes that were simply unacceptable for winemaking, jumped in price while more refined—but less portable—vinifera grapes could hardly be sold.[191]

The result was the wholesale disappearance of dryer wines, replaced by highly alcoholic, fortified wines (wine with an added distilled beverage, usually brandy). America's wine culture went into steep decline and cheap, sugary wines became the norm.[192] Decades would pass, until the 1960s and 1970s, before American consumers would again demand more delicate, refined wines produced from vinifera varieties. As Virginia wine consultant Lucie T. Morton would write in 1985, "The eastern wine industry was so effectively ruined by Prohibition and its aftermath that today the region's vineyards and estate wineries are objects of surprise and curiosity in areas where local wines were once taken for granted."[193]

The great promises of social reform and national sobriety that underlay the best of the arguments advanced by Prohibition's advocates were quickly forgotten, and by the early 1930s America was thoroughly fed up with the experiment.

By 1932, in the grip of the Great Depression, both major political parties abandoned Prohibition in their national platforms, while powerful unions began supporting repeal in the hopes of creating new jobs. Repeal advocates argued that ending Prohibition would create those jobs and produce needed tax revenue.[194]

Congress submitted the Twenty-First Amendment to the states in February 1933, and it was ratified in December of that year. It also passed the Cullen-Harrison Act in April 1933, which legalized the sale of beverages containing not more than 3.2 percent alcohol by weight.[195]

Prohibition was on its deathbed as a national policy, and the prospect of repeal had its effect in Virginia where statewide Prohibition remained the law. After initial refusals to consider statewide repeal, the state's dry governor, John G. Pollard (1930–1934), was persuaded by his fellow Democrat, the influential United States Senator Harry F. Byrd, that there was enough support for repeal. Pollard called the General Assembly into a special session in August 1933 with the intent of legalizing alcoholic beverages. During the special session, the General Assembly legalized the sale of beverages containing not more than 3.2 percent of alcohol, and called for a special referendum on the issue of statewide repeal. Virginians would decide whether to continue statewide Prohibition in the event national Prohibition was repealed or, in the alternative, direct the General Assembly to fashion a so-called "plan of liquor control" to replace Prohibition. The legislature also appointed a committee to draft legislation in the event Virginians voted to end Prohibition.[196]

On October 3, 1933, Virginians reversed course in a vote that mirrored the one imposing statewide Prohibition nearly two decades earlier. 99,640 Virginians voted for repeal, while 58,518 voted against it. The vote to direct the General Assembly to devise an alternative statewide liquor control program also passed, 100,445 to 57,873. Virginia was once again "wet." On October 25, 1933, delegates to a constitutional convention made the state the twenty-ninth to ratify the Twenty-First Amendment. With the approval of the thirty-sixth state, Utah, voting to ratify, the Amendment became effective on December 15, 1933. The nation's "noble experiment" had come to an end.[197]

While most Americans were happy to see Prohibition in the rearview mirror, an altogether different reality soon set in. The second section of the Twenty-First Amendment began to figure into everyday American life. While section one repealed the Eighteenth Amendment, section two was a continuing affirmative grant to states and territories to ban the importation of alcohol: they retained unfettered authority over the regulation of alcoholic beverages. Each state could legalize alcohol, ban it, or restrict its production, consumption, or access.[198]

This authority resulted in a profusion of alcohol control laws across the nation, with each state serving as a laboratory for alcohol regulation. Some states, including Kansas and Georgia, remained in the grip of Temperance sentiment and opted to continue their enforcement of statewide Prohibition for years; others retreated to the "local option" concept, thereby leaving the issue in the hands of each community. Still others opted for a private-licensing system whereby a state granted licenses to businesses to purchase and distribute alcohol at the state's discretion.

With each state granted the authority to devise its own alcohol control policies, the result was a nationwide mishmash of rules, licensing requirements, and distributional controls. The federal government, for its part, opted to retain some of its authority in the Treasury Department's Bureau of Alcohol, Tobacco, and Firearms.[199]

In Virginia, the General Assembly's August 1933 liquor committee reviewed various alcohol control systems in other states, as well as in Canada and European countries. Among its findings, the committee discovered that higher alcohol levels in beverages led to increased danger, and that in fashioning a liquor control plan, "the private profit motive, with its incentive to encourage sale and consumption of alcoholic beverage, should be minimized." In addition, the committee observed that "in order to encourage temperance, [Virginia's alcohol] plan should discourage use of hard liquor and give relative encouragement to use of lighter alcoholic beverages."[200]

The committee produced a January 1934 report, known as "Senate Document 5," that set forth eight principles deemed indispensable for Virginia's future liquor control plan, and established the state's most-comprehensive alcohol regulations to date. Senate Document 5 recommended the establishment of a new regulatory agency to be called the "Department of Alcoholic Beverage Control" as well as a three-man "Alcoholic Beverage Control Board" to oversee the department's functions.

The committee also recommended the creation of a hybrid monopoly and state licensure system, similar to that found in the Canadian province of Quebec, where lower-content alcoholic beverages (i.e., beer and wine) would be available to select state licensees, while all hard liquor would be sold exclusively by the state, in state-owned stores.[201]

Central as well to the committee's recommendations was the establishment of a three-tiered regulatory system, wherein alcohol industry groups were divided into three components: manufacturers (i.e., distillers, vintners, and brewers), wholesalers, and retailers—each of which required a state license. The committee envisioned that each tier would remain separate from the others:

manufacturers must sell only to wholesalers; retailers must buy beverages only from a wholesaler; and wholesalers must collect excise taxes from the producer. Key to the three-tiered system was that beverage manufacturers—including winemakers and wineries—were prohibited from selling directly to consumers.[202]

Senate Document 5 was submitted during the 1934 General Assembly session and was adopted—almost as presented—in March 1934. The Virginia Department of Alcoholic Beverage Control and its Alcoholic Beverage Control Board were established later that month, replacing the Department of Prohibition, and Virginia began a new chapter as a "liquor control state." While the local option regime was maintained by statute, the new Virginia ABC Board set prices and controlled the manufacturing and distribution of alcohol across the state.[203]

During the 1936 General Assembly session, Virginia's ABC agents were conferred full police powers to enforce state laws against bootlegging and moonshining. The ABC opened its first state-owned hard liquor store in Richmond in May 1934, and opened forty-nine more by August of that year. The ABC also granted licenses to sell beer and wine to more than 5,200 private establishments by the close of 1934. Though it had been one of the first states to institute statewide Prohibition, the commonwealth now found itself firmly injected into the alcohol trade a mere three months after Prohibition's repeal.[204]

While Virginia's post-Prohibition alcohol control laws were uniform and predictable after 1934, the flexibility and practicality of the state's three-tiered system would be called into question half a century later in light of the changing needs of the commonwealth's growing wine industry. Beginning in the 1980s—and particularly after the dawn of the new millennium—the commonwealth's three-tiered system of distribution was met with increasing resistance and arguments over its outright futility, as Virginia wineries sought to distribute their wines directly to consumers both at wineries and at home.

The growing opposition to ABC laws gave rise to an unprecedented army of lobbyists representing the interests of manufacturers, wholesalers, retailers, and an increasing number of wine producers—all of whom found themselves at odds with one another, and all of whom were interested in self-preservation under what would become a decades-old alcohol control system. While an uneasy truce would be reached in 2008, even today no easy answer has been found, and Virginia's alcohol industry participants continue—as in so many things in Virginia history—to maintain an uneasy status quo.[205]

## —*An Ignoble Rebirth: Depression and War*—

Prohibition had an enduring, if not catastrophic, effect on the American wine industry, both in terms of quality and regulation. It solidified the notion that wine was primarily an alcoholic rather than agricultural product, and it halted research in viticulture. Prohibition also diminished America's taste for drier and less alcoholic wines and, following repeal, consumers clamored for mediocre sweet and fortified "belly wash" wines. Given that high-quality wine could not be produced overnight, it took decades for American consumers once more to refine their tastes, and it would take just as long for the nation's wine producers to replant vineyards, relearn the winemaking trade, and manufacture high-quality wine.[206]

Even following repeal, residual Prohibitionist sentiments remained firmly entrenched in the United States Congress, which blocked practically all federal government efforts to revive viticulture. One post-Repeal casualty of Prohibitionist politics was President Franklin D. Roosevelt's attempt to reestablish the Department of Agriculture's role in viticultural research. Roosevelt proposed building wine experimentation facilities at Beltsville, Maryland and Meridian, Mississippi. An influential dry congressman on the House Appropriations Committee, however, threatened to block all funding for the Department of Agriculture unless the "wicked work on 'fermentation' was halted."[207]

While Prohibition was the most significant cause of the demise of the wine industry in the United States, mention must also be made of the Stock Market Crash of 1929, and the onset of World War II. Each of these played its role in stifling the prospects for the commonwealth's wine industry rebirth. Those effects lasted for nearly two decades. The crash, which began in October 1929, gave birth to the Great Depression, the most devastating economic collapse in American history. It immediately ended the "Roaring Twenties," and its effects would be felt until the end of the war.

Remarkably, the commonwealth found itself able to avoid the Depression's more destructive elements. The Old Dominion continued to enjoy higher incomes and an economy that was diversified between manufacturing, agriculture, and trade. Following Roosevelt's 1932 election, Virginia also took advantage of an unprecedented infusion of federal funding and programs. While these helped Virginia recover, in relative terms, by the mid-1930s, investment in more recreational pursuits—including winemaking—largely took a back seat to the planting of staple crops and mere survival.[208]

The Depression did not, however, entirely halt winemaking in Virginia. To the contrary, Virginian's post-Prohibition penchant for sweeter, fortified wines resulted in the limited success of several smaller wine operations across the state. The Petersburg area, for example, was home to at least three wineries: Connolly's Winery, Chesterfield Winery, and Old Dominion Winery, the last of which produced "fair wines" from Virginia grapes that one observer, however, found to be "too high in Concord content."[209]

In Richmond, New York native Antoine L. Alaj opened his small Alaj Wine Company early in the 1930s, while a significant wine bottling and distribution company, Dixie Wine Company, opened in 1935 in the city's Northside neighborhood. Boasting a production capacity of 600,000 gallons, Dixie Wine bottled some 3,500 cases per day and produced a variety of dessert, table, and fruit wines under the "Virginia Lee," "Imperial Reserve," and "Royal" labels. Acquired by the Canandaigua Wine Company in 1975, Dixie's wines had been good enough to be served on the Chesapeake & Ohio Railroad's cars by the 1960s. In the Shockoe Valley area of downtown Richmond, the Southland Wine Company opened in 1937 and produced a variety of low-grade, high-alcohol-content varietals, including "Velvet Rose," "Madison House," "Pine Hurst," "Three Bears," "Black Ranger," "3 Little Pigs," and "Old Homestead."[210]

In Charlottesville, two Depression-era businesses took advantage of the region's abundant apple farms by specializing in the production of apple wines. The better-known of the two, Laird & Company's "Distillery No. 5," opened as early as 1934 in the Albemarle County hamlet of North Garden. Headquartered in northeastern New Jersey, Laird enjoyed historical distinction as being both the nation's first licensed commercial distillery, as well as a major manufacturer of apple-based distilled products. As New Jersey's apple farms succumbed to development in the 1930s, the company looked south to supply its operations.

Following Repeal, Laird produced a sweet cider-based liquor, known as "Applejack," at the North Garden distillery, while under the proprietary name of "Virginia Fruit Brandy Distilling Company" and "Virginia Wine Cellars," the facility also produced an apple wine as well as a cheap, fortified, Labrusca "bum wine" known as "Sly Fox."[211]

Elsewhere in Charlottesville, the Piedmont Apple Products Company was founded in 1937 in the city's Belmont neighborhood. Piedmont possessed a storage capacity of some one million gallons and bottled 1,500 cases per day of table, dessert, and fruit wines as well as brandies under the brand names "Shady Lane," "Gold Crown," and "Old Piedmont." Like the wines produced by Richmond's Dixie Wine Company, Piedmont's apple wines were also offered to riders on the Chesapeake & Ohio and Southern Railways.[212]

In Danville, K. C. Arey & Company opened a large winery in 1933 with a storage capacity of 100,000 gallons on the south side of the city where it began bottling and distributing so-called "vinouse beverages." Primarily distributed in southern Virginia, North Carolina, and Tennessee, and overseen by K. C. Arey, Jr., the winery produced 1,000 cases of wine daily under the "Old Plantation," "Kay-Cee," "Old 97," "Three Buds," "Old Colony," "Dan Valley," and "Old Pete" labels.[213]

One standout among the myriad low-grade Depression-era winery operations was the remarkable, but little-known, Woburn Winery, which was founded in 1940 in the Ivy Hill area of Mecklenburg County. Owned and operated by John June Lewis, Woburn is believed to be the first winery to have been owned by an African American in the United States. Lewis, a veteran of World War I, initially learned the art of winemaking as a child from the owner of the plantation on which his mother was once a slave. He gained a further appreciation for viniculture in 1919 while serving in the army in the Rhine Valley of Europe.

After his return to Virginia, Lewis bought a farm and planted 10 acres of wine grapes in 1933. He opened Woburn in 1940 with a storage capacity of 5,000 gallons. Lewis produced sweet native and hybrid wines for his neighbors and friends and at least one of his wines, which he bottled under the "Virginia Car" label, was sold to Southern Railway passengers at the railroad's nearby Clarksville station. Noted wine writer Leon Adams has attested that Woburn's wines were "sound," and that they used yeast cultures from California. Woburn operated well into the early 1970s before closing.[214]

With production costs at an all-time high during the Great Depression, home winemaking became ever more popular. Anecdotal evidence suggests that Virginians produced wine out of practically anything that would ferment, including dandelions, blackberries, strawberries, and even beans. In Fairfax County, William Davidson imported grapevine stock and operated a fruit orchard at his property, Hunter House. Davidson used the grapes and fruits to open Northern Virginia's first licensed winery and produced wine under the "Virginia Maid" label. Hunter House—no doubt like countless other homes, farmsteads, mansions, and plantations across the commonwealth—featured a cellar stocked with wine likely produced from grapes grown on the property.[215]

While Virginia's Depression-era vintners struggled to produce wines from native grapes, or grapes procured from out of state, an ambitious effort to revive the former Monticello Wine Company and produce high-quality wine began outside of Charlottesville. Following the creation of a special wine-growing committee by the Charlottesville and Albemarle Regional Chamber of Commerce, several area businessmen founded the Monticello Grape Growers

Cooperative Association in 1934, hoping to reduce Virginia's downward trend in wine grapes, promote the acceptance of light table wines, and revive the region's once-flourishing grape industry.

With the benefit of early organizational assistance from grape researcher William B. Alwood and winemaker Paul Garrett, the Cooperative was created as a statewide organization that sought to represent viticultural interests, provide education as to the benefits of wine consumption, reduce wine excise taxes, and encourage the planting of grapes. Participants executed a marketing agreement that obligated them to deliver wine grapes to the Cooperative. In exchange, the Cooperative agreed to store and market members' grapes.[216]

Charlottesville attorney Bernard Peyton Chamberlain was the leader behind the Cooperative's creation and was selected as its president. At once an amateur author, local historian, and one-time candidate for the Virginia House of Delegates, Chamberlain found that his attraction to the promotion of Virginia wine came about quite honestly. In 1931, during the waning days of Prohibition, Chamberlain self-published a short treatise on home winemaking, *The Making of Palatable Table Wines,* that served as a bible for Virginians who had suffered from a decades-long deficiency in winemaking expertise.

Chamberlain printed at least 400 copies of the book and, perhaps seeking to avoid a run in with the law, prefaced it with a history of temperate wine drinking, cautioning against overindulgence. "We believe that moderate use of food and drink gives greater enjoyment to life," Chamberlain later noted, "and that temperance in the use of alcoholic beverages is facilitated by the opportunity to procure easily and cheaply light wines of good quality."[217]

While Chamberlain's Cooperative supported the planting of almost any grape variety, it encouraged particularly the cultivation of Norton and Ives wine grapes that could produce "high grade" red wine capable of being manufactured, and primarily sold, in Virginia. "It is this Norton wine," Chamberlain noted, "which will be a light dry red wine… for which the public is waiting."[218]

After receiving Paul Garrett's promise to locate a winery in central Virginia once the Cooperative produced 500 tons of wine grapes annually, Cooperative members scurried to demonstrate the viability of the enterprise. The Cooperative encouraged its members to plant at least forty new acres of grapes annually and grape plantings grew rapidly.[219]

In its first two years, the Cooperative planted some twenty acres of grapes of fifteen varieties in Halifax and Nelson Counties, and by 1936, thirty acres were under cultivation. It sold its first commercial crop and manufactured wine for its members in 1938. The following year, nearly fifty acres were under cultivation and by 1940, the Cooperative had established a small winery where it produced 3,000 gallons of dry red wine of "fair quality."[220]

Once again, however, the Cooperative's success proved short-lived and its goal of developing large quantities of refined table wines manufactured from native grapes never materialized. The ghost of Prohibition, which had eviscerated market demand for more refined, higher-grade red wine, haunted the Cooperative's efforts. Moreover, even though it was encouraged by the plantings of grape growers in Fredericksburg, Halifax County, and other Virginia locales, the scarcity of grapes ultimately forced the Cooperative to buy California grapes for wine processing. By the outbreak of World War II, the Cooperative was all but defunct.[221]

## —Virginia Wine in the Postwar Era—

The outbreak of the Second World War again delayed developments in the state's wine industry. The national market for fresh grapes collapsed in the face of a need to focus attention on the production of food and other material for the war effort. By the time of the Japanese surrender in September 1945, Virginia's wine industry had suffered through more than a quarter century of interruption from disease, Prohibition, and postponements. In addition, by the end of the war national wine tastes had come to favor sweeter alcoholic beverages, and Americans displayed a pronounced preference for distilled spirits, martinis, cocktails, and highballs.

The face of Virginia agriculture had also changed; by 1950, more than half of the commonwealth's agricultural revenues were generated from the raising of livestock, including cows, turkeys, and chickens. Tobacco, long the state's dominant agricultural enterprise, had been joined by new crops, including potatoes and peanuts. Opportunities for grape growing were nonexistent, as Virginia's fruit producers focused on the large-scale production of apples, peaches, and strawberries. While Virginia's Depression-era wineries continued to churn out cheaper wines, the production of higher-quality Virginia wine remained of little significance.[222]

The history of commercial winemaking in Virginia from the 1950s to the 1980s must inevitably include mention of Richard's Wine Cellars in Petersburg. It not only dominated Virginia's wine scene for more than two decades but, just as Captain Paul Garrett had accomplished some four decades earlier, it also generated a national sensation with the popularity of some of its scuppernong brands.

Despite its relatively recent predominance, information on the history of Richard's is limited. The company's genesis can be traced to a family patriarch, Mordecai E. "Mack" Sands. A Brooklyn native, Sands is thought to have been a bootlegger during Prohibition, running illegal liquor along the Canadian-U.S. border. Following Repeal, Sands began his affiliation with the wine industry by working as a partner at a small, low-grade winery, located in Long Island City, New York. There, from relatively few grapes and despite Sand's limited expertise, the winery managed to produce large quantities of low-quality wine.[223]

After World War II, Sands purchased a former sauerkraut factory in Canandaigua, New York, and renovated it into a winery. He placed his son, Marvin Sands, in charge of the winery's operations and founded the "Canandaigua Industries Company" to specialize in the manufacture of bulk wines for bottlers in the eastern United States. With his Canandaigua operation in his son's capable hands, Mack Sands headed to Petersburg in 1951, where he opened Richard's Wine Cellars named in honor of his infant grandson.[224]

Richard's location in the Southeast was Sands's attempt to address the beverage needs of a region largely neglected by the national wine industry. To satisfy the sugary taste preferences of the region's wine drinkers, Richard's began producing copious amounts of cheap wine from sweet native scuppernong grapes. Following in Paul Garrett's footsteps, Sands established scuppernong grape-buying stations in North Carolina to assure alternative sources of income in rural areas. Also like Garrett, Sands's operation expanded rapidly, purchasing competing wine operations and becoming the largest winery in the Southeast.[225]

Acquisitions and expansions continued into the 1970s and afforded Richard's the ability to offer an unparalleled line of low-quality fortified varietals with alcohol content varying between 12 percent and 20 percent by volume. While most of Richard's wines were produced from grapes grown outside of Virginia, every Richard's label was replete with colorful graphics including apple farms, Native Americans, pigs' heads, boars' heads, cowboys, cartoon bears, plantation houses, and more. Several wines were sold aboard the Atlantic Coast Line Railroad, which served southeastern states from Virginia to Florida.[226]

The most famous of the company's line of bargain-priced beverages, "Richards Wild Irish Rose," was a low-end, fortified, very sweet, Concord-flavored varietal, introduced in 1954 and nicknamed "The Happy Wine." Given its high alcohol content and liquor bottle–style packaging, Richards Wild Irish Rose was soon dubbed a "bum" or "wino" wine.[227]

In 1967, Mack Sands again shadowed Paul Garrett's path when he reintroduced the "Virginia Dare" label to the market after purchasing the naming rights. While the reintroduction of the wine not only reconnected the "Virginia

Dare" brand to scuppernong grapes and the commonwealth, wine writer Leon Adams noted that the reconstituted Virginia Dare wine fell far short of offering the same historical and geographical connection envisioned by Garrett:

> [Sands has] ignored one of the key's to Garrett's original success, which was to make the name mean only an individual, distinctive wine with Scuppernong wine of the South as part of its blend. Instead, Virginia Dare now represents a "complete line" of generic types, from sauterne and burgundy to port and sherry. Only two of the "line," Virginia Dare White and Rosé, contain some Scuppernong wine. And whether the white closely resembles the wine Captain Paul Garrett served me in 1934, I cannot, after a lifetime, be sure.[228]

Regardless of the quality and appeal (or lack thereof) of Richard's wines, by the mid-1970s, the Sands family was overseeing the largest winemaking empire in eastern North America operating multiple wineries in four states and producing more than two million gallons annually. The family consolidated its enterprises into the "Canandaigua Wine Company, Inc." in 1972, and instantly became the nation's second-largest wine producer, after California's mammoth bulk wine producer, E&J Gallo Winery.[229]

Late in the 1980s, a recession—combined with Canandaigua's failed foray into the wine cooler business, and the national development of more refined tastes that demanded higher-quality, drier wines—led to falling sales for the company. Canandaigua cut some twenty percent of its workforce and shuttered several wineries, including Richard's Wine Cellars in Petersburg. The company survives, however, and has once again prospered. In 2000, Canandaigua changed its name to "Constellation Brands, Inc.," and remains today the country's second-largest wine producer.[230]

While the company's early Virginia roots have long since been forgotten, and though the original Richard's Wine Cellar building has been demolished, Richard's can properly be remembered as the company that revived interest in scuppernong wine, devoted attention to long-neglected southeastern wine drinkers, and recaptured the "Virginia Dare" name for the Old Dominion.[231]

Not all Virginia wines produced during the 1950s and 1960s were manufactured from native grapes, nor were all wines of low quality. One Prince William County winery, Sciutto Winery, became notable for its unique wines, distinctive promotions, and the irrepressible personality of its founder, John Sciutto. Located twenty-six miles west of Washington, D.C., near the community of

Groveton, Sciutto Winery was situated on one of the few remaining privately held properties in the middle of Manassas National Battlefield Park.

An Italian who immigrated to the United States in 1931 to escape the fascist government of Benito Mussolini, Sciutto had previously worked for several years in the Northern Virginia real estate industry before purchasing the property in August 1948 with the intention of opening a winery. Once operational, the small winery complex featured a one-story winery facility and several smaller buildings for vats and storage space.[232]

Sciutto hailed from a long winemaking tradition; his forebears had produced wine in Savona, Italy, for more than five centuries, and he had repeatedly professed a desire to replicate his ancestor's winemaking methods. Unlike most Virginia winemakers of the day, Sciutto sought to manufacture pure vinifera wine with a lower alcohol and sugar content. He produced at least four varieties of red and white table wines made from the Freisa (a red Italian grape wine), Norton, Dolcetto (a red wine grape), and Moscato varieties. Each bottle proudly featured the Sciutto family name and crest, along with the phrase "Made in Virginia"—despite the fact that the scarcity of Virginia-grown grapes forced him to procure fruit from California.[233]

Ever the socialite, Sciutto displayed a jovial public persona and frequently hosted chicken and spaghetti suppers for his neighbors. Even more impressively, the winery hosted an annual "old country" Italian grape stomping festival each October—perhaps the first in Virginia history—that was described by observers as "half Bacchanalian, half Neapolitan." After a blessing of the fruit by local priests, John Sciutto selected a few eager young ladies—dressed in their Sunday finest and described as "beautiful of face with pedal extremities"—to hop, stomp, and crush the ice-cold refrigerated grapes in large troughs. The dazzling, barefooted women, one of whom was annually crowned the "Queen of Grapes," squealed, winced, and laughed as they stomped the grapes long enough for reporters to snap a few choice photographs.[234]

Following the "dance of the grapes," the stomping models and their anointed queen dipped their numb, purple-dyed toes in a tub of steaming hot water. "No good if the pretty girls catcha cold," Sciutto explained to a reporter in his thick Italian accent. Afterwards, guests were treated to a sumptuous buffet of Italian delicacies, including salami, antipasto, and crushed garlicky olives, as they raised glasses of red and white wine from the previous year's vintage. A bonfire roared as singers and folk bands entertained a crowd that danced and sang into the night.[235]

Sciutto's lively festival became something of an annual tradition in Prince William County during the 1950s, turning him into a local folk hero and attracting families, local officials, ambassadors, congressmen, judges, and generals. Despite his charming public persona however, observers noted that Sciutto was inwardly a lonely man who longed for his wife, Mary Sciutto, and his two sons—who had chosen to stay in Italy.[236]

In the fall of 1956, however, the Virginia ABC Board rescinded his wine-making license after finding that one of his test batches had gone awry. Insisting that the batch could have only turned bad from "sabotage," the incident nonetheless devastated Sciutto and brought about his first heart attack. Though the winery's license was reinstated several weeks later, Sciutto shortly thereafter suffered a second heart attack, which his friends asserted was likely a direct result of the problem. It was said that "heartbreak failed the proud little Italian."[237]

Emotionally and physically exhausted by 1957, Sciutto turned his winery into a grocery store. He died the following February following a third heart attack suffered after a head-on collision in a snowstorm on Route 29, less than a quarter mile from his winery. The winery property was subsequently incorporated into Manassas National Battlefield Park, and today, all that remains of the winery is the original parking lot on the north side of Route 29. Older Park Service staff continue to refer to the property as the "winery parking lot," though park tourists today would find nothing to remind them of the once joyous times made possible by its late clever and merry Italian owner.[238]

Page County's Lorelei Vineyards, which operated in the Shenandoah Valley in the 1950s and 1960s, was yet another short-lived commercial winery that experienced difficulties with Virginia's ABC inspectors. Founded by Urban Westenberger, a German who immigrated to Virginia 1948, Lorelei was located along the southern slope of Massanutten Mountain on the western banks of the Shenandoah River. The property contained a handsome red brick home with high ceilings, as well as a courtyard and a wine cellar. Coincidently, it also featured a small vineyard that had been established by the previous owner of the property, none other than Prince William County's John Sciutto.

Rumored to be a recluse as well as somewhat argumentative with neighbors (not to mention a heavy drinker), Westenberger was a native of Germany's famous Rheingau wine region, where he spent his childhood surrounded by the area's extraordinary vineyards. In Virginia, Westenberger had expanded the farm's grape acreage, which he named "Lorelei Vineyards," and by 1953 he had begun manufacturing wine without permits from the Virginia ABC Board. Westenberger continued to bottle and sell more than 8,000 gallons annually, if quietly and illegally, making him one of the commonwealth's largest wine producers.[239]

Westenberger produced three wines under the "Virginia Rhine," "Virginia Vin Rosé," and "Virginia Burgundy" labels, each of which carried the phrase, "A Superior Product of Virginia." Lorelei's wines enjoyed remarkable regional success; they could be found at the Lorelei Lodge in Luray (which he owned), a store along Lee Highway in Manassas (perhaps owned by John Sciutto), the Mess Hall in Quantico, the McLean Delicatessen, Falls Church's Red & White Supermarket, and Arlington's Carrier Drug Center.

Production ground to a halt in 1955, however, when the Virginia ABC Board finally shuttered Westenberger's unpermitted operation. Three years later, in April 1958—still mired in bureaucratic red tape and attempting to reopen—Westenberger wrote to federal officials to complain:

> The [Federal] Government pays farmers to take crop land out of production and the [Virginia] A.B.C. Board seems determined to make me put land back into crop production, or go bankrupt. This is a very unhealthy situation. How much longer can a man remain law abiding, while keeping him not only economically down, but making him pay the federal wine taxes and then refusing, to let him sell his produce.[240]

Despite the ABC's view that Westenberger had demonstrated "a lack of respect for law and order, and... has maintained an unsanitary establishment," the ABC Board nevertheless granted him a winery license in August 1958. Three months later, Westenberger had obtained the necessary federal licenses for his labels and he again began to market his wines.[241]

But the operation was once more forced to stop in October 1960, when the ABC Board informed Westenberger that his Burgundy and Rhine wines "did not equal the quality and characteristics of the original approved samples and [were], therefore, condemned for sale in the State of Virginia." In what must have appeared to Westenberger as a bureaucratic vendetta, the ABC notice was followed by an on-site inspection by representatives of the state's Division of Chemistry and Foods, who found that Lorelei Vineyards did not meet cleanliness codes. In December 1960, the ABC again inspected Lorelei's wines only to find that they failed state standards. After unsuccessfully contesting the inspectors' findings for more than a year, Westenberger saw his federal permits revoked in March 1962.[242]

By late in the 1960s, Westenberger had sold his Page County property and moved to Florida, where he died in Key West in 1977. Left in his wake were an abandoned winery, vineyards, records, and a manor house, failed dreams, and perhaps as many as 2,800 gallons of bottled wine. Sadly, the deserted manor house and a small mausoleum Westenberger had constructed for his parents became a convenient spot for vandalism by looters and partiers. As former *Washington Post* reporter Hank Burchard poetically wrote of the abandoned property in 1977,

> For a decade vandals have been smashing the bottles of unsold wine of Lorelei Vineyards. They smash them by the case and by the hundred, bottle after bottle, against the walls and against each other, so that the ruins reek of sour wine…. And still thousands of bottles remain, dressed in handsome labels, filled with awful wine. No one who has made wine, or simply loves it, could help being saddened by the sight.[243]

Burchard, who had stumbled onto the property during a canoe trip, surmised that had Westenberger devoted more time toward producing higher quality wine rather than forcing to market manifestly inferior wine, events may have played out differently for the German immigrant.

## —Optimism Suddenly Abounds—

The nearly two centuries between the close of the American Revolution and the late 1960s was one of conflict, contrast, and change for winemaking in Virginia. Without any governmental or significant academic support, enterprising Virginians experimented with grape growing, Dr. Daniel Norton had discovered a native red grape that produced a high-quality wine, and a budding fruit industry increased the opportunities for Virginia's grape growers.

The commonwealth's viticultural industry had shown remarkable resilience, particularly following the Civil War. The state's first grape advocacy organizations were formed, the Old Dominion's wine companies received national and international recognition for their products, one studious academic professor in Blacksburg developed a national reputation for grape research, and Charlottesville emerged as the center of Virginia's first wine industry.

Despite these isolated and occasional successes, one would have had difficulty recognizing the state of the Virginia wine industry as hopeful as America entered the 1960s. While Virginians consumed an estimated 2.8 million gallons of wine annually by 1960, it had only six licensed wineries, and a paltry sixteen acres of grapevines planted—none of which were vinifera varieties, and nearly all of which were table grapes unsuitable for wine production. By the end of that decade, the state's commercial vineyards fared only marginally better; fifteen commercial vineyards cultivated only some fifty acres of grapes. The

135

state's fruit industry remained dominated by apples, strawberries, pears, plums, and figs. Even more disconcerting, Virginians continued in their preference for sweeter, fortified beverages rather than more delicate wines.[244]

An honest assessment of conditions would have led an observer to think that the state's wine industry was almost as nonexistent as it had been when the settlers first landed at Jamestown. Successive traumatic events—be it war, grape disease, Prohibition, the Great Depression, or a highly restrictive liquor control plan—had exacted a terrible toll on one of the Old Dominion's most historically-significant horticultural endeavors. Battles had been fought over personal liberties, whether wine should be treated as an agricultural product or as the drink of the devil, and indeed over the very definition of alcohol. Anticipation of a renewed wine industry would have seemed little more than a misguided fantasy.

Hope, though, still sprang eternal. Optimism as to the potential for the future, if badly battered and bloodied by long experience, had served as the driving force for progress through it all. Whether this was found in the confidence shared by dozens of German families who engaged in viticulture after the Civil War, in the spirit of the Monticello Wine Company that continued operating into the waning hours prior to Prohibition, or in the devotion shown by Captain Paul Garrett to assure that his company outlived the Eighteenth Amendment, a handful of Virginians seemed perpetually eager to envision what was next in store for their hometown winemaking team.

It was an enthusiasm shared by the redoubtable Bernard P. Chamberlain, who noted in 1936, on the second anniversary of the founding of his Monticello Grape Growers Cooperative Association,

> We have come far, but really only a short part of the way to our goal of giving to the world a really good Virginia wine derived from a prosperous viticulture. The faint hearted may falter, but those who have the patience and the courage to hold the time and persevere can…make our grape growers the envy of all farmers in the state and the wine from our grapes the delight of a grateful nation.[245]

It would take the tremendous dedication and foresight of many if the state's wine industry was ever to revive. Fortunately, much to the surprise of everyone, even the most stalwart wine industry advocate, that revival was not far in the future. For over the next forty years, Virginia's wine industry would rise in prominence and reputation in a manner that exceeded even the wildest dreams of Thomas Jefferson.

# 3

## Against All Odds:
## Emergence of Virginia Wine
## in the Modern Era, 1967–1990

THOSE INTERESTED IN wine production in the late 1960s Virginia would have found little inspiration. Thanks to the legacy of Prohibition and the historically conservative nature of the state's politics and culture, the status of Virginia's wine industry was moribund. The Old Dominion boasted few vineyards and scant governmental support, was almost devoid of the expertise needed to produce high-quality wines, and most of the state's wine was produced by mass-production, generic, industrial producers in Richmond and Petersburg.

That all began to change in 1967, when Charles J. Raney, a former United States Navy and commercial airline pilot, founded a small vineyard on an eighty-six-acre property outside of Amissville in rural Rappahannock County. There on a hillside overlooking the end of a long, secluded driveway, he and his wife Virginia planted 110 French-American vines in an old peach orchard. They intended to open an artisanal winery.

The following year, they planted an additional 1,400 French-American and vinifera vines, which were the first to be cultivated successfully in modern Virginia. While growers had experimented with vinifera elsewhere, all documented attempts to grow vinifera in Virginia since the seventeenth century had failed. Raney, though, was a determined sort. His time in the U.S. Navy afforded him the chance to visit several European wine regions, where he developed an appreciation for wine and became enamored with the concept of starting his own vineyard in Virginia. Once back in the United States, Raney consulted with several northeastern growers on varieties and growing techniques.[1]

Though the Raneys' property was climatically- and topographically-challenged, they thought it had potential for a vineyard and future winery. It boasted a Frank Lloyd Wright–inspired home, a 130-year-old barn and corncrib, a deck, a generous lawn suitable for games, and a trail along the Rappahannock River.

Given their extraordinary undertaking, it was befitting that the Raneys settled on naming their operation "Farfelu," meaning "eccentric" or "crazy" in Old French.[2]

Farfelu's first bottling occurred in 1967 and, eight years later, it became Virginia's first licensed farm winery—a moniker that lawfully permitted the Raneys to both produce and sell wine. In June 1976, after an investment of nearly $20,000 in tanks, vats, and a French wine press, the Raneys sold their first vintage in a matter of days. "There's no question now that we can grow the grapes," Raney prophetically told a reporter. "From here on out, it's just a matter of economics."[3]

Whether observers of the day appreciated it or not, the Raneys' initial plantings would serve as a much-needed catalyst for the rebirth of Virginia's modern wine industry. One by one, in the aftermath of Farfelu's great gamble, pioneering and enterprising individuals surfaced across the state hoping to accomplish a feat that had not been attempted in more than a century: to plant and cultivate the state's first significant French-American and vinifera vineyards. Most possessed no prior experience in growing grapes or making wine; many held full-time occupations in industries far removed from viticulture. Nearly all failed to grasp the nature of the arduous task that lay ahead.

Given the relative lack of expertise as to the state's suitability for growing vinifera, these innovators relied on their own fortitude, capital, and common-sense to experiment with varieties, master grape growing conditions, and, in the end, produce drinkable wine. Widely panned by critics both outside the Old Dominion and within for pursuing entirely unprecedented goals at great financial risk, their actions resulted in a surprisingly resurgent movement that would sweep across the commonwealth between 1967 and 1990. Their efforts would finally provide the momentum needed to accomplish more in the name of Virginia wine in less than four decades than throughout the previous four centuries combined.

In short, a wine revolution had begun.

## — The Vinifera Wine Growers Association —

The success of all human causes—just, unjust, or even célèbre—inherently relies on the loyalty of a critical mass of determined individuals to carry forth the mission of the day. The same held true in Virginia in the late 1960s where, were there to be any rebirth of winemaking, an army of dedicated grape growers and winemakers would need to join the cause of producing high-quality wine. At that time, however, the cultivation of such sentiments required something that could spark the imagination of dormant, would-be winemakers: propaganda.

To that end, the story of Virginia's revolutionary wine era would be incomplete without mentioning the efforts of the indefatigable Robert de Treville Lawrence—a man who was not particularly celebrated for his viticultural or vinification skills (though he certainly grew grapes and attempted to make wine) but rather for his talents in the art of promotion.

Committed to public service for most of his life, Lawrence became something of a one-man marketing machine for the cause of Virginia wine. Between the late 1960s and early 1990s, Lawrence capitalized on his unique talents not only by experimenting with different vinifera varieties at his home, but also, more importantly, by organizing like-minded Virginia wine enthusiasts into Virginia's first modern wine advocacy organization, the Vinifera Wine Growers Association, which was formally established in 1973.

A Georgia native, Lawrence graduated from the University of Georgia in 1937 with a journalism degree, writing briefly for the former *Atlanta Georgian* newspaper before becoming a public relations officer for the U.S. Army Air Corps. Later, he would serve in the foreign service, where his belief in the advantages of a free press for purposes of advancing democracy led him to help establish numerous small newspapers across the world, earning him the nicknames "Lawrence of Monrovia" and "Lawrence of Calcutta" from his African and Indian friends.[4]

It was during Lawrence's decades abroad that he first cultivated his taste for fine wine. After his retirement to northern Fauquier County in 1967, he immersed himself in Virginia's viticultural history, often slipping into long-winded after-dinner tales of early Virginia wine pioneers. His obsession with mastering the history of the state's viticultural industry mirrored an equally passionate desire to ensure its revival in the modern era.[5]

Lawrence believed that Virginia's climate and soil—with its moisture, mild winters, and proximity to many of the East Coast's wealthiest wine-drinking markets—was ideal for establishing a new fine wine industry. To do so, however, he felt strongly that the state's wines must evolve beyond traditional native American grapes like scuppernong and Concord.

A man of extraordinary opinion, he reasoned that if the Old Dominion stood any chance of developing a reputation for fine wine, Virginia's growers must move even beyond the prevalence of French-American varieties. "The key to quality," he told a *TIME* magazine reporter in 1977, "is vinifera. There is no other way to make a good wine. Other wines are simply hamburger wines." Indeed, he reasoned, it was only through growing vinifera and applying advanced scientific knowledge to counteract the devastating effects of destructive mildew and fungi, that Virginia's growers could shatter the myth that Americans lacked the ability to produce fine American wines.[6]

Lawrence began implementing his grand vision at home. In 1968, he planted a small vineyard of 100 vines next to his stone house, Highbury. But merely planting and tending to his vines did little to satisfy Lawrence's itch; his compulsion for organization and promotion nagged at him. As he had so many times during his writing career in the Foreign Service, Lawrence wanted to inspire others to act.[7]

In October 1973, the ever-restless Lawrence persuaded some fifty other Virginia wine enthusiasts—each of whom believed in the promise of vinifera as the salvation of Virginia's wine industry—to meet at Grace Episcopal Church in the small Fauquier County town of The Plains. There, beneath the church's historic wooden roof and stained-glass windows, Lawrence led a lively discussion on the need to attract out-of-state viticultural experts to visit the Virginia Piedmont and provide seminars on winemaking. He also persuaded those assembled to collaborate and found a nonprofit organization, the Vinifera Wine Growers Association, to create a positive legal and political climate to spearhead the growth of vinifera grape growing along the East Coast.[8]

Armed with the slogan "Better Wines Through Better Vines," the new Association would disseminate information on viticultural developments, provide technical information on grape growing and winemaking, sponsor educational courses, advocate for better wine laws, and call attention to the need for better government-sponsored research. Though conceived as a Virginia-based organization, the group sought to represent the interests of all winegrowers east of the Mississippi. One could not help but notice that the list of the group's founders—not to mention most of its general membership—was filled with prominent Northern Virginia families from the rolling hills of rural Loudoun and Fauquier Counties.[9]

For an initial $10 membership, Association members could attend winegrowing seminars in different Virginia locales that featured notable authors and speakers from across the country. Association membership also entitled one to a subscription to the *Vinifera Wine Growers Journal*, a no-frills, text-heavy compilation of materials edited by Lawrence himself. The *Journal* was one of the primary publications of the time dedicated to "expanding technology in the premium wine growing field" and promoting the cultivation of vinifera in eastern North America. While it included articles culled from other periodicals and placed a heavy emphasis on coverage of the nascent Virginia wine scene, the *Journal* accepted topical commentaries covering viticultural history, growing techniques, soil conditions, foreign markets, grape diseases, and more.[10]

The Association did not dedicate its efforts solely toward the promotion of grape growing. It also actively encouraged viticulture as a means to improve farm incomes and preserve Northern Virginia's rolling Piedmont landscape from the suburban sprawl creeping outwards from Washington, D.C. "Economics, without question," read one *Journal* article, "is the primary cause of our beautiful farms being subdivided into small pieces with little unattractive buildings." It was not surprising, therefore, to see conspicuous in the new Association's objectives the "preservation of the rural countryside and old stone structures." In the coming years, representatives would routinely partner with local environmental and historic preservation organizations and regularly appear at public hearings in opposition to encroaching development and highways.[11]

To promote wine and stop uncontrolled sprawl, the Association needed first to tackle structural deficiencies that had hampered the revival of Virginia's wine industry. Chief among these was the public sector's manifest lack of enthusiasm for the growing of high-quality wine grapes in the mid-Atlantic region. In some cases, the Association even found that its goals were in direct conflict with those of the U.S. Department of Agriculture and the scientists at Virginia Tech—two entities that, more than any others, the Association felt should encourage grape growing and winemaking in the Old Dominion.

The Association argued that the USDA should play a major role in providing educational support and attracting investors to establish vineyards across the nation—and not just in California. The Department, however, was ill-equipped to assist. Despite the emergence of a booming wine industry in California by the mid-1970s, the USDA's oenology programs were still recovering from the devastating effects of Prohibition four decades earlier. Its viticultural research and development work suffered from a substantial technology gap and, even by the mid-1970s, a one-man "Fruit and Nuts Office" conducted the whole of the department's oenology research.[12]

In the Association's view, the agency had been "shortsighted and negligent in not going all out for quality where such a great potential gain lies for our farmers." The Association maintained that the USDA should monitor foreign wine imports and inform the public of how it could produce high-quality wine to halt the "great loss in dollar flow out of the country." The USDA's failure to provide farmers and consumers with valuable viticultural information during the recessionary economics of the 1970s was, the Association argued, tantamount to "agricultural censorship."[13]

The USDA persisted in its refusal to assist and, in many instances, criticized the Association's efforts. In its defense, the criticism lobbed at Virginia's experimental wine grape growers was based on the best information available to a hidebound bureaucracy; the department was mired in a status quo that was, for the most part, outdated and erroneous. One USDA grape scientist, for example, believed that unpredictable frosts and hurricanes around harvest time would make grape growing east of the Mississippi River too risky. Another administrator of the USDA's Agricultural Research Service claimed that, because California and Europe were overproducing grapes and because vinifera varieties were susceptible to meteorological phenomena and diseases, the USDA could not recommend the planting of wine grapes *anywhere* on the East Coast.[14]

Many more USDA representatives simply maintained that the planting of additional vinifera grapes should be discouraged entirely. In 1975, the Association requested that the agency produce a brochure on grape growing. In response, one senior USDA administrator captured a familiar refrain heard during the 1970s:

> We cannot justify research to promote vinifera wine grape production in the East. Among other facts to support this position are the adverse climate, high incidence of insects and diseases, high cost of production, non-competitive position of eastern regions…and the present world surplus of wine grape plantings and wine stocks…. There is extremely little commercial production of vinifera wine grapes in the Eastern United States at the present time, [and] there is no economic opportunity for the development of such an industry, and…we foresee no future potential…. Such a publication might be useful to prevent innocent but well meaning commercial growers from investing, and losing, their money in such an enterprise but this should be obvious.[15]

The Association fared no better with researchers at Virginia Tech, the commonwealth's principal state-supported land-grant institution. Long a seat of horticultural experimentation as well as a leader in the state's first wine industry of the late 1800s, the institution shared the USDA's pessimism. Its researchers asserted that Virginia's extreme temperatures and excessive rainfall presented poor grape-growing conditions. In fact, it went so far as to list vinifera and other high-quality wine grape varieties on official lists that, the institution asserted, would lead to "disaster" for investors. During a particularly contentious 1978 meeting, one Virginia Tech professor reportedly told a hopeful vinifera grower, "As long as you throw away the money of the people you work for that is perfectly all right with us. The moment you get a Virginia farmer excited about something that does not make any sense we have the duty to step in and stop you."[16]

Lawrence and the Association felt the time was ripe to reverse course. Thus, beginning in October 1973, the Association began a coordinated campaign to petition the USDA, the U.S. Secretary of Agriculture, senators, and even the White House's Council of Economic Advisors to have the USDA dedicate funds to viticultural research. At a minimum, the Association sought an informational pamphlet regarding the cultivation of grapes east of the Rocky Mountains. The Association also asked that the USDA consolidate its wine-growing efforts in the eastern states and coordinate fungicide development with national chemical companies. This set off heated arguments between the Association, bureaucrats, and politicians.[17]

The USDA simply declined to accede to any of the Association's requests. By 1978, after five years of unsuccessful attempts to make any ground with the USDA, the Association conceded the failure of its federal efforts, noting in its *Journal*, "Man, unlike other animals, is able to exist and prosper because he can adjust to his environment. Whether the [USDA's] problem is professional jealousy, stubbornness, or a strong California grape lobby, it is immaterial. The [USDA] gives as the excuse, 'lack of funds.' This is unacceptable."[18]

## —Rebirth of State Support—

Though the Association's federal lobbying efforts did not bear fruit, its experience with state officials was quite different. In December 1976, Association representatives secured a meeting with Virginia Governor Mills E. Godwin (1966–1970; 1974–1978) and his Commissioner of Agriculture and Consumer Services, S. Mason Carbaugh, to discuss the status of Virginia's wine industry. In a state in which apples had become the dominant agricultural fruit, this was truly remarkable. During the meeting, Godwin and Carbaugh heard the Association representatives' arguments as to how increases in the state's wine imports from other regions and countries were hurting Virginia's businesses, farmers, and taxpayers. They also heard how, with the proper state encouragement, high-quality vinifera wine grapes could be grown in the commonwealth.

Following the meeting, Carbaugh's Virginia Department of Agriculture and Consumer Services (VDACS) unveiled a series of promotional efforts designed to support the fledgling Virginia wine industry. VDACS's efforts sparked the beginning of what would become a perpetually increasing, unbroken chain of official support by Virginia's government to promote Virginia's modern wine industry. This support was not only exceptional in the country, but represented the first time since the colonial era that politically-conservative Virginia had officially taken a proactive stance in favor of the entirely unproven industry of wine grape growing.

The first, albeit minor, effort by Virginia's government began in the summer of 1977 with VDACS's publication of the *Grape Newsletter*, designed both to assist with Virginia's grape-marketing efforts and stimulate an interest in Virginia wine. Hoping to ease "the rather frantic search for juice right at harvesting time…[and] aid the vineyardist in selling all his grapes," the *Newsletter* provided names, contact information, and directions to the state's known grape-producing facilities. Carbaugh's personal brainchild, the *Newsletter* also contained a map of Virginia's vineyards, a list of growers, and a list of wineries.[19]

Publication of the newsletter was followed in September 1977 by the creation of an official, state-level, and state-sponsored "Grape Growers Advisory Committee," that consisted of twelve Virginia wine industry pioneers who would advise state government on promotional efforts to assist the nascent industry. As with the *Newsletter*, the idea for the committee was Carbaugh's. After conducting a statewide survey of vinifera vineyards, he had called a one-day statewide conference at Elizabeth Furness's Piedmont Winery outside of Middleburg. There, he proclaimed that the promotion of vinifera grapes was a significant state agricultural policy, called for the committee's creation, and set a statewide goal of establishing 175 commercial vineyards and four new wineries over the next five years.[20]

In the autumn of 1979, VDACS published its first winery guide featuring six wineries. It was replaced the following autumn by a twenty-page *Guide to the Virginia Estate Wineries and Their Wines*, which included wine-tasting tips and a winery map, as well as information on the state's existing and future wineries and the commonwealth's viticultural history. In the same year, as part of a larger revamping of VDACS's agriculture publicity efforts, the agency reorganized its "Product Promotion Section," which, thereafter, began marketing Virginia wineries alongside the state's more-traditional agricultural commodities.[21]

VDACS's promotional efforts were soon bolstered by a major legislative initiative that rewrote nearly all of Virginia's wine regulations. Like most of Virginia's sister states, whose laws dated to the end of Prohibition, by the late 1970s, Virginia's wine laws were archaic and costly to winemakers. Grape growers had significant difficulty making and selling their finished, fermented product as compared to other nonalcoholic agricultural products like corn and wheat.

Previously, Virginia's outdated wine regulations had required the enactment of special laws dealing with the sale and use of wine for practically any application. The commonwealth compounded the problem by imposing an array of duplicative retailing and wholesale license fees that could total nearly $2,000 per year for the average Virginia winemaker and impeded the establishment of new wineries. Further, the commonwealth's taxes and fees of $1.73 per gallon were among the highest in the country, and were double those of California. As the *Winchester Star* reported in 1980, "Virginia wineries operate in the dregs of the tax collector's barrel.... The taxman collects three times on every bottle of wine corked in Virginia."[22]

It would not be accurate, however, to suggest that Virginia was entirely out of step with the rest of the nation. Practically every state regulated wine through a variety of confusing laws meant to curb underage drinking, ensure the collection of excise taxes, and, most important, to protect the three-tiered wholesaler-friendly alcohol-distribution regime that had been in place since the repeal of Prohibition.

While many had long called for the overhaul and harmonizing of the nation's wine laws, it was not until April 1979, during a meeting of the newly appointed Grape Growers Advisory Committee, that Virginia wine supporters began rallying in earnest for revised, updated state wine laws. Several Virginia winemakers reviewed existing statutes and drafted model amendments. The purpose was to unshackle Virginia's nascent winemaking industry from laws and regulations that strangled it at birth, to relieve it of outdated constraints, to eliminate nonproductive costs, and to lower permit fees without reducing overall tax revenue.[23]

By 1980, the call was loud enough for the General Assembly to pass the Virginia Farm Winery Act, signed into law by Governor John Dalton (1978–1982) on March 24, 1980. Perhaps the most important structural improvement in the history of Virginia's modern wine industry, the new law represented a major legislative step toward the support of the production of table wines in Virginia. More important, the act created two categories of wineries: "farm wineries" and "commercial wineries," each distinguished by the source of each winery's grapes. To qualify as a farm winery, a minimum of 51 percent of the winery's fruit must have been grown on land owned or leased by the vintner, and no more than 25 percent of the wine's fruit or juice could be purchased from out of state. By contrast, a "commercial winery" could bottle wine with fruit or grape juice from any source.[24]

The legislation offered a host of tax and distribution advantages to the growers to encourage farm wineries. The act simplified licensing requirements by establishing a single license for all farm wineries, and lowered the licensing fee from $1,000 to $100. The act also eliminated state wines from wine-liter taxes. In addition, the legislation explicitly classified vineyards and wineries as "agricultural" rather than "commercial" operations, which allowed a winery's equipment, buildings, and land to be taxed at lower levels than other commercial concerns. Funds generated through wine fees and taxes were to be reinvested in the state's wine research, marketing, and educational programs, including the funding of oenology and viticulture research and staff positions at Virginia Tech.[25]

Recognizing that Virginia's small wine producers could ill afford to distribute their wines only through wholesalers, the legislation allowed farm wineries to bypass the traditional three-tiered system of distribution that regulated most other alcoholic beverage commerce. This allowed small wineries to act as their own wholesalers and distributors and to transfer wine from production to their retail tasting rooms without additional licenses, and to directly distribute their wines to restaurants, grocery stores, and shops. The state's wineries thus gained needed exposure and began to develop relationships with restaurants, retail outlets, and consumers.

Over the next three decades, the 1980 Farm Winery Act proved to be a profound boon to Virginia's wine industry. Within two years, the number of farm wineries doubled, and this in turn prompted Virginia's government further to increase its support to the industry.[26]

Lawrence, who died in 2007 at the age of ninety-one, would serve as president of the Association until his retirement in 1989, when he was replaced by an equally-gifted California native, Gordon W. Murchie. While Lawrence was a highly controversial and opinionated figure in the Virginia wine narrative, and though the original experimental vines he planted at his Highbury estate have long since withered, those planted by countless others who followed him have taken their place.[27]

— *Revolutionary Planters* —

Among those who joined Treville Lawrence and the efforts of the Vinifera Wine Growers Association were a handful of charismatic individuals who persisted in their support despite a near-total lack of viticultural knowledge, winemaking infrastructure, or positive governmental assistance. Some simply planted grapes on their farms—irrespective of whether the location was good for grape growing; others boasted independent sources of income.

148

While they came from different backgrounds and largely attempted grape growing for pleasure, they were all singularly driven to advance the cause of Virginia wine. They were, simply, the vanguard generation of Virginia's winegrowers—an elegant, refined, hard-working, and congenial set—one that was not only unafraid of getting their hands dirty in the vineyards, but also all-too-enthusiastic about staking what, for some members, were great personal fortunes and reputations in the quest for high-quality winemaking.

One of the more active participants in Virginia's renascent industry was a man who could only be described as the quintessential gentleman farmer: Archibald M. "Archie" Smith, Jr. A retired advertising executive and Marine who had served as a dive bomber pilot at Guadalcanal and Okinawa during World War II, Smith and his wife, Dody Smith, purchased the 215-acre Stirling Farm outside of Middleburg in 1952 where they began raising corn and cattle.[28]

By the late 1960s, however, falling livestock prices and rising land values threatened the farm's future. Not wanting to leave the property, the Smiths began searching for an alternative crop that would help pay the bills. Their pursuit led them to multiple New York wineries where they observed growing techniques and engaged various wine consultants to review the potential for producing wine in Virginia.

After more than a year of investigation, the Smiths decided in 1972 to try their hand at wine. They planted 6,000 French-American vines in a five-acre vineyard that, almost overnight, made Stirling Farm the largest vineyard in the commonwealth. The Smiths increased their acreage the following year, and in 1974 the two planted their first vinifera varieties. While waiting for the vines to mature, Smith experimented with making wines from concentrates, apples, and grapes from other growers. In 1975, they obtained a license for a farm winery—the second such permit issued in Virginia after Farfelu some three months earlier. Stirling Farm was rechristened Meredyth Vineyards, named in honor of Archie's grandmother, and the Smiths opened for business.[29]

By July 1976, Meredyth had sold its first 325 cases of wine and later that year, the Smiths sold their 1975 Villard Blanc at the newly constructed Yorktown Victory Center in conjunction with the nation's bicentennial celebrations. In the decades that followed, Meredyth continued to expand and to enjoy remarkable success. It counted forty acres under vine by 1980 and ten more by 1987. It was by far the largest vineyard in the state by volume throughout the 1980s, producing some 40,000 gallons annually and offering consumers an assortment of more than fifteen red and white wines.[30]

What distinguished Meredyth from other early Virginia wineries, however, was its operational philosophy, marketing strategy, and commitment to family involvement. Smith insisted that Meredyth's grape processing and winemaking should be done on the property, so that the quality and profitability of Meredyth's wines could be controlled from grape to glass. "I wanted this place to become a viable economic unit," Smith told a reporter in 1983. "I wanted to take one single product—wine—and process [it] and sell it not only to distributors and retailers, but to the consumers." And that's just what he did.[31]

Meredyth also became known for its entrepreneurial spirit and extensive marketing efforts. Smith relied heavily on his prior advertising experience to promote Meredyth's wines through a strong retail program—immensely important for a young winery. Smith maintained direct contact with retailers and distributors who helped Meredyth create brand recognition and sell its wines through a broad distribution network across several states. The winery also hosted festivals, special events, daily tours, private and public tastings, and special restaurant-style food pairings known as "Dinner with Meredyth." Smith's marketing efforts even helped secure his Seyval Blanc a place at a White House dinner in 1976—a first for Virginia wine—where it received high praise.[32]

Though a thriving business concern, Meredyth was also intensely family-oriented. The entire Smith family was involved in the Meredyth operation; Dody Smith handled Meredyth's paperwork and assisted with marketing and promotion, while the Smiths' daughter, Susan, served as the winery's marketing director.

The Smith's son Robert Smith, an architect, helped with plans for the expansion of the winery and at times with harvests.[33] In 1981, the Smiths welcomed home their other son, Archie Smith III, as winemaker. Young Archie had initially assisted his parents in establishing Meredyth during his summer months while studying in Oxford, England. Following graduation, he served as a lecturer and a coach for wine-tasting competitions before returning to Virginia.

Once back at Meredyth, Archie Smith III became the first Virginia winemaker to use the French technique of carbonic maceration, which fermented juice while inside the grape skin. Archie III's winemaking methods helped Meredyth's wines garner multiple awards and ensured strong sales at nearby stores and local restaurants. "It would be hubristic to say we expect to make some of the great wines of the world," Archie Smith III told *The New York Times* in 1985. "But we've been able to demonstrate we can grow good grapes and make good wine."[34]

In March 1989, the Smiths reluctantly listed the winery for sale. Smith said that he and Dody Smith were approaching retirement age, and that the operation needed an infusion of funds to stabilize it and to "expand in the right direction." Others observed that the winery had simply overplanted and over-relied on

French-American varieties, while failing to keep pace with changes in consumer tastes. Smith turned down multiple offers to sell Stirling Farm to real estate developers and pledged to sell to someone who would maintain the operation as a vineyard. "We've put a hell of a lot of heart and soul in this business," Smith said. "It's been demonstrated that Virginia wineries can grow grapes as well as any around the country, or the world, for that matter."[35]

Meredyth finally closed its doors in 2000. In the end, the winery and its founder secured positions as preeminent leaders in the early Virginia wine industry. The winery grew alongside the industry for more than a quarter of a century and helped secure Virginia a spot on the map as a wine-growing state. In 1998, Smith passed away at the age of seventy-eight after long battling amyotrophic lateral sclerosis (Lou Gehrig's Disease). He is still remembered by industry insiders as one who promoted the cause of Virginia wine, having been named Virginia's "Agriculture Person of the Year" in the 1980s.[36]

During his life, Smith also served as the founder and first president of the Virginia Wineries Association, led the fight to pass the 1980 Farm Winery Act, and served as president of both the Association of American Vintners and of the Virginia Food Processors Association. Archie III would follow in his father's footsteps by serving as president of the Virginia Wineries Association. He died in 2009.[37]

By diversifying Stirling Farm's agricultural products and marketing aggressively, the Smiths not only expanded their family business, but demonstrated to Virginia's farmers that wine grapes could be a profitable alternative agricultural enterprise in the face of the poor economic performance of many traditional crops. "If people want to keep land rural, it has to support itself agriculturally," said Archie Smith in 1987. "Grape growing and wine making enable you to get a higher yield per acre.... Plus, grape-growing itself is an attractive thing."[38]

As wine writers Hilde Gabriel Lee and Allan E. Lee noted in their 1986 book *Virginia Wine Country,* "There is more to the story of Archie Smith.... It is more than experimentation with grape growing in unknown soils and climates. He is doing his part to save a way of life—the agricultural life—which he feels is too quickly disappearing from the American countryside."[39]

Less than a mile from Meredyth, midway between Middleburg and The Plains in northern Fauquier County, sat an equally important contributor to Virginia's wine renaissance: a 500-acre dairy farm, Waverly. Waverly was the home of Treville Lawrence's erstwhile partner in the Vinifera Wine Growers Association, Middleburg socialite and horsewoman Elizabeth Furness. Affectionately remembered as the "Grande Dame of the Wine Industry," Furness was a well-traveled native of Duluth, Minnesota, who attended finishing schools in England, France, Germany, Washington, D.C., and Boston.[40]

An accomplished horsewoman, Elizabeth Merrill married her second husband, Thomas Furness, in 1941 and two years later moved to Waverly during the height of the Second World War. The Furnesses renovated Waverly's circa-1730 Greek Revival manor house (a project that included the installation of electricity and plumbing) and, following the war, the two comfortably established themselves in the Middleburg community, frequently hosting hunt breakfasts at their restored home.[41]

Like Archie Smith, Jr. at Stirling Farm, the Furnesses recognized by the late 1960s that maintaining Waverly's dairy operation would prove increasingly unprofitable. Searching for ways to preserve the property for future generations, Elizabeth discovered viticulture and, like Treville Lawrence, became captivated with the writings and success of vinifera advocate Dr. Konstantin Frank. In the spring of 1973, after completing wine appreciation courses taught by Dr. Frank, the seventy-five-year-old converted part of Waverly's declining dairy operation into what became Virginia's first commercial vinifera vineyard.[42]

Building on her experiences in France during her youth, Furness ordered vines from California and, with assistance from Dr. Frank and renowned Maryland vineyardist G. Hamilton Mowbray, she followed her staff around the property—in a folding chair—to personally observe their planting of five acres of Chardonnay, five acres of the Sémillon grape, and, just in case of a severe winter, five acres of a French-American grape, Seyval Blanc.[43]

Furness directed her staff—then accustomed only to dairy operations—to receive winemaking and grape growing instruction from Mowbray. She also hired her grandson, Walter Luschinger, a real estate broker and graduate of the University of California at Davis's viticultural program, as winemaker. By 1974, Waverly boasted nearly 25 acres of grapevines; more were planted in 1976, and, that year, Furness converted Waverly's former dairy barn into a winery building and launched Piedmont Vineyards.[44]

As was the case with so many young Virginia wineries in the 1970s, Piedmont was an enterprise of "firsts." It was, for example, the first to use deep plowing techniques prior to planting, and perhaps the first in Virginia to produce wine from the Sémillon grape. The wines produced from the winery's first crush in 1977 became modern Virginia's first commercial vinifera wines. In 1978, Furness sold seven bottles to a Washington, D.C., wine shop and immediately purchased all seven of the bottles back for her own wine cellar. For this, she was recognized by Governor John N. Dalton and VDACS Commissioner S. Mason Carbaugh as the first Virginia vintner to sell wine outside of the commonwealth. "They told me Jefferson couldn't do it so I couldn't either," Furness repeatedly told visitors to her estate. "Jefferson's been dead a long time. He didn't have the sprays we have, he didn't have the chemicals."[45]

Elizabeth Furness died in February 1986 at the age of eighty-seven. At the time of her passing, Piedmont boasted vinifera and French-American vineyards, and enjoyed a well-established reputation for producing quality white wines. During her life, Furness served on the Board of Directors of the Vinifera Wine Growers Association and would leave behind a legacy as the first grower and producer of vinifera wine in modern Virginia history. Her daughter, Elizabeth "Sis" Worrall, who had assisted Furness in running the winery since the early 1980s, assumed full responsibility for the operation until her own death in 1996.[46]

Following Sis Worrall's passing, a new owner, German native Gerhard von Finck, purchased Waverly, which by that time comprised only 95 acres of the original 500-acre tract the Furnesses had purchased some five decades before. Von Finck renovated the Waverly manor house, established a new tasting room in the property's horse barn, updated the winemaking facility, and replanted many of the vines that had fallen into disrepair. Piedmont later closed in 2013.[47]

Of the handful of Virginia vineyards that began experimenting with vinifera and French-American plantings in the early 1970s, one small enterprise, Morland, deserves special mention. The vineyard was first planted with 1,800 French-American and Zinfandel grapes in 1973, on land bordering the Potomac River in King George County at the family home of W. Brown Morton, Jr. While Morland's vineyard would produce more than 2,000 flourishing vines by 1975, it would best become known for the unique personality of one woman: Lucie T. Morton. She would eventually develop a reputation as the nation's foremost freelancing viticultural consultant and ampelographer (one who is concerned with the identification and classifications of grapevines).[48]

Born and raised in Alexandria, Lucie Morton obtained a degree in history from the University of Pennsylvania and subsequently studied nineteenth-century theology at Oxford. In 1972, Lucie Morton's father asked her to consider running her grandfather's farm for one year and to plant a vineyard there. Not only was her father in search of a profitable agricultural crop for the farm's limited open acreage, but he believed the Potomac River exhibited similar characteristics to the Gironde Estuary in France's Bordeaux region.[49]

Without any knowledge of cultivating wine grapes, Lucie Morton accepted the challenge, and proceeded to plant 1,800 grapevines of thirteen different varieties in the spring of 1973. Over time, she learned to manage the vineyard, including operating a grape hoe on her grandfather's 1948 Ford tractor, but recognized that she needed to formally study viticulture. Lucie Morton's long-held desire to improve her French and study vineyard management encouraged her to look for opportunities to study in France.

During her time in Europe, Morton spent one month working at two famous Bordeaux wineries, Lafite Rothschild and Fourcas-Hoston, studied for two months as the first American student at one of France's grand schools, the École Nationale Supérieure d'Agronomique de Montpellier, and went on a seven-month tour of vineyards in Italy, France, Spain, and Switzerland. She subsequently wrote a fifty-page thesis—in French, no less—on grape growing in the eastern United States.[50]

Morton came away from her sojourn in France not only able to speak French fluently, but also able to identify grapes by their leaves. In 1974, she returned to the United States and immediately began touring American vineyards with, among others, famed American wine writer Leon D. Adams. At Morland, Morton offered classes in winemaking and pruning to Virginia vineyard and winemaking enthusiasts. In 1979, she translated *A Practical Ampelography*, a study of grape leaf identification originally written in French by one of her Montpelier professors, Pierre Galet. In 1985, Morton published her own book, *Winegrowing in Eastern America*, the first volume dedicated solely to the grape varieties and winemaking history of the eastern two-thirds of the United States.[51]

Morton—a self-professed "grape nerd"—continued to advise vineyards on varieties to plant and how to maintain and pick them. She developed an international reputation for her no-frills approach to wine consulting and to even cultivate fungi in her refrigerator to study its impact on grape varieties. She enjoys revitalizing neglected vineyards and, unlike some Virginia wine industry followers, who suggest that the state focus on a handful of varieties, Lucie has consistently advocated for experimentation and a diversity of grape species, including both vinifera and European American varieties.[52]

Perhaps more than anything, Morton became a devout advocate of European-style, high-density planting and cane pruning in the mid-Atlantic region. "Everybody bought into this idea that we have a terrible climate to grow grapes," Morton told a reporter in 2010. "Sure, we get hurricanes. What wine region doesn't get messed up once in a while?"[53]

Just east of Lucie Morton's vineyard at Morland, the Northern Neck's first winery, Ingleside Plantation Vineyards, opened in 1980. Overlooking the Rappahannock River on the historic 2,500-acre Ingleside Plantation in Westmoreland County, the winery was the creation of Carl Flemer, Jr., a longtime dairy farmer who learned about grapes and wine on annual visits to Europe.[54]

Flemer began experimenting with alternative agricultural ventures in the 1940s, hoping to discover a new source of income that would also encourage his fellow Northern Neck planters to diversify their agricultural crops.[55]

In 1976, after extensive reading on winemaking, including studies by the pioneering Maryland grape grower Philip M. Wagner, and participating in Lucie Morton's winemaking classes, Flemer planted a five-acre vineyard and devised plans to establish a larger winery. "I don't know if we can compete with California wines, because there is a different climate here," Flemer told a reporter. "The object is to have a small regional winery where people will be proud to say it's our product." By 1981, Flemer's small vineyard had grown to 18 acres. He began winemaking in earnest and converted the property's former dairy barn into a winery, and that year, Ingleside Winery opened to customers; Flemer's son Doug Flemer served as manager while another son, Carl Flemer III, managed Ingleside's more established nursery business.[56]

Doug Flemer had worked alongside his father at the property's nursery before going to college and serving in the U.S. Coast Guard. After graduating from North Carolina State University with a degree in horticulture, he traveled to Europe, where he fell in love with wine. Doug Flemer's friendship with Lucie Morton allowed him to visit and experience some of France's most famous vineyards and wineries. Like his father, Doug Flemer was optimistic about the promise of Virginia's wine industry: "It will be a long time before we catch California and New York, but there is no reason we can't be number three," he told a reporter. "It takes time and a lot of money, but Virginia has money. It's a matter of expertise and experience."[57]

Such expertise and experience practically landed on Ingleside's doorstep in July 1980, while Doug Flemer was in Europe. That month, Flemer hired Jacques Recht, a retired wine technology professor from Belgium's University of Brussels, as Ingleside's consulting winemaker. Recht was more than qualified: he held a doctoral degree in oenology and had served as a winemaker and consultant in North Africa and Europe. He had also worked to reestablish vineyards in Algiers following World War II, and taught wine technology at the prestigious Institute of Fermentation in Brussels.[58]

What makes Recht's story truly exceptional, however, was the unusual manner in which he arrived at Ingleside. He happened to be traveling with his wife, Liliane, along the last leg of a nearly two-year sailing journey around the world in a thirty-six-foot catamaran. Setting out from Europe, the two visited Spain, the Canary Islands, Barbados, the Virgin Islands, the Bahamas, and the Atlantic Intracoastal Waterway.[59]

Enthralled by James Michener's classic *Chesapeake*, the Rechts headed for Colonial Beach, a small Potomac River town. Before reaching port, however, the two briefly docked near Ingleside in the riverfront community of Kinsale, where they were charmed by the welcoming attitude of the locals. "The more we went north," Recht later recounted, "the more we lost time because of American hospitality."[60]

It was during their stopover in Kinsale that the Rechts met Carl Flemer at a party. Flemer lost no time explaining that Ingleside's first big harvest was at hand and that his son Doug Flemer had not yet returned from Europe to help. The Rechts reluctantly accompanied Flemer back to Ingleside where, over a glass of Ingleside's Seyval Blanc, Flemer persuaded Recht to stay in Virginia for three weeks—through the end of the harvest—as a temporary consulting winemaker.[61]

As Doug Flemer later recounted his father saying, "Here's a fellow who knows how to make wine already. If we could keep him here, it would make things go faster than if we were self-taught." Enthralled with the idea of partic-ipating in a new Virginia wine tradition, Recht stayed on after the harvest and served as Ingleside's winemaker for fifteen years.[62]

An expert on French and European wines, Recht used his observations of the emerging American wine industry to guide the types of wines he made during his career. Recht observed that Americans were enjoying wine with dinner more frequently and selecting dryer, more sophisticated wines. He also predicted that this cultural trend would encourage better local wines in Vir-ginia. "Who knows," he said, "maybe Virginia will be the Beaujolais of the United States." Recht found that, relative to California wines, Virginia's wines were lower in alcohol content and offered more delicate flavors. "I can't see why Virginia can't produce a distinctly 'Virginia' type of wine. Most Europeans won't say it... but I will: American wines can compete with the top French wines."[63]

Thanks to Recht's expertise, Ingleside was the first Virginia winery to pro-duce a *méthode champenoise* sparkling wine, and its 1980 champagne received a bronze medal at the 1981 Wineries Unlimited Eastern Wine Competition. Ingleside won several other awards (including the 1984 Governor's Cup), which helped secure its reputation for producing quality wines. "It's a damn good thing for Westmoreland County," boasted one taster of Ingleside's impact on both the Virginia wine industry and the Northern Neck's economic development.[64]

Recht retired from Ingleside in 1995, but stayed involved until his death in 2009. While he would go on to consult at other wineries across the country, he particularly encouraged the planting of vinifera grapes in eastern Virginia. He authored more than 120 articles for the industry trade magazine *Wine East*, and assisted Old Dominion University professor Roy L. Williams in establishing that school's oenology program. "Europe's loss was our gain," said Doug Flemer. "Jacques was one of the first professionals to come into the area and share his knowledge and experience. Without his expertise and help in the early days, we would not be as far along as we are today."[65]

Ingleside later grew to produce more than 15,000 cases annually under four labels and, as the only winery with property fronting on a river, Ingleside welcomed visitors both by car and by boat, including cruises from the Tangier Island and Rappahannock River Cruise Line. In 1990, Carl Flemer turned Ingleside's management over to Doug Flemer, who replanted and expanded the vineyards. "We're a family business," Doug Flemer told a reporter. "I don't ever see it being sold to another family."[66]

While considerable portions of Virginia's modern wine revival occurred in the northern and eastern parts of the state, much of the commonwealth's early wine history was written in its quieter western counties, where unique climates, terrains, and consumer tastes necessitated different growing and marketing techniques. Two early growers in Virginia's Blue Ridge region, Al and Emily Weed, experienced these challenges firsthand when they established La Abra Farm Winery—later Mountain Cove Vineyards—in the early 1970s.

Al, a Brooklyn native and Yale and Princeton graduate, served as a Green Beret during the Vietnam War and an investment banker before he and Emily moved to a farm just west of Lovington in Nelson County in 1973. The Weeds embarked on their dream and, between 1974 and 1975, they planted a 12-acre vineyard at La Abra entirely with French-American grapes, which Al had earlier concluded would prove hardier and more resistant to fungal diseases in the area's unpredictable climate conditions.

In 1976, while waiting for the grapes to mature, the Weeds produced their first vintage—several thousand gallons of apple wine. The following year, they constructed a small, rustic two-story log-cabin winery and tasting room. The Weeds again produced wines, this time made from grapes grown elsewhere as well as a peach wine from peaches grown by a neighbor. All of these new wines were, for ease of marketing, produced under the proprietary label "Mountain Cove."[67]

As the years passed, the Weeds also planted other varieties, including Norton, Cabernet Franc, Cabernet Sauvignon, Chambourcin, Traminette, and Vidal Blanc. Though Emily and Al Weed had realized their vision, Al Weed, it seemed, resisted settling into a contemplative lifestyle. Consequently, he not only established himself as a winemaker, but also pursued business and politics, running unsuccessfully for Congress in 2004 and 2006. He served as a cofounder and president of the Virginia Wineries Association, a lobbyist for Virginia wine interests in Richmond, and a trustee for the Virginia Land Conservation Trust.[68]

By 2000, Mountain Cove's vineyard comprised some nine acres, and the Weeds were satisfied with their accomplishments and lifestyle. "It's been hard work," Al told an author, "but we have achieved our dream to live on a farm and produce a farm product."[69]

Another western Virginia couple, James and Emma Randel, opened Shenandoah Vineyards in the northern Shenandoah Valley in July 1979. Emma Randel was a native farm girl from Shenandoah County who, after obtaining an economics degree from Duke University, landed a job in Washington, D.C., where she met James Randel. After marriage, they moved to New Jersey, where James Randel, then a public relations executive, began experimenting with home winemaking.

In 1974, the couple returned to Virginia after James Randel suffered a heart attack. During his recuperation, the Randels read of Virginia's growing wine industry and began to consider growing grapes as a nontraditional retirement plan. In 1976, following extensive soil and climate studies, the Randels found a property nestled between Edinburg and Woodstock in Shenandoah County. Their return to the commonwealth proved to be a homecoming of sorts; Emma Randel's mother had been born in a log house on the property. There, the two deep plowed the ground and planted more than seven acres of vinifera and French-American grapes.

The Randels made wine in 1977 using a neighbor's French-American grapes but, unable to obtain help from Virginia Tech, the two turned to wineries in Pennsylvania and New York for advice. Two years later, they opened Shenandoah Vineyards in a converted barn that dated to the Civil War. "We are convinced," said James Randel, "that the [Shenandoah] Valley is destined to become one of the great wine grape growing regions of the United States, not for quantity, but for quality."[70]

James Randel died in 1985, after which Emma Randel became more involved in the winery, supervising nearly every aspect with the help of her small staff. The winery eventually won numerous awards and boasted more than 35 acres under vine, including Chambourcin, Cabernet Sauvignon, Cabernet Franc, Riesling, and Chardonnay.[71]

The revival of Virginia wine also brought a resurgence of grape growing in the cultural and historic home of Virginia's wine industry, Albemarle County. The county had previously led the production of Virginia wine in the late 1800s, earning Charlottesville its moniker "Capital of the Wine Belt of Virginia." One

Albemarle vineyard, Burnley Vineyards, began in 1977, cofounded by a U.S. Army colonel, Claire J. "C. J." Reeder, his wife, Pat, and their son, Lee.[72]

C. J. Reeder, a California native who grew up on an Oregon dairy farm, purchased forty acres northeast of Charlottesville in 1976 while overseeing the nearby U.S. Army Foreign Science and Technology Center. The following year, the Reeders planted a three-acre vineyard of Cabernet Sauvignon and Chardonnay. Shortly thereafter, they expanded the vineyard to twelve acres, including other vinifera and French-American varieties. In 1983, Lee Reeder graduated from Virginia Tech (where he studied winemaking), and the family hired him as winemaker.

In 1984, Burnley Vineyards opened to the public in a new winery building largely constructed by C. J. and Lee Reeder. By the mid-1980s, the boutique winery produced 500 cases per year, and had garnered multiple medals at various competitions. Building upon past experience in California, and to compensate for their property's relatively low elevation (only 650-feet above sea level), the Reeders installed a thirty-five-foot, high-powered, twin-bladed wind machine to assist in creating artificial thermal inversion. The machine—the first installed in a Virginia vineyard—directed warm air above the vineyard to the vines below to help prevent frost damage.[73]

By 1992, the vineyard grew grapes on twenty acres, which were hand-harvested and used to produce 7,000 cases of wine annually. The Reeders were also actively involved in supporting the young Virginia wine industry; Pat Reeder helped found and served as president of the Virginia Vineyards Association and, along with C. J. Reeder, helped establish the Jeffersonian Wine Grape Growers Society. Lee Reeder would later serve as president of the Virginia Wineries Association.[74]

Among the most recognizable, and indeed infamous, of Virginia's early wineries, Oasis Winery has met with much success and equal controversy since its founding in 1982. The winery's founder, Dirgham Salahi, was a Jerusalem-born Palestinian who came to the United States in 1955 to study at Louisiana State University and, subsequently, at George Washington University. He later served as a gemologist with the American Geological Institute and cofounded the Montessori School of Alexandria with his wife, Corinne Salahi, in 1970.[75]

In 1976 to escape the pressures of urban life, the Salahis purchased 108 acres in the Hume area of Fauquier County, located 65 miles from Washington, D.C. There, they constructed a French-inspired home and later that year, after searching for a hobby, Dirgham used some of his geological training to plant a ten-acre French-American vineyard, which he dubbed "Oasis." The following spring, Salahi planted an additional twenty-five acres of vinifera varieties and, in 1979, purchased custom-made concrete Italian fermentation tanks.[76]

Like many of Virginia's early vintners, Salahi had to learn grape-growing techniques from the ground up, and, though he found the exercise demanding, Salahi relished learning new skills. While he initially made wine in his garage for private use, by 1980 the property produced more grapes than could be used for his home winemaking. Encouraged by winning multiple home winemaking awards, the Salahis obtained a winery license in 1980 and opened Oasis Winery. That year, the family produced some 2,000 gallons of wine, which included a 1981 Sauvignon Blanc that received a silver medal at the 1981 Wineries Unlimited Competition. The win, as well as the property's enviable location not far from Interstate 66, persuaded the Salahis to invest more heavily in the operation.[77]

The Salahis subsequently began construction of a larger, two-story, partially underground winery building. Once open, the larger facility was capable of producing between 100,000 and 200,000 gallons annually and featured a 10,000-square foot underground wine cellar with unique Italian epoxy-lined concrete tanks, a banquet room, a tasting room with high ceilings, and a large fireplace.[78]

Like Meredyth, Oasis became known for its marketing efforts, offering numerous special events and tourist amenities through its Oasis Enterprises wine-event business, which eventually grew to include part-ownership of a Potomac yacht, a fleet of limousines, and a bus for "wine-country tours." Much of this entrepreneurial pizzazz, while successful, earned Oasis the enduring enmity of neighbors who believed that such activities spoiled the serenity of the surrounding area.[79]

Of course, the Oasis story is not complete without the mention of Dirgham Salahi's well-known son, Tareq Salahi. Tareq Salahi obtained a degree from the University of California at Davis, where he studied winemaking. He would later be credited by observers with being one of the most influential personalities in the wine industry in the 1990s and 2000s. Unfortunately, the Salahi name—and that of Oasis—would become widely known following a 2006 dispute between Tareq Salahi and his parents over Tareq's Oasis Enterprises company. Oasis's notoriety increased further when Tareq Salahi and his then-wife, Michaele Salahi, attended (allegedly uninvited) a White House state dinner in 2009. Neither incident should, however, overshadow Oasis Winery's early history and the hard work and dedication required of the Salahis to make Oasis a reality. Oasis was later sold following the longstanding family dispute.[80]

After Dirgham Salahi died in October 2010 at the age of eighty-one, *The Washington Post* reprinted his apt 1984 statement describing the family property and winemaking generally: "When you work here, it's so quiet you talk to your vines. It's very peaceful."[80]

## —*Foreign Investment*—

Joining the growing chorus of Virginia's revolutionary winemakers were foreign wine investors, increasingly convinced Virginia vines could produce fine vinifera grapes. Many of Europe's great wine houses began purchasing properties across the United States in the early 1970s—most notably in California—when they noticed the increase in America's post-World War II wine consumption and believed that producing American wine could reduce shipping costs. The foreign investment trend was not lost on Virginia, where major investors from Italy, Germany, and France as well as Canada searched for locations to provide much-needed financing, encouragement, and legitimacy to the Old Dominion's fledgling wine industry.[81]

In the spring of 1976, news broke that a British investment and land development company, Western American Finance, would partner with Italy's largest wine producer, the Zonin Wine Company, to invest approximately $5 million over 10 years to construct a new vinifera winery and chateau north of Charlottesville in Orange County.[82]

The winery investment—astonishing to most at the time—was by far the most significant in Virginia history, and is believed to be the largest vinifera planting project east of California. "We want to establish Virginia as a place of high-quality wine production ...producing wine as good as or better than anything in California," said Western American Finance's Jonathan A. Todhunter at the time. "I'll be proud to tell my grandchildren I had a part in that."[83]

Western American Finance asked Zonin's founder, the Italian Gianni Zonin, to find a suitable American location offering the right soil and conditions to enable Zonin to become the top local wine producer. While Zonin initially considered land in California, the Golden State was ultimately ruled out because it already had too many growers. Zonin concluded, however, that Virginia offered a climate like that of his native northern Italy, and that the state held the promise of an emerging wine industry that was gaining traction. He also shared Treville Lawrence's goal of attracting foreign investment and turning the Piedmont into a "vineyard-studded new world Bordeaux."[84]

Zonin eventually settled on a 700-acre former sheep farm, known as the Barboursville Estate, located north of Charlottesville in southern Orange County. Placed on the National Register of Historic Places in 1969, the property featured the ruins of a manor once owned by Virginia governor James Barbour.

Designed by Thomas Jefferson, the ruins were located midway between Jefferson's home at Monticello and James Madison's Montpelier.[85]

The home burned on Christmas Day 1884, and its ruins formed a picturesque and historic backdrop that captivated Zonin's imagination. "The history of the place, the Jefferson connection, the ruins all interested him, too …. He's an Italian," said Luca Paschina, who was hired in 1990 as the winery's general manager. Zonin and his wife Silvana Zonin were also interested in the fact that Barboursville featured two connected historic structures built in 1804, which the couple refurbished and converted into a second home and a boutique hotel, dubbed the 1804 Inn.[86]

To oversee the winemaking venture, Zonin hired Gabriele Rausse, a thirty-year-old, Italian-born, plant pathologist and expert oenologist who was well-versed on the potential for grape-crop threats, including the effects of winter cold, fungus, pests, Phylloxera attacks, black rot, and Japanese beetles. While he acknowledged that Virginia's soils and climate did not resemble that of the Bordeaux region, Rausse was convinced that the right variety of grape—including certain vinifera varieties—could grow in almost any soil.[87]

Later in 1976, Rausse oversaw the planting of 3,300 Chardonnay, Riesling, Cabernet Sauvignon, and Merlot vines. Early goals, which called for the planting of 10,000 vines, were overly ambitious, if not completely unrealistic, and aroused both excitement and suspicion in observers. Barboursville's 1976 planting was perhaps the most serious effort yet by a Virginia vineyard and was widely publicized, including in *The Washington Post* and *The New York Times*. "It was as if the President of Kenya had decided to plant bananas in Alaska," Rausse told an author in the 1980s. "Everybody thought we were crazy."[88]

Zonin's Barboursville investment was not without its challenges, the most fundamental of which was the lack of the most basic winemaking infrastructure. The lack of a winery facility, for example, forced Rausse to convert a former sheep-shearing barn into a temporary winery until a more substantial winery could be completed. Rausse insisted on using Italian-style concrete trellising posts that would last as long as the lifespan of an average vine; local manufacturers, however, had never seen such a product and quoted him outrageous production prices. Zonin was thus compelled to spend large sums to import the concrete posts directly from Italy. Barboursville also imported a special deep-trenching plow that was unavailable in the mid-Atlantic, but that allowed Barboursville's vines to thrive in the property's dense clay soils.[89]

Finding skilled laborers knowledgeable in planting, handling, and processing grapes was also problematic. "It's difficult to find people here who know or can quickly learn the wine-growing side, who are familiar with viticulture," said then-assistant winemaker Tim Bradshaw. "So much of winemaking is tradition … that people in Europe have grown up with." Rausse also had difficulty securing quality grape cuttings and discovered that the mid-Atlantic region was entirely devoid of nurseries that offered certified virus-free vinifera plants. Rausse accordingly established his own nursery to remedy this and to offer certified grafted vinifera grape stock for sale.[90]

The Barboursville effort also had to struggle against political skepticism and opposition. As with the experience of Treville Lawrence a few years before, Rausse was roundly panned by USDA and Virginia Tech representatives, who admonished him for planting vinifera grapes in Virginia and instead suggested that native Concord and French-American grapes were the only suitable varieties. Virginia Tech further advised against the use of Barboursville's deep-trenching plow. But Rausse dug in his heels and welcomed the possibility of failure: "I have been a loser all my life, starting from school," he later recalled to a reporter. "So the idea of coming here and doing something which didn't work was very attractive to me."[91]

Added to these challenges were two major setbacks. First, in 1977, Rausse lost much of his initial crop, which prompted Western America to pull out its investment. Rausse and Zonin chugged along, however, and the following year, Barboursville managed to produce its first, now historic, vintage of 2,500 gallons of wine. While a meager quantity relative to the number of vines planted, Rausse and Zonin had again proven that vinifera wine could be made in Virginia. Emboldened by their success, Rausse grafted an additional 33,000 vines, added new staff, and purchased additional equipment. Their enthusiasm soured, however, in September 1979 when the winery building sustained severe damage stemming from a fire that destroyed the facility, crushers, bottling equipment, and presses.[92]

Barboursville, though, stayed the course, growing with the wine industry it helped spur. By 1985, the winery produced an estimated 81,000 bottles per year, many of which garnered national recognition, from premium vinifera wine grapes grown on the property. The following September, two Barboursville wines became the first in Virginia to be sold abroad. A decade later, in 1986, the "temporary" converted sheep-shearing winery was replaced by an attractive and impressive facility featuring a unique blend of European flair and genteel, colonial Virginia architecture. Barboursville opened a full-service destination wine restaurant in 1999—*Palladio*—which featured traditional Italian fare in an atmosphere that evoked an Italian country villa. The winery eventually earned a reputation for producing high-quality wines and attracted more than 80,000 visitors per year—all of whom could stroll freely around the property and investigate the historic ruins that first captured Zonin's imagination.[93]

Sensing that he and his family needed a break from the lifestyle of work for a large company, Rausse left Barboursville in 1981 and was replaced by a succession of young professionals, including Claudio Salvador, Adriano Rossi, and, finally, Luca Paschina. Paschina, a native of Piemonte, Italy, was a graduate of the Umberto I Institute of Oenology near Turin, Italy, and initially came to Barboursville as a consultant in July 1990 at the age of twenty-nine. Though he intended to return to his home country when his contract expired, he became enchanted with Barboursville's orderly, well-tended vines just before leaving. When his contract was over, he returned to Italy to deliver a final report to Zonin and, only three days later, came back to Barboursville as the winery's manager.[94]

Building on Rausse's legacy, Paschina made significant changes to the Barboursville operation. By listening "to what the territory tells [him] to grow," Paschina—like Rausse before him—gradually developed an understanding of grape-growing techniques suitable for Virginia. For example, he changed the system of trellising, tore out lower-quality vines, and oversaw the construction of the new winery building and administrative offices, as well as the expansion of the vineyards.[95]

Rausse would go on to become a formidable force in the Virginia wine industry in his own right. Following his departure from Barboursville, Rausse was hired to begin a new winemaking venture at the home of Stanley Woodward, Sr., a former ambassador and White House chief of protocol under Presidents Franklin Roosevelt and Harry Truman, who owned a large, 750-acre farm located just south of Charlottesville in Albemarle County. Woodward's property befittingly included grounds that once housed Colle, the former home of Thomas Jefferson's longtime friend Philip Mazzei, an Italian wine enthusiast and fellow patriot. Woodward, who had purchased the property in 1939, had long sought a profitable agricultural venture and endeavored to resurrect Mazzei's vintner's legacy. The Woodwards converted a former stable into a tasting room and, perhaps in a nod to history (or simply business acumen), tapped Rausse to oversee their new venture, which they dubbed Simeon Vineyards.[96]

Simeon's first ceremonial planting occurred in October 1981 in conjunction with the first Albemarle Harvest Wine Festival, during which Lapo Mazzei—a direct descendant of Philip Mazzei—was in attendance to watch the rebirth of the vineyard first planted by his ancestor. The vineyard expanded, and in 1983 Rausse began producing wine in a small farm building on the property. By 1986, a larger winery was constructed. After Woodward died in 1992, his son, Stanley

Woodward, Jr., assumed management of the operation and changed the name of the enterprise to Jefferson Vineyards.[97]

Woodward's death also prompted Rausse's departure and his own purchase of a 220-acre property in southeastern Albemarle County. There he planted a small, one-acre vineyard and constructed a home and winery. In 1995, Rausse was hired as assistant director of gardens at Monticello, where he oversaw the replanting and management of Monticello's vineyards. Two years later, he introduced his own line of wine under his Gabriele Rausse label. He continues to work at Monticello and his personal wine operation produces approximately 1,200 cases annually. He is widely praised as the "godfather" of the Virginia wine industry and has served as a knowledgeable consultant to countless Virginia wineries and winemakers.[98]

The Italian investment at Barboursville was followed two years later by another Orange County entrepreneurial endeavor, this time led by Germans: Rapidan River Vineyards. The idea for Rapidan began as the hobby of a German surgeon, Dr. Gerhard Guth, who had originally purchased the 1,800-acre Island View Farm outside Culpeper along the Rapidan River as a business venture in 1974. On the advice of German viticulturalists, who asserted that vinifera vines could indeed flourish in Virginia, Guth planted a small, experimental five-acre vineyard of German wine grapes, and ultimately envisioned the planting of 250 acres by 1990.

After investing $1 million to plant twenty-five acres of Riesling, Gewürztraminer, Chardonnay, and other vinifera varieties, Guth converted an old brick building on the property into a winery. He also constructed additional brick buildings, including a winemaker's house, which formed a small courtyard with picnic tables. The Rapidan project represented what was then believed to be the nation's largest German-owned viticultural investment. The location was particularly appropriate considering that Island View Farm was located near the seventeenth-century settlement of Germanna, where German settlers once labored to produce red and white Virginia wines.[99]

To oversee planting, Guth contacted Germany's University of Geisenheim, which recommended that he hire Joachim Hollerith, a young graduate and German native. Originally from the Pfalz region of Germany, Hollerith was descended from a German winemaking family. He also boasted nearly three years' experience in vineyards and had turned down offers to start wineries in Tanzania and Mississippi.[100]

Philosophically, while Hollerith believed that Virginia's wine industry should focus on grapes that would grow best given its soil and climate characteristics, he thought he could build on Germany's 2,000-year history of winegrowing to produce uniquely Virginia vintages from German grapes. Guth subsequently hired Hollerith in 1978 as winemaker and, by the close of his first year, Hollerith had planted 2,500 Riesling and Chardonnay vines.[101]

Hollerith built on the legacy of the Germans who came before him at nearby Germanna. The Rapidan venture would become one of the most ambitious, expansive, and prototypical hobby-turned-business wineries during the industry rebirth period in Virginia winemaking. By 1979, the property had produced its first vintage of Riesling, and by 1981, the farm boasted twenty-five acres under cultivation, including Chardonnay, Pinot Noir, and Gewürztraminer varieties. By 1985, an additional twenty-five acres featuring 36,000 vinifera vines had been added, and the winery joined Meredyth, Oasis, and Ingleside in producing a sparkling wine.[102]

While one of Virginia's most ambitious undertakings, Rapidan was also short-lived. Hollerith would remain at Rapidan only until 1983, when he was lured away by the prospect of overseeing a new winemaking venture in northern Madison County, Prince Michel Vineyards. Guth would subsequently sell the entire enterprise to Prince Michel two years later.[103]

Founded by Frenchman Jean Leducq, Prince Michel Vineyards comprised a $2.5 million investment that saw the conversion of a former cattle farm along Route 29 south of Culpeper in Madison County into a world-class winery. A university professor by training and an entrepreneur by inclination, Leducq purchased the 400-acre property with an American business partner, Norman Martin, after being priced out of the French market for winery land.[104]

Planting began in 1983, following Joachim Hollerith's arrival from Rapidan River Vineyards, and development proceeded quickly. By 1984, Prince Michel's vineyards boasted ninety acres under vine and more than 100,000 vinifera vines. The following year, 110 acres were under cultivation and Leducq's purchase of Rapidan River made Prince Michel the state's largest winemaking operation. Leducq opened a winery in 1986 that included a visitor center, gift shop, and a museum of European winemaking equipment, as well as big-screen televisions and a small theater that showed a twelve-minute film about the Virginia wine industry.[105]

Like Barboursville, Prince Michel was a winery of "firsts." It was the first in Virginia to feature a state-of-the-art mechanical harvester, which was capable of harvesting four tons of grapes per hour. In 1987, Prince Michel became the first Virginia winery to have its wines served on an international airline when Germany's Lufthansa Airlines contracted to supply Prince Michel's wines for its first-class passengers. In 1992, the winery became the first to incorporate a restaurant into its operation with the opening of the Prince Michel Restaurant, a

Parisian-café-inspired eatery offering French cuisine. Later, Prince Michel even offered overnight lodging to guests.[106]

With 157 acres under cultivation by the mid-1990s, Prince Michel maintained its position as Virginia's largest winemaking enterprise. It's parent company, New Vavin, Inc., also boasted a twenty-acre vineyard outside the Napa Valley town of St. Helena, California, which served as a reserve vineyard in the event of crop damage in Virginia. By 2000, Prince Michel produced some 40,000 cases annually, including an entire line of wines under three different labels: the higher-end Prince Michel label; German-style Riesling and Gewürztraminer wines under the Rapidan River label; and a more moderately priced line under the Madison label.[107]

Leducq passed away in 2002, and proceeds from his estate and businesses were dedicated to a heart disease foundation he established in his will. Hollerith stayed at Prince Michel for fourteen years before leaving in 1991.[108]

The European investments at Barboursville, Rapidan River, and Prince Michel were joined in 1979 by that of the world's largest wine and distilled spirits producer and marketer, Canadian-based Seagram Company, Ltd. Reports first surfaced in late 1979 that Saratoga, California–based Paul Masson Vineyards, a division of Seagrams's United States subsidiary, had purchased the 190-acre Ivy Creek Farm just west of Charlottesville in Albemarle County for a large-scale experimental winery investment.[109]

The property, formerly an apple and peach farm, included a circa-1875 manor house with barns, sheds, and beautiful views of the Blue Ridge Mountains. Seagrams' investment represented the first by a major California and Canadian wine company, and Ivy Creek's new owners anticipated opening a full-scale winery to the public by 1985. The idea for the purchase came directly from the company's chairman and chief executive officer, Edward Bronfman, who had previously planted an experimental vineyard at his estate, Georgetown Farm, a few miles away in the Free Union area of Albemarle County.[110]

In 1980, Seagrams hired Paul Mierzejewski, a graduate of California State University, Fresno, who had studied under viticultural pioneer Vince Petrucci and had worked for both Paul Masson in Fresno and Gold Seal Winery in Hammondsport, New York. While the company was hesitant to commit to producing wine until vineyard experiments could be done, Seagrams built two contemporary homes for vineyard staff and, in 1981, planted ten acres of vinifera and French-American grapes. The following year, another twenty-five acres of vines were added, from which small amounts of Riesling wine were produced under their own private Georgetown label. Plans for the winery, however, never materialized.[111]

## —*Early Battles*—

While Virginia's pioneering vintners encountered criticism or even misinformation from public-sector researchers in the 1970s, by the 1980s the political landscape had indeed changed for the better. Industry enthusiasts found increasing support from private entrepreneurs and investors, as well as renewed assistance from Virginia's government. But during the new enthusiasm of the early 1980s the young industry was forced to respond to two episodes that struck simultaneously and affected its commercial viability.

The first came in the form of a 1981 wine labeling controversy over use of the name Shenandoah. This not only thrust Virginia's vintners into the national spotlight, but placed them directly in the crosshairs of the well-funded California wine lobby. The second witnessed wine advocates standing shoulder-to-shoulder with environmental and historic preservation groups to oppose uranium mining plans. Fortunately, these events served as a call to arms and a catalyst, which unified Virginia's winemakers around common goals and, for the first time, showcased their increasing political prowess.

The Shenandoah labeling affair began following the 1978 adoption of a new national wine-labeling law. The congressional legislation authorized the U.S. Treasury's Bureau of Alcohol, Tobacco, and Firearms to designate certain wine-growing regions as American Viticultural Areas, or AVAs, if they offered unique historic, geographic, and viticultural characteristics. Anyone could petition the bureau to designate their region as an AVA and the law authorized use of the geographical name of the particular AVA on bottle labels if at least 85 percent of fruit in each bottle had been grown in the AVA.[112]

California struck the first blow. In September 1980, the Amador County Wine Grape Growers Association of Sacramento, California, petitioned the bureau to designate a fifteen-square-mile growing area in Amador County—known locally as the Shenandoah Valley—as the Shenandoah Valley AVA. The petition requested exclusive use of the name Shenandoah Valley on all wine labels and in wine advertisements for the valley's ten wineries and 1,400 acres of grapes.[113]

That California's Shenandoah Valley shared a name identical to Virginia's most famous geological formation was no coincidence; California's Shenandoah Valley had been founded by nineteenth-century Virginians who had moved west searching for gold and were reminded of their native state. California's Valley also boasted a rich viticultural history, with its first winery having been founded as early as 1856. "When you talk about history, we agree that Virginia's

Shenandoah Valley is tops over us," said Shirley Sabon, owner of California's Shenandoah Vineyards. "But if you're talking about viticulture area and Zinfandel, you could go a long ways away from us and people back East have heard about our Shenandoah Valley and its grapes."[114]

In its petition, the Amador County wine growers even went so far as to assert that Virginia's Shenandoah Valley "isn't really a valley at all, just a depression between two ridges." History-minded Virginians were cold to the idea that the name of their Shenandoah might be conscripted by upstart westerners. The Shenandoah name, they felt—the place where Stonewall Jackson fought and that George Washington and Thomas Jefferson surveyed—was rightly theirs. Several of Virginia's vintners rushed to file a competing petition to claim the Shenandoah name for the Old Dominion, and to protect the Virginia Shenandoah Valley's sixteen commercial vineyards and three wineries.[115]

"The Shenandoah Valley in Virginia has spent generations investing millions in promoting the valley name," said Meredyth Vineyard owner Archie Smith, Jr., who by that point was president of the Virginia Wineries Association. "[Union cavalry general] Phil Sheridan did indeed march through the Shenandoah Valley of Virginia and lay it waste.… But even he didn't try to take the name away from us," he said. James Randel, co-founder of Shenandoah Vineyards and the author of the Shenandoah AVA petition, agreed: "Sure, we're just getting started producing wine in [Virginia's] Shenandoah Valley. But I don't think California should be entitled to use the name 'Shenandoah,' which everyone associates with Virginia."[116]

California's wine producers and politicians fired back. "We were making wine in the Shenandoah Valley of California long before they were making it in Virginia," asserted an aide to Alan Cranston, then a California senator. "We feel we had it first." California congressman Norman D. Shumway wrote to the bureau in support of the Amador petition: "My constituents seek only to take advantage of a well-deserved reputation for fine wines, which has come to be associated with California's Shenandoah Valley over the past 100 years.… Virginia's Shenandoah Valley does not have a reputation for wine production." One Amador grower asked, "Why do they think it's their name? They stole it from the Indians."[117]

Such claims prompted Virginia governor John Dalton to issue a strongly worded letter to the bureau, which included a history of the Shenandoah Valley and the evolution of the name. "We recognize that Virginia's wine industry has not yet reached the same level of development as California's," the governor wrote. "However, we also recognize and sincerely hope that everyone else realizes that there is no comparison between the 2.4 million acres in the

Shenandoah Valley of Virginia and the 20,000 acre 'depression between two ridges' in Amador County." Virginia's General Assembly followed the governor's appeal and unanimously passed a resolution opposing the Amador petition asserting that the Shenandoah Valley name should be reserved to the commonwealth in perpetuity.[118]

After conducting public hearings in California in late 1981, the bureau held a two-day hearing in Harrisonburg in January 1982. The hearing, which took place during a raging snowstorm, was nevertheless attended by Virginia's two United States senators, members of congress, Governor-elect Charles S. Robb (1982–1986), key state officials, and industry representatives. Most speakers argued that Amador County's petition ignored history and would forever prohibit winemakers in Virginia's Shenandoah Valley from using their own geographical and historical name.[119]

"The federal government has no business creating new Shenandoah Valleys to market California wines," thundered Winchester-born United States senator Harry F. Byrd, Jr., who saw the new AVA regulations as nothing more than bureaucratic aggravation. Others argued that the petition would rob the growing Virginia wine industry of an important commercial asset, confuse customers, and exacerbate the very problems the new labeling regulations were meant to discourage.[120]

"The Virginia Shenandoah Valley is known throughout the world as a Virginia location," said VDACS commissioner S. Mason Carbaugh. "Even in California the average citizen associates the Shenandoah Valley with Virginia first… only those in Amador County associate it with California."[121]

The battle between the two Shenandoahs raged on for another eleven months, until December 1982, when the bureau issued its determination: The result was a draw. On one hand, the decision permitted vintners from Virginia and West Virginia to label their wine bottles with Shenandoah Valley AVA labels. Wine from California could also use the Shenandoah Valley name, but only if qualified by the word "California."[122]

The announcement pleased California's wine producers but brought far more robust responses in Virginia, ranging from delight to disappointment and denunciation. "I have nothing against the wine producers of Amador County," said Virginia congressman J. Kenneth Robinson, who at the time represented much of the state's Shenandoah Valley wine-growing region. "But I continue to object strongly to their effort to appropriate for their own commercial use a name which has national recognition as that of a Virginia area."[123]

Other Virginians detected in the bureau's reasoning the sour odor of indecent compromise. "It sort of reminded me of the King Solomon episode in the Bible," said Archie Smith, Jr. in reaction. "He said we'll just split the baby down the middle." Still others tried to put the best possible face on the decision, noting that it gave the commonwealth's wine industry free advertising. "Virginia was surprised to find California had a Shenandoah area," said VDACS's wine-market specialist, Leeanne Ladin. "But California was surprised to hear Virginia had a wine industry. It did us a lot of good."[124]

The battle certainly resulted in the creation of Virginia's first AVA. As established, the Shenandoah Valley AVA stretched from three counties in the panhandle of West Virginia southward through nine Virginia counties bounded by the Blue Ridge Mountains to the east, and the Allegheny and Appalachian Mountains to the west. It would be the first of six AVAs to dot the Virginia map in the years to come.[125]

While Virginia's wine industry fought for the Shenandoah Valley's reputation, another menace emerged in 1981—potentially far more significant and damaging than a battle for pride of place. Beginning as early as 1978, the Marline Uranium Corporation, working with Union Carbide, began exploring uranium deposits in Virginia. They had managed to quietly secure several mineral leases on nearly 15,000 acres across Madison, Orange, Culpeper, and Fauquier Counties. In October 1981, the company announced both its purchase of an additional 40,000 acres in Pittsylvania County and its intent to begin mining.

This announcement caught Virginia's legislature entirely off guard. In 1982, the General Assembly, unprepared to regulate or legislate for a nuclear industry that had scant presence east of the Mississippi, hurried to place a temporary moratorium on uranium mining that would last until 1984. With the partial nuclear meltdown at Three Mile Island in 1979 still in recent memory, the legislature directed a group to study the effects and implications of uranium mining and to produce regulatory recommendations.[126]

Marline responded by contending that uranium mining and milling would present "an almost negligible risk of radiation pollution," and that, in preparation for drilling, Marline would *improve* the productivity of the land by constructing gates, repairing fences, and clearing brush. It also highlighted the potential benefits to Virginia's economy and the impact of "hundreds of millions of dollars" that would flow into the state if large commercial deposits were found. "Get involved. Regulate the hell out of us. But don't hide from the problem," Marline's vice president, Norman W. Reynolds, told elected officials.[127]

Though Marline claimed that its proposed drilling operations would have little effect on the environment or public health, the Vinifera Wine Growers Association, the Virginia Vineyards Association, and the Virginia Wineries Association each adopted resolutions in opposition. The three groups were concerned that, because grapes are particularly susceptible to pollutants, and because some of Marline's leaseholds were adjacent to, directly upwind, or upstream from existing or planned vineyards, uranium extraction might directly threaten vineyards, wildlife, and the overall productivity of agricultural land. The three organizations were joined by several other environmental advocacy groups that called for an immediate ban on uranium mining until independent studies had been conducted to ensure the safety of radiation levels.[128]

Marline hoped to placate the wine industry and paid special attention to it by producing a glossy eight-page color brochure that included a map depicting the location of vineyards near uranium mines in France as well as a large photo of a French vineyard with an arrow pointing to a nearby uranium mine. Virginia's wine industry representatives rebuffed such attempts: "It is also obvious," the *Vinifera Wine Growers Journal* remarked, "that Marline has employed someone knowledgeable about vineyards in its efforts to convince us all that wine and uranium go as well together as wine and cheese." The opposition continued.[129]

In December 1981, Marline voluntarily agreed not to seek permits for 18 months to allow the General Assembly time to study the issue and enact appropriate laws.[130] The following September, Marline abruptly canceled all of its Northern Virginia Piedmont leases—the location of the most vocal opposition to its efforts—and elected instead to focus its activities on the company's holdings in Pittsylvania County, where it had uncovered a 30-million-ton uranium deposit—potentially the largest in the United States. The company would later assert publicly that the Northern Virginia leases had been canceled not because of public opposition, but rather because no economically viable deposits of uranium ore were ever discovered there.[131]

Marline's announcement was perhaps premature. In 1983, the General Assembly's uranium task force issued its report and, after exhaustive studies, concluded that the temporary ban could be lifted if certain regulations were enacted. Subsequent votes by the General Assembly to lift the 1982 moratorium, however, were never taken, and the "temporary" ban remains in effect. No permits have ever been issued, nor, indeed, has legislation been passed authorizing any permits.[132]

## —The Matriarch of Central Virginia—

An often-overlooked aspect of Virginia's modern wine narrative is the crucial role played by women in the rebirth, growth, and promotion of the industry. Whether in the role of a proprietor, such as Elizabeth Furness at Piedmont or

Shenandoah Vineyards' Emma Randel; as a consultant like Lucie Morton; or in a more supportive capacity such as Meredyth's Dody Smith or La Abra's Emily Weed—women, to a large degree, led wine's rebirth in modern Virginia. This was certainly true in the greater Charlottesville region, where one determined person, Felicia Warburg Rogan, worked tirelessly to promote the cause of central Virginia's winegrowers.

Rogan, a native New Yorker, had observed that wine's best allies were invariably women. Men, after all, frequently held to distilled spirits at parties, leaving the more delicate taste of wine to the fairer sex. Rogan had herself been a collector of fine wines while living in New York and had long cherished wine as an essential element of fine dining. Though her Scotch-drinking husband, John B. Rogan, was not a wine drinker, Rogan looked forward to making it herself. "There is a special elation in producing a bottle of your own wine which transcends the end products of all other kinds of vegetative plantings," Rogan once told a reporter. "Homemade jams and kitchen cookies don't evoke the same amazement as a glass of your own wine."[133]

Such thinking would eventually propel Rogan to serve as the founder of the Charlottesville area's first large-scale wine advocacy group, as well as the organizer of the area's first wine festival. She also became the driving force behind the establishment of the Monticello American Viticultural Area and the proprietor of one of the state's best-regarded wineries. Certainly, her hard work and enthusiasm spurred the rebirth of central Virginia's wine industry, much of which was undertaken during her marriage to her husband, John Rogan.[134]

Rogan moved to Virginia in 1976 from New York to marry John Rogan—then a successful land developer, as well as the owner and creator of the famous Boar's Head Inn—and join him on their 250-acre Oakencroft farm just west of Charlottesville in Albemarle County. The idea for a winery began after a meeting with Lucie Morton, who was then cultivating a vineyard at her family farm, Morland, in King George County. Rogan and her husband subsequently purchased several Seyval Blanc grapes from Morton and transported them back to Oakencroft, where they attempted to produce wine in their garage. John "spent a year and a half trying to make wine from these grapes," Rogan later recounted, noting that the results were less than spectacular. "I called it garage wine."[135]

The Rogans persisted, and planted twenty-five French-American varietals in 1978 under Lucie's direction. Based on the success of these second-generation grapes, the Rogans planted a one-acre vineyard in 1979 and bottled their first wine the following year. "When we realized that we could grow and make good wines, we really started to get involved," Felicia later told a reporter. The Rogans subsequently planted a commercial vineyard and harvested their first crop of grapes in 1981. By 1983, they had received a winery license, and the following year they converted a large, red barn into a tasting room and winery, which they named Oakencroft.[136]

Felicia Rogan's proprietorship of Oakencroft formed only a part of a much larger drive to support the growing Virginia wine industry. Not only did her Jaguar sport a Virginia vanity license plate that read "WINES," but her various endeavors would result in the achievement of many firsts and the promotion of Virginia wine in untraditional venues.[137]

For example, in March 1987, to commemorate the 200th anniversary of Thomas Jefferson's 1787 three-month trip across the Burgundy region of France, Felicia Rogan gave a lecture in French at a university in Dijon concerning Jefferson's passion for wine and the growing Virginia wine industry. The lecture also featured a Virginia wine tasting—the first ever to be conducted in Europe. In 1991, Oakencroft became the first Virginia winery to sell its wines in an Asian market when it shipped 140 cases of wine to Taiwan. In the early 1990s, Rogan even capitalized on her New York connections to secure a plum spot for Virginia wines in a promotional effort at Bloomingdales in New York City, where she had a friend in top management.[138]

Rogan also fancied herself an author. In 1988, she published a thirty-two-page pamphlet, *Virginia Wines: A Vineyard Year*, as a promotional piece that offered a short history of Virginia wine, including a discussion of Thomas Jefferson, his vintner friend Philip Mazzei, and Dr. Daniel N. Norton, as well as a snapshot of the Virginia wine industry in the mid-1980s. Rogan's work was followed in 2001 by *Virginia Wines and Wineries*, a short volume that included a summary of Virginia's winemaking heritage, as well as a brief synopsis of, and map to, each of Virginia's wineries.[139]

It was Rogan's passion to carry the promise of Virginia wine beyond Oakencroft's gates, however, that allowed her to achieve her most lasting legacy. While Treville Lawrence's Vinifera Wine Growers Association was making remarkable strides in stimulating a wine industry in Northern Virginia, Rogan hoped to make the Charlottesville region once again the wine capital of Virginia and promoted it as Virginia's chief region for wine production.[140]

In 1981, Rogan invited seventy vineyardists, along with Ivy grape grower Frederick E. Gignoux, to her husband's Boar's Head Inn just west of Charlottesville. There, Felicia Rogan and Fred Gignoux formed the Jeffersonian Wine Grape Growers Society. The Society was overseen by an eight-member board of directors led, unsurprisingly, by Rogan. The Society's goals included, among other things, promoting central Virginia wines, conducting winemaking and grape-growing forums, holding wine harvest festivals, and organizing a bus tour of wineries. With an eye toward the important role played by the native Norton grape in creating central Virginia's first major wine industry during the late nineteenth century, the Society declined to discriminate between native, French-American, and vinifera varieties. Any grape was good—as long as it aided in the production of local wine.[141]

Membership in the Society grew rapidly; by 1982, the Society counted more than 150 members, including ten of the nineteen licensed Virginia wineries. By March 1983, the Society offered the state's first "advanced" oenology course, which featured a six-day course at the Boar's Head Inn covering chemistry, microbiology, fermentation, and diseases. To raise funds, the Society produced an entire line of cocktail napkins, scarves, tote bags, wine-bottle ties, and bumper stickers that read "Conserve Water, Drink Virginia Wines." They even offered postcards with a picture of Wine Street in Charlottesville—the site of the former Monticello Wine Company.[142]

Many of the Society's activities were educational, offering seminars, for example, including critiques of small family vineyards, and advanced oenology courses featuring Virginia and international winemakers. In 1986, the Society raised funds at the request of newly-hired state oenologist Bruce Zoecklein, and dedicated the funds toward a new oenology analytical laboratory and a small processing lab.[143]

In April 1985, the Society founded a Virginia Wine Museum in the upper level of the historic Michie Tavern near Monticello. Consistent with other exhibitions at Michie Tavern, the wine museum featured many artifacts, including old wine bottles and seals that had been excavated from Jamestown and Williamsburg, copies of letters and materials from Jefferson and Philip Mazzei, an audio/visual presentation on the winemaking process, and a description of modern-day Virginia winemaking.[144]

From a promotional perspective, the Society also assumed responsibility for the Albemarle Harvest Wine Festival in 1982 and introduced a Bacchanalian Feast as the kickoff for the event. The Society's promotional efforts also led to the adoption of a joint resolution in August 1987 issued by the City of Charlottesville and Albemarle County that declared Charlottesville the Wine Capital of Virginia.[145]

One of the Society's more notable accomplishments was the January 1984 establishment of the Monticello AVA. The Society originally struggled with geographic limits and name of the proposed AVA, which was originally conceived as the Thomas Jefferson AVA. A steering committee of the Society—headed by Rogan herself—initially drew up a map of the proposed AVA that left out much of western Albemarle County, under the assumption that the soils were poorer and that the proposed AVA would be too large. The committee told western Albemarle's winery and grape growers that they should join with growers in Waynesboro and Augusta County to form their own AVA—an assertion that was met with strong objections. Indeed, some of the objections were so severe that the matter threatened the continued existence of the newly created Society.[146]

Eventually, however, the Society agreed on the name Monticello. As approved, the Monticello AVA consisted of approximately 1,250 square miles and approximately 300 acres of vineyards. It included most of Albemarle County as well as portions of Orange, Greene, and Nelson Counties. To promote this newly created AVA, the Society distributed brochures to participating wineries and state visitors' centers, and erected highway signs throughout the AVA with a trademark silhouette of Thomas Jefferson and James Madison.[147]

The Society paid close attention to the ways in which local government regulations affected the wine industry. For example, Society members opposed a 1981 effort by the Albemarle County Board of Supervisors requiring winery owners to pay a $1,000 annual local license fee in addition to state fees. In 1983, Society members also monitored the adoption of Albemarle's first winery laws related to land use, tastings, tours, and licenses for festivals. Later, they helped persuade the Board to amend the zoning ordinance to allow wine-tasting rooms and wine tours without a county permit.[148]

Key to the success of Oakencroft, the Society, and central Virginia wineries was the unique role played by the Boar's Head Inn. This inn, thanks to the efforts of John and Felicia Rogan, developed into the veritable home of central Virginia's wine activities in the 1980s. Not only did the Boar's Head serve as the location of the annual Albemarle Harvest Wine Festival, it also offered winemaking seminars, hosted the Society's events, offered balloon tours of Virginia vineyards, and featured Virginia wines on its restaurant wine lists. The resort even began offering wine tour packages in 1990 that featured accommodations, breakfast, and tours of Oakencroft Winery.[149]

With an eye toward recognizing advancements in the wine industry, the hotel, in conjunction with the Society, created an Award for Outstanding Achievement in the Advancement of the Virginia Wine Industry in January 1981—the first of which was conferred by Governor John Dalton on Meredyth Vineyards' Archie Smith, Jr.[150]

Also in that year, the Boar's Head began publishing a quarterly promotional periodical, the *Boar's Head Grape Vine Press,* distributed at the hotel, which offered timely updates on developments in the Virginia wine industry. The Society assumed responsibility for the publication in fall 1982, renaming it *The Boar's*

*Head Virginia Grapevine.* Each issue concluded with the phrase, "Save Water. Drink Virginia Wines!"[151]

John Rogan died in 1988, after years of generously working with his wife to promote central Virginia wines. The Society, like its principal founder, Felicia Rogan, would continue to promote the cause of central Virginia wineries for more than three decades. In June 2008, after three decades at the forefront of Virginia's wine industry and twenty-five vintages at Oakencroft, Felicia Rogan announced both her retirement and the closing of the winery. In the years between her first 1978 planting and her retirement, she had arguably accomplished more than anyone else in the commonwealth to promote the cause of Virginia wine. During her career, she served on multiple state and local wine promotion boards, including the Virginia Wine Grape Advisory Committee and the Virginia Winegrowers Advisory Board, and she received numerous small business and tourism awards, including the Virginia Wine Industry Person of the Year award in 1995.[152]

Although Oakencroft's new buyers were not interested in maintaining Oakencroft as a winery, its existence, coupled with Rogan's efforts, had nevertheless yielded countless dividends for the wine industry. Her role in the rebirth of Virginia's young wine industry cannot be understated, nor can it be measured solely by the number of promotional events, wine "firsts," or countless hours she spent at the helm of central Virginia's most prominent wine advocacy group.

Rather, Rogan's legacy should be measured by the indelible impact she made on those who came under her influence. Through her devotion to the industry, she legitimized Virginia wine and reestablished central Virginia's wine tradition. She has bequeathed a priceless heritage—not only for the cause of wine promotion in the Charlottesville area, but for the commonwealth. While traveling alongside Governor Gerald L. Baliles (1986–1990) during various trade missions abroad, the governor referred to Rogan as the "matriarch" of the Virginia wine industry—a well-deserved title.[153]

## — The Voice of the Industry —

The Vinifera Wine Growers Association and the Jeffersonian Wine Grape Growers Society were not alone in their advocacy for better recognition, state support, and sensible regulation. Other groups emerged during the rebirth period that were equally passionate about the promotion of Virginia wine and its positive effect on the state's agricultural sector.

In the early 1980s, several licensed wineries and industry supporters formed a nonprofit trade organization, the Virginia Wineries Association, to address issues related to commercial winemaking at Virginia's licensed wineries as well as to provide the needed social community infrastructure among winery owners. Formed chiefly to advocate for the interests of winemakers, the VWA sought to provide education on Virginia wines and promote an appreciation for their distinctive qualities. The group advocated for high-quality viticultural practices as well as continued research into the relationship between wine and health. Based in Richmond, the VWA was responsible for advocating for farm winery legislation during the 1980s, as well as hosting both the annual Vintage Virginia wine festival and the Governor's Cup competition.[154]

Addressing the specialized needs of the commonwealth's grape growers, the Virginia Vineyards Association was formed in 1979 as a joint effort to exchange information and improve cooperation between the state's viticulturists, winery owners, and Virginia Tech. The organization's goals included the promotion of the state's viticultural interests, the cultivation of grapes, increased recognition for Virginia grape products, improved relationships with government officials, and more.[155]

These two organizations joined an increasing chorus of similar groups from other eastern states that were formed to advocate for research, modern laws, and dissemination of information. Of course, it was not enough to just *form* an advocacy organization; rather, members needed to articulate their positions effectively and influence decisions. This meant developing a thorough understanding of the legislative process and budgetary constraints, as well as cultivating meaningful relationships with key decision makers. For Virginia's wine organizations, knowing the industry's personalities, challenges, and products was also critical.

During Virginia's wine revolution, Treville Lawrence, Felicia Rogan, and Archie Smith, Jr. led the way in fiercely advancing the interests of Virginia's wineries and grape producers. Few, however, possessed as agreeable a personality and grasped the legislative advocacy process better than Gordon W. Murchie. A California native, Murchie became involved with the Vinifera Wine Growers Association's board of directors in the early 1980s as he neared his retirement from the U.S. Department of State. He would later succeed Treville Lawrence as president of the Association in August 1989 and serve in that capacity until 2008.[156]

Like his predecessor, Murchie established himself as a powerful advocate for quality winemaking in Virginia. He not only led the Association's legislative lobbying efforts in Richmond, on Capitol Hill, and in several foreign countries, but he later served as the executive director of both the Virginia Wineries Association and the National Wine Coalition.[157]

Along with the support of his wife Anita, Murchie's work over the course of more than thirty years provided invaluable assistance and expertise to Virginia's nascent wine industry. He also consulted with several wineries and worked to establish Mount Vernon's first wine festival in 1997. Lucie Morton later likened Murchie to a grape rootstock in terms of Virginia's wine revolution. "Rootstocks are not apparent to the naked eye but are the indispensable underpinnings of viticulture," Morton said. "Gordon's faith in the future of local wines and his work to promote them deserves our gratitude."[158]

Murchie received the 1998 Virginia Wine Industry Person of the Year award as well as the Virginia Wineries Association's first lifetime achievement award, in 2005, for his work. He also received the Award of Merit from the American Wine Society, the nation's largest consumer-based wine organization. Winemaker Dennis Horton noted that Murchie had "made an enormous contribution to the growth of the Virginia wine industry over the last thirty years and more importantly, he ...cares deeply about it."[159]

## —Celebrating Viticulture: Early Wine Festivals—

The art of extracting grape juice and producing wine has been part of cultural and religious celebration since at least the days of ancient Greece. In more recent times, most of the world's wine regions conducted annual harvest festivals in the fall months to celebrate the grape harvest. Such occasions are frequently accompanied by regional foods and music.

The same has been true in Virginia since the 1950s, when, during each October of that decade, Prince William County winemaker John Sciutto held what were likely to have been the commonwealth's first grape-stomping, wine, and food festivals, at his Manassas winery. Following the rebirth of the state's modern industry in the 1970s, winemakers and advocacy groups discovered that their desire to generate enthusiasm for Virginia's wines required more than what could be mustered by even the enterprising spirit of individual planters, substantial foreign investment, and government support. Spreading knowledge and educating consumers in a state that had all but lost its tradition for winemaking and the enjoyment of wine required significant promotion, education, and, frankly, fun.

The advent of wine festivals in the Old Dominion thus came during the revolutionary period of industry rebirth—a trend mirrored by the national rise of festivals as a sophisticated regional marketing tool. Virginia's early wine festivals not only helped to promote Virginia wine, but provided critical exposure and financial rewards to the state's wineries, large and small alike. Festivals allowed attendees—most of whom were largely unaware of the growing Virginia wine industry—to sample several of the state's wines over the course of an afternoon, enjoying the company of friends and, perhaps, getting a bit tipsy. Proceeds from the festivals went to support wine industry publications, conferences, journals, and other activities.[160]

Emblematic of the diverse interests in Virginia's nascent viticulture industry, it was common to see farmers in overalls observing tractors and machinery alongside the preppy sort in tweed jackets and Bermuda shorts at Virginia's early wine festivals. Virginia boasted nearly twenty separate festivals by the close of the 1980s and had emerged as a leader along the East Coast in numbers of wine-related celebrations; two important festivals nevertheless deserve special mention: the Virginia Wine Festival and the Albemarle Harvest Wine Festival.[161]

As with many other early promotional efforts during the 1970s and 1980s, the commonwealth's first wine festivals were largely the province of the Vinifera Wine Growers Association in Northern Virginia. In August 1976, in conjunction with the celebration of the nation's bicentennial, the Association held its first Wine Festival and Vineyard Tour, which provided more than 800 attendees a wine tour route beginning in Middleburg with stops at Elizabeth Furness's Piedmont Winery and Treville Lawrence's Highbury Estate.[162]

Along the way, attendees were treated to multimedia presentations, vineyard tours, a chicken lunch, live music, and, of course, free wine. At Piedmont, the region's most popular weatherman, Willard Scott, emceed a spirited grape-stomping contest for children, while U.C. Davis viticulture professor A. Dinsmore Webb provided a winemaking seminar. The festival raised money for the Association, which touted it as the first "full blown wine festival with a tour of vineyards and grape stomping ever held in the East."[163]

The celebration was renamed the Virginia Wine Festival in 1978, and included tours of Piedmont Vineyards, Treville Lawrence's Highbury, and Melrose Vineyard, as well as a grape-stomping contest, a live auction, and races in which waiters balanced filled wine glasses to win a case of Virginia wine. The 1978 jubilee also offered films on French, German, and American winemaking at the Middleburg Community Center, with additional seminars offered at Piedmont Winery.[164]

Festival attendance increased as the years passed and in 1980 the Association completed a new festival center at Piedmont Vineyards. It offered an ever-expanding series of attractions, including the running of foxhounds, live music, wagon rides provided by the Virginia Draft Horse and Mule Association, jousting tournaments, a wine auction, cork-throwing contests, and children's pony rides.[165]

The Association unveiled its new home in the recently restored railroad depot in The Plains, duly renamed the Virginia Enovit Center, in conjunction with the 1984 festival. The Enovit Center was intended to serve as a clearing-house for the Association's activities, including assistance to and promotion for winegrowers. It also housed a "bottled wine library," which sought to preserve the first releases of Virginia wines for posterity. The Festival Center was moved in 1985 to Wayne and Juanita Swedenburg's Valley View Farm just east of Middleburg and, for the first time, the event offered seminars by the new Virginia oenologist, Bruce Zoecklein, and the state's new viticulture extension advisor, Tony K. Wolf.[166]

By 1989, the event attracted twenty-two of the state's forty-one licensed farm wineries, and, two years later, the festival was held over a two-day period and moved to Great Meadow, an outdoor events center located just south of The Plains that had been developed by publishing magnate Arthur W. "Nick" Arundel. By then the festival welcomed some 11,000 attendees and 110 vendors and craftsmen. By 1994, the number of attendees approached 20,000.[167]

Northern Virginia was not alone in its fostering of wine festivals. In October 1981, central Virginia commemorated its first Albemarle Harvest Wine Festival on the lakefront grounds of John Rogan's Boar's Head Inn. Sponsored jointly by the Boar's Head and Felicia Rogan's Jeffersonian Wine Grape Growers Society, the festival was inspired by Jefferson's role in experimenting with vinifera varieties at Monticello. Unlike the Virginia Wine Festival, however, the Albemarle Harvest Festival emphasized Charlottesville-area wineries rather than Virginia wineries at large.[168]

Organized chiefly by Felicia Rogan and Charlottesville-area vineyardist Fred Gignoux, the festival offered its 2,500 patrons nearly forty exhibitors, free wine tastings, hot air balloon rides, and discussions by wine experts, including wine writers Leon D. Adams and Bern C. Ramey, as well as by representatives of Paul Masson Vineyards, which had just purchased land for an experimental vineyard at nearby Ivy Creek Farm. Also featured were tours at nearby Barboursville Vineyards, Montdomaine Cellars, and the vineyard of Albemarle County Circuit Court Judge E. Gerald Tremblay.[169]

Rose Bower Vineyards' Tom O'Grady offered poetry readings and a premiere showing of a recently produced movie about his winery, *The Land Is a Woman*. In a nod to history, the festival also featured a meeting between descendants of Philip Mazzei and Thomas Jefferson at Monticello, nearly two centuries after their ancestors' winemaking efforts. The modern-day Mazzeis—Fillipo and his son, Lapo—also joined Simeon Vineyard's Gabriele Rausse the Friday before the event for a ceremonial vine planting at the site of Philip Mazzei's original Colle vineyard at the home of former ambassador Stanley B. Woodward.[170]

The Society assumed sole responsibility for the festival in 1982 and added a Bacchanalian Feast, which featured a family-style dinner of several gourmet courses of delicacies paired with Virginia wines, all of which were presented per culinary traditions drawn from ancient Greece through Virginia's colonial era. The feast, held in the Boars Head's Grand Ballroom, featured herb and flower essences, harvest decorations, and entertainers in lavish period costumes, and was frequently sold out two months in advance. The Society began a professional wine tasting at the 1985 festival, which later evolved into the Monticello Cup competition.[171]

In later years, the Albemarle festival featured self-guided vineyard tours and live music, as well as lectures by Gianni Zonin, Lucie Morton, and international wine connoisseur Peter M. F. Sichel. By 1986, the festival had been rechristened the Monticello Wine and Food Festival, and featured seventeen participating wineries and wine and crafts from thirty-five Charlottesville-area food vendors and businesses.[172]

Other wine festivals were held across Virginia in the early 1980s. Another early event, sponsored by the Virginia Wineries Association, was Vintage Virginia, held for the first time in 1981 in Front Royal. Later moved to the Culpeper 4-H center and later still to the 300-acre Great Meadow Field Events Center in The Plains, Vintage Virginia offered more than 250 wines for sampling and had grown into one of the largest wine festivals on the East Coast by the late 1990s, attracting tens of thousands of attendees over a two-day period.[173]

Smaller festivals proved popular, too. The first Tri-Mountain Winery and Vineyard Festival, held in September 1984, was reputed to be the first two-day wine festival east of California. The Vinifera Wine Growers Association conducted its first Showcase of Virginia Wines at the Middleburg Community Center in conjunction with the Town of Middleburg's 200th anniversary in March 1987, where eight Virginia wineries presented their vintages while an ensemble played on stage.[174]

By the dawn of the 1990s, Virginia's wine festivals expanded beyond Charlottesville and Northern Virginia. After attending several Northern Virginia wine festivals, and sensing that southwest Virginia might appreciate a similar event, two couples, Lee and Mary Lynn Tucker and Phil and Margaret Hager, financed the first Smith Mountain Lake Wine Festival in 1989 with their own funds. Originally held at the Tuckers' home, a bed and breakfast in Floyd County, the festival featured ten wineries and regional craft and food vendors. Attendees were offered grape stomping, hot air balloon rides, and educational lectures on wine tasting and music.

In 1992, the Tuckers and Hagers partnered with the Smith Mountain Lake Chamber of Commerce and the festival eventually grew to more than 7,000 attendees, more than twenty wineries, and some seventy arts and crafts exhibitors annually. The festival's success even spawned an offshoot organization, the Smith Mountain Lake Wine Tasters, and encouraged the establishment of other festivals in the area. For example, the Roanoke Valley Wine Society offered tastings in Salem; the Christiansburg Voluntary Action Center held its annual Virginia Wine and Food Festival at the New River Valley Mall; and in 1996, Mill Mountain Theatre raised an estimated $50,000 from auctions of Virginia wines, wine dinners, trips, and more to support live theater.[175]

None of Virginia's first wine festivals featured professionally judged competitions. As early as 1979, however, the state government's Grape Growers Advisory Committee began exploring the idea of developing wine judging at state and local fairs. Its ideas were realized in 1981, when the Vinifera Wine Growers Association inaugurated its Virginia Wine Competition, the first statewide competition to recognize quality Virginia vintages.[176]

The following August, in conjunction with the 1982 Virginia Wine Festival and the first Virginia Vineyard Day proclaimed by Governor Charles S. Robb, the Vinifera Wine Growers Association renamed the contest the Virginia Governor's Cup at a competition held at Middleburg's Red Fox Inn. For an entry fee of only $15, forty-six wines from eleven Virginia vineyards competed for the first Governor's Trophy. The first such prize was awarded by Lieutenant Governor Richard Joseph Davis, Jr., to Piedmont Vineyards for its 1981 Chardonnay.[177]

In 1983, sixty-seven wines from fourteen Virginia wineries entered the contest. The tasting took place in Philadelphia, Pennsylvania, and was held by members of L'Ecole du Vin, a Pennsylvania wine enthusiast society. The 1983 Governor's Cup was presented by Mel Jefferson, then director of the Virginia Department of Agriculture and Consumer Services' Division of Marketing, to Ingleside Vineyards owner Carl Flemer, Jr., for its 1981 Chardonnay.[178]

With an eye towards increasing the reputation of Virginia wines, the Association reduced the number of categories from twenty-two to five in August 1984 and, that year—two weeks before the Association's annual festival—the Association ceded use of the name Governor's Cup Wine Competition to the Virginia Wineries Association, which was conducting its first festival and wine competition that year.[179]

Tastings and the award of Governor's Cup competitions in subsequent years were held at a variety of historic properties and other venues in the mid-Atlantic area. The Governor's Cup eventually evolved into the commonwealth's most prestigious and professionally organized annual wine competition. Contest categories ranged from specific grape varieties to broad classes, such as red and white vinifera blends. Wines were judged on color, aroma, body, balance, finish, and overall quality. After every wine was judged and scored, the best were re-tasted by experienced wine judges to select the winner. Representing varied backgrounds within the ranks of wine professionals, judges also served as hotel food and beverage directors, retail wine shop and restaurant owners, and wine writers.[180]

By the close of the 1980s, festivals had become an indispensable part of the state's wine tourism model and served as much more than occasional acknowledgements of a beverage. While vintners promoted their wares, these festivals permitted artists, musicians, and food vendors to offer a variety of products, entertainment, and culinary treats.[181]

Wine festivals not only assisted the state's wine industry with much-needed advertising and money; they encapsulated the very best of the young industry. With more than 30,000 attendees annually, they became robust and celebratory affairs, ultimately warranting British wine critic Michael Broadbent's assertion that "drinking good wine with good food in good company is one of life's most civilized pleasures."[182]

## —Government Support in the 1980s—

As noted earlier, governmental support at the dawn of the 1980s was rather limited in the wake of the passage of the 1980 Farm Winery Act. The Virginia Department of Agriculture and Consumer Service's actions were largely limited to publishing brochures, the most notable being a 1982 pocket guide to Virginia wineries and a 1983 "How to Get Started" pamphlet on grape growing and winemaking for home vineyard enthusiasts. This limited support, however, was expanded significantly in 1984, when a series of substantial public-sector initiatives offered more substantial and sustainable encouragement to winemakers. This civic boost—which came in the form of legislative, gubernatorial, and academic encouragement—helped ensure the young industry's viability, and distinguished the Old Dominion from its sister states.[183]

Beginning in 1984, the General Assembly adopted a series of legislative initiatives that greatly benefited the industry. For example, the legislature exempted farm winery equipment from the personal property tax, which classified it along with other farm machinery and emphasized grape growing and winemaking as chiefly agricultural pursuits. To promote Virginia wines and to increase the number of retail outlets where Virginia wines were available, the legislature passed a law mandating the sale of only Virginia wine in the state's approximately 250 state-run ABC stores. By the mid-1990s, ABC sales accounted for approximately 10 percent of all Virginia wine sales.[184]

Most significantly, the 1984 General Assembly appropriated $190,000 to fund three full-time state government positions to assist the wine industry. Funding the positions—which signaled the most potent support yet by a southern state towards the stimulation of a quality wine industry—provided for a state oenologist and state viticulturalist to be based at Virginia Tech, as well as one full-time wine marketing specialist to be located in a new Wine Marketing Office at VDACS's headquarters in Richmond.[185]

Lou Ann Whitton (later Leeanne Ladin) was hired as Virginia's first wine marketing specialist in 1984. Ladin, formerly a product promotion specialist in VDACS's Division of Markets, had worked closely with the state's fledgling wine industry since the late 1970s. In her new position, Whitton rolled out a Virginia Wine Country promotional campaign by 1985, replete with a new industry logo and slogan, as well as a wine guide. She was succeeded in June 1987 by Annette Ringwood Boyd, a former marketing director for Richmond on the James and an expert who boasted an impressive background in public relations and promotion. Boyd was followed by Wendy C. Rizzo in 1992. By the late 1980s, the VDACS Wine Marketing Office had directed the preparation of countless reports and surveys, responded to public inquiries, and furnished reports to the Virginia Winegrowers Advisory Board.[186]

The hiring of an official state oenologist had long been championed by industry supporters, most notably the Vinifera Wine Growers Association. As early as 1973 the Association had requested that Virginia Tech reestablish its viticultural program and replace a part-time horticultural specialist with a "younger, progressive minded, full time" viticulturalist and oenologist. Twelve years later, in 1985, the state's first professional oenologist, Bruce Zoecklein, was hired.[187]

A native of California, Zoecklein studied microbiology and biochemistry at California State University at San Diego and received a master's degree in horticulture and a Ph.D. in food science from Virginia Tech. After serving as Missouri's state oenologist, Zoecklein was lured to Virginia, in part, thanks to the tremendous public and private sector investment in the state's wineries. Zoecklein joined Virginia Tech as head of its Oenology-Grape Chemistry Group, and proceeded to offer professional chemistry assistance to Virginia's winemakers, many of whom could not afford such expertise. He also provided winemakers with information on winemaking styles, aromas, and the chemical consistency of their wines.[188]

Zoecklein would later be honored with emeritus status from Virginia Tech in 2010, but during his twenty-five-year career with the institution, few experts would make such lasting contributions to the Virginia wine industry. He became an internationally respected chemist, giving more than 400 lectures and thirty-three international presentations, writing four books on wine chemistry (including one that has been translated into Spanish), and providing oenological assistance to several governments around the world. Zoecklein also served as a section chair of the American Society of Enology and Viticulture, a conference organizer, an editor for two wine journals, and publisher of *Enology Notes*, a widely distributed oenological newsletter.[189]

One year after Zoecklein was hired, Dr. Tony K. Wolf joined Virginia Tech's Cooperative Extension Service as state viticulturist. A graduate of West Virginia University, Wolf earned his master's degree from Pennsylvania State University and a doctorate from Cornell University. While at West Virginia, Wolf worked in that school's experimental vineyard—an experience he would repeat at Virginia Tech's Alson H. Smith Jr. Agricultural Research and Extension Center (AREC) south of Winchester, where he oversaw a two-acre experimental vineyard. The vineyard, first planted in 1989, was conceived to identify grape varieties that would prove useful in terms of blending, developing a market niche, resistance to fruit rots, winter hardiness, and good wine quality.[190]

During his tenure with Virginia Tech, Wolf helped generate technical knowledge and support for the state's grape growers, providing them with information on vineyard locations and how best to navigate through problems created by climates, pests, and fungi. He produced multiple studies on grape-growing techniques in Virginia—including variety selection, low-yield problems, and disease research—and taught graduate-level grape-growing courses. Wolf was also responsible for assisting area growers with the identification and promotion of unique wine grape varieties that work well with Virginia's varying climates and soils. By 2010, he had organized more than one hundred grape-growing related workshops, received the 2009 Alumni Award for Excellence in Extension from the Virginia Department of Education, and coauthored *The Mid-Atlantic Winegrape Growers Guide*, first published in 1996, which provided production and business-related information for grape growers.[191]

The General Assembly's 1984 actions were complemented that year by VDACS's creation of a Viticultural Technical Advisory Committee. Appointed by VDACS commissioner S. Mason Carbaugh, the committee was tasked with developing a grapevine certification program and adopting a series of regulations governing the planting of grapevines across the state. Calls for just such a group began, unsurprisingly, with the Vinifera Wine Growers Association, which, as early as 1973, had noted the potential threat of grapevine viruses. By August 1985, the committee had adopted a series of rules, and the following year worked with Virginia Tech to establish the Virginia Grapevine Certification Program to provide virus-free grapevine materials to Virginia nurseries. The committee also worked with Virginia Tech to establish a Foundation Plant Materials Service in 1986, which provided for the sale of certified vinifera clones and rootstock selections.[192]

The General Assembly built on its 1984 actions during the following year's legislative session, when it created the Virginia Winegrowers Advisory Board and allocated a $140,000 Winegrowers Productivity Fund. Ever since the 1977 creation of the original Grape Growers Advisory Committee, VDACS had intermittently tinkered with the committee's name, membership, funding, and responsibilities. As reorganized in 1985, the new Winegrowers Advisory Board was tasked with coordinating Virginia's growing wine industry with other segments of Virginia's economy, establishing quality assurance methods for the industry, increasing productivity in grape and wine production, and engaging in research and promotion. Highlighting its increased stature, the Advisory Board was the first Virginia wine organization to be appointed by the governor. The group, led by Oakencroft's Felicia Rogan as its first chairman, was also charged with making recommendations on the use of the Winegrowers Productivity Fund to the VDACS commissioner.[193]

As established by the legislature, the Winegrowers Productivity Fund was to receive an annual appropriation from the General Assembly, derived from excise taxes paid by Virginia's farm wineries to the Department of Alcoholic Beverage Control. In its first year, the Advisory Board's recommendations resulted in the disbursement of more than $112,000 to projects and, by 1989, it funded sixteen research, technical, and marketing projects at a cost of nearly $650,000.[194]

The Advisory Board and the Productivity Fund continue to lead state efforts to promote Virginia wines and improve their quality. The Advisory Board serves as the chief advisory arm of state government dedicated to promoting the interests of vineyards and wineries through research, education, and marketing.[195]

Critical to the success of the growing wine industry was the encouragement expressed by the state's legislature as well as by its chief executive. Beginning with the enthusiasm shown by the Godwin administration in the late 1970s, each of Virginia's governors since has endorsed the cause of Virginia wine to a greater or lesser degree.[196]

Throughout the 1980s, executive support came in the form of gubernatorial endorsements of marketing initiatives, support for legislative enactments that benefited the industry, and the appointment of qualified individuals enthusiastic about the wine industry to positions of public trust. This, naturally, included the seemingly-perpetual reappointment of the able S. Mason Carbaugh as VDACS commissioner.

Among the more notable wine promotion measures spearheaded by Virginia's governors was their annual decree—issued at the start of each year's grape harvest season—that recognized the state's growing wine industry and its contributions to Virginia's economy. The first such proclamation came during the 1982 Vinifera Wine Growers Festival, when Governor Charles S. Robb proclaimed August 28, 1982 as Virginia Vineyard Day. In August of the following year, Governor Robb proclaimed the first Virginia Farm Winery Week and noted the great economic development potential of the wine industry and the improvement in the quality of the state's wines.[197]

Virginia Farm Winery Week was proclaimed annually for two more years until VDACS persuaded Governor Gerald L. Baliles to designate August 1986 as the first Virginia Farm Winery Month. In conjunction with highlighting and celebrating the accomplishments of the industry over an entire month, VDACS encouraged retailers and restaurants to offer Virginia wine by the glass, and distributed materials, posters, and table tent cards to selected restaurants across the state to aid waiters in wine-food pairing selections. Baliles renamed the celebration Virginia Wine Month in 1988 and moved it to October to take advantage of the cooler weather, brighter fall foliage, and the fact that it fell closer to the time of the grape harvest.[198]

Virginia's governors have proclaimed October as Virginia Wine Month ever since, and it remains the state government's most significant period of industry marketing. During the month-long celebration, a series of festivals, events, travel packages, and tours are offered across the commonwealth, and it continues to be the most eagerly anticipated part of the year for winery owners and patrons alike.[199]

Governors during the 1980s also spearheaded initiatives aimed at bolstering the industry. Governor John N. Dalton, for example, signed the significant 1980 Farm Winery Act into law. Governor Charles S. Robb attended many wine festivals during his tenure and signed the important wine-related legislation from the 1984 and 1985 legislative sessions. Even before he assumed the oath of office, Robb passionately argued for the rights of Shenandoah Valley vintners during the 1981 Shenandoah AVA controversy. In spring 1985, Robb used a bottle of Barboursville's Cabernet Sauvignon to christen a reproduction of the *Godspeed*, one of three ships that brought settlers and casks of wine to Jamestown in 1607.[200]

Robb's successor, Gerald L. Baliles, was even more passionate in his support of Virginia wine; not only did he enthusiastically endorse the various promotional campaigns of the late 1980s, but he believed Virginia wines could become a signature export. During his administration, Baliles hosted dozens of receptions for wine industry representatives and often gave remarks on the industry's importance. He routinely touted Virginia wines during his international economic development trips and persuaded some major air carriers, including Japan's All Nippon Airways, to serve Virginia wines on its flights.[201]

Baliles made frequent trips to Virginia's wineries, the most notable being an eleven-stop, three-day tour of nine Virginia wineries in June 1988. The journey—unprecedented for any sitting American governor—was envisioned to show strong executive support for Virginia's emerging wine industry and its growing economic impact. At each stop, Baliles stressed that Virginia wines were taking their place in the "pantheon of American and international wines." Back in Richmond that October, Baliles unveiled a new wine cellar in the Governor's Mansion, conceived and designed by the Virginia Winegrowers Advisory Board to showcase Virginia wines during official events.[202]

Baliles also challenged the Virginia Winegrowers Advisory Board to review the status of the industry and provide recommendations for raising its visibility. His five-point "charge" to the Advisory Board in September 1988 included, among other things, requests to develop a wine marketing initiative in cooperation with the state's Division of Tourism; undertake a wine market study for Virginia wines; develop industry standards for quality, inventory, and merchandising; increase the advisory board's responsibilities; and review the potential for an academic program on wine. The result was the first comprehensive study of the Virginia wine industry, published in January 1989, which provided an overview of the industry and made short- and long-term recommendations for future growth.[203]

Baliles' successor, L. Douglas Wilder (1990–1994), promoted Virginia wines as well, but to a lesser degree. This must be contrasted, however, with Baliles' unparalleled support of the state's more general economic development initiatives. Wilder nevertheless promoted Virginia wines during a trip to Japan in the early 1990s along with Oakencroft's Felicia Warburg Rogan. Wilder also penned a letter to the Jeffersonian Wine Grape Growers Society and noted, "just as I strive to meet Jeffersonian ideals in public service, I hope to build upon Mr. Jefferson's contributions to the wine industry in Virginia."[204]

189

Aside from annual decrees and economic development efforts, public sector support during the 1980s consisted of a series of major marketing campaigns that either featured or primarily focused on Virginia wine. For example, the state's first major promotional effort to feature Virginia wines, "We Have It Made in Virginia," was developed by the Secretary of Commerce, Dr. Betty J. Diener, launched in early 1983 by VDACS to promote a variety of Virginia products.[205]

VDACS's 1983 campaign was complemented in the autumn of 1985 by a more aggressive $1 million marketing effort by the Virginia Division of Tourism called "These Are Exciting Times in Virginia." This campaign was a cooperative effort between VDACS, the Virginia ABC Board, and what was then called the Virginia Department of Highways. Not only did the initiative provide information to tourists on restaurants and country inns, it also placed full-page ads promoting Virginia products in the New York, Baltimore, Philadelphia, and Washington, D.C., markets. As part of the campaign, the Division of Tourism produced a thirty-two-page color booklet that featured notable tourist attractions and wineries.[206]

In 1984, the Division of Tourism also coined a new term, Virginia Wine Country, and began promoting its "Visit Virginia Wine Country" campaign as a way for tourists to plan a romantic getaway. The following year, the division unveiled its "Virginia is Wine Country" promotion, which featured sixteen Virginia wineries clustered around five tour routes in the Charlottesville, Fredericksburg, Northern Virginia, Shenandoah Valley, and Roanoke regions.[207]

In conjunction with this effort, the Department of Highways erected grape cluster logo signs that had been placed within ten miles of all Virginia wineries by 1987. The markers—popular with wineries and tourists alike—made finding wineries along Virginia's roads considerably easier, as they included directional markings, vineyard routes, and turnoffs. Estimates following the 1985 campaign showed that tourism improved in the targeted areas and visitors at wineries increased between 20 and 200 percent.[208]

The 1985 campaign was followed in July 1986 by yet another wine industry–exclusive marketing promotion when Governor Baliles unveiled "Virginia Wines—A Growing Tradition." The effort, largely funded with a $50,000 grant from the Winegrowers Advisory Board, included a new logo with two bottles forming a wine glass. The campaign materials included not only tent table cards for restaurants, but also so-called "shelf-talkers" for retail stores and handsome pinewood wine bottle holders for retail displays. The materials proved very popular with retailers. "I felt the industry needed a cohesive image, something that would help the wines be recognized where they were sold," VDACS wine market specialist Lou Ann Whitton said at the time. "We feel like we've finally created an image and it's getting people excited."[209]

The Baliles administration continued its economic development efforts in January 1989, when VDACS's Division of Marketing launched a new trade-marked logo, Virginia's Finest. Designed to replace the division's 1983 "We Have It Made in Virginia" campaign, the effort featured a new logo designed to increase buyer motivation. By the close of 1990, Virginia's Finest had become the nation's largest quality-based trademark program, and Virginia wines were prominently featured alongside other Virginia-made products.[210]

Efforts by the legislative and executive arms of Virginia's government were eventually complimented by academic developments at some of Virginia's state-supported universities. While initially resistant to support early vinifera growing efforts in the 1970s, Virginia Tech became a leader in the nascent Virginia wine movement and shed its former oppositionist attitude as the 1980s unfolded.

In addition to serving as the official host institution for the state's new oenologist, Bruce Zoecklein, and its new viticulturalist, Tony Wolf, Virginia Tech began offering meaningful courses in wine grape growing and marketing. The school had initially offered a Virginia Grape Short Course as early as 1975, but the course did not encourage vinifera nor did it extensively discuss wine grape growing. As one disappointed student lamented of those early classes, "In all honesty, the course at VPI on grapes did not encourage the growing of vinifera grapes. Of course, the sad thing was that the instructors were from New York, [Pennsylvania], and Ohio. No one from Virginia seemed to have anything to say."[211]

As course attendance doubled in the late 1970s, however, Virginia Tech revamped its academic offerings. In 1981, the university began offering grape courses in Northern Virginia and revised the curriculum to discuss winemaking practices, trellis systems, wine marketing, and development of wine cellars. At the request of VDACS Commissioner Carbaugh, and in response to increasing demands for information about grape growing, it began providing two-day grape courses for the county agricultural extension agents. The courses covered the industry, site selection, training systems, varieties, cultural and nutrition information, and production costs. Such early classes quickly established Virginia Tech as the state's foremost institution for wine grape research, winemaking, and vineyard site selection.[212]

Another direct result of Virginia's growing wine industry was the 1991 creation of a new University Enological Research Facility at Old Dominion University. The new facility—the brainchild of ODU chemistry professor Roy L.

Williams—was inaugurated following Williams' 1989 receipt of a grant from the Virginia Wine Advisory Board, intended for research into the health effects of wine.[213]

Williams, a 1960 graduate of what was then the College of William & Mary's Norfolk Division (later Old Dominion University), returned to the school in 1965 as an organic chemistry professor. Inspired by the work of Jacques Recht at Ingleside, Williams hoped to turn the facility into Virginia's second major wine research center (after Virginia Tech) and envisioned partnering with wineries and other industry organizations to identify beneficial wine agents and grape-seed extracts that would prove useful to that state's winemakers.[214]

In conjunction with the opening of the facility, Williams published a bimonthly *Virginia Wine Journal* and sponsored wine education courses. The center studied topics such as natural phytochemicals in grape plants, how to address the black goo grapevine disease, how to enhance wine's positive health effects, beneficial reuse of leftover grape seeds, and research into the health, anti-aging, and cardiovascular factors in wine.[215]

Beyond the confines of ODU, Williams and his wife Sherry Williams administered the Town Point Virginia Wine Competition, which, for many years, was the only wine competition in the Tidewater region. Held at the Town Point Club in downtown Norfolk beginning in 1987, the Williamses personally subsidized the event and handled the logistics of the competition. All Virginia wineries were invited to participate, and of the 35 typical entrants, only three awards (gold, silver, and bronze) were awarded for each category.

Williams also created a highly-rated twelve-session college wine appreciation course. While teaching students about wine through the lens of organic chemistry, Williams used charts and maps to distinguish the sometimes confusing array of wines and varieties. "He makes an intimidating, overwhelming subject fun and easy," said student Karen Winters. Randy Wyatt, a student from Norfolk, said, "He is passionate about the subject. We are not just sipping, we are learning."

Williams' course, like that of his research facility and wine festival, was highly rated by students, business executives, and wine industry representatives. He would go on to publish numerous papers in peer-reviewed journals, give lectures at local restaurants and civic clubs, present his research at national and international conferences, write for the Newport News *Daily Press*, and even appear on *Meet the Press*. His work eventually earned him the title of Virginia Wine Industry Person of the Year in 2001 from the Virginia Winegrowers Advisory Board.[216]

Despite new academic programs and offerings, studies showed that salaries for degree-holding oenologists and viticulturists at Virginia's public institutions were not competitive with those of their counterparts in other states, which hampered efforts to attract top-tier educators in wine-related fields. The totality of the state government's efforts during the 1980s, however, resulted in an unprecedented, multidimensional level of public sector support for Virginia's wine industry that was far more substantial and durable than could ever have been predicted by industry observers two decades before.[217]

Through the direct contribution of financial, infrastructural, marketing, and research resources, the state's entrepreneurial public sector cultivated favorable policies and a structural climate that not only attracted winemakers, but unequivocally signaled that the development of Virginia wine—yes, even as an alcoholic beverage in a politically-conservative state—was something that ought to be, and henceforth would be, encouraged.

## *— Vanguard Wineries —*

The fervor surrounding Virginia's wine revolution surged in the 1980s as foreign companies invested millions of dollars in new wine ventures and Virginia's government offered substantial assistance to help foster the new industry. As repeatedly observed in this chapter, the attempt to grow vinifera grapes in a southern state was unprecedented, and the Old Dominion's new wine-friendly environment attracted newcomers excited about the potential to be at the forefront of what appeared to be the East Coast's most promising new wine region.

Carving out their own small wineries to join the cadre of wine pioneers at Farfelu, Meredyth, Piedmont, and elsewhere, these adventurous entrepreneurs boasted diverse backgrounds that made for a variety of wine styles and winery experiences. Between 1979 and 1991, the number of Virginia wineries increased dramatically from six to forty-three. Vineyard acreage increased from 286 to 1,220 acres during that same period.[218]

Despite growth, there were signs that the state's wine industry was still in its infancy: the quality of Virginia wines was uneven and the sheer distance between wineries required the dedication of multiple weekends to get a sense of the local wine scene. Geographic location proved critical not only for growing grapes but for getting the finished product to market and distributors.

Lastly, a visit to a typical Virginia winery during its modern rebirth wasn't just *like* a visit to someone's home—in most instances it *was* someone's home. Converted garages, living rooms, and kitchens served as settings for tasting rooms; visitors were often encouraged to call ahead to make sure winemaking families were in town. On the positive side, few wineries charged fees, as it was largely accepted practice at the time that tours and tastings were free unless otherwise noted. Forced to learn by trial and error like many emerging industries, some wineries succeeded while others failed. Several early wineries operating in the 1970s and 1980s later closed or were renamed; they would in time, however, be replaced by dozens more.

Loudoun and Fauquier Counties quickly emerged as Northern Virginia's most promising winemaking areas. Wineries in both counties greatly benefited from the 1982 completion of Interstate 66, which provided a direct connection to consumers in Washington, D.C. Loudoun County's winery growth—which would outpace all other counties by the 2000s—began quietly enough in 1981 along the southern tip of the Catoctin Mountain range outside of Leesburg when Lew and Cindy Parker founded Willowcroft Farm Vineyards.[219]

The Parkers, who boasted neither viticultural nor farming expertise, purchased an early 1800s farmhouse and barn in 1979 for the benefit of their daughters' 4-H club activities. Lew Parker, a graduate in engineering with a master's degree in business administration from Lehigh University and Wharton respectively, explored an assortment of agricultural ideas for the property and learned of new technology that made it possible to grow quality wine grapes in Virginia.

During the spring of 1980, the Parkers planted forty vines in an experimental, one-acre plot, most of which died because of poor sunlight exposure. The Parkers persisted and, in 1984, manufactured a winemaking apparatus from the farm's old dairy equipment, converting their two-story horse stable into a cozy winery. In time, Willowcroft boasted more than twelve acres of vinifera and French-American vineyards scattered about the property and on nearby lands.[220]

East of Leesburg, tucked away on a picturesque expanse just south of Waterford, Loudoun Valley Vineyards was founded by New York natives Hubert and Delores Tucker. Like Gabriele Rausse at Barboursville, the Tuckers initially sought to address the region's need for high quality, certified vinifera wine grapes by establishing a grape root stock nursery. In 1983, following several soil and climate studies, the Tuckers began planting four acres of vinifera vines with the intent of opening their own winery. The couple constructed a winery building that included a tasting room, kitchen, and visitor center with enviable views of the surrounding countryside. Opened in the fall of 1987, Loudoun Valley Vineyards later boasted twenty-eight acres of vines.[221]

Another Loudoun establishment, Tarara Winery, was opened in 1988 by Whitie and Margaret Hubert on their 475-acre farm along the Potomac River. Whitie, founder of a successful Gaithersburg, Maryland-based construction company, spent his Ohio youth picking Concord grapes for Welch's Grape Juice Company. In 1985, the Huberts planted an experimental plot of six rows of grapes on their property. They increased their small vineyard the following year to fifty acres of vinifera and established a sixty-acre nursery with blackberries, asparagus, and fruit trees.[222]

By 1988, the Huberts had constructed a winery and, using his prior construction industry experience, Whitie Hubert drilled a 230-foot long man-made wine cave—the first in Virginia. While the business expanded fast, it quickly became better-known for its festivals and events rather than the caliber of its wine. Attempts to change perceptions began in the early 2000s when a new winemaker, Jordan Harris, embarked on an attempt to reinvigorate the winery as a "wine-first" operation.[223]

To the south, in Fauquier County, a pair of home winemakers, Robert and Phoebe Harper, started Naked Mountain Winery and Vineyards in 1976. Robert, a former sales representative for Texaco, was a longtime winemaker at the couple's home in Falls Church. Phoebe, a former computer systems analyst for the federal government, was an agricultural economics major in college. In 1973, after trying unsuccessfully to cultivate an experimental plot of grapes on a friend's farm near the Rappahannock River, the couple purchased forty-two acres of rolling land situated in a small valley in northwestern Fauquier, where they built a small home and cleared land for a vineyard.

Despite objections from neighbors who suggested the property was more appropriate for apples, the Harpers planted Riesling, Chardonnay, and Sauvignon Blanc vines in 1976 and 1977. After three years of selling grapes to other wineries, the Harpers built a small winery in 1981 and opened Naked Mountain, constructing a large chalet-style winery building in 1984. In August 2010, the Harpers sold Naked Mountain to Randy and Meagan Morgan, who bought Naked Mountain while in their late twenties, becoming overnight the youngest winery owners in the state, and the history of Naked Mountain began anew.[224]

One Fauquier winery that relished its quaintness and focused on quality wine—perhaps more than any other in Virginia—is Linden Vineyards. The winery was founded in 1983 by Jim and Peggy Law, the former of whom was often described as an archetypal wine practitioner. An Ohio native, Jim spent time in the Peace Corps in Zaire (now the Democratic Republic of the Congo) helping with fruit production. On his return to the Buckeye State, Law spent two years as an apprentice at an Ohio winery, where he learned basic winemaking techniques. In 1981, he headed south, and took a job as winemaker at Joseph C. Geraci's Tri-Mountain Winery. There, he met Peggy, a former zoologist who had recently joined Tri-Mountain's staff. The two were married the following year, and in 1983 the couple, in partnership with Jim Law's parents, purchased seventy-six acres of quiet hillside land in the Linden area of northwestern Fauquier County.[225]

Situated at elevations between 1,200 and 1,400 feet, the property featured well-drained soils, the intermittent thermal inversion of warm air, and areas suitable for grapes. After planting vinifera and French-American grapes in a vineyard Jim Law referred to as "Hardscrabble," the couple obtained a winery license and opened Linden Vineyards in spring 1987. The Laws constructed a winery with space for a tasting room, equipment, and a seminar room.[226]

The intent from the beginning was for Linden to remain small, allowing the Laws to be integrally involved in all aspects of the agricultural process. Central to Linden's success has been Jim Law's belief that the best wine is made from the best grapes. To this end, Linden was the first to employ a lyre trellising system (a Bordeaux method in which vines are cut and trained to extend toward the sun in order to double the vines' exposure), and a de-juicing tank that permits gentler extraction of the grape juice from berries.[227]

Law was initially an advocate of the work of Australian viticulturalist Dr. Richard Smart and his book, *Sunlight into Wine*. Dr. Smart advocated the use of mathematical calculations with empirical observations to support strong canopy management and routine pruning to produce an optimal balance between a vine's foliage and the amount of fruit produced. Later, Law switched to close spacing and higher density plantings[228]

While Linden produced its own wines, Jim Law also bottled private-label wines for some of his growers. He traveled abroad extensively to observe winemaking and vineyard techniques, and routinely read English and French newspapers about both. The winery developed a reputation for focusing on perfecting its viticultural practices, with Law viewing winemaking as a continually evolving process that one is unlikely to ever master. As the Laws noted to an author,

> The land is our partner and we are still learning to understand it…. Slowly we have begun to understand our land in terms of flavors, aromas, nuances, and the style that contributes to our wine. Our job as winegrowers is to nurture these flavors in the vineyard and to allow them to develop in the cellar. This is what gives personality and character to wine. It is the thumbprint and signature of our land.[229]

A humble steward of the art of winemaking, his thoughts on grape growing were later printed in many wine publications, through which he has counseled countless growers, both experienced and not, earning Jim frequent recognition as Virginia's best wine grape grower and the state's "high priest of viticulture."[230]

## Central Virginia

Far from the hustle and bustle of the Washington, D.C., suburbs, wine activity during the industry's modern rebirth was also fermenting in Central Virginia, where U.S. Route 29 provided easy mobility between Washington, D.C., Charlottesville, and Lynchburg. Joining Barboursville, Prince Michel, Rapidan, Mountain Cove, Burnley, and Oakencroft were several smaller operations that helped bolster the region's reputation as the cultural center of Virginia's wine industry.

Just west of Charlottesville along the southeastern face of the Blue Ridge Mountains in Nelson County, Richmond chemist David Mefford and his wife, Betty Mefford, planted one of the earliest vinifera vineyards in the commonwealth in 1978. In 1984, they opened Bacchanal Vineyards and constructed a winery. Later renamed Afton Mountain Vineyards, the Meffords sold the property to Tom and Shinko Corpora in 1987, who spent nearly two years rehabilitating the vineyards, enlarging the tasting room and retail area, and upgrading the winery. In April 2009, after twenty-one years of running Afton Mountain, the Corporas retired and sold the property to Elizabeth and Tony Smith.[231]

In 1979, another early vineyard—Autumn Hill Vineyard—was started on a ninety-acre hillside southwest of Stanardsville in Greene County. The winery was the idea of two couples, Ed and Avra Schwab and Gunther and Anita Gaede, looking to abandon their frantic New York lifestyles. The four selected the Greene County property after searching for suitable sites and being encouraged by Virginia's wine-friendly environment. The couples planted five acres of Chardonnay, Riesling, and Cabernet Sauvignon—all varieties recommended to them by Gabriele Rausse. Autumn Hill released its first wines in 1986 and, after outgrowing its garage, constructed a winery building in 1989.[232]

One farm that epitomized the call for agricultural diversification was Madison County's Rose River Farm. The winery began after the 1976 purchase of the historic 175-acre Rose River Farm by a Washington, D.C.–based pathologist, Dr. Kenneth L. McCoy. McCoy had long sought a peaceful life in a rural setting and he was attracted to Rose River's circa-1770 log cabin. Though the land was rocky and covered with underbrush, McCoy's son Ken, Jr., planted an experimental plot of 2,000 vinifera and French-American vines in 1976. The McCoys then converted the log cabin into a winery, while Ken McCoy, Jr. consulted with Gabriele Rausse on winemaking. The farm was purchased by Douglas Dear and his family in 2002.[233]

Elsewhere in Madison County, Misty Mountain Winery was founded in 1984 by J. Michael Cerceo and his wife. The Cerceos moved to a 350-acre farm just west of Madison in 1982 and, on the advice of Jacques Recht and Gabriele Rausse, the couple planted vinifera and French-American grapes in 1983. The Cerceos converted a barn into their winery in 1984 and celebrated their first grape harvest in 1986. By the mid-1990s, the vineyard had grown to twelve acres of vinifera, and the winery specialized in producing dry table wines. In 2000, Misty Mountain was purchased by Larry Christensen and J. D. Hartman, and renamed Christensen Ridge. Further south along the Route 29 corridor, south of Charlottesville, retired U.S. Navy captain John O. "Josh" Sherman began Chermont Winery in 1981—perhaps the first irrigated vineyard in the commonwealth.[234]

In the greater Lynchburg area, one of Virginia's smallest wineries, Rebec Vineyards, opened in December 1987. Founded by retired engineer Richard Hanson and his wife, Ella Hanson, the two decided to open the winery on a 600-acre tobacco farm previously owned by Ella's father. The farm had been in Ella's family for more than 150 years, and the winery, named for a medieval string instrument, opened in 1987, following Richard's enrollment in winemaking and grape growing courses at Virginia Tech.

In October 1991, Rebec began a small wine festival at the suggestion of a nearby herbologist who advocated the use of garlic as a natural antibiotic. The festival evolved into the annual Virginia Wine and Garlic Festival, which attracted up to 20,000 attendees. The annual festival's early years featured vendors, wines, and a garlic-eating contest (which was, alas, eventually canceled thanks to the number of attendees taken to the emergency room two years in a row). By 2010, the festival had secured a position as one of central Virginia's fall wine traditions. To make the event more family friendly, Hanson added clowns, magicians, and a petting zoo.[235]

To the east of Lynchburg in western Appomattox County, Stonewall Vineyards opened in 1983. The winery was started by Howard and Betty Bryan, who planted an experimental French-American and Chardonnay vineyard in 1972. After experimenting with varieties and trellising systems, the Bryans expanded their vineyard in 1980; in 1991, Larry and Sterry Davis, with their son Bart Davis purchased the winery, which later closed.[236]

## The Shenandoah Valley

The otherwise peaceful Shenandoah Valley was alive with viticultural action during the 1980s, particularly in the wake of the 1981 American Viticultural

Area naming controversy. The hard work of James and Emma Randel at Shenandoah Vineyards—the valley's undisputed wine leader—stirred the entrepreneurial spirits of several other winemakers as well. Preceding the Randels' planting at Shenandoah were several smaller growers in the northern Shenandoah Valley who attempted winemaking and opened wineries, but whose efforts subsequently ended.

One of the earliest plantings of wine grapes in Virginia, for example, occurred in 1971, when John Gerba planted four acres of French-American grapes on an eighty-five-acre farm just north of Stanley in Page County. The planting, while small, comprised the commonwealth's second largest vineyard at the time (after Farfelu). Gerba sold his grapes principally to home winemakers until 1983, when he and his business partner Harland Baker began producing wine under the proprietary name Guilford Ridge. Guilford Ridge's production was quite small—no more than 400 cases annually—and, to supplement their income, Gerba and Baker raised llamas on the property and even produced musical and theatrical productions at the winery.[237]

In 1976, five years after Gerba planted his first grapes, two brothers, Steve and Scott Smith, planted a five-acre vineyard on their family's ninety-three-acre hay farm, Cedar Lane, southwest of Winchester in Frederick County. In 1984, the Smiths opened Winchester Winery in a two-level winery building that included space for a tasting room, office, and winemaking equipment. By the mid-1980s, Winchester Winery boasted eighteen acres of grapes, producing Seyval Blanc, Vidal Blanc, Johannisberg Riesling, Chambourcin, and blended wines.[238]

Another short-lived but ambitious concern, Tri-Mountain Winery and Vineyards, was opened in 1981 by a colorful entrepreneur, Joseph C. Geraci. A New York native who moved to Alexandria in his youth, Geraci bought a 112-acre farm in southeastern Frederick County outside of Middletown in 1973, where he planted fifteen acres of grapes of eighteen varieties and began making wine in honor of his family's Italian heritage. While Geraci initially sold grapes to other winemakers, in 1980, he began devoting himself full-time to the vineyard and opened Tri-Mountain, named for the three mountain ranges that surround his property.[239]

Geraci constructed a four-acre lake to moderate the temperature and reduce frost damage, and converted a barn on the property into the winery building. He hosted a Tri-Mountain Winery and Vineyard Festival in September 1984, reputed to be the first two-day wine festival in the eastern United States. Regrettably, Geraci died later that year at the age of seventy-six. By that time, the winery produced approximately 8,000 gallons of vinifera and French-American wine made from a thirty-acre vineyard. Though his daughters initially intended to continue the winery operation, it was subsequently closed.[240]

On the opposite side of Frederick County from Tri-Mountain, Deer Meadow Vineyard opened in 1987 southwest of Winchester. The winery was the brainchild of Charles and Jennifer Sarle, who planted an experimental five-acre French-American and Chardonnay vineyard in 1983. Four years later, the pair opened their two-story winery built by hand over a two-year period, and constructed with timbers reclaimed from the property. By the mid-2000s, Deer Meadow's vineyard had grown to eight acres, and the winery produced wines made from both vinifera and French-American grapes. Notably, Deer Meadow was one of Virginia's only growers of the Stueben grape—a table variety developed at the New York State Agricultural Experimentation Station in Geneva, New York.[241]

Just south of Deer Meadow, North Mountain Vineyard opened in 1989 outside Tom's Brook in Shenandoah County. North Mountain's first plantings date to 1982, when Richard McCormack planted ten acres of grapes on his property, and the winery remains operational. McCormack, a former public affairs specialist for the Pentagon, purchased the property in 1981 after talking with Jim and Emma Randel at nearby Shenandoah Vineyards. The following year, McCormack planted ten acres of Chardonnay, Vidal Blanc, and Chambourcin grapes. In 1988, after selling grapes to other wineries for four years, McCormack completed a winery in the style of a Norwegian farmhouse. He operated the winery until 2002, when he sold it to Texas resident John Jackson and Jackson's mother and stepfather, Krista and Brad Foster. The three moved to Virginia to run the winery and have since revamped North Mountain's aging equipment and vineyards.[242]

In the early 1980s, a small vineyard in the southern Shenandoah Valley, MJC Vineyards, was established in the Catawba Valley of Montgomery County outside of Roanoke. MJC was the creation of Dr. Karl T. Hereford, who was then dean of Virginia Tech's College of Education. Plantings at MJC began in 1974, and by 1984 Hereford had produced 3,000 gallons of wine annually—nearly all of it in their garage and kitchen.

The Herefords often hosted Virginia Tech students during harvest, and Karl taught courses in winemaking and small vineyard development at the university. Hereford, who became interested in home winemaking as a hobby, was an early believer in what he termed the "inescapable" destiny of the emergence of Virginia as an important winegrowing state. As he told VDACS's marketing specialist Leeanne Ladin, "Not even the threat of a depression could impede the progress, chiefly because of the innate stability of the people in the industry."[243]

## Other Early Wineries

Pioneering Virginia vineyards and wineries were not just limited to the state's Piedmont and Shenandoah Valley regions. One of the state's more popular wineries, Lake Anna Winery, was founded by Anne and Bill Heidig near Lake Anna in southern Spotsylvania County. In 1981, the Heidigs began planting grapes following Bill Heidig's return from a business trip to France. With the help of consultants, including Linden Vineyards' Jim Law, the Heidigs sold their first crop in 1986. In 1990, after seeing several wines made with their grapes garner awards, the two opened Lake Anna Winery. The winery was located on the ground level of a circa-1940s dairy barn and, after adjustments to the floor and roof, the Heidigs located the tanks and other winemaking equipment on the barn's second level.[244]

The Heidigs' sons, Jeff Heidig and Eric Heidig, would later help run the winery, while Anne Heidig established herself as a civic leader and a force in the Virginia wine industry. She would eventually serve as, among other things, president of the Virginia Wineries Association, representative to the National Grape and Wine Initiative, a Spotsylvania County supervisor, and more. Throughout her professional career, however, she never underestimated the effort involved in the winemaking process. "People see it as a way to make a living in agriculture," Heidig said of winemaking in 1997. "People see vineyards as romantic and fun—but that is because they don't have one yet."[245]

A few years before Anne and Bill Heidig planted their first vines, nearby resident James Livingston planted an experimental vineyard in his backyard near Lake Anna in 1975. Grapevines purchased from a home gardening catalog, unsurprisingly failed miserably. Undeterred, Livingston enrolled in viticultural courses taught by Linden Vineyards' Jim Law and Ingleside Vineyards' Jacques Recht.[246]

In 1984, after experimenting with grape growing on a friend's property, Livingston purchased a twelve-acre hayfield in the Hartwood area of Stafford County, where he planted 2,300 Cabernet Sauvignon vines. The vines were subsequently replaced with French-American vines and, in 1989, he opened Hartwood Winery. Livingston constructed a winery building that mimicked many of the rural houses found in the Hartwood area, complete with a porch, tasting room, and barrel and fermenting rooms.[247]

Virginia's often overlooked and geographically isolated Eastern Shore offered at least one winery in the 1980s. As early as 1986, James D. "Jim" Keyes opened Accomack Vineyards outside the town of Painter in Accomack County.

In 1979, after restoring their 150-year old house, Keyes and his wife, Gerry Keyes, conducted numerous soil and climate tests. This prompted Keyes to plant an experimental plot of grapes and, by the late 1980s, he had two acres of 1,800 vinifera vines under cultivation. Regrettably, Keyes's flirtation with viticulture—which forced him to serve as sales manager, winemaker, and vineyard manager—was short-lived; in September 1992, Keyes announced that the winery would be closed due to a lack of capital and sheer exhaustion.[248]

South of the Appomattox River, in Virginia's "Southside," two wineries opened in the 1980s, Tomahawk Mill Winery and Rose Bower Vineyards. (Discussed later.) One of Southside's first wineries, Tomahawk Mill operates just north of Danville in Pittsylvania County. The winery was founded by a former environmental research scientist, Walter Crider, who purchased a former grist mill along Tomahawk Creek in 1975. Originally built in the 1880s by James Anderson, the mill ground corn and wheat for area residents until 1974, when Crider, Anderson's great-grandnephew, acquired the property. Crider operated the mill until 1988, when he planted a two-acre Chardonnay vineyard overlooking a nearby pond. Crider converted a portion of the mill into a tasting room, making the facility a unique attraction.[249]

## Mixed-Use Wineries

Because most of Virginia's wines were sold at the wineries themselves during the industry's rebirth, it was critical for wineries to develop unique ways to attract visitors and tourists. Meredyth Vineyards, for example, offered winery tours, outdoor murder-mystery dinner parties, and live music. Beginning in 1990, Barboursville Vineyards offered annual Shakespeare plays performed under the stars during the summer. Wineries also hosted weddings and other banquet-type events.[250]

Few early Virginia wineries successfully capitalized on wine-industry tourism more than Williamsburg Vineyard and Winery, which opened in 1988. The winery, founded by Belgian native Patrick Duffeler and his wife, Peggy Duffeler, is situated on a 290-acre farm located only a few miles from colonial Williamsburg. Duffeler, an entrepreneur and former president of a New York luxury perfume and soap importer, had fallen in love with Virginia during a visit as an exchange student as early as 1961. Once settled at their farm, which they named Wessex Hundred, the couple restored the grounds as well as its 250-year-old farmhouse. The Duffelers also planted a small three-acre Chardonnay vineyard in 1985 in coordination with Prince Michel's winemaker, Joachim Hollerith. After the Duffelers found that the temperatures across the property were moderated by its proximity to the York and James Rivers, the initial 1985 vinifera planting was quickly followed by the rapid construction of a winery.[251]

Williamsburg Winery released its first wine for sale in December 1987 and the winery opened to the public the following year. Though the Duffelers had "no ambition of being the premier-size winery in Virginia," over the next 25 years, the winery would grow into Virginia's largest, producing nearly 80,000 cases annually by 2010. During their ownership, the Duffelers have capitalized on Williamsburg Winery's access to the nearby, and lucrative, Williamsburg tourist market. The Winery complex was later expanded to include the wood-paneled Gabriel Archer Tavern, a full-service restaurant that evoked colonial charm and is named for Virginia's first lawyer and co-captain of the *Godspeed* (which landed in 1607).

In the early 2000s, the winery opened Wessex Hall, a reception venue with a large central hall, terra cotta tiles, and an 800-plus barrel storage room. The winery also features two rooms dedicated to American wine history. Perhaps the most significant expansion since the winery's founding was the 2007 opening of Wedmore Place, a twenty-eight-room European-style boutique luxury inn. The hotel features a full-service restaurant and a pool, as well as conference and wedding venues. The winery later obtained grapes from multiple vineyards across the state, including a twenty-four-acre vineyard in the Somerset area of Orange County and a fifteen-acre vineyard on the property of James Madison's Montpelier plantation. In 1991, the winery took over Culpeper's Dominion Wine Cellars (see below), and obtained grapes from that cooperative's growers until 2004. The winery's market share has grown into several eastern states. Patrick Duffeler, for his part, found himself immersed in the politics of the Virginia wine industry, serving on the Virginia Winegrowers Advisory Board and as president of the Virginia Wineries Association.[252]

In the southwestern region of the state, another ambitious multiuse winery, Chateau Morrisette, began to take shape in the late 1970s. In the foothills of the Blue Ridge Mountains in Floyd County, William and Nancy Morrisette purchased 1,000 acres in 1978. The property sat at an elevation of 3,000 feet, boasted enviable views of the surrounding Blue Ridge Mountains, and featured cool nights and warm days—perfect for grape growing. Hoping to help preserve southwest Virginia's rural landscape, the Morrisettes began growing a variety of crops, including Christmas trees, cauliflower, and two acres of French-American grapes.[253]

The couple's son David Morrisette subsequently enrolled in oenology and viticulture programs at Mississippi State University and, after his graduation in 1982, helped his parents construct a small winery that resembled a miniature

Rhine castle, using native stones on the property. With David Morrisette as winemaker, the family produced its first 2,000 gallons of commercial wines in 1982 under the label Woolwine Winery.[254]

Later renamed Chateau Morrisette, the winery expanded rapidly throughout the 1980s, largely thanks to its quality wines and striking location along the Blue Ridge Parkway. Sensing the need to offer a more complete wine experience, David Morrisette converted the original winery building into a restaurant in 1989, which he called Le Chien Noir at Chateau Morrisette ("The Black Dog at Chateau Morrisette"). The restaurant features stained-glass windows, outdoor dining, and locally produced American cuisine.[255]

Chateau Morrisette underwent a major renovation and expansion in 1999, including a new 32,365-square foot, 54-foot-tall wine production facility and hospitality center. "We're real excited about it... I've mortgaged myself for the next forty years for it," said David Morrisette of the expansion. The structure, at that time the largest-ever constructed of reclaimed timber in the United States, was built using local businesses and architects, could accommodate 150,000 gallons of wine in steel tanks and 50,000 gallons in oak barrels, and offered a twenty-two-ton grape press and a bottling press. The winery eventually grew into one of Virginia's largest, producing more than 60,000 cases of wine annually.[256]

## —Days of Wine & Poets—

It has been said that wine is bottled poetry. Perhaps no Virginia winemaker took that sentiment to heart more than Tom O'Grady, who founded Rose Bower Vineyards outside Hampden-Sydney in Prince Edward County. A Baltimore native, O'Grady joined the "back to the land" movement of the early 1970s and arrived in rural Prince Edward County in 1973 to serve as a part-time English lecturer at Hampden-Sydney College. Once in Virginia, O'Grady and his wife, Bronwyn O'Grady, moved to a 214-year-old farm that featured a home named Rose Bower, built by an Irish family in the 1750s.[257]

When he learned that vineyards had once flourished in the Hampden-Sydney area in the 1800s, O'Grady planted an experimental grape nursery in 1973. The following year, the O'Gradys planted a vinifera and French-American vineyard with the intent of growing grapes for home winemaking. Tom soon learned, however, that the type of wine he wished to produce would require extensive knowledge, so he proceeded to teach himself the art of viticulture. "I made myself read at least an hour a day," he told a reporter in 1983. "I also visited all the wineries I could see in California, Germany, New York, and France."[258]

The O'Gradys' Rose Bower Winery opened in 1979 and, by the late 1980s, the small winery produced a series of wines including the popular Hampden Forest Red—which he sold directly from his cellar. Rose Bower also hosted the Festival Aoutement (Harvest Festival) every August. In 1988, O'Grady constructed a chalet in the style of a small, oak timber-frame lodge. Featuring a French-style champagne cave in the basement, the chalet was rented to visitors for summer banquets and Hampden-Sydney students for lodging in the winter months.[259]

Following in the footsteps of Virginia's seventeenth-century poet and winemaker George Sandys, O'Grady is distinguished by his combination of work as a winemaker and literary talent as a poet. "The life of the vintner is not an activity for the timid at heart," O'Grady told a reporter in 1981. "Like poetry, winemaking takes someone who is three-quarters mad who has the courage to follow something through to completion."[260]

Indeed, O'Grady was first attracted to winemaking because of its symbolic language. "I see the vine as a metaphor for man," he once told a reporter. "It punctuates his life; it represents time, youth, suffering, and love." O'Grady believed that one could parallel any portion of one's life with work in a vineyard, choosing to see oneself as a voyager from subterranean caves of the fermenting room to the meadowlands of the vineyard.[261]

O'Grady authored a major poetry collection in 1978, *Establishing a Vineyard*, which consisted of sonnets that reflected on his efforts to create Rose Bower Vineyard. Self-described as a "book of marriages," the book was written in English and French. Many of the sonnets were penned for his wife, Bronwyn O'Grady, following their successful move to Virginia and their planting of the vineyard. Poems from the book were included in the narration for independent filmmaker Charlotte Schrader's 1981 short film *The Land Is a Woman*, which originally premiered at the Smithsonian Institution and later at the Albemarle Harvest Festival, and featured scenes filmed at the winery.[262]

A subsequent National Endowment for the Arts award encouraged Hampden-Sydney to name O'Grady a "Poet in Residence," which encouraged him to publish other works, including a 1986 essay on winemaking, *Wine Making Itself*. "You can't write poetry every day," he told a reporter, adding, "It's good to tend the vines and think about poems."[263]

In reviewing O'Grady's works, the *Vinifera Wine Growers Journal* penned a fitting tribute in one issue, "Most of us can find little poetry in digging trellis post holes or cultivating the earth, but Tom does, and it gives one more joy to viticulture dreams." O'Grady retired from Hampden-Sydney in 2008. As he told a reporter, "John Donne once said there is no great poetry without a great audience, and it's the same thing with wine. People must find out more about the wine, experiment, and embrace it …there needs to be tremendous local pride in the whole affair."[264]

## — *Cooperatives & Corporations* —

While Virginia witnessed an explosion of wineries during the 1970s and 1980s, few possessed the capital needed to purchase winemaking equipment, much less to construct, open, and operate a winery. Countless individuals were undoubtedly dissuaded from founding wineries due to the significant start-up costs, including the price of land, site preparation and development, infrastructure, and expertise—all of which could place winemaking dreams out of reach.

To address these shortcomings, two entities—Dominion Wine Cellars and Montdomaine Cellars—emerged in the early 1980s, composed of individuals who banded together to fund, establish, and run their own winery collectives. While neither entity persisted into the 2000s under its original design, these collectives symbolized the eagerness and ingenuity, shared by many during the industry's rebirth, to go to great and creative lengths to produce quality Virginia wine.

In June 1984, twelve central Virginia grape growers from diverse backgrounds met in Culpeper to discuss the legal aspects of forming a cooperative. The group had long contemplated a way to pool resources from multiple growers to finance a winery that would produce high-quality wine at a low cost. During the meeting, the attendees pledged capital totaling $190,000 to lay the groundwork; the growers also set forth three goals: the establishment of a safe market, a fair profit for the members' crops, and a fair profit for the cooperative's wines.[265]

After crafting the necessary legal documents, the Virginia Winery Cooperative, Inc., was born. Known better by its proprietary name, Dominion Wine Cellars, it became the nation's first cooperative formed with the intent to produce premium wine. Under its bylaws, profits made from Dominion's wines would be used to satisfy loans and provide income to the cooperative's shareholders.[266]

Pooling their resources, Dominion's members purchased a twenty-acre site outside Culpeper along Route 29 and secured a $750,000 loan from the Culpeper Industrial Development Authority to construct a winery. In May 1987, the cooperative completed an impressive $1.5 million, multistory winery complex featuring a Swiss chateau–style building with arches and gables, a walled courtyard entrance, and a three-acre demonstration vinifera vineyard.[267]

The cooperative counted some fifty-five acres under cultivation by the late 1980s, spread across its members' vineyards. This assortment of vineyards ensured the cooperative's access to different wine regions and growing conditions, and bestowed on its members the honor of overseeing Virginia's fourth-largest vineyard proprietorship. Dominion hired a professional winemaker, Steve Reeder, in 1986, and held its first crush later that year. The cooperative's first bottles of wine, which included Chardonnay, Cabernet Sauvignon, Riesling, and blends, were produced in 1987 under the Dominion Wine Cellars name.[268]

In 1991, after suffering financial difficulties in the wake of an economic recession and sensing the need for more professional oversight, Dominion entered into a management agreement with Williamsburg Winery. The marriage was particularly fortuitous for Williamsburg Winery, which needed additional grapes for its booming enterprise in the eastern part of the commonwealth. Under the agreement, Dominion's grapes were to be either processed at Dominion Wine Cellars in Culpeper or shipped to Williamsburg, while some of the juice would continue to be bottled under the Dominion label.[269]

In 1993, Williamsburg Winery purchased Dominion Wine Cellars outright and replaced the cooperative's small experimental vineyard with eleven acres of Vidal Blanc grapes. Though the Williamsburg Winery produced about 5,000 cases of wine under the Dominion label by 2001, all of the grape juice was transported to Williamsburg for winemaking. Difficulties in managing two winemaking facilities in different regions of the state forced Williamsburg Winery to shutter Dominion Wine Cellars in 2004.[270]

Dominion's winemaking equipment was subsequently transferred to Williamsburg and the chalet-style winery demolished to make way for a community college building. "The saddest thing, from my point of view," Williamsburg Winery owner Patrick Duffeler remarked to a reporter, "is seeing eleven acres of beautiful vineyards bulldozed down." The original cooperative members almost certainly would have agreed.[271]

Another response to the high cost of opening a winery was the 1980 establishment of Montdomaine Cellars, located south of Charlottesville in Albemarle County. The concept for the winery—Albemarle County's first farm winery—was generated by Steve Bowles, who, after selling his construction business, apprenticed with Gabriele Rausse and quickly came to believe that Virginia's red wines needed improvement.[272]

After Bowles planted a forty-acre vinifera vineyard in 1977 and worked with his brother Michael Bowles to manage its growth, Bowles and five other grape growers founded Montdomaine Cellars, Inc. Under its governing documents,

Montdomaine's members were obligated to sell their then-combined forty-eighty acres' worth of grapes to Montdomaine and, in return, members would benefit from group policies on vineyard management.[273]

In 1984, Montdomaine constructed a large warehouse-style winery built into a hill on Bowles's property, with a tasting room and offices located in a large nearby trailer; guests could take a one-hour tour of the vineyards and winery. In a nod to Virginia's viticultural heritage, Montdomaine's labels incorporated historically-significant imagery drawn from wine labels produced by the defunct Monticello Wine Company. Montdomaine even named one of its wines in honor of the former enterprise.[274]

The company hired Fresno State–trained oenologist Steve Warner as winemaker in 1984. Warner stayed until 1986, when he was succeeded by Shep Rouse. A Williamsburg native and one of the first University of California-Davis–trained viticulturalists to work in Virginia, Rouse got his start in the wine industry in his youth when he found a 1718 glass wine bottle near his home. After attending Washington and Lee University and studying in Germany, he worked in Williamsburg before heading to California for his master's degree in oenology.[275]

Early wines produced by Montdomaine enjoyed success. By 1988 its wines were not only the first Virginia wines to be featured in all Giant and Safeway grocery stores, but were featured on the Waldorf Astoria's "wine of the week" list—a first for a Virginia wine. That fall, two Montdomaine wines were selected by *The Washington Post* as the best on the East Coast. The company received the 1988 Governor's Cup for its 1984 Merlot, and in 1989, the White House selected Montdomaine's 1986 Chardonnay for a state dinner held at Monticello.[276]

By the late 1980s, Montdomaine's production levels had increased to 20,000 gallons and the property boasted a fifty-acre multi-site vineyard that was planted using advice found in Thomas Jefferson's *Garden Book*. In 1991, Montdomaine engaged a Springfield, Virginia, entrepreneur, Dennis Horton, to manage the winery's operations. Horton, who had long overseen his own vineyards, expanded Montdomaine's vineyards, constructed a large barrel room, and eventually purchased the outfit in January 1992 with an associate, Joan Beida. Thereafter, Horton and his wife Sharon Horton oversaw Montdomaine's vineyard management and research, while Beida and her son Tony Beida assumed responsibility for the winery's marketing and management.[277]

In 1996, Montdomaine was sold to former Jefferson Vineyards winemaker Michael Shaps, who would sell Montdomaine's grapes to other wineries for more than a decade until 2007, when he opened a custom crush winery at the facility and renamed Montdomaine Cellars as Virginia Wineworks, discussed below.

The Montdomaine label resurfaced in 2008 when Bowles and Shaps released a limited number of Viognier, Chardonnay, Cabernet Sauvignon, and Meritage wines. From Virginia Wineworks, Montdomaine's wines continue to be distributed statewide, where they evoke the spirit of both its original founders and the former Monticello Wine Company.[278]

## —Synergistic Benefits—

Virginia's maturing wine industry unexpectedly paid handsome dividends to the state's tourism sector in the 1980s, as out-of-state visitors flocked to the Old Dominion to experience an ever-expanding list of wineries and wine-related events. Virginia's developing "wine country"—nonexistent two decades before—provided an added amenity to the state's traditional tourist attractions of beaches, historic sites, and scenery. The industry's primary and secondary sectors—the production of grapes and the production of wine—inexorably led to the creation of ancillary services and goods, which, by the close of the 1980s, demonstrated that the industry comprised far more than a bulwark of wineries and vineyards.

Indeed, the young industry spurred a new soft economy of unique goods, trends, events, and jobs that revolved around the making and promotion of wine. New businesses developed to maintain the state's ever-growing winemaking infrastructure; new services were offered to help tourists identify and experience Virginia's wine country; and existing restaurants and retailers found it increasingly beneficial to feature Virginia wines on their menus and store shelves.

In 1982, for example, a full-time professional balloonist, Rick Behr, was brought to Charlottesville by the Boar's Head Inn owner John Rogan; there he offered hot air balloon tours from the resort above Albemarle County's vineyards. Behr piloted the resort's 140,000-cubic-foot balloon and after each tour—often dependent on where and when the balloon decided to land—guests were treated to champagne and Virginia wines.[279]

To familiarize consumers with the increasing quality of Virginia's wine offerings, the Virginia Wine of the Month Club was started in Fredericksburg in August 1988 by three brothers, Tommy, John, and Berkley Mitchell.[280]

The first of its kind in the commonwealth, the Wine of the Month Club sent members bottles of Virginia wine selected by a tasting panel of industry representatives. Members received recipes that paired well with the wines, discounts on purchases, wine-related gifts, and a subscription to the *Virginia Wine*

*Journal,* a concise newsletter detailing information about the state's wine industry and background information on each wine shipped.[281]

Dozens of specialty wine stores began offering Virginia wines. Among the most prominent was the Leesburg Vintner, which opened in downtown Leesburg in 1988. Founded by McLean native Mike Carroll, the store was among the first in the Commonwealth to carry a large selection of local wine.[282]

In addition, Virginia wines could increasingly—though still inconsistently—be found on the shelves of grocery stores. They enjoyed shelf space at one large, all-wine outlet, Total Beverage, which opened in Chantilly in 1992. The store, which featured approximately 4,000 wines, shook up the local retail wine market by helping to legitimize Virginia as a wine consumption market and breaking the habit of Northern Virginians venturing to nearby Washington, D.C., to purchase wine.[283]

The hospitality industry slowly followed suit, with some owners finding it advantageous to offer patrons a unique local tasting experience. During the 1980s, for example, the Homestead Resort offered annual wine competitions, seminars, tastings, and wine-pairing banquets during its Virginia Wine Weekend each April. Scottsville's High Meadows Inn offered complimentary Virginia wines, cheese, and crackers to guests—something later emulated by Albemarle County's prestigious Clifton Inn in the 1990s.[284]

The Virginia Winegrowers Advisory Board led efforts to encourage restaurants to carry Virginia wines through its "Virginia Wine Masters Course" and "Wine and the Bottom Line" restaurant training seminars. Two restaurants in Middleburg, the Red Fox Inn and Windsor House, put an array of Virginia wines on their wine lists, while the Colonial Williamsburg Foundation began offering the state's wines in its taverns.[285]

One of the more notable attempts to insert Virginia wine onto wine lists was made by the Trellis Restaurant in Williamsburg, which began hosting Virginia Vintners Barrel Tastings in 1981. The event, conceived to distinguish the restaurant from others in Hampton Roads, invited representatives of Virginia wineries to enjoy a gourmet meal prepared by head chef Marcel Desaulniers. Desaulniers and his diners discussed the pairing of wine and food selections as well as Virginia winemaking trends and personal experiences.[286]

Despite increased acknowledgement, it would be incorrect to suggest that most restaurants or stores were jumping at the chance to feature Virginia wines. It was an untested proposition for fledgling restaurateurs, as many of Virginia's young wines were yet subpar compared to their French and California counterparts. Washington, D.C.'s major liquor stores largely ignored Virginia wines and, if they stocked them, carried them only in small quantities on out-of-the-way shelves.

"As a restaurateur, I'd love to support them and I'd love to have more on my list," John Sherman, former owner of the Ashby Inn in Fauquier County, told a reporter in the mid-1990s of his decision not to feature Virginia wines. "But I've got a small list, and I've got to be fairly choosy. If I can't sell a wine, neither love of my state nor anything is going to argue to keep it on the list." This reluctance eventually dissipated as the quality of the state's wines improved.[287]

The revival of Virginia wine breathed new life into several of the state's historic public-trust properties. In 1989, George Washington's Mount Vernon unveiled private-label wines produced by Oasis Winery and Montdomaine Cellars, with bottles featuring a 1792 illustration of the mansion. Though growing grapes was almost certainly a low-priority pastime for the first president, the popular keepsake wines were sold in the estate's gift shop and its adjacent restaurant.[288]

In August 1985, the Thomas Jefferson Memorial Foundation announced the successful restoration of Jefferson's quarter-acre northeast vineyard at Monticello. The restoration followed a 1984 archaeological investigation that confirmed the vineyard's location and required experts, including Lucie Morton and Gabriele Rausse, to translate Jefferson's colonial-era terminology and variety descriptions. The investigation resulted in the Foundation's planting of some 250 vines of various varieties that Jefferson had first planted on the same land in 1807.[289]

The estate's vineyard restoration effort was followed three years later, in 1988, by Monticello celebrating its first grape harvest in nearly two centuries. Following Rausse's advice, Monticello's director of grounds and gardens, Peter J. Hatch, turned the nearly 1,350 pounds of healthy grapes into wine. The success of the vineyard restoration stimulated a new interest in Thomas Jefferson's love affair with wine, and led the estate to reestablish Jefferson's larger, 16,000-square-foot southwest vineyard in 1993, as well as to recreate his wine cellar in 2010. Wine later played a prominent role in Monticello's attractions, lectures, and cultural offerings. Tourists, for example, could often be seen strolling through both vineyards and the cellar, and buying wine made from the estate's grapes at the gift shop.[290]

## —*Increased Publicity & Literary Notoriety*—

Among the earliest proponents of Virginia's wine revolution were writers, journalists, and authors whose work publicized Virginia wine industry developments to a broad audience. They chronicled the rebirth of the state's wine industry in books, magazines, and newspapers. Prior to the industry's rebirth, little, if anything, had been written about Virginia wine. Where such accounts had appeared they were often negative, and referred either to the state's pre-Prohibition industry glories or to the low-budget wine empires of Captain Paul Garret or Richard's Wine Cellars.[291]

Perceptions began to change in 1973, with the publication of Leon D. Adams's critically acclaimed book *The Wines of America*. A native of Massachusetts, living in California at the time, Adams was a prolific wine writer and advocate for the American wine industry. Adams's book was widely read and cited by oenophiles and provided, for the first time, a comprehensive survey of North American wines. The work was the product of nearly two decades of travel across the continent, with a trained eye toward discovering large and small wine regions.[292]

Though Virginia's wine industry was in its infancy, Adams was persuaded by Lucie Morton to include a section on the Old Dominion, including a brief history of Virginia wine, colonial winemaking efforts, Jefferson's failed attempts, the discovery of the Norton grape, and more. Most important for the state's budding vinifera planters—many of whom still faced continuing governmental opposition—Adams asserted that premium wines could be made in the state. With Virginia's wine revolution in full bloom by the time of the book's third edition in 1985, Adams lent further encouragement to Virginia's industry by noting that the most rapid spread of winegrowing on the East Coast was occurring in the commonwealth.[293]

Adams passed away in September 1995, and was considered by the nation's wine connoisseurs to be *the* seminal wine historian of his era. His 1973 work heralded the beginning of a nationwide trend in promotional wine writing—one that would increase markedly over the following decades. That Virginia received recognition in such a volume is notable, for it provided welcome attention to the state at a time when its wine industry was in dire need of legitimacy. Henceforth, the commonwealth would increasingly find itself included in national wine guides, articles, magazines, surveys, books, atlases, and more.[294]

National and regional newspapers began carrying articles on Virginia wine increasingly throughout the 1970s and 1980s; mention was found in *The*

*Washington Post,* the *Richmond Times-Dispatch,* the *Washington Business Journal, The Washington Times, The Fredericksburg Free Lance–Star, The Hill,* and even *The New York Times.* Articles on Virginia wine could be found in magazines such as *Southern Living, Gourmet, Metropolitan Home,* and *Bon Appetit.* Montdomaine Cellars was featured in the February 28, 1989, issue of *Wine Spectator,* the first time a Virginia winery had been mentioned in that prestigious publication.

Much of the rebirth of the modern Virginia wine industry was cataloged by Pennsylvania writers Hudson Cattell and Linda Jones McKee in their magazine, *Wine East,* which was published between 1981 and 2008. The only magazine exclusively devoted to covering the wine industry in eastern North America, *Wine East* was an outgrowth of two earlier publications that had begun covering the industry as early as 1974. *Wine East* covered topical articles and results of wine competitions across eastern North America, was notable for its accuracy, and for being the first wine magazine to include a series of academic articles on varietals, wine, and vineyard development by Meredyth Vineyards' Archie Smith III, Ingleside Vineyards' Jacques Recht, and Linden Vineyards' Jim Law.[295]

Virginia's wineries also came to be well-represented in national wine books. In 1982, several wineries were selected for inclusion in Hudson Cattell and Lee Miller's *Wine: East of the Rockies,* which focused on the wine revolution occurring in the eastern United States. In a first, the book included photographs of the state's wineries and winemakers, including Shenandoah Vineyards' Emma and Jim Randel, Ingleside's Jacques Recht, Rapidan's Joachim Hollerith, and Barboursville's Gianni Zonin. Several Virginia wineries were also featured in Suzanne Goldenson's 1985 wine guide, *Vintage Places,* which, with the help of Leon Adams, noted that Virginia had already solidified its position as the "richest" area for wine touring in the Southeast.[296]

In 1985, Lucie Morton authored her pivotal work on eastern North American wine culture, *Winemaking in Eastern America,* which provided the first in-depth review of the revival of modern viniculture across the eastern two-thirds of the nation. Morton detailed winegrowing efforts in several states, discussed Virginia's wine history and the 1980 Virginia Farm Winery Act, and listed several of the state's relatively new wineries.[297]

Six Virginia wineries—Naked Mountain, La Abra, Barboursville, Montdomaine, Prince Michel, and Rapidan River—were selected for inclusion in Thomas K. Hardy's 1988 *Pictorial Atlas of North American Wines.* Another survey text published that year, Barbara Ensrud's *American Vineyards,* included a section on winegrowing in Virginia and contained many photographs from Oakencroft Vineyards and Monticello.[298]

In conjunction with its 1976 wine festival, the Vinifera Wine Growers Association produced *Jefferson and Wine*, a 200-page volume that provided what is believed to be the first comprehensive review of Jefferson's love of wine and his unsuccessful efforts to grow grapes in Virginia. The book, edited by Association founder Treville Lawrence, focused on Jefferson's work at Monticello, his association with Phillip Mazzei, and his correspondence with other viticulturalists.[299]

The most comprehensive volume of Virginia wineries came in 1987 with the publication of *Virginia Wine Country* by Hilde Gabriel Lee and Allan E. Lee. The Lees—then living in California—had just completed their first book, *Vintner's Choice*, when Leon Adams suggested the two write a volume on the growing Virginia wine industry. After some initial skepticism, the couple traveled to Virginia, where they found themselves entranced by the state's beauty and its growing wine industry. Their book catalogued the history of each of Virginia's then-thirty-five wineries and represented the first volume dedicated solely to Virginia's wineries. It also included recipes with wine pairings (many provided by the wineries themselves) as well as suggestions on restaurants and lodging destinations to complement a Virginia wine tour.[300]

In 1993, the Lees produced a second edition of their work, *Virginia Wine Country Revisited*, an account of Virginia's then-forty-six wineries. The following year, in 1994, the Lees published *Serve with Virginia Wine*, written to provide Virginia wine consumers with food pairing ideas for wines made from each of the thirty-seven varieties then known to be under cultivation in Virginia. Finally, in 2004, the Lees published *Virginia Wine Country III* after visiting more than eighty of the state's wineries. The Lees' four works remain perhaps the most important volumes in tracing the early revival of the modern Virginia wine industry. Such publicity helped to educate the public as to the increasing quality of Virginia wines and the significance of the state's wine industry.[301]

## —Virginia's Wine Revolution: Twenty Years On—

By the end of the twentieth century, the prospect of Virginia's emergence as a major wine producing state had been anticipated—repeatedly—for nearly four centuries. Neither trial and error during the colonial period nor a native variety industry during the nineteenth century had provided the type of lasting, successful wine industry envisioned by the state's earliest founders. The state's cheap wine industry flourished in years following Prohibition, but changing consumer preferences were fast rendering that business model outdated by the late 1960s.

When Virginia commenced its wine revolution, however, things were different. Thanks to modern technology, chemical sprays, and experimentation with grape varieties that worked well with the state's climate, Virginia managed to develop a growing cottage industry centered on quality wine grapes, and had done so in just two decades. From virtually nothing in 1967, the Old Dominion had solidified its position as the most promising wine-growing state in the Southeast by 1990.

Growth in the state's industry was dramatic, the rise in the number of wineries and vineyard acres nothing short of remarkable. From six licensed wineries and 286 acres of plantings in 1976, by 1991 Virginia would boast forty-three wineries. More than 170 commercial grape growers produced more than 2,000 tons of grapes from some 1,500 acres spread across more than half of Virginia's ninety-five counties. Public requests for information on the wine industry grew from 20,000 in 1982 to more than 125,000 in 1988.[302]

During this period, the young industry demonstrated tremendous improvement in the quality of its wine, and the state's wineries now ranged from large operations such as Prince Michel, to small farm wineries such as Farfelu—the winery that started it all. Vinifera plantings, led by Chardonnay, Riesling, and Cabernet Sauvignon, accounted for more than two-thirds of grape acreage across the state, while French-American and native varieties made up an ever-decreasing percentage of the balance. Prominent wine writers gave high ratings to several Virginia wines, and Virginia's production was rising rapidly.[303]

Industry groups such as the Vinifera Wine Growers Association, the Jeffersonian Wine and Grape Growers Society, the Virginia Wineries Association, and Virginia Vineyards Association advocated for better wine laws, reduced licensure fees, and increased state support. After years of opposition to and cynicism about growing wine grapes in the commonwealth, the public sector finally recognized that money spent supporting research, marketing, and promotion of the state's wines could yield significant benefits for Virginia's agricultural, tourism, and hospitality sectors.

Indeed, cooperative efforts by Virginia's government to aid the young industry distinguished Virginia from other states and provided an unmatched level of technical support. After the resistant attitudes of earlier years, Virginia winemakers credited both the state viticulturist and the state oenologist for playing a crucial part in improving the quality of wines, and they appreciated the work of the state's Wine Board Marketing Office in increasing the national relevance of the young industry. Through it all, Virginia winemakers persevered, often with remarkable results.

The industry began attracting a diverse group of entrepreneurs that included estate owners seeking additional income to maintain their hold on land, retired professionals looking for second careers, farmers seeking diversification, and wine lovers simply living out their oenological fantasies. With increasing land values and new residents hungry for specialty products, growing wine grapes also provided tremendous potential for a value-added alternative for farmers who were weary of traditional agricultural commodities such as beef, tobacco, corn, and apples.[304]

Virginia's wineries were increasingly seen as tourist attractions, drawing a record 220,000 visitors during 1991—nearly half from outside the state. Tourists found Virginia's unmatched array of historic attractions to be the perfect complement to their wine experience, with the state's peaceful back roads and rolling countryside equally as lovely as California's green and blond valleys. Virginia might not be Napa Valley, but the state's wine country proved as superb a setting for a few self-indulgent days.

Colorful wine festivals drew hordes of residents each weekend while introducing attendees to Virginia's wines. Immensely successful, they also afforded attendees the opportunity to meet the winemakers, stomp grapes, and explore the mystery of how wine is made. The 1985 Virginia Wineries Festival, sponsored by the Virginia Wineries Association, drew an estimated 10,000 people in sweltering ninety-degree July heat to stomp grapes and taste the best of nineteen Virginia wineries. By the late 1980s, cars with California license plates could be been seen prowling the festival parking lots.[305]

Amid such optimism, however, were doubts and questions. On which varieties should producers focus? What was needed to increase production and competitiveness? Would the state's wine industry persist, or would it vanish as suddenly as it had a century before?

Virginia's cottage wine industry, which produced 273,700 gallons of wine in 1991, posed no threat to California, the industry giant that produced some 330 *million* gallons a year. The quality of Virginia wines was yet uneven and the state's hot, wet, often unpredictable continental climate continued to pose challenges as winemakers attempted to grow varieties more accustomed to a Mediterranean environment.

Virginia wineries also wrestled with their ability to market themselves and attract new customers, both within the state and beyond. The commonwealth's wines remained curiosities to Virginians and non-Virginians alike and, despite increased recognition and showings at competitions, most remained unaware of the state's viticultural offerings. No national wine magazine had yet dedicated an issue to the state's wine industry and no international wine critic had yet paid a visit to the state.

Getting Virginians to try their own wines remained a perpetual challenge. Those who purchased Virginia wines were largely those already familiar with them or who had personal connections to the wineries. Virginians drank a mere ten million gallons of wine each year—a fraction of the estimated 127.7 million sipped by Californians. Even more alarming was the lack of loyalty to Virginia wines: less than 4 percent of all wine purchased in the commonwealth consisted of state wines.[306]

Most Virginia wines were sold at the wineries themselves, with distribution largely limited to in-state stores and some smaller stores and restaurants in metropolitan Washington, D.C. Despite an increasing recognition in supermarkets, specialty stores, and restaurants of Virginia wines, European, California, and New York vintages continued to dominate the bulk of wine lists, and there had been almost no market penetration outside of the state.[307]

Virginia's wines were also expensive, and represented a gamble for prospective purchasers who typically opted for better-known and cheaper brands. Virginia's wineries produced no bulk wines, which excluded them from a major portion of the cheaper wine market dominated by California's giants.

Many had suggested that the industry may have grown too fast in too short a time; the state was producing wine at one-third of its capacity and quality grape yields were roughly half of recommended production levels. Nearly a quarter of the state's grape acreage suffered from poor site selection, and it was clear that more expensive and comprehensive crop-management techniques were needed.[308]

Despite these setbacks, Virginia's winemakers and industry observers persisted: something magical was happening, and by 1990 a new wine industry had been created and a proper foundation had been laid for its sustainable future. Such potential had been nearly unimaginable just two decades earlier, but all it took was a weekend visit to what was now known as "Virginia wine country" to change the perception of even the most hardened disbeliever.

Virginia's two-decade wine rebirth may have been varied and unpredictable, but was nevertheless an exciting time and place to be for those who participated. It was a period when newly created wine advocacy groups fought for increased recognition and when the state's government finally answered the call. It was a place filled with entrepreneurial growers and winemakers who relished the challenges presented by Virginia's terrain and climates. And, yes, it was a time when Virginians first envisioned that someday their state might actually compete successfully against the nation's largest wine producers.

Just as Virginia has perhaps always been "revolutionary," the commonwealth during this period was a place for those willing to fight—and fight hard—for Virginia's spot among the world's great wine regions. Much work remained and much more would be accomplished in the years to come. But, finally, thanks to the tireless efforts of Virginia's revolutionary wine pioneers, the Old Dominion appeared to be waking to the viticultural promise that was Thomas Jefferson's dream.

49. Cardinal Point winemaker and vineyard manager Tim Gorman.

50. Chrysalis Vineyards' owner Jennifer McCloud inspecting her beloved Norton grapes.

51. Wine-themed promotional sign in downtown Purcellville highlighting Loudoun County's self-branded, if not well-deserved, position as "DC's Wine Country."

52. Wine entrepreneur Chris Pearmund.

53. Former Governor Bob McDonnell, left, speaks with British wine writer and consultant editor of Decanter magazine Steven Spurrier at the Executive Mansion in Richmond as Maureen McDonnell looks on.

54. Future President of the United States Donald Trump announcing the purchase and rechristening of Kluge Estate Winery and Vineyard in October 2011 as (left to right) Patricia Kluge, William Moses, and Governor Bob McDonnell look on.

55. After a protracted zoning battle, the Wiles Family and members of the Fairfax County Board of Supervisors celebrate the opening of Paradise Springs Winery in Clifton in 2010.

56. Swedenburg Estate Vineyard owner Juanita Swedenburg.

57. Viticultural experimenters Sharon and Dennis Horton standing in front of their award-winning Viognier vineyard in 1993.

58. From left to right, Veramar Vineyard owners Della and Jim Bogaty, Delegate J. Randall Minchew, Senator Jill Holtzman Vogel, and Commissioner of Agriculture Todd Haymore unveil the new Shenandoah Valley American Viticultural Area highway sign, part of a 2012 McDonnell administration initiative.

59. Former Governor George Allen (center, back row) with representatives of the Winegrowers Advisory Board in the mid-1990s.

60. Virginia's historic trust properties, like Monticello above, have increasingly looked to wine-themed events to generate visitors and revenue for historic preservation efforts.

61. Luca Paschina, winemaker at Barboursville Vineyards.

62. David King founded King Family Vineyards with his wife Ellen in the mid-1990s.

63. Skip and Cindi Causey's impressive Potomac Point Winery in Stafford County is reflective of the changing physical and experiential characteristics of Virginia wineries in terms of tasting room design, special events, and culinary offerings.

64. By the early 2000s, Virginia's wine festivals had grown into major promotional events often attracting tens of thousands at a single event. Shown here is the Town Point Wine Festival, in downtown Norfolk.

65. Breaking away to wineries along the Blue Ridge Parkway, such as Chateau Morrisette Winery, is a popular pastime across the commonwealth.

66. The Virginia Wine booth at the 2014 London International Wine Fair signaled the wine industry's broader international appeal and marketing efforts.

67. Wine bottles at Albemarle County's Jefferson Vineyards.

68. Rendering of the unbuilt Virginia French Winery, first proposed by French investors in 1987.

69. New Kent Winery, located east of Richmond, is the centerpiece of a larger mixed-use development project featuring golf courses and 2,500 homes set among vineyards.

70. A new community breaks ground adjacent to Bull Run Winery in Northern Virginia, highlighting the industry's broader appeal to homebuyers, and harkening back to Virginia's colonial era viticultural settlements.

71. Loudoun County winemaker Doug Fabbioli has worked to establish a sustainable rural economy in Northern Virginia through his winery, establishment of the Piedmont Epicurean and Agricultural Center, leading educational classes, and more.

72. Veteran winemaker Michael Shaps.

73. Several wineries, such as Madison County's Early Mountain Vineyards, have raised expectations in terms of quality architectural design and furnishings as well as the movement of visitors between indoor and outdoor spaces.

74. Acknowledging the benefits of wine-related tourism as a key component of the commonwealth's overall economic development strategy, a Virginia wine scene was, at long last, featured on the front cover of the state's travel guide for the first time in 2011.

# 4

# *End of the Beginning: 1990–Present*

BY THE BEGINNING of the 1990s, it seemed that the long years of struggle simply to establish a viable wine industry in Virginia were over. The challenges that would face the commonwealth's vintners would be of a different nature but the future looked bright.

Indeed, Sunday, November 17, 1991, was a watershed moment for the wine industry around the world. That evening, as the United States was reeling from an economic recession, the end of the Cold War, and the beginning a "hot war" in the Persian Gulf, millions of Americans tuned in to the popular prime-time television show *60 Minutes* to hear a story on the "French Paradox." The report described the altogether curious phenomenon of the French experiencing exceptionally low rates of coronary heart disease, despite their fatty diets and notoriously high levels of cigarette usage. The premise of the story was that the French people's moderate consumption of wine, and especially red wine, cut their risk of cardiovascular heart disease by up to 50 percent.[1]

Almost overnight, Americans stocked up on their favorite vintages. The *60 Minutes* report, while not in and of itself singularly responsible for boosting wine sales nationwide, lent a hand to an American alcohol industry that, at the time, was in the throes of a public relations battle over the evils of drunk driving. The story also offered positive signs for Virginia's wine industry, as increased sales, combined with the entrepreneurial spirit that had led to the industry's modern rebirth in the 1970s and 1980s, allowed the commonwealth's winemakers to continue experiencing steady growth into the 1990s.[2]

After the dawn of the new millennium, the expansion of Virginia's wine industry went into overdrive, and winemakers from beyond the state's borders began to look to Virginia with increased respect and optimism. The industry had evolved, in fits and starts, into a valued component of the state's economy, the number of wineries had grown nearly six-fold since 1991, and the amount of wine produced more than quadrupled.

For all the positives during this period of expansion, however, it was easy to overlook the myriad challenges that threatened the industry's continued development. The truly modern industry was barely thirty years old. As a result of its impressive pace of growth—especially rapid after 2000—the Virginia wine industry confronted issues commonly faced by older, more established wine regions—but without their experience. There was a need to increase the sheer quantity of high-quality fruit, for example, and to find better ways to market to in-state residents. Of utmost concern was the question of how to deal with the state's rigid alcohol distribution laws in the face of the changing needs of wine producers and consumers, and how to expand the industry in times of economic troubles. Questions arose as to how the industry would participate in the digital marketplace, whether and how it would heed calls for environmental sustainability, and ways Virginia wine might be promoted outside the state. Each problem, of course, generated an array of potential answers, personal opinions, and legal ramifications.

By 2017, any lingering doubts about the long-term viability of the commonwealth's modern wine industry, or concerns over its ability to overcome challenges and rise to the occasion, were answered by a growing legion of more than 8,200 winemakers, winery owners, seasonal laborers, marketing specialists, lobbyists, filmmakers, writers, artists, and an estimated 2.25 million annual tourists, who could affirmatively agree on one thing: Virginia's wine industry was, finally, here to stay—and it was prospering.

## —Growing Pains—

The optimism surrounding the industry's expansion nevertheless masked complex issues such as the compatibility between the increasing number and size of Virginia wineries and their sometimes-annoyed neighbors. Industry advocates had long argued that wineries were perfectly harmonious with the tranquility of the Virginia countryside, that they reinvigorated rural economies, and that they played a central role in thwarting suburban development. "It's an agricultural product, but it's one that integrates nicely with our environment," said Mary Davis-Barton of the Virginia Wine Marketing Office. "Most people don't mind having a vineyard or a winery next door."[3]

As the industry grew, however, conflicts emerged between those who saw winemaking as a genteel undertaking, and those who saw wine as "rock and roll." Many wineries continued to eschew activities other than wine production, while others expanded beyond bottling and tasting businesses into ever-larger operations, attracting thousands of visitors and hosting well-attended events that might include loud music, wine dinners, harvest festivals, car or pet shows, even the occasional helicopter tour—all of which increased traffic on rural roads. There was a reason: in some cases, these events could provide more than half of a winery's annual income and were seen by owners as critical to the solvency of their operations.[4]

Special events varied as much as the wineries themselves: some offered polo matches, kayak tours, even yoga workouts, followed by outdoor wine tastings and tours. Barboursville Vineyards, Williamsburg Winery, and Chateau Morrisette opened full-service restaurants, while others were designed from the outset to incorporate restaurants, conferences, and other large events. Weddings, naturally, proved particularly lucrative; some "wedding factory" wineries were booked for grape-centered nuptials every Saturday from April to October. They scrambled to hire full-time event managers and wedding coordinators during the spring and fall months, and purchased catering equipment, chairs, tents, and more. "Either more folks are getting married or there are fewer places to host them," Ingleside Vineyards owner Doug Flemer happily observed in 2009.[5]

As wineries diversified from a primary focus on beverage production to larger business operations centered (and sometimes not so centered) on wine, worries rose that the reputation of Virginia wine might suffer if the industry came to be associated with noisy events and traffic jams. "These extraneous activities would trash the reputation of Virginia wines along with the countryside and have a disastrous effect upon agriculture and communities," wrote *Washington Post* wine critic James Conaway, who was particularly critical of promotional events at Fauquier County's (now abandoned) Oasis Winery. Event proponents countered that the functions brought in tourist dollars and helped Virginia become a wine and food destination. "If [the complaining neighbors] want to live in a desert, let them live in a desert…. They knew we were here when they moved here," said Oasis Winery's Dirgham Salahi. Barboursville's general manager, Luca Paschina, agreed: "If I have cows that howl at the moon all night, I don't want to have neighbors tell me, 'Hey, move your cows.'"[6]

Cries over winery events were perhaps loudest in Fauquier County, where, in 2000, citizens persuaded the Board of Supervisors to impose strict noise limits on the county's wineries. The adoption of Fauquier's regulations served as the opening salvo in what became a contentious, ongoing statewide debate over what special events, if any, should be permitted at rural wineries. Things came to a head in 2006 when the General Assembly sided with winery owners and passed legislation that all but exempted farm wineries from local regulations governing noise and private parties. Three years later, the legislature provided yet further protections for those wineries.[7]

Seeking a way around the statutory changes, Albemarle and Fauquier counties amended zoning ordinances to limit winery activities without regard to the state legislation. In November 2009, Albemarle County considered an ordinance that would have limited large events to no more than fifty people, restricted event hours, and allowed only one special event per year. In response to strong resistance from the wine industry, the proposal was revised to require special permits for events with attendance of more than 200. The proposal was subsequently adopted by the Board of Supervisors in May 2010.[8]

Matters remained more contentious in Fauquier, where, beginning in 2009, county supervisors held public hearings to consider a long list of restrictive rules that would limit wine tasting hours, prohibit outdoor amplified music, and limit winery events based on size, frequency, and time of day. During hearings on the proposed changes, supervisors heard from residents weary of crowds and noise, including Linden Vineyards' Jim Law: "I'm a farmer. I'm not an entertainment person," he said. "You don't need to be doing all this. You can be profitable simply by farming."

In July 2012, after nearly five years of study, public hearings, and deliberations, the Board of Supervisors voted to limit wineries to two large events per month depending on the size of a winery's property and road access. One month later, Richmond attorney Philip Carter Strother (himself owner of Philip Carter Winery) filed a lawsuit against the county on behalf of ten wineries challenging the regulations. As Strother noted of the new regulations, "It's all grossly unfair and driven by a group of super-wealthy people who don't care about small business, only about maintaining the views from their 1,000-acre estates." A second lawsuit was filed by Barrel Oak Winery, but settled in February 2013 after the county granted it the right to hold an additional twelve special events per year.[9]

While many wineries, neighbors, and localities deliberated noise ordinances and special-event limitations, others struggled in jurisdictions that prohibited wineries altogether. This proved particularly true in the late 2000s in Northern Virginia, as would-be winemakers crept ever closer to the sophisticated and wealthy populations of metropolitan Washington, D.C. Until 2005, Northern Virginia's wineries were located a healthy distance from the nation's capital; more adjacent communities like Fairfax and Prince William counties had never considered that their jurisdictions might one day be home to wineries. However, in March of that year, Rappahannock Cellars' vintner John Delmare and Pearmund Cellars' owner and entrepreneur Chris Pearmund approached Prince William County's government with the idea of opening the county's first winery.

The two proposed to open the Winery at La Grange, a boutique winery to be located on twenty scenic acres northwest of Haymarket. The proposal caught Prince William County off-guard. While the county's zoning ordinance had long permitted a host of separately-listed uses traditionally found at wineries, including vineyards, winemaking, and food establishments, the zoning ordinance did not include a "winery" as a single, all-encompassing use; wineries were thus determined by the county to be prohibited. Delmare and Pearmund worked with Prince William officials to amend the ordinance, and after the zoning change, the two moved forward with their plans. They renovated a stately circa-1790s brick farmhouse to serve as their tasting room and constructed a barrel room behind the farmhouse. La Grange's choice location was successful; situated just north of heavily traveled Interstate 66, La Grange instantly became the closest winery to the nation's capital, virtually guaranteeing immense market exposure.[10] Since La Grange opened, wineries have blossomed in suburban locales across Virginia. While each came to understand the nuances of living in proximity to neighbors, noise, and suburban sprawl, few wineries have experienced a closer call with zoning regulations and the resistance of suburban homeowners than Fairfax County's Paradise Springs Winery.

A partnership between Kirk Wiles and his mother, Jane Kincheloe Wiles, Paradise Springs was proposed for a quiet corner of southwest Fairfax County near the town of Clifton, until the Wileses received a letter from Fairfax County's zoning staff claiming that the operation was the functional equivalent of industrial manufacturing and was, therefore, not permitted. The Wileses appealed the letter, arguing, among other things, that the General Assembly's actions protecting wineries trumped Fairfax County's prohibition of same. The matter received scant notice until *The Washington Post* blasted the story across the region in December 2008. The article caught the immediate attention of the county's Board of Supervisors, which at their next meeting publicly rebuked zoning officials and voted to amend the county's zoning ordinance to permit wineries.[11]

Plans for Paradise Springs divided not only Fairfax County's government, but the surrounding community. Several neighbors in nearby subdivisions objected to the Wileses' plans out of fear that the winery would bring traffic, drunk drivers, and large events. One local environmental advocacy organization, which had previously spoken out against additional residential development in the area, suggested its preference for new homes on the Wileses' property rather than a winery. "[New homes are] the devil we know," said Occoquan Watershed Coalition president Jim Bonhivert, "The winery is the devil we don't know."[12]

In January 2009, the Wileses received preliminary approval for a state license from the Virginia Alcoholic Beverage Control Board. In its ruling, the

ABC hearing examiner said that state law trumped local ordinances, and that concerns about unsafe roads were unfounded. Paradise Springs' ribbon-cutting ceremony was held in January 2010, and in its first year in operation, the winery's Chardonnay was awarded the 2010 Virginia Governor's Cup. A second Fairfax County winery, the Winery at Bull Run, opened in 2012 near Manassas National Battlefield Park. The Civil War–themed winery, which featured several Civil War relics collected by proprietors Jon and Kimberly Hickox, was spared the zoning struggles of their sister Fairfax County winery.[13]

In addition to the need to abide by local zoning ordinances, wineries sometimes found themselves struggling against the sometimes-ambiguous but powerful private agreements between property owners that take the form of conservation easements and restrictive property covenants. Such was the experience of Kate and Charles Marterella, who purchased property in Bellevue, a large-lot subdivision in Fauquier County in 2000. Comprising hundreds of acres, Bellevue's lots were encumbered by private covenants that restricted land uses in the neighborhood. In 2004, Bellevue's homeowners' association granted the Marterellas approval to operate a vineyard and winery on their property. Concerned about traffic and visitors, however, the association explicitly prohibited the couple from selling wine from their house. The Marterellas opened their winery to the public in 2006. They also advertised in the media, erected signs on their property, and opened a tasting room that included a restaurant, a gift shop, and an entertainment area.[14]

The homeowners' association issued warnings to the Marterellas and, when those warnings were ignored, the association filed for an injunction in the Fauquier County Circuit Court. The Marterellas cited the example of a nearby winery also located in Bellevue, Mediterranean Cellars, which had received the association's approval to operate in 2002. In June 2009, following a three-day trial, the jury found for the Marterellas. The judge, however, set aside the jury verdict, a rarely taken step, finding that covenants prohibited the commercial elements of the Marterellas' operation and that Kate Marterella was not a credible witness. The Marterellas mothballed their business, appealing the judge's ruling to the Supreme Court of Virginia, which upheld the jury's verdict, in May 2012.[15]

Another case related to private restrictions came about after Loudoun County's Chrysalis Vineyards constructed a new farm building on land that was subject to a conservation easement. Chrysalis intended to include a creamery, bakery, and tasting room within the building. The holder of the easement, Ducks Unlimited, filed a lawsuit in January 2013 alleging that the building and its intended use was contrary to the easement's terms. Chrysalis responded that the building and its use were explicitly permitted commercial agricultural uses under the easement. The winery won in circuit court and again before the Virginia Supreme Court, which ruled in 2016 that any ambiguities within conservation easements, unless explicitly prohibited in the easement, should be resolved with deference to the free use of land.*

Whether at the state, local, private homeowners' association, or conservation organization level, increased complaints and growing resistance to some wineries demonstrated a rising sentiment that wineries could disrupt the Virginia countryside rather than foster its preservation. While this fractured an otherwise congenial industry, many of Virginia's winemakers, such as Tarara's Jordan Harris, took note, fearing that their craft might one day be relegated to a secondary position behind special events. No matter where one stood on the issue, almost everyone agreed that skirmishes between neighbors and wineries was, as vineyard consultant Lucie Morton once noted to a reporter on the subject, "the last thing that the wine industry in Virginia needs."[16]

## —Prohibition's Ghost: Challenges to Direct Shipping—

As the 1990s progressed, Virginia's vintners not only faced zoning and restrictive covenant battles with local governments and neighbors, they occasionally tussled with Virginia's ABC system and its roots in Prohibition. Since Prohibition's repeal in 1934, the commonwealth had prohibited distilleries, breweries, and wineries from selling directly to consumers, restaurants, and retailers. Virginia's "three-tiered system" stipulated that beverage producers could sell only to wholesalers and retailers could buy beverages only from a wholesaler. The consumer was obliged to buy from the retailer.[17]

With the passage of the 1980 Farm Winery Act, however, Virginia allowed its wineries—and its wineries alone—to bypass the three-tiered system and act as their own wholesalers and distributors, so long as they were conducting business inside the commonwealth. This exemption permitted Virginia's wineries to sell directly to in-state consumers and retailers, and provided much-needed exposure as the industry grew. Despite this special treatment, Virginia's wineries were still prohibited from directly shipping wine to consumers outside Virginia, while the commonwealth's residents were forbidden from receiving wine directly from out-of-state wineries. Wholesalers were still essential for interstate sales, a practice that proved costly and problematic for Virginia's smaller wineries.[18]

* *Wetlands America Trust v. White Cloud Nine Ventures*, L.P. Attorneys Andrew Burcher and Michael Kalish represented the winery and are members of author's law firm.

As the 1990s ended, the growing popularity of the Internet, coupled with a nationwide demand for wine, increased tension between the commonwealth's wineries, distributors, and government. Virginia's struggles with its anachronistic three-tiered system mirrored a national reality: by the dawn of the new millennium, wineries faced a confusing nationwide puzzle of often-conflicting regulations. Not only did this welter of requirements make it difficult for the state's smaller wineries to find wholesalers willing to distribute their wines outside Virginia, the smaller wineries viewed wholesalers as unnecessary middlemen who drove up costs, sometimes as much as 25 percent per bottle, and made Virginia wines less competitive. With their very existence threatened, Virginia's wholesalers, together with other advocates of interstate shipping bans, rallied around the retention of the three-tiered system, expressing concern about underage drinking and the reduced ability of states to collect excise and sales taxes via the Internet, and claiming that nationwide self-distribution by small wineries would lead to industry-wide chaos. [19]

Smaller wineries found the wholesaler's assertions specious, constituting nothing more than state-sponsored economic protectionism. They pointed out that little evidence existed of widespread sales to underage drinkers, and that such arguments made no sense considering that direct shipments of Virginia wine to in-state consumers was legal. "I can't order wine directly from Caymus in California, but I can order it directly from Prince Michel in Culpeper?" asked George Mason University economics professor Donald Boudreaux. "Unless the politicians can explain why Virginia wine is less harmful to minors than is non-Virginia wine, the [wholesalers'] 'we-want-to-protect-our-children' argument is nothing more than a ruse."[20]

These conditions could not last forever. Across the nation at the close of the 1990s, America's small wine producers forged strategic alliances with free-trade consumer groups, both of which sought the elimination of shipping and distribution hurdles for a wide range of consumer products. Wine wholesalers teamed up with social conservatives and economic protectionists to retain direct shipping bans. Both sides initiated lawsuits hoping to generate conflicting rulings and compel either the Supreme Court of the United States or Congress to address the issue on a national scale.

One of the first of these legal challenges came in November 1999, when Williamsburg resident Robin Heatwole and Clint Bolick, a Northern Virginia attorney with a commitment to free enterprise, joined three wineries in Texas, California, and Oregon to sue Virginia's ABC Board, challenging the constitutionally of Virginia's direct shipping laws. The suit arose after Heatwole tried to order wine directly from the three wineries by mail, and was politely refused by each one. The case, *Bolick, et al. v. Roberts, et al.*, was decided in March 2002 when District Court Judge Richard L. Williams ruled that Virginia's ban on the shipment of wine from out-of-state alcohol producers to Virginia residents violated the Commerce Clause of the U.S. Constitution and was unconstitutional. Judge Williams ordered the commonwealth to halt enforcement of its direct shipping ban and, at the same time, declared unconstitutional a 1984 law that permitted only the sale of Virginia wines in ABC stores, concluding that the law improperly gave an advantage to Virginia producers of alcoholic beverages over out-of-state producers. [21]

The wholesaler lobby quickly condemned Williams's decision, arguing it ignored the Twenty-First Amendment to the U.S. Constitution, which gave states plenary control over the alcohol trade within its borders. "If [Judge Williams's ruling] were sustained, there would be no such thing as an illegal sale of alcohol by anybody to anybody else, regardless of age or other circumstances," claimed the Virginia Wine Wholesalers Association's attorney, Walter A. Marston. He added that the judge's ruling would eventually lead to the proliferation of "nip joints and bootleggers." The Wine and Spirits Wholesalers of America released a similar statement claiming that allowing direct shipping would undermine Virginia's ability to collect taxes on alcoholic beverages and result in sales to minors. [22]

Unsurprisingly, Virginia's smaller wineries and wine enthusiasts hailed Judge Williams's ruling. Attorney Matthew Hale, who had represented the plaintiffs in the case, praised the decision as "a slap in the face to the beer and wine wholesalers who, for years, have had a state-authorized monopoly on the sale of alcoholic beverages in Virginia." State officials filed an appeal to the United States Court of Appeals for the Fourth Circuit, and Judge Williams agreed to a stay of his ruling, pending the outcome of the appeal or, alternatively, to allow time for consideration of a legislative remedy at the 2003 General Assembly Session. [23]

During that session, the legislature passed a bill that permitted Virginia wineries to ship directly up to two cases of wine or beer per month to consumers in thirteen specific states with which Virginia enjoyed direct reciprocal shipping rights, including California, Washington, and Oregon. Commonly referred to as "reciprocity," the new law was seen as a loss for the commonwealth's wine and beer wholesalers. In light of the new reciprocity law, the Fourth Circuit remanded the case to Judge Williams for review in light of the new statute. However, in April 2005, Judge Williams held that Virginia's reciprocity legislation insufficiently addressed his earlier ruling. He ruled it to be unconstitutional, among other things, for Virginia to allow its wineries to be treated differently than out of state wineries. [24]

Williams's ruling on remand alarmed the commonwealth's smaller wineries, who, in turn, feared that the General Assembly might cave in to the wholesale lobby and eliminate all direct shipping licenses. Two competing bills were thus introduced during the 2006 General Assembly Session: one by Staunton delegate Christopher B. Saxman and one by Fairfax delegate David B. Albo. Saxman's bill would have permitted small wineries (which the legislation classified as those that produced fewer than 100,000 cases annually) to distribute their products directly to Virginia consumers. It would have applied to 98 percent of the nation's wineries, including all of Virginia's wineries.[25]

Fearing the potential destruction of their industry, the wholesale lobby vigorously campaigned against Saxman's proposal. This time, though, the wholesalers downplayed their oft-repeated arguments that their industry protected children and ensured excise tax transparency. Instead, the wholesalers maintained that they, like small wineries, were also small, family-owned businesses. They elected to rally around Delegate Albo's bill, which—as the vintners had feared—proposed the elimination of all self-distribution rights for Virginia's wineries. Albo's bill also included the *expansion* of the wholesale industry by creating a new class of smaller distributors in which wineries would be forbidden from holding an ownership interest.[26]

After vigorous lobbying by the wholesalers, the General Assembly approved a version of Albo's bill, which forbade Virginia wineries from selling directly to restaurants and retailers. Signed into law by Governor Tim Kaine (2006–2010), the new law reversed years of self-distribution rights afforded under the 1980 Farm Winery Act, and for the first time placed Virginia's wineries at a competitive disadvantage with its northern neighbor, Maryland, which had recently acted to permit all small in-state and out-of-state wineries to self-distribute.[27]

Winery owners, nearly all of whom had developed business models predicated on the right to self-distribute to retailers and restaurants, expressed dismay: "We don't have the lobbyists or the money to fund the lawyers that distributors do," said Jack Weaver, co-manager of Dye's Vineyards, a four-acre operation in Russell County. "It sounds like good ol' boys taking care of some good ol' boys." Christensen Ridge winemaker J. D. Hartman agreed: "It's just outrageous that it got away from us," he said. "We used to self-distribute in sixty markets, Richmond, Charlottesville, Virginia Beach, and Northern Virginia. Now all that's completely shot." The wholesalers, of course, were thrilled. Wholesaler attorney Walter Marston responded that most small wineries failed to account for the costs of self-distribution. "If [the wineries] want to change the system, they've got to show something is wrong…something needs to be fixed."[28]

But something was indeed wrong, and as 2006 wore on, it became clear that the law benefited only the wholesale lobby. By that winter, Virginia's wineries were selling their wines through distributors, if they could find them, at lower prices. Virginia's restaurants and retailers also saw their stocks of Virginia wines dwindle while the price of Virginia wines increased. Newspaper editorials and letters to editors across the state, nearly all of which called for corrective action during the 2007 General Assembly session, began to appear with some frequency.[29] As noted in one editorial from the influential *Richmond Times-Dispatch*,

> Virginia's wineries are willing to compete for business fair and square. Virginia's wholesalers evidently are not. The Assembly's eagerness to prop up the latter at the expense of the former suggests some sour-grape legislators' minds have turned to vinegar. Next year they should come to their senses and allow all to compete through self-distribution.[30]

A more-impassioned plea came from Jim Vascik, co-owner of Valhalla Vineyards near Roanoke, who wrote in an op-ed piece in the *Roanoke Star*:

> As to the ability of foreign wineries to sell and compete in Virginia, I say Virginia wineries first, wineries in the rest of the United States next, and be damned to any help to the foreigners…. Call or write your Virginia legislators and tell them: Free Virginia grapes![31]

The chorus of those opposing the 2006 law grew so loud that the General Assembly once again visited direct distribution during its 2007 session. Contrary to its somnambulance just the year before, the wine industry came to Richmond prepared to fight against the influence of the wholesale lobby, organizing grass-roots campaigns and collecting thousands of petition signatures for a change.

During the session, Senator Emmett Hanger concieved, and Delegate Chris Saxman and Powhatan Senator John Watkins proposed what could only be described as an entirely novel idea: the creation of a nonprofit corporation within the Virginia Department of Agriculture and Consumer Services that would provide distribution services for up to 3,000 cases annually for all wineries, regardless of their location or size. Reaction from wholesalers was dismissive. Even before he had read the bill, Charles Duvall of the Virginia Wine Wholesalers Association admitted his organization would probably oppose it, and that it was nothing more than "[s]ame horse, different color," comparing it to Saxman's proposal the previous year.[32]

By the close of the session though, the General Assembly had adopted Saxman and Watkins's proposal, and gave the new distribution entity a name:

the Virginia Winery Distribution Company. Launched in April 2008 at a ceremony at King Family Vineyards, the VWDC allowed smaller wineries to make direct sales of up to 3,000 cases per year to stores and restaurants by acting as their own distributors, as agents of the state, thus without running afoul of the three-tiered ABC system.

The VWDC distribution model was relatively simple: any store or restaurant looking to purchase Virginia wine could place an order through VWDC, which would forward the order to the winery. Upon receipt, winery employees would place the wine "at rest" in a space that was technically leased to VWDC. While the 2007 law was silent on the standards required for the "come to rest" areas, most wineries chose small areas—a room, a shelf, a closet, or even dog cages—each of which was specifically marked as being leased to the VWDC. The act of "coming to rest" formally transferred the wine from the producer (the winery) to the distributor (the state-run VWDC). Once the product had been technically transferred by this method, the same winery employees who placed it there then acted as official VWDC distributors and delivered the product directly to the customer.[33]

More than seventy wineries joined VWDC within its first month of operation, and by 2017, more than 180 wineries had signed on. VWDC's implementation was closely watched by industry observers nationwide, and the organization has grown with the industry and responded effectively to changes in the marketplace. Governed by a board composed of two wholesalers, two winery representatives, and the VDACS commissioner, VWDC ushered in a modest détente between the Old Dominion's wholesaler and winery industries—mutual victims of antiquated Prohibition-era laws. Instead of feuding, both industries proved that with the right leadership and cooperation between the private and public sectors, Virginia could again serve as an innovative leader for its wine industry.

Despite the fervor surrounding the VWDC's creation, the great national question of the constitutionality of direct-shipping bans by and from out-of-state producers had been left unanswered. A case from Virginia, however, ultimately wound its way to the United States Supreme Court with striking effect. In February 2002, three months after *Bolick v. Roberts* was filed in Virginia, Middleburg vintner Juanita Swedenburg joined a California winery and several New York customers in filing a lawsuit against members of the New York State Liquor Authority. The case, *Swedenburg v. Kelley*, filed in a New York federal court, sought a declaration that New York's prohibition on direct shipment of wine from out-of-state wineries to New York customers, as well as the Empire State's ban on advertising by out-of-state wineries, violated the Commerce Clause.[34]

A gracious person, Juanita Swedenburg seemed an unlikely combatant. She and her husband, Wayne Swedenburg, were certainly viticultural pioneers; they had hosted many of the early Virginia Wine Festivals and sold fewer than 2,000 cases per year, most of which was sold at their Swedenburg Estate Vineyard. A staunch advocate of conservative principles and free enterprise, however, Swedenburg was prompted to file the lawsuit in the wake of President Bill Clinton's October 2000 signing of the Twenty-First Amendment Enforcement Act, a federal statute that permitted federal courts, rather than state courts, to police interstate alcohol sales. "I'm so convinced that the Founding Fathers meant for us to have trade between the states," she noted to reporters, adding that state-centric Prohibition laws were of a type that "brought down the first American government, the Articles of Confederation: State lines were barriers to trade, and it just didn't work."[35]

Swedenburg won in trial court, but the United States Court of Appeals for the Second Circuit reversed the ruling, claiming that New York's interest in ensuring accountability in alcohol transactions was constitutional under the Twenty-First Amendment. Swedenburg appealed the case to the Supreme Court of the United States, where it was consolidated with two similar Michigan cases under the caption *Granholm v. Heald*. The *Granholm* case galvanized American wine drinkers and attracted opinions from some of the nation's most respected legal minds. On it turned the fate of entire industries centered on the sale of wine.[36]

In May 2005, the Supreme Court struck down all New York and Michigan laws that criminalized the direct shipment of beverages from out-of-state wineries. The majority opinion, written by Justice Anthony Kennedy, observed that while states possessed broad authority to regulate the sale of alcohol under the Twenty-First Amendment, that power did not permit states to ban or severely restrict the direct shipment of out-of-state wine while simultaneously authorizing direct shipment to consumers by in-state producers. "The patchwork of laws," wrote Justice Kennedy, was "essentially the product of an ongoing, low-level trade war" between the states, in direct contravention of the Commerce Clause.[37]

The *Granholm* ruling required states to level the playing field and to either ban direct shipping altogether or permit in-state and out-of-state wineries to ship directly to consumers. Swedenburg was elated, viewing the decision as a "very great win for small wineries" and "a 100 percent win for consumers." States scrambled to address the implication of the court's ruling by revisiting and revising a variety of taxes, rules, permits, paperwork, and fees. In the wake of the decision, twenty-seven states loosened their requirements, bringing to thirty-seven the number of states that permitted various extents of direct shipment to consumers. As noted above, Virginia created its VWDC in 2008, and Swedenburg had changed history.[38]

## —*Into the New Century*—

As Virginians celebrated the eleventh anniversary of Virginia Wine Month in October 1999, the commonwealth's wine industry prepared to close the door on the twentieth century and enter its next period of development. In that year, the Old Dominion counted fifty-four wineries among its ranks, vineyard acreage had increased from 286 acres in 1979 to more than 1,609 acres, retail sales were approaching $25 million annually, and the commonwealth produced some 214,000 cases of wine per year. While vinifera varietals had been rare in the 1970s, they comprised some 71 percent of total Virginia plantings by the late 1990s, outstripping French-American hybrids and native varieties.[39]

An estimated 500,000 people toured Virginia wineries annually and viticulture had evolved into the Old Dominion's fastest-growing agricultural sector. Consumers were spending more time savoring wine at tasting rooms and festivals, while entrepreneurs planted vines and opened tasting rooms across the commonwealth at a lightning pace. The new millennium was to prove an era of hypergrowth that presented opportunities and challenges alike.[40]

Among the industry's more pressing concerns was the simple but critical need for more grapes. Wine production had soared from 75,000 cases in 1985 (the earliest year for which records exist) to 205,000 cases in 1997, and sales had more than tripled between 1985 and 1997, from $7.5 million to $25 million. By 1998, Virginia's wineries found themselves scrambling for additional fruit to meet growing demand. The need to increase vineyard acreage and the search for high-quality grapes were particularly pronounced in years of unpromising harvests. Part of the need for additional Virginia grapes derived from statutory requirements for farm wineries that forced them to obtain at least 75 percent of their fruit from Virginia vineyards. Adding new vines, however, was no easy task given the locational, financial, political, and weather requirements and the three to five years typically needed to produce a full crop of grapes. "The industry is growing too fast," said David Morrisette, owner of Chateau Morrisette in Floyd County. "There's no way we could survive unless we're able to buy grapes from out of state or there's enough planted in Virginia."[41]

To address the problem, the Virginia Department of Agriculture and Consumer Services established a Grape Production Initiative Task Force in

December 1997 to publicize the need for additional grapes and offer technical advice to prospective grape growers. The task force was formed at the urging of assistant VDACS commissioner William P. "Bill" Dickinson, Jr., and was composed of representatives from the Virginia Wineries Association and the Virginia Vineyards Association, as well as VDACS staff and Virginia Tech personnel. It set a goal of increasing Virginia's grape plantings by 500 acres and sought to reach out to large landowners, hobby grape growers, and experienced farmers looking to diversify their crops. The task force met between 1997 and 1999, and produced significant technical data, grape recommendations, and vineyard suitability maps.

By the close of 1998, the commonwealth's vineyard acreage had increased eight percent over the previous year, and by 1999 grape acreage had increased an additional 22 percent. This resulted in a record 1,963 acres of grapes planted and a harvest of 4,563 tons of grapes in 1999, the highest production to that date in Virginia history. Despite this rather moderate success in increasing grape acreage, the equivalent need for high quality fruit continued to vex the industry. Over time, industry advocates, including Secretary of Agriculture Todd Haymore, continued to urge industry leaders to plant more vines, and Governor Robert F. McDonnell (2010–2014) worked to institute a reimbursable tax credit program for establishing or expanding vineyards and wineries.[42]

As grape acreage increased, so too did the sheer number of wines produced. With winemakers possessing widely varying degrees of experience in vinification, the quality of Virginia wines ranged from those with the proper balance of alcohol, flavor, and tannins to those that proved too sugary, too acidic, watered-down, or just undrinkable due to technical flaws. Inconsistency affected the reputation of the Virginia wine industry as a whole. "I'm convinced that some of the winery folks in Virginia honestly don't know when they've got a flawed wine," said Rockbridge Vineyards winemaker Shepherd "Shep" Rouse. "There is amazing naiveté in the industry," he added. "There are people who've got no palate…and no real training."[43]

Beginning in the late 1980s, state enologist Bruce Zoecklein, Williamsburg Winery's Patrick Duffeler, and others began to champion the idea of improving the technical aspects of Virginia vintners and their wines by establishing a quality assurance program. The idea was first broached in a 1989 report by the Virginia Winegrowers Advisory Board, which advocated the implementation of a "seal of quality" program to improve wine quality and identify enological shortcomings before bottling.[44]

Absent such a program, the only way consumers could gauge wine quality was through the marketplace and an increasing number of wine competitions.

Several vintners, though, had grown frustrated with both the proliferation of competitions and the large number of medals awarded, phenomena that did little to provide consumers with useful information about individual wines. Zoecklein advocated a program based on Ontario's Vintners Quality Alliance system, whereby winemakers voluntarily submitted their wines to certified tasting panels for technical review and criticism. Under the Canadian program, those wines that met the standards received a stamp of approval intended to assure customers that the wine was of high quality.[45]

The concept of a voluntary quality assurance program in Virginia was not met with universal acclaim. Some vintners did not want to submit their products to a costly analysis and feared that their wines would fail to meet the requisite tests. Others believed efforts could be better spent on expanded marketing. Though a quality assurance program had long been discussed, and even proposed by Governor Mark R. Warner's Wine Study Work Group in 2004, no program had yet been established by the mid-2000s.

By 2008, Zoecklein had all but abandoned his call for higher standards, citing a lack of funds and opposition from winery owners. Beginning in 2009, however, with financial assistance from a U.S. Department of Agriculture specialty-crop block grant, members of the Virginia Wineries Association formed the Commonwealth Quality Alliance, a technical study committee to develop and implement a quality control program for Virginia wineries. The program was formally launched in November 2012 with the support of the Virginia Wineries Association, the Virginia Vineyards Association, and the Virginia Winery Distribution Company. Under the CQA program, wines submitted for review were required to use Virginia-grown grapes exclusively, and the use of commercial concentrate grape juice was prohibited. The CQA system subjected entries to a laboratory and sugar analysis at Virginia Tech, as well as to a tasting panel; entries were then graded, and those without oenological flaws were approved and permitted to use the CQA logo on their wine bottles.[46]

Concurrent with the need to ensure quality wine production, another challenge faced by the industry was the need to identify those grape varieties that offered Virginia the best chance to distinguish itself from other wine regions. Nearly two-thirds of the commonwealth's wine grape acreage was planted with European varieties by 1990, and though experts predicted that Virginia's future market growth would undoubtedly lie in vinifera cultivation, they also pointed to examples of other emerging wine regions, such as Oregon, New York, New Zealand, and Argentina, that had focused on only one or two signature grapes to drive market interest, tourism, and industry expansion.[47]

At the suggestions of those who warned that over-reliance on the state's workhorse vinifera plantings could stifle innovation, several vineyardists experimented with alternative grape varieties, including some with obscure names. For the first time, Barbera, Marsanne, and Malbec were planted in the Old Dominion, as were Malvaxia, Mourvédre, Tannat, Tempranillo, and Pinotage. The most popular proved to be Traminette, Petit Manseng, Petit Verdot, Chambourcin, Norton, and Viognier, the latter two largely owing their position in modern Virginia to the man who was perhaps the greatest Virginia grape experimenter of all, Dennis Horton.[48]

A native of Hermann, Missouri, a small town with a rich history of German winemaking, Horton and his wife Sharon Horton purchased land in Madison County in 1977 and commenced experimentation with different varieties, seeking exotic niche wine grapes. Each of Horton's methodical trials was premised on a desire to identify varieties that grew well in Virginia, produced quality wine, and, of equal importance, could be grown and used profitably. In time, Horton turned his vineyards and later his winery, Horton Vineyards, into laboratories for wine-grape trials. "If my claim to fame is anything," Horton once told a reporter, "it's probably that I've ripped out more vines than most people have put in." Horton's curiosity would lead him to test more than forty varieties, earning him a well-deserved reputation as Virginia's most progressive and adventurous vintner.[49]

Horton is perhaps most widely known for his experimentation with the Viognier grape, a variety he found could flourish in Virginia's hot, sticky climate. The rare, white variety was all but extinct worldwide by the mid-1960s; even as late as 1986 it could only be found on some eighty acres in France's Rhône Valley. Viognier was not only scarce, it was also difficult to grow. Its cultivation required it to remain on the vine long enough to develop optimal flavors, and it could only be picked within a narrow window of time to avoid losing its unique attributes. Horton planted his first Viognier vines in 1989 and found the grape to be extremely consistent in terms of ripeness between vintages.

Horton's first successful Viognier planting led him to bottle 300 cases of Viognier wine in 1993. The wine quickly became Horton Vineyards' flagship offering, lauded as the crown jewel of Virginia viticulture for its extraordinary peach and vanilla notes. Thanks to Horton, Virginia attracted national attention for the consistent quality and finesse of its Viognier wines, which offered a premium bottle price for Virginia's winemakers and proved crisper, less fruity, and lower in alcohol content than their California counterparts. This encouraged the Virginia Wine Board to designate the variety as Virginia's signature white wine grape in 2011. By that time, Horton Vineyards had fortified its position as one of Virginia's largest wineries.

Around the time he began experimenting with Viognier grapes, Horton also turned to a native grape that served as the backbone of the first Virginia wine industry in the nineteenth century: the redoubtable Norton. In 1989, he planted eight acres of the variety, the largest such planting since Prohibition, and five years later, he reintroduced the Norton to commercial production. The reappearance of Norton wine in Virginia, dubbed "Horton's Norton," was an instant success. Aided by its memorable, rather Dr. Seuss–like name, Horton sold more than 100 cases within the first month, and by 1996 the wine could be found on retail shelves in a dozen states.[50]

By the early 2000s, several Virginia wineries followed in Horton's footsteps and produced their own Norton wine. One vocal advocate of the variety, Chrysalis Vineyards' Jennifer McCloud, had founded Chrysalis in 1997 outside Middleburg and developed a winery that specifically focused on the Norton. McCloud planted more than forty acres of the grape, the largest such planting in the world, attempting to restore the Norton grape to a position of prominence in American viticulture. She even trademarked a slogan, "Norton, the Real American Grape!" that she featured on Chrysalis' labels. She worked with other vintners in Virginia and Missouri to promote the cultivation of the variety. Her enthusiasm for the Norton was eloquently captured in Todd Kliman's 2010 book, *The Wild Vine*. McCloud remains confident in the future of the grape and her role in its cultivation: "I would rather be a bigger fish in a small pond and produce the world's best Norton than the 400th Merlot," she told a reporter.[51]

Enthusiasm over the Viognier and the Norton was matched in the mid-2000s by the arrival of another rather obscure grape, the Petit Verdot. The red vinifera variety had long suffered from a reputation—well-deserved though it was—as an expensive, late ripener with irregular quality that yielded a spicy, peppery juice. Few regions around the world attempted to grow the grape; fewer still dared to bottle it on its own. Beginning in 1991, however, state viticulturalist Dr. Tony K. Wolf began testing the variety at Virginia Tech's Alson H. Smith Jr. Agricultural Research and Extension Center south of Winchester. Linden Vineyards' owner and winemaker, Jim Law, also experimented with the grape and began using it for blending in the middle 1990s.[52]

Wolf and Law, among others, found that the Petit Verdot's small berry size resulted in a higher skin-to-juice ratio during production than comparable varieties, a characteristic that equated to deeper color and richer flavor. Its thicker skin also meant that the grape was, like the Viognier, more resistant to Virginia's humid summers and grape rot, problems long experienced with the commonwealth's dominant red vinifera varieties. Tests on the grape continued, and in 1996, Wolf, along with state enologist Bruce Zoecklein, issued a report concluding that the Petit Verdot could become an important grape for Virginia, both as a blending grape and as one that could be bottled separately.[53]

Acceptance of the grape was slow until 2007, when, much to the surprise of nearly everyone, Petit Verdot wines won several top awards at various prestigious competitions. The wins supported the notion that the grape could develop into a signature red variety for Virginia.[54]

For years, Virginia's winemakers had focused on red and white wines for the general consumer. But as with other emerging American wine regions, many of the commonwealth's early wines were decidedly sweet. Though consumer tastes later yielded to drier varietals, the development of the historic, if underappreciated, art of crafting fine dessert and fruit wines continued. Popular since Virginia's colonial period, fruit wines made from elderberry, pear, apple, apricot, blackberry, raspberry, and blueberry proved particularly popular in more rural areas of the commonwealth.[55]

In the 1990s, the Peaks of Otter Winery emerged as one of Virginia's largest fruit wine producers. Danny and Nancy Johnson diversified their Bedford County orchard by producing a variety of fruit wines made from pears, plums, and apples, taking advantage of a glut of apples on the 1990s market. The Johnsons opened their winery in 1995 and used the farm's former apple-packing house for the sale of jams, relishes, and some thirty varieties of fruit wine. Fruit wines also helped diversify Nelson County's Hill Top Berry Farm and Winery. Founded late in the 1970s by Marlyn and Sue Allen, Hill Top was originally conceived as a "pick-your-own" operation to take advantage of the fruits grown there, including raspberries, blueberries, peaches, plums, and apples. In 1998, the Allens began manufacturing more than a dozen fruit wines and honey mead. Horton Vineyards, not to be outdone, produced a separate line of inexpensive fruit wines under its Chateau Le Cabin label, while Nelson County's Wintergreen Winery offered patrons a variety of fruit wines made from apples and raspberries.[56]

Another industry trend, driven largely by the infusion of new winemaking talent and increasing demand for more delicate wines, was the evolution of the commonwealth's sparkling wines. Though "the bubbly" had existed for centuries in the Americas as a celebratory drink, it was not until the early 2000s that Virginia's sparkling wines began drawing national attention. Sparkling wines had been produced in Virginia as early as the mid-1980s, when Ingleside Vineyards' Jacques Recht crafted a Chardonnay brut-style wine. While others followed, few Virginia wineries were due more credit for advancing the reputation of Virginia's sparkling wines than the former Kluge Estate Winery and Vineyard. Before the operation was shuttered in 2010 (as described in detail below), owner Patricia Kluge maintained several sparkling wine consultants from France's Champagne region on her staff, and produced four award-winning sparkling wines. One of her more prominent winemakers, Claude Thibaut, was a fifth-generation winemaker who spent half of his career producing sparkling wines across the world. Thibaut had studied the traditional *méthode champoise* at France's University of Reims, and came to Virginia with his wife in 2003 to help Kluge produce high-quality sparkling wines.[57]

Thibaut remained with Kluge for nearly three years, and thereafter consulted with several Virginia winemakers on the production of sparkling wine. In 2005, he partnered with critically acclaimed French Champagne maker Manuel Janisson to launch a new joint-venture label, Thibaut-Janisson. Their mission was to produce the best sparkling wine in the world, one that combined the *méthode champoise* style with the distinctive features of Virginia's terroir. They leased space at Veritas Winery to make sparkling wines, and released their first vintage, an all-Chardonnay nonvintage sparkling wine, Blanc de Chardonnay Brut, in 2007. It received widespread acclaim on its release and was served by President Barack Obama at state dinners in 2009 and 2014.[58]

One of the more visible trends in the late 1990s and early 2000s was the increased production of custom-label wines for corporate, educational, and promotional organizations. With an eye toward generating additional profits, cultivating customer loyalty, and improving marketing, groups and businesses began to commission specially labeled wines from Virginia wineries to be sold or given away as gifts. Meredyth Vineyards was among the first to issue custom-labeled wines for companies early in the 1980s, but by the dawn of the new millennium, the idea had spread to educational institutions as well, driven largely by the need for schools to raise money and to cater to an increased interest in wine among younger alumni. Among the most prolific custom wine producers was Chateau Morrisette, which partnered with Virginia Tech and Roanoke's Hollins College to produce red and white vintages that proved popular for tailgating at football games and benefited each school's alumni association.

Personalized wines proved particularly popular with the commonwealth's tourist and hospitality industries. Hotels, resorts, and other attractions saw them as a way to boost their marketing efforts and to distinguish themselves from competitors. The Homestead, for example, as well as Albemarle County's Keswick Hall, James Madison's Montpelier, Mount Vernon, and the Colonial Williamsburg Foundation, partnered with Virginia winemakers to produce their own private-label wines. This personalized label trend allowed Virginia winemakers to reach a broader market and produce a product that possessed cachet as a novelty item. More important, it spread the word of the quality of Virginia wines to discerning consumers, many of whom purchased the specially labeled wines for novelty purposes and had likely never before tasted a wine produced in the commonwealth.[59]

The new millennium also sparked a renewed worldwide appreciation for environmental stewardship and the responsible management of natural resources. This was not lost on Virginia's wine industry. From waste reduction and recycling, to minimizing the use of disposable food-service products, many of Virginia's wineries sought to incorporate environmentally-sustainable components into their businesses. Wineries promoted water and energy efficiency, limited use of chemicals and fertilizers, integrated pest management and fungicide techniques, incorporated solar energy, and instituted crop rotation. Attention also focused on energy conservation, natural cooling, the strategic placement of trees, and natural ventilation.[60]

Sustainable practices extended to winery infrastructure. Madison County's DuCard Vineyards used lighter-weight wine bottles and featured a 1,200-square-foot, solar-powered facility with floors made from century-old reclaimed barn wood. Geothermal heating and cooling systems were used at two Fauquier County wineries, Pearmund Cellars and Barrel Oak Winery, as well as at Albemarle County's Pippin Hill Farm and Vineyards, which also made use of rainwater harvesting.[61]

Efforts to achieve Leadership in Energy and Environmental Design (LEED) certification were also at the forefront of wineries' environmental initiatives. Louisa County's Cooper Vineyards opened the East Coast's first LEED-certified tasting room in April 2011, featuring reclaimed wood, solar panels, low-voltage lighting, a rainwater collection system, a geothermal heating and cooling system, low-flow water fixtures, and energy-efficient lighting. LEED certification was awarded to Loudoun County's North Gate Vineyard for its tasting room, which incorporated locally sourced stone and countertops manufactured from epoxy resin, recycled glass, and porcelain chips.

These private-sector efforts were complemented in 2009 by Virginia Green, a statewide environmental program for the commonwealth's tourism sectors created by the Virginia Tourism Corporation, in conjunction with the Virginia Department of Environmental Quality and the Virginia Hospitality and Travel Association. Those wishing to be certified as a Virginia Green Winery were required to self-certify compliance with a series of initiatives. Wineries rushed to be certified, incorporating everything from insulated wine tanks, to recycling programs, to efficient heating and air conditioning.[62]

One of the commonwealth's more-remarkable environmental initiatives came in 2009, when a Charlottesville flooring company, Carpet Plus, announced the launch of a wine cork recycling program known as Re-Cork C-Ville. Hoping to salvage some of the nearly 15 billion wine corks that end up in landfills annually, Carpet Plus provided cork collection boxes to more than sixty local restaurants and vineyards across central Virginia. The program collected more than 1.7 million corks by 2017, all of which were reused for flooring, building insulation, soil conditioner, shoes, sports equipment, or automotive gaskets. That year, cork recycling programs could also be found at Whole Foods grocery stores across the commonwealth. Recycling extended to reusing bottles as well. Goochland County's Byrd Cellars, for example, sanitized and reused wine bottles donated by customers.[63]

## — Established Wine Areas Grow —

Virginia's established wine regions, including the Shenandoah Valley, greater Charlottesville, and Northern Virginia, grew tremendously during the 1990s and 2000s, fueled by increasing tourism and growing fame. By 2017, the state boasted some 260 wineries of all shapes and sizes, with nearly twenty new wineries opening each year; even skeptical observers had to admit that the state's wine industry was experiencing a unique time.

In the Shenandoah Valley, wineries popped up along busy Interstate 81. Jane and Shep Rouse opened Rockbridge Vineyards on a 158-acre former dairy farm north of Lexington. As the 2000s progressed, the Valley saw the addition of several other wineries as well. The greater Charlottesville area remained dominant. In the pristine horse country east of town, two Michigan natives, Al and Cindy Schornberg, opened Keswick Vineyards at their historic 400-acre Edgewood estate in 2004. After hiring South African Stephen Barnard as winemaker, they received the 2009 Governor's Cup for their 2007 Cabernet Sauvignon.[64]

South of Charlottesville, Mary and Jamie Lewis opened Totier Creek Vineyard in 1992, later purchased by Randolph McElroy, Jr., and renamed First Colony Winery. That same year, Tony and Edith Champ opened White Hall Vineyards on a 300-acre farm in northeastern Albemarle County, where they worked with winemaker Brad McCarthy to capture the 1997 and 1998 Governors Cups for their 1995 Cabernet Sauvignon and 1997 Gewürztraminer wines, respectively. Nearby Nelson County also emerged as a winery leader. There, in 2000, Claude DelFosse and his family opened DelFosse Vineyards and Winery on their 330-acre property. Nearby, Paul and Ruth Gorman opened Cardinal Point Winery in 2002 on a 90-acre former peach farm in the Afton area, along with their daughter Sarah, Paul's son Tim, and Tim's wife, Susan Gorman. Just west of Cardinal Point, Andrew and Patricia Hodson converted a historic cattle farm into Veritas Vineyard and Winery, where they planted vinifera grapes, turning winemaking responsibility over to their daughter, Emily Hodson Pelton. In central Nelson County outside Lovingston, Ed and Janet Puckett opened Lovingston Winery in 2005, where they hired former Oakencroft winemaker Riaan Rossouw as winemaker.[65]

The Charlottesville region's wine industry received a boost in 2013 when Albemarle County received a $20,000 state matching grant to evaluate the potential for a Virginia wine heritage center, proposed to help solidify the area's importance to the industry. It was conceived to include space for Virginia wine history exhibitions, seminar classrooms, and potentially an experimental vineyard and processing facility.

Though greater Charlottesville may have retained its title as the cultural center of Virginia's wine industry into the new millennium, Northern Virginia witnessed lightning growth as well. Dozens of wineries popped up in Loudoun County and near Interstate 66. In the Delaplane area of Fauquier County, Holli and John Todhunter opened Three Fox Vineyards in 2006 on fifty acres. Nearby, Brian and Sharon Roeder opened their impressive Barrel Oak Winery in 2008, on a scenic hillside overlooking Delaplane and Interstate 66. Just north of Barrel Oak, longtime home winemaker Jim Dolphin and his wife, Betsy Dolphin, opened Delaplane Cellars in 2009, after consulting with Linden Vineyards' Jim Law on grape varieties and planting techniques. Immediately east of Delaplane Cellars, one of Jim Law's former apprentices, former U.S. Marine Rutger de Vink, opened RdV Vineyards in 2011. Touted in local media as "the next generation of Virginia wine," RdV Vineyards enjoyed great acclaim and positive media coverage, despite its comparatively high prices.[66]

In Clarke County, James and Della Bogaty realized their winemaking dream when they opened Veramar Vineyard early in the 2000s, while in nearby Rappahannock County, John Delmare, with his wife and children, opened Rappahannock Cellars in 2000. Not far from Rappahannock Cellars, Dave and Joann Hilty produced red vinifera wines at their Berry Hill Vineyard, and in the Fort Valley area of southwestern Rappahannock County, David and Marilyn Armor opened Sharp Rock Vineyards in 1998. Rappahannock County's northernmost winery, Chester Gap Cellars, launched in 2000 overlooking a small valley, after its owners, former German World Games water skier Bernd Jung and his wife, Kristi Jung, conducted a five-year search for a property offering high quality terrior.[67]

Perhaps no Virginia jurisdiction worked harder to craft an economic development strategy based on wine, tourism, and rural business than Loudoun County. Nestled on the western cusp of greater Washington, D.C., Loudoun recognized early on the need to protect the rural splendor of its western two-thirds, where farms and fields give way to unparalleled views of the Blue Ridge Mountains. Once primarily known for dairy, wheat, and horse farms, the county's land values had risen dramatically in the 1980s and 1990s as the population soared, causing Loudoun's farmers to struggle.

Preserving western Loudoun County and reinvigorating its agricultural sector, however, would take patience and commitment. Beginning in 1984, the county worked to support niche agricultural markets and capitalize on immense tourism opportunities provided by Loudoun's proximity to the national capital area's consumer market. The Board of Supervisors established a Rural Economic Development Council in 2000 to provide advice and recommendations for prospective farmers, and county planning policies emphasized the importance of so-called "rural economy" uses, which included wineries. Loudoun also adopted policies calling for the expansion of rural businesses through reduced regulation, incentive-based programs, and assistance for farm wineries.[68]

Together with efforts to attract high-tech and manufacturing firms, Loudoun's Department of Economic Development prioritized rural economic growth. It hired a full-time agricultural development officer to help vintners identify available land and grape growers, navigate zoning laws, and secure business licenses. The department produced a series of local farm maps and a website that advertised rural-related events. The county even offered wine education seminars and produced a Loudoun Wine Trail brochure as early as 1998. The county also supported a full-time horticultural agent to assist grape growers with grape production, disease identification, and pest control.[69]

Key to Loudoun's wine promotion efforts was the Loudoun Convention and Visitors Association, also known as Visit Loudoun. A taxpayer-supported, not-for-profit organization, Visit Loudoun worked to market the area as a destination location and adopted marketing strategies to promote the county's wineries and restaurants through print and online media. The spectacular growth of Loudoun's wine industry spurred Visit Loudoun to rebrand its tourism efforts as "D.C.'s Wine Country" in 2008, and to produce a glossy winery and restaurant touring guide to serve as the county's primary marketing piece.[70]

Visit Loudoun's focus on wine helped the county attract more than 2,000 runners to the 2011 Virginia Wine Country Half Marathon, as well as a partnership with *Saveur Magazine* to produce a 2013 wine and culinary event dubbed "Epicurience." Investments made by the county's public and private sectors resulted in a tight-knit community of growers, vineyards, and wineries, which provided mutual assistance and education to Loudoun's wine industry participants. As a result of its efforts, Loudoun's agriculture industry stabilized, the county's traditional agricultural sectors gave way to a variety of newer commodities, and Loudoun turned itself into a center for the commonwealth's winemaking industry. The number of Loudoun County wineries doubled between 2008 and 2011, so that by 2017 the county produced more grapes on more acres of vineyards, while claiming more wineries (forty-four), than any other jurisdiction in Virginia.[71]

As might be expected from such a rapid proliferation, the wineries that blossomed in Loudoun during the 1990s and 2000s were as varied as the county's landscape. Much of the inspiration for Loudoun's new wineries came from one exceptionally gifted and forward-thinking winemaker, vineyard manager, and winery owner, Doug Fabbioli. A New York native who inherited his passion for winemaking from his paternal grandfather, Fabbioli worked at a number of wineries before opening his own venture, Fabbioli Cellars, outside the village of Lucketts. Fabbioli generously offered his consulting services to several wineries, and to help the next generation of Loudoun winery and agricultural enthusiasts create a sustainable rural economy, in 2012 he launched the Piedmont Epicurean and Agricultural Center in Leesburg with his friend James Koennicke. The small center provided wine-related consulting services as well as collaborative education courses on winemaking, vineyard management, and tasting-room operations.[72]

## — *Virginia's Emerging Wine Regions* —

Few at the outset of Virginia's modern wine revolution could have imagined that wineries would eventually reach all corners of the commonwealth. As wineries crowded into Northern Virginia and greater Charlottesville, attention turned to the Old Dominion's lesser-known regions, including Southwest Virginia, Southside, Greater Richmond, the Eastern Shore, and the Northern Neck. These areas had largely been left out of the commonwealth's viticultural rebirth, but advances in research and technology increased their potential for quality winegrape growing. Through trial and error, vineyardists and winemakers discovered that viticulture offered potential to meet the demands of an underserved rural consumer base while providing alternative economic development and tourism opportunities.[73]

In the undulating hills and valleys of Southwest Virginia, a small but remarkable wine industry emerged in the 1990s. Although the area was home to two American Viticultural Areas, the Rocky Knob AVA and the North Fork of Roanoke AVA, development of Southwest Virginia's wine industry had long lagged behind its eastern counterparts. Part of the reason was meteorological: Southwest Virginia frequently bore the brunt of the cool mountain air and early frosts that swept through the region, sometimes a full month before the rest of Virginia. Equally important, much of the region remained difficult to traverse, and the mountainous landscape often restricted the supply of land for vineyards. For all its drawbacks, Southwest Virginia offered advantages, including well-drained, rocky soils and higher elevations that provided thermal inversions, milder winters, and cooler summers.[74]

For years beginning in the 1980s, Floyd County's Chateau Morrisette served as the Virginia wine industry's western terminus. This lasted until Ken Dye opened Dye's Vineyards on a former tobacco farm in 1989 in Russell County. Though a third winery, Boundary Rock Farm and Winery later opened in Floyd, it was not until the late 1990s that Southwest Virginia's wine industry really ramped up. The close of the decade brought significant investment to the region with three new wineries: Villa Appalachia, founded by Dr. Stephen Haskill and his wife, Dr. Susanne Becker, in 1997; Valhalla Vineyards, founded by Jim and Debra Vascik in 1998; and AmRhein's Wine Cellars, founded by Russell and Paula Amrhein in 1999. The region received accolades and competition wins that boosted Southwest Virginia's reputation as an emerging wine region. Valhalla, for example, received the 2000 Governor's Cup and garnered national attention in *Wine Spectator* and *Decanter* magazines, while the 2001 and 2002 Governor's Cups were awarded to wines produced by AmRhein's Wine Cellars.[75]

The new millennium witnessed the openings of an unprecedented number of additional wineries in the region, most of which were family-run operations founded by local residents. Few family wineries symbolized the economic hurdles facing Southwest Virginia and the promise of its wine industry more than David Lawson's MountainRose Vineyard. Opened in 2004 outside the tiny coal-mining town of Wise, MountainRose was situated atop reclaimed coal-mining land. Though rich in minerals, the property's compacted soils were devoid of organic material and the microorganisms needed to create nutrients. Consequently, Lawson prepared and regraded the site, added compost around the property, and adjusted the soil's acidity levels. "People migrated from this region in the 1930s and the 1960s and they come back home to visit family," MountainRose's vice president Suzanne Lawson told a reporter. "Their relatives bring them here to the winery, and we take them on a tour and they really enjoy it."[76]

Many of Southwest Virginia's wineries found a welcome home for their products at the Heartwood, Southwest Virginia's Artisan Gateway, which opened in Abingdon in 2011. Funded in part by the General Assembly, Heartwood featured a state tourism office, workspace for local artisans and crafters, and a culinary area that showcased Virginia wines and regional foods. The advent of wineries in an underserved area of the commonwealth helped improve Southwest Virginia's economic development prospects and provided another avenue for tourists to experience the region's unique history and heritage.

Much as Southwest Virginia's wine industry evolved from smaller, family-run enterprises, the same proved true of Virginia's Southside region. An area bounded on the north by the James River and on the west by the Blue Ridge Mountains, Southside had long been synonymous with tobacco farming, textile production, and furniture manufacturing. By the late 1990s, with the tobacco industry in turmoil because of cigarette tax increases, globalization of the tobacco market, and tobacco-related lawsuits, many Southside farmers turned to corn, cotton, and soybeans.

Viticulture in the region began as early as 1978, when longtime tobacco farmers Arthur and Ercelle Hodges transformed their Rocky Mount tobacco farm into Chateau Naturel Vineyard. In tobacco-rich Halifax County, growers planted eight vineyards between 2002 and 2007, which eventually led to the opening of four wineries. One of them, Shirley and Boyd Archer's Bright Meadows Farm, produced eleven wines, including Bright Leaf White and Burley Red, which paid appropriate homage to the area's tobacco heritage. In neighboring Pittsylvania County, one of Southside's oldest wineries, Tomahawk Mill Vineyard and Winery, opened late in the 1980s. Purchased by Nancy and Corky Medaglia in 1996, the Tomahawk complex included a historic circa-1890 mill, former country store, and post office. By the late 2000s, interest in Southside's wineries had developed sufficiently to encourage several of the region's wine producers to form the Southern Virginia Wine Trail promoting Southside's counties. In February 2012, the group produced its inaugural event, SoVa Wine Fest, at the newly constructed Olde Dominion Agricultural Complex in Chatham. Though the region continued to suffer economically, prospects for its grape culture seemed bright.[77]

Virginia's capital city of Richmond also witnessed the rebirth of a budding wine industry. Richmond, of course, had been home to nineteenth-century viticultural pioneer Dr. Daniel Norborne Norton, and in the twentieth century, the city found itself host to wine and wholesale lobbyists, major wine festivals, and the crowning event of each year: the Virginia Governor's Cup competition. Hints of physical participation in Virginia's wine industry, though, remained elusive in the capitol region until 1997, when Randy and Judith Rocchiccioli opened Windy River Winery in nearby Hanover County. Four years later, Ray Lazarchic opened James River Cellars Winery outside Ashland, perhaps the closest winery to the State Capitol. In the 2000s, three small wineries opened south of the James River, and winery growth was strong west of Richmond, in Goochland and Louisa Counties. East of the city, New Kent Winery and Vineyards opened in 2007 as an amenity for a major residential community, and four years later, Saudé Creek Vineyards opened on the site of a former colonial tavern along the Pamunkey River.

Another latecomer to the Virginia wine industry was the 662-square-mile Eastern Shore. An area of a seemingly endless tidal marshes, the Eastern Shore was home to the Virginia's Eastern Shore AVA, offering flat topography, sandy loam soils, and a climate moderated by the Chesapeake Bay and Atlantic Ocean, with cool springs and long, sunny summers. Despite such advantages, and though it enjoyed a strategic location along busy U.S. Route 13, the region was separated from the nearby Hampton Roads community by the Chesapeake Bay and a twenty-three-mile toll bridge-tunnel complex.[78]

The Eastern Shore's first winery, Jim Keyes's Accomack Vineyards in Accomack County, operated between 1986 and 1992. Twelve years would pass before Robert and Francesca Giardina opened the peninsula's second winery, Bloxom Vineyard and Winery, in 2004. Two years later, Jon and Mills Wehner opened Chatham Vineyards in Northampton County. Wehner, a Fairfax County native, spent much of his childhood tending grapes and making wine on his family's Great Falls dairy farm, which included a three-acre vineyard. His parents, Joan and Harrison Wehner, produced wine, some of which was served as a house blend at a top-rated Washington, D.C.–area restaurant, L'Auberge Chez Francois, in the 1970s and 1980s. Wehner hired Lucie Morton to serve as vineyard consultant, and tapped Prince Michel winemaker Brad Hansen to serve as winemaking consultant. Just north of Chatham Vineyards, John H. "Rock" Stephens, along with his wife, Kris Stephens, founded a twelve-acre vinifera vineyard, the Vineyard at Pointe Breeze, in 1999 outside the small community of Belle Haven. One of Virginia's leading commercial grape growers, Stephens was a retired U.S. Navy captain, and served as president of the Virginia Vineyards Association and chairman of the Virginia Wine Board.[79]

Across the Chesapeake Bay from the Eastern Shore, nestled between the Potomac and Rappahannock Rivers, the largely rural peninsula known colloquially as the Northern Neck also spawned a small but growing wine industry by the late 2000s. Though the region had enjoyed a long, if modest, history of viticulture dating to the colonial period, it was not until the arrival of winemaker

Jacques Recht at Ingleside Plantation in 1980 that modern winemaking along the Northern Neck began in earnest.

By 2017, the Northern Neck was home to ten wineries and its own American Viticultural Area, the Northern Neck George Washington Birthplace AVA, which was proclaimed in 1987. The rapid growth of the wine industry along the Northern Neck, particularly after 2005, prompted several of the peninsula's vineyards to form the Northern Neck Wine Trail (later renamed the Chesapeake Bay Wine Trail) late in the 2000s. To promote the Neck's viticultural and historic offerings, participating vineyards also collaborated on a commemorative book published in 2012, *Virginia: First in Wine and History.*[80]

## —Winemaking on a Personal Level—

Along with the growing number of Virginia wineries came an increased interest in home winemaking, a trend that had been evident for some time. In the 1970s and 1980s, Lucie Morton taught home winemaking classes, television weatherman Willard Scott cultivated his own French-American grape at his home in The Plains, and Albemarle County Circuit Court Judge E. Gerald Tremblay made wine at his home. The types and quality of home-produced wine were as varied as the personalities responsible for their production.

The art of home winemaking not only provided a creative outlet for committed oenophiles, in some cases it also led to the creation of full-fledged winery operations. One notable example, Gray Ghost Vineyards, opened in 1994 in Rappahannock County after its founders, Al and Cheryl Kellert, had experimented with home winemaking behind their Woodbridge home in 1981. Five years later, they moved to Rappahannock, where they converted an old horse barn into a tasting room and winery named in honor of Confederate colonel John Singleton Mosby, the "Gray Ghost." Another example of a home-winemaking hobby gone wild was Stafford County's Potomac Point Winery. Skip and Cindi Causey opened Potomac Point in 2007 after long dreaming of going into business for themselves. Early in the 2000s, they purchased a home winemaking kit, enrolled in viticulture and oenology classes at Piedmont Virginia Community College, and toured several Virginia vineyards. The Causeys eventually purchased property in Stafford, where they constructed a large Mediterranean-inspired winery.[81]

By the late 1990s and early 2000s, the advent of "custom crush" facilities provided emerging wineries with a way to bottle wines that didn't require investing in expensive winemaking equipment. Custom crush facilities engaged in everything from winemaking consulting, business plan and goal development, to grape processing and bottling. Virginia's first custom crush facility, Virginia Wineworks, opened in 2007 at the site of the former Montdomaine Cellars south of Charlottesville. The brainchild of veteran Virginia winemaker Michael Shaps and businessman Philip Stafford, the facility was conceived as a way to assist would-be winemakers by providing winemaking space, equipment, and expertise. Virginia Wineworks was not Shaps's first encounter with Virginia wine; formerly a winemaker at Jefferson Vineyards, Shaps later moved to King Family Vineyards where proprietors David and Ellen King helped him found his own label. After spending several years studying winemaking in France, Shaps later partnered with French winemaker Michel Roucher-Sarrazin in 2003 to create a boutique winery in France's Mersault region, known as Maison Shaps et Roucher-Sarrazin.[82]

Two years after Virginia Wineworks' opening, a hybrid small winery and custom crush facility, Vint Hill Craft Winery, opened in eastern Fauquier County on the site of a former military base. Vint Hill was founded by veteran Virginia winemaker and entrepreneur Chris Pearmund, who began his viticultural career in 1990 while working for Naked Mountain Winery and Vineyards. He purchased Fauquier County's Meriwether Vineyards in 1993, and ten years later opened Pearmund Cellars, where he produced an entire line of vinifera wines.

At Vint Hill, Pearmund offered anyone—winery operators or private individuals—the chance to make his or her own barrel of wine under the guidance of a professional winemaking team. Prospective winemakers could, for a fee, customize their own barrel of wine after selecting from multiple grape varieties and barrel types, different yeasts, and wine processing options. "This is a new concept: for people to be participatory," Pearmund told a reporter at Vint Hill's opening in 2009, hoping that Vint Hill would help spur the proliferation of urban wineries across Virginia.[83]

In addition to custom crush facilities, Virginia wineries borrowed from a West Coast trend and began offering their wares at so-called "off-site tasting rooms." Such facilities, which elaborated on a concept built into the 1980 Farm Winery Act, allowed wineries to expand their direct-marketing reach, recognizing that vineyards and farm wineries were sometimes located in remote areas. Virginia's first off-site tasting room, and first urban-style winery, opened in the small southwestern town of Rural Retreat in 2007, where in the heart of downtown owner Scott Mecimore opened a tasting room for his winery, Rural Retreat Winery and Vineyards, in two renovated historic buildings. Off-site tasting rooms could later be found in downtown Middleburg, Berryville, Staunton, Norfolk, and Charlottesville.

As popular as off-site tasting rooms proved, they were not uniformly welcomed. In an industry in which personal sacrifice, quality, and craft are key, some observers felt that the facilities diminished visitors' ability to see where the grapes were grown, learn how the wines were made, and meet the winemakers. Others questioned the labeling integrity of the wines; some off-site tasting rooms explicitly promoted themselves as appendages to the parent winery, while others, often in an attempt to create a separate identity, relabeled their wines under the proprietary name of the off-site tasting operation.

This latter criticism extended far beyond facilities that self-identified as off-site tasting rooms; indeed, by the 2000s, some of the more dubious practices included procuring off-site grapes and then producing wines at other wineries or relying on custom crush operations. Of course, many nascent wineries simply lacked mature vines and vinification know-how at their birth, choosing instead to rely on the skills and facilities of veteran consulting winemakers elsewhere to assist with production and guide them through infancy. Reliance on others was often necessary for new wineries to pay down hefty construction and capitalization loans and build quality brand loyalty.

While most wineries gradually weaned themselves from such practices as the years progressed, others continued to rely on off-site production as a means and an end. In some cases, the only discernible evidence of the pedigree and location of a wine's origins was to be found on the bottle in tiny print next to the Surgeon General's Warning. Unsuspecting consumers had little clue that no wine was actually made at the place they were visiting, or that the grapevines that lined the winery's entryway were merely for show. This led some observers to criticize many Virginia wineries as little more than fancy off-site wine bars with ornamental vines. For the most part, tourists and patrons did not seem to care; most were pleased to spend a day in the countryside or tasting room, taking in the views and enjoying a good drink with friends or family.

## — Wine Festival Fever —

During the 1990s and into the new millennium, the pace of Virginia's wine-industry growth was outmatched by the profusion of more than 300 annual wine festivals, street festivals, county fairs, and farmers' markets, each of which celebrated the cultivation of the vine. While earlier celebrations during the 1970s and 1980s had featured only a handful of wineries because there were so few of them at the time, by the 1990s festivals had progressed into major tourism and economic development events, often attracting tens of thousands of attendees, national music acts, arts and crafts vendors, gourmet food, and corporate sponsorships. For the price of admission, attendees could now taste hundreds of Virginia wines, sometimes more than 400 in a single event. Festival goers could also purchase a wide variety of accessories from vendors, ranging from cigars and gourmet cutlery to pet wear, jewelry, and rhinestone-studded T-shirts. It was not uncommon to see dedicated attendees sporting small leather-and-string pouches that permitted them to carry a wine glass around the neck like a Saint Bernard. For those festivals held on hot summer days, festival planners provided cooling tents where people gathered, worn out and flushed, to sip wine and mop their faces.[84]

All of the state's early wine festivals survived into the 1990s and 2000s, growing along with the industry. By the 2000s, for example, the Vinifera Wine Growers Festival held annually in The Plains had morphed into the Virginia Wine Festival, the largest outdoor wine festival in the state. It featured wine tastings from fifty Virginia wineries, as well as food, crafts, concerts, and seminars. The Virginia Wineries Association's keynote celebration, Vintage Virginia, also grew into a biannual celebration and moved to Bull Run Regional Park in Centreville, where it offered nearly 20,000 attendees more than 350 wines from nearly 60 wineries, with seminars and nearly 100 arts and crafts exhibitors.[85]

Virginia Beach hosted its first annual Neptune Festival Wine Tasting in 1997 in conjunction with that year's Neptune Festival along the city's oceanfront. The city also launched its first "Where the Wines Meet the Sea" wine week in September 2007, which attracted more than thirty city restaurants and featured tastings, wine dinners, and seminars. In nearby Norfolk, where the Town Point Virginia Wine Festival was as popular as ever, the city added a "Made in Virginia" wine-tasting bar to the thirtieth anniversary of the Norfolk Harborfest waterfront festival in June 2006.[86]

At the other end of the state, Roanoke hosted its first Roanoke Valley Wine Festival in 1992 at the Hotel Roanoke and Conference Center. By 2012, the event had been supplanted by the Toast of the Valley, which featured wine, craft beers, music, and art and food vendors. Next door in Salem, the local chamber of commerce launched the Wine and Unwind Festival in 2008, which featured fifteen area wineries. In nearby Blacksburg, Virginia Tech hosted its first wine festival in April 2009 and celebrated its first annual Fork and Cork celebration the following month. Wine festivals were also popular in nearby Bedford County, where Peaks of Otter Winery and the Bedford County Hunt co-hosted the first annual Horse and Hound Wine Festival on a sweltering day in July 2005.[87]

In Northern Virginia, the Farm Wineries Council Inc., a farm winery advocacy organization, spearheaded the annual Virginia Wine Showcase, which featured pourings from boutique farm wineries, along with authors, retailers, chocolatiers, and seminars from chefs. Carl and Donna Henrickson, owners of Rappahannock County's Little Washington Winery, helped organize the event and, through a related organization, printed the annual *Virginia Winery-Hopping Guide*, a free, printed guide to Virginia wineries.

Wine-related fêtes also exploded in Richmond. As early as 1991, the James River Wine Festival was held downtown before moving to the Innsbrook Pavilion in nearby Henrico County. Beginning in 2004, however, Richmonders also flooded Cary Street, an area full of eclectic shops and restaurants, for the annual Carytown Food and Wine Festival, which featured tastings from multiple wineries and local restaurants. Just west of Richmond, the Powhatan County Chamber of Commerce sponsored the first annual Festival of the Grape in 2003 in Powhatan's historic Courthouse Village.[88]

Richmond also became home to the Virginia wine industry's largest annual trade and consumer event, the Virginia Wine Expo, which was held at the Greater Richmond Convention Center beginning in 2008. The idea for the two-day event came from savvy promoter Alex Papajohn. The Wine Expo's first year was a rousing success, and by 2009 was one of the state's largest wine events. Governor Bob McDonnell provided opening remarks for the 2010 event, and the following year it incorporated the Virginia Wineries Association's Governor's Cup competition award ceremony. By then, the Virginia Wine Expo had evolved into one of the nation's most-respected wine industry trade shows, and had become a much-anticipated event on Richmond's social calendar.

Wine events proved particularly lucrative for Virginia's historic trust properties. Often in need of additional funding, the properties increasingly turned to such events to generate visitors and revenue for their preservation efforts. The events introduced a new generation of Virginians to the state's past and showcased the complementary nature of history and wine tourism. At George Washington's Mount Vernon, visitors participated in the Wine Festival and Sunset Tour, held each spring and fall, which included tours of the mansion and its wine cellar as well as conversations with George and Martha Washington reenactors. Monticello, which held its first wine festival in May 2010, invited guests to visit the mansion, Jefferson's wine cellar, and the estate's restored vineyards. Other historic properties, including Orange County's Montpelier estate, home to President James Madison, Ashlawn-Highland, the home of James Monroe, George Mason's home at Gunston Hall, the Lee ancestral home of Stratford Hall, and Thomas Jefferson's Bedford County retreat at Poplar Forest, each held their own festivals.[89]

The explosion of wine festivals highlighted the fact that people were anxious to enjoy wine in the company of others. Though the agritourism days of chicken box-lunches, driving tours, tractor displays, and draft-horse exhibits were long gone, by the mid-2000s the Old Dominion's wine festival circuit easily ranked among the best in the nation.

## — State Government Support —

Beginning with the administration of Governor Mills E. Godwin, Virginia's wine industry relied to a greater or lesser degree on Virginia's government to support its growth. The active support of the state's governors was of both symbolic and substantive importance in persuading the General Assembly to enact legislation favoring the industry. As noted in the preceding chapter, Governors Robb, Baliles, and Wilder had each played a key role in promoting Virginia's wine industry. During the 1990s, the industry counted on the cooperation of Governors George F. Allen (1994–1998) and James S. Gilmore (1998–2002), both of whom continued the efforts of their predecessors, though perhaps more intermittently. Allen, a longtime Charlottesville resident and graduate of the University of Virginia School of Law, was particularly supportive of the industry, largely thanks to his representation of portions of winery-laden Albemarle and Nelson counties in the House of Delegates before his gubernatorial election.

With the wine industry growing ever faster into the new millennium, this sometimes episodic gubernatorial backing evolved into full-out support for the industry. By then, the wine industry had emerged as the commonwealth's fastest-growing agricultural sector. Whether governors were announcing wine industry initiatives or crowning the winner of the annual Governor's Cup competition, the wine industry provided Virginia's chief executives with a pleasurable respite from their otherwise difficult duties. Promotion of Virginia wine not only made for good publicity, it made financial sense, too: by the late 2000s, the commonwealth received approximately five dollars in tax revenues for each dollar Virginia spent to attract visitors to wineries.[90]

The industry counted among its biggest supporters Virginia's sixty-ninth governor, Mark R. Warner (2002–2006). What set Warner apart from his predecessors was his ownership of a fifteen-acre King George County vineyard known as Rappahannock Bend. Although he came into office without a formal wine policy, Warner presided during a time of phenomenal industry expansion, and was engaged and effective during key challenges to Virginia's Prohibition-era wine laws. He also oversaw the reorganization of the Virginia Winegrowers Advisory Board into the Virginia Wine Board, and, during the 2004 Governor's Cup ceremony, he unveiled *Vision 2015*, an aggressive eleven-year strategic plan for improving the state's wine industry and doubling its market share.[91]

*Vision 2015* represented the first comprehensive statewide strategy for the development of Virginia's wine industry. It called for an industry quality-assurance and image-enhancement program through more aggressive branding and marketing, proposed increasing wine research and development, and set goals for improvement in six areas: quality and uniqueness, image and reputation, market share, profitability, preservation of Virginia's rural character, and supply and service industries.[92]

Under *Vision 2015*, Virginia wines were to be aggressively marketed to restaurants, retailers, and distributors in an attempt to capture more space on store shelves and menus. The plan suggested that Virginia Tech offer wine-industry courses at off-campus locations, including online and at community colleges. It also recommended experimenting with niche market grapes, such as Viognier, that might help Virginia distinguish itself from other emerging wine regions. Warner charged the newly created Virginia Wine Board with implementation of the plan, and, since its adoption, *Vision 2015* has been periodically revisited and updated into a larger strategic marketing plan.[93]

Warner's lieutenant governor, Timothy M. Kaine, succeeded to the governor's chair in January 2006. Like his predecessor, Kaine did not enter office with a wine industry policy, but events during his tenure ultimately guided his approach. Kaine assumed office in the midst of several court cases challenging Virginia's direct-shipping laws, as well as the significant winery-wholesaler battles that took place during the 2006 and 2007 General Assembly sessions. While he approved a controversial 2006 bill that greatly restricted the rights of wineries to self-distribute, Kaine also signed into law legislation creating the Virginia Winery Distribution Company in 2007, a step that was widely welcomed by the industry.

Few Virginia governors, however, made wine promotion a centerpiece of their administration more than Robert F. McDonnell. Sworn into office in 2010 during a time of great worldwide financial unrest, McDonnell made Virginia's economic development his top priority. Among his efforts, McDonnell championed wine industry initiatives and singled out the commonwealth's wine industry as a "dynamic and growing" agricultural sector during his first State of the Commonwealth address in 2010.[94]

McDonnell sought to make Virginia the center of winemaking on the East Coast, proposing sharp increases in funding for new and expanding wineries, tourism promotion, and marketing. He called for a portion of Virginia's wine liter tax to be directed to the state's Wine Promotion Fund, and approved a reimbursable tax credit program for establishing or expanding vineyards and wineries. His Commission on Economic Development and Jobs Creation recommended various policy changes to boost Virginia's wine industry to national prominence.[95] Governor McDonnell aggressively promoted Virginia wine to international business leaders during foreign trade missions, and served only Virginia wines during events at the Executive Mansion as part of his "Choose the Commonwealth!" initiative.

McDonnell also relied on the efforts of his secretary of agriculture, Todd P. Haymore. Haymore, who had previously served as commissioner of the Virginia Department of Agriculture and Consumer Services, was appointed secretary of agriculture in December 2009 by Governor Kaine. A Pittsylvania County native, Haymore served as the Kaine and McDonnell administrations' chief liaison to the wine industry, and he could often be found talking with winery owners and advocacy groups, attending winery tours with foreign delegations, and issuing press releases about the industry's growth.[96]

McDonnell's wife, Maureen McDonnell, was an important advocate for the industry. Through her "First Lady's Initiatives Team Effort," she promoted Virginia wines through a seemingly endless circuit of tours, campaigns, and events. In May 2010 she visited Charlottesville-area vineyards, and that August she led representatives of several Washington, D.C.-area retail stores and restaurants on a two-day blitz of Fauquier and Loudoun County wineries. In conjunction with Virginia Wine Week in March 2011, she planted ten Chambourcin vines, the first at Virginia's Executive Mansion. To mark the 200th anniversary of that building two years later, the McDonnells introduced a blended red wine dubbed "1813," made from those Chambourcin grapes and three vintages procured from the vineyards of members of the Virginia Wine Board. A total of 1,813 bottles were produced, all of which were designated for a specific use by the Virginia Wine Board Marketing Office.[97]

Reaction from Virginia's vintners to the McDonnell administration's overtures was positive. "This is actually the first time that I've felt that kind of connection with our government, that they are really promoting this like I think they should," said John Higgs, owner of Barren Ridge Vineyards. "What it shows me is that this administration is serious about helping local industry," Tony Champ, owner of White Hall Vineyards, told a reporter. "In California, people tend to drink more California wines, but we don't seem to do the same in Virginia. Efforts like this could help change that."

McDonnell's successor, Terry R. McAuliffe (2014–2018), was no stranger to Virginia wine; as a gubernatorial candidate in April 2010, he launched a four-day personal trade mission to Cuba with several Virginia businessmen, where he persuaded the Cuban government to accept Virginia wine imports. As governor, McAuliffe retained Todd Haymore as secretary of agriculture, a move welcomed by the wine industry, but he was criticized for relaxing Governor McDonnell's practice of serving exclusively Virginia wines at the Executive Mansion.[98]

Downstairs from the governor's ceremonial office in the State Capitol, legislators continued their perennial struggles over the wine industry. Though forced to resolve the pitched battles between wholesalers and wine producers over direct distribution rights in the early 2000s, the General Assembly found time to address less contentious issues, too. In 2000, the legislature approved an increase in the maximum alcohol content of wines produced by Virginia farm wineries from 14 to 18 percent. Three years later, it approved an increase in the number of off-site retail sales and tasting privileges a winery could use on any given day, yet another chink in the rusting armor of Prohibition.

A substantial change for the industry came in 2004, when the General Assembly accepted Governor Warner's recommendations and reorganized the Virginia Winegrowers Advisory Board into the Virginia Wine Board, the first update to the state's primary wine governing body since 1985. The Virginia Wine Board would henceforth be headed by the commissioner of VDACS, along with nine wine industry representatives appointed by the governor. While the new Board continued to serve as the coordinator of the commonwealth's wine industry initiatives, it was also granted new authorization to raise money, enter contracts, conduct research, publish, and engage in marketing and promotion. The 2004 legislation also eliminated the wine liter tax as a funding mechanism, and replaced the former Winegrowers Productivity Fund with a new Virginia Wine Promotion Fund, one-third of which was to be spent on research, with the balance to be allocated for promotion and administrative expenses.[99]

In 2008, with the wholesaler-winery battles largely resolved by the creation of the Virginia Winery Distribution Company a year before, the General Assembly passed the so-called "Sangria Bill," which permitted restaurants, bars, and wineries to serve mixed drinks consisting of wine, beer, and distilled spirits. That summer, Virginia's wineries began providing samples of sangria wines and cold, slushy mixed drinks in tasting rooms.

Two years later, the legislature passed two key bills. The first permitted representatives from distilleries and wineries to conduct tastings at Virginia's ABC stores. The second, even more consequentially, doubled the sums contributed to the Virginia Wine Promotion Fund to $1.35 million, and rededicated a portion of the wine liter tax as a long-term funding source. In 2011, the General Assembly passed a law that permitted restaurants, at their discretion, to allow customers to consume wine purchased elsewhere. To help offset potential lost profits, restaurants could charge up to a seventy-five-dollar corkage fee to open each bottle, though most set their price based on the average bottle price or even less. While some restaurateurs initially expressed misgivings about potential revenue losses, others welcomed the move. Winemaker Chris Pearmund offered to refund half of the corkage fee on any Virginia wine, not just his own, and the Tuskies Restaurant Group waived the corkage fee at their five affiliated Northern Virginia restaurants for any Virginia wine purchased the same day.[100]

Though the General Assembly's wine-related actions generated mostly positive outcomes for the industry, not every initiative met with success. In 2005 the General Assembly authorized the Virginia Department of Motor Vehicles to issue a wine-themed license plate if the DMV received 350 prepaid applications. The proposal for the plate, which would have featured two clusters of grapes with the phrase "First in Wine," was abandoned in 2008 when too few people applied.[101]

Much of the wine industry's legislative accomplishments during the 2000s came as a result of the efforts of a small cadre of winery owners, attorneys, and government affairs consultants, each of whom developed strategies, built personal relationships, and championed industry causes before the General Assembly. The industry benefitted from the legal and political skills of Richmond lawyer Terri C. Beirne, who began representing the Virginia Wineries Association in 2002 as a lobbyist. Before her 2008 appointment to serve as counsel to the California-based Wine Institute, Beirne worked with the legislature on matters related to direct shipping and helped establish the Virginia Winery Distribution Company.

Joining Beirne in the fight was David King, an Albemarle County winery owner who spent much of the 2007 session seeking a way out of the wine industry's distribution quagmires. A Texan by birth, King and his wife, Ellen, relocated from Houston to a 327-acre farm in the Crozet area of Albemarle County in the middle 1990s. Two years later, after attending grape seminars and hiring veteran Virginia vineyard consultant Chris Hill and winemaker Michael Shaps, the Kings planted an eight-acre vineyard and later opened King Family Vineyards.

King was first attracted to the public policy aspects of the wine industry during Albemarle County's winery zoning ordinance battles in the mid-2000s, and later came to believe that the growing demands of the Virginia wine industry necessitated a permanent physical presence in Richmond. He therefore formed the Virginia Wine Council, which contracted with a Richmond lobbying firm, Alliance Group, to represent the industry before the state government. Alliance assigned the capable Matthew A. Conrad as the Virginia Wine Council's first lobbyist, and he served until 2010.[102]

Alongside Virginia's governors and legislature, some of the commonwealth's executive branch agencies intensified their efforts to promote Virginia wine. Responsibility for wine publicity during this period primarily fell to the Virginia Wine Marketing Office, which coordinated an increasing number of events, festivals, and promotions. In 1999 the Wine Marketing Office, in coordination with the Virginia Tourism Corporation and VDACS, unveiled Virginia wine country vacation packages to introduce the Old Dominion's wineries to new markets with high per-capita wine consumption rates and significant disposable income. For a starting price of $199 per person, travelers could visit the state's wine regions and receive special discounts and bonuses at wineries, hotels, and participating restaurants.

The Wine Marketing Office's efforts played an increasingly important role as the industry matured and the number of wineries and wine events swelled. Much of the credit for the office's work was due to its capable staff, including Mary Davis-Barton, who succeeded Wendy C. Rizzo as director of the Wine Marketing Office in 1994. Davis-Barton, who had previously worked for six years marketing other agricultural products, worked with wine marketing specialist Barbara Payton until her departure early in the 2000s. The Wine Marketing Office was reconstituted in 2007 after a brief hiatus, when the Virginia Wine Board contracted with Ringwood Boyd Marketing to manage the Wine Marketing Office's efforts. Annette R. Boyd, who had served as the Wine Marketing Office's second director from 1987 to 1992, set about reinventing the office's promotional efforts and worked to implement the goals of the *Vision 2015* strategic plan. By spring 2008, she had created an impressive website, produced online guides to wine events throughout the state, and opened a new Wine Marketing Office in Richmond's historic Old City Hall. Boyd also coordinated with the state's various wine organizations, including the Virginia Wineries Association, to develop logos, advertising campaigns, tasting booklets, and public relations efforts for the annual Governor's Cup competition.[103]

In 2008, Boyd's office partnered with the Virginia Tourism Corporation on several promotional events to commemorate both the twentieth anniversary of Virginia Wine Month and the fortieth anniversary of VTC's stupendously successful "Virginia is for Lovers" slogan. Virginia Wine Month continued to be the largest program sponsored by the Wine Marketing Office, and that year VTC featured Barboursville winemaker Luca Paschina it its "Portraits of

Passion" campaign. It included a feature spread in VTC's 2009 state travel guide as well as an online video clip. VTC also spearheaded a "20 Ways to Celebrate 20 Years of Virginia Wine Month" advertising campaign on the state's website, which featured more than sixty wine-related events.[104]

In October 2008, the Wine Marketing Office held two promotional wine tastings to draw attention to the state's improving wine quality over the previous two decades. The events were retrospective: the first, a "Heritage Tasting," featured fourteen award-winning wines from vintages between 1988 and 2000; the second, held at the Capitol during a celebration of Virginia Wine Month, featured wines from twenty-four wineries and attracted nearly 200 people, including Governor Kaine and former governor Gerald Baliles, the latter of whom signed the proclamation in 1988 designating the first Virginia Wine Month.[105]

Commemorative wine events continued into 2010 when, as part of the celebration of the 150th anniversary of the Civil War, Virginia's Commonwealth Transportation Board awarded $3.5 million to fund a Civil War tourism partnership between the Virginia Department of Transportation, VTC, and the Virginia Wine Board. While a majority of the partnership's funds were designated for multimedia information terminals at highway rest areas, the Wine Marketing Office worked with twenty-nine wineries to develop thirty-two specially labeled Civil War–themed wines. Participating wineries either added a Civil War image to their labels or created new wines with names like General's Battlefield Red, Brothers at War, or Sunrise Surrender. To encourage collaboration with battlefield parks, the Wine Marketing Office developed a wine passport program for each of the participating wineries featuring images of the special labels and a pullout map of the wineries and nearby battlefields.[106]

In March 2010, the Wine Marketing Office and VTC announced a weeklong promotion, "Love by the Glass." Taking place at the end of March to promote Virginia wines during a slow part of the year, Love by the Glass featured promotions by Virginia restaurants and retailers that offered at least two Virginia wines for sale by the glass. Enthusiasm for the new wine week proved so popular that, by 2012, the entire month of March had been rechristened "Virginia Wine and Dine Month," with retailers featuring specials and hotels offering wine-related packages with names like "Winter Wine and Romance Package," "Wine, Dine, and Get Pampered with the Girls Package," and "Shared Wines and Treasured Times."[107]

Work continued into September 2010, when the Wine Board hosted a delegation from the Circle of Wine Writers, a British organization of wine journalists and broadcasters. The group visited eleven Virginia wineries and attended several wine-pairing dinners, regional tasting events, and tours of Monticello and Williamsburg. Circle members came away from the tour impressed not only by the quality of the wines, but by the integrated efforts and offerings of Virginia's wine-related tourism. "I was utterly captivated by Virginia: its scenery, history, people, and wines," noted wine expert and Circle member Peter F. May. "Up to now, the natural destination for those interested in American wines has been California. However, Virginia has the advantage for Europeans of being much closer and having wines that are restrained and elegant."[108]

The Circle of Wine Writers event signaled the Wine Marketing Office's new emphasis on generating "buzz" about the Virginia wine industry by soliciting the support of domestic and international wine writers, authors, and journalists. In April 2011, for example, the Wine Marketing Office attracted the 2011 Wineries Unlimited trade show to the Greater Richmond Convention Center. The second-largest winery conference in North America, Wineries Unlimited had long been held in Pennsylvania, and its relocation to the Old Dominion was viewed as a major victory. The three-day event resulted in $1.3 million in revenue and attracted some 2,100 visitors, twice as many as in previous years. "The outpouring of enthusiasm and excitement we've received in the State of Virginia, from the wine industry up to the governor, has been tremendous," said Robert Merletti, publisher of *Vineyard & Winery Management* magazine, which produced the conference.[109]

Joining the ever-expanding list of events were two VTC tourism commercials unveiled in 2011. The first ran in eight out-of-state media markets and depicted views of beaches, mountains, battlefields, vineyards, and wineries. The second, a thirty-second Virginia Wine Month commercial, showed a 360-degree time-lapse view of wine being poured into a wine glass during which a dulcet voiceover told viewers that,

> In every glass of Virginia wine, there is a note of devotion, the spice of infatuation, instant attraction, and just a hint of true love. Follow your heart to Virginia's wineries, and the whole state is your tasting room. It's time to discover your local crush.

One of the more visible signs of state support for the wine industry came in April 2012, when Governor McDonnell unveiled a new wine signage program along Virginia's highways. Jointly funded by federal and state grants, the program placed large highway markers acknowledging the state's winemaking regions at key entry points along major roads. The attractive signs were among the only such state-funded markers in the nation, and were similar to the "World Famous Wine Growing Region" signs that had long dotted California's Napa

Valley. Not since the 1987 installation of the first, now ubiquitous, grape-cluster road signs had there been such explicit official endorsement of the Virginia wine industry.[110]

To kick off Virginia Wine Month in October 2012, the Wine Marketing Office and VTC partnered with Fairfax County–based Reston Limousine and Whole Foods grocery stores in Northern Virginia and Richmond to promote the "Discover Your Local Crush" promotion. This unique (for Virginia) public-private campaign offered day-trip tours of Loudoun County and Charlottesville-area wineries, tastings with various Virginia winemakers at Whole Foods, and an eye-catching, colorful vineyard-themed vehicle, dubbed the "Virginia Crush Bus." That same month, the Wine Marketing Office coordinated its inaugural Virginia Wine Summit, which attracted industry enthusiasts and featured sessions about Virginia's wine varieties and trends. The British wine writer and consultant editor of *Decanter* magazine Steven Spurrier provided a keynote address for the event, during which he lauded the growth of Virginia's industry:

> Before coming out here, I knew already that Virginia could stand tall for the product. But in just three days I now know that the place and the people fit perfectly into the equation and that Virginia stands tall on all three and will continue to do so for the foreseeable future.[111]

As the keynote speaker for the 2013 Wine Summit, famed British wine writer Oz Clarke praised Virginians for their uniqueness, urging the commonwealth's vintners to explore niche Virginia grapes like Nebbiolo and Petit Manseng.

As the wine industry matured, Virginia's public institutions of higher education continued its steadfast support, initiated long before. Efforts were most substantial at Virginia Tech, which worked to enhance its regional and national reputation by increasing its enological research. One brief initiative came in 2000, when formal grape evaluations were launched at the school's Southern Piedmont Agricultural Research and Extension Center (SPAREC) in Blackstone. Overseen by Dr. Jeremy A. Pattison, the tests recorded the performance of grape varieties in relation to the soil and climatic conditions of the southern Virginia Piedmont. To assist winemakers in identifying and correcting deficiencies in wine, Virginia Tech launched a new Enology Services Laboratory in 2006, providing chemical, physical, microbiological, and sensory analyses.[112]

In 2010, Virginia Tech's College of Agriculture and Life Sciences received a $3.8 million grant from the U.S. Department of Agriculture to lead a five-year, multistate effort to improve grape and wine quality in the eastern United States. Project goals included encouraging research-based wine evaluations and determining optimal crop-leaf balance to promote wine grape quality. Virginia Tech's geospatial information students assisted with the effort, creating a computer program to evaluate climactic and soil characteristics of properties for appropriate grape varieties.[113]

At Virginia Tech's sister land-grant institution, Virginia State University, researchers established the commonwealth's first experimental organic vineyard at Eppington, a historic tobacco plantation in southern Chesterfield County. There, in 2012, the school planted 225 vines and either declined to treat the vines for fungi or treated them with organic elements, including sulfur and copper.[114]

These research efforts were complimented by the more moderate attempts of Virginia Tech's chief collegiate rival, the University of Virginia. Despite its 1819 founding by oenophile Thomas Jefferson, and though located in the heart of Central Virginia's wine country, the university offered no programs on Virginia wine prior to 2007. That year, however, the university's School of Continuing and Professional Studies launched a five-day program, "Virginia's Wine Legacy: From Jefferson to the Present," which traced the evolution of winemaking from Thomas Jefferson to the modern era. Program participants spent each morning learning about Virginia's wine history, visited Charlottesville-area wineries each afternoon, and enjoyed a gourmet dinner each evening.[115]

UVA also began offering noncredit social science courses in Virginia wine history during the 2008–2009 academic year, and in 2010 its Department of Science, Technology, and Society offered a unique three-credit course, the Curious History of Wine in Virginia: A Sociotechnical Systems Approach, which examined the pre–Revolutionary War history of Virginia wine and activities associated with grape-growing, winemaking, and wine sales. That same year members of the public were invited to attend the university's More Than the Score pre-game lecture series. Held on the days of home football games, the series featured discussions on Virginia wine history and the state's future growth. In January 2011, the Darden School of Business's Wine and Cuisine Club sponsored a one-day food and beverage conference that focused on Virginia as an emerging alcoholic beverage production center.[116]

Promotion of Virginia wine was also an increasing priority for the University of Virginia Alumni Association, which in 2009 held a small wine festival during its annual reunions weekend. During the event, more than 300 alumni sampled and rated wines from twelve Charlottesville-area wineries. The winning wines became the first offered under the association's new Virginia wine program, which offered wines to alumni at a discounted price. In April 2012 the association also announced "1819 Wine," a private-label vintage commemorating the school's founding. The label featured the Rotunda and the bottle came in a commemorative wooden gift-box. Much to the chagrin of alumni who preferred that Mr. Jefferson's university honor its Virginia roots, however, the wine was actually crafted and bottled in California by an alumnus who was a former owner of Napa Valley's Screaming Eagle Winery.[117]

The Old Dominion's community college system joined its four-year brethren in promoting the wine industry by offering courses that filled its institutional mission and addressed the need for a more experienced cadre of wine industry workers. In 2005, Piedmont Virginia Community College launched a workshop series in winemaking, soil preparation, grape planting and harvesting, and marketing. These noncredit courses were held in classrooms and at local vineyards; interest was so strong that PVCC converted the seminars into two certificate programs in viticulture and enology the following year. PVCC also attracted international recognition through its unique ten-week internship program in conjunction with the South African wine industry, which offered a select group of disadvantaged South Africans the ability to study Virginia and California winemaking.[118]

Other Virginia community colleges also offered introductory courses in viticulture and vineyard management, including Virginia Western Community College, Patrick Henry Community College, and Rappahannock Community College. At Dabney S. Lancaster Community College in Clifton Forge, Covington resident Judson Howard taught a noncredit introductory winemaking course. Northern Virginia Community College, Virginia's largest, partnered with Lord Fairfax Community College in 2006 to offer a popular wine fundamentals course at Clarke County's Veramar Vineyard. In 2015, NVCC began offering viticultural, vineyard management, and pest and disease management courses.[119]

## —Star Power—

For decades, actors, entertainers, athletes, and other famous or wealthy people with an affection for wine had made substantial investments in vineyards. They launched personalized wine brands, produced small batches for friends and family, and lent their names to limited-edition wines. Many dabbled in the wine industry as a hobby, for an encore career, to maintain name recognition, or simply because they enjoyed making wine. This trend was not lost on the Old Dominion, where the wine industry attracted a growing number of well-known individuals eager to bring about their own signature class of Virginia wines.

In 1999, five years after his band scored a hit with the song "What Would You Say," musician and Charlottesville resident Dave Matthews purchased

Blenheim Vineyards and its surrounding 1,260-acre farm in southern Albemarle County. Blenheim had long operated as a winery under the direction of former Ohio grain farmer John Marquis, Sr., whose son planted ten acres of vinifera grapes as early as 1979. After Matthews' purchase, the singer attempted to convert Blenheim into a model organic operation that complimented his other artistic pursuits. In time, Blenheim featured grass-fed livestock, organic vegetable gardens, and a recording studio. After planting a five-acre vineyard in 1999, Matthews reopened Blenheim Winery in 2001. He hired a longtime friend, veteran Virginia winemaker Brad McCarthy, as general manager and winemaker. Matthews and McCarthy developed creative differences, and in 2008 Matthews hired University of Virginia graduate Kristy Harmon as winemaker. Harmon, who had previously worked at wineries in Virginia, France, New Zealand, and California, was later promoted to general manager.[120]

In 2004, John Kent Cooke, son of the former owner of the Washington Redskins, alongside his wife, Rita Cooke, announced his intention to build a state-of-the-art winery at his 150-acre Boxwood Farm just south of Middleburg. Cooke's initial plans called for a boutique winery that would produce high-end, Bordeaux-style wines to appeal to exclusive restaurants and sophisticated oenophiles. Boxwood Winery was designed from the outset to be an architectural treasure. Its four sleek buildings were made from glass, concrete, and Virginia fieldstone, and each was dedicated to a different part of the winemaking process. Stainless steel pipes transferred grape juice from one building to the next, while a unique circular underground wine cave housed French oak barrels. Cooke tapped his stepdaughter, Rachel Martin, to manage Boxwood's operations and, on her advice, planted cloned French grapevines under the supervision of viticultural consultant Lucie Morton. Martin also hired a relatively young but experienced Canadian winemaker, Adam McTaggart, and brought on famous French wine consultant Stéphane Derenoncourt as an advisor. Boxwood quickly developed a reputation for quality wine, and beginning in 2009, Martin petitioned the U.S. Alcohol and Tobacco Tax and Trade Bureau to create Virginia's seventh American Viticultural Area around Middleburg. The Middleburg AVA was approved in 2012.[121]

The same year Cooke announced his plans for Boxwood Winery, Jess and Sharon Sweely opened a high-end vineyard and winery in Madison County called Sweely Estate Winery, with the intention of producing between 25,000 and 30,000 cases annually. They built a nearly $7 million, 18,000-square-foot winery and event center, and purchased modern computerized equipment, an on-site bottling system, and wind machines for the vineyards. For all their investment, though, the Sweelys announced in October 2010 that their property would be sold at a foreclosure auction the following month. Much of the problem apparently stemmed from the winery's inability to sell its product to wholesalers during trying economic times. "If I'd had known there was a recession, we wouldn't have built what we built at this point in time," Jess Sweely told a reporter about the foreclosure. The lack of a market for their wine was apparently so bad that their winemaker, Frantz Ventre, was forced to sell his 2010 harvest to other winemakers, instead of producing a 2010 vintage.[122]

After twice going to auction over a two-year period, the winery was purchased in November 2011 by businessman and former America Online chief executive Steve Case and his wife, Jean Case. The Cases, who had become enamored with Virginia wine following visits to Charlottesville-area wineries, renovated the facility and replanted several acres of underperforming vines. They rechristened the winery Early Mountain Vineyards. "Our goal is for us and our team to be out in some markets in Virginia and building exposure for Virginia wines," Jean Case told reporters following the purchase. "There's a beautiful opportunity to be out there with a wine, and show people the quality it represents."[123]

Though the investments made by Dave Matthews, John Kent Cooke, Jess and Sharon Sweely, and Steve and Jean Case were indeed substantial, they were exceeded by those of one Charlottesville vintner, Patricia Kluge. As an outcome of a 1990 divorce settlement from media mogul John W. Kluge, Patricia Kluge acquired some 1,800 acres southeast of Charlottesville. The property featured a 23,500-square-foot mansion known as Albemarle House, as well as an Arnold Palmer–designed golf course, staff lodging, a croquet lawn, a multilevel formal English garden, a log cabin, and a Gothic-inspired chapel.[124]

Living a mere stone's throw from Thomas Jefferson's Monticello, Kluge attempted to create an economic powerhouse that combined wine, gourmet foods, tourism, and residential real estate into a new standard for Virginia winemaking. Together with her second husband, Bill Moses, Kluge adopted a business model largely borrowed from California's Robert Mondavi, one that sought to compete against the finest wines in the world. "We did months of research and travel and decided we could either be a regional winery or a world-class winery," said a determined Kluge in 2006. "We are in the great-wine business."[125]

The centerpiece of her efforts was the creation of one of the most notable wineries in Virginia history, Kluge Estate Winery and Vineyard, which opened in the autumn of 2002. Kluge invested a reported $50 million into the winery, with a plan to bottle between 50,000 and 60,000 cases per year from the outset. She hired a first-rate staff, including Gabriele Rausse as winemaking consultant, and appointed brand managers in Hong Kong and Paris. A fan of European wines, Kluge hired internationally renowned wine consultant Michel Rolland and employed equally capable French winemakers Claude Thibaut, Laurent Champs, and Charles Gendrot.[126]

Kluge threw a lavish fête in New York City to celebrate the opening, attended by luminaries including former vice president Al Gore. At a separate ceremony at the winery a few days later, Governor Mark Warner cut the ribbon on the winery's tasting room, known as the Farm Shop. "I don't do anything halfway," Kluge said to a reporter. "So to enter into the wine business with anything less than 100 percent commitment, the utmost passion, and excitement never crossed my mind."[127]

Her winery investments were matched by other ventures, including the 2003 opening of Fuel Co., a retro bistro located in a converted gas station in Charlottesville. In the autumn of 2006, she commenced the conversion of a former carriage museum into a 37,500-square-foot visitor center and sparkling wine operation. As discussed later in this chapter, Kluge also began planning a large luxury residential subdivision adjacent to her winery, dubbed Vineyard Estates, where homebuyers could own their own vineyard.[128]

Amid the buzz, however, ran a current of anxiety that Kluge's lavish spending bordered on reckless. The prices charged for her wines were also of concern, sometimes being twice that of other Virginia wines. During one CNBC television interview in 2002, the interviewer expressed surprise that Kluge would charge eighty dollars for her wine. Veteran winemaker Jim Law of Linden Vineyards, who welcomed Kluge's investment in the state's wine industry, also offered a caution: "She's got to be concerned. I'm concerned. What happens if the [*Wine Spectator*] gives her sixty-dollar red an 82 [a mediocre score]? Will she be a laughingstock? And will the publicity she's getting for the Virginia industry backfire?" To such criticism and reservations, Kluge responded, "They won't." She claimed in a May 2003 issue of *W Magazine* that she could command higher prices because hers were the only superior wines in Virginia. "Our success will affect the other winemakers," she told the magazine. "They know that Virginia has the potential to be a major wine region, but they need someone to be the catalyst." Few, however, could bicker with Kluge's goal: to build a major wine company that could compete with any in the world.[129]

This is not to say that Kluge failed to value other Virginia wines; indeed, she and Moses publicly commended other Virginia wines at every opportunity. Her goal was simply to improve the state's wine reputation. "Whenever you have a winery like Kluge Estate Winery that's producing top quality wines that are reaching folks at the national level, it helps everyone in the Virginia wine

267

industry," said Wine Marketing Office director Annette Boyd. Or, as Bill Moses put it, "A rising tide lifts all boats."[130]

By the mid-2000s, with a vineyard covering more than 160 acres and a winery producing approximately 35,000 cases annually, it appeared Kluge's investment was paying off. The Farm Shop provided hundreds of wine tastings per day; the winery produced multiple blends sold in fifteen states. Kluge pressed forward with her blitzkrieg-like expansion plans, working to sell her wines in Europe and the other thirty-five American states. Kluge's "rising tide," however, was about to fall.[131]

For years, rumors had quietly circulated that the winery and other operations suffered from a string of bad managerial decisions. Multiple winemakers left and the world economic crisis that began in September 2008 threatened the winery's long-term stability. Things had indeed begun unraveling in July 2007, when, to the surprise of many, Kluge's Fuel Co. bistro suddenly closed. That same month, Kluge was sued by a Charlottesville-area upholstery-cleaning service for unpaid bills dating back to April 2006. Then, in early October 2009, Kluge announced that she was auctioning some of her prized silver collection. Later that October, *The Wall Street Journal* broke the news that 300 acres of her estate, including her beloved Albemarle House, were listed for sale by Sotheby's International Realty for a stratospheric $100 million, making the offering one of the most expensive listings in the country. Kluge and Moses said they simply had too many pressing commitments, were merely looking to downsize, and that the sale of the property would not jeopardize the winery.[132]

As though the potential sale of Albemarle House were not proof enough of Kluge's worsening financial situation, in April 2010 Sotheby's auctioned Kluge's jewelry for $5 million. Two months later, it auctioned additional furniture and fine art that had graced Albemarle House during a two-day on-site home-auction extravaganza attended by some 2,000 people. Still, Kluge remained silent as to her financial health, electing only to say that the winery would not be affected.[133]

Conditions worsened further in November 2010, when reports surfaced that Kluge owed more than $86,000 in unpaid real estate taxes as well as an estimated $34.8 million to Farm Credit Bank for a loan secured by the winery and vineyard. "There is no doubt we overleveraged the company," a distraught Moses told a reporter, noting that the winery's struggles were the result of a perfect storm of a bad economy, highly paid consultants, a high-profile national sales team, and substantial investments in the vineyard and winemaking process. Unable to renegotiate its loans, Farm Credit seized control of the winery's operations in 2011, dismissed employees, and began mothballing the operation.[134]

Farm Credit announced a foreclosure sale for the winery property, the largest in Albemarle County history, which excluded Albemarle House. Though Kluge and Moses pressed the bank to postpone the sale and renegotiate the loan, the auction took place on the steps of the Albemarle County Courthouse on December 8, 2011. The bank took back the property after waiting fifteen minutes to see if one of the registered bidders would outbid its own $19 million opening bid. Left now with the unenviable task of offloading the property, Farm Credit subsequently sought a buyer at $20 to $25 million, a fraction of the estimated millions that Kluge and Moses had invested in the property.[135]

Three days after the foreclosure, some 10,000 cases of unsold Kluge wine were auctioned off at bargain-basement prices in nearby Madison County. Industry insiders were concerned that the flood of low-priced Kluge wine would glut the market, devalue other Virginia wines, and make the state's wine industry "look amateurish." Many feared that a fire sale would send the message that the Virginia wine industry was not yet ready for major outside investment.[136]

With her winery now shuttered, the nail in the Kluge wine coffin was driven in January 2011 when Bank of America initiated foreclosure proceedings on Albemarle House and ninety-eight surrounding acres. For a short while no one knew what would become of the former Kluge property. And then, in April 2011, real estate businessman, longtime Kluge friend, and future United States President Donald Trump purchased the winery property for $6.2 million, substantially below Farm Credit's asking price. The following September, Trump negotiated the purchase of Albemarle House for $6.5 million, again, substantially below the bank's asking price.[137]

Trump unveiled his plans for a rechristened Trump Winery at a press conference in October 2011, attended by Governor Bob McDonnell, First Lady Maureen McDonnell, and Secretary of Agriculture Todd Haymore. "I think we can make this one of the finest, if not the finest, winery anywhere, really, in the country," Donald Trump said. Patricia Kluge herself was present and remarked, "What was paramount to me was seeing that what I built [will] be saved, because the loss of the winery would have had a negative impact on Virginia's wine industry."[138]

Trump tasked his son, Eric Trump, with overseeing the renovation and refurbishment of the winery. Many of Kluge's former wines were relabeled with Trump Vineyards labels, and Kluge's former Farm Shop tasting room was renovated with Trump's signature gilded touch. It offered sit-down wine tasting flights and gourmet foods served by a wait staff. Trump retained Kluge as the winery's manager on a one-year contract to help the Trump family take over the winery.

Though Trump may have saved the winery, the Kluge foreclosures reverberated across the Virginia wine industry. It had lost not only one of its top producers, but also one of its most recognizable names. "Any loss of anyone in the wine industry is a loss to the state," said J. "Rock" Stephens, then-chair of the Virginia Wine Board. Pamela Margaux, a Charlottesville-area distributor married to former Kluge winemaker Claude Thibaut, noted to a reporter that while there was "no love lost" between her and Kluge, she was nevertheless "sad for the Virginia wine industry."

In hindsight, explanations and excuses for the winery's downfall were legion. Some blamed Kluge's undoing on poor winery and vineyard management decisions. Others suggested Kluge was a victim of simply trying to do too much, too fast. "Just like the rest of the economy, there are ups and downs in the wine industry," Annette Boyd told a reporter. "Kluge tried to grow very quickly and then the economy bottomed out." Richmond wine shop owner Bob Kocher offered a more critical assessment:

> Napa started in barns, they didn't start in tasting rooms. [Kluge] was trying to make a fast dime when they should have made a slow nickel....
> I don't think she was a person that really knew the wine industry, in general, and I think she just went overboard telling people she would go global before even she went Virginia-wide.[139]

Nearly everyone agreed that the Kluge story was a cautionary tale about the pitfalls involved with running a high-risk venture like a winery. Many concluded she had overleveraged her business and paid top dollar for everything, all in the faith that doing so would produce the best wines and ensure automatic success. What became clear, however, was that simply spending money as a way to ensure positive results, absent the critical ingredients of a strong business acumen, knowledge of the winemaking process, and financial restraint, ultimately led to the winery's downfall. Sadly, the phrase "Don't Kluge it," became a popular refrain among prospective and experienced Virginia winemakers alike.

Following the foreclosures, Bill Moses pondered aloud to reporters whether he and Kluge would have made the same business choices again knowing the outcome. "It's hard to say," he said to a reporter, "but everything that has been lost has been lost because Patricia was dedicated to the winery. We wanted it to succeed and she put everything she had into it." Moses's words rang true, for despite the soured relationships, managerial decisions, and outcomes, Patricia Kluge was willing to sell everything, including most of her personal fortune and possessions, to keep her winery going and find ways to produce Virginia wines that rivaled the world's best.

## —Telling the Virginia Wine Story—

Throughout the 1990s, and especially after 2000, Virginia's wine industry gained increasing recognition in top lifestyle magazines, news publications, books, and even the movies. This was largely due to the state's improved wine quality and its eclectic mix of new restaurants, appealing accommodations, and historic attractions, all of which made the commonwealth a valued travel destination. Governmental support through marketing efforts was often cited as a primary reason for the dramatic improvement in Virginia's wine quality. Such publicity helped introduce outsiders to Virginia's viticultural offerings and spread the word about an industry on the rise.

One of the world's two leading wine magazines, *Wine Spectator*, singled out Virginia as "America's most promising emerging wine region" in September 1992, while *Travel and Leisure* ranked the Old Dominion as one of the top five new wine travel destinations in the world in 2007. *Gourmet Magazine*, along with the International Culinary Tourism Association and the Travel Industry Association, ranked Virginia eighth in the nation for wine tourism in 2007, and in 2008, *Coastal Living* magazine named Ingleside Vineyards' four-bedroom Leeds Cove cottage as one of its Top 10 Wine Getaways. Another accolade came late in 2011 from the world's other great wine magazine, *Wine Enthusiast*, which named Virginia a Top 10 Wine Destination for 2012. Although many people, over many years, had proclaimed Virginia as the next great wine region, by the middle of the 2000s it appeared that the promise had been realized.

Virginia's newspapers also increased their coverage of Virginia wine developments and events. There were those, however, who felt the need for new publications specializing in Virginia's wine industry. The first privately funded newsletter devoted purely to Virginia wine was launched in 1997. *Virginia Wine Gazette* featured stories of relevance to both consumers and industry insiders. A second, and short-lived publication, *Flavor Magazine*, covered the Washington, D.C.–area's growing local food and sustainable agriculture movement, and featured a Virginia wine section in each issue. The best-known and most widely circulated Virginia wine magazine, *Virginia Wine Lover*, debuted in May 2008. Unveiled during troubling times for American print media, the concept came from Randy Thompson and Frank Britt, both of whom believed that a high-quality magazine could fill a niche for Virginia-based wine tourism. The magazine, which was later rebranded to *Savor Virginia*, premiered in 2008, and counted an award-winning Hampton Roads food writer and chef, Patrick Evans-Hylton, as its first editor.[140]

Other books, too, figured prominently in spreading information about the Old Dominion's wine industry. While many only scratched the surface with wine tour routes, pricing information, and the like, other books provided more thoughtful reviews. Author James Gabler, for example, offered an introspective look into Thomas Jefferson's wine preferences in his 1995 book, *Passions: The Wines and Travels of Thomas Jefferson*, while Faye Chewning Weems poetically detailed Virginia's wineries in her 2001 book, *Virginia Wineries: Your Complete Tour Guide*. In 2001, Oakencroft Vineyard and Winery's Felicia Warburg Rogan authored a sixty-four-page volume, *Virginia Wines and Wineries*, and in 2009, Chiles T. A. Larson published a pictorial history of Barboursville Vineyards. Baltimore writer Paul Lukacs offered detailed descriptions of Virginia wine and winemaker Dennis Horton in his 2000 work, *American Vintage*, and in *The Great Wines of America*, published in 2005.[141]

Perhaps the most extensive volume on Virginia wine history published in the early 2000s was Walker Elliott Rowe's *A History of Virginia Wines: From Grapes to Glass*, released in December 2009. Rowe's book was joined in 2012 by Richard G. Leahy's *Beyond Jefferson's Vines*, which discussed the development of Virginia wine in the modern era. Leahy, a writer who had long covered Virginia wines since the mid-1980s, had freelanced as a writer for the *Charlottesville Business Journal* and the *Virginia Wine Gazette*, among others, and maintained a widely-read Virginia wine blog. Andrea E. Saathoff, whose Albemarle Limousine company began offering Virginia winery tours under the trade name "Blue Ridge Wine Excursions" in 2009, authored *Blue Ridge Wine Excursions* in 2014, which provided wine tasting and historic information on wineries in the greater Charlottesville area. By 2017, most books which covered wine regions across the world included at least a passing mention to the Old Dominion.

Books covering the industry were not limited to nonfiction accounts. In September 2006, Ellen Crosby published *The Merlot Murders*, a murder mystery set in Northern Virginia's wine country. Crosby, a longtime freelance feature writer for *The Washington Post*, detailed the life of a fictional character, Lucie Montgomery (loosely based, it would seem, on the real-life Virginia vineyard consultant Lucie Morton), who returned to her parent's vineyard and her dysfunctional siblings after studying in France. Crosby's five sequels, published between 2007 and 2012, told the tales of Lucie's adventures across the Old Dominion. Each included information on Virginia winemaking, local lore, weather, grape cultivation, and the winemaking legacy of Thomas Jefferson.[142]

The wine industry also found itself prominently featured in two documentary films in the 2000s. The first, *The Cultivated Life: Thomas Jefferson and Wine*, released in 2005, chronicled the life of the third president and his passion for fine wine. In 2010, Virginia wine served as the focus of a ninety-minute PBS documentary, *Vintage: The Winemaker's Year*, which chronicled the making of the commonwealth's 2008 vintage, the rapid development of the state's wine industry, and its impact on Virginia's economy and culture. *Vintage* featured stunning high-definition widescreen cinematography and interviews with a dozen central Virginia winemakers and consultants.[143]

Along with its use of traditional print media, Virginia's wine industry found itself contending with a new force for advertising and publicity: the Internet. While nearly all Virginia wineries had created websites by the mid-2000s, the Internet also forced wineries to embrace nontraditional ways of marketing through the use of social media sites. In contrast with established marketing methods, social media provided wineries with an economically efficient tool for brand advocacy and allowed wineries to create a loyal following, broadcast their message to potential customers, and focus on target markets with millions of participants.

Such features were viewed as critical to accommodate the habits of younger wine drinkers, who had grown up with the Internet, were less attached to conventional media, and held fewer regional wine prejudices. These new drinkers displayed a preference for their own opinions and for newer media, characteristics that provided a youthful wine region like Virginia with immense opportunities.

One social media platform, "blogging," generated regular entries on Internet-based logs (or "blogs"), which could be written by essentially anyone with a computer. Worldwide, wine blogging competed with wine writing in traditional print media, and helped spread news of changes in the wine industry. Virginia wine blogging exploded by the late 2000s, attracting not only novice wine drinkers, but skilled professionals as well. Multiple wine blogs appeared covering the state's wine industry with names like "Cellar Blog," "Virginia Wine Time," "Wine About Virginia," "Virginia Pour House," "My Vine Spot," "Swirl, Sip, Snark," "Virginia Wine In My Pocket," "Hagarty On Wine," and "Virginia Wine Dogs." Blog entries described visits to wineries, shared interviews with winemakers and winery owners, and offered personalized takes on Virginia wine history and reviews of industry events.

The popular social media platform Twitter also played an increasingly important role in sharing the latest news about the Virginia wine industry, allowing users to send, receive, and re-"tweet" 140-character instant messages to thousands of readers. It turned participants into "brand ambassadors" for Virginia wine, and the industry worked to capture the attention of "tweeters."

The power of social media was not lost on the Virginia wine industry, which worked to capture the attention of Internet writers, often through large invitational conferences and gatherings. To kick off Virginia Wine Month in September 2009, for example, the Virginia Tourism Corporation organized an online campaign, Vintage Tweets, which used Twitter to target a group of forty D.C.-area bloggers, consumers, and media representatives who had significant followings and were passionate about Virginia wine. The event featured a two-hour Virginia wine reception during which participants tweeted about their tastings. In March 2010, Clarke County's Veramar Vineyard sponsored its own wine-tasting event for bloggers; and in December 2010, TasteLive.com, a wine-and-beer-themed social website, partnered with the Virginia Wine Marketing Board, various Virginia wine bloggers, and five Loudoun County wineries to host a virtual tasting event.[144]

Approximately 300 wine bloggers participated in a three-day Wine Bloggers Conference in Charlottesville in July 2011. The event, which included a keynote address from British wine expert and *Financial Times* columnist Jancis Robinson, resulted in an astonishing forty-three million potential "marketing impressions," a term measuring the number of times an online advertisement or message is displayed. In May 2012, forty Internet wine writers and bloggers on the East Coast participated in "Taste Camp," a weekend-long "immersion" event designed to introduce wine writers to emerging wine regions. Over three days, wine writers visited eight wineries, tasted wines complemented by local foods, and met dozens of winemakers. Co-organized by Lenn Thompson, creator of a New York wine-related website, and blogger Frank Morgan, editor of "Drink What You Like," a Virginia wine blog, the concept had been developed in 2009.[145]

Though the Internet offered Virginia's wine industry rapid worldwide exposure, much of the emphasis of social media was decidedly local. In April 2010, for example, the Virginia Wine Board, the Maryland Wineries Association, and the Loudoun Convention and Visitors Association partnered with DrinkLocal Wine.com, a website founded by *Washington Post* columnist Dave McIntyre and Texas wine blogger Jeff Siegel, to produce the Drink Local Wine Conference. Held at Loudoun County's Lansdowne Resort, the event featured discussions on issues facing the Virginia and Maryland wine industries, lectures on the promotion of wine through social media, and a "Twitter Taste-Off," which allowed participants to tweet about Virginia wines they tasted.[146]

Concurrent with the rise in blogging and tweeting was the emergence of the immensely popular YouTube.com. Launched in 2005, YouTube quickly emerged as the most significant Internet-based site for sharing user-generated video content. VTC and the Virginia Wine Board Marketing Office had created YouTube profiles by 2009, which they used to upload short videos of interviews with winemakers and overviews of the state's wine history. Multiple Virginia wine-related videos were also uploaded by wineries, wine promotion companies, and endless private individuals who wanted to showcase their Virginia wine experiences. Among the more prominent was the 2011 creation of "Virginia Wine TV," which featured several short episodes covering a host of wine industry topics and interviews with winemakers.[147]

Along with increased Internet usage was the advent and proliferation of smartphones early in the 2000s, offering new opportunities to connect to customers through "apps." By April 2010, the Virginia Information Technologies Agency had launched a Virginia wine app for smartphone users showcasing Virginia wineries and events. That October, Lieutenant Governor Bill Bolling unveiled a tourist app for Apple iPhones, which provided listings for accommodations, wineries, and restaurants. Relying on increasingly accurate GPS maps, each app provided driving directions, winery descriptions, and information on nearby attractions. The development of such apps provided a fresh, interactive way for wine enthusiasts to locate and access wineries, resulting in perhaps the biggest improvement in Virginia winery wayfinding since the advent of "grape cluster" directional roadway signs in 1987.[148]

With improved recognition, more diverse publicity, and an expanding market, Virginia wineries were featured at a number of high-profile events in Washington, D.C., in the 2000s, all of which reflected the acceptance of Virginia wine by the District's chefs, critics, and wine enthusiasts. In an effort to increase collaboration between area wineries and local restaurants, the Washington, D.C., chapter of Women Chefs and Restaurateurs held a series of Virginia wine tastings in March 2003 pairing seven Washington, D.C., restaurants with seven Virginia wineries. "Restaurants are great promoters of our product, and pairing it with food is extremely important," said Horton Vineyards' Dennis Horton, who partnered with a high-end Washington restaurant, Equinox, for the event. "No one makes a killing at [these tastings], but we're introducing new people to the product."[149]

In June 2003, Virginia's senior U.S. Senator John Warner arranged for use of the elegant Senate Armed Services Committee hearing room for a "Virginia Wine Day on Capitol Hill" luncheon. Organized by the Vinifera Wine Growers Association, the event was attended by Virginia Congressman Robert

Goodlatte, members of the Congressional Wine Caucus, and Governor Mark Warner, the latter of whom toasted the industry with a quote from the Bible (1 Timothy 5:23): "Drink no longer water, but use a little wine for thy stomach's sake and thine often infirmities." That September, on the roof of the John F. Kennedy Center for the Performing Arts, the National Capital Area Chapter of the American Institute of Wine and Food partnered with the Virginia Wine and Food Society to host a Virginia wine showcase in which Kennedy Center restaurant chef Michel Fitoussi paired local foods with thirteen wineries.[150]

Virginia wines also featured prominently in the administration of President Barack Obama. Wine from Veritas Vineyard, for example, was served at a February 2010 International Women of Courage Awards event hosted by First Lady Michelle Obama and Secretary of State Hillary Clinton. In January 2009, the White House selected three wines from Barboursville Vineyards to be served at Obama's inaugural ball, and that December, Virginia winemaker Claude Thibaut's 2007 sparkling wine was selected to be served at President Obama's first state dinner. The event was not the first time a Virginia wine had been served in the White House; indeed, a wine from Meredyth Vineyards had been served at a White House dinner as early as 1976, while Montdomaine's 1985 Chardonnay had been served at a state dinner for President George H. W. Bush, and Horton Vineyards' 1993 Viognier had been served at a state dinner for President Bill Clinton in 1995. Thibaut's sparkling wine was, however, the first to be served often at the White House, as it was again chosen for a February 2014 state dinner honoring French President François Hollande.[151]

That Virginia wines were selected by Washington, D.C., restaurateurs and politicos as representative of the nation's best reverberated within the Old Dominion and beyond. Their selection proved advantageous for marketing and introduced the commonwealth's wines to sophisticated Washingtonians and national lawmakers alike.

Not all publicity was positive. While awkward and unpleasant moments have proved blessedly scarce in Virginia's modern wine narrative, there was a moment of pause in November 2009 when Tareq Salahi (son of Oasis Winery founder Dirgham Salahi) and his wife, Michaele, allegedly made an uninvited appearance at President Obama's first state dinner in honor of the prime minister of India; coincidentally, the same state dinner during which Thibaut-Jannison sparkling wines were served. Secret Service officials later alleged the two were not on the guest list and that the Salahis should not have been allowed entry. The "White House Gate-Crashers" as Tareq and Michaele Salahi were branded, made their names a national meme; images of the couple were blasted across newspapers and in the television media for several days."[153]

The American public ate it up; for several weeks, it seemed impossible to turn on a television without seeing the couple. Many observers, though, were unhappy with what they perceived to be damage to the state's wine reputation. The press speculated that Michaele and Tareq Salahi had staged the gate-crashing event to enhance their chances of being selected as characters for a reality cable-television series, *Real Housewives of Washington, D.C.* The Salahis were ultimately selected for the show, and several episodes mentioned Tareq Salahi's connection to the wine industry. One August 2010 episode, in particular, showed the cast traveling to Oasis in a white limousine for a tasting and a celebratory grape-stomping. Sadly, the episode also vividly portrayed a shuttered Oasis Winery, and its aging infrastructure, leading one *Washington Post* columnist to write,

> If you don't live inside the Beltway, Episode 3 [of *Real Housewives*] would have left you with the impression that all Washingtonians do is pop bottles of Virginia wine and engage in esoteric (slightly buzzed, perhaps?) dissections of international politics…. The show appears to regard winemaking as a close second to politics in Washington…. The Salahis can't stop plugging their connection to Northern Virginia's Oasis Winery…. Ugh, It was like one big ad, paid for by Virginia's wine industry.[154]

The circus surrounding the Salahis died down by late in 2010. Although the affair left a sour taste in the mouths of many industry observers, most recognized that it proved nothing more than a momentary blip in the otherwise positive trajectory of the industry.[155]

## —Business Deals—

As might be expected from an industry that was growing by leaps and bounds, Virginia wine spurred a host of other industries and innovations. Businesses sprouted up in all corners of the commonwealth to meet the demands of both consumers and the industry. Many innovations were driven by wineries themselves. In 2009, for example, three Virginia wineries, Pearmund Cellars, the Winery at La Grange, and DelFosse Vineyards and Winery, teamed with a Minneapolis company to offer wine cruises to Italy and Spain. The next year, Veramar Vineyards and Philip Carter Winery offered their own Mediterranean cruises, and in October 2011 a nonprofit educational organization, the

Washington Wine Academy, sponsored Virginia wine dinner cruises on the Potomac River.[156]

There were wine excursions on land, as well. Beginning late in the 1990s, several Washington, D.C., Richmond, and Charlottesville transportation companies began offering wine tourism packages by limousine, bus, mini-coach, and sedan. Each package included a variety of services, including boxed lunches, winery tours, and designated drivers. Land cruises even came in nonmotorized form. In 2013, the Charlottesville-based Indian Summer Guide Service began offering horseback tours at select Albemarle County vineyards.[157]

Wineries also ventured into the hospitality business. Though Barboursville Vineyards was the first Virginia winery to offer overnight accommodations, starting in the 1970s, by the 2000s, lodging was offered at Williamsburg Winery, Fincastle Vineyard and Winery, Veritas Vineyard and Winery, Ingleside Vineyards, Jacey Vineyards, Beliveau Estate Winery, Belle Mount Vineyards, The Hague Winery, General's Ridge Vineyard and Winery, Philip Carter Winery, and the Hope and Glory Inn (which purchased a vineyard in the 2000s).[158]

Industry growth also sparked interest in the fine arts. Goochland County artist Christopher Mize captured the beauty of Virginia wines and vineyard scenes in a series of oil paintings, while Richmond-area artist Melanie Haislip, and Roanoke artist Donna Tuten used their talents to depict a variety of landscape, food, equestrian, and wine-themed images. Their works could be found for sale at Virginia's many wine festivals, and quickly made their way into art galleries, restaurants, and homes. Similarly, Arthur Roberts, the founder of an etching and imprinting company in the town of Lively, decorated personalized glassware with wine-themed imagery.[159]

Not all business innovations were quite so decorative; one discreet trend that nevertheless proved critical to Virginia's wineries was the growth of the commonwealth's winery insurance market. During the 1990s, Virginia's insurance underwriters rushed to develop specialized insurance endorsements for the risks peculiar to the industry, including wine leakage, contamination, tasting-room risks, bottle shipping, and equipment malfunctions. Such coverage had rarely been available before, and with increased Internet usage in the 2000s there emerged a need for cyber-liability and intellectual property coverage, particularly with respect to winery names, wine labels, and advertising.[160]

Another vital business innovation was the advent of mobile bottling services. To address the costly process of bottling, companies moved large trailers from winery to winery, carrying state-of-the art bottling lines that filtered wine, and sterilized, filled, and corked bottles. Virginia's first such service, The Filling Station, was launched by Naked Mountain Winery and Vineyards owners Bob and Phoebe Harper in 1991, and a second, Landwirt Bottling, was founded by one-time vintner Gary Simmers outside Harrisonburg in 1999. Two other mobile services were started in Fauquier County in the 2000s: Mark and Elizabeth Lacy's Virginia Wine Bottling, and Blue Moon Mobile Bottling, founded by Oley and Judy Olsen in consultation with veteran bottler Joe Sullivan. [161]

Enterprising changes were seen as well in how the wine grape itself was used. Nelson County–based Virginia Vinegar Works, launched by Jay and Steph Rostow in 2006, combined varietal-specific Virginia wine with a vinegar starter culture to produce high-quality vinegar. At Felicia Rogan's former Oakencroft Vineyard and Winery, which had closed in 2008, John and Amy Griffin worked with longtime Oakencroft vineyard manager Philip Ponton to turn the former winery into an artisanal grape juice operation.[162]

Retailers, of course, played an important role in introducing consumers to Virginia wines. While larger grocery chains steadily improved their Virginia wine selections throughout the 1990s, smaller retailers and restaurants played an equally critical role. As early as 1991, Annette and Sonny Fleischer carried an ever-increasing line of Virginia wines at their Sumdat Farm Market in downtown Roanoke, while Janet Carper and Mari Spragins, opened Ye Olde Dominion Wine Shoppe, the first store devoted exclusively to Virginia wines, in Occoquan, in November 2000. In downtown Fredericksburg, Edwin Wyant opened Virginia Wine Experience in 2005, which offered select Virginia wines as well as vintages from other regions.[163]

Virginia wines were increasingly found on the wine lists of Virginia's top restaurants and hotels. The trend was aided by the Virginia Wine Marketing Office's creation of its Crystal Stem Awards, a program that recognized restaurants based on the number of Virginia wines served. Restaurants found out-of-state guests particularly curious about the novelty of trying Virginia wine, and, in some instances, the commonwealth's wines were served as the central theme of the establishment. One of the earliest restaurants to specialize in Virginia wines, 235: A Virginia Wine Country Restaurant, opened in March 1995 in the Omni Hotel on Charlottesville's historic downtown mall. A decade later and a few blocks away, King Family Vineyards owner David King and winemaker Michael Shaps opened VAVino, the first full-scale wine bar dedicated exclusively to Virginia wines. The short-lived venture closed in 2007, however, in the wake of 2006 General Assembly legislation that rescinded the right of wineries to self-distribute.[164]

Virginia wine served as a central theme for other restaurants as well, including downtown Norfolk's Vintage Kitchen, which opened in 2005, and Warrenton's Iron Bridge Wine Company, which opened in 2007. In 2011, Michael

Matthews and Michael Sawyers, the operators of Winchester's Vino Curioso winery, opened Virginia Wine Factory in Loudoun County, and the following year, Sheila C. Johnson opened the Gold Cup Wine Bar at her ultra-luxurious Salamander Resort and Spa outside Middleburg.[165]

In some cases, sales of Virginia wine had something of an altruistic touch; in April 2010, Richmond's Wine Loft bar partnered with the Central Virginia Food Bank to promote the "Virginia Wine Backpack Challenge." For every bottle of Virginia wine purchased, the Wine Loft contributed a backpack full of food for at-risk school children to take home from school on the weekends.

Perhaps no restaurant demonstrated an appreciation for Virginia wines as did Leesburg's Tuscarora Mill restaurant. "Tuskies," as the restaurant was famil-iarly known, along with its four affiliated restaurants not only offered Virginia wines on their menus but also made space available for wineries to display their literature. In February 2010, Tuskies launched a series of Loudoun Winemaker Luncheons, and that July started the Tuskies Wine Trail, which featured a color-ful map and coupon book for Loudoun County restaurants and wineries.

Tuskies' Wine Trail efforts were a part of a larger wine-trail trend across Vir-ginia, which saw the advent of partnerships between multiple wineries designed to enhance marketability and provide tourists with a broader wine experience than that typically found by visiting just one winery. With nearly thirty large and small trails mapped by 2017, these routes inspired patrons to visit multiple wineries and sample several wines that shared a larger geographic or cultural identity. Several encouraged participants to visit related restaurants, art galleries, lodging establishments, museums, and battlefields.[166]

## —Emerging International Markets—

Business deals concerning Virginia wine spread beyond the state's boundaries and, with increasing frequency, outside of the United States. Though governors Gerald Baliles and Douglas Wilder had promoted Virginia wine in Asia in the 1980s and 1990s, more recent attempts to publicize the industry abroad began in 2007 with celebrations organized around the 400th anniversary of a seminal event in American history, the founding of Jamestown in 1607. The festivities, which were preceded by significant Virginia Tourism Corporation promotions, featured an Executive Mansion dinner with Great Britain's Queen Elizabeth. Barboursville Vineyards winemaker Luca Paschina was tasked with selecting three highly-prized vintages for the occasion. "If your best bottle is in the cellar waiting for an occasion to open it, this was the occasion," Paschina noted of his selections. Despite a first-class enological rollout for Her Majesty, time constraints prohibited the Queen from tasting the wines.[167]

In the run-up to the 400th anniversary celebrations, six Virginia wineries, Keswick Vineyards, Kluge Estate Vineyard and Winery, Pearmund Cellars, White Hall Vineyards, Williamsburg Winery, and Veritas Vineyard and Winery, formed the Virginia Wine Experience in London, devoted to improving the reputation of Virginia wines with Great Britain's highly-discerning and influential wine critics. In May 2007, VWEL invited members of Britain's wine media to an exclusive tasting of sixty-five high-quality Virginia wines at Vinopolis, a large viticultural tasting venue in wine-savvy London. "Since this is the 400th anniversary of the Jamestown settlement," said VWEL executive director Richard G. Leahy, "now is an excellent time to highlight the fact that Virginia was the first place in North America where English settlers deliberately set out to produce wine."[168]

The VWEL tasting, entitled "Virginia, First in Wine," was attended by several British critics including famed wine writers and *Decanter Magazine* columnists Hugh Johnson and Steven Spurrier. Noting the elegance and low alcohol content of the Virginia wines, Johnson wrote glowingly of the tasting, describing it as "mind-altering," and that "Viognier, Riesling, and Petit Verdot (esp. Veritas) were the wines that surprised and impressed me most." Spurrier echoed Johnson's sentiments: "It was certainly an eye-opening tasting. I think my view was just about the general view: Best varietal was Viognier; some nice Chardonnays; best reds were the Meritage blends." British columnist Andrew Jefford, who also attended the tasting and came away pleasantly surprised, penned a review of Virginia wines in the London's *Financial Times* aptly titled "Vineyards to make a founding father proud."[169]

The following year, another wine promotion organization, New Horizon Wines, launched in Northern Virginia to export select Virginia wines to England and offer visiting Britons wine lifestyle tours across the Old Dominion. New Horizon was the creation of Christopher Parker, a British-born entrepreneur who believed that the combination of Virginia's landscapes, history, and wines would appeal to British consumers. New Horizon was quickly retained as the British representative of several Virginia wineries, and in May 2009 it worked with the VDACS and secretary of agriculture Todd Haymore to serve as an exhibitor at the London International Wine Fair. There, they showcased eleven Virginia wines, the largest number ever from Virginia to be featured at the fair, which later led to marketing agreements in London and Oxford.[170]

While some Virginians focused their wine promotion efforts on Great Britain, others concentrated their energies on additional emerging markets. In April

2008, for example, several South Korean officials visited Culpeper County's Old House Vineyards and Madison County's Prince Michel Vineyard and Winery, where they tasted wine and learned about the winemaking process. The visit came after the group learned of a small crossroads community in Culpeper County named Korea, which was originally a post office established in 1899. The discovery prompted both the Korean Embassy and the Korean-American Association to establish economic, social, and cultural ties with Culpeper County. "They've really locked on to this community, and they like it," said longtime Culpeper Supervisor Bill Chase. "[They] specifically asked to tour the wineries."[171]

A wine partnership also blossomed with Hong Kong beginning in 2009, when Virginia Senator Jim Webb met with Hong Kong financial director John Tsang. Early in 2008, the semiautonomous Chinese region had eliminated tariffs on imported wine in an attempt to improve its cosmopolitan image and become the first free wine port among major economies. Tsang later joined Webb on a tour of Shenandoah Valley wineries, where the two discussed opportunities for introducing Virginia wine to Southeast Asia. In March 2010, Hong Kong's commissioner for economic and trade affairs also visited Richmond and met with Wine Marketing Office director Annette Boyd to promote Hong Kong as a regional center for wine-related businesses.[172]

Virginia wines were even promoted in Cuba. Beginning in 2007, secretary of agriculture Todd Haymore led a series of successful trade missions to the communist island, during which he promoted Virginia wine. Governor Bob McDonnell also heavily promoted Virginia wine during his eleven-day trade tour to Japan, South Korea, and China in May 2011. Asian interest in Virginia wine was especially strong in China, and by the close of that same year the first commercial shipment of Virginia wine (from Barboursville Vineyards) had been delivered to Tianjin, China. Success in China led McDonnell to proclaim 2012 as the year of "Virginia Wine's Emergence on the International Stage," and he led several more successful trade missions to Europe, Canada, Israel, and India during the year.[173]

## —All in the Alcohol Family—

By the mid-2000s, advances in the Old Dominion's wine industry were matched by a growing public acceptance of the production and responsible consumption of alcoholic beverages. Such receptivity, combined with a growing desire for locally sourced foods and beverages, encouraged younger Virginians to experiment with four craft beverage "cousins" of the wine industry: meaderies, distilleries, cideries, and breweries. This resurgence late in the 2000s aimed to revive their historic roles in the commonwealth's spirituous artisan traditions.[174]

Meaderies were winery-type facilities that produced a fermented honey wine known for millennia as mead. Believed to be man's oldest fermented beverage, mead dates to antiquity and was an early way to preserve water for long periods. It was brewed using techniques handed down by honeybee keepers and then by clergy in Africa, Europe, and Asia. By the 2000s, a new generation of mead makers had opened several meaderies across Virginia, each with the potential to infuse modern styles and flavors into ancient recipes.[175]

John Hallberg opened Virginia's first meadery, Smokehouse Winery, in Rappahannock County in 1999. Smokehouse, which later closed, was followed in 2005 by Richard Copeland's Misty Mountain Meadworks in Frederick County. Steve and Joanne Villers opened Blacksnake Meadery in Carroll County in 2006, and Betsy and Rusty East opened White Oak Mountain Meadery in Pittsylvania County six years later. De Rustica Meadery also opened in Culpeper in 2012, and the following year, retired U.S. Department of Agriculture employee Colonel Locklear opened Stonehouse Meadery in Loudoun County, after completing a one-year internship with winemaker Doug Fabbioli.[176]

Several traditional wineries also offered mead. Marlyn and Sue Allen produced mead infused with flowers, fruits, and vegetables at their Hill Top Berry Farm and Winery in Nelson County, while mead could be found at Pittsylvania County's Tomahawk Mill Vineyard and Winery and Madison County's Rose River Farm. Though randomly scattered throughout the commonwealth, most mead makers were passionate about sharing their product's history with the public. Few took that mission more seriously than Richmond resident and beekeeper Bill Cavender, who in 2013 launched RVA Meadlab, a unique educational and collaborative laboratory for mead makers that provided space for both winemakers and brewers to learn about beekeeping and mead production.[177]

Such dedication was shared by Virginia's new crop of distilleries, which enjoyed a renaissance of their own in the 2000s. The commonwealth had a long tradition of distilling whiskey. George Washington operated one of the nation's most successful distilleries at Mount Vernon in the late eighteenth century, and two hundred years later countless illegal moonshine operations still dotted the foothills outside Roanoke, perhaps most spectacularly in Franklin County. The commonwealth's oldest legal distilleries, Laird and Company in Albemarle County, and the A. Smith Bowman Distillery in Fredericksburg, were founded shortly after the repeal of Prohibition. They were joined in 1987 by Chuck and Jeanette Miller's Belmont Farm Distillery in Culpeper.

Though the Millers enjoyed success using a circa-1933 copper pot still to create their White Lightning and Kopper Kettle whiskies, the craft distillery movement did not take off until 2004, when Paul McCann began concocting his award-winning potato-based Cirrus Vodka in a small Richmond distillery. McCann's enterprise folded, but it was replaced in 2010 by another Richmond concern, Reservoir Distillery, which produced small batch whiskies.[178]

One of Virginia's more prominent microdistillers, Rick Wasmund, opened Copper Fox Distillery in 2005 in Rappahannock County, where he produced single malt whiskey in a rustic tractor-powered barley mill. Malt whiskeys could also be found at Nelson County's Virginia Distillery Company, while corn-based vodkas were the trade at Chris Richeson's Chesapeake Bay Distillery in Virginia Beach. In Loudoun County, Becky and Scott Harris's Catoctin Creek Distilling Company turned out organic and kosher whiskies, brandies, and seasonal specialty liqueurs. Perhaps most appropriate for a state that often honors history above all else, Mount Vernon restored the first president's distillery in 2009 to demonstrate colonial-era whiskey making, and bottles of the distillery's high-end whiskeys are now available at the site.[179]

The Old Dominion's distillery industry received a major boost in 2015, when the General Assembly adopted legislation creating a "limited distiller's license" for small craft distillery operations producing less than 36,000 gallons of spirits per year. By 2017, Virginia boasted nearly 30 craft distillers and more licensed distilleries than any other state in the nation, manufacturing all manner of distilled products from local herbs, berries, and other ingredients.

Virginia's engagement with distilled products was more than matched by the revival of its hard cider industry, which also traces its roots to the earliest days of the colony. George Washington and Thomas Jefferson both enjoyed cider, and many settlers turned to its production after frustration with their inability to grow quality wine grapes. Hard cider was perhaps the most common drink in the Americas by the late 1700s, and with Virginia's standing as the nation's sixth-largest apple producer two centuries later, would-be cider makers found renewed inspiration in the quality of Virginia's apples.[180]

The Old Dominion's first modern commercial cider-making operation, Spotted Tavern Winery, opened in 1995 in Stafford County. Founded by Cathy and John Harris, Spotted Tavern featured an enormous circa-1912 commercial cider press, which produced "Moonbeam." While Spotted Tavern closed in the 2000s, in 2006 Diane and Chuck Flynt opened Virginia's second cidery, Foggy Ridge Cider, in Floyd County. The Flynts planted their first heirloom apples in 1997 and later produced a line of six ciders made from American, French, and English cider apples.[181]

Hard cider's revival was concentrated in the greater Charlottesville area, where, just south of town, Chuck Shelton opened Albemarle Ciderworks, producing ciders made from the approximately 3,000 fruit trees on his property. Northeast of Charlottesville, Castle Hill Cider opened in July 2011 in an impressive barn boasting enviable views of the Southwest Mountains. Two former home beer brewers, Tim Edmond and Dan Potter, founded Potter's Craft Cider in a renovated horse veterinarian clinic northwest of the city, and in nearby Nelson County, John Washburn partnered with internationally acclaimed New Zealand orchardist Brian Shanks to open Bold Rock Cidery in 2012. Bold Rock's hard ciders, perhaps the most widely distributed of any in the state, could be found in many mid-Atlantic grocery stores in standard six-packs.[182]

Elsewhere in Virginia, Shannon and Sarah Showalter founded Old Hill Hard Cider in 2012 on their forty-acre family orchard north of Harrisonburg, while Stephen Schuurman and Joshua Ussel opened Winchester Ciderworks in orchard-laden Frederick County. In 2013, former Albemarle Ciderworks apprentice Courtney Mailey opened Virginia's first urban cidery, Blue Bee Cider in Richmond.[183]

As might be expected from a state that had long embraced its wine and apple industries, Virginia's government offered support to its budding cider movement. In 2011, the General Assembly relaxed limitations on the allowable levels of alcohol in hard cider, and the following year VDACS helped Nelson County secure a U.S. Department of Agriculture grant to study the profitability of hard cider production. By November 2012, with seven active cideries and several more in development, Governor Bob McDonnell proclaimed the first Virginia Cider Week, which was also the first week-long hard cider celebration in the nation. By 2017, Virginia's cider industry sold more than 556,500 cases of hard cider, and the industry was poised for phenomenal growth.

The Old Dominion's cideries, meaderies, and distilleries joined its wineries and more than 206 licensed breweries operating across the state by 2017 (a 468 percent increase since 2012). Among the more well-known artisan breweries included Lexington's Devil's Backbone Brewing Company, Goochland County's Lickinghole Creek Craft Brewery, Charlottesville's Starr Hill Brewery, Port City Brewing Company in Alexandria, and Richmond's Hardywood Park Craft Brewery, which is located in the capital city's historic German brewing district.

The General Assembly boosted the craft brewery industry in 2012 when it allowed brewers to directly sell their products in on-site taprooms, similar to Virginia's farm wineries, which had received such permission 32 years earlier. The first Virginia Craft Beer Month was proclaimed in August of that year, and additional legislation was passed in 2014 to ease regulations for farm breweries which grew their own hops. Between 2014 and 2017, Virginia lured four large west coast craft breweries, Stone, Deschutes, Green Flash, and Ballast Point, to open their east coast facilities within the state. Each received public funding incentive packages, sometimes to the chagrin of the Old Dominion's home-grown craft brewers. Nevertheless, by 2017, the commonwealth's beer industry contributed more than $9.34 billion to the state's economy and employed more than 8,000 Virginians.

When taken together, this growing family of craft alcoholic beverages found itself connected to Virginia tourism and agriculture through the local sourcing of products, opening new markets for Virginia farmers, and investing millions in jobs. They also happened to render Virginia "wetter" than at any time since Prohibition.[184]

## — Real Estate Developments —

A booming real estate market, coupled with wine industry growth, captured the fancy of real estate developers in the 1990s and 2000s, many of which capitalized on the industry's growing cachet by incorporating wine themes and elements into their projects. The Colonial Heritage community in Williamsburg promoted the first annual Williamsburg Wine and Food Festival in 2010—in part as a community sales promotion—while Albemarle County's Estates at Keswick Hall prominently featured images of vineyards and barrels in its mar-keting brochures. Loudoun County's Tarara Winery produced custom-labeled red and white wines for the developers of Willowsford, a large residential com-munity that emphasized local foods in its marketing materials and named some streets after hybrid grape varietals.

Such promotional efforts were augmented by more elaborate plans of vine-yard-inspired Virginia real estate developments that emphasized viticulture.[185] The idea for Virginia's first major wine-related real estate development, Old Dominion French Winery, was generated by four French investors in 1987. Backed by a major French insurance company, Garantie Mutuelle des Fonction-naires, supported by Governor Gerald Baliles, and represented by Williams-burg Investment Group Ltd., the initial proposal called for a $10 million winery located on ten acres in York County. The consortium received zoning approval for a large winery capable of bottling 250,000 cases per year, as well as approval from the Peninsula Ports Authority for industrial development bonds. The investors' representative, Philip C. Poling, observed to reporters of the venture, "I think that this project could very possibly be the thing that puts Virginia on the map as a wine state."[186]

In April 1989, the French investors announced their intent to abandon the York County site because of land-title issues, and instead to build their winery as the major focal point of a larger, $96 million, 492-acre residential and office development known as the Williamsburg Corporate Campus in neighboring James City County. The size of this project worried nearby neighbors, concerned that the development would clog roads and deplete area wells. In response, the French investors scaled back their plans to construct a three-story, 103,800-square-foot French chateau-inspired winery and restaurant on twenty-three acres.[187]

In October 1991, while their James City County rezoning application was pending, the investors announced that they were considering yet another location, this time, a virgin 315-acre site back in York County. There, the investors proposed a winery and restaurant, 500 timeshare units, a 150-room hotel, and one million square feet of industrial development. The project vaporized with the onset of an economic recession in the early 1990s.[188]

Nearly a decade after plans for the Old Dominion French Winery were abandoned, Albemarle County winemaker Patricia Kluge began marketing a large real estate project known as Vineyard Estates on 500 acres adjacent to her Kluge Estate Winery and Vineyard. Hoping to combine what she perceived as a growing demand for ultra-luxurious lifestyles with Virginia's growing wine culture, she envisioned the project as a private enclave of twenty-four custom luxury homes on large lots, each with their own vineyard.[189]

Billed as a "community for the ages," and a development for the "gentleman vintner," Vineyard Estates' plans were impressive, if not ostentatious. Residences were to feature Federal, Georgian, Gothic, and Beaux-Arts architecture as well as twenty-four-hour concierge service. Prospective purchasers could select from a range of options, including professionally designed formal gardens, orchards, greenhouses, stables, putting greens, and ice-skating rinks. Residents would also have access to the Kluge Winery's private rooms, including a ballroom pavilion on the property. Kluge even offered purchasers the option of having their vineyards professionally managed by Kluge Winery personnel in order to produce private-label wines.[190]

To promote the project, Kluge advertised in high-end markets and even produced an online promotional video, *Awaken to America's Eden*. She produced a lavish online brochure featuring views from Thomas Jefferson's Monticello estate, and created marketing materials exclaiming that residents could "reside with others who share this idealism and aspire to the best that life has to offer." As might be expected, the price for such a lifestyle was staggering; Vineyard Estates' lots and homes were marketed at anywhere from $6.8 million to $23 million. Ultimately, the onset of an international recession doomed the project. In March 2010, the 6,600-square-foot Glen Love Cottage, originally built in 2006 as a spec house for the subdivision, was foreclosed on after two of Kluge's original partners went bankrupt. That December, the bank foreclosed on the entire project.[191]

An equally ambitious vineyard-inspired community, but ultimately far more successful, the Farms of New Kent and its New Kent Vineyards, broke ground in New Kent County in 2006. Initially developed by Kitty Hawk Land Company, the project included 2,500 homes as well as a park, a golf course, an equestrian center, polo fields, and a retail town center. Plans called for more than forty acres of vineyards throughout the community, some near golf courses, others near homes and the winery. The centerpiece of the community was a new $4 million, 12,000-square-foot winery, New Kent Winery and Vineyards, which opened in 2007 and served as a key promotional draw. Designed to replicate the feel of a historic building, the winery was constructed with reclaimed historic materials, including reused pine trusses, vintage cobblestones, salvaged cypress shingles, and antebellum bricks. "We studied wineries for five to six years," developer Pete Johns said in 2006. "We included all the neat and functional ideas from wineries in California, Canada, and all of Virginia."[192]

While new home sales in the community were slowed by the same economic recession that doomed Kluge's Vineyard Estates project, New Kent Vineyards proved more popular with homebuyers, no doubt influenced by lower prices and the developer's heavy promotion of the winery. The winery was awarded the 2011 Virginia Governor's Cup for its 2009 Reserve Chardonnay; the developer's promotional events included hosting the first annual Taste of New Kent wine and food festival; and personalized wine casks could be stored at the winery.[193]

A two-hour drive northwest of New Kent Vineyards in Warrenton, Chris Pearmund partnered with Dallas-based Centex Homes in 2007 to propose Arrington Knolls, a winery-inspired, age-restricted community on a lush 483-acre farm outside the town. Through an agreement between Pearmund and Centex, Arrington Knolls would have nearly 300 homes, while a vineyard and winery, both of which would be owned and operated by Pearmund, would have formed a key marketing component of the community.

Under an agreement with the farm's owner, Arrabelle Arrington, Pearmund planted some 4,000 white grape vines, with plans to ultimately plant 40,000 vines, before the zoning of the property was complete. In the process of seeking approvals for the community in the midst of an economic recession, however, Centex abruptly announced in January 2008 that it was abandoning the development, which prompted Pearmund to cancel his winery plans as well.

He told reporters that he wanted to continue maintaining the vines until the housing market rebounded. Pearmund, however, acknowledged, "That's up to Mrs. Arrington. If she wants me to take out the vineyard, I will take it out." Mrs. Arrington requested that the vines be removed, and nothing more came of the project.[194]

In 2013, the concept for a fifth Virginia vineyard community, Vineyard Terraces, began taking shape alongside the Virginian Golf Club in Bristol. Upon completion, the project was to include single family homes and multifamily villas overlooking the golf course interspersed with table grape and wine vineyards. Four years later, another developer, NV Homes, broke ground on Stoneridge at Bull Run Winery, which featured homes adjacent to the popular Fairfax County winery.

## — Virginia Wine: Four Centuries On —

Cultivation of the grape—whether for agriculture, curiosity, or the production of fine wine—has absorbed the ambition of countless Virginians since the commonwealth's earliest days. No American state can claim a longer history of experimentation with and promotion of viticulture, nor can any boast a more spectacular record of initial failure followed by eventual success, than can Virginia.

It is perhaps surprising that the commonwealth's winemaking development proved distressingly erratic for nearly four hundred years, given the extraordinary effort and assembled talent involved. Colonial-era disappointments, including the efforts of that committed oenophile Thomas Jefferson, were followed by the adventurous, but doomed, efforts of an antebellum and post-Civil War wine industry. Even into the latter half of the twentieth century, Virginia winemaking was moribund thanks largely to the disastrous and lingering effects of Prohibition.

Beginning in the early 1970s, however, Virginia's wines and wineries commenced a striking rise in prominence and reputation that would surely have exceeded the wildest dreams of the state's earliest vintners. One by struggling one, pioneering and enterprising men and women proved willing to gamble on the cultivation of the state's first significant European grape and French hybrid vineyards. Their revolutionary work was matched by a new and surprising level of governmental encouragement, including critical support by Virginia's institutions of higher education, most notably Virginia Tech. To this was added the importation and growth of modern, and essential, viticultural expertise, a growing interest in locally-produced foods, cooperation among industry members, and improvements in grape and wine quality. . Thanks to these combined efforts, more has been accomplished in the name of Virginia wine over the span of four short decades than during the preceding four centuries, resulting in historical, political, geographical, and social changes to Virginia's history and culture—changes that continue in an agricultural and industrial sector itself unique in world commerce.

Today, the commonwealth's position as a high-quality winemaking state has arrived. While the industry is still in its relative infancy, its growth has proven steady and strong and, at present, shows no sign of abatement. The industry grew by 82 percent between 2010 and 2015 and, by 2017, Virginia boasted more than 260 wineries which produced more than 556,000 cases of wine (or more than six million bottles) annually. More than 8,000 tons of grapes were cultivated across 3,300 acres, and more than 2.25 million tourists visited Virginia's wineries each year. The industry contributed to the full-time employment of nearly 8,200 people and added $1.37 billion annually to the commonwealth's economy.

Many of the original workhorse wineries from the 1970s and 1980s continue to flourish, their walls decorated with posters and photographs from an earlier era, reminders of the essential role they played in delivering a viticultural, political and economic climate in which the newer wineries could succeed. Virginia now offers a wealth of wine tourism experiences attracting enthusiasts and connoisseurs from across the world. With few exceptions, Virginia's wine industry remains as congenial as ever, basking in a fraternal spirit of cooperation that has set Virginia apart from other winemaking regions.

The wine industry has also figured prominently in the commonwealth's overall tourism strategy. Aggressive public sector marketing and financial assistance have enhanced Virginia's reputation for wine tourism, and its cornucopia of historic attractions and ineffably bucolic countryside have proven remarkably complementary.

Despite this success, there are those who doubt the sustainability of the commonwealth's current progress. Most fundamentally, the need for new fruit continues to be a major public policy problem for an industry that has seen a proliferation of wineries and wine sales, only to be faced by inadequate growth in grape acreage. Equally disconcerting is the sense that the industry has grown too fast and without consistency, leaving wine enthusiasts excited about Virginia's prospects yet often frustrated in their search for truly fine vintages.

There also appears to be no easy way to reduce the retail price of Virginia wines, a consideration that necessarily diminishes the ability for the commonwealth's vintages to compete with other regions. The high markups on

Virginia's wines no doubt reflect multiple difficulties faced by Virginia winemakers, including a lack of reliable seasonal labor, higher marketing costs, and increased up-front investment expenditures, but their combined effects put Virginia wines at a competitive disadvantage.

There is, thus, a concern that the industry could be facing a period of stagnation, and that further production, distribution, and marketing are required to match international expectations of quality and uniqueness.

Virginia's modern wine industry appears, however, fully equal to the task.

As an observer who knew little of the wine industry before embarking on this journey into history—and this unique aspect of both human, and American, culture—I posit that the best way for the industry to move forward would be to follow that noblest of Virginia virtues; that is, to have the capacity to remember the lessons and experiences of those who proceeded us, while freeing ourselves from their grasp. It is clear, for example, that the winemakers and winery owners who have proven the most successful and admired are those which have focused on the people in the winemaking process and emphasized the strengths of their human capital. Those who surround themselves with family and friends, mentor others, and create an atmosphere in which employees are respected, will continue to enjoy the greatest competitive position.

Essentially, however, those in the industry must be grounded in reality; they must develop effective business models and succession plans, be frugal and prudent and live within their means, for as much as wine is an art, it is a business and must act as one to thrive. It is wise to remember that Virginia's wine industry has taken 400 years to mature. Financial success in winemaking—if it comes—will emerge from measured steps and wise investment over the course of decades. Respect for one's land is equally important, and an emphasis on sustainability and wine quality in the vineyard and winery must be paramount, for the ever-present necessity of attention to detail is crucial. Every owner and winemaker must strive to do better with their next vintage.

It should also be remembered that Virginia's unpredictable weather makes it an oddly illogical place for large winery capital investment, as generations of other winemakers can attest. Therefore, as the industry moves forward, it may be best comprised in the main of families that can create and market an agricultural farm-to-table product at the local level. Such families were the key to the rebirth of Virginia's modern wine industry, and they will most assuredly be the key to the industry's continued success.

Virginia's wine history has consisted of a series of separate events over the course of more than four centuries. Change has proven the only constant in this narrative. As the commonwealth progresses deeper into the new millennium, the story of its wine industry will continue to evolve. Future generations will improve upon the work contained within these pages, painting an ever-shifting mosaic symbolic of Virginia's historic land and determined people.

Reflective in each step forward will be the experiences of the dreamers of long ago who searched for opportunity, defied prevailing beliefs and a challenging climate, and eventually made the impossible possible. The Virginia wine industry will continue to redefine itself, and it will continue to bring to one of life's great pleasures the same spirit that infused a small company of travel-weary Englishmen, who stepped ashore among the dunes of Cape Henry more than four centuries ago, and from whom sprang a great people and a great land.

# Photo credits

1. Library of Congress, Geography and Map Division
2. Portrait by Jacques-Louis David (c.1790), Wikimedia Commons
3. STC 22790, Houghton Library, Harvard University
4. Courtesy Library of Virginia, image altered from original
5. Courtesy Library of Virginia
6. Courtesy John P. Barden
7. Author's collection
8. Author's collection
9. Photo by author
10. Courtesy Robert de Treville Lawrence, IV
11. Courtesy Susan M. Smith
12. Courtesy Susan M. Smith
13. Courtesy Hudson Cattell
14. Courtesy Gordon and Anita Murchie
15. Courtesy Hudson Cattell
16. Courtesy Hudson Cattell
17. Courtesy Al Weed
18. Courtesy Lucie Morton
19. Courtesy Hudson Cattell
20. Courtesy Hudson Cattell
21. Courtesy Pat Reeder, Burnley Vineyards
22. Courtesy Lew Parker
23. Courtesy Gordon and Anita Murchie
24. Courtesy Virginia Tourism Corporation (Virginia.org)
25. Courtesy Hudson Cattell
26. Courtesy Felicia Warburg Rogan
27. Courtesy Virginia Wine Marketing Office
28. Courtesy C-VILLE Weekly
29. Courtesy Al Weed
30. Courtesy Sherry Williams
31. Courtesy Tom O'Grady
32. Courtesy Jim Livingston
33. Courtesy Gabriele Rausse
34. Courtesy Hudson Cattell
35. Courtesy Gordon and Anita Murchie
36. Courtesy Luca Pascina
37. Courtesy Hudson Cattell
38. Courtesy Hudson Cattell
39. Courtesy Gordon and Anita Murchie
40. Courtesy Robert de Treville Lawrence, IV
41. Courtesy Hudson Cattell
42. Courtesy Robert de Treville Lawrence, IV

43. Courtesy Pat Reeder, Burnley Vineyards
44. Courtesy Hudson Cattell
45. Courtesy of Virginia Tech
46. Courtesy Hudson Cattell
47. Courtesy Virginia Wine Marketing Office
48. Courtesy Virginia Wine Marketing Office
49. Courtesy Cardinal Point Winery
50. Courtesy Jennifer McCloud
51. Photo by author
52. Courtesy Chris Pearmund
53. Courtesy Virginia Wine Marketing Office
54. Courtesy Library of Virginia
55. Courtesy Kirk Wiles
56. Photo by Don Wilson, Institute for Justice
57. Courtesy Dennis and Sharon Horton
58. Courtesy Cindy Bridgman
59. Courtesy Pat Reeder, Burnley Vineyards
60. Courtesy Virginia Tourism Corporation (Virginia.org)
61. Courtesy Virginia Tourism Corporation (Virginia.org)
62. Courtesy Library of Virginia
63. Courtesy Potomac Point Winery
64. Courtesy Virginia Tourism Corporation (Virginia.org)
65. Courtesy Virginia Tourism Corporation (Virginia.org)
66. Courtesy Virginia Wine Marketing Office
67. Courtesy Virginia Tourism Corporation (Virginia.org)
68. Courtesy Philip C. Poling, Williamsburg Investment Group, Ltd.
69. Courtesy Virginia Tourism Corporation (Virginia.org)
70. Photo by author
71. Courtesy Fabbioli Cellars
72. Courtesy Michael Shaps
73. Photo by Andrea Hubbel, courtesy of Early Mountain Vineyards
74. Courtesy Virginia Tourism Corporation (Virginia.org)

# Chapter 1 Notes

1. Nicholas Barber, Lyndsey Hutchins, and Tom Dodd, "A History of the American Wine Industry: History and Development" (Lubbock: Texas Tech University Technical Report No. 07-02, June 2007), 7–8 (http://www.depts.ttu.edu/hs/texaswine/docs/wine_history.pdf) (accessed Apr. 3, 2014) (hereafter cited as Barber, "American Wine Industry").
2. Peter J. Hatch, *The Fruits and Fruit Trees of Monticello* (Charlottesville: University Press of Virginia, 1998), 140–141.
3. Barber, "American Wine Industry," 16.
4. U. P. Hedrick, *The Grapes of New York* (Albany, N.Y.: J. B. Lyon Company, 1908), 6.
5. At the time, Virginia formed a portion of a poorly defined and unexplored Spanish territory known as "Ajacán," in the La Florida colony, which spanned from Florida to Newfoundland. It was claimed by the Spanish pursuant to the Treaty of Tordesillas of 1493. *Virginia Magazine of History and Biography* 96, No. 2 (Apr. 1988): 133.
6. The only survivor, a young boy named Alonso, was spared by Don Luis's brother. W. Stitt Robinson, Jr., Review of *The Spanish Jesuit Mission in Virginia, 1570–1572*, in *Journal of Southern History* 20, No. 2 (May 1954): 241–243; *Virginia Magazine of History and Biography* 96, No. 2 (Apr. 1988): 144–147.
7. Carrera also noted that the vineyard included plum, cherry, and persimmon trees. Clifford M. Lewis and Albert J. Loomie, *The Spanish Jesuit Mission in Virginia, 1570–1572* (Chapel Hill: University of North Carolina Press, 1953), 138, 141.
8. Carrera also noted that the vineyard included plum, cherry, and persimmon trees. John Smith, "The Spanish in Virginia," in *The Spanish Jesuit Mission in Virginia, 1570–1572*, ed. Clifford M. Lewis and Albert J. Loomie [and the following:] (Chapel Hill: University of North Carolina Press, 1953), 138, 141.
9. Located in what is today the modern-day city of Hampton, Kecoughtan would serve in 1607 as the site where English explorers first interacted with Native Americans. Thomas Pinney, *A History of Wine in America: From the Beginnings to Prohibition* (Berkeley: University of California Press, 1989), 16.
10. The Spanish had attempted viticulture in the West Indies as early as 1516 and in New Spain (today northern Mexico and the American southwest) by 1524. Success in New Spain led to Spanish fears that its wine industry might be threatened by a New World viticultural industry. This led to Spain's outlawing of planting vineyards in the colonies by 1595. Close in time, France explored the idea of establishing vineyards in Florida and New France, which stretched from Louisiana to Quebec; similar fears about the damage to France's domestic wine industry caused that country to outlaw the planting of vineyards in Louisiana in the late 1600s. Both empires feared the competition from colonial wines. In part to forestall a glut on the wine market and ensure higher prices for the commodity, in 1567 France began restricting the excess planting of vineyards and ordered that two-thirds of France be reserved for the planting of grains. David Joel Mishkin, *The American Colonial Wine Industry: An Economic Interpretation* (New York: Arno Press, 1975), 73–176; Todd Kliman, *The Wild Vine: A Forgotten Grape and the Untold Story of American Wine* (New York: Clarkson Potter, 2010), 25.
11. Most Britons believed that their treasury would be enhanced by producing many of the raw materials England was forced to purchase from her sometimes hostile neighbors, as well as those friendlier nations in the Mediterranean, the Baltics, and Russia, from which the purchase of such commodities required great risk and cost. Such goods included wine, oil, silk, and other luxury products that England had traditionally paid for in bullion. Dr. Beer notes that England experienced bad relations or geopolitical realities with several other European countries: war with Spain prevented direct commercial relations with that nation and its ally Holland, and the Spanish confiscated English ships seeking to do business with the Barbary states; Algerian pirates and opposition from Venice prevented trade with Turkey; trade with France was stifled by heavy taxes and competition; trade with Germany and Russia was declining and hampered by a disfavored-trading status. Louis B. Wright, *Dream of Prosperity in Colonial America* (New York: New York University Press, 1965), 26; Kliman, *Wild Vine*, 22, 25, 30; Louis B. Wright, *The Colonial Search for a Southern Eden* (Birmingham: Univer-

sity of Alabama Press, 1953), 27; Mishkin, *American Colonial Wine Industry*, 177; George Louis Beer, *The Origins of the British Colonial System, 1578–1660* (New York: Macmillan, 1908), 57–77. Mishkin notes that most writings from the period highlight the need to secure gold, silver, pearls, spices, silk, wine, and fishing grounds (Mishkin, *American Colonial Wine Industry*, 178). See also Alfred Leslie Rowse, *The Expansion of Elizabethan England* (Madison: University of Wisconsin Press, 2003), 160–162; E. G. R. Taylor, *Late Tudor and Early Stuart Geography, 1583–1650: A Sequel to Tudor Geography, 1485–1583* (New York: Octagon Books, 1968), 160–167.

12. Mishkin, *American Colonial Wine Industry*, 184; Wright, *Dream of Prosperity*, 25. They were quickly supplanted by more profitable uses of the soil. Mishkin notes that this viticultural revival into the 1600s attempted to mimic French gardening techniques and was driven by British gardening and horticultural tracts that were heavily influenced by, or plagiarized from, French sources. Mishkin concludes that such influences served to introduce French viticultural techniques to the British. (Mishkin, *American Colonial Wine Industry*, 186–187, 189–193, 197–199, 215–219). To dissuade critics who thought that establishing costly, new permanent overseas colonies was a farce, advocates of New World colonialism stressed the secondary benefits of colonialism, including political, religious, military, and economic rewards. Eventually, those advancing imperialism won the day and the frantic search for New World riches, a northwest passage to the Far East, and increased trade exploded. In this way the notion that new, permanent colonies were required to attain these goals was established. "These commodities in this abundant maner," one advocate wrote, "are not to be gathered from thence, without planting and settling there." George Peckham, "Sir George Peckham's true Report of the late discoveries," reprinted in Richard Hakluyt, *The Principal Navigations, Voyages, Traffiques, And Discoveries Of The English Nation, Vol. XIII. America. Part II,* ed. Edmund Goldsmid, F.R.H.S. (Edinburgh: E. & G. Goldsmid, 1889), 22.

13. Without empirical evidence to the contrary, the colonists believed Virginia to be so replete with abundant resources that they could quickly turn a profit and handsomely return to England. Some descriptions were based on direct observations; others were only imagined. Writing in 1588, long before the founding of Jamestown, English mathematician and astronomer Thomas Hariot speculated on the types of grapes that future colonists would undoubtedly encounter in the New World: "There are two kinds of grapes that grow wild there. One is sour and the size of the ordinary English grape; the other is lusciously sweet and much larger. When they are planted and husbanded as they should be, an important commodity in wines can be established." Hariot, *A Brief and True Report of the New Found Land of Virginia* (1588); Hedrick, *Grapes of New York*, 31; Wright, *Dream of Prosperity*, 21–22; Wright, *Colonial Search*, 27–29; Stevenson Whitcomb Fletcher, *A History of Fruit Growing in Virginia* (Staunton, Va.: Beverley Press, 1932), 3.

14. Their profusion also reminded them of European vineyards; This belief in Virginia's promise was so extraordinary that even Britain's clergy were enlisted in what became a veritable crusade to proselytize Virginia as a piece of heaven on earth. Fletcher, *History of Fruit Growing*, 3; Wright, *Dream of Prosperity*, 21–22; Wright, *Colonial Search*, 27–29; Barber, "American Wine Industry," 7.

15. Much of what we know of the early days of the colony comes from William Strachey (1527–1621), a British writer and traveler aboard the ship *Sea Venture*, a colonial supply ship that foundered off the coast of Bermuda in July 1609. Eventually reaching Virginia in May 1610, Strachey would serve as secretary and recorder of the colony for almost three years, during which time he captured his impressions of Jamestown life and his experience aboard the *Sea Venture*. A hopeful writer and critic of the Virginia Company, Strachey borrowed much of his works—and, in some cases, heavily lifted—from that of other writers. Nevertheless, Strachey penned multiple volumes on the history of Virginia, including *Purchas His Pilgrims* (Strachey's chief work written while he was in America) and his 1612 *Historie*. One official Virginia Company promotional pamphlet published in 1610, *A True Declaration of the Estate of the Colonie in Virginia*—ostensibly written to quell doubters of the young colony—described "grapes and walnuts innumerable; the vines being as common as brambles...." See William Strachey, *The historie of travaile into Virginia Britannia* (London, Eng.: Printed for the Hakluyt Society, 1849), 120; William B. Cairns, ed., *Selections from Early American Writers, 1607–1800* (New York: Macmillan, 1909), 19. It is believed that Strachey's powerful and detailed account of the storm

and wreck served as the inspiration for William Shakespeare's play *The Tempest*; the wreck certainly led to the unanticipated colonization of the Bermuda Archipelago and is memorialized in the coat of arms for the archipelago territory. Alden T. Vaughan, "William Strachey's 'True Repertory' and Shakespeare: A Closer Look at the Evidence," *Shakespeare Quarterly* 59, No. 3 (Fall, 2008): 245–273; Charles Richard Sanders, "William Strachey, the Virginia Colony, and Shakespeare," *Virginia Magazine of History and Biography* 57, No. 2 (Apr. 1949): 115–132; Raymond Phineas Stearns, *Science in the British Colonies of America* (Urbana: University of Illinois Press, 1970), 74–75; published in London under the title, "A true repertory of the wrack, and redemption of Sir Thomas Gates Knight..."; *A True Declaration* was written to justify continued support for the colony in the wake of negative accounts following the Starving Time. *A True Declaration* is noted as being perhaps "the most distinguished piece of propaganda for the colony and its best apologia." David Quinn, ed., *New American World: A Documentary History of North America to 1612* (New York: Arno Press, 1979), 5:248–262.

16. Their profusion also reminded them of European vineyards; Fletcher, *History of Fruit Growing in Virginia*, 3. U. P. Hedrick noted that such writings were "not considered to be of great intrinsic value but only suggested to the explorers that the grape of the old home might be grown in the new home." Mishkin notes that such accounts conceived winemaking in America as merely the "barreling of a ready vintage." Mishkin, *American Colonial Wine Industry*, 244–245; *Vinifera Wine Growers Journal* 14, No. 4 (Winter 1987): 211 (hereafter cited as *VWGJ*); Hedrick, *Grapes of New York*, 29, 31; Philip Alexander Bruce, *Economic History of Virginia in the Seventeenth Century* (New York: Macmillan, 1907), 32; Earl A. Hart, "Winemaking in Colonial Virginia: The Lure and the Demise," published in the *American Wine Society Journal* and reprinted in *VWGJ* No. 1 (Jan. 1994): 1 (hereafter cited as Hart, "Winemaking"); Hatch, *Fruits and Fruit Trees of Monticello*, 140; English poet Michael Drayton (1563–1631), writing in his patriotic "Ode to the Virginian Voyage," celebrates the Virginia voyages and encapsulates what he saw as Britain's great dream, noting that Virginia was "Earth's only Paradise," and that the New World offered gold, pearls, fowl, deer, none of which required "toyle." See Mishkin, *American Colonial Wine Industry*, 205. Mishkin notes that only the site of paradise remained unresolved, with some preferring Virginia and others preferring Bermuda and Guyana. See Mishkin, *American Colonial Wine Industry*, 206, 244; Mishkin notes that the late economic historian Dr. John U. Nef found that wage increases in Elizabethan England and Britons' willingness to pay higher prices for imported wine to satisfy their increasing desire for wine as a common beverage meant that the English devoted a larger proportion of their salaries to wine. He also notes that excises on beer and cider production stimulated wine production; only prohibitive wine taxes (i.e., the Wine Act of 1688) resuscitated beer consumption by the lower classes. See Mishkin, *American Colonial Wine Industry*, 207–209; *VWGJ* 1, No. 1 (Spring 1974): 39.

17. Hart, "Winemaking," 4.

18. George Percy, *Discourse of the Plantation of the Southern Colony in Virginia by the English, 1606* (London, Eng., 1608). Indeed, much of the fruit-growing in the colony was in hopes of the production of alcoholic beverages. Largely because of high excise taxes on wine and the inability to produce an abundant source of wine in the colonies, many colonists turned to beer and distilled spirits—primarily whiskey—with the average Englishman drinking some forty gallons of alcohol per year. Believing that alcohol helped maintain strength, many doctors suggested alcohol consumption during hot days and while engaged in physical labor and, through the mid-1800s, many women bathed children in distilled spirits rather than water. Upper-class colonists routinely drank wine, middle-class colonists drank cider, pear cider, peach brandy, and other fermented fruit juices, while lower-class colonists drank apple jack and rum. Stephen A. McLeod, ed., *Dining with the Washingtons: Historic Recipes, Entertaining, and Hospitality from Mount Vernon* (Chapel Hill: University of North Carolina Press, 2011), 97; Sarah Hand Meacham, *Every Home a Distillery: Alcohol, Gender, and Technology in the Colonial Chesapeake* (Baltimore, Md.: Johns Hopkins University Press, 2009), 8, 10; Fletcher, *History of Fruit Growing*, 6; Kliman, *Wild Vine*, 24, 30; Mishkin, *American Colonial Wine Industry*, 250–251.

19. Smith's *Generall Historie*, published in 1624, is perhaps the earliest-written history of the colony; *The Generall Historie of Virginia, New-England, and the Summer Isles* was first printed by I. D and I. H. for Michael Sparkes in 1624. Other editions followed in 1625, 1626, 1627, 1631, and 1632. Captain John

Smith, *The Generall Historie of Virginia, New-England and the Summer Isles* (Glasgow, U.K.: James MacLehose and Sons, 1907), 2:53–54; *VWGJ* 14, No. 4 (Winter 1987): 211.

20. Smith, *Generall Historie*, 53–54; *VWGJ* 14, No.4 (Winter 1987): 211.

21. Barber, "American Wine Industry," 10.

22. *VWGJ* 1, No. 1 (Spring 1974): 39; Kliman, *Wild Vine*, 26; Barber, "American Wine Industry," 8. Francis Maguel, a Spanish subject who was Irish by birth, recorded in his July 1619 *Report* that Virginia by 1609 had boasted "many forest grapes, of which the English make wine that resembles much the wine of Alicante, according to the opinion of the narrator who has tasted both." Also known as Francisco "Miguel," "Manuel," and "Maguer." Maguel lived in Virginia for eight months before returning to Spain in July 1610. J. Leander Bishop mistakenly writes in *A History of American Manufacture* that wine samples were sent to Britain in 1612, and likely confused it with 1609. Alexander Brown, *The Genesis of the United States* (Boston: Houghton Mifflin, 1890), 395; Bruce, *Economic History*, 243–246; Mishkin, *American Colonial Wine Industry*, 163.

23. Hart, "Winemaking," 1; Fletcher, *History of Fruit Growing*, 8.

24. Historian Thomas Pinney speculates that, prior to his arrival, De La Warr must have known of Virginia's wine-growing capacity as he issued "Instructions for such things as are to be sente from Virginia" to London, which included both grapes to be packed in sand and "a hoggeshead or two" sample of wine, even if the wine was sour. *VWGJ* (Winter 1981): 221; Brown, *Genesis of United States*, 385; Lord De La Warr to Virginia Company (July 7, 1610), reprinted in Strachey, *Historie of Travaile*, xxxii; James J. McDonald, *Life in Old Virginia*, ed. J. A. C. Chandler (Norfolk, Va.: The Old Virginia Publishing Company, 1907), 265.

25. Even where accurate horticultural advice was available, its distribution was often limited to the nobility and England's literate population. Reprinted in Ainsworth Rand Spofford, "Virginia Three Hundred Years Ago," Records of the Columbia Historical Society, Washington, D.C., Vol. 11, 1908, 108. What is evident from these tracts is not only the enthusiasm with which the colonists anticipated a flourishing wine industry, but also the role that colonists from France played in attempting to found such an industry. While agricultural reports from the colony detailed Virginia's abundance of wild grapes, they failed to provide any meaningful discourse on how to cultivate the vine in the New World. (Mishkin, *American Colonial Wine Industry*, 246–247). Reports by the Virginia Company issued in 1609 and 1610 listed the need for skilled laborers, including six "Vine-dressers," six "Coopers," and two "Presse-makers." One February 1609 letter written by the Spanish ambassador to England, Don Pedro de Zuñiga, also pleaded for the assistance of workmen who "know how to plant vineyards," and for them to enlist with the treasurer of the colony in London. (Letter of Don Pedro de Zuñiga, reprinted in Brown, *Genesis of United States*, 248–249). As Robert Johnson (1586–1626) wrote in *Nova Britannia*, "Wee doubt not but to make there in a few yeares a store of good wines, as any from the Canaries, by replanting and making tame the vines that grow there in great abundance; onely send men of skill to doe it, and Coopers [barrel makers] to make caske, and hoopes for that and all other uses, for which there is wood enough at hand." Reprinted in Mishkin, *American Colonial Wine Industry*, 247–248; John Stepney, "A True and Sincere Declaration…," reprinted in Brown, *Genesis of United States*, 352–355; Hart, "Winemaking," 1; Mishkin, *American Colonial Wine Industry*, 162; James B. Stoudt, *Nicolas Martiau, the Adventurous Huguenot: The Military Engineer, and the Earliest American Ancestor of George Washington* (Norristown, Pa.: Norristown Press, 1932), 26–27; Arthur Henry Hirsch, *The Huguenots of Colonial South Carolina* (Columbia: University of South Carolina Press, 1999), 3–43; Bertrand Van Ruymbeke, *From New Babylon to Eden: The Huguenots and Their Migration to Colonial South Carolina* (Columbia: University of South Carolina Press, 2006).

26. Margaret Vowell Smith, *Virginia, 1492–1892* (Washington, D.C.: W. H. Lowdermilk & Company, 1893), 47–49; Strachey, "Purchas His Pilgrims," 4:1755; "A Declaration of the State of the Colony and Affairs in Virginia," in Peter Force, *Tracts and other papers relating principally to the origin, Settlement, and progress of the colonies in North American, from the discovery of the country to the year 1776* (Gloucester, Mass.: Peter Smith, 1963), Vol. 3, No. 5, P. 15 (hereafter cited as Force, *Tracts*); Richard L. Maury, *The Huguenots in Virginia* (N.p.: N.p., 1902?), 15; *Stith's History of Virginia*, 118; Smith, *Historie of Virginia*, 208; *True Declaration of the Estate of the Colony of Virginia*, 23; *VWGJ* (Fall 1980):

178.

27. Writing of his experience in July 1611, he noted, "There are many Vines planted in divers places and do prosper well." Regrettably, he never stayed long enough to see the industry to fruition. (De La Warr, "A Short Relation" (1611), in Brown, *Genesis of United States*, 482). Bohune was later described as "one of the most colorful of the early Virginia doctors." He was reportedly "a man of talent, of an investigative nature, full of robust enthusiasm for the sea and for adventure." Wyndham B. Blanton, *Medicine in Virginia in the Seventeenth Century* (Richmond, Va.: William Byrd Press, 1930); Sidney E. Negus, "Physicians at Early Jamestown," *Virginia Journal of Science* 8, No. 1, ([Jan.] 1957): 65–73; (written elsewhere as "Bohun," "Bootie," or Boone") Negus, "Physicians at Early Jamestown," 65–73; Caleb Clarke Magruder, Jr., *Dr. Lawrence Bohune: First Physician-General to the Colony of Virginia, and Dr. John Pott, His Successor*, reprinted from the *Interstate Medical Journal* 17, No. 6 (1910): 1; Brown, *Genesis of United States*, 412–413; he experimented with sassafras, rhubarb, and gums of local trees. Stearns, *Science in British Colonies*, 74–75; Strachey, *Historie of Travaile*, 120 (emphasis in the original).

28. Justin Winsor, ed., *Narrative and Critical History of America* (Boston: Houghton Mifflin, 1889), 3:137; Negus, "Physicians at Early Jamestown," 65–73; Magruder, *Dr. Lawrence Bohune*, 2; Blanton, *Medicine in Virginia*, 11–15; Pinney, *History of Wine*, 14.

29. Martha W. McCartney, *Virginia Immigrants and Adventurers, 1607–1635: A Biographical Dictionary* (Baltimore, Md.: Genealogical Publishing, 2007), 616.

30. Ralph Hamor, *A True Discourse of the Present State of Virginia* ( London: Printed by John Beale for W. Welby, 1615), 22. Henricus is alternatively known as "Henricopolis" and "Henrico." *See* Hamor, *True Discourse*, 22.

31. Brown, *Genesis of United States*, 248–249; reprinted in John William Reps, *Tidewater Towns: City Planning in Colonial Virginia and Maryland* (Williamsburg, Va.: Colonial Williamsburg Foundation; Charlottesville: Distributed by the University Press of Virginia, Charlottesville, 1972), 40.

32. Bruce, *Economic History*, 219.

33. Henricus boasted the first hospital in the British colonies of North America and land that was set aside for what would have been the New World's first college. Dale, for his part in hoping to resurrect the struggling colony, had wanted to found a 2,000-plus-acre town at Point Comfort (located today in the City of Hampton) to grow corn and plant vines. "Vines growe naturallie there, in great abundance," Dale wrote to Lord Salisbury in August 1611. Letter to Lord Salisbury from Thomas Dale, August 1611, reprinted in Warren M. Billings, ed., *The Old Dominion in the Seventeenth Century* (Chapel Hill: Published for the Institute of Early American History and Culture at Williamsburg, Va., by the University of North Carolina Press, 1975), 33-34; Hamor, *True Discourse*, 22; Charles E. Hatch, Jr., "A True Discourse of the *Present State of Virginia* by Ralph Hamor," *The Virginia Magazine of History and Biography* 65, No. 4 (Oct., 1957), 490–491; Bruce, *Economic History*, 219; Robert Johnson, *The New Life of Virginia* (London, 1612), in Force, *Tracts*, 1:14.

34. Article 1.31 of the laws. The law and its proscribed penalty underscore the importance of wine and its potential in securing an optimistic future for the colony. Compiled and published by William Strachey in 1612, his "For the Colony in Virginea Britannia. Lawes Divine, Morall and Martiall, &c." represents the earliest compilation of English-language laws in the New World. The laws consisted largely of edicts issued by the colony's various governors between 1610 and 1612. The laws, which regulated the conduct of Virginia's settlers, did not recognize British common law, jury trials, or other rights previously guaranteed by the Virginia Company. William Strachey, "For the Colony in Virginea Britannia, Lawes Divine, Morall and Martiall, Etc.," in Force, *Tracts*, Vol. 3. No. 2, Pp. 16–17; Mishkin, *American Colonial Wine Industry*, 163; Hart, "Winemaking," 1.

35. Susan Myra Kingsbury, ed., *The Records of the Virginia Company of London* (Washington, D.C.: Government Printing Office, 1906–1935), 3:166 (hereafter cited as Kingsbury, *Records of Va. Co.*).

36. *Colonial Records of Virginia*, 22; Hedrick, *Grapes of New York*, 7.

37. Report of Sandys in 1620, reprinted in *Stith's History of Virginia*, 177; Virginia Brainard Kunz, *The French in America* (Minneapolis, Minn.: Lerner Publications Co., 1966), 144; Virginia Historical Society, Abstract of the Proceedings of the Virginia Company of London, 1619–1624 (Richmond, Va.:

The Society, 1888), 1:67–68, 92; Hedrick, *Grapes of New York*, 7; "Discourse of the Old Company," reprinted in *Virginia Magazine of History and Biography 1* (1893–1894): 159; Kingsbury, Records of Va. Co., 1:353; Kliman, *Wild Vine*, 26.

38. Today a historic marker WY-92 located in the Buckroe area of Hampton reads, "In 1620, Frenchmen sent over to plant mulberry trees and grape vines settled here. The name was taken from a place in England." The Company also sought vignerons from the Rhineland and Spain. Mishkin, *American Colonial Wine Industry*, 164–165; Kingsbury, Records of Va. Co., 1:392, 466, 627; Pinney, *History of Wine*, 15. The colony had also requested "men skillfull in the plantinge and dressing of Vynes outt of [France] and from the [Rhein]" as well as "plants as likewise from the Canaries" in July 1620. Kingsbury, *Records of Va. Co.*, 1: 392; These were two niche industries in southern France at the time. William Waller Hening, ed., *The Statutes at Large…*(New York : Printed for the editor, by R. & W. & G. Bartow, 1819–1923), 1:115; Maury, *The Huguenots in Virginia*, 15, 19; Alexander Brown, *The First Republic in America* (Boston: Houghton Mifflin, 1898), 458; reports indicated that the Frenchmen "were so in love with their new country that the character they then gave of it…was very much to its advantage." See Kingsbury, *Records of Va. Co.*, 3:254–256; "A Declaration of the State of the Colony and Affairs in Virginia," in Force, *Tracts*, Vol. 3, No. 5, P. 15. Bonoeil's name is spelled elsewhere as "Bonnall" or "Bonnell." This area is located just south of the area advocated for settlement and vineyards by Sir Thomas Dale in 1611 and where Father Juan de la Carrera claimed to have witnessed vineyards in 1572. *William and Mary Quarterly*, 1st Series, Vol. 9 ( 1900–1901): 86; "Jamieson-Elegood-Parker," *William and Mary Quarterly*, 1st Series, Vol. 13 (1904): 289; "Abstracts of Virginia Land Patents," *Virginia Magazine of History and Biography 2* (1894–1895): 310–311; Letter of George Sandys to John Ferrar, Apr. 8, 1623, reprinted in *Virginia Magazine of History and Biography 6*, No. 3 (1898–1899): 241–242, also found in United Kingdom, Public Record Office; Calendar of State Papers, Colonial Series, 1574–1660, Apr. 8, 1623, ed. William Noel Sainsbury et al. (London: Her Majesty's Stationery Office, 1860), 42; Warren M. Billings, *Sir William Berkeley and the Forging of Colonial Virginia* (Baton Rouge: Louisiana State University Press, 2010), 71. Thomas Pinney has noted that budding the following spring "is easily possible if the cutting includes a fruitful bud or buds from the parent vine. But the grower should remove the clusters that grow from any such buds until the vine is mature enough to sustain them. That the Virginia French apparently did not suggests that they had little experience in viticulture." Pinney, *History of Wine in America*, 454, n. 48; Beverley, *History of Virginia*, 107; Samuel Purchas, *Hakluytus posthumus, or Purchas his Pilgrimes: contayning a history of the world in sea voyages and lande travells by Englishmen and others* (Glasgow: J. MacLehose and Sons, 1905–1907), 19:152–153.

39. John Pory, who arrived in Virginia late that year to serve as the colony's secretary, wrote of the colony's potential for wine production in light of the Company's recent investments: Vines here are in suche abundance, as where soever a man treads, they are ready to embrace his foote. I have tasted here of a great black grape as big as a Damascin, 3 that hath a true Muscatell-taste; 4 the vine whereof now spending itselfe to the topps of high trees, if it were reduced into a vineyard, and there domesticated, would yield incomparable fruite. The like or a better taste have I founde in a lesser sorte of black grapes. 5 White grapes 6 also of great excellency I have hearde to be in the country; but they are very rare, nor did I ever see or taste of them 1619 Letter of John Pory, Secretary of Virginia, to Sir Dudley Carleton, reprinted in Lyon Gardiner Tyler, ed., *Narratives of Early Virginia*, 1606–1625 (New York: Charles Scribner's Sons, 1907), 281–287; Purchas, *His Pilgrimes*, 19:152–153.

40. The growth of silk and wine continued. Kingsbury, *Records of Va. Co.*, 4:142, 2:349; Billings, *Sir William Berkeley*, 71; Company reports reprinted in Maury, *The Huguenots in Virginia*, 15; Charles E. Hatch, Jr., "Mulberry Trees and Silkworms: Sericulture in Early Virginia," *Virginia Magazine of History and Biography 65*, No. 1 (Jan., 1957): 3; Mishkin, *American Colonial Wine Industry*, 250–251; Kingsbury, *Records of Va. Co.*, 3:641; Calendar of State Papers, Colonial, America and West Indies, Volume 1: 1574–1660 (1860), 28–29 (hereafter cited as Calendar of State Papers, Colonial, 1574–1660); Hedrick, *Grapes of New York*, 7.

41. Barber, "American Wine Industry," 15.

42. Kliman, *Wild Vine*, 27; Mishkin, *American Colonial Wine Industry*, 164, 254; Bruce, *Economic History*,

238–239.

43. Wright, *Dream of Prosperity*, 33. As writer James E. "Jim" Mays has argued, "Tobacco, not wine, was to provide the wealth that would enable the great-great grandsons of the first settlers to indulge in what would become their passion for politics and philosophy and thus set the stage for the American Revolution." *VWGJ 1*, No. 1 (Spring 1974): 39.

44. Exports to England grew from 60,000 pounds in 1622 to 500,000 pounds by 1628 and to 1,500,000 pounds by 1639. By the close of the 1600s, England was importing more than 20 million pounds annually. See J. Thomas Scharf, *History of Maryland: From the Earliest Periods to the Present Day* (Hatboro, Pa.: Tradition Press, 1967), 47, 94; Arthur Pierce Middleton, *Tobacco Coast* (Newport News, Va.: Mariners' Museum, 1953), 35; Mishkin, *American Colonial Wine Industry*, 227; http://www.tobacco.org/History/colonialtobacco.html; John Solomon Otto, *The Southern Frontiers, 1607–1860: The Agricultural Evolution of the Colonial and Antebellum South* (New York: Greenwood Press, 1989), 12; Melvin Herndon, *Tobacco in Colonial Virginia: "The Sovereign Remedy"* (Williamsburg, Va.: Virginia 350th Anniversary Celebration Corporation, 1957), 38.

45. There were periodically ruinous tobacco price collapses between 1629 and 1630, 1638 and 1639, in 1642, and from 1650 to 1667. During the 1620s, tobacco planting in the colony evolved from exporting 40,000 pounds at three shillings per pound to producing 1,800,000 pounds valued at less than one pence per pound. Mishkin, *American Colonial Wine Industry*, 224, 228–230.

46. Richard Lee Morton, *Colonial Virginia* (Chapel Hill: Published for the Virginia Historical Society by the University of North Carolina Press, 1960), 1:40–41, 93; Edward L. Bond, *Damned Souls in a Tobacco Colony: Religion in Seventeenth-Century Virginia* (Macon, Ga.: Mercer University Press, 2000), 194; Mishkin, *American Colonial Wine Industry*, 226–228.

47. The king blamed Native Americans for tobacco's presence in Europe. King James, Counterblaste; "Sovereign Remedies: Natural Authority and the Counterblaste to Tobacco," by Michael Ziser, *William and Mary Quarterly*, 3rd Series, Vol. 62, No. 4 (Oct. 2005): 719–744; Jeffrey Knapp, "Elizabethan Tobacco," Representations No. 21 (Winter 1988): 26–66.

48. Billings, *Sir William Berkeley*, 70–71; Calendar of State Papers, Colonial, 1574–1660, July 2, 1624, 1:263; *VWGJ* (Winter 1981): 222; Hatch, "Mulberry Trees," 3–61. In March 1623, colony treasurer George Sandys, wrote to [Samuel] Wrott requesting "two Frenchmen skilfull in silkeworms and the planting of vines," each to be fed and paid at 20 marks annually. Kingsbury, Records of Va. Co., 4:68.

49. John Bonoeil, "His Maiesties Gracious Letter to the Earle of South-Hampton...commanding the present setting up of Silke works, and planting of Vines in Virginia" (London, 1622), 85–86; Mishkin, *American Colonial Wine Industry*, 291. This idea from Bonoeil was shared by Sir William Alexander, Earl of Stirling (ca. 1570–1640) in his 1624 work *An Encouragement to Colonies* (London: Printed by Nathaniel Butter, 1630), 38; the king had earlier appointed him in 1614 as the keeper of the royal gardens, vines, and silkworms at Oatlands Palace. Billings, *Sir William Berkeley*, 71; Hatch, "Mulberry Trees," 21; the king also encouraged the diversification of Virginia's economy and the creation of a trade zone between England and its colonies. Believing there to be a shortage of available labor in the colony, he advocated for the enslavement of Native Americans for viticultural pursuits. Linda Levy Peck, *Consuming Splendor: Society and Culture in Seventeenth-Century England* (Cambridge, Eng.: Cambridge University Press, 2005), 100–103.

50. Bonoeil largely premised his findings on prior reports from the colony. See John R. McGrew, "Some Untold Episodes in the History of Virginia Grapes and Wine," *American Wine Society Journal* (Fall 1986): 82–83 (hereafter cited as McGrew, "Untold Episodes"); Bonoeil, "His Maiesties Gracious Letter." Endeavoring to possess an understanding of the subject, London-based colonial administrators heavily cited such works and admonished their colonists to do the same. In the face of the strong desire by colonists to grow tobacco—not to mention some glaring mistakes that were clearly indicative of armchair academics who had never visited the colonies—such works were disregarded and often scorned as being unsuitable for the American climate. Bonoeil's pamphlet was no exception. In 1620, Sir Edwin Sandys requested that the Virginia Company provide an English translation of a French book on silkworms. Kingsbury, *Records of Va. Co.*, 1:422. As one John Laurence wrote, "Indeed it seems to me...that we suffer so many French Books of Gardening to be obtruded upon

us, containing Rules calculated for another climate, and which tend to lead us into many Errors." Laurence, *The Fruit-Garden Kalendar*, iii, reprinted in Mishkin, *American Colonial Wine Industry*, 161.

51. McCartney, *Virginia Immigrants and Adventurers*, 616; Pinney, *History of Wine*, 19; McGrew, "Untold Episodes," 82–83. Wine historian Thomas Pinney has argued that Bonoeil's recipe would have likely resulted in unattractive wine: "The boiling would have extracted an intense color, but the water would have diluted the already inadequate proportion of sugar in the native grapes." Nevertheless, Pinney suggests that Bonoeil was likely motivated out of charitable concern to provide "every man in Virginia... 'reasonably good' wine to drink." Pinney, History of Wine, 17; John Bonoeil, "His Maiesties Gracious Letter."

52. Hatch, "Mulberry Trees," 3–61; Joan Thirsk, *Alternative Agriculture: A History from the Black Death to the Present Day* (Oxford, Eng.: Oxford University Press, 1997), 126–128. Historian Louis B. Wright has opined, "Like many other theorists who never stir from their libraries, the king believed that bookish directions would be enough to ensure success, especially if reinforced by royal command." John Bonoeil, "His Maiesties Gracious Letter"; the king's and the Earl of Southampton's letters were reprinted by Samuel Purchas in *Purchas His Pilgrims* (1625); Wright, *Dream of Prosperity*, 34–35.

53. Kingsbury, *Records of Va. Co.*, 3:661–664, 2:102; Peck, *Consuming Splendor*, 100; Wright, *Dream of Prosperity*, 35.

54. One 1622 report noted that "the French Vignerons had conceived great Hopes of speedily making Plenty of good Wine whereof they had already made an Experiment and sent home a taste." William Stith, "Records of the Company," 218, reprinted in Maury, *The Huguenots in Virginia*, 15."

55. Pinney, *History of Wine*, 16; Captain Butler, "Dismasking of Virginia" (1622), in Kingsbury, *Records of Va. Co.*, 2:375. Such observations appear more believable than the Company's official reports. As historian Louis B. Wright observed, even if a settler were literate and could comprehend Bonoeil's tract, "the practical difficulties he faced with all of the other labor he had to perform made silk production and the care of vineyards mere fantasies of dreamers back in London." Wright, *Dream of Prosperity*, 36.

56. Butler, "Dismasking of Virginia," 2:384: Kingsbury, *Records of Va. Co.*, 1:107.

57. "An Answer to a Declaration of the *Present State of Virginia*" (1623), in Kingsbury, *Records of Va. Co.*, 4:142.

58. James Ellison, *George Sandys: Travel, Colonialism, and Tolerance in the Seventeenth Century* (Cambridge, Eng.; Rochester, N.Y.: D. S. Brewer, 2002), 117.

59. Sandys's translation has been cited as "the first utterance of the conscious literary spirit articulated in America." Literary historian Moses Coit Taylor has noted that while there were undoubtedly other early writings from early Virginia by John Smith, William Strachey, and more, these were produced for immediate, practical purposes. Moses Coit Tyler, *A History of American Literature during the Colonial Time* (New York: G. P. Putnam's Sons, 1897), 1:54–55; Ellison, George Sandys, 83.

60. George Sandys to John Ferrar, March 1623, Kingsbury, *Records of Va. Co.*, 4:24.

61. This law had apparently first been proposed in 1619, and was dispatched by Governor Yeardley to the Virginia Company for approval. It was not until 1623 that approval was granted, perhaps owing to the great distance between the colony and London, changes in governors, and Indian attacks. Hening, *Statutes at Large*, 1:126; VWGJ 14, Issue 4 (Winter 1987): 212; Kingsbury, *Records of Va. Co.*, 4:583; Hedrick, *Grapes of New York*, 7; Bruce, *Economic History*, 246.

62. "Minutes of the Council and General Court, 1622–1624," reprinted in *Virginia Magazine of History and Biography 20*, No. 2 (Apr. 1912): 156.

63. Sandys's home, the Treasurer's Plantation, consisted of one square mile and, aside from a vineyard, included a frame house for raising silkworms and a 1.5-acre garden. See Brown, *First Republic*, 626; Hatch, "Mulberry Trees," 21; Historic Marker K-234 "History At Crouch's Creek"; A. W. Bohannan, "Jamestown Island and The Surry Side," *Virginia Magazine of History and Biography 55*, No. 2 (Apr. 1947): 132; McCartney, *Virginia Immigrants and Adventurers*, 41; Pinney, *History of Wine*, 21; Taylor, *History of American Literature*, 1:83. Ellison, *George Sandys*, 83; James D. Kornwolf and Georgiana W. Kornwolf, *Architecture and Town Planning in Colonial North America* (Baltimore, Md.: Johns Hopkins

University Press, 2002), 2:552.

64. Mishkin, *American Colonial Wine Industry*, 166; Bruce, *Economic History*, 239–247; Kingsbury, *Records of Va. Co.*, 3:646–647.

65. Including Sherry wine (a fortified white Spanish wine), Canary wine (a sweet wine from the Canary Islands), Malaga wine (a sweet fortified Spanish wine), Alicante wine, Tent wine (a red wine chiefly from Galicia or Malaga in Spain), Muscadel wine, and Bastard wine (a sweet Iberian-blended wine). Violators were to forfeit the price paid, with half going to the buyer and half to the government. Kingsbury, *Records of Va. Co.*, 4:271–273.

66. Whether such a motion was passed in the hopes of raising money or further to encourage planters to experiment with winemaking is not known. This effort, of course, acted as a significant deterrent to planting vineyards. Kingsbury, *Records of Va. Co.*, 1:627–628; Mishkin, *American Colonial Wine Industry*, 254; *Abstract of the Proceedings of the Virginia Company of London*, 1:170; Brown, *First Republic*, 561–562.

67. McCartney, *Virginia Immigrants and Adventurers*, 616; Pinney, *History of Wine*, 19; McGrew, "Untold Episodes," 82–83.

68. Presumably because sea captains asserted that only sour casks would make the voyage without spoiling. Kingsbury, *Records of Va. Co.*, 4:453.

69. The General Assembly replying to questions from the king, reprinted in Maury, *The Huguenots in Virginia*, 15.

70. Wyatt sounded a pragmatic note, suggesting that the colony pursue a limited number of only the most hopeful and beneficial industries, including wine, silk, salt, fish, and iron, rather than the pursuit of a great number of alternative industries "as Adventures which are esteemed such in populous countrys." "Affairs in Virginia in 1626," *Virginia Magazine of History and Biography 2*, No. 1 (July 1894): 53; Mishkin, *American Colonial Wine Industry*, 252–253.

71. Hoping to dissuade them from abandoning their task, the Company in 1619 ordered its new governor, Sir Francis Wyatt, to encourage the French settlers to "plant an abundance of vines," and not to let them "forsake their [wine and silk] trades for planting tobacco or any useless commodity." The French, however, gave up winemaking and increasingly focused their attention on tobacco. The move engendered hostility from the desperate colonial government, a reaction perhaps understandable given the money and effort with which the Company had procured the men from France. See Mishkin, *American Colonial Wine Industry*, 168; David Hackett Fischer and James C. Kelly, *Bound Away: Virginia and the Westward Movement* (Charlottesville: University of Virginia Press, 2000), 108; Hening, *The Statutes at Large*, 1:135–136; Hart, "Winemaking," 3. The Company also sought vignerons from the Rhineland and Spain. Mishkin, *American Colonial Wine Industry*, 164–165; Kingsbury, *Records of Va. Co.*, 1:392, 466, 627; Pinney, *History of Wine*, 15. The colony had also requested "men skillfull in the plantinge and dressing of Vynes outt of [France] and from the [Rhein]" as well as "plants as likewise from the Canaries" in July 1620. Kingsbury, *Records of Va. Co.*, 1:3; Hening, *The Statutes at Large*, 1:115; Maury, *The Huguenots in Virginia*, 15, 19; Brown, *First Republic*, 458; "Answer of the Governor, Council, and Burgesses to the King," March 26, 1628, reprinted in *Virginia Magazine of History and Biography 7*, No. 3 (Jan. 1900): 262; Hening, *The Statutes at Large*, 1:134–136.

72. Hening, *The Statutes at Large*, 1:161.

73. Edward Williams, "Virginia…Richly and Truly Valued," in Force, *Tracts*, 3, no. 11, p. 17. Others have ascribed Virginia…Richly and Truly Valued to be the work of John Ferrar. See Winsor, *Narrative and Critical History*, 168.

74. Williams's premise is today supported by others who believe that while diseases may have played a role in the cause of viticulture failure, blame could also be shared by other natural predators (i.e., deer, raccoons, etc.), the 1622 Indian attack, and a lack of financial motivation by the French vignerons. Williams, "Richly and Truly Valued," 17; McGrew, "Untold Episodes," 83; John Lawson wrote in *A New Voyage to Carolina* that "These French Refugees have had small Encouragement in Virginia, because, at their first coming over, they took their Measures of Living, from Europe; which was all wrong." Lawson also identified six kinds of grapes growing in the Carolinas. See John Lawson, *A New Voyage to Carolina*, ed. Hugh Talmage Lefler (Chapel Hill: University of North Carolina Press,

1967), 108–114; the assembly also instituted a requirement for each person to plant a prescribed number of mulberry trees and forbade the destruction of any. Maury, *The Huguenots in Virginia*, 19; see also Calendar of State Papers, Colonial, 1574–1660, 267–273, item 98.

75. Hening, *The Statutes at Large*, 1:162.

76. Ibid., 1:192; Hedrick, *Grapes of New York*, 7.

77. Act of Assembly, 1639, Conway Robinson Transcripts of Early Virginia Records, Ca. 1860, from the Robert Alonzo Brock Collection at The Huntington Library, San Marino, California, Acc. 41008, Miscellaneous Reel 5316, p. 216; Hening, *The Statutes at Large*, 1:469–470; historians speculate it is unlikely anyone ever claimed the prize. See Pinney, *History of Wine*, 24.

78. Brocas was evidently a member of the colony's Council of State serving under Governor Sir John Harvey between 1636 and 1658. Ferrar, "Perfect Description of Virginia," in Force, *Tracts*, 2, no. 8, 14; Horace Edwin Hayden, *Virginia Genealogies: A Genealogy of the Glassell Family of Scotland and Virginia* (Wilkes-Barre, Pa.: E. B. Yordy, 1891), 230.

79. Philip Alexander Bruce, *Social Life of Virginia in the Seventeenth Century* (Richmond, Va.: Whittet and Shepperson, 1907), 178–179; "Sons of the Revolution in the State of Virginia," *Virginia Quarterly Magazine 1–2* (1922): 78; Thomas Glover, "An Account of Virginia, Its Scituation, Temperature, Productions, Inhabitants, and their Manner of Planting and Ordering Tobacco, etc. Communicated by Mr. Thomas Glover, An Ingenious Chirurgion that Hath Lived Some Years in That Country," Royal Society of London, *Philosophical Transactions* (1665–1678) No. 163 (June 20, 1676): 623–636; Dr. Kent Mountford "Siren song of Chesapeake grasses lure occasional manatee to Bay," *Bay Journal* (Oct. 2011) at http://www.bayjournal.com/article/siren_song_of_chesapeake_grasses_lure_occasional_manatee_to_bay (accessed Apr. 4, 2014).

80. See Edward Ayers, "Fruit Culture in Colonial Virginia," Unpublished Manuscript, Collections of the University of Virginia, 1973, p. 64, Charlottesville (hereafter cited as Ayers, "Fruit Culture"). Such calls typically blamed the colony's overreliance on tobacco as the main impediment to developing a wine industry. Others called for diversification in Virginia's economy. Writing in 1649, for example, London-based William Bullock asserted wine to be one of Virginia's "natural commodities," and that the production of great quantities of wine would assist the state economically. He urged Virginians to experiment with useful crops other than tobacco. Bullock's suggestions were largely based on available printed works and conversations he had in London with visiting Virginia planters. William Bullock, *Virginia Impartially Examined* (London, Eng.: Printed by John Hammond, 1649), 8; Peter Thompson, "William Bullock's 'Strange Adventure': A Plan to Transform Seventeenth-Century Virginia," *William and Mary Quarterly*, 3rd Series, Vol. 61, No. 1 (Jan. 2004): 107–128; "The Use and Abuse of Forests by the Virginia Indians," by Hu Maxwell, *William and Mary Quarterly*, 1st Series, Vol. 19, No. 2 (Oct. 1910), 73–103.

81. Hedrick, *Grapes of New York*, 7; Edward Williams in Hatch, *Fruits and Fruit Trees of Monticello*, 140, quoting Williams in Sandra Raphael, *An Oak Spring Sylva: A Selection of the Rare Books on Trees in the Oak Spring Garden Library* (Upperville, Va.: Oak Spring Garden Library; New Haven: Distributed by Yale University Press, 1989), 84.

82. Historian Thomas Pinney notes that while Williams's work may rank as the second instructional pamphlet (after Bonoeil's) written for an American audience, "his argument that grapes from one latitude in Europe should grow on the same latitude in North America is…quite fallacious." Nevertheless, such arguments justifying the concurrency of botanical success would be repeated by later writers on the topic and can be found in advertisements today. See Williams, "Virginia…Richly and Truly Valued," 16–18; Pinney, *History of Wine*, 23–24.

83. The absence of such high-level political direction—which diverged with a longstanding practice ever since 1621 to diversify Virginia's economy—coincided with the coronation of King James II and VII of England and in the face of lower tobacco revenues. Presumably, the new king did not want to distract Virginians from any enterprise that might lessen the tobacco's value to England. Lyman Carrier, *Agriculture in Virginia, 1607–1699* (Williamsburg: Virginia 350th Anniversary Celebration, 1957), 24. By 1649, Virginia boasted six breweries. See Kliman, *Wild Vine*, 28; Hart, "Winemaking," 3; "Instructions to Sir Francis Wyatt," reprinted in "Virginia in 1638–39 (Continued)," *Virginia Magazine*

*of History and Biography 11*, No. 1 (July 1903): 56; "Instructions to Berkeley, 1642," reprinted in *Virginia Magazine of History and Biography 2*, No. 3 (Jan. 1895): 287; "Virginia in 1681–82: Instructions to Lord Culpeper," *Virginia Magazine of History and Biography 28*, No. 1, (Jan. 1920): 47.

84. The penalties included a death penalty on all Protestant pastors and required young boys to be kept in Catholic schools until they professed the Catholic religion. Protestant women caught leaving France were to be imprisoned for life in secret convents or until recantation; older men were sent to the galleys as prisoners on ships. Maury, *The Huguenots in Virginia*, 93; Mishkin, *American Colonial Wine Industry*, 169; Van Ruymbeke, *From New Babylon to Eden*, 15–16; Oscar Theodore Barck, Jr. and Hugh Talmage Lefler, *Colonial America*, 2nd ed. (New York: Macmillan, 1968), 274; Huguenots also poured into South Carolina, Massachusetts, Rhode Island, and New York.

85. This was particularly true after 1700, when France felt increasingly threatened by the potential for British wines to impede on the sanctity of France's wine industry. The English had, by 1698, imposed exorbitant taxes on French wine imports. The military and commercial Treaty of Methuen of 1703 between England and Portugal placed France's wines at a disadvantage to those of Portugal as wines imported from the latter were subject to one-third less duty than those from France. The shift was apparently dramatic as colonial tastes shifted from drier French wines to sweeter Madeira wines imported from Portugal. See Mishkin, *American Colonial Wine Industry*, 173; *VWGJ* 1, No. 1 (Spring 1974): 40. David E. Lambert, *The Protestant International and the Huguenot Migration to Virginia* (New York: Peter Lang Publishing, 2010), 38–39; Mishkin, *American Colonial Wine Industry*, 170; Charles W. Baird, *History of the Huguenot Emigration to America* (New York: Dodd, Mead, and Company, 1885), 2:171.

86. The idea for setting aside land for a settlement of foreign immigrants was not new; Virginia's colonial government had long favored enticing colonists to the interior of the colony to create a buffer between Virginia's eastern settlements and plantations. For more perilous settlements, the Crown encouraged foreign immigrants as they would be less aware of "real and imagined dangers of the frontier." Mishkin, *American Colonial Wine Industry*, 169; L. Scott Philyaw, *Virginia's Western Visions: Political and Cultural Expansion on an Early American Frontier* (Knoxville: University of Tennessee Press, 2004), 10.

87. Maury, *The Huguenots in Virginia*, 27–31; Calendar of State Papers, Colonial, 1574–1660, 98; Van Ruymbeke, *From New Babylon to Eden*, 2; letter, available in Baird, *History of Huguenot Emigration*. The idea of importing French Huguenots for purposes of winemaking was also supported by William Penn, who wrote in "England's Present Interest Discovered" (London, Eng.: N.p., 1675), 44–45, that it would be good to have "Prudent Forreigners" to populate the colonies, "especially at this Time of Day, when our Forreign Islands yearly take off so many necessary inhabitants from us." McCartney, *Virginia Immigrants and Adventurers*, 616.

88. Leon Adams, *The Wines of America* (New York: McGraw-Hill, 1985), 16; Barck, *Colonial America*, 753; Maury, *The Huguenots in Virginia*, 37; Mishkin, *American Colonial Wine Industry*, 169–170.

89. Commentators, including Gilbert Chinard—one of the first chroniclers of French Huguenots in America—edited du Dauphiné's work and came to the conclusion that it was a disguised promotional pamphlet. Van Ruymbeke, *From New Babylon to Eden*, 45–46; Durand de Dauphiné, *A Huguenot Exile in Virginia*, ed. Gilbert Chinard (New York: Press of the Pioneers, 1924), 60; de Dauphiné, *A Frenchman in Virginia; being the memoirs of a Huguenot refugee in 1686, translated by a Virginian* ([Richmond]: Privately printed, 1923), 61.

90. Nan Netherton et al., *Fairfax County, Virginia: A History* (Fairfax County Board of Supervisors, 1978), PG. 161-163; Charles Knowles Bolton, *The Founders: Portraits of Persons Born Abroad Who Came to the Colonies in North America Before the Year 1701* (Boston: Boston Athenaeum, 1919), 1:135; Pinney, History of Wine, 100–101; Fairfax Harrison, *Landmarks of Old Prince William: A Study of Origins in Northern Virginia* (Berryville, Va.: Chesapeake Book Company, 1924), 1:188; du Dauphiné, *Huguenot Exile*, 126; William Fitzhugh to Nicholas Hayward, May 20, 1686, *William Fitzhugh and His Chesapeake World, 1676–1701: The Fitzhugh Letters and Other Documents*, ed. Richard Beale Davis (Chapel Hill: University of North Carolina Press, 1963), 189. Colonial law required those who obtained patents to "seat and plant" their land within three years and to pay an annual quitrent fee of

one shilling per fifty acres. Those who failed to seat and plant within three years (or beyond six years with an extension) could be sued in General Court. Philyaw, *Virginia's Western Visions*, 10; Willard Sterne Randall, *Thomas Jefferson: A Life* (New York: Henry Holt and Company, 1993), 67. Fitzhugh had inherited the 21,996-acre Ravensworth from his great-grandfather William Fitzhugh, who had purchased it in 1685. The tract was later confirmed by a direct grant from the colonial government in 1694. Eleanor Lee Templeman, *Northern Virginia Heritage: A Pictorial Compilation of the Historic Sites and Homes in the Counties of Arlington, Fairfax, Loudoun, Fauquier, Prince William and Stafford, and the Cities of Alexandria and Fredericksburg* (Arlington, Va.: Privately published by E. L. Templeman, 1966), 82.

91. François Durand du Dauphiné, "Un Français En Virginie," reprinted in *Virginia Magazine of History and Biography 41*, No. 3 (July 1933): 268–270; Pinney, *History of Wine*, 100–101; Harrison, *Landmarks of Old Prince William*, 188; du Dauphiné, *Huguenot Exile*, 126; Netherton, *History of Fairfax*, 14. Fitzhugh died in 1701 a prosperous lawyer, merchant, planter, and father of a well-known Virginia family. He left behind a large family and some 54,000 acres at Bedford in what was then Stafford County, Virginia. Today this area is known as King George County (Ernest Ludlow Bogart and Charles Manfred Thompson, *Readings in the Economic History of the United States* [New York, Chicago: Longmans, Green and Co., 1916], 35). Another Northern Virginia property owner, George Brent, unsuccessfully attempted to settle Huguenots on his 30,000 acres in Prince William County (all of whom eventually moved to Maryland). Nicholas Hayward, for his part, went into a partnership with a George Brent, a surveyor and lawyer, to purchase property in the Stafford backwoods (now a part of Prince William County) that became known as Brenton, later corrupted to Brent Town. Hayward promoted the property as "healthy, good and fertile, producing all sorts of…vines and all sorts of fruit." du Dauphiné, *A Frenchman in Virginia*, 69.

92. Klaus Wust, *The Virginia Germans* (Charlottesville: University Press of Virginia, 1989), 17.

93. Beverley, *History of Virginia*, 282; George Thomas Surface, *Studies on the Geography of Virginia* (Philadelphia: University of Pennsylvania, 1907), 42; James L Bugg, Jr., "The French Huguenots Frontier Settlement of Manakin Town," *Virginia Magazine of History and Biography 61*, No. 4 (Oct. 1953): 386. Manakin Town was unique as it was "set aside for a community planned by the Virginia Council for an alien, dissimilar culture, to be set within the much larger, more dominant Anglican Colony in the frontier wilderness of Virginia. These distinctly French people were to be colonized within a completely English colony, yet remain free to retain their French language, customs, characteristics, and more importantly, their religion."

94. Historical Magazine of the Protestant Episcopal Church 55 (1986): 205; John Lawson, *A New Voyage to Carolina*, ed. Hugh Talmage Lefler (Chapel Hill: University of North Carolina Press, 1967), 83; Bugg, "French Huguenots," 387. Optimistic settlers believed that improvements in transportation would allow the industrial nature of the community to expand greatly. The General Assembly aided the settlement by granting it donations of money and provisions, and exempting it from taxes. Beverley, History of Virginia, 282; Maury, *The Huguenots in Virginia*, 91; Charles Campbell, *History of the Colony and Ancient Dominion of Virginia* (Philadelphia: J. B. Lippincott, 1860), 370.

95. Beverley pondered, "Now if such may be made of the wild Vine in the Woods, without Pruning, Weeding, or removing it out of the Shade, what may not be produc'd from a Vineyard skillfully Cultivated?" In 1705, Beverley found that the settlers had resolved themselves to the making of wine and brandy. Beverley wrote that the French made their claret from an "early Ripe common grape" that was "common to the whole Country, some of which are black, and some blue on the Outside, but are both red within. They grow upon vast large Vines, and bear very plentifully. The nice Observer might, perhaps, distinguish them into several Kinds, because they differ in Colour, Size, and Relish; but I shall divide them only into Two, viz. The early, and the late ripe. The early ripe common Grape is much larger, sweeter and better than the other. Of these some are quite black, and bother blue; some also ripen Three Weeks, or a Month before the other. The Distance of their ripening, is from the latter End of August, to the latter End of October. The late ripe common Grapes are less than any of the other, neither are they so pleasant to the Taste. They hang commonly till the latter End of November, or till Christmas." Beverley, *History of Virginia*, 133–134, 282; Bugg, "French Huguenots,"

359–394; John Lawson, *History of North Carolina* (Charlotte, N.C.: Observer Printing House, 1903), 85; Louis Michel, "The Journey of Francis Louis Michel," *Virginia Magazine of History and Biography* 24 (1916): 123.

96. Bugg, "French Huguenots," 359–394. According to explorer and historian John Lawson, those that resettled in North Carolina intended to "propagate Vines, as far as their present Circumstances would permit; provided they could get any Slips of Vines, that would do." http://nationalhuman-itiescenter.org/pds/becomingamer/growth/text4/frenchvirginia.pdf (accessed Apr. 4, 2014); Lawson, New Voyage to Carolina, 114.

97. "Eventually their surplus products were exchanged for the manufactures which they had once dreamed of producing in their wilderness home." Bugg, "French Huguenots," 359–394, 387–388; H. R. McIlwaine, ed., *Executive Journal of the Council of Colonial Virginia*, June 11, 1680–May 3, 1775 (Richmond: Virginia State Library, 1925–1966), 2:227–228, 231, 247, 258, 353, 401; McIlwaine, ed., Journal of the House of Burgesses, 1702–1712 (Richmond: Virginia State Library, 1912), 60–61.

98. Wust, Virginia Germans, 3, 18–19; Fischer and Kelly, Bound Away, 367. These settlers were not the first of German stock in Virginia; indeed, as early as 1608, one year after the arrival of the English at Jamestown, eight "Dutchmen and Poles" disembarked from the Mary and Margaret to join the seventeen-month settlement. S. J. Quinn, *The History of the City of Fredericksburg, Virginia* (Richmond, Va.: The Hermitage Press, 1908, 23.

99. Fischer and Kelly, Bound Away, 366; John Fiske, *Old Virginia and Her Neighbours* (New York: Houghton Mifflin, 1897), 2:372, 385; Wust, Virginia Germans, 20. The area is still known today as Germania Ford.

100. Hugh Jones, *The Present State of Virginia: From Whence Is Inferred a Short View of Maryland and North Carolina*, ed. Richard L. Morton (Chapel Hill: University of North Carolina Press, 1956), 91; Ray K. Saunders, "A Taste of the 'Old World' Being Nurtured near Culpeper," Culpeper Star-Exponent, July 29, 1981; Mort Hochstein, "Right Spot Still Eludes Virginia Wine Pioneers," Wine Spectator 7, No. 16 (Nov. 16–30, 1982): 30. John Fontaine, *The Journal of John Fontaine: An Irish Huguenot Son in Spain and Virginia, 1710–1719*, ed. Edward P. Alexander (Charlottesville: University Press of Virginia, 1972), 88; Wust, *Virginia Germans*, 21.

101. Pinney, *History of Wine*, 65. Historians differ as to whether Jones was describing Germanna or a later German settlement. Jones, *Present State of Virginia*, 59–60. See also John Blankenbaker's series of Short Notes on Germanna History Notes and Genealogy Comments, which were originally posted to the "Germanna_Colonies" discussion list. Each page contains 25 notes. http://homepages.roots-web.ancestry.com/~george/johnsgermnotes/index.html

102. Fontaine, *Journal of John Fontaine*, 106.

103. Fontaine was an Englishman born to French Huguenot refugees who traveled across Virginia between 1715 and 1719. Wine historian Thomas Pinney notes that, given their likely inebriated condition, it is unlikely they were in a position to make discriminating judgments. Pinney, *History of Wine*, 65; Fiske, *Old Virginia*, 372, 385.

104. Ferrar, "Perfect Description of Virginia," 6.

105. Beverley, *History of Virginia*, 260; Hedrick, *Grapes of New York*, 33.

106. Berkeley was removed as governor during the English Interregnum (1649–1660), but was reappointed when the restoration of Charles II was viewed as inevitable, and shortly thereafter received a royal commission officially appointing him as governor once more. See Beer, *Origins of the British Colonial System*, 112.

107. Billings, *Sir William Berkeley*, 167–170; Alan Taylor, *American Colonies: The Settling of North America* (New York: Penguin, 2001), 146–151. Berkeley penned numerous correspondences to the Crown asking them to encourage the production of other commodities in the colony. While tobacco provided a handsome profit to London, Berkeley felt that encouraging other industries would, in the long run, pay even larger dividends. See William Berkeley, *A Discourse and View of Virginia* (London, Eng.: N.p., 1662), 2; J. Leander Bishop, *A History of American Manufactures from 1608 to 1860* (London, Eng.: Sampson Low, Son and Company, 1864), 1:31.

108. Warren M. Billings, "Sir William Berkeley and the Diversification of the Virginia Economy," *Virgin-

ia *Magazine of History and Biography 104*, No. 4 (Autumn 1996): 433–454; Virginia B. Price, "Constructing to Command: Rivalries between Green Spring and the Governor's Palace, 1677–1722," *Virginia Magazine of History and Biography 113*, No. 1 (2005): 2–45; Peter Martin, *The Pleasure Gardens of Virginia: From Jamestown to Jefferson* (Charlottesville: University Press of Virginia, 2001), 7; Billings, *Sir William Berkeley*, 433–454.

109. Edward Hyde estimated that Green Spring contained approximately 1,500 fruit trees; Berkeley planted fruit trees throughout the 1640s during his first tenure as governor (1642–1652). Martin, *Pleasure Gardens*, 7–8; Ferrar, "Perfect Description of Virginia," 14; Billings, *Sir William Berkeley*, 66–67; Louis R. Caywood, "Green Spring Plantation," *Virginia Magazine of History and Biography 65*, No. 1 (Jan. 1957): 70.

110. Beverley, *History of Virginia*, 135.

111. Berkeley biographer Warren M. Billings has suggested that Berkeley's pledge to Hyde may have been more of an aspiration than a reflection of reality, given the lack of authenticating accounts. See Library of Congress British Transcripts, Egerton MSS, 2395, fol. 365, reprinted in Warren M. Billings, "Sir William Berkeley and the Diversification of the Virginia Economy," *William and Mary Quarterly*, 2nd Series, Vol. 18, No. 2 (Apr. 1938): 170; Billings, *Sir William Berkeley*, 66–67.

112. Clayton also wrote that "there be 3 or 4 Sorts of grapes, that grow wild, yet there be no vineyards in the Country." "Another 'Account of Virginia': By the Reverend John Clayton," *Virginia Magazine of History and Biography 76*, No. 4 (Oct. 1968): 427.

113. Clayton penned "Another 'Account of Virginia'" as a letter to British scientist Robert Boyle in June 1687—a decade following Berkeley's death. *The Reverend John Clayton, A Parson with a Scientific Mind: His Scientific Writings and Other Related Papers* by Edmund Berkeley and Dorothy Smith Berkeley (Charlottesville, Published for the Virginia Historical Society by the University Press of Virginia, 1965); Review by Conway Zirkle, *Virginia Magazine of History and Biography 74*, No. 2 (Apr. 1966): 210–211; Review by Richard M. Jellison, *William and Mary Quarterly*, 3rd Series, Vol. 23, No. 4 (Oct. 1966): 656–658; Clayton, "Another Account," 415, 427.

114. Wine bottles were recovered at Bacon's Castle by its former owner, Arthur Allen, indicating that Bacon may have produced wine there as well. Caywood, "Green Spring Plantation," 68.

115. Beverley was the son of wealthy immigrants and served as the clerk of the General Assembly and as a member of the House of Burgesses. Considered the most accurate history of early life in Virginia at the time, Beverley's *History*, historian Louis B. Wright noted, was "a readable work, simple and vigorous in style, with flashes of ironic and satirical humor." While critiquing an unpublished history of English historian John Oldmixon's British Empire in America in June 1703, Beverley was persuaded to write his own account of Virginia after finding Oldmixon's to be inadequate and inaccurate. (Beverley, *History of Virginia*.) In it, Beverley vigorously mixes an enthusiasm for Virginia, shrewd insight, and vivid descriptions of the natural world and the political and social histories of the colony. He largely drew from Captain John Smith's *Generall Historie of Virginia*. Beverley participated in then-lieutenant governor Alexander Spotswood's "Knights of the Golden Horseshoe" expedition in 1716. "Robert Beverley, the Historian of Virginia," *Virginia Magazine of History and Biography 36*, No. 4 (Oct. 1928): 333–344; "The Quest for Freedom: Style and Meaning in Robert Beverley's 'History and *Present State of Virginia*," *Southern Literary Journal 8*, No. 2 (Spring 1976): 79–98. Although there is no full-length biography of Beverley, one can gather a sketch of him in the introduction to Louis B. Wright's edition of Beverley's work *The History and Present State of Virginia* (reprint, 1947). Louis B. Wright, *The First Gentlemen of Virginia: Intellectual Qualities of the Early Colonial Ruling Class* (1940), gives a sympathetic and lively account of Beverley and his contemporaries. Genealogical data are in John McGill, T*he Beverley Family of Virginia: Descendants of Major Robert Beverley (1641–1687) and Allied Families* (1956). Valuable for an understanding of the historical background are Bruce, *Social Life of Virginia* (1964), and Thomas J. Wertenbaker, *Patrician and Plebeian in Virginia* (1910), and *The Planters of Colonial Virginia* (1922); "Louis B. Wright, Beverley's History…of Virginia (1705): A Neglected Classic," *William and Mary Quarterly*, 3rd Series, Vol. 1, No. 1 (Jan. 1944): 49.

116. Beverley described six native varieties that grew in Virginia and claimed to have seen "great Trees covered with single Vines almost hid with the Grapes." Frances Mossiker, *Pocahontas: The Life and the*

*Legend* (New York: Da Capo Press, 1996), 48; historian Edward Ayers has noted that, given available evidence, it is not possible to identify with precision the species of grapes Beverley highlighted. See Ayers, "Fruit Culture," 1; Beverley, *History of Virginia*, 315–316.

117. He also critiqued efforts by a one Isaac Jamart, a French immigrant merchant who arrived in 1705 and attempted to grow grapes along the lowlands of Archers-Hope Creek (later renamed College Creek) near the James River outside of Williamsburg as well as Sir William Berkeley's efforts of using mulberry trees as espaliers. "The Pine-Tree and Fir are naturally very noxious to the Vine; and the Vine is observed never to thrive, where it is any ways influenced by them," he asserted. Beverley, *History of Virginia*, 134–135.

118. Alfred Bagby, Jr., "Beverley Park and the Knights of the Golden Horseshoe," *William and Mary Quarterly*, 2nd Series, Vol. 20, No. 4 (Oct. 1940): 508; Various, "Robert Beverley," 333–344, 339; Beverley, *History of Virginia*, 315–316.

119. De Kocherthal noted, however, that Beverley's attempts were unsuccessful because of inexperience and skill. De Kocherthal also observed that French and German methods of planting were "disagreeable" with North America's climate and soils. From Cecil Headlam, ed., *Calendar of State Papers Colonial, America and West Indies, 1708–1709* (London, Her Majesty's Stationery Office, 1922), 24:932.

120. Fontaine, *Journal of John Fontaine*, 85–86; W. G. Stanard, "Major Robert Beverley and His Descendants (Concluded)," *Virginia Magazine of History and Biography 3*, No. 2 (Oct. 1895): 169–176; Bagby, "Beverley Park," 509; Hatch, *Fruits and Fruit Trees of Monticello*, 142; Louis B. Wright, *The First Gentleman of Virginia: Intellectual Qualities of the Early Colonial Ruling Class* (Huntington, Calif.: The Huntington Library, 1970), 90.

121. Fontaine wrote that "Mr. Beverley gave a hundred guineas upon the above-mentioned terms, and I do not in the least doubt but next year he will make the seven hundred gallons and win the thousand guineas." Fontaine, *Journal of John Fontaine*, 86. Beverley provided anecdotal evidence in his 1722 edition of his History that, prior to 1722, there were vineyards that produced 750 gallons per year. At least one historian has surmised that this evidently meant Beverley's own. At least one jug of wine has been reported to have been recovered on the property. Bagby, "Beverley Park," 508–510; Jones, *Present State of Virginia*, 91, 139–140; Fontaine, *Journal of John Fontaine*, 86; Stanard, "Major Robert Beverley," 171.

122. Alan Gallay, ed., *Voices of the Old South: Eyewitness Accounts, 1528–1861* (Athens: University of Georgia Press, 1994), 152.

123. Framed by large poplar trees, dogwoods, and boxwoods, Westover is today located midway between Richmond and Williamsburg in Charles City County. Westover remains today perhaps the premier example of colonial Georgian architecture in the United States. William Byrd II, the founder of Richmond, was thought to have built the mansion circa 1730. This date was part of the 1960 designation of the house as a National Historic Landmark. Recent dendrochronologic testing on boards and planks in the house showed, however, that they dated to the 1750s. The house was thus probably built and first occupied by William Byrd III, not his father. The National Park Service has accepted the revised construction date. See http://www.westover-plantation.com/about.htm (accessed Apr. 4, 2014). Byrd visited the Duke of Buckingham's New Hall, Felix Hall, Brackley Lodge, Audley End, and Euston Hall. Martin, *Pleasure Gardens*, 64–66. Many plantations were far removed from ports and cities, and they were dependent on cultivating their own wine from their own vineyards. By early in the 1700s, Virginia's colonial gardens began to have a more pastoral, less formal appearance, perhaps a result of the rise of agrarianism in the colony and an attempt to replicate the English countryside. By the time of the American Revolution, Virginia's pleasure gardens had taken on their own aesthetic spirit with an increased reliance on native species. Some of these gardens, including that of the Governor's Palace in Williamsburg, had developed a new paradigm in which urban and rural settings were joined. J. A. Osborne, *Williamsburg in Colonial Times* (Richmond, Va.: Dietz Press, 1935), 101–102; Fletcher, *History of Fruit Growing*, 8, 13. The gardens, the ideas for many of which came from European gardening books, included imported European and native species, nurseries, terraces, sunken gardens, paths, and bowling greens. Kliman, *Wild Vine*, 30; Mishkin, *American Colonial Wine Industry*, 255. For native grapes, see Bullock, *Virginia Impartially Examined*, 8; du Dauphiné,

*Huguenot Exile,* 126; Beverley, *History of Virginia,* 134, 282; Richmond Croom Beatty and William J. Mulloy, *William Byrd's Natural History of Virginia; Or, the Newly Discovered Eden* (Richmond, Va.: Dietz Press, 1940), 32–33; Bruce, *Economic History,* 410–411; for imported grapes, see Beverley, *History of Virginia,* 19, 21, 46; Jones, *Present State of Virginia,* 52, 59–60, 140–141; VWGJ (Summer 1984): 124; Fletcher, *History of Fruit Growing,* 17. As one commentator noted, "If ever Virginia gardening and changing English norms of taste discoursed with each other intimately in the early eighteenth century, it was in the mind and art of Byrd." Westover's was similar to the homes of several other prominent Virginians, many of which boasted lavish gardens ostensibly established for ornamental and productive purposes. Mimicking the gardens of formal European estates, these gardens were often laid out on an axis and boasted geometric formal designs that provided a sense of English formality on an otherwise unsettled continent. Martin, *Pleasure Gardens,* 64–65.

124. Marion Tinling, ed., *The Correspondence of the Three William Byrds of Westover, Virginia, 1684–1776,* foreword by Louis B. Wright (Charlottesville: Published for the Virginia Historical Society by the University Press of Virginia, 1977), 1:380, 408–410; Martin, *Pleasure Gardens,* 71–72, 76; Pierre Marambaud, *William Byrd of Westover, 1674–1744* (Charlottesville: University Press of Virginia, 1971), 159; Ayers, "Fruit Culture," 67.

125. Byrd likely began collecting grapevines in the 1720s—particularly French varieties. Martin, *Pleasure Gardens,* 71–72, 76; Tinling, *Correspondence,* 408–409; Pinney, *History of Wine,* 67.

126. Letter to Mr. Collenson, July 18, 1736, reprinted in "Letters of the Byrd Family (Continued)," *Virginia Magazine of History and Biography 36,* No. 4 (Oct. 1928): 353–354; *Virginia Magazine of History and Biography 36,* No. 2 (Apr. 1928): 116.

127. It is possible that Westover boasted a vineyard as early as 1712 or as late as 1726. Returned from England and now living comfortably in Virginia, Byrd noted to Charles Boyle, the fourth Earl of Orrery, "Like one of the patriarchs, I have my flocks and my herds, my bondmen, and bond-women…we sit securely under our vines, and our fig-trees without any danger to our property." Byrd also noted that a neighbor, Colonel Henry Armistead, and his son had attempted to grow vines in their lowland property. Martin, *Pleasure Gardens,* 71; William Byrd to Peter Colinson, July 18, 1736, "Letters of the Byrd Family (Continued)," *Virginia Magazine of History and Biography 36,* No. 4 (Oct. 1928): 353–354.

128. Between 1731 and 1743 Catesby published his *Natural History of Carolina, Florida and the Bahama Islands,* the first published account of the flora and fauna of North America. It included 220 plates of birds, reptiles and amphibians, fish, insects, and mammals. See Tinling, *Correspondence,* 518.

129. Byrd also paid frequent visits to Sir William Berkeley's Green Spring gardens following Berkeley's death. *The History of the Dividing Line* mixes geographical surveys with Byrd's views of the American frontier, relations between the boundary commissioners, and his own remarkable impressions of the area he surveyed. Martin, *Pleasure Gardens,* 7; Hatch, *Fruits and Fruit Trees of Monticello,* 142; Maud Carter Clement, *The History of Pittsylvania County, Virginia* (Baltimore, Md.: Genealogical Publishing, 1999), 35; As one commentator noted, "From the outset, Byrd's writing embellishes this geographical line with a profusion of human plots that effectively eclipse the survey's nominal purpose." Douglas Anderson, "Plotting William Byrd," *William and Mary Quarterly,* 3rd Series, Vol. 56, No. 4 (Oct. 1999): 701–722.

130. Byrd also recounted that he encountered black grapes that were sweet but small, and concluded that such wild grapes were small because of the energy required by the wild vine in climbing the trees. Letter to Mr. Collenson, July 18, 1736, reprinted in "Letters of the Byrd Family (Continued)," 353–354; William Byrd, "History of the Dividing Line," October 12, 1728, in *The Prose Works of William Byrd of Westover: Narratives of a Colonial Virginia,* ed. Louis B. Wright (Cambridge, Mass.: Belknap Press, of Harvard University Press, 1966), 244; "because the Strength of the Vine spends itself in the Wood; tho' without Question a proper Culture would make the same Grapes both larger and Sweeter." William Byrd, *The Writings of "Colonel William Byrd, of Westover in Virginia, esqr.,"* ed. John Spencer Bassett (New York: Doubleday, Page & Co, 1901), 12 (hereafter cited as Byrd, *Colonel William Byrd*); Martin, *Pleasure Gardens,* 71.

131. Byrd's 1737 Swiss settlement scheme followed a June 1735 plan in which he successfully petitioned

the Virginia legislature to give him 100,000 acres located near the confluence of the Dan and Irvine Rivers in what is today southern Pittsylvania County. William Byrd to Sir Hans Sloan, May 31, 1737, Sloan MS 4055, f. 112 (British Museum), reprinted in Ayers, "Fruit Culture," 69 n. 87; Byrd, *Colonel William Byrd*, 208. As he wrote to a Swiss friend in July 1736, "If I should fail in my Intention, of planting a Swiss Colony, in this delightful part of the World (which are the People of the Earth I wou'd choose to have) I must then Seat my land with Scots-Irish, who crowd from Pennsylvania in such numbers, that there is no Room for them. We have already a pretty many of them settled on the River." Reprinted in "Letters of the Byrd Family (Continued)," 353.

132. Letter to Mark Catesby, reprinted in Byrd, *Colonel William Byrd*, ix–xix; Charles E. Kemper, "The Early Westward Movement of Virginia, 1722–1734, As Shown by the Proceedings of the Colonial Council (Continued)," *Virginia Magazine of History and Biography 13*, No. 3 (Jan. 1906): 281–297, 232 n.; http://www.victorianvilla.com/sims-mitchell/local/clement/mc/abb/03.htm; Byrd, *Natural History of Virginia*. A copy can be found in the John Carter Brown Library, Providence, R.I. This book is extremely scarce and was not retranslated into English until 1940 (Beatty, William Byrd's Natural History). See William J. Hinke and Charles E. Kemper, "Moravian Diaries of Travels through Virginia (Continued)," *Virginia Magazine of History and Biography 11*, No. 4 (Apr. 1904): 370–393; Conway Zirkle, "John Clayton and Our Colonial Botany," *Virginia Magazine of History and Biography 67*, No. 3 (July 1959): 284–294.

133. Byrd's impression of Scotsman and Irishman must not have been high, as he noted, "They swarm like the Goths and Vandals of old & will over-spread our Continent Soon." Letter to Mr. Collenson, July 18, 1736, reprinted in "Letters of the Byrd Family (Continued)," 353–354. Byrd was forced to petition the assembly for 12-month settlement extensions in 1737, 1738, and 1739. Clement, *History of Pittsylvania*, 35.

134. William Hunter, *The Virginia Almanack for the Year of our Lord God 1753* (Williamsburg, Va.: Printed and sold by William Hunter, [1752], 1753).

135. "The Will of Charles Carter of Cleve," *Virginia Magazine of History and Biography 31*, No. 1 (Jan. 1923): 39–40; Barbara Burlison Mooney, *Prodigy Houses of Virginia: Architecture and the Native Elite* (Charlottesville: University of Virginia Press, 2008), 138–140; Robert A. Lancaster, *Historic Virginia Homes and Churches* (Philadelphia, Pa.: J. B. Lippincott, 1915), 346–347; Thomas Allen Glenn, *Some Colonial Mansions and Those Who Lived in Them: With Genealogies of the Various Families Mentioned* (Philadelphia, Pa.: Henry T. Coates, 1900), 250; Helen Bryan, *Martha Washington: First Lady of Liberty* (New York: John Wiley and Sons, 2002), 82.

136. His education in Britain also led him toward the growing of smaller Old World grains that required different horticultural and processing techniques based on European methods—something he believed would set him apart and enhance his prestige. Such methods included plowing, manuring, crop rotation, and advocacy of better tools. Rhys Isaac, *Landon Carter's Uneasy Kingdom: Revolution and Rebellion on a Virginia Plantation* (Oxford, Eng.: Oxford University Press, 2004), 85–103; Lorena S. Walsh, *Motives of Honor, Pleasure, and Profit: Plantation Management in the Colonial Chesapeake, 1607–1763* (Chapel Hill: University of North Carolina Press, 2010), 526–527.

137. Robert Carter had attempted to diversify his operations, including raising walnuts, making cider, distilling spirits, and making wine. As one historian notes, "Most of these schemes were labor-intensive, hopelessly unprofitable, and…climatically impossible ventures that only an extremely wealthy man like Carter had the resources to pursue." Walsh, *Motives of Honor*, 535; "Will of Charles Carter," 44; Charles Carter to [Peter Wyche], n.d., received in England by Wyche, May 6, 1761, *Guard Book*, Vol. 6, No. 47 (American Correspondence of the Royal Society of Arts, originals at Special Collections & Rare Books, University of Missouri Libraries), 1–2 (hereafter cited as American Correspondence of the Royal Society of Arts, reprinted in Robert Leroy Hilldrup, "A Campaign to Promote the Prosperity of Colonial Virginia," *Virginia Magazine of History and Biography 67*, No. 4 (Oct. 1959): 415).

138. Hilldrup, "Campaign to Promote," 415.

139. Ibid., 422–423.

140. Formerly shared by the Virginia Company, Sir William Berkeley, and William Byrd II. Hilldrup, "Campaign to Promote," 410–428; Hening, *The Statutes at Large*, 7:288–290; Walsh, *Motives of Hon-*

*or*, 535–536.

141. The Premium Society is today known as the Royal Society for the Encouragement of Arts, Manufacturers and Commerce. The Premium Society consisted of some 200 influential persons, each of whom subscribed to "promote the Grandeur and Welfare of England." See "Williamsburg—The Old Colonial Capital," *William and Mary College Quarterly Historical Magazine*, 1st Series, Vol. 16, No. 1 (July 1907): 23. Historian Edward Ayers has noted that the correspondence between the Virginians and the Premium Society commenced in April 1760, when Philip Ludwell wrote to the society requesting assistance in obtaining foreign grape slips. Ludwell's letter was accompanied by one issued by Governor Francis Fauquier, who outlined the 1759 Act and suggested that Charles Carter be appointed as the primary contact between Virginians and the Society. See Ayers, "Fruit Culture," 71–72; Philip Ludwell to the Royal Society of Arts, April 21, 1760, *Guard Book*, Vol. 4, Item No. 140 (American Correspondence of the Royal Society of Arts); Francis Fauquier to Peter Wyche, April 22, 1760, *Guard Book*, Vol. 4, Item No. 141 (American Correspondence of the Royal Society of Arts); Hilldrup, "Campaign to Promote," 411; the famous Mutiny on the Bounty happened when Captain William Bligh tried for the first time to ship breadfruit from the East to the West Indies, to win a "premium" offered by RSA. Charles Dick, who established a gunnery at Fredericksburg with other Fredericksburg patriotic elites in 1775, attempted to claim a prize from the Premium Society in 1762 for allegedly shipping pearl ash from Virginia to London between 1757 and 1761. In his justification to the Society, Dick expressed his skepticism on the prospects of Virginia wine, but stated that profitable vineyards could thrive along the mountainous and limestone soil areas of the colony. See Charles Dick to [The Society], Fredericksburg, Virginia, June 22, 1762, *Guard Book*, Vol. 7, No. 15 (American Correspondence of the Royal Society of Arts), discussed in Hilldrup, "Campaign to Promote," 426–427; Richard Amrhine, "Venerable Dick House Long a City Landmark," *The Fredericksburg Free Lance–Star*, May 29, 2009.

142. Hening, *The Statutes at Large*, 7:566.

143. Any deficits in subscriptions would be supplied by the government and any surplus funds from subscriptions were to be awarded for the manufacturing of silk and other "articles as should appear to the committee most advantageous to the colony." A list of subscribed "gentlemen" who pledged their support to the cause included several wealthy Virginia planters, including acting-governor Francis Fauquier, Thomas Nelson, Richard Henry Lee, Charles Carter, George Washington, Edmund Pendleton, Richard Bland, and John Blair. See Hening, *The Statutes at Large*, 7:563–570.

144. After learning of the establishment of a similar committee in Virginia, the Premium Society expressed an eagerness to exchange ideas and information concerning ways to promote Virginia's economy; despite being a tobacco producer himself, Carter maintained that oversupply of the golden leaf would ultimately prove ruinous to Virginia and suggested tobacco to be a "poysonous" and "narcotick" plant that farmers should "lay…aside, to preserve their Healths & save their Money." Hilldrup, "Campaign to Promote," 412–413, 415, 421.

145. Peter Wyche to Charles Carter, May 30, 1761, *Guard Book*, Vol. 7, No. 49 (American Correspondence of the Royal Society of Arts), pp. 3–4; Hilldrup, "Campaign to Promote," 422.

146. Hill suggested Virginia growers process her "bruised" grapes over the course of a week in deep vaults in the ground "where the air would be cooled and kept temperate." "The Late Mr. A. Hill's Directions for Cultivating Vines in America," *Annual Register, or a View of the History, Politics, and Literature for the Year 1759*, 6th ed. (London: Printed for J. Dodsley, in Pall-Mall, 1777), 382–383.

147. Hilldrup, "Campaign to Promote," 416; "Grape Culture in America," *Journal of the Society of Arts 13* (June 6, 1865): 499; McGrew, "Untold Episodes," 83. Wyche also suggested that Virginia's inferior native grapes might be useful in producing native brandy, thereby keeping more money in the colony. In August 1763, Wyche wrote that Virginians should attempt the grafting of grapes, peaches, and wild olives to improve fruit quality. For grapes, Wyche borrowed suggestions from the Roman agricultural writer Lucius Junius Moderatus Columella, and suggested repeatedly grafting tissue from the vine on the same vine from which it was taken over a period of three years. He also advised Virginians to clear lees (residual deposits of yeast in wine vats) either by pouring brandy into the wine, by cooling wine in cellars, or by introducing wood shavings and sawdust into wine casks (a

French method). Historian Robert Leroy Hilldrup noted that, like so many of their contemporaries, neither Carter nor Wyche appreciated the impact of the various North American parasites that destroyed European grape vines. "Had [Wyche] proposed cross-grafting of the grape vines of Europe on American stocks, which were resistant to indigenous root parasites," Hilldrup wrote, "a wine industry might have been started in colonial Virginia." See Hilldrup, "Campaign to Promote," 421, 423; Extract of Peter Wyche's letter to Charles Carter, August 1763, *Papers of the Carter and Wellford family of Sabine Hall*, 1650 (1736–1874), 1936, University of Virginia Library, Charlottesville (hereafter cited as Sabine Hall Papers).

148. Derek Hudson and Kenneth W. Lockhurst. *Royal Society of Arts*, 1754–1954 (London, Eng.: John Murray, 1954), 154; Robert Dossie, *Memoirs of Agriculture* (London, Eng.: J. Nourse, 1768), 1:241–242. Envy by these other committee members was apparently so heated that Carter noted to his brother Landon Carter, "They did not take any notice of the Honour done them by the society and all my endeavors were little regarded." Charles Carter Sr., of Cleve to Landon Carter, Cleve, June 3, 1762, Sabine Hall Papers, reprinted in Hilldrup, "Campaign to Promote," 423.

149. Hilldrup, "Campaign to Promote," 427–428.

150. Historian Edward Ayers has speculated that Carter may have used the certified document to claim the £500 premium. Attestation signed by Francis Fauquier and others, dated July 5, 1763, and August 6, 1763, *Guard Book*, Vol. 9, Item No. 28 (American Correspondence of the Royal Society of Arts); Ayers, "Fruit Culture," 75.

151. This document has not survived. *Virginia Magazine of History and Biography 31*, No. 1 (Jan. 1923): 64; Lancaster, *Historic Virginia Homes*, 347; Hilldrup, "Campaign to Promote," 412; Walsh, *Motives of Honor*, 526, 536.

152. Sabine Hall is situated on a ridge overlooking the Rappahannock River. The name is from Horace's villa outside Rome, Sabine Farm, where Horace pursued a life of reflection and contemplation. Martin, *Pleasure Gardens*, 114; William M. S. Rasmussen, "Sabine Hall, A Classical Villa in Virginia," *Journal of the Society of Architectural Historians 39*, No. 4 (Dec. 1980): 286–296; Walsh, *Motives of Honor*, 527–528.

153. Like Byrd before him, Landon Carter was a prolific writer and perhaps the most-published Virginian of his generation. He authored four major political pamphlets (Letter from a Gentleman in Virginia to the Merchants of Great Britain Trading to that Colony (1754), A Letter to a Gentleman in London, from Virginia (1759), A Letter to the Right Reverend Father in God, the Lord B——p of L——n (1760), and The Rector Detected, Being a Just Defense of the twopenny Act, Against the Artful Misrepresentations of the Reverend John Camm (1764), nearly fifty newspaper essays in the *Virginia Gazette* and the *Maryland Gazette*, and a revealing personal diary; Gallay, *Voices of the Old South*, 152; Martin, *Pleasure Gardens*, 114; Hatch, *Fruits and Fruit Trees of Monticello*, 142.

154. Carter's first attempt was apparently so foul-tasting such that he boiled it and added sugar to make it palatable. Virginia planter and statesman Thomas Nelson wrote to Carter in May 1763, noting both his enthusiasm for Landon Carter's viticultural endeavor and his misguided belief that winemaking was not difficult. See Thomas Nelson to Landon Carter, May 26, 1763, Correspondence, Carter Family Papers, 1659–1797, University of Virginia Library Microfilm Project, Charlottesville; Ayers, "Fruit Culture," 76; Walker Elliott Rowe, *A History of Virginia Wines: From Grapes to Glass* (Charleston, S.C.: The History Press, 2009), 50; Jack P. Greene, ed., *The Diary of Colonel Landon Carter of Sabine Hall, 1752–1778* (Charlottesville: Published for the Virginia Historical Society by the University Press of Virginia, 1965), 1:276, 312.

155. *The Diary of Colonel Landon Carter of Sabine Hall* (Oct. 4, 1777), 2:1134–1135

156. Hatch, *Fruits and Fruit Trees of Monticello*, 142.

157. *Journal of the House of Burgesses, 1770–1772*, pp. 17, 19.

158. Estave was to answer to the trustees, which had the power, in their sole discretion, to fire him. See Hening, *The Statutes at Large*, 7:364–366; "Williamsburg—The Old Colonial Capital," *William and Mary Quarterly*, 1st Series, Vol. 16, No. 1 (July 1907): 31–32; J. A. Osborne, *Williamsburg in Colonial Times* (Richmond, Va.: Dietz Press, 1935), 103–104. The committee included Speaker of the House of Burgesses Severn Eyre, future Declaration of Independence signer Thomas Nelson, future

first president of the Continental Congress Peyton Randolph, future United States Supreme Court justice John Blair, Jr., and William and Mary law professor and future signer of the Declaration of Independence George Wythe. Hening, *The Statutes at Large*, 8:364–366.

159. The trustees purchased land a little more than one mile east of Williamsburg along what is now Penniman Road near its intersection with Queens Creek Road. A marker was placed at the site in 1927 commemorating its establishment and reads, "Here was an experimental farm for the culture of grapes established by the Virginia government in 1769. On this tract stood a hospital of the French-American army, 1781." See Historic Marker W-46 "Vineyard Tract"; Osborne, *Williamsburg*, 103; Hening, *The Statutes at Large*, 8:364–366.

160. Unsurprisingly, Estave sought more money and additional apprentices from the trustees. The General Assembly, still confident in the venture, granted him an additional £42 and 15 shillings as compensation for his work to date, as well as an annual payment of £50 for two years, a one-year loan of £50, and money to purchase a new slave. Pinney, *History of Wine*, 72; *Journal of the House of Burgesses, 1770–1772* (Mar. 13, 23, and 26, 1772), 240, 265, 272; H. R. McIlwaine, *Legislative Journals of the Council of Colonial Virginia* (Richmond, Va.: The Colonial Press, Everett Waddey Co., 1918) (Mar. 25, 1772), 1461.

161. This allegedly followed one in which the girl was caught sexually molesting Estave's three-year-old daughter (according to Estave). Dunmore himself had recently fled to a British warship in the York River to avoid rising civil unrest. See Pinney, *History of Wine*, 71; *Virginia Gazette* (Purdie and Dixon) (Quomony) June 20, 1771 (Cuffy) Oct. 22, 1772 (Jack) Nov. 18, 1773 (Saundy) Mar. 23 1776. The account is based on a newspaper notice that Estave published in order to justify what some of his white neighbors had called his "cruel and inhuman treatment" of the enslaved teenager (*Virginia Gazette* [Pinkney], July 20, 1775). See Woody Holton, "'Rebel against Rebel': Enslaved Virginians and the Coming of the American Revolution," *Virginia Magazine of History and Biography 105*, No. 2 (Spring 1997): 181–182.

162. Hatch, *Fruits and Fruit Trees of Monticello*, 142; James Parker to Charles Steuart, Aug. 5, 1770, Charles Steuart Papers 5040, fol. 103, National Library of Scotland, Edinburgh; *Virginia Gazette* (Purdie and Dixon), Mar. 18, 1773.

163. *Virginia Gazette* (Purdie and Dixon), Mar. 18, 1773. As wine historian Thomas Pinney noted, Estave's 1773 letter may not have been the recommendation to use native grapes for American wine, "but it is perhaps the first made by a man who had direct experience of growing both native and European vines experimentally." Pinney, *History of Wine*, 72.

164. *Virginia Gazette* (Purdie and Dixon), May 12, 1774, p. 4, c. 2. The account of fellow viticulturalist Philip Mazzei demonstrates that the frost hit Albemarle, too: "On the night of May 4, 1774, a frost, caused by a northwest wind, ruined the corn and the wheat just above the ground, froze the small oak and other young trees, and caused all other trees to shed their leaves, which did not bud again until the following year. It was horrible to see the woods entirely stripped of leaves in summer, as if it had been midwinter. The bunches of grapes were already quite large, but they froze with the new crop. The old part of the vine, from which the branches had sprung, suffered too. But the vines put out new shoots, which produced about half the amount of grapes of the preceding years, and ripened at the usual season in the woods and gardens." Howard R. Marraro, trans., *Memoirs of the Life and Peregrinations of the Florentine Philip Mazzei, 1730–1816* (New York: Columbia University Press, 1942), 207 (hereafter cited as Marraro, *Mazzei Memoirs*). The severe frost was also noted by George Washington in his diary entry for May 4, 1774. See *The Papers of George Washington Digital Edition*, ed. Theodore J. Crackel (Charlottesville: University of Virginia Press, Rotunda, 2008) (diary entry, May 4, 1774).

165. *Virginia Gazette* (Dixon and Hunter), June 24, 1775, p. 3; Gallus Thomann, *Liquor Laws of the United States: Their Spirit and Effect* (New York: The United States Brewers' Association, 1898), 69.

166. U. P. Hedrick wrote in *The Grapes of New York* that "Estave succeeded in making the wine but it was poor stuff and he had difficulty in getting the authorities to turn over the property which was to be his reward. This was finally done by an act of the Assembly." Given the General Assembly's disbursement of the property, this claim cannot be supported. The property later served as the site

of a Revolutionary War hospital and was given to the College of William and Mary in 1784. The college disposed of it five years later. Today, all that remains of the history of the property is a state highway marker that was placed at the site in 1927 commemorating its establishment. See Hedrick, *Grapes of New York*, 8; Hening, *The Statutes at Large*, 10:239; *Journal of the House of Delegates of the Commonwealth of Virginia, One Thousand Seven Hundred and Seventy-Seven* (Richmond: Printed by Thomas White, Opposite the Bell Tavern, 1827), June 11, 1777, p. 72; *Virginia Gazette* (Purdie), Feb. 28, 1777; "Williamsburg—The Old Colonial Capital," *William and Mary Quarterly*, 1st Series, Vol. 16, No. 1 (July 1907): 31–32; "Papers Relating to the College," *William and Mary Quarterly*, 1st Series, Vol. 16, No. 3 (July 1907): 163; Osborne, *Williamsburg in Colonial Times*, 103–104; Historic Marker W-46 "Vineyard Tract."

167. Estave apparently interacted with General Thomas McCall, who recalled that Estave had emphatically advised McCall to grow native and not European varieties. Thomann, Liquor Laws, 69; Letter of Thomas McCall, *American Farmer*, Feb. 11, 1825, p. 369; McGrew, "Untold Episodes," 85, 102.

168. Bolling was referred to as "Jr." or identified as "of Chellowe, Buckingham county," by his contemporaries to distinguish him from his older cousin Robert Bolling of Blandford, Petersburg, Dinwiddie County.

169. Bolling's readings included European agricultural volumes covering Italian and French viticultural pursuits. Observers noted that he was "the most accomplished litterateur of colonial Virginia." See J. A. Leo Lemay, *Robert Bolling Woos Anne Miller: Love and Courtship in Colonial Virginia, 1760* (Charlottesville: University Press of Virginia, 1990), 25; Lemay, "Robert Bolling and the Bailment of Colonel Chiswell," *Early American Literature 6*, No. 2 (Fall 1971): 103; Ayers, "Fruit Culture," 80; Joseph M. Flora, Amber Vogel, and Bryan Giemza, eds. *Southern Writers: A New Biographical Dictionary* (Baton Rouge: Louisiana State University Press, 2006), 33.

170. Bolling even named a son after the heathen god of wine, Lenæus. See Wyndham Robertson, *Pocahontas, Alias Matoaka, and Her Descendants Through Her Marriage at Jamestown, Virginia, in April, 1614, with John Rolfe, Gentleman* (Richmond, Va.: J. W. Randolph and English, 1887), 61–62; Ayers, "Fruit Culture," 80; *Virginia Gazette* (Purdie and Dixon), Feb. 25, 1773, p. 1.

171. Chellow is interchangeably written as "Chellowe" and "Cello" in various accounts. Pinney, *History of Wine*, 73; *American Farmer*, Feb. 20, 1829, p. 387; Robert Bolling, "A Sketch of Vine Culture for Pennsylvania, Maryland, Virginia and the Carolinas" (N.p.: N.p., [1773–1774]), 36, in Pinney, *History of Wine*, 73–76; McGrew, "Untold Episodes," 84. While U. P. Hedrick credited Bolling as being the first American writer on grapes, Bolling's work was preceded by Edward Antill's "essay of the cultivation of the vine, and the making and preserving of wine, suited to the different climates of North America," *Transactions of the American Philosophical Society 1* (1789): 183 (see Pinney, *History of Wine*, 463 n. 36). The sole copy of the document was apparently "leased" to the publisher of the *American Farmer* periodical in 1829 before being saved from destruction at a Worcester, Massachusetts, paper mill in 1860. A complete copy is at the Huntington Library, portions were copied and are available at the National Agricultural Library. See Robert Bolling, *A Memoir of a Portion of the Bolling Family in England and Virginia* (Richmond, Va.: W. H. Wade, 1868), 42–44; *Historical Magazine and Notes and Queries Concerning the Antiquities, History and Biography of America 4* (1860): 280. First quotation in Pinney, *History of Wine*, 73; Hedrick, *Grapes of New York*, 15; Richard P. Vine, *Commercial Winemaking: Processing and Controls* (Westport, Conn.: AVI Publishing, 1981), 13; Ayers, "Fruit Culture," 86.

172. Bolling's work, like that of Antill, was reportedly meant for publication before Bolling's untimely death "in the hope of…infusing into the minds of his countrymen a desire to engage in the healthy, agreeable and lucrative employment of vine planting."; Pinney, *History of Wine*, 91; *American Farmer*, Feb. 20, 1829 at http://books.google.com/books?id=lIREKu_iM70C&pg=PA387

173. Historian Thomas Pinney notes that Bolling's work also advocated a pruning system—later known as the "Umbrella Kniffin" pruning system—which would become an industry standard. Pinney, *History of Wine*, 75. U. P. Hedrick gave credit to Bolling for the first work, but it was produced between May 1774 and July 1775, and Bolling's work includes quotations from Antill's work. *Bulletin*, Pennsylvania. Dept. of Agriculture, Issue 217 (1912), 13; McGrew, "Untold Episodes," 84; *American Farmer*,

Feb. 20, 1829.

174. To realize his goals, Bolling sought to stir his fellow citizens to advocate for legislation that would support additional grape-growing experiments elsewhere in Virginia. *Virginia Gazette* (Purdie and Dixon), Feb. 25, 1773, p. 1.

175. Arguing for the similarities in the "air" of Tuscany and Virginia, Bolling was particularly supportive of vignerons who could grow Italian grapes. *Virginia Gazette* (Purdie and Dixon), Feb. 25, 1773, p. 1.

176. Estave threatened to consult one Colonel Baker of Smithfield who had apparently grown native and foreign vines in his garden, all of which appeared to have succeeded equally well until the time of ripening. "Then he found that the foreign Grapes were constantly spoiled by Accidents which I have already enumerated," wrote Estave, "while the Natives sustained no Injury, because probably their Skins are of a Nature capable of resisting the Insects, and the Rains; and because, too, they do not ripen until two Months after the foreign Grapes, at a Season more favourable to the Fermentation of Wine." *Virginia Gazette* (Purdie and Dixon), Mar. 18, 1773, p. 2.

177. In publishing details of the statute, the *Virginia Gazette* noted that Bolling had "engaged an [unnamed] Foreigner, thoroughly acquainted with the Business, in all its Branches, to instruct him therein." McIlwaine, *Legislative Journals* (March 11–12, 1773), 3:1482–1483; *Virginia Gazette* (Purdie and Dixon), Mar. 11, 1773, p. 2; *Virginia Gazette* (Purdie and Dixon), July 29, 1773.

178. While withholding judgment of Bolling's own calls for foreign vine experiments, he nevertheless "doubt[ed] exceedingly their success." *Virginia Gazette* (Purdie and Dixon), Sept. 2, 1773.

179. McGrew, "Untold Episodes," 84.

180. In 1774, Chellow boasted several vineyards, and at least two were one acre in size. Ayers, "Fruit Culture," 87. Peter Hatch has written that "Virginia does have about the same latitude of southern France and northern Italy, but the climatic disparity is extreme in terms of rainfall, humidity, and temperature variations." *Virginia Gazette* (Dixon and Hunter), Sept. 9, 1775; Hatch, *Fruits and Fruit Trees of Monticello*, 143.

181. Letter of Lenæus Bolling, *American Farmer*, Feb. 20. 1829, p. 387; *VWGJ* 1, No. 1 (Spring 1974): 41; Ayers, "Fruit Culture," 87.

182. Fletcher, *History of Fruit Growing*, 11; Lemay, *Robert Bolling Woos Anne Miller*; Robertson, *Pocahontas, 61–62*; Letter of Lenæus Bolling, *American Farmer*, Feb. 20, 1829, p. 387; Pinney, *History of Wine*, 77.

183. Much of what is known of Mazzei is gleaned from his personal memoirs, which—though taking some enthusiastic liberties—Mazzei wrote at the age of 80. His memoirs and other writings about him capture both his life story in Virginia and abroad, as well as those of other personalities with whom he came into contact, including Thomas Jefferson. E. C. Branchi, "Memoirs of the Life and Voyages of Doctor Philip Mazzei," *William and Mary Quarterly*, 2nd Series, Vol. 9, No. 3 (July 1929): 162 n. 1; Review by Stringfellow Barr, "Philip Mazzei, Friend of Jefferson: His Life and Letters by Richard Cecil Garlick, Jr." *Virginia Magazine of History and Biography 42*, No. 1 (Jan. 1934): 94–95.

184. Felicia W. Rogan, "The Marvelous Mr. Mazzei," *Shenandoah/Virginia Town & Country* (July–August 1982): 54–56; Albemarle County (Va.) Judgment, Giovanni Antonio Giannini (John Antonio Gianinna) vs. Thomas Jefferson, 1798 Aug., Local Government Records Collection, Albemarle County Court Records, The Library of Virginia, Richmond; H. Christopher Martin, "Jefferson's Italian Vigneron: Philip Mazzei, Revolutionary Patriot," in *Jefferson and Wine: Model of Moderation*, ed. R. Treville Lawrence III (The Plains, Va.: Vinifera Wine Growers Association, 1976), 18; James M. Gabler, *Passions: The Wines and Travels of Thomas Jefferson* (Baltimore, Md.: Bacchus Press, 1995), 4; Barr, "Philip Mazzei," 14–22, 26; Branchi, "Life and Voyages," 162 n. 1; Pinney, *History of Wine*, 77.

185. Margherita Marchione, trans. and ed., Philip Mazzei: Jefferson's "Zealous Whig" (New York: American Institute of Italian Studies, 1975); Martin, "Jefferson's Italian Vigneron," 18–20, 284. To assist in the endeavor, Mazzei proposed the retention of some 50 farmers skilled in wine-making and silk-making for a term of four years. Pinney, *History of Wine*, 78; Barr, "Philip Mazzei," 27–29.

186. Martin, "Jefferson's Italian Vigneron," 20. A note of the arrival was carried in the *Virginia Gazette*, reading, "The Triumph Frigate, Rogers, from Leghorn, are arrived in James river; in the latter, we hear, many gentlemen came passengers, in order to fettle and cultivate [vines] in this colony." See

Gabler, *Passions*, 3; Jefferson to Albert Galatin, Jan. 25, 1793, Library of Congress, Manuscript Collections, Thomas Jefferson Papers, Reel 49, reprinted in Edwin Morris Betts, ed., *Thomas Jefferson's Garden Book* (Charlottesville: Thomas Jefferson Memorial Foundation, 1999), 64; *Virginia Gazette* (Rind), Dec. 2, 1773; Barr, "Philip Mazzei," 32–39.

187. Rogan, "Marvelous Mr. Mazzei," 54–56; Branchi, "Life and Voyages," 163; Marraro, *Mazzei Memoirs*, 191.
188. Pinney, *History of Wine*, 79.
189. Rogan, "Marvelous Mr. Mazzei," 54–56; Jefferson to John Dortie, Oct. 1, 1811 [Betts, Garden Book, 348]; Hatch, *Fruits and Fruit Trees of Monticello*, 133; Martin, "Jefferson's Italian Vigneron," 28.
190. Marraro, *Mazzei Memoirs*, 192–193; Rogan, "Marvelous Mr. Mazzei," 54–56.
191. Martin, "Jefferson's Italian Vigneron," 21; Hatch, *Fruits and Fruit Trees of Monticello*, 133; Barr, "Philip Mazzei," 41–42.
192. Philip Mazzei, *Researches on the United States*, trans. and ed. Constance D. Sherman (Charlottesville: University Press of Virginia, 1976), 245; Frances MacLean, "Through the Grapevine of History," *Country* (Feb. 1982): 4;  Spending much of his life in Tuscany, Mazzei was well-versed in winemaking; he had visited Burgundy and observed vinification, he had learned from his grandfather never to drink Tuscan wines that were less than one year old, and he was a frequent buyer of the beverage. Gabler, *Passions*, 5; Jefferson to Albert Galatin, Jan. 25, 1793, Library of Congress, in Betts, *Jefferson's Garden Book*, 64; Marraro, *Mazzei Memoirs*, 206; S. Eugene Scalia, trans., *Philip Mazzei: My Life and Wanderings*, Ed. Margherita Marchione (New York: American Institute of Italian Studies, 1980), 204. Peter Hatch has attributed this description as a "typical hyperbolic rendering of the prolific, variable, and confusing native grape flora." Hatch, *Fruits and Fruit Trees of Monticello*, 133.
193. Pinney, *History of Wine*, 79; Marraro, *Mazzei Memoirs*, 207.
194. Historian Thomas Pinney notes that such a description of vinifera vines fruiting is quite rare in the eighteenth century. Pinney, *History of Wine*, 79–80; Mazzei, *Researches*, 243–44; Hatch, *Fruits and Fruit Trees of Monticello*, 134; Marraro, *Mazzei Memoirs*, 207; Howard R. Marraro, "Unpublished Mazzei Letters to Jefferson," *William and Mary Quarterly*, 3rd Series, Vol. 1, No. 4 (Oct., 1944): 374.
195. Pinney, *History of Wine*, 79; Mazzei, *Researches*, 243–244; *The Triumph*, which had ferried Mazzei across the Atlantic late in 1773, brought over Italian seeds and cuttings in the summer of 1774. Gabler, *Passions*, 5; Barr, "Philip Mazzei," 43–47; *Virginia Gazette* (Purdie and Dixon), July 28, 1774.
196. Mazzei culled the six varietals from the top of a tree in very dense woods from a vine with a "enormous number of branches." Marraro, *Mazzei Memoirs*, 206; Pinney, *History of Wine*, 79–80; Hatch, *Fruits and Fruit Trees of Monticello*, 134; *Virginia Gazette* (Purdie and Dixon), July 28, 1774; Mazzei, *Researches*, 243–245; Hatch, *Fruits and Fruit Trees of Monticello*, 134; Marraro, *Mazzei Memoirs*, 206; Gabler, *Passions*, 5.
197. Filippo Mazzei, *Philip Mazzei, Virginia's Agent in Europe: The Story of His Mission as related in His Own Dispatches and Other Documents*, ed. Howard Rosario Marraro (New York: New York Public Library, 1935), 72.
198. Rogan, "Marvelous Mr. Mazzei," 54–56; Marraro, *Mazzei Memoirs*, 203. Marchione, *Philip Mazzei: Jefferson's "Zealous Whig,"* 18; Scalia, Philip Mazzei, 207–209. Notably, Jefferson presented Mazzei with one of the five copies he made of the Declaration of Independence. Martin, "Jefferson's Italian Vigneron," 24. The unit was formed after the closure of the Port of Boston in 1774, though never tested in battle. See William E. White, "The Independent Companies of Virginia, 1774–1775," *Virginia Magazine of History and Biography* 86, No. 2 (Apr. 1978): 149–162; Branchi, "Life and Voyages," 166–167; Martin, "Jefferson's Italian Vigneron," 24.
199. Rogan, "Marvelous Mr. Mazzei," 54–56; Jefferson to Albert Galatin. Jan. 25, 1793, Library of Congress, in Betts, *Jefferson's Garden Book*, 64.
200. Jefferson was prompted to write this letter to New York Senator Albert Galatin at the urging of Peter Legaux, a Pennsylvania viticulturalist, Jan. 25, 1793, Library of Congress, in Betts, *Jefferson's Garden Book*, 64. Michael Kranish, *Flight from Monticello: Thomas Jefferson at War* (Oxford, Eng.: Oxford University Press, 2010), 110; Merrill D. Peterson, *Thomas Jefferson and the New Nation: A Biography*

(New York: Oxford University Press, 1970), 163–164.

201. Howard R. Marraro, "The Settlement of Philip Mazzei's Virginia Estate: Unpublished Correspondence and Other Documents," *Virginia Magazine of History and Biography 63*, No. 3 (July 1955): 306, 307; American Philatelist 109, Issues 1–6 (Feb. 1995): 117; Lecture by Sister Margherita Marchione, Conference on Philip Mazzei at the Embassy of Italy, Oct. 6, 2011, available at http://www.youtube.com/watch?v=Cj7Z21WqC1E (accessed Apr. 4, 2014).

202. Stefania Buccini, *The Americas in Italian Literature and Culture, 1700–1825* (University Park: Pennsylvania State University Press, 1997), 144; Mazzei, *Recherches historiques et politiques, sur les États-Unis de l'Amérique septentrionale....* (Colle and Paris: Froullé, 1788). The book has been recognized by several historians as one of the best works on the history of Colonial America and served as one of the sources for the Italian Historian Carlo Botta's History of the War of Independence of the United States of America. Mazzei's work was roundly condemned by James Madison for what Madison felt was Mazzei's misunderstanding of the American democratic system: "I did not approve the tendency of it.... If your plan of a single Legislature, etc. as in [Pennsylvania] were adopted, I sincerly [sic] believe that it would prove the most deadly blow ever given to republicanism." Madison to Jefferson, Dec.r 10, 1788, in William T. Hutchinson et al., *The Papers of James Madison* (Chicago: University of Chicago Press, 1962), 11:388–389; Rogan, "Marvelous Mr. Mazzei," 54–56; Branchi, "Life and Voyages," 162 n. 1.

203. Marraro, "Unpublished Jefferson Letter," 84; Branchi, "Life and Voyages," 162 n. 1.

204. Today, only a Virginia historical highway marker in the vicinity of Colle remains, reading in part, "The house was built about 1770 by workmen engaged in building Monticello. Mazzei, an Italian, lived here for some years adapting grape culture to Virginia. Baron de Riedesel, captured at Saratoga in 1777, lived here with his family, 1779–1780." Marker W-201; Pinney, *History of Wine*, 81; Martin, "Jefferson's Italian Vigneron," 23.

205. In March 1805, prior to Mazzei's passing, Latrobe wrote to Mazzei thanking him perhaps prophetically, "The time is already approaching when our vines & our olives will spread your name & our gratitude over a greate portion of our country. Let us also owe to your kindness the introduction of excellence in the most fascinating branch of the Arts." Letter from Latrobe to Mazzei, Mar. 6, 1805, *Journal of Latrobe* (New York: D. Appleton and Company, 1905), 126–127; Rogan, "Marvelous Mr. Mazzei," 54–56.

206. Sandy Hook is located in Goochland County between Richmond and Charlottesville. Letter of June 3, 1785, to James Madison, in *Philip Mazzei: Selected Writings and Correspondence*, 473, quoted in Buccini, *Americas in Italian Literature*, 144.

207. Hilde Gabriel Lee and Allan E. Lee, *Virginia Wine Country III* (Keswick, Va.: Hildesigns Press, 2004), 14. As Julian P. Boyd, noted, "Among Jefferson's contemporaries in America, if not among all who preceded and followed him, only Franklin could be said to approach him in the extent and variety of his inquiry. To catalogue the areas of his explorations is to list most of the principal categories of knowledge." *The Papers of Thomas Jefferson*, Princeton, N.J., 1950, reprinted in Gabler, *Passions*, xiii.

208. Much of his farming experience was recorded in his Farm Book, which he began in 1774. Filled with technical observations and records of his multiple properties throughout the commonwealth, Jefferson viewed the work to be "the employment of our first parents in Eden, the happiest we can follow, and the most important to our country." Jefferson to Charles Willson Peale, Poplar Forest, Aug. 20, 1811, Edwin M. Betts, ed., *Thomas Jefferson's Farm Book: With Commentary and Relevant Extracts from Other Writings* (Princeton: Princeton University Press, 1953, reprint 1976, 1987, 1999), 572.

209. Except for a brief family sojourn to Tuckahoe plantation outside of Richmond between the ages of two and nine, Jefferson remained at Shadwell, which boasted enviable views of the surrounding Blue Ridge Mountains. See Lawrence, Jefferson and Wine, 220; James McGrath Morris and Persephone Weene, eds., *Thomas Jefferson's European Travel Diaries* (Ithaca, N.Y.: I. Stephanus Sons, 1987), 11 (hereafter cited as *Jefferson's Travel Diaries*); Paul Lukacs, *American Vintage: The Rise of American Wine* (Boston: Houghton Mifflin, 2000), 15.

210. Gabler, *Passions*, xiii. Peter Jefferson, Jefferson's rugged frontiersman father, lacked a formal education, and insisted that Jefferson receive a classical education. No doubt Jefferson came into contact with

Greek and Roman passages from antiquity praising wine and the cultivation of the grape. Lawrence, *Jefferson and Wine*, 2; John Hailman, *Jefferson on Wine* (Jackson: University Press of Mississippi, 2006), 28.

211. Hailman, *Jefferson on Wine* (Jackson: University Press of Mississippi, 2006), 28. Jefferson, writing to his doctor in his last decade, stated, "Wine from long habit has become an indispensable for my health." Jefferson to Dr. J. F. O. Fernandez, Dec. 16, 1815, Library of Congress, Washington, D.C.; Lawrence, *Jefferson and Wine*, 16.

212. *Jefferson's Travel Diaries*, 29.

213. Hailman, *Jefferson on Wine*, 29.

214. A wartime governor, Jefferson later transferred the capital to Richmond. Jefferson still later was forced to flee the capital, eventually to his retreat at Poplar Forest in Bedford County—a decision that would mar his gubernatorial legacy. Lawrence, *Jefferson and Wine*, 295.

215. Jefferson routinely corresponded with sophisticated wine merchants and grape growers, and enjoyed visiting wineries, vineyards, orchards, and farms. *Jefferson's Travel Diaries*, 12, 14; William Howard Adams, *The Paris Years of Thomas Jefferson*, (New Haven: Yale University Press, 1997), 190–191 (hereafter cited as *Thomas Jefferson's Paris Years*).

216. Felicia Warburg Rogan, "Thomas Jefferson's World of Wine," Speech, Mar. 27, 1987, pp. 1, 7; Gabler, *Passions*, 19, 21; Letter from Jefferson to James Monroe, June 6, 1817; William Howard Adams, ed., *The Eye of Th[omas] Jefferson* (Washington: National Gallery of Art, 1976), 119; Hailman, *Jefferson on Wine*, 73.

217. *Jefferson's Travel Diaries*, 15; Ann Mah, "Following Jefferson Through the Vineyards," *The New York Times*, June 10, 2010.

218. He believed his notes would prove useful to American farmers, or could later be incorporated into his theories or practices at Monticello. He followed the advice he would later give to others: "When you are doubting whether a thing is worth the trouble of going to see, recollect that you will never again be so near it, that you may repent the not having seen it, but can never repent having seen it." Anthony Brandt, ed., *Thomas Jefferson Travels: Selected Writings, 1784–1789* (Washington, D.C.: National Geographic Society, 2006), n.p. (see http://books.google.com/books?id=735H5RrVRbQC&pg=PT510&dq=%22When+you+are+doubting+whether+a+thing+is+worth+the+trouble+of+going+to+see,+recollect+that+you+will+never+again+be+so+near+it&hl=en&sa=X&ei=wZUcU-4unCsv20wGFuoGwBg&ved=0CC8Q6AEwAQ#v=onepage&q=%22When%20you%20are%20doubting%20whether%20a%20thing%20is%20worth%20the%20trouble%20of%20going%20to%20see%2C%20recollect%20that%20you%20will%20never%20again%20be%20so%20near%20it&f=false) (accessed Apr. 4, 2014); *Thomas Jefferson's Paris Years*, 108.

219. *Jefferson's Travel Diaries*, 25, 28; *Thomas Jefferson's Paris Years*, 190.

220. Monticello's Christa Dierksheide has observed that even if Americans did develop a taste for the drier wines, it was nearly impossible to get the correct, unadulterated wine because of the corrupt merchants. Because of this corruption, and hot travel conditions, a large amount of the wine Jefferson ordered was spoiled. Rogan, "Thomas Jefferson's World of Wine," 10; Ann Mah, "Following Jefferson Through the Vineyards," *The New York Times*, June 10, 2010; E-mail/Interview between author and Christa Dierksheide Feb. 13, 2014.

221. *Jefferson on Wine*, 232. Jefferson would later import some 550 bottles of the wine to introduce to dinner guests in America.

222. His visit is celebrated in the second-year barrel room. Jefferson's ranking occurred 68 years prior to the Bordeaux Wine Official Classification of 1855, which followed a request from French Emperor Napoleon III to develop a classification system for marketing French Bordeaux wines around the world. The 1855 ranking shared many similarities to Jefferson's 1787 ranking. *Jefferson's Travel Diaries*, 19; Gabler, *Passions*, 95.

223. Gabler, *Passions*, 73; *Jefferson's Travel Diaries*, 16. The excursion would be the first of his journeys across the European countryside; he would later tour the wine regions of Germany and Champagne in March 1788 following a diplomatic mission with John Adams in The Hague. A series of plaques documenting his 1787 visit now dot the French and Italian countryside. The mission was intended to

secure bonds to cover the United States' outstanding debt. He traveled from Paris into Belguim, and into Amsterdam, and then along the Rhine into Germany, visiting Cologne and touring the vineyards of the Moselle Valley, Johannisberg, Hocheim, and more. He toured German vineyards with his friend, Hessian officer Baron von Geismar, who later sent him cuttings of German vines, which he then attempted to cultivate at his home in Paris. He next spent four days visiting Champagne before arriving back in Paris, where he took detailed notes on how to make champagne. *Thomas Jefferson's Paris Years*, 20; Lawrence, *Jefferson and Wine*, 150–160.

224. Jefferson to William Drayton, July 30, 1787; *Jefferson's Travel Diaries*, 28.

225. Despite his aversion to an American wine industry at this point, he continued to experiment with grapes at Monticello. *Jefferson's Travel Diaries*, 28–29; Lee and Lee, *Virginia Wine Country III*, 16; Lawrence, *Jefferson and Wine*, 223.

226. Gabler, *Passions*, 165.

227. *The Autobiography of Thomas Jefferson, 1743–1790*, ed. Paul Leicester Ford (1914; reprint, Philadelphia: University of Pennsylvania Press, 2005), 157.

228. He had been elected by Congress as a special diplomat to assist with the negotiation of treaties between the United States and her allies. In Paris, Jefferson would be an eyewitness to history, including the fall of the French monarchy and the adoption of the French Declaration of Rights.

229. Gabler, *Passions*, 176.

230. Jefferson to James Monroe, Apr. 8, 1817; Gabler, *Passions*, 220; Lawrence, *Jefferson and Wine*, 175.

231. Lee and Lee, *Virginia Wine Country III*, 15; Gabler, *Passions*, 199. In 1803 Jefferson became the first president to introduce 100 bottles of Chambertin burgundy to the President's House. Patrick Phillips-Schrock, *The White House: An Illustrated Architectural History* (Jefferson, N.C.: McFarland & Company, Inc., Publishers, 2013), 33; Rogan, "Thomas Jefferson's World of Wine," 2; Gabler, *Passions*, 200; Lee and Lee, *Virginia Wine Country III*, 15; Hailman, *Jefferson on Wine*, 256.

232. Jefferson to Monsieur de Neuville, Dec. 13, 1818.

233. Gabler, *Passions*, 205; Lukacs, *American Vintage*, 15, 16; Jefferson to William H. Crawford," in *The Writings of Thomas Jefferson*, ed Paul Leicester Ford (New York: G. P. Putnam's Sons, 1899), 10.

234. Jefferson to Pierre-Samuel DuPont de Nemours, Mar. 2, 1809. In The Letters of Thomas Jefferson, 1743–1826 online (http://www.let.rug.nl/usa/presidents/thomas-jefferson/letters-of-thomas-jefferson/jefl192.php) and also at http://yourthomasjefferson.tumblr.com/post/44426565490/never-did-a-prisoner-released-from-his-chains-feel (accessed Apr. 4, 2014).

235. Such a lifestyle, of course, came at a cost. Jefferson's continual social engagements forced him, in part, to sell much of his private library to help reconstitute the Library of Congress after it was burned by the British in the War of 1812. After one extended 1824 visit by the Marquis de Lafayette, Jefferson writes an order to local merchant for emergency replenishment. Gabler, *Passions*; Lawrence, *Jefferson and Wine*, 14.

236. Renovated in 2010, the cellar looks as it did during Jefferson's retirement (1809–1826). To ensure authenticity, Monticello's archaeology and research crews scoured meticulous inventories and notes, along with correspondence, drawings, and other documents. The archaeologists also conducted a dig in the space, unearthing artifacts and other clues to the cellar's appearance two centuries ago.

237. *VWGJ* 16, No. 3 (Fall 1989): 147.

238. He planted another 60 vinifera grape vines in 1802. See Lawrence, *Jefferson and Wine*; "Jefferson's Diary of Philip Mazzei's Affairs," *The Papers of Thomas Jefferson*, 30 Nov. 1789 to 4 July 1790, ed. Charles T. Cullen et al. (Princeton: Princeton University Press, 1961), 16:308–309; Gabler, *Passions*, 34.

239. The 1807 plantings occurred just prior to the effective date of the 1807 Embargo Act, in which the United States embargoed trade between Great Britain and France during the Napoleonic Wars. Rogan, "Thomas Jefferson's World of Wine," 14; Hatch, *Fruits and Fruit Trees of Monticello*, 132. See Lee and Lee, *Virginia Wine Country III*, 14; Hatch, *Fruits and Fruit Trees of Monticello*, 135–137; Andrea Wulf, *Founding Gardeners: The Revolutionary Generation, Nature, and the Shaping of the American Nation* (New York: Alfred A. Knopf, 2011), 288 n. 186; Rogan, "Thomas Jefferson's World of Wine," 10.

240. To encourage the group to experiment with viticulture, Jefferson penned "Object for the Attention

and Enquiry of the Society," in which he singled out the grape for special attention. Hailman, *Jefferson on Wine*, 324; McGrew, "Untold Episodes," 84; American Horticultural Association, *Annual Report of the American Horticultural Association for the Year 1918* (Washington, D.C.: Government Printing Office,), 1:241–261; *Virginia Magazine of History and Biography 3* (1895): 209–210; Jefferson to John Dortic, Oct. 1, 1811 (quotation). One must posit whether the elder Jefferson's palate had devolved to judge American wine to be equal to that of France.

241. As historian Peter J. Hatch has noted, "Such an inelegant, harshly flavored, sweet wine" as scuppernong was equal to that of France. See Lee and Lee, *Virginia Wine Country III*, 16; Lukacs, *American Vintage*, 16.

242. Pinney, *History of Wine*; Jean David to Jefferson, Nov. 26, 1815; Gabler, *Passions*, 219.

243. Indeed, while his *Garden Book* included detailed plans for his garden at Monticello and meticulous notes on plantings and harvests with other commodities, much is missing in the realm of viticulture. As Peter Hatch has noted, "The continual replanting of the Monticello vineyards suggests a perennial and losing struggle with grape cultivation." Hatch, *Fruits and Fruit Trees of Monticello*, 131; *VWGJ* (Fall 1985): 148; Hatch, *Fruits and Fruit Trees of Monticello*, 135–137; Rogan, "Thomas Jefferson's World of Wine," 1, 13.

244. Pinney, *History of Wine*.

245. Lawrence, *Jefferson and Wine*, 2; Rogan, "Thomas Jefferson's World of Wine"; Hatch, *Fruits and Fruit Trees of Monticello*, 131.

246. Washington was aware of the dangers of drinking excessively and, during the American Revolution, discharged soldiers for so doing. McLeod, *Dining with the Washingtons*, 99; Hatch, *Fruits and Fruit Trees of Monticello*, 144.

247. Madeira, a fortified Portuguese port-style white wine, was widely consumed during the 1800s largely because it was capable of surviving long ocean voyages and could be stored for years without souring. Washington's first order for Madeira wine was placed in 1759, during which he ordered an estimated 126 gallons of the beverage. Bill Daley, "Founding Fathers knew they had a good thing when drinking Madeira," *Chicago Tribune*, Feb. 22, 2006; David Hancock, "Commerce and Conversation in the Eighteenth-Century Atlantic: The Invention of Madeira Wine," *Journal of Interdisciplinary History* 29, No. 2 (Autumn 1998): 197–219; GW to Philip Mazzei, July 1, 1790; McLeod, *Dining with the Washingtons*, 98; David Hancock, *Oceans of Wine: Madeira and the Emergence of American Trade and Taste* (New Haven: Yale University Press, 2009), 282, 391–392; Dennis J. Pogue, *Founding Spirits: George Washington and the Beginnings of the American Whiskey Industry* (Buena Vista, Va.: Harbour Books, 2011), 22–24.

248. He was also not the first in his family to attempt to grow wine grapes; his father-in-law, John Custis IV, evidently planted white grape seeds in 1736, but found that wine grapes "do not do well in this hot country." See George Washington to Alexander Spotswood, Feb. 13, 1788, *The Writings of Washington from the Original Manuscript Sources, 1745–1799*, ed. John C. Fitzpatrick (Washington, D.C.: U.S. Government Printing Office, 1944), 2; John Custis to Peter Collinson, [July] 1736, and Peter Colinson to John Custis, Nov. 12, 1736, and Peter Collinson to John Custis, Jan. 25, 1738/39, in *Brothers of the Spade: Correspondence of Peter Collinson of London, and of John Custis, of Williamsburg, Virginia, 1734–1746*, ed. E. G. Swem (Worcester, Mass.: The Society, 1949), 48–53 and 74–77; Ayers, "Fruit Culture," 69.

249. Martin, *Pleasure Gardens*, 135, 144. Located behind the stables on the south slope some fifty yards below the Lower Garden, this space boasted native vines and cuttings from abroad. See Mary V. Thompson, "Grapes," George Washington's Mount Vernon Digital Encyclopedia, at http://www.mountvernon.org/educational-resources/encyclopedia/grapes#note7

250. Lawrence, *Jefferson and Wine*, 19; Fitzpatrick, *Writings of Washington*, 41; Diary entry, Mar. 21, 1763, *The Papers of George Washington Digital Edition*, University of Virginia; Dorothy Twohig, ed., *The Papers of George Washington* (Charlottesville: University Press of Virginia, 1976), xx–vil; George Washington to Lafayette, Feb. 1, 1784; Pogue, *Founding Spirits*, 25; Letter to M. Marbois, July 9, 1783, *The Writings of George Washington, 1782–1785*, ed. Worthington Chauncey Ford (New York: G. P. Putnam's Sons, 1891), 10:279–281 (hereafter cited as *The Writings of George Washington, 1782–1785*

[Putnam's Sons]).

251. John C. Fitzpatrick, ed., *The Writings of George Washington from the Original Manuscript Sources, 1745–1799* (Washington, D.C.: U.S. Government Printing Office, 1944), 27:55.

252. Letter to M. Marbois, July 9, 1783, in *The Writings of George Washington, 1782–1785* (Putnam's Sons), 10:279–281. Washington selected the Winter grape because of its trait of supposedly not ripening until after repeated frosts. Pinney suggests that Washington's description is indicative of the same "winter grape" that Charles Carter had planted a decade before, that the winter grape was likely cordifolia, and that the summer grape was aestivalis. Washington grew not only wine grapes, but also table grapes as well. Pinney, *History of Wine*, 81; Hatch, *Fruits and Fruit Trees of Monticello*, 143; Forrest, *Grounds and Gardens of Mount Vernon*, 83–87; Diary Entries, Nov. 20, 1771, and Dec. 16, 1771, *The Papers of George Washington Digital Edition*, University of Virginia; Letter to M. Marbois, July 9, 1783, *The Writings of George Washington, 1782–1785*, (Putnam's Sons), 10:279–281; Mac Griswold, *Washington's Gardens at Mount Vernon: Landscape of the Inner Man* (New York: Houghton Mifflin Harcourt, 1999), 98; Washington to George Clinton, Nov. 25, 1784, *The Papers of George Washington Digital Edition*, University of Virginia.

253. Evidently, Washington had previously procured the vine cuttings from a French soldier, diplomat, and American sympathizer, Anne-César de La Luzerne, and stored the cuttings in the garden of a "Mr. Beekman" outside of New York City. Washington to George Clinton, Nov. 25, 1784, *The Papers of George Washington Digital Edition*, University of Virginia; Hatch, *Fruits and Fruit Trees of Monticello*, 144; Letter to M. Marbois, July 9, 1783, *The Writings of George Washington, 1782–1785* (Putnam's Sons), 10:279–281.

254. For Washington's visit to Bartram's gardens, see Donald Jackson and Dorothy Twohig, eds. *The Diaries of George Washington*, 6 vols. (Charlottesville: University Press of Virginia, 1976–1979), 5:166–167, 183; http://memory.loc.gov/cgi-bin/ampage?collId=mgw1&fileName=mgw1b/gwpage872.db&recNum=12 (accessed Apr. 2, 2014); Historic American Landscapes Survey, John Bartram House and Garden (Bartram's Garden), HALS No. PA-1, at http://www.nps.gov/history/hdp/samples/HALS/bartram/HALS_PA-1_Hist.pdf (accessed Apr. 2, 2014); George Washington to Anthony Whiting, Oct. 28, 1792, *The Diaries of George Washington*, July 1786–December 1789, 5:183; George Washington to Anthony Whiting, Feb. 10, 1793, *The Writings of George Washington*, ed. John C. Fitzpatrick (Washington, D.C.: U.S. Government Printing Office, 1939), 32, 195, 341; "Catalogue of Trees, Shrubs, & Plants, of Jno. Bartram," Mar. 1792, George Washington Papers, LOC, printed in Philander D. Chase, *The Papers of George Washington: Presidential Series* (Charlottesville: University of Virginia Press, 2002), 10:175–183; List of ninety-seven species sent from Bartram's Garden to Mount Vernon for George Washington, in hand of Bartholomew Dandridge, Washington's secretary, Nov. 7, 1792, George Washington Papers, LOC. It should be noted that at the time of Washington's visit to Bartram's garden it was just outside of the city limits. The city and county of Philadelphia became one during the 1850s so today Bartram's garden is located in southwestern Philadelphia within the city limits.

255. During his travels in Philadelphia during 1792 and 1793, Washington sent grape cuttings and seeds to his overseer at Mount Vernon. Washington also used the space to root all manners of hedge materials to be used in living fences. As he wrote his farm manager in 1793, "And what is called the Vineyard Inclosure, was designed for other [non-grape] articles of experiment, or for seed which required still greater space before they were adopted upon a larger scale." McGrew, "Untold Episodes," 84; *The Writings of George Washington* (Putnam's Sons), 32:216, 298, 306, and 35:207; Archaeological Investigations at the "Vineyard Inclosure" (44Fx763/4), Mount Vernon Plantation, Mount Vernon, Virginia, Mount Vernon Ladies' Association, cited in *Archaeology at George Washington's Mount Vernon, 1931–2006*, by Dennis J. Pogue, available at http://www.mountvernon.org/sites/mountvernon.org/files/Pogue%20Mount%20Vernon%20Archaeology.pdf (accessed Apr. 4, 2014); Diary entry, Jan. 13, 1786, *The Papers of George Washington Digital Edition*, University of Virginia Press.

256. Hatch, *Fruits and Fruit Trees of Monticello*, 143.

257. Writing in April 1776 to George Washington, George Mason prayed for an end to the ensuring conflict with the British, "May God grant us a return to those halcyon Days; when every Man may sit

down at his Ease under the Shade of his own Vine, & his own fig-tree, & enjoy the Sweets of domestic Life!" Kate M. Rowland, *The Life of George Mason, 1725–1792* (New York: G. P. Putnam's Sons, 1892), 216–219; "To cultivate Exotics for the purpose of making Wine, or for my amusement, was never contemplated by me." Letter to M. Marbois, July 9, 1783, *The Writings of George Washington, 1782–1785* (Putnam's Sons), 10:279–281; Griswold, *Washington's Gardens*, 98; Paul Bedard, "George Washington Plied Voters with Booze," *US News*, Nov. 8, 2011; William S. Baker and George Washington, "Washington after the Revolution, 1784–1799 (Continued)," *Pennsylvania Magazine of History and Biography 20*, No. 3 (1896): 334–369; Ayers, "Fruit Culture," 91–92; McGrew, "Untold Episodes," 102.

258. Beginning in 1988, archaeologists at Mount Vernon embarked on a multiyear study of the estate's grounds and gardens. After unearthing several ditches, molds, holes, postholes, and evidence of live hedges that were used for partitioning, the Vineyard enclosure was restored as a fruit garden and nursery in 1996 based primarily on the archaeological findings. These discoveries also led to new wine-related interpretive programs at the estate and today guests can learn of Washington's attempts to create a vineyard, see many wine-related items in the mansion, and purchase a bottle of wine with a Mount Vernon label. At the suggestion of George Mason in 1759, Washington subscribed to the failed endeavors of Maurice Pound; in 1773, Washington joined in supporting Philip Mazzei's efforts in Albemarle County. See Martin, *Pleasure Gardens*, 135–136. Washington posited that Virginia's hot summers and falls invariably hastened the ripening of grapes, which in turn led to excess fermentation and highly acidic wine. Washington to French minister of state, Chretien Guillaume de Lamoignon de Malesherbes, July 9, 1793, http://memory.loc.gov/cgi-bin/query/P?mgw:3:./temp/~ammem_tnYw (accessed Apr. 2, 2014). The engraved image, G. Washington in His Last Illness, was the work of Edward Pember and Samuel Luzader in 1800. See Hancock, *Oceans of Wine*, 324–325; Frank E. Grizzard, *George Washington: A Biographical Companion* (Santa Barbara, Calif.: ABC-CLIO, 2002), 292; Dennis J. Pogue, "Archaeology at George Washington's Mount Vernon, 1931–2006," 172, available at http://www.mountvernon.org/sites/mountvernon/files/Pogue%20Mount%20Vernon%20Archaeology.pdf; "George Washington's Mount Vernon Estate & Gardens: Application For Inclusion On The U.S. World Heritage Tentative List," 14, found at: http://www.nps.gov/oia/topics/worldheritage/Applications/Mount%20Vernon.pdf; http://www.mountvernon.org/more/news-press/release-archive/2010/mount-vernon%E2%80%99s-popular-fall-wine-festival-sunset-tour (accessed Apr. 2, 2014).

259. Robert A. Rutland, ed., *The Papers of George Mason, 1725–1792* (Chapel Hill: University of North Carolina Press, 1970), 757–762 (hereafter cited as Rutland, *Mason Papers*). Pamela C. Copeland and Richard K. MacMaster, *The Five George Masons: Patriots and Planters of Virginia and Maryland* (Charlottesville: University Press of Virginia, 1975), 103–104. Mason purchased a £50 share in Mazzei's company. *The Triumph*, which had ferried Mazzei across the Atlantic late in 1773, brought over Italian seeds and cuttings in the summer of 1774. Gabler, *Passions*, 5; Barr, "Philip Mazzei," 43–47; Pinney, *History of Wine*, 79; *Virginia Gazette* (Purdie and Dixon), July 28, 1774. Mason reserved the right to withdraw his share "in case, any slaves should be purchased on account of the Company." Copeland, *Five George Masons*, 103–104; *Virginia Gazette* (Rind), July 28, 1774; Julian P. Boyd, et al., eds., *The Papers of Thomas Jefferson* (Princeton: Princeton University Press, 1950), 1:156–159.

260. Copeland, *Five George Masons*, 101–102.

261. Also known as "Morris Pountz" or "Maurice Poutz." Pound purchased Lots 18 and 26 along Essex Street. Edith Moore Sprouse, *Colchester: Colonial Port on the Potomac* (Fairfax, Va.: Fairfax County Office of Comprehensive Planning, 1975), 59; Rutland, *Mason Papers*, 44–45; Copeland, *Five George Masons*, 101–102. Mason reserved the right to withdraw his share "in case, any slaves should be purchased on account of the Company." Copeland, *Five George Masons*, 103–104; *Virginia Gazette* (Rind), July 28, 1774; Julian P. Boyd, et al., eds., *The Papers of Thomas Jefferson* 1:156–159; "George Mason—Orchardist," by Susan A. Borchardt, available at http://www.gunstonhall.org/georgemason/essays/gm_orchardist.html (accessed Apr. 4, 2014); Grizzard, George Washington, 292.

262. George Mason, "Subscription for Maurice Pound," Misc. Collection, Historical Society of Pennsyl-

vania, Philadelphia, reprinted in Copeland, *Five George Masons*, 103.

263. Laura Croghan Kamoie, *Irons in the Fire: The Business History of the Tayloe Family and Virginia's Gentry, 1700–1860* (Charlottesville: University of Virginia Press, 2007), 54, 58, 59; *The Papers of George Washington: Colonial Series*, 6:368–437; Pinney, *History of Wine*, 69; Sprouse, *Colchester*, 60. No remnants of Pound's efforts remain; one street in Colchester, however, was named in honor of the wine effort, "Wine Street," located along Old Colchester Road near the entrance to a marina along the Occoquan. When the assets of one of Pound's creditors, Spencer Grayson, were taken over by creditors in 1765, one of Pound's two lots was advertised for sale. Though no record confirms whether Pound ever regained control of the lot, records do indicate that he and his heirs paid taxes on the property through 1782. "A Loan Agreement for Maurice Pound, Oct. 1759," Rutland, *Mason Papers*, 1:45; George William Fairfax to Thomas Fairfax, n.d. (ca. 1716), *Fairfax of Cameron Papers*, Gay's House, Holyport, Berkshire, Eng.; From Chalkley's Augusta County Records, 283; Patrick Willson to George Weaver, £130, 380 acres, art of 5,000 acres patented to Jacob Stover, 3,100 acres thereof being conveyed by Jacob to Christopher Francisco and recorded in Orange County, on Shanando River; corner Morris Pound whereon he lives. Delivered: Geo. Weaver, 20th December, [17]94; Copeland, *Five George Masons*, 103. Washington advanced Pound £15. See George Washington Account Books, Ledger A, fol. 100, Research Library, Mount Vernon, Va.; Grizzard, *George Washington*, 292.

264. William Downman evidently had a vineyard inclosure. See Rawleigh Downman to William Downman, Nov. 15, 1764, *Joseph Ball Letter Book, 1743–1780*, p. 237 (Library of Congress); Isaac Giberne to Landon Carter, Mar. 31, 1772, Correspondence, n.p., *Carter Family Papers, 1659–1797* (University of Virginia Library Microfilm Project); *James Pendleton Memorandum Book, 1782–1802*, n.p; Ayers, "Fruit Culture," 78, 198.

265. Winston was a Hanover County native and captain in the Continental army, who moved to Buckingham County in his youth, where he became sheriff and served as delegate to the Convention of 1775. *Virginia Gazette*, July 13, 1775 (Pinkney), 4; Daughters of the American Revolution, *Lineage Book—National Society of the Daughters of the American Revolution* (Washington, D.C.: National Society of the Daughters of the American Revolution, 1919), 53:146; Willis Brewer, *Alabama: Her History, Resources, War Record, and Public Men* (Montgomery, Ala.: Barrett and Brown, 1872), 530; Alabama Department of Archives and History, Montgomery, Revolutionary Soldiers in Alabama (Montgomery, Ala.: Brown Printing, 1911), 405.

266. Jefferson wrote to Monroe in January 1816, "I have an opportunity of getting some vines planted next month under the direction of Mr. [Jean] David, brought up to the business from his infancy. Will you permit me to take the trimmings of your vines, such I mean as ought to be taken from them next month. It shall be done by him so as to ensure no injury to them." In the White House, most of Mrs. Monroe's recipes contained sherry, brandy, or other spirits, and the Monroes continued the executive branch's tradition of preserving the White House's wine cellar. See note on Hailman, *Thomas Jefferson on Wine*, 389; Debbie Levy, *James Monroe* (Minneapolis, Minn.: Lerner Publications, 2005), 58; Jefferson to James Monroe, Jan. 16, 1816; Pinney, *History of Wine*, 82, 128; *VWGJ* (Fall 1980): 150; Marie D. Smith, *Entertaining in the White House* (New York: Acropolis Americana, 1967), 56; To James Monroe, Monticello, Apr. 8, 1817; see also *VWGJ* (Fall 1978): 149; Bolling to Pleasants Feb. 26, 1775 (MS, Huntington Library. The UVA Special Collections library contains images of wine bottle caps of the Eppes family of Bermuda Hundred, Va., pointing to the fact that the Eppes family manufactured their own wine.

267. Hancock, *Oceans of Wine*, 110–111; Fletcher, *History of Fruit Growing*, 8, 14; Ayers, "Fruit Culture," 64; Strachey, *Historie of Travaile*, 120 (emphasis in the original).

268. Hart, "Winemaking," 4; Wright, *Dream of Prosperity*, 36. Sir William Alexander, Earl of Stirling, noted in his work *An Encouragement to Colonies* that Virginians purchased "their food and rayment from England, in exchange of Tobacco...oherwife that Countrey before this time for Wine, Oyle, Wheate, and other things neceffary for the ufe of man might haue equalled for the like quantitie any bounds within Europe"(29–30). Robert Beverley noted that, though the colonial government attempted to encourage the production of other commodities, they yielded an inadequate return. Meyer Jacobstein, *The Tobacco Industry in the United States* (New York: Columbia University Press,

1907), 22; *VWGJ* (Summer 1984): 124; Ayers, "Fruit Culture," 97.

269. Hart, "Winemaking," 4; *VWGJ* 1, No. 1(Spring 1974): 39; Mishkin, *American Colonial Wine Industry*, 294–295, 297; Peyton Boswell, *Wine Makers Manual: A Guide for the Home Wine Maker and the Small Winery* (New York: Orange Judd, 1935), 31. Had the early colonial settlers understood about phylloxera, and had the European vines that were planted in California arrived there after traversing phylloxera territory, it may have been the American East—rather than the West—that would boast the nation's wine industry today. *VWGJ* (Fall 1980): 150.

270. Mishkin notes that, during the 1620s, tobacco planting in the colony evolved from exporting 40,000 pounds at three shillings per pound to producing 1,800,000 pounds valued at less than one pence per pound. Mishkin, *American Colonial Wine Industry*, 224–233.

271. Mishkin, *American Colonial Wine Industry*, 180, 224, 239–240, 291, 294. Historian Edward Ayers has noted that, while many colonists believed that proper cultivation of vinifera would yield high quality wine, past failed viticultural and vinification attempts had yielded little in the way of success, which dissuaded would-be winemakers. As one colonist, Jabez Whitaker (1595–1626), wrote to Sir Edwin Sandys in 1620, "For vines we can not go about it with courage until such time as we may have such plants as we know are good and will be worth our labor.... I have both the last year and this year planted some young nurseries of vines which live and grow, but I can have no confidence in them that they should ever make good wines." Jabez Whitaker to Sir Edwin Sandys, May [16], 1620, Ferrar Papers, Box 11, No. 1044 (Magdalene College, Cambridge University, Eng.), reprinted in Ayers, "Fruit Culture," 63 n. 75, 64, 97; Beverley, *History of Virginia*, 315–316; *Monticello Farmer and Grape Grower* (Charlottesville), Nov. 1883, p. 12; Hart, "Winemaking," 4; G. Terry Sharrer, *A Kind of Fate: Agricultural Change in Virginia, 1861–1920* (Ames: Iowa State University, 2000), 74. As the 1700s progressed, winemaking was also stalled by changing tastes and an abundance of imports. Tastes in the colony were changing as well, as a desire for sweeter wines from Madeira, the Canaries, and the Azores were gradually replacing drier French wines. These changing tastes were matched by gradually cheaper prices for imported wines, beer, spirits, and rum, all of which depressed wine prices and curtailed the demand for domestic wine production. As Virginia's colonial government increasingly viewed wine imports favorably from a tax perspective, its interest in fostering domestic wine production waned. See Mishkin, *American Colonial Wine Industry*, 173–174; Beverley, *History of Virginia*, 293; Byrd, *Natural History of Virginia*, 89–90. As recorded in the journal of John Bartram and incorporated into William Stork's 1766 treatise *A Description of East Florida*, "The dearness of labour, and the cheapness of foreign vines [wines] in America, have both contributed to prevent the planting of vineyards more frequently...it will, probably, not be owing to any defect either in soil or climate, but to the dearness of labour, or negligence of its inhabitants, if wine is not produced hereafter in some plenty upon this continent." William Stork, ed., *A Description of East-Florida, with a Journal Kept by John Bartram of Philadelphia, Botanist to His Majesty for the Floridas; upon A Journey from St. Augustine up the River to St. John's as far as the Lakes* (London: Sold by W. Nicoll; and T. Jefferies, 1769), 29.

272. Hancock, *Oceans of Wine*, 110.

273. Virginia—and indeed the eastern United States—would experience just such an evolution during the 1800s and it is not too far of a stretch to suggest that Virginia might have realized such a fate a century earlier. Mishkin, *American Colonial Wine Industry*, 242, 256, 290, 292. At least one Virginia governor, Sir William Berkeley—a stalwart supporter of commodity diversification away from tobacco—noted that the Navigation Acts were responsible for the fact that "Wee cannot add to our plantacon any Commodity that growes out of itt [Europe], as oliue trees, Cotton, or vines, besides this wee Cannot procure any skilfull Men." See Beer, *Origins of the British Colonial System*, 113.

274. Concerning Mazzei's efforts specifically, Weld asserted that "the vines which the Italians found growing here were different, as well as the soil, from what they had been in the habit of cultivating, and they were not much more successful in the business than the people of the country." Isaac Weld, Jr., *Travels through the States of North America during the Years 1795, 1796 and 1797*, 2d. ed. (London: J. Stockdale, 1799), 206–209.

# Chapter 2 Notes

1.   John D. Boyer, "Geographical Analysis of Viticulture Potential in Virginia" (Master's thesis, Virginia Tech, 1998), 75, found at http://scholar.lib.vt.edu/theses/available/etd-92198-02524/unrestricted/ Boyer.pdf; W. H. Upshall, ed., *History of Fruit Growing and Handling in the United States of America and Canada, 1860–1972* (University Park, Pa.: The Society, 1976), 139.

2.   John R. McGrew, "The 'Alexander' Grape," *American Wine Society Journal* 8 (1976): 20; Hilda Gabriel Lee and Allan E. Lee, *Serve with Virginia Wine* (Charlottesville, Va.: Hildesigns Press, 1994), 7.

3.   Such travails were often recounted in letters, advertisements, and agricultural journals, but wine writers Hilda and Allan Lee have written, "This process more nearly paralleled that of an Easter egg hunt than scientific research." See Lee and Lee. *Virginia Wine Country III*, 17, 18.

4.   A purported descendant of Pocahontas, Bland was educated in England and returned to Prince George County in 1764 where he settled at Kippax Plantation, a property he inherited located on the south bank of the Appomattox River in the present-day City of Hopewell. Bland represented Virginia in the Continental Congress and in the United States House of Representatives. At Kippax, Bland experimented with germinating Spanish raisins and, by 1774, had distributed grape seedlings to both Thomas Jefferson and Colonel Robert Bolling. See John R. McGrew, "Some Untold Episodes in the History of Virginia Grapes and Wine," *American Wine Society Journal* (Fall 1986): 84–85; A. F. M. Willich and James Mease, *The Domestic Encyclopaedia* (Philadelphia: W. Y. Birch and A. Small, 1804), p. 291; Alden Spooner, *The Cultivation of American Grape Vines, and Making of Wine* (Brooklyn, N.Y.: A. Spooner and Company Printers, 1846), 53; William Robert Prince, *A Treatise on the Vine: Embracing Its History from the Earliest Ages to the Present Day* (New York: T. & J. Swords, 1830), 178–179; Thomas G. Fessenden, *The New England Farmer and Horticultural Journal* 12, No. 49 (Boston: Geo. C. Barrett, 1834): 331. The grape was also called a host of names, including the "Bland," "Bland's Madeira," the "Virginia Muscadel," "Bland's Fox Grape," and the "Red Bland" grape. D. J. Browne, *The Trees of America* (New York: Harper and Brothers, 1846), 134; Edmund Ruffin, ed., *The Farmers' Register* 1 (Petersburg, Va.: Edmund Ruffin, 1834): 457; Robert Bolling, *A Sketch of Vine Culture for Pennsylvania, Maryland, Virginia and the Carolinas* (N.p.: N.p., [1773–1774]), 36, in Thomas Pinney, *A History of Wine in America: From the Beginnings to Prohibition* (Berkeley: University of California Press, 1989), 73–76.

5.   Indeed, Bland's Madeira is a grape of great dispute, both as to its genus and the legend of its discovery. Bolling wrote in his *Sketch of Vine Culture* that Bland created the varietal from the seeds of raisins: "witness the fine grapes raised by Theodorick Bland Esq. from the seeds of raisins…. He has known vines, raised the seeds to grow to the length of three feet the first year. And that, with proper pruning, they will bear fruit the third or fourth year at farthest. Prince, *Treatise on the Vine*, 178; Edward Ayers, "Fruit Culture in Colonial Virginia" (Unpublished Manuscript, Collections of the University of Virginia, 1973), 96. Of the 35 varietals Dufour had planted, it is often thought that the Bland Grape proved productive. Pinney, *History of Wine*, 148; Willich, *Domestic Encyclopaedia*, 291; Ruffin, Farmers' Register, Vol. 5, No. 6, 378; McGrew, "Untold Episodes," 84; "Transactions" by the Massachusetts Horticultural Society (1915), p. 61; Prince, *Treatise on the Vine*, 178; *Sketch of Vine Culture*, in Lineaeus Bolling, Buckingham County, to the editor, Feb. 2, 1829, "On the Cultivation of the Vine," reprinted in *American Farmer* 10, No. 43 (Feb. 20, 1829): 387.

6.   William Bartram, an American naturalist and writer, noted that the Alexander grape was a cross between the common bunch grape (*Vitis sylvestris*) and *Vitis vinifera*. The grape was popularized by the Bartram family of Philadelphia after the American Revolution. See William Bartram, *An Account of the Species, Hybrids, and Other Varieties of the Vine in North America* (New York: Medical Repository, 1804), 1:19–24; Pinney, *History of Wine*, 85–86; McGrew, "'Alexander' Grape," 21.

7.   The grape was also widely distributed early in the 1800s by Peter Legaux. John McGrew has noted that "contemporary descriptions lack sufficient detail to distinguish among the possible many chance hybrids grown under the single name [of Alexander]." See McGrew, "'Alexander' Grape," 21; Pinney, *History of Wine*, 110.

8.   Jefferson to Adlum, Oct. 9, 1809 (*The Papers of Thomas Jefferson: Retirement Series: Volume 1: 4 March*

*1809 to 15 November 1809* (Princeton: Princeton University Press, 2004– ). Jefferson would later acclaim the wine as "good as the best Burgundy." Jefferson to Adlum, Jan. 13, 1810 (Jefferson Papers, Retirement Series, Vol. 2); Jefferson to Adlum, Apr. 10, 1810 (Jefferson Papers, Retirement Series, Vol. 2); Peter J. Hatch, *The Fruits and Fruit Trees of Monticello* (Charlottesville: University Press of Virginia, 1998), 152.

9. The Alexander grape may be extinct, and it is not known exactly if any live material of the variety still exists; McGrew, "'Alexander' Grape," 21; A. J. Downing, *The Fruits and Fruit Trees of America* (New York: Wiley and Halsted, 1958), 152, 154; J. L. Phillips, "History and Development of the Commercial Orchard Industry in Virginia," *Proceedings of the Thirtieth Session of the American Pomological Society*, Volumes 27–30 (Newark, N.Y.: Published by the Society, 1907), 166.

10. The origins of the grape, as well as its first propagator are unknown. While the grape may have originated in the Carolinas, the 19th century wine historian Dr. U. P. Hedrick wrote in his 1908 book *The Grapes of New York State* that the South Carolina growers who corresponded regularly with Adlum never once mentioned the grape in their letters. Adlum to Jefferson, Mar. 24, 1823 (Jefferson Papers, Founders Online, Library of Congress, Washington, D.C., at http://founders.archives.gov/documents/Jefferson/98-01-02-3412 [accessed Apr. 9, 2014]); Pinney, *History of Wine*, 142.

11. Jefferson to Adlum, Apr. 11, 1823, *American Farmer* 5 (May 16, 1823): 63. Adlum is often cited as the first American writer to publish a book about American grapes. The Catawba became the first American hybrid to garner national and international acclaim for an American grape, and the American Pomological Society later noted that it "marked an important epoch in American grape growing and helped to draw attention to the native vine." See Vinifera Wine Growers Association, *Vinifera Wine Growers Journal* (Spring 1977): 308, 310 (hereafter cited as *VWGJ*); Lucie T. Morton, *Winegrowing in Eastern America* (Ithaca, N.Y.: Cornell University Press, 1985), 26. See Phillips, "History and Development of the Commercial Orchard Industry in Virginia," 166; Pinney, *History of Wine*, 145.

12. Believed to have substantial *Vitis vinifera* parentage, the grape is susceptible to fungal diseases and produces a slightly pinkish grape that proved suitable for sparkling wines and dessert wines. See Pinney, *History of Wine*, 208–209.

13. Boyer, "Geographical Analysis of Viticulture Potential in Virginia," 75.

14. Pinney, *History of Wine*, 82; Prince, *Treatise on the Vine*, 186.

15. While Norton's practice was located at the intersection of Ninth and Broad Streets in downtown Richmond, Magnolia Farm was situated more than one mile west of downtown Richmond along the Richmond Turnpike (today known as Broad Street). Using landmarks in modern Richmond, Magnolia Farm is believed to have been bounded by Broad Street (Route 250) to the south, Bowe Street to the west, Clay Street to the north, and between Harrison and Hancock Streets to the east. Today, "Norton Street" crosses the former farm property. Henrico County Deed Book 17, 1818, Reel 19, pp. 163–165, Library of Virginia, Richmond; wife's death in *Richmond Daily Mercantile Advertiser*, Dec. 21, 1821, p. 3, c. 2; "Dr. Daniel Norborne Norton and the Origin of the Norton Grape," Rebecca K. R. Ambers, Ph.D. and Clifford P. Ambers, Ph.D., *American Wine Society Journal*, 36 (Fall 2004) pp. 81-82, at http://chrysaliswine.com/AWS-V36-No3-2004.pdf (accessed Apr. 10, 2014). See Ambers and Ambers, "Dr. Daniel Norborne Norton," 83; T. J. Macon, *Life Gleanings* (Richmond: W. H. Adams, 1913), 9.

16. Observers have noted that he seemed to have practiced medicine out of necessity rather than a genuine interest in the profession. Ambers and Ambers, "Dr. Daniel Norborne Norton," 79. As Norton showed a particular fondness toward vineyard planting, his brother was kind enough to forward slips and cuttings of European table and wine grapes. Daniel Norton to John Jaquelin Ambler, in William Prince, *A Treatise on the Vine* (1830), 178, reprinted in part in Ambers and Ambers, "Dr. Daniel Norborne Norton," 78–79.

17. Prince, a horticulturalist and proprietor of the Linnean Botanic Garden in Flushing, New York, noted that there were six varietals of grapes that had originated in Virginia, including the Red Bland, Norton's Virginia Seedling, Carter's Favorite, Henrico [Cunningham, Woodson], Beaverdam, and Early Black Summer. See Prince, *Treatise on the Vine*, 177–178; Ayers, *Fruit Culture*, 96.

18. Hedrick also noted that Norton "probably" originated the Norton varietal, a thought echoed by

George Hussman in 1866. See Prince, *Treatise on the Vine*, 186–187; U. P. Hedrick, *Manual of American Grape-Growing* (New York: Macmillan, 1919), 11; George Hussman, *The Cultivation of the Native Grape and Manufacture of American Wines* (New York: George E. Woodward, 1866), 98; Ambers and Ambers, "Dr. Daniel Norborne Norton," 78.

19. Peter B. Mead, ed., *The Horticulturist, and Journal of Rural Art and Rural Taste* (New York: C. M. Saxon, 1861), 286–287; Upshall, *History of Fruit Growing*, 139; Ambers and Ambers, "Dr. Daniel Norborne Norton," 80. Following publication of Lemosy's account, an increasing number of observers attributed to Lemosy, rather than Norton, the grape's founding. T. V. Munson, for example, credits Lemosy with finding the grape in 1835, but also credits Dr. Norton with its public introduction. See also Bush and Son and Meissner, Vinegrowers, *Illustrated Descriptive Catalogue of American Grape Vines* (St. Louis: R. P. Studley & Co., Printers, 1895), 163–164; T. V. Munson, *Foundations of American Grape Culture* (Denison, Tex.: T. V. Munson & Son, 1909), 141; L. H. Bailey, *Sketch of the Evolution of our Native Fruits* (New York: Macmillan, 1898), p. 78; Ambers and Ambers, "Dr. Daniel Norborne Norton," 80; Todd Kliman, *The Wild Vine: A Forgotten Grape and the Untold Story of American Wine* (New York: Clarkson Potter, 2010), 59–63. U. P. Hedrick cast doubt on Norton and Lemosy's accounts in his 1908 volume *The Grapes of New York* and concluded by saying, "It is probable that the true history of the variety will never be known." See U. P. Hedrick, *The Grapes of New York* (Albany, N.Y.: J. B. Lyon Company, 1908), 367. There exists today no known firsthand documentation evincing Norton's direct role in discovering or developing the variety. A third story of the Norton grape originated as recently as 2004, when *Sauce Magazine*, a culinary periodical, suggested that the first Norton grapes to be grown under "controlled conditions" occurred not at Magnolia Farm, but rather at Monticello. *Sauce*'s contention is largely based on the actions of a gentleman named Bernard Peyton, Thomas Jefferson's Richmond "agent," who in 1824 reportedly sent "a Box of Grape cuttings" of the Norton varietal to Thomas Jefferson's grandson, Thomas Jefferson Randolph, at Monticello. While *Sauce*'s suggestion is based on Randolph's alleged planting of the Norton cuttings at Monticello, no records exist of such cuttings being sent, much less planted, and this claim cannot be supported by available evidence. Indeed, one observer has noted that *Sauce*'s misinterpretation is nothing more than a nod to the currently fashionable trend of linking Jefferson with all facets of Virginia wine history and "an attempt to use the Jefferson-Monticello connection as a marketing tool. See Ambers and Ambers, "Dr. Daniel Norborne Norton," 77, 80–81, 86; Bernard Peyton to Thomas Jefferson, Mar. 22, 1824, reprinted in Edwin Morris Betts, ed., *Thomas Jefferson's Garden Book* (Charlottesville, Va.: Thomas Jefferson Memorial Foundation, 1999), 613; Andrew Garfunkel, "Norton: Missouri's State Grape Harbors Juicy Little Secrets," *Sauce Magazine*, June 1, 2004.

20. Ambers and Ambers, "Dr. Daniel Norborne Norton," 85. J. Downing, in his 1955 book *The Fruits and .Fruit Trees of America*, noted that the Norton was a cross between the Bland and Miller's Burgundy grapes. Others have suggested that the grape is a hybrid of the Bland and either the Pinot Meunier (a vinifera variety) or the native "Summer" grape, the latter of which grew near Dr. Norton's Miller's Burgundy plantings at his Magnolia Farm. Still more have thought the grape to resemble the nearly identical Cynthiana grape—a variety believed to have originated in Arkansas. Observers have noted that the Cynthiana offers higher-quality fruit than the Norton with sweeter pulp, and U. P. Hedrick has observed that the Cynthiana is more discriminating when it comes to soil type, that it prefers gravelly or sandy soils, and does not thrive in clay or limestone soils. See Downing, *Fruits and Fruit Trees*, 342; Peter B. Mead, ed., *The Horticulturist, and Journal of Rural Art and Rural Taste* (New York: C. M. Saxon, 1861) 287; *VWGJ* 1, No. 1 (Spring 1974), 43; Ambers and Ambers, "Dr. Daniel Norborne Norton," 80, 85; *VWGJ* (Summer 1991): 126, 127; Prince, *Treatise on the Vine*, 178–179; Hedrick, *Grapes of New York*, 228; William Kenrick, *New American Orchardist* (Boston: Otis, Broaders, and Company, 1844), 259–260.

21. Letters and articles from Norton endorsing the grape's use appeared in agricultural journals (even after his death). See Kenrick, *New American Orchardist*, 259–260. Plantings were particularly pronounced in Ohio, Missouri, and Arkansas. See Kliman, *Wild Vine*, 59, 136; George Hussman, *American Grape Growing and Wine Making* (New York: Orange Judd, 1880), 57; Hussman, *Cultivation of*

*the Native Grape*, 98.

22. This fact was aided by an 1852 disease attack on the Catawba in which the hardy Norton emerged as a favored varietal. See Kliman, *Wild Vine*, 103, 105. Indeed, U. P. Hedrick noted that the Norton was viewed as the hardiest, best wine grape grown in the eastern United States, and it grew the best in the Piedmont areas of Virginia. See Leon D. Adams, *The Wines of America*, 3rd ed. (New York: McGraw-Hill, 1985), 65 (hereafter cited as Adams, *Wines of America* [1985]); U. P. Hedrick, *Grapes and Wines from Home Vineyards* (Oxford, Eng.: Oxford University Press, 1945), 192.

23. Francis Norton Mason, ed., *John Norton and Sons, Merchants of London and Virginia* (New York: Augustus M. Kelley, 1968), 515; obituary of Daniel Norborne Norton, *Richmond Whig & Public Advertiser*, Jan. 28, 1842; *Richmond Enquirer*, Jan. 28, 1842. Norton's grave is located in the northwestern corner of Shockoe Hill Cemetery, near the intersection of Second and Hospital Streets. See Ambers and Ambers, "Dr. Daniel Norborne Norton," 79.

24. C. S. Rafinesque, *American Manual of the Grape Vines and the Art of Making Wine* (Philadelphia: Printed for the Author, 1830), 43, 44; Bailey, *Sketch*, 49; Hedrick, *Grapes of New York*, 47–48; *Proceedings of the Thirtieth Session of the American Pomological Society, 166*; *VWGJ* (Spring 1977), 309.

25. A veteran of the War of 1812, Lockhart was also a stockholder in the North-western Road Company, incorporated by the General Assembly in 1827 to construct present-day Route 50 from Winchester to the Ohio River. See Pinney, *History of Wine*, 149; *American Farmer* 9, No. 49 (Feb. 22, 1828): 388–389; Thomas Kemp Cartmell, *Shenandoah Valley Pioneers and Their Descendants: A History of Frederick County, Virginia (Illustrated) from Its Formation in 1738 to 1908* (Winchester, Va.: Printed by the Eddy Press Corporation, 1909), 478; McGrew, "Untold Episodes," 102; "Old Northwest" Genealogical Society, *"Old Northwest" Genealogical Quarterly* 10 (1907): 53–54; Archer Butler Hulbert, *Historic Highways of America–Index* (Cleveland, Ohio: Arthur H. Clark, 1905), 16:30-33.

26. B. F. D. Runk, "John Patten Emmet," *Magazine of Albemarle County History* 8 (1953): 55, 58; Thomas Addis Emmet, *A Memoir of John Patten Emmet, M.D* (New York: Bradstreet Press, 1898), 27.

27. The house was reportedly built in 1830 and is currently owned by the University of Virginia. It is located along Emmet Road, and the name "Morea" comes from the Latin phrase *morus*, meaning mulberry. Emmet, *Memoir*, 38-41; Runk, "John Patten Emmet, 63–64.

28. Emmet, *Memoir of John Patten Emmet*, 38-41.

29. Stevenson Whitcomb Fletcher, *A History of Fruit Growing in Virginia* (Staunton, Va.: Beverley Press, 1932), 15; Upshall, *History of Fruit Growing*, 139.

30. Fletcher, *History of Fruit Growing*, 20.

31. Ibid., 24.

32. Upshall, *History of Fruit Growing*, 139; *Proceedings of the Thirtieth Session of the American Pomological Society* (1907), 166–167; Shermand & Smith's Gazetteer of the United States, which contains the results of the 1840 census, included in Henry Howe, *Historical Collections of Virginia* (Charleston, S.C.: Babcock, 1845), 129; Hedrick, *Grapes and Wines*, 192.

33. Morton, *Winegrowing in Eastern America*, 26.

34. "Report of Brig.-General A.R. Wright," reprinted in Frank Moore and Edward Everett, *The Rebellion Record* (New York: G. P. Putnam, 1867), 288; Civil War Trails Marker Series, "Upperville: Drama At Vineyard Hill," located on Route 50 in Upperville Park; Clarence Thomas, "In the Rear: The Recollections of a Boy During the Civil War," printed in Thomas E. Watson, *Watson's Jefferson Magazine* 4, No. 1 (Jan. 1910): 76–79.

35. Robert N. Scott, *The War of the Rebellion: A Compilation of the Official Records of the Union and Confederate Armies* (Washington, D.C.: Government Printing Office, 1902), 185, 195; Duane Schulz, *The Dahlgren Affair: Terror and Conspiracy in the Civil War* (New York: W. W. Norton & Company, 1999), 118; Edward G. Longacre, *Lincoln's Cavalrymen: A History of the Mounted Forces of the Army of the Potomac* (Mechanicsburg, Pa.: Stackpole Books, 2000), 240; Joseph Wheelan, *Libby Prison Breakout: The Daring Escape from the Notorious Civil War Prison* (New York: Public Affairs, 2010), 202; Katharine M. Jones, *Ladies of Richmond, Confederate Capital* (Indianapolis, Ind.: Bobbs-Merrill, 1962), 204.

36. Following the rebirth of the Virginia wine industry late in the twentieth century, the names of at least two wineries would honor the commonwealth's struggle during the Civil War: Gray Ghost Vineyards

(named in honor of Confederate colonel John Singleton Mosby—the "Gray Ghost"). One winery, The Winery At Bull Run, opened in 2012 immediately adjacent to Manassas National Battlefield Park. Sciutto Winery, which operated between 1948 and 1956, was located in the heart of what is now Manassas National Battlefield Park. The now-defunct "Stonewall Vineyards" was not named in honor of Thomas J. "Stonewall" Jackson but rather a small unincorporated hamlet in western Appomattox County. William Henry Seamon, *Albemarle County (Virginia): A Hand Book Giving a Description of Its Topography, Climate, Geology, Minerals, Fruits, Plants, History, Educational, Agricultural and Manufacturing Advantages, and Inducements the County Offers the Industrious and Intelligent Farmer and Manufacturer* (Charlottesville, Va.: Jeffersonian Book and Job Print. House, 1888), 54.

37. Upshall, *History of Fruit Growing*, 139; Boyer, "Geographical Analysis of Viticulture Potential in Virginia," 75.

38. It was estimated that some 500,000 Virginia slaves had been freed. William E. Hemphill et al., *Cavalier Commonwealth: History and Government of Virginia* (New York: McGraw-Hill, 1957), 342; Pinney, *History of Wine*, 413. Farmers still grew tobacco in quantity, but they began experimenting with higher-quality tobacco and alternative crops as well, including vegetables and fruits, to serve demand in northeastern cities. Hemphill, *Cavalier Commonwealth*, 358–360.

39. Pinney, *History of Wine*, 413; Fletcher, *History of Fruit Growing*, 25; S. M. Janney, "Virginia: Her Past, Present and Future," printed in *Report of the Commissioner of Agriculture 1864* (Washington, D.C.: GPO, 1865), 38–39; William C. Lodge, "Wine-Making and Vine Culture in the Middle States," printed in *Report of the Commissioner of Agriculture, 1866* (Washington, D.C.: GPO, 1867), 124; G. Terry Sharrer, *A Kind of Fate: Agricultural Change in Virginia, 1861–1920* (Ames: Iowa State University Press, 2000), 74.

40. Fletcher, *History of Fruit Growing*, 24; Adams, *Wines of America* (1985), 65; "William Hotopp and William Ward Minor: Post–Civil War Pioneers of the Grape, exhibition at the Albemarle Charlottesville Historical Society, available at http://albemarlehistory.org/index.php/Historical_Society/exhibits_detailed/exhibits_04._william_hotopp_and_william_ward_minor_post-civil_war_pioneers_/ (accessed Apr. 10, 2014); *Monticello Farmer and Grape Grower* (Dec. 1886): 23.

41. Janney, "Virginia: Her Past, Present and Future," 38–39.

42. Upshall, *History of Fruit Growing*, 140.

43. Creighton Lee Calhoun, Jr., *Old Southern Apples: A Comprehensive History and Description of Varieties for Collectors, Growers, and Fruit Enthusiasts* (White River Junction, Vt.: Chelsea Green Publishing, 2010), 9; *Proceedings of the Thirtieth Session of the American Pomological Society* (1907), 164; Maynard A. Amerine and Axel E. Borg, *A Bibliography on Grapes, Wines, Other Alcoholic Beverages, and Temperance: Works Published in the United States Before 1901* (Berkeley: University of California Press, 1996), 87; Fletcher, *History of Fruit Growing*, 29; *Monticello Farmer and Grape Grower* (Feb. 1887): 1.

44. *First Report of the Michigan State Pomological Society, by Authority* (Lansing, Mich.: W. S. George & Co., 1872), 362; Secretary of the Commonwealth, *Annual report of the Secretary of the Commonwealth to the Governor and General Assembly of Virginia for the year ending Sept. 30, 1903* (Richmond: J. H. O'Bannon, 1903), 289; Amerine and Bork, *Bibliography on Grapes*, 75; *Southern Cultivator and Dixie Farmer* 45 (J. W. & W. S. Jones, 1887): 449; Fletcher, *History of Fruit Growing*, 28-29.

45. Most of these organizations ceased functioning following the depression in the 1880s. The Catoctin Farmers' Club, however, was established in 1868 and continued to advocate on behalf of agricultural interests through the early 1980s. Fletcher, *History of Fruit Growing*, 28.

46. Fletcher, *History of Fruit Growing*, 28; Upshall, *History of Fruit Growing*, 140.

47. United States, Department of the Treasury, Bureau of Statistics, *Report on the Internal Commerce of the United States* (Washington, D.C.: U.S. Government Printing Office, 1886), 175–176, 177.

48. *Monticello Farmer and Grape Grower* (Nov. 1883): 11, 13; *Proceedings of the Thirtieth Session of the American Pomological Society*, 166–167.

49. Other varietals included Mish, Flowers, Hartford, Ives, and Telegraph. U.S. Commissioner of Agriculture, Special Report No. 36. *Report Upon Statistics of Grape Culture and Wine Production in the United States for 1880* (Washington, D.C.: Government Printing Office, 1881), 102; *Report on the*

*Internal Commerce of the United States* (1886), 178; Pinney, *History of Wine*, 414.

50. *Monticello Farmer and Grape Grower* (Nov. 1885): p. 14, 24; Interview by author with Eugene Scheel, Dec. 23, 2013; *Proceedings of the Thirtieth Session of the American Pomological Society*, 166–167; Fairfax County Board of Supervisors, *Industrial and Historical Sketch of Fairfax County, Virginia* (Falls Church, Va., Newell Ptg. Co., 1907), 34; Commissioner of Agriculture, Special Report No. 36. *Report Upon Statistics of Grape Culture and Wine Production in the United States for 1880*, 102.

51. Commissioner of Agriculture, Special Report No. 36. *Report Upon Statistics of Grape Culture and Wine Production in the United States for 1880*, 102; *Fairfax Herald*, May 1895, quoted in *Prince William Reliquary* 1, No. 3 (July 2002): 57.

52. *Monticello Farmer and Grape Grower* (Feb. 1886): 24; Randolph Harrison, Commissioner of Agriculture, *Hand-Book of Virginia* (Richmond: Johns & Goolsby, 1885), 18; *Report on the Internal Commerce of the United States* (1886), 175.

53. Virginia Department of Agriculture and Immigration, *Annual Report of the Commissioner and the Board of Agriculture and Immigration* (Richmond: R. F. Walker, Superintendent of Public Printing, 1881), 15; United States Department of Agriculture, *Monthly Reports of the Department of Agriculture* (Washington, D.C.: Government Printing Office, 1873), 78; *Southern Cultivator*, 45 (J. W. & W. S. Jones, 1887): 146; *Monticello Farmer and Grape Grower* (Apr. 1886): 11, 25.

54. Refined palates disdained its heaviness and sweetness. See Hedrick, *Grapes and Wines*, 239; Thomas Pinney, *The Makers of American Wine: A Record of Two Hundred Years* (Berkeley: University of California Press, 2012), 107; "Norfolk to Have the Largest Clock in the World," *The Washington Post*, Dec. 16, 1906, p. B3.

55. Commissioner of Agriculture, Special Report No. 36. *Report Upon Statistics of Grape Culture and Wine Production in the United States for 1880*, 102. Dodge also grew small quantities of other native varietals, including Salem No. 14, Hartford Prolific, scuppernong, Worden, and Mish. *Annual Report of the Commissioner and the Board of Agriculture* (Richmond, 1881), 15.

56. *Annual Report of the Commissioner and the Board of Agriculture* (Richmond, 1881), 15; Commissioner of Agriculture, Special Report No. 36. *Report Upon Statistics of Grape Culture and Wine Production in the United States for 1880*, 102, 103; Sir William Crookes, *Chemical News and Journal of Industrial Science* 32 (London: Chemical News Office, 1875): 160; *First Report of the Michigan State Pomological Society*, 362; California Board of State Viticultural Commissioners, *Directory of the Grape Growers, Wine Makers and Distillers of California, and of the Principal Grape Growers and Wine Makers of the Eastern States* (Sacramento: A.J. Johnson, Superintendent of State Printing, 1891), 250.

57. Harrison, *Hand-Book of Virginia*, 70.

58. Moseley grew Concord, Hartford Prolific, Delaware, Martha, and Wilder varietals. Commissioner of Agriculture, Special Report No. 36. *Report Upon Statistics of Grape Culture and Wine Production in the United States for 1880*, 103. It was reported that Walker had plans to plant an additional 50,000 vines in the mid-1880s. Harrison, *Hand-Book of Virginia*, 94–95, 132. Other pioneering winemaking Virginians whose names appear in various listings include J. B. Carnaga of Richmond, F. Lentz of Nelson County, William Hilliers and Henry Harman of Albemarle County, S. G. Walker of Lynchburg, T. Lentz & Co. of Livingston, S. T. B. Higginbotham of Grantland, C. Shiverchart of Gordonsville, Van Opstal and Charles E. Hunter of Fredericksburg, and Fred Byers of Afton. See *Directory of the Grape Growers, Wine Makers and Distillers of California*, 250; Home of Alexander and Thomas Beggs, Rockbridge County, Virginia, at http://freepages.genealogy.rootsweb.ancestry.com/~qvarizona/Vineyard%20Hill.html (accessed Apr. 10, 2014).

59. Upshall, *History of Fruit Growing*, 139; "Virginia Offerings Trickle into California's Push For America's Business," *Cavalier Daily*, April 13, 1983, p. 3; Fletcher, *History of Fruit Growing*, 26; Sharrer, *Kind of Fate*, 73; Thomas Whitehead, Virginia Department of Agriculture, *Virginia, A Hand-Book: Giving Its History, Climate, and Mineral Wealth....* Volumes 81–893 (Richmond: Everett Waddey Co., 1893), 196.

60. *American Farmer: Devoted to Agriculture, Horticulture and Rural Life* 5, No. 2 (Baltimore: S. Sands & Son, 1876):70; Sharrer, *Kind of Fate*, 73; Herrmann Schuricht, *History of the German Element in Virginia* (Baltimore: T. Kroh & Sons, Printers, 1900), 2:132, 133; Seamon, *Albemarle County (Virginia)*,

55; Pinney, *History of Wine*, 413.

61. Special Report No. 36. *Report Upon Statistics of Grape Culture and Wine Production in the United States for 1880*, 102, 103; Society for the History of the Germans in Maryland, *Annual Report of the Society for the History of the Germans in Maryland*, Volumes 13–22 (1900–1908): 133. Other calculations placed Albemarle's grape acreage at 1,500 acres and 2,500 acres. See *Monticello Farmer and Grape Grower* (1888): 10; Seamon, *Albemarle County (Virginia)*, 34–35, 47, 55, 56; Fletcher, *History of Fruit Growing*, 4-6; Pinney, *History of Wine*, 414; Adams, *Wines of America* (1985), 65; Hedrick, *Grapes and Wines*, 193.

62. *Monticello Farmer and Grape Grower* (Mar. 1887): 11.

63. *Monticello Farmer and Grape Grower* (Nov. 1884): 12, 15–16, 26–27, 33.

64. Adams, *Wines of America* (1985), 65; Sharrer, *Kind of Fate*, 73; Hedrick, *Grapes and Wines*, 193; Fletcher, *History of Fruit Growing*, 26. Early officers in the Association included R. H. Stratton (president), R. M. Newton (vice president), Frank Lovelock (secretary), and T. R. McCleod (treasurer). See *Monticello Farmer and Grape Grower* (Aug. 1888): 2, 4–5, 21.

65. Stevens, William T. *Virginia House Tour*. Charlottesville, Virginia: William T. Stevens, 1962, p. 116; "Windie Know," Magazine Section, *Richmond Times-Dispatch*, Jan. 1, 1905; Albemarle Charlottesville Historical Society, "William Hotopp and William Ward Minor: Post-Civil War Pioneers of the Grape," at http://albemarlehistory.org/index.php/Historical_Society/exhibits_detailed/exhibits_04._william_hotopp_and_william_ward_minor_post-civil_war_pioneers_/ (accessed Apr. 11, 2014). 66.        It was reported that Germans had cultivated vineyards in Charlottesville, Cobham (Albemarle County), Warren County, Nelson County, Fairfax, Madison, Goochland, Appomattox, Hanover, Brunswick, Greensville, Lunenburg, Middlesex, Spotsylvania, and Surry Counties. See Schuricht, *History*, 132.

67. Schuricht, *History*, 52; Seamon, *Albemarle County (Virginia)*, 55.

68. Edward W. Hase II and Robert M. Hubbard, "Adolph Russow and the Monticello Wine Company," *Magazine of Albemarle County History* 46 (May 1988): 18-19; "Tariff hearings before the Committee on Ways and Means: Second Session, Fifty-fourth Congress, 1896–97" (Washington, D.C.: Government Printing Office, 1897), 1864 at http://catalog.hathitrust.org/Record/001122539 (accessed Apr. 11, 2014); see also Schuricht, *History*, 132; *Kaufman v. Charlottesville Woolen Mills*, 93 Va. 673; 25 S.E. 1003 (1896).

69. Hotopp also oversaw a thirty-five-acre vineyard on the north side of the Rivanna River in Albemarle County and obtained grapes from other vineyards elsewhere in Albemarle County and in Orange County. "House Documents, Otherwise Publ. as Executive Documents: 13th Congress, 2d Session–49th Congress, 1st Session" (Washington, D.C.: Government Printing Office, 1872), 147; *Directory of the Grape Growers, Wine Makers and Distillers of California*, 250. Hotopp died in May 1898 and portions of his Pen Park property and vineyard were later incorporated into what is today known as Pen Park in the City of Charlottesville. Hotopp was the first to produce commercial wine in Albemarle County. Oscar Reierson of the Monticello Wine Company alleged Hotopp manufactured perhaps as much as 50,000 gallons in 1885. It is rumored that Hotopp developed the idea for a large-scale wine industry in central Virginia after talking with an older Swiss gentleman, a "Sol. Seiler." Hotopp maintained his soil's fertility by using spreading wood ashes, loam, and manure annually. See *Annual Report of the Commissioner and the Board of Agriculture and Immigration* (1881), 14; *Report on the Internal Commerce of the United States* (1886), 177, 178; Seamon, *Albemarle County (Virginia)*, 55, 59; Harrison, *Hand-Book of Virginia*, 66; John Hammond Moore, *Albemarle: Jefferson's County, 1727–1976* (Charlottesville: University Press of Virginia, 1976), 249; Hase and Hubbard, "Adolph Russow," 18; Whitehead, *Virginia, A Hand-Book*, 195; Schuricht, *History*, 132; Commissioner of Agriculture, Special Report No. 36. *Report Upon Statistics of Grape Culture and Wine Production in the United States for 1880*, 103; *Annual Report of the Society for the History of the Germans* (1900): 132; "Thomas Jefferson's Unsuccessful Idea May Yet Work in His State," UPI, *Ludington (*Michigan) *Daily News*, July 23, 1976, p. 9.

70. *Annual Report of the Commissioner and the Board of Agriculture and Immigration* (1881), 14; Schuricht, *History*, 133; Special Report No. 36. *Report Upon Statistics of Grape Culture and Wine Production in the*

*United States for 1880*, 103; *Directory of the Grape Growers, Wine Makers and Distillers of California*, 250; *Monticello Farmer and Grape Grower* (Aug. 1886): 5–7.

71. *Monticello Farmer and Grape Grower* (Nov. 1884): 7–11, 22l; *Report on the Internal Commerce of the United States* (1886), 178.

72. John Toler, "German Immigrants Brought the First Wineries to Western Prince William," *Haymarket Lifestyle Magazine*, November 2010, pp. 8–14. By 1871, one vineyard, owned by a "Captain Herald," was evidently large and prosperous, as was a ten-acre vineyard owned by a German immigrant, Otto Witticher, which boasted "flourishing" vines after only two years of cultivation. *Annual Report of the Commissioner and the Board of Agriculture and Immigration* (1881), 15 n*; Jock Elliot, letter to the editor, *Alexandria Gazette*, Sept. 4, 1871; Ronald R. Turner, *Prince William County Virginia, 1865–1875, Newspaper Transcripts* (Manassas: R. R. Turner, 2001) p. 98; Raymond V. Olszewski, *A Taste of Prince William County, Virginia, Wine History* (Farmington, Minn.: Olszewski Enterprises, 2011) 32–33.

73. Portner's estate eventually grew to some 2,000 acres, and featured orchards, lakes, a dairy farm, a castle tower, and three houses. Much of the timber used in the houses' construction came from the Black Forest of Germany. Tom Weil, *Hippocrene USA Guide to America's South: A Travel Guide to the Eleven Southern States* (New York: Hippocrene Books, 1990), 11; Michael Gaines, *The Shortest Dynasty, 1837–1947, The Story of Robert Portner: A History of His Brewing Empire, and the Story of His Beloved Annaburg* (Bowie, Md.: Heritage Books, 2002), 218, 219; Olszewski, *Taste of Prince William County*, 49. Peter Valer and Peggy E. M. Porter, "Golden Days at Annaburg," *Prince William Reliquary* 2 No. 3 (July 2003): 52; Ethel M. Byrd, "Annaburg and Robert Portner," in *Town of Manassas and Old Prince William* ([Manassas: E. M. Byrd, n.d. [1965–1977]), 34; unpublished typescript, reprinted in Olszewski, *Taste of Prince William County*, 49-51; Gaines, *Shortest Dynasty*, 275.

74. *Washington, D.C. with Its Points of Interest, Illustrated* (New York: The Mercantile Illustrating Company, 1894), 148; Christian Xander letterhead graphic, reprinted in Olszewski, *Taste of Prince William County*, 52. The company included the phrase "Producer of Virginia Wines" in its advertisements. See William Henry Boyd and Andrew Boyd. *Boyd's Directory of the District of Columbia* (Washington, D.C.: R. L. Polk, 1909), 1350 (advertising section); Classified Ad, *The Washington Post*, Aug. 9, 1891, p. 6; "Wine Making in This City: Grapes Brought From Albemarle, Prince William, and Other Counties of Virginia," *The Washington Post*, Sept. 24, 1905, p. E7.

75. "About People You Know," *The Washington Post*, Sept. 22, 1895, pp. 6, 8; "Paris Medals," *The Washington Post*, Sept. 23, 1900, p. 10; "Wine Making in This City," p. E7.

76. Xander's one-time vice president, F. Pohndorff Sr., asserted (mistakenly) that the first Norton wine was commercially made by Xander, and *The Washington Post* credited Xander with being the "initiator of the industry of sweet wine of the character of Port from Norton, Va., grape. "About People You Know," p. 6; "Paris Medals," p. 10. Xander trademarked the name "Pride of Virginia" in 1905. As Prince William County wine historian Raymond V. Olszewski has noted, "Whether the [Annaburg] grapes won a bronze or gold medal at the1900 Paris Exposition is irrelevant. What is relevant is that wine made from Portner's grapes and his vineyard in Manassas was internationally recognized. See H. W. Wiley, "American Wines at the Paris Exposition of 1900: Their Chemical Composition and Character," *Bulletin No. 72* (Washington, D.C.: U.S. Department of Agriculture, Bureau of Chemistry, 1903), 18; Valer and Porter, "Golden Days at Annaburg," 52.; Olszewski, *Taste of Prince William County*, 49, 65; *Report of the Commissioner-General for the United States to the International Universal Exposition, Paris, 1900* (Feb. 28, 1901), 2:323; U.S. Patent Office, *Official Gazette of the United States Patent Office, Volume 116, Part 2* (Washington, D.C.: The Office, 1905), 2242.

77. Shannon published articles on Washington and vicinity. See The Rambler [J. Harry Shannon], "Portner Vineyard at Manassas, Grew Concord Grapes," *Washington Star Sunday Magazine*, Aug. 9, 1925, reprinted in Olszewski, *Taste of Prince William County*, 66–67.

78. Sarah McD. Turner, *Haymarket, A Town in Transition: Highlights of the History of the Town* ([Haymarket, Va.]: Prepared by the Haymarket Historical Commission, 1998), p. 156. Peters had been educated at Trinity College in Oxford, England and had served in the German army before selling pharmaceuticals in the 1850s. Toler, "German Immigrants Brought The First Wineries to Western

Prince William," 8–14; 1880 U.S. Census, Prince William County, Virginia, Agricultural Schedules, p. 345, National Archives Micro Publication T-1132, Roll 28, reprinted in Olszewski, *Taste of Prince William County*, 35–36. Todd Kliman in his book, *The Wild Vine*, 131, suggests that the "Martha" varietal is one of several red wines. Charles Hovey suggests that the vine had a deeper green foliage than that of the Concord, was later to bloom, and created superior quality to the Concord in terms of foxiness, pulp, and flavor. Charles Mason Hovey, *Magazine of Horticulture, Botany, and All Useful Discoveries and Improvements in Rural Affairs* 34 (Hovey and Co., 1868): 236–237.

79. Records indicate that Peters would eventually marry Heineken's eldest daughter. Gayle M. Daniels, *St. Paul's Episcopal Church Parish Records, 1837–1995: Baptisms, Marriages and Deaths* (Manassas: Prince William Genealogical Society, 1996), 96, and Ronald R. Turner, *Prince William County Virginia Marriages, 1854–1938* (Manassas: R. R. Turner, 2002), 282, reprinted in Olszewski, *Taste of Prince William County*, 33. Heineken had purchased Mill Park in 1866 at the suggestion of his father, who recommended the property as suitable for a "gentlemen farmer." Heineken's father was a German consulate to Baltimore, Maryland, during the Civil War. Toler, , "German Immigrants Brought the First Wineries to Western Prince William," 8–14; "History and Sundry Notes on Mill Park," http://millpark.org/historical_notes/history_millpark.html (accessed Apr. 11, 2014); Prince William County Deed Book 88, p. 257, Prince William County Courthouse, Manassas, Va.; Turner, *Prince William County Virginia, 1865–1875, Newspaper Transcripts*, 98, latter two reprinted in Olszewski, *Taste of Prince William County*, 33, 34, 42; Elliot letter to editor, Sept. 4, 1871.

80. Mill Park Wine Company Letterhead, http://millpark.org/millpark_docs/letter_head_undated. html (site no longer working, Apr. 11, 2014); Turner, *Haymarket, A Town in Transition*, 152; Daniels, *St. Paul's Episcopal Church*, 96, and Turner, *Prince William County, Virginia, Marriages*, reprinted in Olszewski, *Taste of Prince William County*, 33; Olszewski, *Taste of Prince William County*, 42–43.

81. Song quoted in Ray Olszewski, "Haymarket—Prince William County's Viticulture Center: Who Knew?" *Prince William Reliquary* 5, No. 4 (Oct. 2006): 80; Olszewski, *Taste of Prince William County*, 44; Turner, *Haymarket*, 162; Henry Mazyck Clarkson, *Songs of Love and War* (Manassas, Va.: Manassas Journal Publishing, 1910), 71.

82. Harrison, *Hand-Book of Virginia*, 55–59.

83. Juice quality was determined by a "saccharometer"—a hydrometer that measured sugar in solutions. One author suggests that this might be the first time that readings from an objective instrument was used for marketing purposes. See Sharrer, *Kind of Fate*, 73; Lisa Provence, "Wine Roots: Lost History Gets Marker," *The Hook*, Apr. 14, 2004, at https://www.readthehook.com/96759/news-wine-roots-lost-history-gets-marker (accessed Apr. 12, 2014).

84. The company's wine cellar was built on land presently owned by the Holy Transfiguration Greek Orthodox Church along Perry Drive, near 2nd Street NE and Wine Street in Charlottesville. See *Report on the Internal Commerce of the United States* (1886), 177; Sharrer, *Kind of Fate*, 73; Eryn S. Brennan and Margaret Maliszewski, *Charlottesville* (Charleston, S.C.: Arcadia, 2011), 27; Hase and Hubbard, "Adolph Russow," 19, 22. The company also obtained a small number of grapes from the Richmond area as well. The company's wine cellar was built on land presently owned by the Holy Transfiguration Greek Orthodox Church along Perry Drive, near 2nd Street NE and Wine Street in Charlottesville. See *Report on the Internal Commerce of the United States* (1886), 177; Sharrer, *Kind of Fate*, 73; Harrison, *Hand-Book of Virginia*, 90; Whitehead, *Virginia, A Hand-Book*, 196; Pinney, *History of Wine*, 413; Letter, *Richmond Dispatch*, May 5, 1885, found at http://www.amherstcounty-museum.org/viticulture.html

85. Adams, *Wines of America* (1985), 65; *Report on the Internal Commerce of the United States* (1886), 177; Hase and Hubbard, "Adolph Russow," 21. Its Phylloxera resistance led to its being planted in small amounts in the eastern Alps. J. Henry Chataigne, comp., *Chesapeake & Ohio Railway Directory, Containing an Illustrated History....* ([Richmond]: J. H. Chataigne, 1881), 204 ½.

86. The *Stephens City Star* (Stephens City, Va.), Sept. 17, 1881, reported a total loss of $26,000 and more than 25,000 gallons of wine. The *Star* reported again on Sept. 24, 1881, that the company had made arrangements to acquire a building, casks, vats, fixtures, and machinery so as to resume operations;

"Our city's history," manuscript, 1940–1941, Glenn Curtis, Smith, Jan. 30, 1941, Special Collections.
87. Hase and Hubbard, "Adolph Russow," 21; Moore, *Albemarle*, 250; Seamon, *Albemarle County (Virginia)*, 55, 59–60.
88. Hase and Hubbard, "Adolph Russow," 17, 19; *Annual Report of the Society for the History of the Germans* (1900): 133; Adolph Russow and the Monticello Wine Company," Albemarle Charlottesville Historical Society, available at http://albemarlehistory.org/index.php/Historical_Society/exhibits_detailed/exhibits_07._adolph_russow_and_the_monticello_wine_company/ (accessed Apr. 12, 2014); Schuricht, *History*, 133.
89. J. G. Pollard et al., *Virginia Law Register* 8, No. 2 (Charlottesville, Va.: Michie Co., June 1922), 1; Letter, *Richmond Dispatch*, May 5, 1885.
90. *Report on the Internal Commerce of the United States* (1886), 176, 177; *Monticello Farmer and Grape Grower* (Apr. 1884): 17, 22, 24–25.; *Directory of the Grape Growers, Wine Makers and Distillers of California*, 250.
91. Pinney, *History of Wine*, 413; Chataigne, *Chesapeake & Ohio Railway Directory*, 2401/2; Adams, *Wines of America* (1985), 65. Norton Claret was the only American wine—including those from California—deemed worthy to receive a silver medal and diploma. Virginia State Board of Agriculture, *Report of the State Board of Agriculture, Virginia, 1890* (Richmond: J. H. O'Bannon, Superintendent of Public Printing, 1891), 217; Charlottesville/Albemarle Almanac "Virginia Wine Line" by Felicia Warburg Rogan, March 1984, p. 3. The company's Norton Claret won two first class medals at the 1884–1885 New Orleans World Cotton Centennial, as well as an award at the 1888 Virginia State Fair. *Annual Report of the Commissioner and the Board of Agriculture* (Richmond, 1881), 14.
92. Monticello Wine Company wines were among the only Virginia products submitted to the 1893 World's Columbian Exposition in Chicago. The company also received an award at the 1904 "Louisiana Purchase Exposition" in St. Louis. See *Reports of the United States Commissioners to the Universal Exposition of 1889 at Paris* (Washington, D.C.: Government Printing Office, 1891), 4:731; *Report of the State Board of Agriculture, Virginia, 1890*; *Proceedings of the Thirtieth Session of the American Pomological Society*, 166–167; Department of Agriculture and Immigration of the State of Virginia, Geo. W. Koiner, Commissioner, *A Hand Book of Virginia* (Richmond: Everett Waddey Co., 1911), 41; *Report of the State Board of Agriculture, Virginia, 1892*, 117. Finally, the Norton Claret received a gold medal at the 1907 Jamestown Exposition in Norfolk, Virginia. H. W. Wiley, *American Wines at the Paris Exposition of 1900: Their Chemical Composition and Character*, (Washington, D.C.: U.S. Dept. of Agriculture, Bureau of Chemistry, 1903), 14, 18; Hase and Hubbard, "Adolph Russow," 23.
93. The company sold wine in New York, Philadelphia, Baltimore, as well as Jacksonville, Florida, New Orleans, and more. *Annual Report of the Commissioner and the Board of Agriculture and Immigration* (1881), 14; *Report on the Internal Commerce of the United States* (1886), 177; *Monticello Farmer and Grape Grower* (Apr. 1884): 17. Roosevelt was speaking to the University of Virginia's alumni association as the first distinguished speaker in the university's Cabell Hall. Five years later, the company's Virginia Champagne was used to christen the USS *Virginia* (BB-13), a lead battleship in the United States Navy's famed "Great White Fleet." See Moore, *Albemarle*, 250; *Albemarle County Handbook*, p. 339; Hase and Hubbard, "Adolph Russow," 23; *Charlottesville Daily Progress*, Apr. 3, 1904.
94. Moore, *Albemarle*, 250; *Albemarle County Handbook*, p. 122; Seamon, *Albemarle County (Virginia)*, 55, 61.
95. *Report of the State Board of Agriculture, Virginia, 1892*, 117; "Adolph Russow and the Monticello Wine Company," Albemarle Charlottesville Historical Society, available at http://albemarlehistory.org/index.php/Historical_Society/exhibits/exhibits_07._adolph_russow_and_the_monticello_wine_company/; Hase and Hubbard, "Adolph Russow," 24.
96. Virginia Historic Marker Q31. The bottle was a present of Bernard P. Chamberlain, Honorary President of the Historic Society and a member of the Jeffersonian Wine Grape Growers Society, UVA, which he gave in 1982 as an "emblem of good will for [the Society's] revival of viticulture in Albemarle County. The company was active politically on behalf of wineries. For example, it petitioned the General Assembly in 1978 to reduce wine taxes. See Boar's Head Inn Press Release, The Boar's Head Grape Vine Press, March 1982, Papers of the Jeffersonian Wine Grape Growers Society, UVA;

Letter to the Albemarle County Historic Society from Bernard P. Chamberlain, Honorary President, Mar. 1, 1982, Papers of the Jeffersonian Wine Grape Growers Society, UVA; Virginia General Assembly, House of Delegates, *Journal of the House of Delegates of the State of Virginia for the Session of 1878–9* (Richmond: R. E. Frayser, Superintendent of Public Printing, 1878), 52.

97. Seamon, *Albemarle County (Virginia)*, 52, 55.

98. Sharrer, *Kind of Fate*, 72, 73; Walker Elliott Rowe, *Wandering Through Virginia's Vineyards* (Baltimore, Md.: Apprentice House, 2006), 81; Morton, *Winegrowing in Eastern America*, 29–31.

99. Lee and Lee, *Serve With Virginia Wine*, 7; Morton, *Winegrowing in Eastern America*, 27.

100. Rowe, *Wandering Through Virginia's Vineyards*, 81–82.

101. For Riley's efforts, Riley received the French Grand Gold Medal and was named a Chevalier of the Legion of Honor in 1884. Lee and Lee, *Serve With Virginia Wine*, 7–8; Sharrer, *Kind of Fate*, 72–73.

102. DVR: French Hybrids, "The French Hybrids," at http://davisvines.com/Frenchhybrids.html (accessed Apr. 14, 2014).

103. Lee and Lee, *Serve With Virginia Wine*, 7.

104. *Report of the Commissioner and the Board of Agriculture and Immigration* (1881), 15.

105. The wines included the Monticello Wine Company's Norton Claret, Delaware (a white wine), and hock wines (a white Concord wine), Laurel Hill Vineyard's bacchantees (a light red Concord wine), "Dry Norton's Virginia wine, sweet Delaware, and sweet Concord wines, Belmont Vineyards' Ives wine, Delaware wine, Catawba wine, and red Concord wine." See Crookes, *Chemical News and Journal of Industrial Science* (1875): 160.

106. Ibid., 161.

107. The Morrill Act provided grants of land for institutions of higher education in every state, with a focus on agriculture and mechanical arts. Virginia Tech opened on the campus of the former Preston and Olin Institute. Emily J. Salmon and Edward D. C. Campbell, Jr., *The Hornbook of Virginia History: A Ready-Reference Guide to the Old Dominion's People, Places, and Past*, 4th ed. (Richmond: The Library of Virginia, 1994), 266.

108. Virginia Tech, "About VAES," at http://www.vaes.vt.edu/about/index.html (accessed Apr. 14, 2014); Upshall, *History of Fruit Growing*, 140–141.

109. The father accolade is attributed to a speech given by Samuel Woods, president of the Virginia State Horticultural Society in 1898. See Virginia Tech, Pesticide Programs, "W. B. Alwood: Education and Training," at http://vtpp.ext.vt.edu/museum-of-pest-management/pioneers-of-pest-management/w.-b.-alwood/education-and-training (accessed Apr. 14, 2014); Virginia Tech, Pesticide Programs, "W. B. Alwood: Stonehenge Laboratories–Charlottesville, VA," at http://vtpp.ext.vt.edu/museum-of-pest-management/pioneers-of-pest-management/w.-b.-alwood/charlottesville-va-stonehenge-laboratories (accessed Apr. 14, 2014); Virginia Tech, Pesticide Programs, "Donors Needed," http://vtpp.ext.vt.edu/museum-of-pest-management/we-need-your-help-donors../alwood-plaza (accessed Apr. 14, 2014); "Special Citation Honoring Professor William Bradford Alwood," Aug. 29, 2011, found at http://www.bov.vt.edu/minutes/11-08-29minutes/attach_x_08-29-11.pdf; Virginia Tech, Virginia Tech News, "Bur Oak dedication, Hokie Bugfest festival to honor legacy of William Alwood," at http://www.vtnews.vt.edu/articles/2011/10/101011-cals-alwood.html (accessed Apr. 14, 2014).

110. He was also one of only a few of VPI's original faculty not to have a building named in his honor. "W. B. Alwood: Education and Training," at http://vtpp.ext.vt.edu/museum-of-pest-management/pioneers-of-pest-management/w.-b.-alwood/education-and-training (accessed Apr. 14, 2014); Upshall, *History of Fruit Growing*, 141. Prior to his appointment, Alwood had served as superintendent of the Ohio Experiment Station as well as a special agent for the USDA. He had also served as a botany and entomology professor. See University Archives of Virginia Tech, "A History of Plant Pathology in Virginia: The Alwood Era (1888–1904)," at http://spec.lib.vt.edu/arc/ppws/alwood.htm (accessed Apr. 14, 2014).

111. Virginia Tech, Pesticide Programs, "W. B. Alwood: The First Arboretum at VPI—Planting the Alwood Oak," at http://vtpp.ext.vt.edu/museum-of-pest-management/pioneers-of-pest-management/w.-b.-alwood/the-first-arboretum-at-vpi (accessed Apr. 14, 2014); "Special Citation Honoring

Professor William Bradford Alwood," Aug. 29, 2011, found at http://www.bov.vt.edu/minutes/11-08-29minutes/attach_x_08-29-11.pdf (accessed Apr. 14, 2014); Upshall, *History of Fruit Growing,* 141.

112. The Japy sprayer was originally developed by the Japy brothers of Beaucourt, France, and was lauded for its effectiveness and durability. See "The Improved Japy Knapsack Sprayer," published in the *Journal of Mycology* 7, No. 1 (Sept. 1891): 39; *Southern Planter,* Aug. 1889, pp. 125–126. The *Southern Planter* was published in Richmond. One researcher has identified a statement contained in the Dec. 1893 issue (p. 667) of the *Southern Planter:* "The Southern Planter is the official journal of the Virginia State Board of Agriculture and of the Virginia State Experiment Station." This statement was reprinted in subsequent issues through 1893, but the researcher could find nothing in Experiment Station records to support that statement. The Southern Planter, however, each month carried articles prepared by various Experiment Station researchers). Alwood undertook subscriptions from farmers to assist in the importation of these sprayers. *Southern Planter* (Jan. 1891): 14–15; University Archives of Virginia Tech, "A History of Plant Pathology in Virginia: The Alwood Era (1888–1904)," *Southern Planter* (Oct. 1891): 552–553.

113. *Annual Report of the Experiment Station* (1890–1891), 43, cited in University Archives of Virginia Tech, "A History of Plant Pathology in Virginia: The Alwood Era (1888–1904)," at http://spec.lib.vt.edu/arc/ppws/alwood.htm (accessed Apr. 14, 2014). Virginia Tech, Pesticide Programs, "W. B. Alwood: Stonehenge Laboratories–Charlottesville, VA," at http://vtpp.ext.vt.edu/museum-of-pest-management/pioneers-of-pest-management/w.-b.-alwood/charlottesville-va-stonehenge-laboratories (accessed Apr. 14, 2014). At least one Virginia Tech historian has noted that Alwood's expressions may have been overly boastful: Today, even with more fastidious fungicides and equipment, we are hesitant to speak with such confidence. See University Archives of Virginia Tech, "A History of Plant Pathology in Virginia: The Alwood Era (1888–1904)."

114. In March 1894, in the wake of the introduction of an invasive and particularly damaging fruit pest, the San Jose Scale, Alwood, along with twelve Albemarle County grape growers, founded the Virginia State Horticultural Society that heavily lobbied the General Assembly to ensure that research efforts would focus on problems of fruit growers and for pest eradication laws. Alwood first noted the appearance of the Scale in an Albemarle County orchard in 1892. These efforts "bore fruit" when, in May 1896, the General Assembly passed the first crop pest eradication law in the eastern United States, known as the "San Jose Scale Law." Alwood was noted in the law as the "state entomologist" and was charged with the inspection and eradication. Much to the detriment of other agricultural commodities, including tobacco, cotton, peanuts, and grains. See University Archives of Virginia Tech, "A History of Plant Pathology in Virginia: The Alwood Era (1888–1904)," at http://spec.lib.vt.edu/arc/ppws/alwood.htm (accessed Apr. 14, 2014); Virginia Tech, Pesticide Programs, "Donors Needed," http://vtpp.ext.vt.edu/museum-of-pest-management/we-need-your-help-donors../alwood-plaza (accessed Apr. 14, 2014); Virginia Tech, Pesticide Programs, "W. B. Alwood: Virginia State Horticultural Society," at http://vtpp.ext.vt.edu/museum-of-pest-management/pioneers-of-pest-management/w.-b.-alwood/virginia-state-horticultural-society (accessed Apr. 14, 2014); Upshall, *History of Fruit Growing,* 141. The law also created nursery and orchard inspection and noncompliance called for the destruction of infested crops. *Southern Planter* (May 1896): 228, act approved Mar. 5, 1896. 1900 U.S. Census, Bedford County, Roll 1700, p. 20B; Enumeration District, 0008, National Archives, Washington, D.C.; Duncan Lyle Kinnear, *The First 100 Years: A History of Virginia Polytechnic Institute and State University* (Blacksburg: Virginia Polytechnic Institute Educational Foundation, 1972); Virginia Tech, Pesticide Programs, "W. B. Alwood: A Change in Venue," at http://vtpp.ext.vt.edu/museum-of-pest-management/pioneers-of-pest-management/w.-b.-alwood/a-change-in-venue (accessed Apr. 14, 2014); Upshall, *History of Fruit Growing,* 144

115. Alwood was appointed Chief of Enological Investigations. William Bradford Alwood Papers, 1854–1927, Ms1960-003, Special Collections, Virginia Polytechnic Institute and State University, Blacksburg, Va. See online guide at http://ead.lib.virginia.edu/vivaxtf/view?docId=vt/viblbv00651.xml (accessed Apr. 14, 2014).

116. In one instance, Alwood's experiments empirically demonstrated that artificial sweeteners and sugars

need not be added to properly produced wine to reduce acidity. The addition of such sweeteners was commonplace among New York and Ohio growers who insisted that such sugars were necessary to reduce a wine's acidity. As the Bureau's chief and Alwood friend Harvey Washington Wiley, noted, "These investigations of Alwood show that the makers of wine in New York and Ohio can no longer scientifically claim the privilege of stretching their wines with sugar. Sugared wines are essentially adulterated, even if labeled as such. The rigid investigations of Alwood have also shown that there is no basis for the belief that the acidity of properly made American wines is excessive. I have lately (1917) tested a bottle of pure Virginia red wine made by Alwood in 1904 and found it has kept perfectly and has qualities which entitle it to rank among the good red wines of the Médoc." Harvey Washington Wiley, *Beverages and Their Adulteration* (Philadelphia: P. Blakiston's Son & Company, 1919), 192–193.

117. Virginia Tech, Pesticide Programs, "W. B. Alwood: Alwood—Always a Loyal Hokie," at http://vtpp. ext.vt.edu/museum-of-pest-management/pioneers-of-pest-management/w.-b.-alwood/alwood-always-a-loyal-hokie (accessed Apr. 14, 2014); "Special Citation Honoring Professor William Bradford Alwood," Aug. 29, 2011, at http://www.bov.vt.edu/minutes/11-08-29minutes/attach_x_08-29-11. pdf (accessed Apr. 14, 2014).

118. Alwood was also awarded a "Certificate of Merit" by VPI in 1923. One writer notes that this certificate does not reflect an honorary degree. VPI did not have a policy to bestow honorary degrees nor is this practice commonplace today. But at some point people started referring to Professor Alwood as "Dr. Alwood." It is unclear as to whether this reflected an honorary doctorate or just a coincidence. Virginia Tech, Pesticide Programs, "W. B. Alwood: Stonehenge Laboratories–Charlottesville, VA," at http://vtpp.ext.vt.edu/museum-of-pest-management/pioneers-of-pest-management/w.-b.-alwood/charlottesville-va-stonehenge-laboratories; "Special Citation Honoring Professor William Bradford Alwood," Aug. 29, 2011, found at http://www.bov.vt.edu/minutes/11-08-29minutes/attach_x_08-29-11.pdf (both accessed Apr. 14, 2014).

119. Professor Alwood and his family are buried in Riverview Cemetery. If one goes there they will take note of the prominent "Merite Agricole" medal etched into the grave marker. See Find a Grave, Riverview Cemetery, Charlottesville, Virginia, at http://www.findagrave.com/cgi-bin/ fg.cgi?page=pv&GRid=8945942&PIpi=21364304 (accessed Apr. 14, 2014). Much of this work was the work of entomology professor Mike Weaver, who had spent countless hours investigating Alwood's contributions in the university's archives. In Nov. 2011, Virginia Tech announced plans for the construction of "Alwood Plaza," a small memorial built on the site of the original Experiment Station that will include a plaque as a tribute to Alwood, the Experiment Station, and the history of the Alwood bur oak. The Department of Entomology's Alwood Society was established to encourage student to perform public outreach in the way Alwood did. Virginia Tech, Pesticide Programs, "Donors Needed," http://vtpp.ext.vt.edu/museum-of-pest-management/we-need-your-help-donors../ alwood-plaza (accessed Apr. 14, 2014).

120. The varietal was developed by R. C. Moore, Virginia Tech's horticulturalist who retired in 1964. See "Virginia Grape Draws Praise from Tester," *The Fredericksburg Free Lance–Star*, Nov. 14, 1966, p. 11; Robert Pool, Keith Kimball, John Watson, and John Einset, "Grape Varieties for New York State," *Plant Sciences: Pomology and Viticulture* 27, No. 80, (July 1979): 4–5, at http://ecommons.library. cornell.edu/bitstream/1813/5087/1/FLS-080.pdf (accessed Apr. 15, 2014).

121. *Southern Planter* (Dec. 1890): 573–574.

122. See, generally, American Clan Gregor Society, *Year Book of the American Clan Gregor Society* (Charlottesville: The Society 1920), 37–44; see also Virginia Tech, Pesticide Programs, "H. M. Magruder," at http://vtpp.ext.vt.edu/museum-of-pest-management/pioneers-of-pest-management/h.-m.-magruder (accessed Apr. 15, 2014); Ibid., "Walker Bowman," at http://vtpp.ext.vt.edu/museum-of-pest-management/pioneers-of-pest-management/walker-bowman-m.a.-ph.d; Albemarle Charlottesville Historical Society, "Other Early Local Advocates of Modern Viticulture," at http:// albemarlehistory.org/index.php/Historical_Society/exhibits_detailed/exhibits_05._other_early_local_advocates_of_modern_viticulture/; *Southern Planter* (Mar. 1889): 129–131, 134 (Apr. 1889), and

(Dec. 1890): 573–574. Alwood wrote a tribute to him in the Southern Planter (1891): 376-377.

123. United States, Census Office, 11th Census, 1890, *Report on the Statistics of Agriculture in the United States* (Washington, D.C.: Government Printing Office, 1895), 602; *Report of the State Board of Agriculture, Virginia, 1890,* 217; *Directory of the Grape Growers, Wine Makers and Distillers of California,* 249–252.

124. Letter by Thomas Whitehead, Commissioner of Agriculture, Sept. 21, 1891, to A. L. Masurier, Consular Agent of France, reprinted in *Report of the State Board of Agriculture, Virginia, 1890,* 221; Letter by Henry L. Lyman to Thomas Whitehead, Commissioner of Agriculture, Sep. 17, 1891, reprinted in *Report of the State Board of Agriculture, Virginia, 1890,* 222.

125. United States Department of Agriculture, *Monthly Reports of the Department of Agriculture* (Washington, D.C.: Government Printing Office, 1873), 78; "Wine Making: Much-Needed Enterprise," Letter to the Editor, *Richmond Dispatch*, May 13, 1885. Chartered with a capital stock of $25,000, the Virginia Seal Wild Cherry Wine Company was charged by the Ohio Dairy and Food Commissioner in December 1897 with selling wine that had been "…adulterated with salicylic acid" (known for its ability to reduce fevers and ease aches). The founders of the company included S.C. Whitaker (president), W.W. Jeter (vice president), Bruce Worthington (secretary), Edgar Worthington, and W.B. Hancock (treasurer). Secretary of the Commonwealth, *Annual report of the Secretary of the Commonwealth to the Governor and General Assembly of Virginia for the Year Ending Sept. 30, 1903* (Richmond: J.H. O'Bannon, Superintendent of State Printing, 1903), 291; Charles W. Parsons, ed., *Pharmaceutical Era (Weekly)* 18 (July 15, 1897): 85–86; Dec. 16, 1897, p. 922.

126. Margaret Vowell Smith, *Virginia, 1492–1892* (Washington, D.C.: W. H. Lowdermilk & Company, 1893), 488: *Report of the State Board of Agriculture, Virginia, 1892,* 11.

127. Upshall, *History of Fruit Growing,* 140.

128. Kliman, *Wild Vine,* 145–147; Hedrick, *Grapes and Wines,* 193; Upshall, *History of Fruit Growing,* 139; Lee and Lee, *Virginia Wine Country III,* 19.

129. Boyer, "Geographical Analysis of Viticulture Potential in Virginia" 76 Upshall, *History of Fruit Growing,* 140.

130. Morton L. Wallerstein, annotator, *Liquor Laws of Virginia, Including Also Federal Laws Relating to Interstate Shipments, Issued from the Office of the Attorney General of Virginia, as of December 31, 1915* (Richmond: D. Bottom, Superintendent Public Printing, 1916), 8–11; C. C. Pearson and J. Edwin Hendricks. *Liquor and Anti-Liquor in Virginia 1619–1919* (Durham, N.C.: Duke University Press, 1967), 167.

131. *Report on the Internal Commerce of the United States* (1886), 178. In February 1886, the Monticello Grape and Fruit-Growers Association passed a resolution opposing the passage of the law. See *Monticello Farmer and Grape Grower* (Apr. 1886), p. 22, 29.

132. *Proceedings of the Thirtieth Session of the American Pomological Society,* 166–167; Boyer, "Geographical Analysis of Viticulture Potential in Virginia, 76.

133. The diseases often destroyed entire crops and affected practically every vineyard in the eastern United States. William B. Alwood, *Enological Studies: The Chemical Composition of American Grapes Grown in Ohio, New York, and Virginia* (Washington, D.C.: U.S. Government Printing Office, 1911), 18; Hedrick, *Grapes and Wines,* 193; *Monticello Farmer and Grape Grower* (Oct. 1883): 25; Sharrer, *Kind of Fate,* 74.

134. *Report of the State Board of Agriculture, Virginia, 1890,* 217.

135. Henry Lyman made repeated efforts to discover remedies for grape crop diseases and pests including mildew, rot, and anthracnose. See *Report of the State Board of Agriculture, Virginia, 1890,* 217; United States. Department of Agriculture, Report of the Commissioner of Agriculture (Washington, D.C.: Government Printing Office, 1889), 882; Alwood, *Enological Studies,* 18, 35; Letter by Henry L. Lyman to Thomas Whitehead, Commissioner of Agriculture, Sept. 17, 1891, reprinted in *Report of the State Board of Agriculture, Virginia, 1890,* 222.

136. Letter by Henry L. Lyman to Thomas Whitehead, Commissioner of Agriculture, Sept. 17, 1891, reprinted in *Report of the State Board of Agriculture, Virginia, 1890,* 217.

137. The state's wine production levels were one-tenth of what they had been only a decade earlier and

by 1910, wine production levels were up, though only marginally, to 50,000 gallons annually. Of that amount, 41,336 gallons, most of which was produced by the Monticello Wine Company, could still lawfully operate in Albemarle County as long as the company's wines were not sold therein. See Pinney, *History of Wine*, 415; U.S. Bureau of the Census, Edward Dana Durand, *Agriculture 1909 and 1910* (Washington, D.C.: Government Printing Office, 1913), 717; U.S. Bureau of the Census, 12th Census, 1900, *Census Reports* (Washington, D.C.: Government Printing Office, 1902), 6:619; *Proceedings of the Thirtieth Session of the American Pomological Society*, 166–167; Upshall, *History of Fruit Growing*, 140; Fletcher, *History of Fruit Growing*, 26, 31; Upshall, *History of Fruit Growing*, 140.

138. Alexia Jones Helsley, *A History of North Carolina Wine: From Scuppernong to Syrah* (Charleston, S.C.: History Press, 2010), 49; Emerson Klees, *Paul Garrett: Dean of American Winemakers* (Rochester, N.Y.: Cameo Press Imprint, 2010), 20; Pinney, *Makers of American Wine*, 111.

139. Pinney, *Makers of American Wine*, 109, 112, 114; Klees, *Paul Garrett*, 44–46; Pinney, *History of Wine*, 415.

140. Klees, *Paul Garrett*, 30; Virginia Commissioner of Agriculture, *Report of the Commissioner of Agriculture, 1902* (Richmond: J. H. O'Bannon, Superintendent of Public Printing, 1902), 140.

141. Garrett did so to ensure also that consumers understood there was no "foreign influence" surrounding the sale of his wines. Advertisement, *Appleton's Booklovers Magazine Advertiser* 6, No. 1 (July 1905): 157; "Norfolk to Have the Largest Clock in the World," *The Washington Post*, Dec. 16, 1906, p. B3.

142. Indeed, Garrett was so trusted in the superiority of native grapes that he priced his champagnes equivalent to the prices of imported champagnes, but with the guarantee to the consumer that if the champagne was not "altogether and in every respect as satisfactory as the patron's favorite brand of imported [champagne], his selection of foreign wine [would be] served without additional cost." Pinney, *History of Wine*, 416; "Norfolk to Have the Largest Clock in the World," *The Washington Post*, Dec. 16, 1906, p. B3; Helsley, *History of North Carolina Wine*, 52; Clarence Louis Frank Gohdes, *Scuppernong: North Carolina's Grape and Its Wines* (Durham, N.C.: Duke University Press, 1982), 47; *York Legal Record* 36 (1922): 146; *Metropolitain* 21, No. 6 (Sept. 1904–Mar. 1905); Pinney, *Makers of American Wine*, 119–120; *Garrett & Co. v. A. Schmidt, Jr., & Bros. Wine Co.*, 256 F. 943 (1919); *Wine and Spirit Bulletin* 19 No. 10 (Oct. 1, 1905): 57–58.

143. Klees, *Paul Garrett*, 6, 38. Garrett trademarked the Virginia Dare brand and logo in 1912, and re-registered it in 1917, claiming the use of both since 1891. See U.S. Patent Office, "Trade-marks Published March 20, 1917," *Official Gazette of the United States Patent Office* 236, No. 3 (Mar. 20, 1917): 880; Helsley, *History of North Carolina Wine*, 52; Lee and Lee, *Virginia Wine Country III*, 19; Pinney, *Makers of American Wine*, 118.

144. Advertisement for Virginia Dare, *Life Magazine*, Sept. 5, 1941, p. 87.

145. Gohdes, *Scuppernong*, 79; UPI, "Thomas Jefferson's Unsuccessful Idea May Yet Work in His State," *Ludington Daily News*, July 23, 1976, p. 9; Klees, *Paul Garrett*, 30.

146. Pinney, *Makers of American Wine*, 118; Sallie Southall Cotten, *The White Doe: The Fate of Virginia Dare*. (Philadelphia: J. B. Lippincott, 1901), title page; Martin Hussobee, "Divides Product and Discovers Parts Are Greater Than Whole," *Printers' Ink Monthly* 2, No. 5 (Apr. 1921): 38; Advertisement for Virginia Dare, *Life Magazine*, Sept. 5, 1941, p. 87; *Garrett & Co. v. A. Schmidt, Jr., & Bros. Wine Co.*, 256 F. 943 (1919); "Virginia Dare Wine," North Carolina History Project, at http://www.northcarolinahistory.org/commentary/199/entry (accessed Apr. 16, 2014).

147. *Metropolitain* 21, No. 6 (Sept.–Mar. 1904–1905); Insert found in Cotten, *White Doe*, opposite title page.

148. Helsley, *History of North Carolina Wine*, 52; Gohdes, *Scuppernong*, 51, 63. Consequently, Garrett was increasingly forced to mix grapes from California into the wine such that, by the time that he died in 1940, Virginia Dare featured only a small amount of scuppernong to "tincture the flavor." Pinney, *History of Wine*, 416; Hussobee, "Divides Product and Discovers Parts Are Greater Than Whole," 38; *Fortune Magazine* 8 (May 1933): 8.

149. Adams, *Wines of America* (1985), 66; "Norfolk to Have the Largest Clock in the World," *The Washington Post*, Dec. 16, 1906, p. B3; Klees, *Paul Garrett*, 63.

150. "Norfolk to Have the Largest Clock in the World," *The Washington Post*, Dec. 16, 1906, p. B3; Gohdes,

*Scuppernong*, 51; Pinney, *Makers of American Wine*, 115. The building was torn down in the 1930s. The winery building was 300 feet long by 112 feet wide. The company obtained much of their product from the Southern Vineyard Company, which boasted approximately 1,000 acres in grapes located south of Rocky Mount in Sandy Cross, North Carolina. *Proceedings of the Thirtieth Session of the American Pomological Society*, 166–167. See Raymond L. Harper, *South Norfolk, Virginia, 1601–2005: A Definitive History* (Charleston, S.C.: The History Press, 2005), 1:116, 119.

151. Pinney, *History of Wine*, 416; Virginia Tech, Pesticide Programs, "W. B. Alwood: Stonehenge Laboratories–Charlottesville, VA," http://vtpp.ext.vt.edu/museum-of-pest-management/pioneers-of-pest-management/w.-b.-alwood/charlottesville-va-stonehenge-laboratories (accessed Apr. 17, 2014); Pinney, *Makers of American Wine*, 120.

152. Pinney, *History of Wine*, 416.

153. Robert A. Hohner, "Prohibition Comes to Virginia: The Referendum of 1914," *Virginia Magazine of History and Biography* 75, No. 4 (Oct. 1967): 483 n. 51; Virginius Dabney, *Dry Messiah: The Life of Bishop Cannon* (New York: Alfred A. Knopf, 1949), 81; "Norfolk to Have the Largest Clock in the World," *The Washington Post*, Dec. 16, 1906, p. B3.

154. Promotions for "Vine-Glo" included a service representative delivering the concoction to the purchaser, assisting with the fermentation, and subsequently returning to bottle the wine. Ultimately, in the waning days of Prohibition, Vine-Glo was removed from the shelves in response to protest from prohibitionists. Pinney, *Makers of American Wine*, 123; Hussobee, "Divides Product and Discovers Parts Are Greater Than Whole," 37; Garrett Peck, *The Prohibition Hangover: Alcohol in America from Demon Rum to Cult Cabernet* (Piscataway, N.J.: Rutgers University Press, 2009), 104; Klees, *Paul Garrett*, 6, 65, 66; *Simmon's Spice Mill: Devoted to the Interests of the Coffee, Tea and Spice Trades*, Sept. 1919, p. 1270; *Good Housekeeping*, Apr. 1922, p. 123.

155. *Fortune* article quoted in Pinney, *Makers of American Wine*, 108.

156. Adams, *Wines of America* (1985), 67; Pinney, *Makers of American Wine*, 106, 126; Klees, *Paul Garrett*, 6, 75; Gohdes, *Scuppernong*, 73, 80; Hussobee, "Divides Product and Discovers Parts Are Greater Than Whole," 37.

157. Lee and Lee, *Virginia Wine Country III*, 19; *Report on the Internal Commerce of the United States* (1886), 178; Victor W. Geraci, *Salud! The Rise of Santa Barbara's Wine Industry* (Reno: University of Nevada Press, 2004), 30.

158. For a general discussion of the history of alcohol regulation in Virginia, see Pearson, *Liquor*, 3–5. Whatever enforcement existed was largely found at the local county level. Pearson, *Liquor*, 22.

159. Virginia boasted five temperance societies in 1827 and 250 by 1836. See Pearson, *Liquor*, 27, 59-60, 73; "Virginia ABC's 75th Anniversary, 1934–2009," available at http://www.abc.virginia.gov/admin/abc75th/abc75th_history.html [see http://archive.today/IpIo for a chached copy]. For the 80th anniversary see http://www.abc.virginia.gov/admin/anniversary/abc80th.html] (accessed Aug. 8, 2014); Fletcher, *History of Fruit Growing*, 14; Pinney, *History of Wine*, 427.

160. Thomas Jefferson to Baron Hyde de Neuville, Dec. 13, 1818, *The Thomas Jefferson Papers*, Series 1, Library of Congress, found at http://www.encyclopediavirginia.org/media_player?mets_file-name=evr6516mets.xml (accessed Apr. 17, 2014). For a transcription of the letter, see http://www.encyclopediavirginia.org/Letter_from_Thomas_Jefferson_to_Baron_Hyde_de_Neuville_December_13_1818 (accessed Apr. 17, 2014).

161. Mike Veseth, *Wine Wars: The Curse of the Blue Nun, the Miracle of Two Buck Chuck, and the Revenge of the Terrorists* (Lanham, Md.: Rowman & Littlefield, 2011), 80–81; *Wines & Vines* 16, No. 1 (Jan. 1935): 12.

162. Jack, Temple Kirby, "Alcohol and Irony: The Campaign of Westmoreland Davis for Governor, 1901–1917," *Virginia Magazine of History and Biography* 73, No. 3 (Jul. 1965): 266; Alexander Hamilton Sands, *The Liquor Legislation of Virginia* (Richmond, Va.: C. H. Wynne, 1852). The organization was perhaps the most important women's movement by the turn of the century. See Mark Benbow, "The Old Dominion Goes Dry: Prohibition in Virginia," *Brewery Journal*, No. 138 (Winter 2010–2011): 20–53, at http://www.breweryhistory.com/journal/archive/138/Bendow.pdf (accessed

Apr. 17, 2014); Colman, *Wine Politics*, 30.

163. Wallerstein, *Liquor Laws of Virginia*, 8–11; Pearson, *Liquor*, 167; Henry C. Ferrell, Jr., "Prohibition, Reform, and Politics in Virginia, 1895–1916," in *Studies in the History of the South, 1875–1922* (Greenville: East Carolina College Dept. of History, 1966), 176.

164. *Report on the Internal Commerce of the United States* (1886), 178. Companies in wet counties rushed to fulfill the needs of their dry brethren. For example, the advertisement of one Orange County wine manufacturer, Joel M. Cochran & Co., read, "All orders for Wine and Liquors are shipped the same day as received, with no marks thereon to denote contents." See *Charlottesville Daily Progress*, Sept. 12, 1907; Ferrell, *Prohibition, Reform, and Politics in Virginia*, 175; Kirby, "Alcohol and Irony," 266.

165. Hohner, " Prohibition Comes to Virginia," 473; Benbow, "Old Dominion," 20–53; Virginius Dabney, *Virginia: The New Dominion* (New York: Doubleday, 1971), 443; Pearson, *Liquor*, 193.

166. The history of Cannon is well documented in *Prohibition and Politics: The Life of Bishop James Cannon, Jr.*, by Robert A. Horner (Columbia: University of South Carolina Press, 1998). See also Hohner, "Bishop Cannon's Apprenticeship in Temperance Politics, 1901–1918," *The Journal of Southern History* 34, No. 1 (Feb. 1968): 33–49; Hohner, "Prohibition Comes to Virginia," 473, 474, 480; Michael S. Patterson, "The Fall of Bishop Cannon: James Cannon, Jr., Versus Carter Glass," *Journal of Southern History* 39, No. 4 (Nov. 1973): 493.

167. Kirby, "Alcohol and Irony," 266. See generally Hohner, *Prohibition and Politics*; Pearson, *Liquor*, 231–232.

168. The Mann-Byrd Act resulted in the closure of some 500 of the commonwealth's 2,500 saloons. *Acts and Joint Resolutions Passed by the General Assembly of the State of Virginia during the Session of 1908* (Richmond, Davis Bottom Superintendent of Public Printing, 1908), 275; Dabney, *Virginia*, 443; Benbow, "Old Dominion," 20–53; Lee and Lee, *Virginia Wine Country III*, 20; Pearson, *Liquor*, 257.

169. Pearson, *Liquor*, 211; Hohner, "Bishop Cann's Apprenticeship," 34, 36.

170. Pinney, *History of Wine*, 433; Kirby, "Alcohol and Irony," 266.

171. The General Assembly had successfully rebuffed such attempts during the 1910 and 1912 sessions. The House of Delegates approved the measure overwhelmingly while the Senate passed the measure on a 21–20 split after one absent and hung-over senator was dragged out of bed to vote "dry." Lindsay Rodgers, "The Virginia Prohibition Law and the Commerce Clause of the Federal Constitution," *Virginia Law Review* 3, No. 7 (April, 1916): 483; Dabney, *Virginia*, 461; *Acts and Joint Resolutions (Amending the Constitution) of the General Assembly of the State of Virginia; Session Which Commenced at the State Capitol on Wednesday, January 14, 1914* (Richmond, Davis Bottom, Superintendent of Public Printing, 1914), 20–25; Hohner, "Prohibition Comes to Virginia," 475; *Acts and Joint Resolutions* (1914), Chapter 15; Patterson, "Fall of a Bishop," 493; Jack Temple Kirby, *Westmoreland Davis: Virginia Planter-Politician, 1859–1942* (Charlottesville: University Press of Virginia, 1968), 56–58, 62; Hohner, "Bishop Cannon," 39.

172. Hohner, "Prohibition Comes to Virginia," 474; Valdimer Orlando Key, *Southern Politics in State and Nation* (New York: Alfred A. Knopf, 1949), 19; Hohner, "Bishop Cannon," 46.

173. Hohner, "Prohibition Comes to Virginia," 476.

174. Dabney, *Virginia*, 462; Colman, *Wine Politics*, 29; Kirby, "Alcohol and Irony," 266; Hohner, "Prohibition Comes to Virginia," 476, 481; Dabney, *Virginia*, 461.

175. Historian Virginius Dabney notes that Cannon "wielded an acide pen," and often referred to the wets as "high society folks." See Dabney, *Virginia*, 461; Hohner, "Prohibition Comes to Virginia," 476.

176. Hohner, "Prohibition Comes to Virginia," 483; Ronald L. Heinemann, John G. Kolp, Anthony S. Parent, Jr., William G. Shade, *Old Dominion, New Commonwealth, A History of Virginia 1607-2007*, pp. 283-285.

177. Just three months before the vote, one newspaper publisher from Danville, and chairman-elect of the State Democratic Central Committee, Rorer A. James, reportedly ordered some sixteen gallons of whiskey for, as he asserted, "I believe in looking ahead. I don't know what the pro-hibs will do in September, but I do not mean for them to catch me high and dry in any event." See Hohner, "Prohibition Comes to Virginia," 483; Rorer A. James to William A. Garrett, May 21, 1914, Papers of William Allen Garrett, 1905–1950, Accession #6356, Special Collections, University of Virginia

Library, University of Virginia, Charlottesville.
178. Rodgers, "Virginia Prohibition Law," 483.
179. Wets further argued since that temperance could not be imposed, the Anti-Saloon League's tactics amounted to nothing more than "distressing pictures, tears and other devices of the professional sentimentalist." Almost in the mold of the Anti-Saloon League, the Association distributed literature and founded a newspaper, the *Trumpeter*. Whereas the Prohibitionists capitalized on the support of children, the Association for Local Self-Government relied on statements and promotions by prominent political figures, the most prominent of whom was distinguished attorney and Democratic politician, Henry St. George Tucker. As Cannon historian Robert Hohner has observed, "Instead of lobbying for coercive and unwise prohibition laws, [the Wets said], clergymen should concentrate upon the moral training of Virginia's youth." See Hohner, "Prohibition Comes to Virginia," 478, 479; Ben P. Owen, Jr. to R. L. Ailworth, July 31, 1914, Tucker Family Papers, Southern Historical Collection, University of North Carolina Library, reprinted, in part, in Hohner, "Prohibition Comes to Virginia," 479–480. Historian Thomas Pinney was even more forceful: "Prohibition is everything temperance is not: exclusive, violent, dogmatic, and simple. It is achieved, if at all, not by the free consent of the individual, but by the communal imposition of external control." Pinney, *History of Wine*, 425-426. Charlottesville, Richmond, Williamsburg, and Arlington County stayed wet. *Richmond Times-Dispatch*, Sept. 23, 1914, p. 1, reprinted in part in Hohner, "Prohibition Comes to Virginia," 488; Benbow, "Old Dominion," 20–53.
180. *Acts and Joint Resolutions (Amending the Constitution) of the General Assembly of the State of Virginia; Session Which Commenced at the State Capitol on Wednesday, January 12, 1916* (Richmond, Davis Bottom, Superintendent of Public Printing, 1916), Chapter 146 (hereafter cited as *Acts of the Virginia General Assembly, 1916*). "Ardent spirits" were defined as alcohol, brandy, whiskey, rum, gin, wine, porter, ale, beer, all malt liquors, all fruits preserved in ardent spirits, all liquids, mixtures or preparations which will produce intoxication, all beverages containing more than 1/2 of 1 percent of alcohol by volume. "A Guide to the Records of the Virginia Prohibition Commission," found at: http://ead.lib.virginia.edu/vivaxtf/view?docId=lva/vi01055.xml (accessed Apr. 17, 2014). Like statewide Prohibition statutes elsewhere, Virginia's original Prohibition legislation allowed adult males to transport from outside the state up to one quart of distilled spirits, one gallon of wine, or three gallons of beer for their personal use. This feature was, however, nullified by the Reed "Bone-Dry" Amendment of 1917, federal legislation that prohibited the interstate transportation of liquor into any dry state. Prior to national Prohibition, the regulation of interstate sale of alcohol were deemed to be under the federal purview by virtue of the Commerce Clause of Article 1, Section 8, Clauses 1–3 of the Constitution. See *Acts of the Virginia General Assembly, 1916*, 216; John K. Graves, "The Reed 'Bone-Dry' Amendment, *Virginia Law Review* 4, No. 8 (May 1917); 634; Barbara C. Beliveau and M. Elizabeth Rouse, "Prohibition and Repeal: A Short History of the Wine Industry's Regulation in the United States," *Journal of Wine Economics* 5, No. 1 (2010): 54; Colman, *Wine Politics*, 30.
181. Beliveau and Rouse, "Prohibition and Repeal," 55.
182. Pearson, *Liquor*, 86–87.
183. The 158,137 votes cast in the 1914 referendum represented approximately 7.67 percent of Virginia's 1910 census-reported population 2,061,612; 4.57 of the state's population percent casted votes in favor of Prohibition.
184. "Virginia ABC's 75th Anniversary 1934-2009," available at http://www.abc.virginia.gov/admin/abc75th/abc75th_history.htm (no longer working on Apr. 17, 2014); Pinney, *History of Wine*, 425.
185. Benbow, "Old Dominion," 20–53.
186. Colman, *Wine Politics*, 32. The Department's commissioner as well as the commission's deputies and inspectors were conferred powers similar to sheriffs of the Commonwealth. These same personnel were also authorized to administer oaths, take affidavits, examine records and enter buildings with a warrant. "History of ABC Law Enforcement," at http://www.abc.virginia.gov/enforce/history.html (accessed Apr. 17, 2014).
187. "A Guide to the Records of the Virginia Prohibition Commission," found at: http://ead.lib.virginia.edu/vivaxtf/view?docId=lva/vi01055.xml (accessed Apr. 17, 2014); "Virginia ABC's 75th Anniver-

sary 1934-2009," available at http://www.abc.virginia.gov/admin/abc75th/abc75th_history.htm (no longer working on Apr. 17, 2014); Heinemann, et al., *Old Dominion, New Commonwealth*, p. 304.

188. Robert Portner's Tivoli Brewery in Alexandria closed immediately after the passage of the Mapp Act. Benbow, "Old Dominion," 20–53.

189. Lee and Lee, *Virginia Wine Country III*, 20; Colman, *Wine Politics*, 31; Kliman, *Wild Vine*, 163.

190. "Can wine become an American habit? (Fortune, 1934)," found in *CNN Money* at http://features. blogs.fortune.cnn.com/2012/03/25/american-wine-fortune-1934/ (accessed Apr. 17, 2014).

191. Ultimately, cheaper grapes flooded the market, providing a boost to growers which glutted the market late in the 1920s. Fortune Magazine, 1934 in *CNN Money* at http://features.blogs.fortune.cnn. com/2012/03/25/american-wine-fortune-1934/ (accessed Apr. 17, 2014); Pinney, *History of Wine*, 438; Veseth, *Wine Wars*, 80–81; Dabney, *Virginia*, 485.

192. Lee and Lee, *Serve With Virginia Wine*, 9.

193. Morton, *Winegrowing in Eastern America*, 41; Ronald L. Heinemann, *Harry Byrd of Virginia*, (University of Virginia Press, 1996), pp. 163-165.

194. Colman, *Wine Politics*, 233; Joseph R. Gusfield, *Symbolic Crusade: Status Politics and the American Temperance Movement* (Urbana: University of Illinois Press, 1963), 127.

195. "History of Virginia ABC," found at http://www.abc.virginia.gov/admin/hist1.htm (accessed Apr. 17, 2014).

196. Pollard was apparently also persuaded by then-congressman and future Virginia governor William M. "Bill" Tuck. "History of Virginia ABC," found at http://www.abc.virginia.gov/admin/hist1.htm (accessed Apr. 17, 2014); Benbow, "Old Dominion," 20–53; "History of Virginia ABC," found at http://www.abc.virginia.gov/admin/hist1.htm (accessed Apr. 17, 2014).

197. Benbow, "Old Dominion," 20–53.

198. Beliveau and Rouse, "Prohibition and Repeal," 55.

199. Veseth, *Wine Wars*, 82; Colman, *Wine Politics*, 34.

200. "ABC Powers & Eight Principles: Eight Principles recommended for state liquor control, Senate Document 5 - January 1934," available at http://www.abc.virginia.gov/admin/hist2.htm (accessed Apr. 17, 2014).

201. Once again, wine was included, while suggesting that the "food" aspects of wine were lost in the emergency need to establish an alcohol control program. Wine promoters argued that it should not be confused or regulated like distilled spirits. *Wines & Vines* 16, No. 1 (Jan. 1935): 12.

202. The three-tier system was most likely a reaction to the need to minimize the potential for a criminal element in the legal distribution system. See A. C. Grafstrom, "Commerce—Intoxicating Liquors: Wine Lovers Rejoice! Why Vineyards Can Now Ship Directly To Consumers And Why Everyone Else Should Care *Granholm v. Heald*, 544 U.S. 460 (2005)," *North Dakota Law Review* 82 (2006): 557–558; Beliveau and Rouse, "Prohibition and Repeal," 57.

203. On April 3, 1934, ABC issued its first license to the Pullman Company for the sale of wine and beer on six of its railroad dining cars. Until 1969, customers at ABC stores placed orders for bottles from clerks behind a counter. "Virginia ABC's 75th Anniversary 1934-2009," available at http://www.abc. virginia.gov/admin/abc75th/abc75th_history.htm (no longer working on Apr. 17, 2014).

204. "History of Virginia ABC," found at http://www.abc.virginia.gov/admin/hist1.htm (accessed Apr. 17, 2014).

205. As of the time of this writing, 35 of Virginia's 95 counties are officially "dry," with the retail sale of mixed beverages subject to local option laws by public referendum. Va. Code Section 4.1–122.

206. Colman, *Wine Politics*, 29, 35; Virginia Tech, Pesticide Programs, "W. B. Alwood: Stonehenge Laboratories–Charlottesville, VA," at http://vtpp.ext.vt.edu/museum-of-pest-management/pioneers-of-pest-management/w.-b.-alwood/charlottesville-va-stonehenge-laboratories; "Can wine become an American habit? (Fortune, 1934)," found in *CNN Money* at http://features.blogs.fortune.cnn. com/2012/03/25/american-wine-fortune-1934/ (accessed Apr. 17, 2014). By 1935, American consumers drank nearly as much wine as they had prior to the start of national Prohibition, but many consumers continued to make their own wine or buy it from bootleggers. See Kliman, *Wild Vine*, 165. Virginia's consumption was the seventh-lowest per-capita consumption level of any state. See Robert

D. Rossi, "Post-Repeal Wine Consumption," *Wines & Vines* 16, No. 1 (Jan. 1935): 3; *Wines & Vines* 17, No. 6 (Jun. 1936): 17.

207. It was Missouri congressman Clarence Cannon. "Not one cent of Federal money will go to the fermentation industry," Cannon asserted. The Agriculture Department capitulated, scuttled the plans, sold the machinery, and withdrew from any viticultural activities dealing with wine for decades. *VWGJ* 16 (1989): 214; Pinney, *History of Wine*, 441; Adams, *Wines of America* (1985), 30–31; Colman, *Wine Politics*, 34-35; Lee and Lee, *Virginia Wine Country III*, 20.

208. Pinney, *Makers of American Wine*, 108. While these elements served to delay and minimize the Depression's impacts overall, Virginia experienced markedly lower rainfall levels, above-average unemployment, starving cattle, budget cuts, textile strikes, a tobacco glut, and rental problems with tenant farmers. Dabney, *Virginia*, 495–496; Ronald L. Heinemann, *Depression and New Deal in Virginia: The Enduring Dominion* (Charlottesville: University Press of Virginia, 1983).

209. Chesterfield Winery was owned by Adolph E. Horecka and had a storage capacity of 2,000 gallons. Virginia State Corporation Commission, *Annual Report of the State Corporation Commission of Virginia for the Year Ending 1936* (Richmond: Division of Purchase and Printing, 1936), 34:362; Frank Schoonmaker and Tom Marvel, *American Wines* (New York: Duell, Sloan and Pearce, 1941), 184–185; *Wines & Vines* (1949); Dabney, *Virginia*, 488; Hemphill, *Cavalier Commonwealth*, 450.

210. Dixie was owned by Albert L. Furman, Alec Meyers, R. J. Cheatwood, and Archie Straus. The former Dixie Wine Company building still stands at 1600 Valley Road, Richmond, Virginia. See Monticello Grape Growers Co-Operative Association, Inc., *Officers and Members, Certificate of Incorporation, Bylaws, Annual Report of President, Membership Marketing Agreement* (Charlottesville: Jan. 1935), 2–3, found in Special Collections, UVA; *Wines & Vines* 56 (1975): 20; Pinney, *History of Wine*, 467; California Vineyardists Association, Associated California Fruit Industries, *Wines & Vines* 33, No. 9-A (Sept. 15, 1952): 106, 107; *Wines & Vines* 45, No. 9-A (Sept. 30, 1964): 67; "Directory of the Wine Industry," *Wines & Vines* (1965): 71; Wines & Vines Yearbook of the Wine Industry, *Wines & Vines* (1949): 102. The winery was located at 415–421 17th Street in Richmond. One of nine buildings in a cold storage complex, the former building was converted into loft apartments in 2011. Old Homestead brand label (after it had been purchased by Southland Wine Company in Petersburg) was a scuppernong wine that boasted 20 percent alcohol by volume. "Foster Wheeler is Seeking Raygo," *The New York Times*, Jan. 10, 1974.

211. While Distillery No. 5 no longer produces wine, it remains Laird's sole producer of Applejack. Laird's nearly 230-year old "Applejack" was a staple beverage during the Revolutionary War, and George Washington asked for and was given the recipe. Adams, *Wines of America* (1985), 67. See Maggie Dutton, "Before there was Bourbon, there was Applejack," *Seattle Weekly*, Jan. 9, 2008; "Jersey Lightning," *New Jersey Monthly*, July 13, 2009; Senate Joint Resolution 460, Commending Laird and Company, Agreed to by the Senate, Feb. 25, 2009, agreed to by the House of Delegates, Feb. 27, 2009, 2009 Virginia General Assembly Session, found at: http://leg1.state.va.us/cgi-bin/legp504.exe?091+ful+SJ460ER+pdf (accessed Apr. 18, 2014); Pinney, *History of Wine*, 467; Walter Nichols, "Renewed Spirits," *The Washington Post*, Nov. 2, 2005, p. P1.

212. The company was overseen by Eleanor J. Rothwell and David M. Rothwell. The company's facilities were located at 516 South First Street, Charlottesville. *Virginia Record* 77 (Oct. 1955): 43.

213. The winery was located at 760 Holbrook Avenue and though no longer producing wine, a sign on the building today refers to it as "The Winery Building." Directory of the Wine Industry, *Wines & Vines* (Jan 1, 1965): 71; *Wines & Vines* 33, No. 9-A (Sept. 15, 1952): 106; Winfield Scott Downs, ed., *Encyclopedia of American biography: New series* (New York: American Historical Society, 1963), 32:119.

214. UPI, "Thomas Jefferson's Unsuccessful Idea May Yet Work in His State," *Ludington Daily News*, July 23, 1976, p. 9; Leon D. Adams, *The Wines of America* (Boston: Houghton Mifflin, 1973), 57, 59 (hereafter cited as Adams, *Wines of America* [1973]); *Wines & Vines* 33, No. 9-A (Sept. 15, 1952): 107; John J. Baxevanis, *The Wine Regions of America* (Stroudsburg, Pa.: Vinifera Wine Growers Journal, 1992), 157.

215. Some of the imported grapevine stock, now gone wild, can still be found at the front woodland edges

of the Hunter House property, much of which has been preserved as Nottoway Park. Most other sizeable residential buildings at this time—including Robert E. Lee's former residence at Arlington House—had wine cellars in which homemade wine or brandy was stored; or, at a minimum, cellars in which copious amounts of wine could be kept. Fairfax County, Virginia, "Historic Properties Rental Services: Hunter House," at http://www.fairfaxcounty.gov/parks/hprs/hunterhouse.htm (accessed Apr. 18, 2014); "Hunter House: From Residence to Historic Rental Property," *Resources* 6, No. 3 (Summer 2006), at http://issuu.com/fcpa/docs/resourcessu06/8 (accessed Apr. 18, 2014); http://testffx.fairfaxcounty.gov/parks/resources/Downloads/ResOURcesSu06.pdf (no longer working as of Apr. 17, 2014); interview by author with Eugene Scheel Dec. 23, 2013;Schoonmaker and Marvel, *American Wines*, 184, 188.

216. Monticello Grape Growers Co-Operative Association, Inc., *Officers and Members*, 2–3, 11, 15–16; *Wines & Vines* (1981).

217. The balance of the book included information on equipment, materials, fermentation, aging, and making wine. In a nod to posterity, Chamberlain managed to collect the only two bottles believed to be in existence from the former Monticello Wine Company. The bottles of "Extra Virginia Claret" Norton Red Wine were later donated to the Albemarle County Historical Society and the Jeffersonian Wine Grape Growers Society as the first relics for the society's museum in Historic Michie Tavern. He gave the wine as an "emblem of good will for [the Society's] revival of viticulture in Albemarle County." UPI, "Thomas Jefferson's Unsuccessful Idea May Yet Work in His State," *Ludington Daily News*, July 23, 1976, p. 9; Boar's Head Inn Press Release, The Boar's Head Grape Vine Press, Mar. 1982, Papers of the Jeffersonian Wine Grape Growers Society, UVA. Letter to the Albemarle County Historic Society from Bernard P. Chamberlain, Honorary President, Mar. 1, 1982, Papers of the Jeffersonian Wine Grape Growers Society, UVA. See Bernard Peyton Chamberlain, *A Treatise on the Making of Palatable Table Wines: Recommended to Gentlemen, Especially in Virginia, for Their Own Use* (Charlottesville: Self-Published, 1931), 188.

218. Chamberlain quoted in Schoonmaker and Marvel, *American Wines*, 187.

219. Schoonmaker and Marvel, *American Wines*, 186-187.

220. Monticello Grape Growers Co-Operative Association, Inc., *Officers and Members*, 3, 13; Letter from Bernard P. Chamberlain to Dr. Freeman, Feb. 15, 1939, Papers of Bernard Chamberlain, Manuscript, 1810–1988, Special Collections, UVA.

221. The Association was perhaps the first wine trade organization to lobby the General Assembly and the newly created Alcoholic Beverage Commission to reduce taxes on wine sales and permit wine beverages with 12 percent alcohol to be classified as a "food" and regulated separately from other alcoholic beverages and fortified wines. In response, the ABC Board agreed to reduce taxes on Virginia wines made from Virginia grapes. See Adams, *Wines of America* (1973), 57; Schoonmaker and Marvel, *American Wines*, 188–198; Monticello Grape Growers Co-Operative Association, Inc., *Officers and Members*, 13.

222. Kliman, *Wild Vine*, 165; Hemphill, *Cavalier Commonwealth*, 342; Pinney, *History of Wine*, 470; Jean Gottman, *Virginia in Our Century* (Charlottesville: University Press of Virginia, 1969), 341–343; *Wines & Vines* 33, No. 9-A (Sept. 15, 1952): 143; Upshall, *History of Fruit Growing*, 142; Hedrick, *Grapes and Wines*, 192.

223. At least one writer has speculated that federal wine regulations were adopted, in no small part, in response to Geffen Industries' large-scale production of cheap wine. See Julia Flynn Siler, *The House of Mondavi: The Rise and Fall of an American Wine Dynasty* (New York: Penguin, 2008), Chapter 21, "Brothers, 2004"; Lawrence M. Fisher, "Marvin Sands, Winery's Chairman, Dies at 75," *The New York Times*, Aug. 31, 1999; Adams, *Wines of America* (1973), 58.

224. Adams, *Wines of America* (1973), 66; Siler, *House of Mondavi*; Constellation Brands, "Company History and Heritage of Constellation Brands," at http://www.cbrands.com/about-us/our-heritage (accessed Apr. 18, 2014).

225. The winery was located at 120 Pocahontas Street. In 1948, Sands purchased Mother Vineyard Winery, a historic Manteo, North Carolina, scuppernong winery, and moved its operations to Richard's Wine Cellar in Petersburg. Sands subsequently purchased a Patrick, South Carolina, vineyard and

winery, Tenner Brothers, in 1965 and, in 1976, Sands purchased Richmond's Southland Wine Company and California's Bisceglia Brothers Wine Company and winery. *See* Pinney, *History of Wine*, 256; *Wines & Vines* 33, No. 9-A (Sept. 15, 1952): 106; "North Carolina Growers Double Grape Acreage," *Star News*, June 12, 1972, p. 5; Siler, *House of Mondavi*; "Wine Company Buys Bisceglia," *Petersburg Progress Index*, Mar. 13, 1974.

226. Richard's produced several wines, each of which carried the names of the company that had initially bottled the wine, but were subsequently acquired by Canandaigua, including Mother Vineyard Wine Company, Southland Wine Company, Dixie Wine Company, , and K. C. Arey & Company. The winery produced including Kay-Cee Sherry, Virginia Lee American Peach Wine, Richards Blackberry Wine, Three Bears American Red Grape Wine, Big John Home Style American Red Grape Wine, Red Man American Red Grape Wine, Hostess Reserve American Red Grape Wine, Eleven Star American Grape Wine, Hoghead Apple Wine, Old Homestead American Scuppernong Wine, Golden Suppertime Wine, Peach Wine, Imperial Reserve Brand American Scuppernong Wine, Adams Apple Wine, Boar's Head Apple Wine, Imperial Brand Apple Wine, and more. Richard's Wine Cellars produced "Old Mr. Mack," "Old Duke," "Sun Ray," "Old Maude," "Red Man," "Parade," "Mother Vineyard Scuppernong," and "Suppertime," among others. Southland was acquired in 1974, Dixie in 1975. The winery also offered "Mother Vineyard Southern Scuppernong," a very sweet pink port-style white wine. See *Wines & Vines* 45, No. 9-A (Sept. 30, 1964): 67; labels in the hands of the author; *VWGJ* 9, No. 4 (Winter 1982): 247; "From Virginia's Vineyards: Some Surprising Little Wines," *The Washington Post*, Nov. 9, 1981, p. 1.

227. The brand currently sells about two million cases annually. The brand is available in 13.9 percent and 18 percent alcohol by volume. As Thomas Pinney has noted, the name of the winery was "Richard's," while the name of the wine was "Richards" without an apostrophe. Fisher, "Marvin Sands," 18; Richard's Wild Irish Rose Commercial on YouTube at http://www.youtube.com/watch?v=Pu8Ot-VDkk4k (accessed Apr. 18, 2014); Pinney, *History of Wine*, 256, 461–462; Julian Kingsley and Karen Bachman, *Insiders' Guide to North Carolina's Outer Banks, 30th Anniversary Edition* (Guilford, Conn.: Insiders' Guide, 2009), 196.

228. The Sands family acquired the Guild in 1991. Sands used the "Virginia Dare" name for a "complete line" of wine products, including generic white wine, a Labrusca wine, and blackberry wine, each of which were bottled at Canadiagua. The scuppernong wine was subsequently produced at the Tenner Brothers winery in South Carolina. Adams, *Wines of America* (1973), 67; Fisher, "Marvin Sands," 18; Adams, *Wines of America* (1973), 59, 111; Pinney, *History of Wine*, 462.

229. Adams, *Wines of America* (1973), 66.

230. Pinney, *History of Wine*, 256; AP, "Company News: Canandaigua Wine To Cut 20% of Jobs," *The New York Times*, Nov. 19, 1988.

231. Pinney, *History of Wine*, 256.

232. As noted in Raymond V. Olszewski, *A Taste of Prince William County*, little is known of John Sciutto, save several The Washington Post news articles that were produced between 1953 and 1958. Sciutto formed "Sciutto Properties, Inc." "Vintner Sciutto Dies In Manassas Crash," *The Washington Post & Times Herald*, Feb. 16, 1958, p. A3; Olszewski, *Taste of Prince William County*, 75.

233. "The Ladies Get Chilbains In Ancient Grape Gavotte," *The Washington Post & Times Herald*, Oct. 30, 1955, p. E2. Sciutto also imported Norton grapes, but it is unclear whence they were procured. Sciutto evidently sold his wines for $0.98 per bottle, or $11.50 per case. Olszewski, *Taste of Prince William County*, 78; "Vintner Sciutto Dies," A3; "Grapes Stomped Italian Style in Ceremonies at Bull Run," *The Washington Post*, Nov. 3, 1953, p. 21; Sciutto wine bottle in author's hands.

234. One reporter noted that the hilarious and awkwardly sensuous sight of women crushing grapes was apparently so intense that men "risked blindness—refusing for long periods to blink their eyes." Sciutto selected his stomping participants from across Northern Virginia. See "The Ladies Get Chilbains In Ancient Grape Gavotte," E2; Olszewski, *Taste of Prince William County*, 79–80.

235. Responding to one inquisitive reporter who suggested Sciutto use a crushing machine instead, John Sciutto replied, "Mashing machine? What do you mean mashing machine? We use feet, pretty girls' feet, to crush 'em." Once the last flashbulb had flashed, however, Sciutto did, however, use a hand-op-

erated crushing machine out of the eye of the journalists. He evidently brought the crushing machine with him when he immigrated to the United States. See Aubrey Graves, "You Handle Grapes Just So to Give Wine its Bouquet," *The Washington Post*, July 5, 1953, p. B2; "It's a Lot of Fun, This Making Wine at Bull Run," *The Washington Post & Times Herald*, Oct. 25, 1954, p. 22; Olszewski, *Taste of Prince William County*, 83; "Grapes Stomped Italian Style in Ceremonies at Bull Run," *The Washington Post*, Nov. 3, 1953, p. 21; "The Ladies Get Chilbains In Ancient Grape Gavotte," E2; "Vintner Sciutto Dies In Manassas Crash," A3.

236. While he persuaded one artistic son to relocate to Virginia, the son quickly returned to Italy even though his father had enlarged his home and introduced him to important D.C. artists. See "John Leaves Choice Toast to Yule He'll Spend Abed," *The Washington Post & Times Herald*, Dec. 16, 1956, p. E2.

237. "John Leaves Choice Toast to Yule He'll Spend Abed," E2.

238. The wreck was caused by a soldier who attempted to pass two cars on the two-lane road. "Vintner Sciutto Dies In Manassas Crash," A3; Olszewski, *Taste of Prince William County*, 74.

239. Earl D. Schnell served as winemaker. Wines & Vines Annual Directory Issue, *Wines & Vines* (1960): 100.

240. Apr. 1958 letter from Urban Westenberger to the A&TTD Cincinnati Office, reprinted in *VWGJ* (Summer 1977): 339.

241. Despite these high times, Westenberger was not without his setbacks. In Aug. 1959, a laboratory analysis found that Westenberger's "Virginia Burgundy" had "an extremely high total acid content" and it was condemned by the Virginia ABC. Despite this setback, he had a bottle approved three weeks later. *VWGJ* (Summer 1977): 339.

242. Inspectors found the area where wine was made to be dirty with unscreened windows, improper disposal of waste, a nonprotected water supply, and filled with chicken tracts and fruit flies. In 1963, Westenberger applied for federal permits to allow his manufacturing of wine as head of a household rather than as a commercial enterprise. *See VWGJ* (Summer 1977): 340–341.

243. In Westenberger's small mausoleum, he placed two glass coffins to house the bodies of his parents. The mausoleum, once a center for local partying, was badly vandalized and partially burned. Today, the site is rumored to be haunted. It remains unclear as to the whereabouts of his parent's bodies. See Pinney, *History of Wine,* 287; L. B. Taylor, Jr., *The Big Book of Virginia Ghost Stories* (Mechanicsburg, Pa.: Stackpole Books, 2010), 98–99; *VWGJ* (Summer 1977): 336.

244. Anthony Dias Blue, *American Wine: A Comprehensive Guide* (New York: Harper & Row, 1988), 479; *Wines & Vines* 45, No. 9-A (Sept. 30, 1964): 67; Letter from Bernard P. Chamberlain to Dr. Freeman, Feb. 15, 1939, Special Collections, UVA; Lee and Lee, *Virginia Wine Country III*, 23; Upshall, *History of Fruit Growing*,143.

245. Monticello Grape Growers Co-Operative Association, Inc., "Report of Bernard P. Chamberlain, President," Jan. 18, 1936, p. 7.

# Chapter 3 Notes

1. Hilda Gabriel Lee and Allan E. Lee, *Virginia Wine Country* (White Hall, Va.: Betterway Publications, 1988), 53.
2. Ken Ringle, "Businessman Starts Chateau in Virginia," *Tri-City Herald*, October 10, 1976.
3. Though the economic investment merited a per-bottle price more than twice its selling price of $2.90, Raney priced his first offering of 113 cases of Seyval Blanc white wine at $2.90 per bottle to stay competitive. By 1976, Farfelu's vineyard had grown to 3,000 vines and, by the mid-1980s, the vineyard had grown to seven acres. As constructed, Raney located the winery in a converted 1860s barn and horse stable, where he offered guests a host of activities, including bocce ball and horseshoes. Ringle, "Businessman Starts Chateau in Virginia," 34; Vinifera Wine Growers Association (hereinafter cited as "VWGA"), *Vinifera Wine Growers Journal* (hereafter cited as "*VWGJ*") 1, no. 1 (Spring 1974): 53; Lee and Lee, *Virginia Wine Country*, 53; "Harvest time sparkles at Virginia's wineries," *The Washington Times*, September 28, 2005; VWGA, *The Wine Exchange: The Vinifera Wine Growers Newsletter* (July 1994), 13.
4. "Morris Levin Businessman," *The Washington Post*, January 30, 2007.
5. Ellen Robertson, "R. de Treville Lawrence III dies at age 91," *Richmond Times-Dispatch*, January 30, 2007; *VWGJ* 5, no. 1 (Spring 1978): 35.
6. Lawrence would later state at a wine conference, "We could argue all day, all week, all year about the comparative taste qualities of wines made from different grapes, and probably get nowhere…[B]ut there is no disputing in the market place, the prices on the bottles in the wine stores tell the clear story: Vinifera wines bring the highest prices." "Living: Shaking California's Throne," *Time*, November 21, 1977; Daniel C. Riker, "Small Wine Industry Underway in the East," *Ludington Daily News*, January 22, 1975, p. 16; *VWGJ* 5, no. 1 (Spring 1978): 24–30.
7. Lawrence continually invited guests to tour Highbury to learn about grape growing techniques for free. Guests usually left with a bottle of Highbury vintage. Lawrence, later president of the Rockley Farm Trust, a private preservation organization, was also heavily involved in attempts to preserve land in Fauquier County. Lawrence moved to Marietta, Georgia, in 1997 and died of pneumonia in 2007 at the age of 91. "Morris Levin Businessman," *The Washington Post*; Robertson, "R. de Treville Lawrence III dies at age 91," *Richmond Times-Dispatch*; *VWGJ* 1, no. 1 (Spring 1974): 53; Riker, "Small Wine Industry Underway in the East," 16; Drena Culbertson, "State vineyards getting a push," *The Free Lance–Star*, May 5, 1975; *VWGJ* 11, no. 5 (Spring 1985), 58.
8. Ellen Crosby, "She Vinified, Testified and Changed the Law," *The Washington Post*, June 20, 2007, Arts & Living section; *VWGJ* 1, no. 1 (Spring 1974): 52.
9. The organization fostered communication among research institutions in other states by visiting multiple state agricultural colleges in Florida, Georgia, and South Carolina. The VWGA supported any effort to increase education and cultivation of grapes, be they vinifera, French-American, or table grapes, whether for fun or profit. *VWGJ* 1, no. 1 (Spring 1974): 52–54; Laura Boswell, "Winemaking Assumes Festive Air in Region," *The Washington Times*, September 18, 2003; *VWGJ* 2, no. 1 (Spring 1975): 1; *VWGJ* 5, no. 1 (Spring 1978): 1; *VWGJ* 2, no. 1 (Fall 1974): 6; Culbertson, "State vineyards getting a push," 13; *VWGJ* 3, no. 3 (Fall 1976): 201.
10. Courses were held in The Plains, Charlottesville, Winchester, and Middleburg. Personalities included Dr. Konstantin Frank, author Leon D. Adams, Carl W. Haeseler (Pennsylvania State University), A. D. Webb (University of California, Davis), Donald H. Petersen (plant pathologist), John P. Tomkins (Cornell University), Dr. Harold P. Olmo (University of California), professor Cornelius S. Ough (Chair, Viticulture & Oenology, University of California, Davis), Boris J. Stojanovic (University of Mississippi), Dr. Helmut Becker (Geisenheim Institute of Viticulture). To assist with collecting knowledge about planting vinifera along the East Coast, the *VWGJ* also encouraged readers to experiment with grape planting and to report the results. The *VWGJ* was published quarterly beginning in 1976 and, by the mid-1980s, it had become the oldest wine periodical in the nation outside of California. *VWGJ* 13, no. 1 (Spring 1986): 13; *VWGJ* 1, no. 1 (Spring 1974): 52; *VWGJ* 2, no. 2 (Fall 1975): 44–45; *VWGJ* 2, no. 1 (Spring 1976): 44; *VWGJ* 5, no. 1 (Spring 1978): 45; *VWGJ* 11, no. 2

(Summer 1984): 125; "Morris Levin Businessman" *The Washington Post*; Fauquier Historical Society, "History of Virginia's Wine," Your Guide to Warrenton, Va.; http://www.reocities.com/Wellesley/ Garden/1077/vawinehistory.html; *VWGJ* 15, no. 3 (Fall 1988): 141–142.

11. The VWGA spoke out against highway interchanges and development, and assisted efforts to preserve historic sites and Manassas National Battlefield Park. Another article suggested that, "[w]ith a vineyard, [one] could develop a tidy farm enterprise on a few acres, make all the wines for his own table at a few cents a bottle, earn a profit from the surplus grapes, and insure for his family the protection of their green areas from development and a happy nest egg." With the construction of new interstate highways, airports, and recreational lakes pushing their way across Virginia's scenic terrain and raising land values, the VWGA noted its willingness to "help any public spirited people or groups in any way it can to help stop uncontrolled mass-movement and mass-development." *VWGJ* 15, no. 4 (Winter 1988): 279; *VWGJ* 4, no. 4 (Winter 1977): 464–465; Ringle, "Businessman Starts Chateau in Virginia," 34; *VWGJ* 1, no. 2 (Fall 1974): 51.

12. It is notable that, unlike the wine industry, which takes years to produce vines, the United States' beer industry recovered relatively quickly following Prohibition's repeal, largely due to the ability of hop crops to be grown in one year's time. *VWGJ* 1, no. 1 (Spring 1974): 1; *VWGJ* 1, no. 2 (Fall 1974): 1.

13. At the time, VWGA estimated that wine imports were approximately $300 million to $500 million per year, and that American farmers could provide 80 percent of this amount. The VWGA reported that, between 1972 and 1976, total American wine imports jumped from 29 million gallons to 44 million gallons. Not everyone was surprised at the USDA's resistance to growing vinifera grapes. One English grower who toured Virginia vineyards in 1980, Arthur Woods, wrote in the *Vinifera Wine Growers Journal*, "What I find even more amazing is that the Vinifera Wine Growers Association should be surprised by this attitude of the USDA. It is a rare government department that shows initiative and flair. It might be argued that such attitudes endanger promotion. For let it be remembered that your average civil servant throughout the world is concerned less with the pursuit of truth than the avoidance of error." *VWGJ* 1, no. 1 (Spring 1974): 1; *VWGJ* 1, no. 2 (Fall 1974): 1; Culbertson, "State vineyards getting a push," 13; *VWGJ* 5, no. 1 (Spring 1978): 1; *VWGJ* 2, no. 1 (Spring 1975): 7; *VWGJ* 7, no. 3 (Fall 1980): 177.

14. Riker, "Small Wine Industry Underway in the East," 16; Letter from USDA Administrator T. W. Edminster to Lawrence, May 1, 1975; *VWGJ* 2, no. 1 (Spring 1975): 3, 7.

15. The USDA's concerns may be interpreted as borderline extreme in hindsight, but, given the times, they were valid and help explain why the pace of Virginia vineyard planting later fell behind the pace of new winery development. The VWGA brought its concerns to the attention of Georgia senator Herman Talmadge, chairman of the Senate Committee on Agriculture and Forestry, who subsequently issued a September 1975 letter to the chairman of the Subcommittee on Agricultural Appropriations, Wyoming senator Gale McGree, urging McGree to "…give due consideration to this problem…" by updating research data and considering the VWGA's requests. The VWGA, mindful of Talmadge's and McGree's politically conservative sentiments, emphasized that they were not in pursuit of additional funding for the USDA, which might result in a larger bureaucracy; rather, they merely sought to reallocate funds to grape research. In March 1975, after lobbying senior members of the U.S. Senate, VWGA president John Berna testified before a United States senate committee asking them to restore the USDA's viticultural and oenological research programs. As in prior attempts to go above the USDA's head, the matter was referred back to the USDA without action. Letter from USDA administrator T. W. Edminster to R. Treville Lawrence, May 1, 1975; *VWGJ* 2, no. 1 (Spring 1975): 3–5, 7; Letter from acting USDA-ARS administrator Ralph J. McCracken, to R. Treville Lawrence; *VWGJ* 2, no. 2 (Fall 1975): 6–8.

16. This is not to say that Virginia Tech did not offer courses in oenology; indeed, beginning as early as 1975, the institution offered a Virginia Grape Short Course in grape growing. By 1979, the course's attendance had doubled, but as one Virginia Tech grape student lamented, Virginia Tech did not encourage vinifera grape growing: "In all honesty the course at VPI on grapes did not encourage the growing of Vinifera grapes. Of course, the sad thing was that the instructors were from New York, Pa. and Ohio. No one from Virginia seemed to have anything to say." This is not to say Virginia Tech

faculty did not experiment with vinifera on their own. Indeed, at least one professor, Dr. Karl Hereford, assisted Blacksburg's MJC Vineyards in the late 1970s and early 1980s with grafting vinifera grapevines. In 1981, VPI began offering the short course at the Dulles Airport Marriott, discussing vintage practices, trellis systems, marketing, and development of cellars. In response to increasing demands for questions about wine grape growing, beginning in 1983, Virginia Tech began offering two-day short courses for their agricultural extension agents, which covered the industry, site selection, training systems, varieties, and production costs. This was at the behest of S. Mason Carbaugh. Ed Crews, "Drought was good for grapes," *The Free Lance–Star*, November 10, 1980, p. 6; *VWGJ* 5, no. 1 (Spring 1978): 49; *VWGJ* 5, no. 3 (Fall 1978): 124; *VWGJ* 6, no. 4 (Winter 1979): 208; *VWGJ* 7, no. 1 (Spring 1980): 3, 67; *VWGJ* 8, no. 3 (Fall 1981): 146; *VWGJ* 10, no. 1 (Spring 1983): 28; Virginia Winegrowers Advisory Board, *Status of the Virginia Wine Industry*, (Richmond, Va.: January 1989) 18–19, 35; Walker Elliot Rowe, *A History of Virginia Wine: From Grapes to Glass* (Charleston, SC: The History Press, 2009), 44–45.

17. The VWGA, whose position was "diametrically opposed" to that of the USDA, issued a letter to the USDA asking for $500,000—less than one quarter of one percent of the USDA's annual research and experimental budget—to be dedicated to viticultural research. The letter read, in part, "Worldwide, of all the fruit, nut and other horticultural crops, grapes are the most widely planted, cultivated and used. It just doesn't make sense that the United States Department of Agriculture does not have a substantive program which would make up for the many scores of years of lost wine growing technology." The VWGA also called on the department to publish an informative pamphlet to replace the USDA's sole viticultural pamphlet, "Growing American Bunch Grapes," as well as feature wine grape growing on the USDA's weekend television series, "Across the Fence." While it did provide a response later that month, USDA staff failed to placate the VWGA. Two months later, in December 1973, the VWGA petitioned the United States' secretary of agriculture, who expressed his satisfaction with the USDA's "low-key" approach, noting that "it would be inconsistent with our present organizational structure to establish a viticultural office to serve the needs of a single commodity." In effect, the VWGA's efforts would be relegated to the limited efforts of the USDA's Fruit and Nut Office, which experimented with one or two vines. *VWGJ* 1, no. 2 (Fall 1974): 2–3; *VWGJ* 2, no. 1 (Spring 1975): 1, 3; *VWGJ* 5, no. 4 (Winter 1978): 163; *VWGJ* 4, no. 1 (Spring 1977): 259; *VWGJ* 2, no. 1 (Spring 1976): 51; *VWGJ* 1, no. 1 (Spring 1974): 2.

18. In a small victory, however, Lawrence and Furness persuaded USDA representatives to attend a two-day VWGA-organized workshop held October 1974 at Paul Mellon's Kinloch Farm outside The Plains. The workshop included representatives from Virginia, Pennsylvania, the USDA, and the VWGA. Again, however, the USDA was adamant and "unconvinced that the nation needs a viticultural program"—attributable, as one attendee suggested, to "an attitude of 'Lingering Prohibition'" on the part of the USDA. "If we were to increase our research efforts to support the existing wine industry," wrote a staff scientist with the Fruit and Nut Office, "we would have to locate this effort in the Western Region rather than in the Eastern States. We must clearly separate the needs of the home owner in the East with the needs of the existing wine industry on the West Coast." This position was quickly reversed by a senior USDA official, claiming that no funds could be allocated towards any form of viticultural research venture. Undeterred by its failure to secure a meaningful commitment from the USDA, the VWGA in 1975 petitioned the U.S. Department of Health, Education, and Welfare (later known as the Department of Health and Human Services) and the National Institutes of Health to undertake a comprehensive research program into the effects of wine on health. The VWGA was convinced, based upon medical studies, that wine had a positive effect on health and that wine's elements should be examined. The VWGA also petitioned newly elected President Ronald Reagan in early 1981 to restore a viticulture office to the USDA. *VWGJ* 1, no. 1 (Spring 1974): 4; *VWGJ* 2, no. 1 (Spring 1975): 2; *VWGJ* 5, no. 1 (Spring 1978): 1; *VWGJ* 4, no. 1 (Spring 1977): 263; *VWGJ* 8, no. 2 (Summer 1981): 72.

19. *VWGJ* 4, no. 3 (Summer 1977): 383; *VWGJ* 6, no. 3 (Fall 1979): 130.

20. Though invited to attend, USDA and Virginia Tech representatives declined; the latter reportedly opposed the gathering. VDACS' Virginia Agricultural Opportunities Commission also issued a re-

port the following year that called for increased viticultural research as well as an updating of the state's wine regulations. *VWGJ* 5, no. 1 (Spring 1978): 2, 29, 35; *VWGJ* 6, no. 3 (Fall 1979): 130; *VWGJ* 6, no. 4 (Winter 1979): 226.

21. *VWGJ* 6, no. 3 (Fall 1979): 130; *VWGJ* 7, no. 3 (Fall 1980): 152; Lou Ann Whitton, "Virginia Wine Country: It's There for the Tasting," *Northern Virginian Magazine* (Summer 1985): 18.

22. In 1978, the General Assembly enacted a special law that permitted licensed wineries to make gifts of wine to friends, hospitality rooms, conventions, and for oenological research. Recognizing the health benefits of wine, the Virginia General Assembly approved the sale and service of wine in hospitals in 1977. The commonwealth was the third state to authorize wine service to patients upon the approval of their doctors. Portsmouth General Hospital was reported to be the first to apply for an ABC license to sell wine in hospital rooms. Gifts of wine may be made by licensed wineries to friends, samples, educational programs, research, conventions, hospitality rooms. This total included $190 per year for a winery license (limited to 5,000 gallons), $450 per year to sell wine to a store, $40 per year to sell to consumers at the winery itself. If a winery produces more than 5,000 gallons, an additional $1,500 must be paid. *VWGJ* 4, no. 3 (Summer 1977): 365; *VWGJ* 5, no. 3 (Fall 1978): 130; *VWGJ* 4, no. 3 (Summer 1977): 365; *VWGJ* 5, no. 3 (Fall 1978): 130; *VWGJ* 5, no. 4 (Winter 1978): 164; Address delivered by Leon D. Adams at the Second Southeastern Winegrowing Conference, March 24, 1979, Spartanburg, S.C., reprinted in *VWGJ* 6, no. 2 (Summer 1979): 60; *VWGJ* 6, no. 3 (Fall 1979): 174.

23. This was a proposition supported by VDACS commissioner S. Mason Carbaugh two years earlier. The VWGA worked with Warrenton attorney Robin C. Gulick to develop a law. By 1979, Fairfax attorney B. Vandenburg Hall attempted to draft a modern farm winery law. *VWGJ* 6, no. 2 (Summer 1979): 64; *VWGJ* 5, no. 1 (Spring 1978): 45; *VWGJ* 6, no. 3 (Fall 1979): 174; Speech by A. E. Kileen at the Wineries Unlimited Conference, November 28, 1979, Lancaster, PA (reprinted in *VWGJ* 7, no. 1 (Spring 1980): 13.

24. *VWGJ* 7, no. 3 (Fall 1980): 203; VWGA, *The Wine Exchange* (July 1994), 13; Archie Smith, Jr., "A Virginian Assays his '80 Vintage," *Wines & Vines*, 1981; *Boar's Head Grape Vine Press* 5 (October-November), 1981.

25. The General Assembly did not, however, limit the licensing fees to only that charged by the commonwealth under § 4-38 of the Code of Virginia. Local governments could charge license taxes on wineries, which made the establishment of small wineries economically unfeasible. Letter to Gerald E. Fisher, Chairman of the Albemarle County Board of Supervisors from John O. Sherman, Capt. USN Ret., Chermont Vinyeard, September 8, 1981, Papers of the Jeffersonian Wine Grape Growers Society, University of Virginia.

26. Many growers credited the law with making Virginia "the easiest state in the country to make wine in." The VWGA renamed itself the Atlantic Seaboard Wine Association (ASWA) in 2008 and, while keeping the same grapevine logo and long-stated objectives of the original association, the new ASWA placed greater emphasis on winemaking along the East Coast. Whitton, "Virginia Wine Country: It's There for the Tasting," 18; "Fine Wines From Virginia Realize a Jeffersonian Dream," *Baltimore Sun*, October 16, 1983, reprinted in *VWGJ* 10, no. 4 (Winter 1983): 268; Linda Jones McKee, "Vinifera Organization Renames Itself," *Wines & Vines*, August 26, 2008.

27. Even after his retirement as director, Lawrence continued as a board member and in a consulting role. *VWGJ* 16, no. 2 (Summer 1989): 130.

28. Archie Smith's mother was born on an adjacent property. Hilda Gabriel Lee, Allan E. Lee, and Edwin Talley, *Virginia Wine Country Revisited* (Charlottesville, Va.: Hildesigns Press, 1995), 47–49.

29. Refusing to be caught in the vinifera vs. French-American grape debate then raging between East Coast winemakers, Archie Smith, Jr. valued both equally. The Smiths converted a former three-stall horse stable into a winery building and celebrated their first grape crush in the autumn of 1975. "112 Commercial Vineyards, 22 Farm Wineries Flourish in State," *Richmond Times-Dispatch*, September 18, 1983, L-23; *VWGJ* 1, no. 1 (Spring 1974): 53; *VWGJ* 6, no. 2 (Summer 1979): 115; Faye Chewning Weems, *Virginia Wineries: Your Complete Tour Guide* (Richmond, Va.: Auburn Mills, 2001), 128; Lee and Lee, *Virginia Wine Country*, 63–65; Suzanne Goldenson, *Vintage Places: A Con-*

*noisseur's Guide to North American Wineries and Vineyards* (Pittstown, NJ: Main Street Press, 1985), 92–93.

30. Blake Green, "Yes, Virginia, There Is Wine in Virginia," *San Francisco Chronicle,* February 23, 1981, p. 19; "Zonin Has 1st Virginia Wine," *Wines & Vines,* August 1981; Ringle, "Businessman Starts Chateau in Virginia," 34; VWGA, *The Wine Exchange* (July 1994), 13; "Smith Heads VA Food Processors," *Eastern Grape Grower & Winery News,* June 1981; Weems, *Virginia Wineries: Your Complete Tour Guide,* 128; "State on Verge of Wine Revolution," *Daily Progress,* October 17, 1982; Lee, Lee, and Talley, *Virginia Wine Country Revisited,* 47–49.

31. Green, "Yes, Virginia, There Is Wine in Virginia," 19; "112 Commercial Vineyards, 22 Farm Wineries Flourish in State," *Richmond Times-Dispatch,* L-23; Jon Palmer, *Wineries of the Mid-Atlantic* (New Brunswick, NJ: Rutgers University Press, 1988), 196.

32. Twelve years later, in 1988, Governor Gerald Baliles paid a personal visit to Meredyth, which highlighted the important role the winery played in the reestablishment of the Virginia wine industry. Weems, *Virginia Wineries: Your Complete Tour Guide,* 128; Lee and Lee, *Virginia Wine Country,* 63–66; Smith, Jr., "A Virginian Assays his '80 Vintage," *Wines & Vines;* "Business Briefs," *Northern Virginian Magazine* (Summer 1985): 15; "Of Vineyards and Visits," *The Washington Post,* September 11, 1981; Rowe, *A History of Virginia Wine: From Grapes to Glass,* 23–24.

33. Rowe, *A History of Virginia Wine: From Grapes to Glass,* 25.

34. Lee and Lee, *Virginia Wine Country,* 63–66; Ringle, "Businessman Starts Chateau in Virginia," 34.

35. Rowe, *A History of Virginia Wine: From Grapes to Glass,* 25; Weems, *Virginia Wineries: Your Complete Tour Guide,* 128.

36. "Archie Smith, 78, Virginia Vintner," *The Washington Post,* September 26, 1998; "Smith Heads VA Food Processors," *Eastern Grape Grower & Winery News;* Boar's Head Grape Vine Press 5 (October–November 1981); "112 Commercial Vineyards, 22 Farm Wineries Flourish in State," *Richmond Times-Dispatch,* L-23; Lee and Lee, *Virginia Wine Country,* 63–66.

37. Lee, Lee, and Talley, *Virginia Wine Country Revisited,* 47–49; Adam Bernstein, "Self-Taught Winemaker Pioneered Loudoun Industry," *The Washington Post,* January 20, 2009.

38. Cathy Jett, "Future Rosy for Virginia's Wineries," *The Free Lance–Star,* June 19, 1987, Lifestyle section.

39. Lee and Lee, *Virginia Wine Country,* 66.

40. Kenan Heise, "Elizabeth Furness: At 75 Took Up Winemaking," *Chicago Tribune,* March 2, 1986.

41. The home was subsequently listed on the Virginia Landmarks Register. Lee and Lee, *Virginia Wine Country,* 74–77.

42. *VWGJ* 8, no. 1 (Spring 1981): 63; *Boar's Head Grape Vine Press* 3 (June–July 1981).

43. Sémillon is a white grape of unknown origin popular in Australia, South Africa, and France. Wine writer Walker Elliot Rowe notes that Furness insisted that the vines be planted as they arrived from the seller—including wrapped in plastic. On reflection, her farm manager and his staff replanted them. "112 Commercial Vineyards, 22 Farm Wineries Flourish in State," *Richmond Times-Dispatch,* L-23; Rowe, *A History of Virginia Wine: From Grapes to Glass,* 23–24.

44. Rumor has it that, at an early meeting between Dr. Konstantin Frank and Furness, Dr. Frank informed her that she was too old to begin grape growing. In response, Furness asked Dr. Frank his age, to which he replied that he was 75. Furness subsequently retorted, "I'm only 72." Palmer, *Wineries of the Mid-Atlantic,* 194; *Boar's Head Grape Vine Press* 3 (June–July 1981); Thomas Lippman "Virginia Has Some Surprising Wines—Now Looks For Markets," *The Washington Post,* November 9, 1981; Lee and Lee, *Virginia Wine Country,* 74–77; *VWGJ* 6, no. 2 (Summer 1979): 98; *VWGJ* 1, no. 1 (Spring 1974): 53; "112 Commercial Vineyards, 22 Farm Wineries Flourish in State," *Richmond Times-Dispatch,* L-23.

45. Apparently Furness sold them to Calvert Woodley Fine Wines & Spirits in Washington, D.C. They came to her and offered her top prices and bought out the entire first vintages. *VWGJ* 7, no. 1 (Spring 1980): 65; Rowe, *A History of Virginia Wine: From Grapes to Glass,* 24.

46. Worrall employed Allan Kinne as winemaker and, by 1998, Piedmont boasted 18 acres of Chardonnay, Cabernet Sauvignon, and Cabernet Franc grapes. *VWGJ* 13, no. 1 (Spring 1986): 59; Lee and

Lee, *Virginia Wine Country*, 74–77; Lee, Lee, and Talley, *Virginia Wine Country Revisited*, 55–56.

47. By the mid-2000s, Piedmont's vineyard comprised 26 acres. Weems, *Virginia Wineries: Your Complete Tour Guide*, 91.

48. Ampelography is the field of botany concerned with the identification and classification of grapevines. Culbertson, "State vineyards getting a push," *The Free Lance–Star*, May 5, 1975; *VWGJ* 1, no. 1 (Spring 1974): 53; Warren Rojas, "VA Wine, From the Ground Up," *Northern Virginia Magazine*, October 2008.

49. Charles Fenyvesi, "If It's a Sports Car or a Vineyard, I'll Take the Grapes Every Time," *The Washington Post*, September 1, 1985, C3.

50. *VWGJ* 1, no. 2 (Fall 1974): 6.

51. Some of her early class participants included Ingleside's Carl Flemmer and Oakencroft's Felicia Warburg Rogan. Fenyvesi, "If It's a Sports Car or a Vineyard, I'll Take The Grapes Every Time," C3; *Boar's Head Grape Vine Press* 3 (June–July 1981); Rowe, *A History of Virginia Wine: From Grapes to Glass*, 32.

52. Morton's refrigerator research led to her research demonstrating that "black goo," a disease affecting American grapevine rootstocks, was spreading in large measure due to vineyards selling vines infected with the fungus. This earned her the accolade for the name *Phaeoacremonium Mortoniae*. Morton also supports the controversial practice of high-density close spacing of vines. In some cases, she advocates twice as many vines per acre as is practiced at most other wineries. Dave McIntyre, "Meet Lucie Morton, Ampelographer," *The Washington Post*, October 12, 2010, Arts & Living section; Rojas, "VA Wine, From the Ground Up," *NVM*.

53. Lucie boasts clients in multiple states, including Minnesota, Texas, and Ohio. In Virginia, she has consulted for Middleburg's Boxwood Winery, La Crosse's Rosemont Vineyards and Winery, and the Eastern Shore's Chatham Vineyards. Rojas, "VA Wine, From the Ground Up," *Northern Virginia Magazine*; McIntyre, "Meet Lucie Morton, Ampelographer," *The Washington Post*.

54. Ingleside Plantation featured a circa-1834 manor home originally built as a boy's school and later used as a Civil War command post. The school, called Washington Academy, was named in honor of the first president. The property was subsequently used as a courthouse, a Civil War garrison, and a component of a dairy operation. Carl Flemer obtained a state historic landmarks register designation for the house in 1978. *VWGJ* 11, no. 3 (Fall 1984): 175; Rusty Dennen, "Plan to Look at Future—And Past," *The Free Lance–Star*, March 9, 1979, p. 15; Hilda Gabriel Lee and Allan E. Lee, *Virginia Wine Country III* (Charlottesville, Va.: Hildesigns Press, 2004), 158.

55. Beginning in 1949, Carl gradually converted the property from a dairy farm into a large wholesale nursery operation. Flemer's great-great-uncle served as the consul general in Bordeaux, France.

56. The winery celebrated its first harvest in 1980 and produced 10,000 gallons of Roxbury Red, Wirtland Rosé, and Seyval Blanc wines in its first year. The barn's hayloft transformed into a wine tasting room, and the former milking room was renovated into a storage room. "Northern Neck Vineyard Starts to Come Into Own," *Richmond Times-Dispatch*, April 27, 1981; Lee and Lee, *Virginia Wine Country III*, 159–160; Rusty Dennen, "Ripening: Ingleside Plantation Stakes its Reputation on the Vine," *The Free Lance–Star*, August 5, 1980, p. 13; Rusty Dennen, "Ingleside Uncorks its Wares," *The Free Lance–Star*, April 27, 1981, p. 15; "Winemaking Ripens in the Northern Neck," *The Washington Post*, June 10, 1983, C5.

57. Cathy Jett, "Vintage winemaker still looking for 'next big fad'," *The Free Lance–Star*, March 28, 2010; Cathy Jett, "Ingleside owner wins state grape award," *The Free Lance–Star*, May 13, 2009; "Winemaking Ripens in the Northern Neck," *The Washington Post*, C5; "Northern Neck Vineyard Starts to Come Into Own," *Richmond Times-Dispatch*; *Virginia Wine Journal* 22, no. 7 (February 2011): 1; "From Virginia's Vineyards: Some Surprising Little Wines," *The Washington Post*, November 9, 1981, p. 1.

58. John D. Clarke, "Winemaking expert Jacques Recht dies," *Richmond Times-Dispatch*, March 12, 2009; Lee and Lee, *Virginia Wine Country*, 169.

59. The catamaran's name, Anabla Atanabla, roughly translated, means "Abracadabra." The idea for the trip was fostered three years prior, when the couple agreed to build a boat, which took 15 months

to complete. "I made everything," Jacques recalled to a reporter. "The only thing I did not make was the sails." Dennen, "Ripening: Ingleside Plantation Stakes its Reputation on the Vine," *The Free Lance–Star*, August 15, 1980, p. 13; Rusty Dennen, "Abracadabra: They're Two for the Sea," *The Free Lance–Star*, August 27, 1980, p. 19; *VWGJ* 11, no. 3 (Fall 1984): 174; "Winemaking Ripens in the Northern Neck," *The Washington Post*, C5.

60. Dennen, "Abracadabra: They're Two for the Sea," 19.

61. Dennen, "Abracadabra: They're Two for the Sea," 19; Clarke, "Winemaking expert Jacques Recht dies," *Richmond Times-Dispatch*; Lee and Lee, *Virginia Wine Country*, 169.

62. Flemer subsequently offered Recht a furnished house, a car, a salary, and assistance (his son, Doug). Jett, "Vintage winemaker still looking for 'next big fad'," *The Free Lance–Star*; "Winemaking Ripens in the Northern Neck," *The Washington Post*, C5; *VWGJ* 11, no. 3 (Fall 1984): 174.

63. Dennen, "Ripening: Ingleside Plantation Stakes its Reputation on the Vine," 13.

64. By 1983, Ingleside produced 12,500 gallons annually and offered patrons 12 different wines. The winery's growing notoriety also prompted the Virginia Department of Tourism to invite Ingleside to participate in a special advertising campaign to promote Virginia wine. *Boar's Head Grape Vine Press* 12 (November–December 1982); *VWGJ* 11, no. 3 (Fall 1984): 175; "Area Wineries Harvest New Crop of Top Awards," *The Free Lance–Star*, July 30, 1984, p. 4; "Ingleside Wins Wine Trophy," *The Free Lance–Star*, August 6, 1984, p. 25; Dennen, "Ingleside Uncorks its Wares," 15; "Winemaking Ripens in the Northern Neck," *The Washington Post*, C5.

65. In 2002, Ingleside hired Bill Swain, a winemaker with extensive experience in California and Venezuela, as winemaker. In 2007, the American Wine Society bestowed on him its Award of Merit—the society's highest honor—in recognition of his work. "Jacques Recht," *The Free Lance–Star*, March 13, 2009; "New Grapes from the Vineyards of Ol' Virginia," *New York Daily News*, September 1983; Clarke, "Winemaking expert Jacques Recht dies," *Richmond Times-Dispatch*.

66. By the late 1980s, Ingleside boasted 53 acres of vinifera and French-American vines, and the winery experimented with more than 30 different varieties. The labels are "Reserve" and "Premium," both of which are traditional wines, and "Blue Crab" and "Chesapeake Wine Company," both of which are designed to pair easily with Chesapeake Bay seafood. In 2009, Doug Flemer was recognized by the Virginia Vineyard Association as its Wine Grower of the Year. He also received the organization's Gordon Murchie Lifetime Achievement Award. Lee and Lee, *Virginia Wine Country*, 170; Jett, "Vintage winemaker still looking for 'next big fad'," *The Free Lance–Star*.

67. La Abra means "the cove" in Spanish. "Grape Growing, Sense of Community, Both Thriving in Nelson County," *Virginia Wine Gazette*, Summer 1998, p. 13; Felicia Warburg Rogan, "Virginia Wine Line," *Charlottesville/Albemarle Almanac*, May 1985, p. 21.

68. Weems, *Virginia Wineries: Your Complete Tour Guide*, 34; Rogan, "Virginia Wine Line," May 1985, p. 21.

69. Lee and Lee, *Virginia Wine Country III*, 89; Palmer, *Wineries of the Mid-Atlantic*, 201–203.

70. In 1979, the Randels hired a young, energetic winemaker, Alan Kinne, who had previously worked at Michigan's Tabor Hill Vineyard before coming to Virginia. Kinne stayed with the Randels until the early 1980s, when he left to consult for numerous Virginia wineries, including Piedmont, Horton, Oasis, Ingleside, Lake Anna, and more, before arriving at Chrysalis Vineyards in 2010. Inne was succeeded by Jack Foster, the former winemaker at Ohio's Cedar Hill Wine Company, who stayed at Shenandoah until 1993. Lee and Lee, *Virginia Wine Country III*, 249–251; Lee and Lee, *Virginia Wine Country*, 248–250; Richard Leahy, "Thinking About Planting Chardonnay in the East?" *Vineyard & Winery Management* (September/October 1997): 28; Lee, Lee, and Talley, *Virginia Wine Country Revisited*, 195–197; *VWGJ* 6, no. 3 (Fall 1979): 154.

71. Weems, *Virginia Wineries: Your Complete Tour Guide*, 110–111.

72. Stevenson Whitcomb Fletcher, *A History of Fruit Growing in Virginia* (Staunton, Va.: Beverley Press, 1932), 4–6; Thomas Pinney, *History of Wine in America, Volume 1* (Berkeley, CA: University of California Press, 2005), 414; Leon D. Adams, *The Wines of America* (New York: McGraw-Hill, 65; U. P. Hedrick, *Grapes and Wines from Home Vineyards* (Oxford: Oxford University Press, 1945), 193.

73. Barboursville and Prince Michel, among others, later installed similar fans. Weems, *Virginia Wineries:*

*Your Complete Tour Guide*, 20.

74. Lee and Lee, *Virginia Wine Country*, 108–109.

75. Lee and Lee, *Virginia Wine Country*, 70–72.

76. The varieties were specifically selected to work well the property's loamy earth soil. Graeme Zielinski, "Neighbors Seek Peace, Owners Seek Growth; Winery Conflict Sours Some in Va.," *The Washington Post*, April 30, 2000; T. Rees Shapiro, "Dirgham Salahi, Virginia winery owner and Montessori school founder, dies at 81," *The Washington Post*, October 10, 2010; T. Rees Shapiro, "Dirgham Salahi, Virginia winery owner, dies," *The Washington Post*, October 7, 2010; *VWGJ* 10, no. 3 (Fall 1983): 182; Lee and Lee, *Virginia Wine Country*, 70–72; Weems, *Virginia Wineries: Your Complete Tour Guide*, 86.

77. *VWGJ* 7, no. 4 (Winter 1980): 279; *VWGJ* 10, no. 3 (Fall 1983): 182; Lee and Lee, *Virginia Wine Country*, 70–72.

78. *VWGJ* 10, no. 3 (Fall 1983): 182.

79. The wine was honored in 1997 by *Wine Enthusiast* magazine as one of the top 10 sparkling wines in the world. "Fine Wines From Virginia Realize a Jeffersonian Dream," *Baltimore Sun*, October 16, 1983, reprinted in *VWGJ* 10, no. 4 (Winter 1983): 266; Patrick Getlein, "Wine List: Selections from Northern Virginia's Winery Tours," *The Washington Post*, September 6, 1998; Weems, *Virginia Wineries: Your Complete Tour Guide*, 87; "Harvest time sparkles at Virginia's wineries," *Washington Times*, September 28, 2005; "Dirgham Salahi, Virginia winery owner, dies," *The Washington Post*; Lee and Lee, *Virginia Wine Country III*, 204–206.

80. "Dirgham Salahi, Virginia winery owner, dies," *The Washington Post*.

81. The trend began with several French champagne companies, which were soon joined by their Spanish, German, and Italian counterparts. "European Vintners Turn to U.S. for New Wineries," *USA Today*, October 6, 1982.

82. Based in Great Britain, Western American hoped to capitalize on the growing American wine market. The company also operated cattle farms in Tasmania and hotels in Fiji and built condominiums in Los Angeles. The Zonin Wine Company, based in Tuscany, held large holdings in the Chianti, Friuli, Piedmont, and Lombardy regions, as well as in Sicily. Ringle, "Businessman Starts Chateau in Virginia," 34; "Wine Company Planning Vineyard in Virginia," *The Dispatch*, 7; R. W. Apple, Jr., "Jefferson Gets His Wish: At Last, a Decent Bottle of Virginia Wine," *The New York Times*, September 13, 2000.

83. Ringle, "Businessman Starts Chateau in Virginia," 34.

84. Wine writers Lee and Lee note that Zonin was also a historic romantic, likely entranced by the possibility of following in the footsteps of another Italian, Philip Mazzei. Additionally, they note that Zonin wanted the property to give him an American bottling site in the event that wine import taxes were to increase. Zonin studied Virginia's climates and soils with Frank Bonnano, president of Francis A. Bonanno, Inc., of Miamisburg, Ohio, at the time Zonin's sole American importer. Nancy McKeon, "For Barboursville's vintner, wine and design bridge Old World and new," *The Washington Post*, November 28, 2009; Ringle, "Businessman Starts Chateau in Virginia," 34; Lee and Lee, *Virginia Wine Country*, 102; "Wine Company Planning Vineyard in Virginia," *The Dispatch*, 7; "Jefferson's Dream Coming True," *Atlantic Control Beverage Journal*, August 1981.

85. Western America Finance paid $800,000 for the estate. The house was constructed on the estate of his friend, Virginia governor and senator James Barbour. Apple, Jr., "Jefferson Gets His Wish: At Last, a Decent Bottle of Virginia Wine," *The New York Times*; Daniel C. Riker, "Thomas Jefferson's Unsuccessful Idea May Yet Work in His State," *Ludington Daily News*, July 22, 1976, p. 9; McKeon, "For Barboursville's vintner, wine and design bridge Old World and new," *The Washington Post*; "Jefferson's Dream Coming True," *Alcohol Control Beverage Journal*.

86. As Zonin himself remarked to a reporter, "[y]ou need something to say on a bottle of wine. You always want a story behind it whether it's true or not." Paschina would be voted Wine Person of the Year in 2002. Zonin's son, Enrico Zonin, would later remark to a reporter, "We chose Virginia because the Zonin family is not only interested in growing vines, but also focuses on the historical value of our properties—for example, the castles in Tuscany and in the Piedmont and in the Roman area in Friuli-Venexia-Giulia." Apple, Jr., "Jefferson Gets His Wish: At Last, a Decent Bottle of Virginia

Wine," *The New York Times*; Lee and Lee, *Virginia Wine Country III*, 49; "Barboursville Vineyards Now Fulfilling Dream Jefferson Once Held for Mazzei," *Virginia Wine Gazette*, Harvest 1998, p. 21; Elissa Vanaver, "Testing the Soil," *The Free Lance–Star*, August 16, 1978, p. 19; McKeon, "For Barboursville's vintner, wine and design bridge Old World and new," *The Washington Post*.

87.  "I'd like to see the Americans do it, and keep the thing in an American context," Treville Lawrence said of foreign efforts to grow grapes. "But it's equally beneficial to have European viticulture scientists giving us an opportunity to learn." Lee and Lee, *Virginia Wine Country III*, 50; Gary Emerling, "Virginia's vineyards mature," *The Washington Times*, September 21, 2008; Vanaver, "Testing the Soil," 19; Ringle, "Businessman Starts Chateau in Virginia," 34; "Barboursville Vineyards Now Fulfilling Dream Jefferson Once Held for Mazzei " *Virginia Wine Gazette*, 21.

88.  The vines were purchased from a vineyard nursery in western Maryland in June 1976, and ordered 19,000 to plant in spring 1977. The vines survived the very dry summer, only to be dealt a heavy blow that winter (1976–1977)—sustaining 121 days of temperatures below the freezing mark. By the vineyard's second year, Barboursville boasted 5,300 vines. The winery began offering 16,000 plants grafted onto rootstocks for vineyardists in 1977. Among the most successful first harvests was Cabernet Franc, which remains ranked among the best in the nation. *VWGJ* 4, no. 1 (Spring 1977): 260; *VWGJ* 4, no. 3 (Fall 1977): 388–391; "Wine Company Planning Vineyard in Virginia," *The Dispatch*, 7; Vanaver, "Testing the Soil," 19; Lee and Lee, *Virginia Wine Country*, 102.

89.  The clay, if not sufficiently trenched, can contribute to the fungal disease powdery mildew. Designed to help vines obtain water in times of draught and to avoid the onset of powdery mildew, the plow was designed to dig four feet into the soil. Rausse eventually purchased a bulldozer to accomplish a better result. Lee and Lee, *Virginia Wine Country*, 101–104; Weems, *Virginia Wineries: Your Complete Tour Guide*, 17; Rowe, *A History of Virginia Wine: From Grapes to Glass*, 44.

90.  The nursery grafted some 100,000 vines the first year and the grape nursery—Virginia's first since Prohibition's repeal—quickly sold out of its product. The nursery sold virus-free cuttings to several Virginia vineyards, including Meredyth and Oasis, which not only helped ensure their success, but also led to the establishment of a joint experimental program between Barboursville, VDACS, and Virginia Tech in 1978. The winery offered Chardonnay, Cabernet Sauvignon, Pinot Noir, White Riesling, Malvasia Bianca, Merlot, Cabernet Franc, and Gewürztraminer. "Fine Wines From Virginia Realize a Jeffersonian Dream," *Baltimore Sun*, October 16, 1983, reprinted in *VWGJ* 10, no. 4 (Winter 1983): 266; *VWGJ* 6, no. 1 (Spring 1979): 45; Rowe, *A History of Virginia Wine: From Grapes to Glass*, 42; Lee and Lee, *Virginia Wine Country III*, 68; *VWGJ* 5, no. 1 (Spring 1978): 37; *VWGJ* 5, no. 2 (Summer 1978): 89, 101; *VWGJ* 6, no. 3 (Fall 1979): 163; "Jefferson's Dream Coming True," *Alcohol Control Beverage Journal*.

91.  Rausse ignored the USDA's suggestions of growing muscadine grapes from North Carolina and low-quality varieties. Lee and Lee, *Virginia Wine Country*, 102; *VWGJ* 11, no. 3 (Fall 1984): 171.

92.  The cause of the fire was determined to be arson; perhaps an act of harassment by a local sheep farmer protesting against the ingenuity of the Barboursville enterprise. Insurance covered the building, but not the equipment. *VWGJ* 11, no. 3 (Fall 1984): 171; Lee and Lee, *Virginia Wine Country*, 101–104; *VWGJ* 4, no. 3 (Fall 1977): 388–391; *VWGJ* 6, no. 4 (Winter 1979): 187; Rowe, *A History of Virginia Wine: From Grapes to Glass*, 44; Lee and Lee, *Virginia Wine Country III*, 68.

93.  Goldenson, *Vintage Places: A Connoisseur's Guide to North American Wineries and Vineyards*, 86–87; *VWGJ* 13, no. 3 (Fall 1986): 259; Jeffersonian Wine Grape Growers Society, *Boar's Head Virginia Grapevine* 29 (Winter 1987); *Vineyard & Winery Management* (January/February 1987): 12; Lee and Lee, *Virginia Wine Country III*, 53; Weems, *Virginia Wineries: Your Complete Tour Guide*, 17; Barboursville Vineyards, "Our People: C-Ville Profiles Chef Melissa Close Hart," June 2010; Brian Chidester, "The Education of Melissa Close-Hart," *C-Ville*, June 22, 2010, News section; Apple, Jr., "Jefferson Gets His Wish: At Last, a Decent Bottle of Virginia Wine," *The New York Times*; McKeon, "For Barboursville's vintner, wine and design bridge Old World and new," *The Washington Post*.

94.  Paschina had served in various winemaking capacities in Italy and the United States. *Boar's Head Grape Vine Press* 3 (June–July 1981); *VWGJ* 11, no. 3 (Fall 1984): 173; Apple, Jr., "Jefferson Gets His Wish: At Last, a Decent Bottle of Virginia Wine," *The New York Times*; Dave McIntyre, "The Wine

Guy Visits Barboursville Vineyards," *Washingtonian*, November 8, 2007; Lee and Lee, *Virginia Wine Country III*, 50.

95. Paschina went on to experiment with other varieties and tore out others, including some of the original vines planted by Rausse that were producing inconsistent yields. Paschina was an advocate of tight vine spacing, and by the 2000s, Barboursville's vineyards were tightly planted—triple the density of the average American winery. At a wine tasting at Charlottesville's Boar's Head Inn a year after his arrival, Luca met his wife, Patricia Yetman. The two were married in front of the Barboursville ruins. Paschina had learned which grapes work well and which needed improvement; in years with poor weather or bad vintages, for example, Paschina declined to bottle wine. "That's what you have to do to keep your reputation," he said. Lee and Lee, *Virginia Wine Country III*, 50–51; Apple, Jr., "Jefferson Gets His Wish: At Last, a Decent Bottle of Virginia Wine," *The New York Times*; Zinie Chen Sampson, "Virginia offers winery destinations," *The Southern Illinoisan*, October 23, 2007; Walker Elliot Rowe, *Wandering Through Virginia's Vineyards* (Baltimore, MD: Apprentice House, 2006), 193.

96. Lee and Lee, *Virginia Wine Country*, 141; the original Colle was demolished in the 1930s, and portions of the structure were used to rebuild nearby Michie Tavern. The Woodwards subsequently built a new house on the foundation of Mazzei's former residence. *Boar's Head Grape Vine Press* 3 (June–July 1981); Weems, *Virginia Wineries: Your Complete Tour Guide*, 32.

97. Simeon's first vineyards were one acre of Cabernet Sauvignon and Chardonnay. "Toast to Local Wines Coming Up Saturday," *Daily Progress*, October 12, 1981, p. 1; Frances MacLean, "Through the Grapevine of History," *Country*, February 1982, p. 4; "A Vintner's Vintner," *Virginia Living*, January 2012; Lee and Lee, *Virginia Wine Country*, 141–142.

98. Rausse produces Chardonnay, Cabernet Sauvignon, Merlot, and Cabernet Franc wines, among others, using grapes grown on-site and from properties under lease elsewhere. Rausse hailed from the Vicenza area of Italy and served as a consultant for, among others, Kluge, Afton Mountain, First Colony, Blenheim, Oak Crest, Stone Mountain, and White Hall. Rowe, *A History of Virginia Wine: From Grapes to Glass*, 40; "A Vintner's Vintner," *Virginia Living*; Lee and Lee, *Virginia Wine Country III*, 68–69; *VWGJ* 4, no. 3 (Fall 1977): 390; Ringle, "Businessman Starts Chateau in Virginia," 34; *VWGJ* 11, no. 3 (Fall 1984): 170.

99. Goldenson, *Vintage Places: A Connoisseur's Guide to North American Wineries and Vineyards*, 89; Robert Brickhouse, "Winegrower Joachim Hollerith Carries on Family Tradition," *Daily Progress*; *VWGJ* 7, no. 3 (Fall 1980): 179; Lee and Lee, *Virginia Wine Country*, 138; *VWGJ* 5, no. 2 (Summer 1978): 58; Ray K. Saunders, "A Touch of the Old World," *Culpeper Star-Exponent*.

100. Hollerith's family not only owned a vineyard in Germany at the time, but his ancestors had cultivated vineyards in southwest Germany along the Rhine since 1687. Brickhouse, "Winegrower Joachim Hollerith Carries on Family Tradition," *Daily Progress*; "Area Vintners Await Promising Harvest," *Daily Progress*, September 5, 1982; Vanaver, "Testing the Soil," 19; Saunders, "A Touch of the Old World," *Culpeper Star-Exponent*; *VWGJ* 7, no. 3 (Fall 1980): 179; "Winemaker Finds Success in Returning to Roots," *Charlottesville Business Journal*, June 1993.

101. Brickhouse, "Winegrower Joachim Hollerith Carries on Family Tradition," *Daily Progress*; Vanaver, "Testing the Soil," 19; *VWGJ* 5, no. 2 (Summer 1978): 58.

102. The vineyard was planted with distance between roads, taut wires, and pruning similar to European styles. *VWGJ* 13, no. 1 (Spring 1986): 30; *VWGJ* 7, no. 3 (Fall 1980): 180; Saunders, "A Touch of the Old World," *Culpeper Star-Exponent*; *VWGJ* 7, no. 3 (Fall 1980): 179; *VWGJ* 8, no. 3 (Summer 1981): 139; *VWGJ* 11, no. 4 (Winter 1984): 230; Lee and Lee, *Virginia Wine Country*, 138.

103. Hollerith would be replaced by Walter Luchsinger, then winemaker at Piedmont Vineyards.

104. Before arriving in the United States, Leducq had served at the helm of a successful linen and uniform business. To finance the purchase, Leducq joined with Culpeper businessman Norman B. Martin to form "VAVIN, Inc.," in 1983, and hired Joachim Hollerith as senior partner and general manager. The winery's namesake was in honor of Leducq's friend and exiled son of the King of Poland, Michel; however, the name also honors several men sharing the "Michel" name, including Byzantium emperor Michel II, who promoted the planting of grapevines in Europe. *VWGJ* 11, no. 5 (Spring 1985): 5; *VWGJ* 10, no. 1 (Spring 1983): 52; Palmer, *Wineries of the Mid-Atlantic*, 217; Weems, *Virginia*

*Wineries: Your Complete Tour*, 38–39.

105. Following the purchase, Leducq reinstated Hollerith as Rapidan's winemaker in an effort to maintain Rapidan's distinct German-style wines. Leducq also hired winemaker Allan Kinne to focus on Bordeaux-style wines at Prince Michel. "Right Spot Still Eludes Virginia Wine Pioneers," *Wine Spectator*, November 1982; Suzanne Hamlin, "Jefferson's vision finally bears fruit," *The New York Times*, September 15, 1996, Travel section; *VWGJ* 11, no. 5 (Spring 1985): 5; Lee and Lee, *Virginia Wine Country*, 134–135; Anthony Dias Blue, *American Wine: A Comprehensive Guide* (New York: Harper and Row, 1988); "Prince Michel...More than a Vineyard, It's a Trip to France," *Virginia Wine Gazette*, Harvest 1998, p. 23; Palmer, *Wineries of the Mid-Atlantic*, 217.

106. Later, the winery offered a full-service casual-elegant restaurant, The Grille, which featured cuisine paired with Virginia wines. Lee and Lee, *Virginia Wine Country*, 97, 135; Greg Ricks, "Old Dominion 'shakin up' grape and wine industry," *Bulletin of the Virginia Department of Agriculture and Consumer Services*, October 1986, p. 6; *VWGJ* 14, no. 4 (Winter 1987); "Prince Michel...More than a Vineyard, It's a Trip to France," *Virginia Wine Gazette*, 23; Judy Colbert, "Makeover for Prince Michel," *Wines & Vines*, November 2007.

107. Leducq purchased the historic 42-acre Ehlers Estate, which later grew certified organic Bordeaux varieties. Lee, Lee, and Talley, *Virginia Wine Country Revisted*, 105; Lee and Lee, *Virginia Wine Country III*, 96.

108. Colbert, "Makeover for Prince Michel," *Wines & Vines*; "Spice of Life," *Culpeper Star-Exponent*, May 6, 2007.

109. Bronfman's grapes grown there had been vinified at Seagram's Gold Seal Winery in Hammondsport, New York. "Viticulture: Seagram Co. Vineyard May Be State's Largest," *Daily Progress*, 1982, F1; "Of Vineyards and Visits," *The Washington Post*.

110. "Paul Masson Winery Buys Farm in Albemarle County," *The Free Lance–Star*, January 4, 1980, p. 15; *VWGJ* 6, no. 4 (Winter 1979): 208; Felicia Warburg Rogan, "Virginia Wine Line," *Charlottesville/Albemarle Almanac*, (March 1984): 3; *Boar's Head Grape Vine Press* 17 (Winter 1983–1984).

111. Paul Mierzejewski would later serve as vice president and treasurer of the Virginia Vineyards Association, conduct several seminars, and serve as vineyard consultant to Annefield Vineyards and Delfosse Vineyards & Winery. Annefield Vineyards, "Paul Mierzejewski, Vineyard Consultant," Annefield Vineyards: Charlotte County, Virginia, http://www.annefieldvineyards.com/story_team_vineyard_consultant.php; Lila Gault, "America's Regional Wines: Virginia, Part Two," *Country Living Magazine*, May 1984, p. 22; "New Grapes from the Vineyards of Ol' Virginia," *New York Daily News*; Leahy, "Thinking About Planting Chardonnay in the East?" 28; "Spice of Life," *Culpeper Star-Exponent*; Rowe, *A History of Virginia Wine: From Grapes to Glass*, 72.

112. BATF was later known as the Alcohol and Tobacco Tax and Trade Bureau. In June 1980, the Augusta AVA, located outside the town of Augusta, Missouri (and historically home to that state's wine industry), became the nation's first AVA. The number of AVAs across the country eventually grew to nearly 200, ranging in size from 26,000 square miles (the Ohio River Valley AVA) to 62 acres (California's Cole Ranch AVA). Regulations concerning appellation of origin became mandatory January 1, 1980. An AVA petition must include evidence that the name of the proposed AVA is historically significant; proposed boundaries; and evidence that the geographic features of the AVA are unique, such as climate, soil, elevation, or physical features that set the area apart from surrounding areas. In 2008, the Alcohol and Tobacco Tax and Trade Bureau (TTB) proposed a rule that would have permitted regional names to be incorporated into the brand name even though the wine may not have any grapes grown or wine made in that region. Critics claimed it would perpetrate fraud on consumers and potentially dilute the names of high-quality growing regions. Under the legislation, an appellation is mandatory if a bottle bears a vintage date, varietal designation, a semi-generic name, or the term "Estate Bottled." Gordon Kendall "Meet wine writer Dan Berger," *Roanoke Times*, June 25, 2008; *VWGJ* 10, no. 1 (Spring 1983): 40; *VWGJ* 13, no. 1 (Spring 1986): 65.

113. California's Shenandoah Valley had been founded in the 1850s by Virginians looking for gold. Amador's petition was filed September 18, 1980. At the time, Virginia's Shenandoah Valley had less than 100 acres of grapes and four wineries. Charles Hillinger, "Winemakers Popping Corks in Name

Battle," *Los Angeles Times*, June 1981, p. 3; "Shenandoah Valley Wine Label Still Up for Grabs," *Lodi News-Sentinel*, August 26, 1982, p. 1. "Shenandoah Wine Battle to Be Uncorked," *The Free Lance–Star*, December 8, 1981, p. 8; Linda Jones Beymer, "Amador Vintners Stake Future on a Name," *Lodi News-Sentinel*, December 8, 1981, p. 1; "Grapes of Wrath from Valleys with Gripes," *Anchorage Daily News*, September 12, 1981, C13.

114. The D'Agostini winery is the fourth-oldest in California. "Disturbing the Peace in the Shenandoah Valleys," *Modesto Bee*, May 14, 1981, A-1; Hillinger, "Winemakers Popping Corks in Name Battle," 3; "Who Owns 'Shenandoah'?" *Alcohol Control Beverage Journal*, August 1981.

115. The petition was filed in August 1981. Virginia's application was filed August 25, 1981. "Shenandoah Valley Is Virginia's: Message Is Clear at Wine Hearing," *The Free Lance–Star*, January 13, 1982, p. 14; "Shenandoah Valley Wine Label Still Up for Grabs," *Lodi News-Sentinel*, 1; "Virginia Wins First Round for 'Shenandoah' Label," *Lodi News-Sentinel*, August 24, 1982, p. 1.

116. One British-born Virginia wine enthusiast noted in the *Vinifera Wine Grower's Journal*, "There is no other [Shenandoah Valley] as far as Europeans are concerned…. You may not be aware that the song 'Shenandoah' which is rooted in the folk history of America as taught in European schools, has had the most potent and profound effect on the minds of Europeans and is better known probably than the 'Star Spangled Banner.' When I left London to come here, my next-door neighbor who is French asked me where I was going to in the U.S.A. I told him the Shenandoah Valley and he immediately began to sing the song at the top of his voice." Winchester resident Lula Williams was even more adamant, "I suggest you send those people in California a map of Virginia and a free ticket to see the Jimmy Stewart Movie 'Shenandoah.'" "Grapes of Wrath from Valleys with Gripes," *Anchorage Daily News*, C13; *VWGJ* 9, no. 3 (Fall 1982): 207; Hillinger, "Winemakers Popping Corks in Name Battle," 3; "Virginia Fights for Shenandoah Valley Name," *Lodi News-Sentinel*, January 14, 1982, p. 10.

117. Shumway also noted to reporters, "…the history and folklore of Virginia is not at issue here. Instead, the controversy must be decided on the region's viticultural heritage." "Amador Vintners Stake Future on a Name," *Lodi News-Sentinel*, 1; "Wine Areas Battle Over Shenandoah Valley Name," *Lodi-News Sentinel*, December 3, 1981, p. 1; "Shenandoah Valley Is Virginia's: Message Is Clear at Wine Hearing," *FLS*, 14; "Amador Folks Are Simmering," *Lodi News-Sentinel*, January 14, 1982, p. 1.

118. Passed January 13, 1982. *VWGJ* 9, no. 3 (Spring 1982): 63.

119. Virginians, noted one BATF assistant director, were more aggressive in their arguments during the hearing. "'Shenandoah' Decision Pending," *The Free Lance–Star*, January 14, 1982, p. 14.

120. "Shenandoah Valley Is Virginia's: Message Is Clear at Wine Hearing," *The Free Lance–Star*, 14; "Virginians Ready for Battle," *Lodi News-Sentinel*, January 14, 1982, p. 1; *VWGJ* 8, no. 4 (Winter 1981): 216.

121. "Shenandoah Valley Is Virginia's: Message Is Clear at Wine Hearing," *FLS*, 14; "Virginia Fights for Shenandoah Valley Name," *Lodi News-Sentinel*, 10.

122. In August 1982, BATF proposed awarding Virginia's Shenandoah Valley the right to use the term on its wines, and opened it up to public comment. In the final decision, ATF director G. R. Dickerson disqualified himself from the BATF's decision because he owned a vineyard in Virginia's Shenandoah Valley. "Wine Areas Battle Over Shenandoah Valley Name," *Lodi-News Sentinel*, 1; "State Wins Round in Wine War," *Daily Progress*, August 24, 1982, B7.

123. Robinson complained that California's Shenandoah was but a "miniscule valley" that had drawn "scant notice through the years, even from map makers." Robinson later petitioned, albeit unsuccessfully, Treasury Secretary Donald T. Regan to overturn the bureau's ruling and reserve the "Shenandoah Valley" label exclusively for Virginia wine and also proposed legislation in the U.S. House of Representatives to deny the "Shenandoah Valley" mark to California vintages. "Robinson Hits Ruling on Shenandoah Wine," *The Free Lance–Star*, December 24, 1982, p. 29.

124. "Disturbing the Peace in the Shenandoah Valleys," *Modesto Bee*, A-1.

125. In February 1983, BATF designated two new AVAs: a mountainous area in Floyd and Patrick counties as the Rocky Knob AVA, and the North Fork of Roanoke AVA located along the eastern slopes

of the Allegheny Mountains in Roanoke and Montgomery counties. BATF would later designate the Northern Neck George Washington Birthplace AVA in 1987 and the Virginia's Eastern Shore AVA in 1991. The Vinifera Wine Growers Association proposed the creation of a Northern Virginia AVA in 1986, but it never came to fruition. *Boar's Head Virginia Grapevine* 31 (Summer 1987); *Boar's Head Virginia Grapevine* 43 (Winter 1991); *VWGJ* 13, no. 3 (Fall 1986): 171.

126. Va. Code Ann. §§ 45.1-274, 1-283; Larry Evans, "Marline Agrees to Hold Off Mining," *The Free Lance–Star*, December 22, 1981, p. 15.

127. Larry Evans, "Uranium Firm Goes on the Offensive," *The Free Lance–Star*, October 31, 1981, p. 13.

128. The VWGA also had preservation of open space and farmland as one of their established goals. Other groups included the Piedmont Environmental Council, the Sierra Club, the Garden Club of Virginia, the Virginia Municipal League, the Virginia Conference of Methodist Churches, the Environmental Defense Fund, the Virginia Wildlife Federation, and various local governments. Statement by the Vinifera Wine Growers Association, Nov. 1, 1981, reprinted in *VWGJ* 8, no. 4 (Winter 1981): 265; Larry Evans, "Winegrowers Group Joins Uranium Mining Opposition," *The Free Lance–Star*, November 2, 1981, p. 34; Larry Evans, "Uranium report 'slanted,' says chairman," *The Free Lance–Star*, December 21, 1983, p. 21.

129. *VWGJ* 9, no. 3 (Fall 1982): 199–200.

130. "Marline Agrees to Hold Off Mining," FLS Dec. 22, 1981 p. 15

131. Evans, "Marline Agrees to Hold Off Mining," 15; Larry Evans, "Marline Cancels Uranium Leases," *The Free Lance–Star*, September 15, 1982, p. 1; *VWGJ* 10, no. 2 (Summer 1983): 80; "Uranium Is in the River Basin, But How Much?," *The Free Lance–Star*, February 6, 1986, p. 10-A.

132. While no applications for uranium mining have ever been filed nor permits for drilling granted, in 2007, a consortium known as Virginia Uranium, Inc., announced that it wished to move forward with mining in Pittsylvania County. Anita Kumar, "Gov. McDonnell opposes lifting ban on uranium mining in Virginia this year," *The Washington Post*, January 19, 2012; John C. Watkins, "Virginia Never Banned Uranium Mining," *Richmond Times-Dispatch*, August 7, 2011.

133. Rogan, "Virginia Wine Line," March 1984, p. 17; Lee and Lee, *Virginia Wine Country III*, 90.

134. Rogan's assertions were backed by studies that found that for every $10 spent on alcoholic beverages, women accounted for $7, often preferring lighter, sweeter beverages. *VWGJ* 11, no. 3 (Fall 1984): 172; *VWGJ* 12, no. 4 (Winter 1985): 267.

135. Gault, "America's Regional Wines: Virginia, Part Two," 22; Lee and Lee, *Virginia Wine Country*, 130; Rogan, "Virginia Wine Line," March 1984, p. 3.

136. Lee, Lee, and Talley, *Virginia Wine Country Revisited*, 101–103; Palmer, *Wineries of the Mid-Atlantic*, 207; Rowe, *A History of Virginia Wine: From Grapes to Glass*, 35; "Felicia Rogan: Wine Lover Becomes Vineyard Owner," *Daily Progress*, 12; Lee and Lee, *Virginia Wine Country III*, 90–91; Weems, *Virginia Wineries: Your Complete Tour Guide*, 37; Laura Broach, "Virginia Wineries: Local Wine Industry Experiences Rebirth," *Cavalier Daily*, September 13, 1984, p. 3; "Six Area Residents Appointed By Robb," *The Free Lance–Star*, July 5, 1985, p. 18; "Felicia Rogan: Wine Lover Becomes Vineyard Owner," *Daily Progress*, 12; Goldenson, *Vintage Places: A Connoisseur's Guide to North American Wineries and Vineyards*, 88.

137. "Toast to Local Wines Coming Up Saturday," *Daily Progress*, October 12, 1981, p. 1.

138. The lecture was held in Gevrey-Chambertin, France, and included samples of Oakencroft's 1986 Seyval Blanc. A subsequent Virginia wine tasting, held by the American consulate in Bordeaux, was held two months later to honor Thomas Jefferson's visit to the Bordeaux region. Samples included wines from Guilford Ridge, Ingleside, Meredyth, Montdomaine, Oakencroft, and Prince Michel. The American Embassy in Paris subsequently ordered 20 cases of Oakencroft wine to be served at important functions. The sale followed Rogan's accompaniment of Governor Gerald Baliles to Taiwan on an economic development mission. *Boar's Head Virginia Grapevine* 31 (Summer 1987); *Boar's Head Virginia Grapevine* 32 (Fall 1987); Speech by Felicia Warburg Rogan, March 27, 1987, Papers of the Jeffersonian Wine Grape Growers Society, Special Collections, University of Virginia; *VWGJ* 18, no. 1 (Spring 1991): 52; *Boar's Head Virginia Grapevine* 42 (Fall 1990); *Boar's Head Virginia Grapevine* 43 (Winter 1991); "An Interview with Felicia Rogan, Virginia Wine Pioneer," *Virginia*

*Wine Gazette* (Summer 1998): 8.

139. Poetically written, Rogan's description of the vineyard and winemaking process was interspersed with beautiful photos of Virginia vineyards and wineries, including several of her Oakencroft. Thanks to Oakencroft's promotional efforts, Rogan received further notoriety. In 1985, Oakencroft became the first Virginia winery to be featured on national television when she appeared as a guest on ABC's *American Almanac* with Roger Mudd. In 1988, President Ronald Reagan presented a bottle of Oakencroft wine as a gift to the Soviet Union's Mikhail Gorbachev during that year's Moscow Summit. In April 1991, Oakencroft wines were served during a Virginia wine symposium given by Felicia Rogan and thrown by *House Beautiful Magazine* at the newly opened Chanel Boutique in Washington, D.C. The wine, one of eleven selected by the White House for a gift, was selected for its historic qualities emanating from the Monticello region. Wines from Oakencroft, Rapdian River, Montdomaine, Prince Michel, and Dominion Cellars were served at a tasting following a discussion on the American Constitution at the University Virginia School of Law in March 1988. The evening, the Seventh National Symposium on Law and Public Policy, featured United States Supreme Court Justice Antonin Scalia and 600 guests. *VWGJ* 18, no. 1 (Spring 1991): 52; *Boar's Head Virginia Grapevine* 34 (Spring 1988); *Boar's Head Virginia Grapevine* 43 (Winter 1991).

140. "Toast to Local Wines Coming Up Saturday," *Daily Progress*, October 12, 1981, p. 1; Felicia Warburg Rogan, *Virginia Wines: A Vineyard Year* (Charlottesville, Va.: Thomasson-Grant, 1987); Felicia Warburg Rogan, *Virginia Wines & Wineries* (Charlottesville, Va.: Howell Press, 2001).

141. The first board members included Bernard P. Chamberlain, John J. Marquis Sr., David Mefford, Col. C. J. Reeder, Felicia Rogan, Capt. John Sherman, Frederick E. Gignoux, and E. Gerald Tremblay. Some discussion ensued at the society's first meeting as to whether to include French-American grape growers. After a lively discussion, it was noted that the Norton grape—the grape that gave the region its first medals in Vienna and Paris in 1878—had been a native or French-American grape and was not vinifera. *Boar's Head Grape Vine Press* 4 (August–September 1981); *VWGJ* 8, no. 2 (Summer 1981): 86. Minutes of the Jeffersonian Wine Grape Growers Society, February 27, 1981, March 10, 1981, and June 2, 1981, Papers of the Jeffersonian Wine Grape Growers Society, Special Collections, University of Virginia; Gault, "America's Regional Wines: Virginia, Part Two," 22.

142. The course was led by Ingleside's Jaques Recht; a subsequent 1984 course would feature Prince Michel Vineyards' Joachim Hollerith (formerly of Rapidan Vineyards). Minutes of the Jeffersonian Wine Grape Growers Society, President's Report, June 7, 1982, Papers of the Jeffersonian Wine Grape Growers Society, Special Collections, University of Virginia; *VWGJ* 10, no. 1 (Spring 1983): 47; *Boar's Head Grape Vine Press* 12 (November–December 1982).

143. "Fall Agenda for the J.W.G.G.S.," June 26, 1981, Papers of the Jeffersonian Wine Grape Growers Society, Special Collections, University of Virginia; "A Unique Opportunity for Members of the Jeffersonian Wine Grape Growers Society," December Press Release by Boar's Head Inn, December 1982, Papers of the Jeffersonian Wine Grape Growers Society, Special Collections, University of Virginia; Annual Report of the Jeffersonian Wine Grape Growers Society, June 6, 1983, Papers of the Jeffersonian Wine Grape Growers Society, Special Collections, University of Virginia; "People Around Town," Charlottesville Observer, found in Papers of the Jeffersonian Wine Grape Growers Society, Special Collections, University of Virginia; "Becker Concludes U.S. Tour in Virginia," *Eastern Grape Grower & Winery News*, October/November 1982; *Wines & Vines*, November 1982; Letter from Bruce Zoecklein, Enologist to Mrs. John B. Rogan, March 3, 1986, Papers of the Jeffersonian Wine Grape Growers Society, Special Collections, University of Virginia; Minutes of the Jeffersonian Wine Grape Growers Society, April 7, 1986, Papers of the Jeffersonian Wine Grape Growers Society, Special Collections, University of Virginia; *Boar's Head Virginia Grapevine* 30 (Spring 1987).

144. Exhibitions and displays for the museum were conceived and organized by Kay Chretien of Black Cat Productions. "Virginia Wine Activity Brisk," *Atlantic Control States Beverage Journal* (April 1985): 3; Minutes of the Jeffersonian Wine Grape Growers Society, President's Report, November 18, 1983, Papers of the Jeffersonian Wine Grape Growers Society, Special Collections, University of Virginia; *Boar's Head Grape Vine Press* 19 (Summer 1984).

145. The proclamation's recitals noted that Charlottesville had been the home of the Monticello Wine

Company in the 1800s, and that it boasted, at the time, Virginia's greatest concentration of wineries and vineyards; that it is home to the Jeffersonian Wine Grape Growers Society (JWGGS) and wine museum at Michie Tavern; that Monticello was the site of Jefferson's original vineyard; and that the city and county fully supported the efforts of the JWGGS to regain the city's place as the Wine Capital of Virginia. Minutes of the Jeffersonian Wine Grape Growers Society, November 17, 1981, Papers of the Jeffersonian Wine Grape Growers Society, Special Collections, University of Virginia; Check Boar's Head Grape Vine; also Vineyard and Winery Management, November/December 1987 p. 15.

146. The effort was also spearheaded from Society board members Michael Bowles and David Mefford. Additionally, use of "Thomas Jefferson" as the name of the proposed viticultural area—while favored by most—failed to relate to a proper geographical area as required by the Bureau of Alcohol, Tobacco, and Firearms' regulations. *Boar's Head Grape Vine Press* 3 (June–July 1981); Letter to Mr. & Mrs. John B. Rogan from Ernst and Francoise Attinger, December 12, 1980, Papers of the Jeffersonian Wine Grape Growers Society, Special Collections, University of Virginia; Memorandum from EGT to MEG, Jr., December 18, 1980, Letter to Mr. & Mrs. John B. Rogan from Ernst and Francoise Attinger, December 12, 1980, Papers of the Jeffersonian Wine Grape Growers Society, Special Collections, University of Virginia; Rob Eure, "Vintners want to offer 'Monticello' label," *Daily Progress*, 1983.

147. *Wines & Vines*, March 1984, p. 15; *Boar's Head Grape Vine Press* 19 (Summer 1984); 1990 Membership Roster, the Papers of the Jeffersonian Wine Grape Growers Society, Special Collections, University of Virginia; *Boar's Head Virginia Grapevine* 34 (Spring 1988); *Boar's Head Virginia Grapevine* 36 (Fall 1988).

148. "Wine Growers Win Tax Battle, Face Second Fight in Albemarle," *Richmond Times-Dispatch*, October 15, 1981, B4; Letter to Gerald E. Fisher, Chairman of the Albemarle County Board of Supervisors from John O. Sherman, Capt. USN Ret., Chermont Vineyard, September 8, 1981, Papers of the Jeffersonian Wine Grape Growers Society, Special Collections, University of Virginia; Minutes of the Jeffersonian Wine Grape Growers Society, June 7, 1982, Papers of the Jeffersonian Wine Grape Growers Society, UVA; *Boar's Head Grape Vine Press* 6 (December 1981); Minutes of the Jeffersonian Wine Grape Growers Society, January 8, 1982, Papers of the Jeffersonian Wine Grape Growers Society, Special Collections, University of Virginia; Albemarle Regulation 5.1.25 to the Zoning Ordinance, adopted by the Board of Supervisors December 21, 1983.

149. *Eastern Grape Grower & Winery News*, February 1981 (Papers of the Jeffersonian Wine Grape Growers Society, Special Collections, University of Virginia); *Boar's Head Virginia Grapevine* 36 (Fall 1988); *Boar's Head Virginia Grapevine* 41 (Spring 1990); *Boar's Head Virginia Grapevine* 38 (Winter 1988–1989).

150. "First Advancement of Virginia Wine Industry Award," The Pennsylvania Grape Letter and Wine News, January 1981, p. 1; "Virginia Winery Earns Top Award," The Wine Spectator, Jan, 16–31, 1981

151. Unlike the *Vinifera Wine Growers Journal*, the *Boar's Head Virginia Grapevine* newsletter placed an emphasis on nontechnical information and focused on the status of wine issues in central Virginia. Following John Rogan's death in 1989, the Boar's Head was purchased by the University of Virginia Real Estate Foundation. The new head manager, Richard M. Stormont, pledged to continue the hotel's support of the Society. "First Advancement of Virginia Wine Industry Award," *The Pennsylvania Grape Letter and Wine News*, January 1981, p. 1; "Virginia Winery Earns Top Award," *The Wine Spectator*, January 16–31, 1981; *Boar's Head Virginia Grapevine* 32 (Fall 1987); *Boar's Head Virginia Grapevine* 40 (Winter 1990).

152. At the request of University Librarian Ray W. Franz, Jr., the Society donated its records and working papers to the university in late 1987 to "help future scholars learn about the reemergence of wine growing and production in the Monticello area in the 1980s." *Boar's Head Virginia Grapevine* 29 (Winter 1987); Rogan, "Virginia Wine Line," March 1984, p. 17; Brian McNeill, "Oakencroft founder to retire after 25 years," *Daily Progress*, June 5, 2008, Business section; Lee and Lee, *Virginia*

*Wine Country III*, 90; "Felicia Rogan: Wine Lover Becomes Vineyard Owner," *Daily Progress*, 12.

153. McNeill, "Oakencroft founder to retire after 25 years," *Daily Progress*.

154. Virginia Wineries Association, "Who We Are," Virginia Wineries Association: First in Wine. http://www.vawine.org; *VWGJ* 8, no. 2 (Summer 1981): 86; VWGA, *The Wine Exchange* (July 1994), 13.

155. Virginia Vineyards Association, "About," Virginia Vineyards Association. http://www.virginiavine-yardsassociation.com.

156. *VWGJ* 15, no. 4 (Winter 1988): 211–214, 273–274; *VWGJ* 16, no. 3 (Fall 1989): 200.

157. It was during Murchie's time with the National Wine Coalition that he worked to create the U.S. Congressional Wine Caucus.

158. *VWGJ* 18, no. 3 (Fall 1991) 207; Dave McIntyre, "Murchie: The Voice for Vinifera on the East Coast," *The Washington Post*, November 23, 2011; John Hagarty, "Gordon W. Murchie and Dave Barber Receive Prestigious Wine Awards," Hagarty On Wine; Dave McIntyre, "American Wine Society celebrates Gordon Murchie for his work promoting Eastern viticulture," Dave McIntyre's WineLine.

159. The organization thereafter named the award in his honor.

160. "Wine Festivals Come of Age as a Marketing Tool," *Vineyard & Winery Management* (September/October 1986): 29.

161. As one commentator noted of the Albemarle Harvest Wine Festival, attendees looked like they could be "refugees from Foxfield," a biannual horse race. Attendees were decidedly "yuppie," wearing tweed and blue jackets and Ray-Ban sunglasses. Julia Wilkinson, "Festival Features Area Wines," *Cavalier Daily*, October 7, 1986, p. 3; "From Virginia's Vineyards: Some Surprising Little Wines," *The Washington Post*, 1; *VWGJ* 10, no. 4 (Winter 1983): 270; *VWGJ* 11, no. 2 (Summer 1984): 125; VWGA, *The Wine Exchange*, no. 2 (April 1994): 2.

162. Along with 25 other Northern Virginia landowners who had hobby vineyards, the Mellon family planted a 15.5-acre vineyard in 1973 at their Kinloch Farm outside The Plains. Under the supervision of the farm's superintendent, David J. Spence, the Mellons' vineyard developed into perhaps the finest experimental vineyard in the mid-Atlantic. The Mellons enrolled Kinloch Farm as the "Patron" of the VWGA, and offered the farm's facilities for Association meetings and grape growing courses. Ringle, "Businessman Starts Chateau in Virginia," 34; *VWGJ* 1, no. 1 (Spring 1974): 53; *VWGJ* 6, no. 1 (Spring 1979): 39.

163. *VWGJ* 3, no. 3 (Fall 1976): 248.

164. To promote the event, the VWGA took out an advertisement in *The Washington Post*. A portion of the festival's proceeds were dedicated to restoring the historic train station in The Plains as studio space for local artists, as well as the as restoration of the Aldie Mill east of Middleburg. The 1978 seminars were led by Cornell University scientist Thomas J. Zabadal and Rapidan River Vineyards' Dr. Gerhard Guth. The 1989 auction benefited the Virginia Outdoors Foundation, an organization dedicated to the preservation of Virginia's open spaces through purchase of conservation easements. *VWGJ* 5, no. 3 (Fall 1978): 157; Robertson, "R. de Treville Lawrence III dies at age 91," *Richmond Times-Dispatch*; *VWGJ* 13, no. 2 (Summer 1986): 129; *VWGJ* 16, no. 3 (Fall 1989): 175; Cathy Jett, "Wine festival should leave a good taste," *The Free Lance-Star*, August 19, 1978, p. 2.

165. The Orange County Hounds provided the dogs. *VWGJ* 6, no. 3 (Fall 1979): 173; *VWGJ* 8, no. 1 (Spring 1981): 9; *VWGJ* 8, no. 3 (Fall 1981): 201.

166. The Virginia Enovit Center would eventually be home to wines from all over the eastern United States. At the time, Tony Wolf was just completing his thesis at the New York State Agricultural Experiment Station in Geneva, New York. Recurring personalities who had attended the first wine festival 10 years earlier, including Willard Scott, and nearly $1,800 was raised to assist with Association's ongoing restoration efforts of the railroad depot in The Plains. *VWGJ* 11, no. 2 (Summer 1984): 126; *VWGJ* 11, no. 2 (Summer 1985): 126–127; *VWGJ* 11, no. 3 (Fall 1985): 190; *VWGJ* 14, no. 2 (Summer 1987): 124.

167. *VWGJ* 18, no. 1 (Spring 1991): 62; VWGA, *The Wine Exchange*, (July 1994): 8–9.

168. "First Virginia Wine Festival Planned for Charlottesville," *Washington Star*, June 21, 1981; "Major Wine Festival in Jefferson Country," *Wine Country*, October 1981; Minutes of the Jeffersonian Wine Grape Growers Society, November 5, 1986, Papers of the Jeffersonian Wine Grape Growers Society,

Special Collections, University of Virginia

169. The festival was written about and advertised in *Bon Appetit* magazine. *VWGJ* 8, no. 3 (Fall 1981): 162; "Virginia Wine Makes News," *Charlottesville Observer*, January 15–21, 1981; "Bon Vivant: Feasts and Festivals," *Bon Appetit*, September 1981, p. 23; *VWGJ* 8, no. 1 (Spring 1981): 66; *Boar's Head Grape Vine Press* 6 (December 1981); "First Annual Albemarle Harvest Wine Festival Held in 'Jefferson Country' Attracts National Attention," *Virginia Record*, 1981, p. 31; Minutes of the Jeffersonian Wine Grape Growers Society, November 17, 1981, Papers of the Jeffersonian Wine Grape Growers Society, Special Collections, University of Virginia.

170. "Albemarle Harvest Wine Festival" brochure, October 15, 1981, Papers of the Jeffersonian Wine Grape Growers Society, Special Collections, University of Virginia; "Wine Festival Coming Up," *Daily Progress*, September 6, 1981, B3; "Toast to Local Wines Coming Up Saturday," *Daily Progress*, October 12, 1981, p. 1; *VWGJ* 8, no. 4 (Winter 1981): 251; "First Virginia Wine Festival Planned for Charlottesville," *Washington Star*, June 21, 1981; Major Wine Festival October 17, 1981, Charlottesville, Va. "Jefferson Country," The Grapevine Beverage Communicator, Fall 1981, p. 1.

171. *Boar's Head Grape Vine Press* 11 (September–October 1982); "Virginia Wine Activity Brisk," *ACSBJ*, 3; "The Boar's Head Inn Vine Festival," supplement to the Daily Progress, October 5, 1984; Minutes of the Jeffersonian Wine Grape Growers Society, May 3, 1983, Papers of the Jeffersonian Wine Grape Growers Society, University of Virginia.

172. "Albemarle Harvest Wine Festival and Bacchanalian Feast" brochure, October 15/16 1982, Papers of the Jeffersonian Wine Grape Growers Society, University of Virginia; Wilkinson, "Festival Features Area Wines," 3; *Boar's Head Virginia Grapevine* 27 (Fall 1986).

173. Lee and Lee, *Virginia Wine Country*, 134–135; "Vintage Virginia 1998: A Success Despite Storm," *Virginia Wine Gazette*, Harvest 1998, p. 28.

174. A new feature also appeared—a six-ounce etched bicentennial commemorative wine glass—which proved very popular. Included were Barboursville, Ingleside Plantation, Oasis, Prince Michel, Rapidan, Montdomaine, Winchester Winery, and Willowcroft Farm. *VWGJ* 11, no. 2 (Summer 1984): 137; *VWGJ* 14, no. 1 (Spring 1987): 62; *VWGJ* 14, no. 4 (Winter 1987): 270–271.

175. Mary Lynn Tucker, "Here's to the Festival's Continued Good Health," *Roanoke Times*, September 28, 2007; Courtney Cutright, "Guide to the 2006 Smith Mountain Lake Wine Festival," *Roanoke Times*, September 22, 2006.

176. *VWGJ* 6, no. 4 (Winter 1979): 226; *VWGJ* 13, no. 3 (Fall 1986): 279; *VWGJ* 15, no. 2 (Summer 1988): 130.

177. Renaming the competition was apparently the suggestion of VGWA member Ronald H. Kuhn, proprietor of the Hunt Country Vineyard outside Middleburg. He was appointed chairman of the VWGA's tasting committee in 1982, which subsequently proposed entry rules, categories, and prizes. The first judges were Kuhn, Dr. Hamilton Mowbray, Michel Buller, Peter M. Sichel, Mrs. Ernest Byfield, William Bullinger, Robert F. Carmody, and Deanna Kuhn. *VWGJ* 11, no. 3 (Summer 1984): 186; *VWGJ* 11, no. 3 (Fall 1984): 186; Lou Ann Whitton, "Virginia Wine Festival," *Bulletin of the Virginia Department of Agriculture and Consumer Services*, October 1982, p. 8.

178. *VWGJ* 11, no. 3 (Fall 1984): 186.

179. VWGA retained the rights to the name "Virginia Wine Competition" but ceded use of the event's most prestigious award—the "Governors Cup"—to the Virginia Wineries Association. *VWGJ* 11, no. 2 (Summer 1984): 127.

180. Judges included *The Washington Post* wine critic James Conaway, *Baltimore Sun* wine expert Michael Dresser, the Beverage Tasting Institute's John Binder, wine writer Craig Goldwyn, and Washington, D.C., wine buyer James Arseneault. *VWGJ* 11, no. 3 (Fall 1984): 187; *VWGJ* 11, no. 2 (Summer 1984): 185; *VWGJ* 13, no. 2 (Summer 1986): 81; *VWGJ* 16, no. 3 (Fall 1989): 147; *Boar's Head Virginia Grapevine* 40 (Winter 1990); *Boar's Head Virginia Grapevine* 38 (Spring 1990).

181. Virginia Wine Growers Advisory Board, *Status of the Virginia Wine Industry*, 23.

182. Ibid.

183. In September 1981, VDACS published a "Pick Your Own Grapes Guide," which listed 12 vineyards from across the state offering pick-your-own grapes. The department also produced "The ABCs

of Grapes" and "A Bunch of Grape Ideas" guides, which provided information on grape picking, varieties, and winemaking. The 1982 brochure consisted of 24 pages describing the state's 21 wineries, along with operating hours and upcoming wineries. The 1983 brochure included information on winemaking sources, equipment, names of consultants, and grapevine sources. VDACS' Product Promotion continued publishing brochures throughout the 1980s, including the 1985 publishing of the "Vintage Virginia" winery guide, which featured 35 Virginia farm wineries that were open or soon to be opened and a list of all festivals and special events. *Bulletin of the Virginia Department of Agriculture and Consumer Services*, September 1981, p. 11; *VWGJ* 10, no. 3 (Fall 1983): 208; "Wine Festival," *Daily Progress*, October 11, 1984, p. 3; *Vineyard & Winery Management* (May/June 1986,): 8.

184. The law carried with it an enactment date of July 1, 1986, and, anticipating the change, ABC stores increased their merchandising and inventory of Virginia wines. The stores increased their inventory to 68 Virginia wines from 16 of the state's 29 wineries by 1986. The legislation, while certainly beneficial to Virginia wines, was not necessarily as altruistic a gesture as it may have seemed. The move was largely seen as a bow to pressure by Virginia's largest grocery stores, retailers, and distributors, who had long complained that the ABC both regulated and competed with the state's 7,250 wine retailers for wine sales. ABC stores also welcomed the legislation—not necessarily for purposes of promoting Virginia wine—but rather for freeing up shelf space for more profitable hard liquor sales. Wines previously took up roughly 25 percent of each ABC store's shelf space, yet accounted for only 3.9 percent of the ABC's total sales. "The Boar's Head Inn Vine Festival," *Daily Progress*, October 5, 1984 p 11; Whitton, "Virginia Wine Country: It's There for the Tasting," 18; "Six Area Residents Appointed By Robb," *FLS*, 18; Virginia Department of Alcoholic Beverage Control. "Virginia ABC's 75th Anniversary 1934–2009; Timeline." VA ABC. http://www.abc.virginia.gov/admin/abc75th/abc75th_timeline.html; "ABC Stores Preparing to Stop Selling All Non-Virginia Wines," *The Free Lance–Star*, June 11, 1986, p. 35; Whitton, "Virginia Wine Country: It's There for the Tasting," 18; *Boar's Head Virginia Grapevine* 27 (Summer 1986); VWGA, *The Wine Exchange* no. 3 (July 1994): 8–9.

185. *Boar's Head Virginia Grapevine* 20 (Fall 1984); Rowe, *Wandering Through Virginia's Vineyards*, 41.

186. "Robb Declares 'Winery Week,' Cites Importance," *Virginia Farmer*, July 1984; "Virginia Wine Activity Brisk," *ACSBJ*, 3; *Boar's Head Virginia Grapevine* 32 (Fall 1987).

187. The VWGA, however, responded somewhat coldly to Zoecklein's being based in Blacksburg by asserting, "Wineries, the great majority of which are in the northern part of the state, are in need of fast action oenology extension assistance…if it involves a 400-mile round-trip there is little need for him to be called." *VWGJ* 1, no. 1 (Spring 1974): 2; *VWGJ* 2, no. 1 (Fall 1974): 6; *VWGJ* 11, no. 2 (Summer 1985): 127.

188. Cathy Harding, "State Enologist Bruce Zoecklein says with winemaking, it's not one or the other," *C-Ville*, October 5, 2010, Living section; Elisabeth Frater, *Breaking Away to Virginia & Maryland Wineries* (Stirling, Va.: Capital Books, 2002), 5.

189. Mark Owczarski, "Bruce Zoecklein honored with emeritus status," *Virginia Tech News*, October 29, 2010. http://www.vtnews.vt.edu/articles/2010/10/102910-cals-emerituszoecklein.html; Rowe, *A History of Virginia Wine: From Grapes to Glass*, 100; Rowe, *Wandering Through Virginia's Vineyards*, 63–67.

190. The center was named in honor of Alson H. Smith, Jr., a longtime member of the Virginia House of Delegates who, while a strong promoter of Virginia's apple industry, encouraged the promotion of the state's viticultural industry. Twenty-four varieties were originally planted in 1989. Tony K. Wolf and Bruce W. Zoecklein, "Performance of Alternative Winegrape Varieties in Virginia," *Vineyard & Winery Management* (September/October 1996): 49; Frater, *Breaking Away to Virginia & Maryland Wineries*, 5.

191. Virginia Wine Growers Advisory Board, *Status of the Virginia Wine Industry*, 34; Rowe, *Wandering Through Virginia's Vineyards*, 41; Michael D. Sutphin, "Tony Wolf receives 2009 Alumni Award for Excellence in Extension," *Virginia Tech News*, April 20, 2009. http://www.vtnews.vt.edu/arti-

cles/2009/04/2009-190.html.

192. *VWGJ* 11, no. 4 (Winter 1984): 253–255. *VWGJ* 11, no. 1 (Spring 1984): 59; *VWGJ* 11, no. 2 (Summer 1984): 114; *VWGJ* 11, no. 5 (Spring 1985): 58, 64; *VWGJ* 13, no. 1 (Spring 1986): 2, 13; *VWGJ* 10, no. 1 (Summer 1983): 129–131; *VWGJ* 10, no. 4 (Winter 1983): 269; Whitton, "Virginia Wine Country: It's There for the Tasting," 18; *Boar's Head Virginia Grapevine* 26 (Spring 1986); *Vineyard & Winery Management* (May/June 1986): 7–8; *VWGJ* 13, no. 3 (Fall 1987): 150–151.

193. For example, in 1983, VDACS reorganized the committee into a 12-member Wine Grape Advisory Committee, which was quickly replaced in November 1984 by a new Virginia Wine Production Board. This continual shifting in members coupled with an uncertain source of permanent funding prompted the General Assembly to supersede the Wine Production Board in 1985 with the creation of a 13-member Virginia Wine Growers Advisory Board. The Wine Grape Advisory Committee was composed of the Department of Agriculture's Markets Division chairman, the presidents of the largest four viticultural organizations (VWGA, Virginia Vineyards Association, Virginia Wineries Association, and the Jeffersonian Wine Grape Growers Society), three experienced industry technicians, ABC members, the Virginia Wine Wholesalers Association, Virginia Tech horticulture, the president of a wine society in Richmond, and the Virginia Horticultural Society. The board's members included five winery owners, two vineyard owners, and representatives from the retail industry, the wholesale industry, and Virginia Tech. Representatives from the Virginia Vineyards Association and the Virginia Wineries Association also received a slot on the board. *VWGJ* 11, no. 2 (Summer 1985): 125; *VWGJ* 13, no. 1 (Spring 1986): 12–13; *Boar's Head Virginia Grapevine* 29 (Winter 1987); *VWGJ* 10, no. 4 (Winter 1983): 269; *VWGJ* 11, no. 4 (Winter 1984): 252; "Six Area Residents Appointed By Robb," *FLS*, 18.

194. The first board members included Virginia Beach retailer Peter Coe, Ingleside owner Douglas Flemer, Virginia Tech representative Tom Fretz, Naked Mountain winery owner Phoebe Harper, Alexandria wholesaler Conrad Koneczny, Richmond resident Maria LeGrand, Falmouth grower Sharon Livingston, and Rose Bower owner Tom O'Grady, Oakencroft owner Felicia Rogan, Meredyth owner Archie Smith, Jr., and VDACS Commissioner S. Mason Carbaugh. Rogan served as the board's first chairman. No slot was reserved for the Vinifera Wine Growers Association. *VWGJ* 11, no. 2 (Summer 1985): 125; Statement of Robert E. Gomperts, Director of the Division of Marketing, VDACS, before the US House Committee on Agriculture, October 23, 1991, reprinted in *VWGJ* 18, no. 3 (Fall 1991): 173; *VWGJ* 13, no. 1 (Spring 1986): 12; *Boar's Head Virginia Grapevine* 24 (Fall 1985); Virginia Wine Growers Advisory Board, *Status of the Virginia Wine Industry*, 9.

195. Virginia Wine Growers Advisory Board, *Status of the Virginia Wine Industry*, 10.

196. In some cases, executive support came even before being sworn in. During the 1981 gubernatorial campaign, for example, Virginia wines were served at two separate fundraisers for Republican candidate Marshall Coleman and his successful Democratic challenger, Charles S. Robb. The two wines selected for Coleman's fundraiser were Rose Bower's Chardonnay and Piedmont's Chardonnay. The event was supposed to feature an appearance by newly elected President Ronald Reagan, who cancelled at the last minute; his wife Nancy attended the event in his stead. Mrs. Reagan took samples of wine home with her. Also present were Governor John Dalton, former governor Mills Godwin, and Senator John Warner.

197. *VWGJ* 11, no. 3 (Fall 1984): 186; Whitton, "Virginia Wine Festival," 8; "Robb Declares 'Winery Week,' Cites Importance," *Virginia Farmer*; "Gov. Robb Announces Virginia Farm Wine Week," *Farm & Country*, August 1983.

198. *Bulletin of the Virginia Department of Agriculture and Consumer Services*, August 1987, p. 13.

199. Virginia Department of Agriculture & Consumer Services, "Have a Happy Virginia Grown Thanksgiving," November 4, 2008; Virginia Department of Alcoholic Beverage Control. "Virginia ABC's 75th Anniversary 1934–2009; Timeline." http://www.abc.virginia.gov/admin/abc75th/abc75th_timeline.html; Virginia Tourism Corporation, "Virginia Wine Month Turns 20 in October," June 25, 2008; Cathy Jett, "State wine industry ripening to maturity," *The Free Lance–Star*, October 2, 2008; VWGA, *The Wine Exchange*, no. 2 (April 1994): 3.

200. Casks of wine were taken aboard the ship during a reenactment of the 1607 voyage in spring 1985.

"The Boar's Head Inn Vine Festival," *Daily Progress*, October 5, 1984.

201. The governor also made a trip to Monticello, hosted a reception for wine industry representatives; heard a briefing by Ron Fonte, president of an international magazine on wines titled *Les Amis Du Vin* (translated: the Friends of Wine); and gave remarks on the importance of Virginia's wine industry. Meredith Cohn, "Buyers and Cellars: The Williamsburg Winery Improves with Age and Savvy Marketing," *Virginian-Pilot*, September 28, 1998.

202. The year after taking office in August 1987, Baliles visited Shenandoah Vineyards proprietor Emma Randel, who complained that her winery could not afford to sell its wine beyond the state's border because other states add their own taxes on to the price of Virginia wine in retaliation for Virginia's imposition of a tax of $.30 per liter on all wine sold in the state. Thomas Pinney has noted that the tour was a "...striking illustration of a new willingness on the part of a high public official to show that he thought wine-growing was a thing to be encouraged. A chief executive with bloodshot eyes and a neon nose would be a dubious endorsement for a Virginia industry that is pushing hard to be taken seriously among the ranks of the world's wine connoisseurs. So Baliles had to pace himself. "I'm very careful," the governor said. "I take small sips, and not very frequently." Pinney, *History of Wine in America, Volume II* (Berkeley, California: University of California Press, 2005), 289–290; *Boar's Head Virginia Grapevine* 36 (Fall 1988); *Boar's Head Virginia Grapevine* 38 (Spring 1989).

203. Virginia Wine Growers Advisory Board, *Status of the Virginia Wine Industry*, January 1989.

204. This would not be the first unveiling of Virginia wines to Japan; in October 1988, the VDACS International Marketing Office visited Tokyo and promoted Virginia wines. "Food Shop taps Japan Markets," *Bulletin of the Virginia Department of Agriculture and Consumer Services*, October 1988, pp. 13–15; Lee, Lee, and Talley, *Virginia Wine Country Revisited*, 103; Weems, *Virginia Wineries: Your Complete Tour Guide*, 37; *Boar's Head Virginia Grapevine* 40 (Winter 1990).

205. Developed by Commerce Secretary Dr. Betty J. Diener, and enthusiastically endorsed by Governor Charles S. Robb. *Bulletin of the Virginia Department of Agriculture and Consumer Services*, April 1983, p. 1; *Boar's Head Virginia Grapevine* 29 (Winter 1987).

206. Wineries that wished to be included helped offset the cost of producing the booklet. Whitton, "Virginia Wine Country: It's There for the Tasting," 18; *Boar's Head Grape Vine Press* 19 (Summer 1984).

207. Virginia Wine Growers Advisory Board, *Status of the Virginia Wine Industry*, 14, 24, 32.

208. In recognition of her efforts, Diener was awarded the Boars Head Inn's silver wine cooler trophy for outstanding contribution to the Virginia Wine Industry by John Rogan during the Jeffersonian Wine Grape Growers Society's wine festival in October 1985. *Boar's Head Virginia Grapevine* 42 (Fall 1990); *Vineyard & Winery Management* (July/August 1987): 7; "The Boar's Head Inn Vine Festival," *Daily Progress*, October 5, 1984; "Wine Festival," *Daily Progress*, October 11, 1984, p. 2–3; Whitton, "Virginia Wine Country: It's There for the Tasting," 18; *Boar's Head Virginia Grapevine* 20 (Fall 1990).

209. "Shelf talkers" are printed cards or other signs attached to a store shelf to call buyers' attention to a particular product displayed on that shelf. Each of the bottle holders were capable of displaying 55 bottles at stores and were stamped with the promotional tag line. *Boar's Head Virginia Grapevine* 28 (Fall 1986); *Bulletin of the Virginia Department of Agriculture and Consumer Services*, August 1986, p. 1; *Bulletin of the Virginia Department of Agriculture and Consumer Services*, October 1986, pp. 11, 13.

210. *Bulletin of the Virginia Department of Agriculture and Consumer Services* (March 1989): 11–12; *Bulletin of the Virginia Department of Agriculture and Consumer Services* (Winter 1990): 11; *Boar's Head Virginia Grapevine* 36 (Fall 1988).

211. This is not to say that Virginia Tech faculty did not experiment on their own. Indeed, at least one professor, Dr. Karl Hereford, assisted Blacksburg's MJC Vineyards in the late 1970s and early 1980s with grafting vinifera grapevines (granted, Dr. Hereford was dean of the College of Education).

212. Crews, "Drought was good for grapes," 6; *VWGJ* 5, no. 1 (Spring 1978): 49; *VWGJ* 5, no. 3 (Fall 1978): 124; *VWGJ* 6, no. 4 (Winter 1979): 208; *VWGJ* 7, no. 1 (Spring 1980): 67; *VWGJ* 8, no. 3 (Fall 1981):

146; *VWGJ* 10, no. 1 (Spring 1983): 28; *VWGJ* 10, no. 3 (Fall 1983): 208.

213. VWGA, *The Wine Exchange*, no. 1 (January 1994): 8.

214. Old Dominion University. "75th Anniversary Celebration: Faculty Remembrance – Roy Williams." Old Dominion University – College of Sciences. http://sci.odu.edu/sci/seventy_five/roy_williams.shtml.

215. VWGA, *The Wine Exchange*, no. 1 (January 1994): 8–9.

216. Phyllis Spiedell, "ODU Professor's Tasting Classes Pass on His Passion for Wine," *Virginian-Pilot*, January 2, 2002; Jim Raper, "Humble steward: Virginia wines grow in quantity, quality," *Virginian-Pilot*, November 2, 2005.

217. Virginia Wine Growers Advisory Board, *Status of the Virginia Wine Industry*, 12

218. Virginia Wine Growers Advisory Board *Status of the Virginia Wine Industry*, 12.

219. Hannah Hager, "The Changing Face of Agriculture," *Loudoun Times*, March 4, 2010.

220. "We didn't know anything about planting in Virginia," Parker later told a reporter. In 2002, he was named the Wine Industry Person of the Year by the Virginia Wineries Association. Hager, "The Changing Face of Agriculture," *Loudoun Times*; Lee and Lee, *Virginia Wine Country*, 78–79; Lee and Lee, *Virginia Wine Country III*, 235–236; Lee, Lee, and Talley, *Virginia Wine Country Revisited*, 62–63.

221. Hubert, an aeronautical engineer with the Federal Aviation Administration, was introduced to winemaking while assisting his father with planting a 30-acre vineyard in the Finger Lakes region of the Empire State. Before the two arrived in Loudoun in 1978, Hubert obtained a physics degree from Cornell, where he took courses in viticulture and oenology. By 1986, the nursery had grown to some 35 acres of 15 different varieties, which the Tuckers shipped to customers in 20 states. The nursery was called the Schloss Tucker-Ellis Nursery. The Tuckers commissioned Rowan LaCompte, a renowned stained-glass artist who designed the windows in the National Cathedral, to design the wine labels. Weems, *Virginia Wineries: Your Complete Tour Guide*, 82–83; Lee and Lee, *Virginia Wine Country*, 60–61; Lee and Lee, *Virginia Wine Country III*, 197–198.

222. The name "Tarara" was backwards for "Ararat," the Turkish mount where Noah's Ark landed after God's 40-day flood. Seemingly holding back the water, Whitie constructed a 100-foot dam to create a 10-acre lake to irrigate the property.

223. In 1993, Tarara's wine cave was doubled to 6,000 square feet, and above the cave, the Huberts converted part of their home into a bed-and-breakfast. By 1991, the venture was producing 2,400 cases annually, and by 2001 the winery produced 7,000 cases. Lee and Lee, *Virginia Wine Country III*, 225–227; Weems, *Virginia Wineries: Your Complete Tour Guide*, 98–99; Rowe, *A History of Virginia Wine: From Grapes to Glass*, 68–69.

224. The name is derived from a vernacular name for the adjacent mountain that appeared on local maps as early as 1765 and appeared in the deed to the property once owned by chief justice John Marshall. The vineyards, situated between 800 and 1,200 feet in elevation, provided the grapes with a significant amount of frost protection. *VWGJ* 10, no. 2 (Summer 1983): 71–74; Palmer, *Wineries of the Mid-Atlantic*, 204; Rowe, *A History of Virginia Wine: From Grapes to Glass*, 36; Palmer, *Wineries of the Mid-Atlantic*, 206; Lee and Lee, *Virginia Wine Country III*, 180–181; Weems, *Virginia Wineries: Your Complete Tour Guide*, 85; Lee, Lee, and Talley, *Virginia Wine Country Revisited*, 50–52.

225. Peggy became interested in wine after becoming interested in horticulture while reading books at a local bookstore. Lee and Lee, *Virginia Wine Country*, 55.

226. Law has often referred to his property, which features rocky and hilly terrain, by the name "Hardscrabble." After clearing the property, the Laws planted seven acres of grapes, consisting of Chardonnay, Cabernet Sauvignon, Cabernet Franc, Vidal Blanc, and Seyval Blanc. In addition to grapes, the couple was interested in producing a variety of agricultural products, including wine grapes and pick-your-own fruits—particularly apples. Lee and Lee, *Virginia Wine Country*, 55–57; Weems, *Virginia*

*Wineries: Your Complete Tour Guide*, 20.

227. Lee and Lee, *Virginia Wine Country*, 80–81.

228. Rowe, *Wandering Through Virginia's Vineyards*, 94–95.

229. Lee, Lee, and Talley, *Virginia Wine Country Revisited*, 42.

230. Rowe, *Wandering Through Virginia's Vineyards*, 70, 89; Rowe, *A History of Virginia Wine: From Grapes to Glass*, 54.

231. At the time of purchase, the Smiths lived full-time in Suffolk, Virginia. Upon learning that Afton Mountain was for sale, the two immediately sold their Suffolk property and took control of the winery's operation. The Corporas continued consulting on the winery through the 2009 growing season. "Afton Mountain Vineyards gets new owners," *Daily Progress*; Elizabeth Roberts Smith, "Tending the Vines," *University of Virginia Magazine*, February 8, 2011; Smith, "Tending the Vines," *University of Virginia Magazine*.

232. Both Ed and Gunther enjoyed ties to the interior decorating business, and Anita, a native of Switzerland, had spent much time working in her family's vineyard abroad. Ed served as winemaker. Lee and Lee, *Virginia Wine Country*, 97–98.

233. Lee, Lee, and Talley, *Virginia Wine Country Revisited*, 110–111.

234. Lee and Lee, *Virginia Wine Country*, 124; Lee, Lee, and Talley, *Virginia Wine Country Revisited*, 95–96; Lee and Lee, *Virginia Wine Country III*, 61–62; Rogan, "Virginia Wine Line," March 1984, p. 3; Gault, "America's Regional Wines: Virginia, Part Two," 22; Lee and Lee, *Virginia Wine Country*, 112–113; Rogan, "Virginia Wine Line," May 1985, p. 21; Lee and Lee, *Virginia Wine Country III*, 98; Weems, *Virginia Wineries: Your Complete Tour Guide*, 42–43.

235. By 2011, the two-day weekend festival boasted a garlic cook-off and more than 20,000 attendees and 80 vendors—many of which have returned the festival annually since its inception. Zach Smith, "Fifteen years of garlic and wine," *News & Advance*, October 12, 2005.

236. Lee, Lee, and Talley, *Virginia Wine Country Revisited*, 172–174; Weems, *Virginia Wineries: Your Complete Tour Guide*, 52–53.

237. Baker was in charge of the productions and wrote some of the scripts. In 2003, the farm faced total crop failure. While the two had plans to replant, they wanted to change the name to Page Luray Cellars. Lee and Lee, *Virginia Wine Country*, 244–245; Lee and Lee, *Virginia Wine Country III*, 244–245.

238. Lee and Lee, *Virginia Wine Country*, 254–255.

239. Geraci was better-known as the founder of Dinosaur Land at White Post in Clarke County.

240. *VWGJ* 11, no. 2 (Summer 1984): 137; Lee and Lee, *Virginia Wine Country*, 252.

241. The Sarles used the grape for their Rosé wine. Lee and Lee, *Virginia Wine Country*, 242; Lee and Lee, *Virginia Wine Country III*, 242–243.

242. Lee, Lee, and Talley, *Virginia Wine Country Revisited*, 191–192; Lee and Lee, *Virginia Wine Country III*, 246–248.

243. Hereford intended the winery to remain small, and running the winery was strictly a family affair: "We don't want to be the Gallo of the East," said Maury Isrealson, Hereford's daughter. "We would rather produce award-winning wines and not have to go outside the family for workers or investment," she added. "Virginia's MJC Vineyards, A Family Winery," *Virginia Farmer*, December 1984, Wittman Publications, Baltimore, MD, reprinted in *VWGJ* 11, no. 5 (Spring 1985): 45; Lou Ann Whitton, "Virginia's Ripe For Grapes, Vintners Find," *Roanoke Times & World News*, Papers of the Jeffersonian Wine Grape Growers Society, University of Virginia.

244. *VWGJ* 13, no. 1 (Spring 1986): 68; Lee and Lee, *Virginia Wine Country III*, 164–165; "Yes, Virginia, you can make wine," *The Washington Times*, July 8, 2007; Lee, Lee, and Talley, *Virginia Wine Country Revisited*, 146–147.

245. Danielle Walker, "Virginia's wine industry is aging well," *Inside Business*, August 13, 2010; "Yes, Virginia, you can make wine," *The Washington Times*.

246. Weems, *Virginia Wineries: Your Complete Tour Guide*, 78–79.

247. Cathy Jett, "Librarian background fruitful for winemaker," *The Free Lance–Star*, June 5, 2009.

248. "Accomack Vineyards in Va. to Close," *The Washington Post*, September 21, 1992; *Boar's Head Virginia Grapevine* 46 (Spring 1992); *Vineyard & Winery Management* (May/June 1987): 12; Lee and Lee,

*Virginia Wine Country*, 165–167.

249. Lee, Lee, and Talley, *Virginia Wine Country Revisited*, 175–176.

250. Staged under the portico of the historic Barboursville ruins, actors and actresses annually performed one of Shakespeare's classics. A local theatrical troupe, the Four County Players, presented different plays each summer. Patrons would come from across the eastern United States. "People plan their entire weekends around our plays," said Audrey Briggs, office manager for the Four County Players. Crickets, small bats, and night birds provide ambiance for the approximately 500 patrons that vie for a prime spot for a picnic near the mansion. The winery offers buffet meals as well, but most bring food from home. Wines are sold by the bottle and by the glass through intermission. The outdoor atmosphere, historic location, quality wine, and dinner performance made for an enjoyable evening. "It has a lot of right ingredients to make it a success," Paschina said. Those sentiments were echoed by a young paralegal from the Washington, D.C., area who remarked that the wine "makes watching Shakespeare much more palatable." Gregory Gilligan, "More than Just Shakespeare," *Richmond Times-Dispatch*, August 15, 2002.

251. Much of the early winemaking at Williamsburg Winery was conducted in coordination with Prince Michel's winemaker, Joachim Hollerith, who advised in planting techniques and provided the vines. Weems, *Virginia Wineries: Your Complete Tour Guide*, 66–68; *VWGJ* 11, no. 2 (Summer 1985): 71; *VWGJ* 14, no. 4 (Winter 1987): 211, 213; Lee, Lee, and Talley, *Virginia Wine Country Revisited*, 148–150; Rowe, *A History of Virginia Wine: From Grapes to Glass*, 83.

252. Reflective of the local zoning and permitting battles encountered by growing wineries, the winery's expansion plans ran into legal hurdles in 2003, when it unexpectedly encountered a dearth of zoning, building, and health code permitting issues in the midst of its physical expansion. Lee and Lee, *Virginia Wine Country III*, 168–170; Weems, *Virginia Wineries: Your Complete Tour Guide*, 67; *VWGJ* 11, no. 2 (Summer 1985): 72; Lee, Lee, and Talley, *Virginia Wine Country Revisited*, 148–150.

253. The family also ran a catfish farm in Newbern, Alabama, as well as a paper-distributing business in Greensboro, North Carolina. The combination of wine and catfish was irresistible to the family. "We had some wineglasses made as a joke," David Morrisette later said. "They had a catfish sticking out of a toilet-paper roll, holding a glass of wine." The pitch: "Finest catfish, wine and toilet paper." Morrisette had previously planted two acres of French-American grapes on Patrick County's Sugar Loaf Mountain as early as 1976 and also oversaw another experimental vineyard in Rocky Knob. The vines in Floyd County, however, were killed by winter frost the first winter. The following year, he replanted them. Lee and Lee, *Virginia Wine Country III*, 126.

254. Lee and Lee, *Virginia Wine Country*, 205–206; "Virginia's Ripe For Grapes, Vintners Find," *Roanoke Times & World News*, Papers of the Jeffersonian Wine Grape Growers Society, University of Virginia.

255. Lee and Lee, *Virginia Wine Country III*, 129.

256. Lee and Lee, *Virginia Wine Country III*, 126–128; Tom Angleberger, "Winery Employs Vintage Method of Construction Like Fine Wine," *Roanoke Times*, March 1, 1998, NV16.

257. Before moving to Virginia, O'Grady served as a freelance writer for a Baltimore newspaper during which he developed an interest in winemaking. O'Grady was introduced to the vineyard owned by an editor of a competing newspaper. The name, Rose Bower, was taken from an Irish period song in the mid-eighteenth century, "Come Back to the Rose Bower," with "Rose Bower" being a code name for Ireland pleading with Irish expatriates to return to the Emerald Isle. O'Grady had initially hoped to develop a winery that produced between 4,000 and 5,000 gallons of wine per year, to be sold to area residents and specialty shops. Sheppard Haw, "Wines and Verses," *Commonwealth Magazine*, October 1981, p. 48; Crews, "Drought was good for grapes," 6; Lee and Lee, *Virginia Wine Country*, 213.

258. Despite warnings from viticultural experts at the USDA and Virginia Tech, O'Grady "…wanted to find a way to use the land to have a small income. Things just seemed to work together," he said. In 1980, O'Grady anticipated an ultimate investment of $200,000 with 4,000 vines and a new crushing room. Crews, "Drought was good for grapes," 6; "112 Commercial Vineyards, 22 Farm Wineries Flourish in State," *Richmond Times-Dispatch*, L-23.

259. The winery by the 1980s boasted 10 acres of grapes capable of producing 1,500 cases of wine per

year. The winery sold its first vintage, a Nouveau, in 1980. Crews, "Drought was good for grapes," 6; *VWGJ* 7, no. 2 (Summer 1980): 137; Lee, Lee, and Talley, *Virginia Wine Country Revisited*, 169–171; "112 Commercial Vineyards, 22 Farm Wineries Flourish in State," *Richmond Times-Dispatch*, L-23; *VWGJ* 16, no. 4 (Winter 1989): 242–248; *Boar's Head Virginia Grapevine* 45 (Fall 1991).

260. Haw, "Wines and Verses," 48.

261. Haw, "Wines and Verses," 48.

262. The book followed O'Grady's publishing of poems in *McCall's Magazine* in 1971 and other small literary magazines in the early 1970s. The title for the movie was derived from a statement from a French vintner in France's Loire Valley who told O'Grady that anyone who works the land knows the land is a woman. The movie premiered at the first annual Albemarle Harvest Wine Festival in October 1981. O'Grady's role in the 1975 founding of *The Hampden Sydney Poetry Review*, the nation's second longest continuously run poetry journal, resulted in his receipt of an award from the National Endowment for the Arts, which assisted his efforts in constructing a wine cellar. O'Grady also was a participant in Virginia's Poet-in-the-Schools program and taught a wine appreciation course. O'Grady founded a poetry magazine, *The Hampden-Sydney Poetry Review*, in 1975. *VWGJ* 9, no. 4 (Winter 1982): 248; *VWGJ* 16, no. 4 (Winter 1989): 242–248; *VWGJ* 16, no. 4 (Winter 1989): 242–248.

263. *VWGJ* 16, no. 4 (Winter 1989): 242–248; Crews, "Drought was good for grapes," 6.

264. *VWGJ* 5, no. 1 (Spring 1978): 33; "112 Commercial Vineyards, 22 Farm Wineries Flourish in State," *Richmond Times-Dispatch*, L-23.

265. Early participants included Francis Sargent of Edinburg's Shenandoah Vineyards, Ltd., and retired naval captain Carl Hilscher of Luray's Valley of Virginia Vineyard, John Finley, and Carlotta Puckett.

266. A charter and bylaws were drafted stipulating each member's financial obligations, and that "Charter" members paid $5,000 per acre of grapes committed to the venture. They were granted, in turn, 50 shares of stock. Because the 1980 Virginia Farm Winery Act did not anticipate the formation of winery cooperatives, the General Assembly passed an amendment in 1984 classifying cooperatives as "Farm Wineries." *VWGJ* 11, no. 2 (Summer 1984): 86; Lee and Lee, *Virginia Wine Country*, 116–118; *VWGJ* 13, no. 3 (Fall 1986): 143; *VWGJ* 11, no. 5 (Spring 1985): 19; Lee and Lee, *Virginia Wine Country III*, 54 (noting that the cooperative was originally formed with 17 members in 1983); *VWGJ* 11, no. 3 (Fall 1984): 187.

267. The demonstration vineyard showcased multiple vinifera varieties, trellising canopies, and spacing systems for the educational benefit of the cooperative's members and the general public. Lee and Lee, *Virginia Wine Country*, 116–118; *VWGJ* 14, no. 1 (Spring 1987): 61; *VWGJ* 16, no. 3 (Fall 1989): 174.

268. The name was picked by Steve Reeder. Participating members could also bottle wine under their own label for personal consumption. Reeder, a University of California-Davis–trained Virginia native, boasted winemaking experience in California, New York, and Pennsylvania, as general manager and winemaker. Cathy Jett, "State Gets First Cooperative Winery," *The Free Lance–Star*, June 18, 1987, Lifestyle section, 37; *VWGJ* 14, no. 2 (Summer 1987): 122; *Vineyard & Winery Management* (July/August 1987): 10.

269. Lee and Lee, *Virginia Wine Country III*, 63, 89–90; Linda Couto, "Williamsburg Winery to Buy Vineyard," *Daily Press*, July 20, 1990, C1.

270. Weems, *Virginia Wineries: Your Complete Tour Guide*, 22–23.

271. The winery was replaced with a technology building for Germanna Community College—an institution named, ironically, for the seventeenth-century Germanna settlement where German settlers produced red and white Virginia wines. In justifying Dominion's closure, Williamsburg Winery owner Patrick Duffeler remarked to a reporter that few of the original growers produced grapes, Culpeper County was witnessing a dwindling grape industry, and Williamsburg Winery could save money by not transporting its products between Culpeper and Williamsburg. Donnie Johnston, "Dominion Wine Cellars closes Culpeper location," *The Free Lance–Star*, July 10, 2004, Business section, D1.

272. While Montdomaine in French means "mountain estate," it is believed to have derived from the "Mont" in Monticello and "domaine" from "Old Dominion." At the time, almost all Virginia red

grapes were French-American grapes, including Chambourcin, Chancellor, de Chaunac, Marechal Foch and more. VWGA, *The Wine Exchange*, no. 1 (January 1994): 17–18.

273. VWGA, *The Wine Exchange*, no. 1 (January 1994): 17–18; Rogan, "Virginia Wine Line," March 1984, p. 3; Gault, "America's Regional Wines: Virginia, Part Two," 22.

274. Goldenson, *Vintage Places: A Connoisseur's Guide to North American Wineries and Vineyards*, 87; Gault, "America's Regional Wines: Virginia, Part Two," 22; *Vineyard & Winery Management* (January/February 1997): 66.

275. Lee and Lee, *Virginia Wine Country III*, 100; Lee, Lee, and Talley, *Virginia Wine Country Revisited*, 193.

276. 1984 and 1985 Cabernet Sauvignon. *Boar's Head Virginia Grapevine* 36 (Fall 1988); *Boar's Head Virginia Grapevine* 38 (Winter 1988–1989); http://www.montdomaine.com/id5.html; *Vineyard & Winery Management* (January/February 1997): 66.

277. In particular, Montdomaine's founders appreciated Jefferson's suggestion concerning the laying out of vineyards on the southeastern slope of Green Mountain, at an altitude of 750 feet above sea level. Beida and Horton hired Owen Smith, also educated in California, as winemaker. Palmer, *Wineries of the Mid-Atlantic*, 199–201; VWGA, *The Wine Exchange*, no. 1 (January 1994): 17–18; "Horton Vineyards/Montdomaine Explores New Growth," *Charlottesville Business Journal*, March 1993; Rowe, *A History of Virginia Wine: From Grapes to Glass*, 38.

278. http://www.montdomaine.com/id5.html

279. *Boar's Head Grape Vine Press* 16 (Fall 1983).

280. John managed the store; Tommy became enthusiastic about Virginia wines after selling California and Virginia wines for an Arlington beverage company for 14 years; Berkley's interest peaked following trips to California and his enrollment in Germanna Community College's wine-appreciation classes in the 1980s, taught by Sharon Livingston, then a partner at Hartwood Winery. Gordon Kendall, "Virginia wines delivered to your door!" *Smith Mountain Laker Magazine*, January 1, 2010; Cathy Jett, "Picking a wine of the month," *The Free Lance–Star*, January 17, 1989, Lifestyle section, 17; "What's new in business," *The Free Lance–Star*, August 8, 1988.

281. After borrowing money to print 15,000 brochures and sending them to individuals on the Virginia Wine Association's mailing list. In the first five months, nearly 350 people signed up. The wines included a mix of recognized award-winning wines as well as newer artisan vintages not typically found in stores. Membership fees or enrollment periods would not be required; members would simply be billed or debited a standard monthly charge. The club's first offering was a nonvintage Sauvignon Blanc from Meredyth Vineyards, which had won the 1987 Governor's Cup. Other selections in the early years included champagnes from Oasis Vineyard, Gewürztraminer wine from Rapidan River Vineyards, and blushes from Willowcroft Farm Vineyards. Management of the club was turned over to Willis Logan, owner of Charlottesville's Virginia Shop in 2002. Jett, "Picking a wine of the month," 17; "What's new in business," *FLS*; Kendall, "Virginia wines delivered to your door!" *Smith Mountain Laker Magazine*.

282. Carroll completed minimal business courses at George Washington University, and got his start in retailing at the former Cheese and Bottle store in Arlington. At the advice of his father, he reluctantly opened his store in Leesburg. Customers routinely note Mike's expertise and personal attention as a critical element of his staying power and experience in visiting the store, and he continuously updates his selections in response to perceived customer tastes, which include many tourist and upper-income residents. Stephanie Stoughton, "Vintner Has Right Touch For Success," *The Washington Post*, April 30, 1998.

283. The store, originally founded and owned by businessman Herbert Haft, was later purchased and renamed Total Wine.

284. On the 256th anniversary of Jefferson's birthday in 1999, Clifton Inn chef Rachel Greenberg prepared a five-course feast paired with Virginia wine. *Boar's Head Virginia Grapevine* 29 (Winter 1987); Hamlin, "Jefferson's vision finally bears fruit," *The New York Times*.

285. Jordan's, a restaurant located in downtown Leesburg, served wines from nearby Willowcroft Farm Vineyards. The popular Bavarian Chef, located outside of Madison, featured several German-style

white wines made in Virginia. Virginia Wine Growers Advisory Board, *Status of the Virginia Wine Industry*, 10, 34.

286. To determine each year's invitees, the restaurant solicited samples from across Virginia. The event proved an instant success that would grow in attendance and ultimately become a critical annual barometer of food and wine trends. As Virginia's wine industry matured, so too did the menus, which showed an evolution in whites from Riesling to Chardonnay and other drier varieties, including Cabernet Franc. Desaulniers, originally from Rhode Island, would ultimately become well-known as a chef and cookbook writer. Jim Raper, "Humble Steward: Creative Meal Accents Best of Virginia's Wines," *Virginian-Pilot*, May 12, 2004; *Boar's Head Virginia Grapevine* 27 (Fall 1986).

287. Ann O'Hanlon, "Virginia's Winemakers Striving to Give Their Grapes Good Press," *The Washington Post*, May 30, 1996.

288. Thomas W. Lippman and Joel Glenn Brenner, "…Stuck a Feather in His Cap and Called it Chardonnay," *The Washington Post*, June 19, 1989.

289. The vineyard's recreation was part of an overall restoration of the mansion and its grounds. Lucie Morton assisted in identifying grape varieties. As Monticello's superintendent of grounds & gardens wrote, "It will not be so much a salute to [Jefferson's] accomplishments as a testament to his vision and the urgent ambition of his great experiment." The varieties included a handful of Italian varieties, including Mammolo, Trebbiano, Toscano, and Malvasia Bianca, as well as the Alexander, and Muscat. Landscape blueprints from 1778 and circa 1811, collated with written documents, helped William L. Beiswanger, then Monticello's director of restoration, find the right site. The plantings following a 1984 archeological investigation that confirmed the existence of four-foot-wide terraces and cramped six-foot spacing between rows, and suggested use of a wooden trellis system for espaliers. Because Jefferson left scantly little to guide those who followed in his footsteps, Hatch recreated the vineyard by looking up the wine and table grapes Jefferson listed in his *Garden Book*, a diary of his horticultural activities from 1766 to 1824. To identify the colonial-era names of the grapes, Hatch pored over 19th- and 20th-century French, Italian, and American viticultural literature. The site's location offered superior protection against late spring frosts, and its restoration, based on the most fully documented planting records available, included 23 varieties of mostly European table grapes, with some European wine grapes as well. These varieties included eight from a Georgetown nurseryman, Thomas Main; seven from Philip Mazzei; and eight dry wine vines from the Florence Botanical Garden by Thomas Appelton, the local ambassador. The varieties were clustered, suggesting the experimental nature of the vineyard rather than a concerted effort by Jefferson to produce wine. *VWGJ* 11, no. 3 (Fall 1985): 148–151; Barbara Ensrud, *American Vineyards* (New York: Stewart, Tabori & Chang, 1988), 71; "A Vintner's Vintner," *Virginia Living*; *VWGJ* 16, no. 3 (Fall 1989): 147.

290. The bottled wine was subsequently distributed to the estate's staff and friends. The 1985, 1986, and 1987 vintages from the young vines yielded skimpy and diseased grapes. But surprisingly, 1988 was, according to Hatch, Monticello's "vintage of the century." Other grapes were crushed into 325 bottles of a white table wine and 75 gallons were crushed into a red blend, both of which bore labels which read "Monticello Gardening" to celebrate the work of the estate's staff. The wines were distributed to employees. Others were used at Board of Trustees meetings. While the estate had to spray in previous years, 1988 was the first year the vineyard was organic (no spraying). Varieties included Muscat of Alexandria, Malaga Rosada, Luglienga, and Olivette Blanc. Gabriele Rausse continues to oversee the estate's vineyards and winemaking process. The vineyard was afflicted with a fungus and had to be replanted. *VWGJ* 16, no. 3 (Fall 1989): 147; "A Vintner's Vintner," *Virginia Living*.

291. While publications internal to the industry, including the *Vinifera Wine Growers Journal*, *The Boar's Head Virginia Grapevine*, and the *Virginia Wine Journal*, offered wine news and happenings, their distribution was limited to their membership.

292. A consummate advocate for wine's place as a health beverage, and with an eye towards reducing the cost of wine, Adams routinely advised winemakers to lobby their respective state legislators to permit wineries and vineyards to be co-located. In 1933, Adams founded a wine trade industry lobbying group, the California Grape Growers League, which helped spur the creation of the Wine Institute in 1934 and the 1938 founding of the Wine Advisory Board. Adams helped run all three

groups for nearly two decades, during which he clamored for improved wine laws and the planting of high-quality varieties. Adams also founded the Society of Medical Friends of Wine, an organization of doctors who promoted the beneficial health effects of wine. Emerson Klees, *Paul Garrett: Dean of American Winemakers* (Rochester, NY: Cameo Press Imprint, 2010), 14; Lucie T. Morton, *Winegrowing in Eastern America* (Ithaca, NY: Cornell University Press, 1985), 47; *VWGJ* 6, no. 1 (Spring 1979): 40; Lucie Morton, "A Farewell to Leon D. Adams," *Vineyard & Winery Management* (November/December 1995): 53; Howard G. Goldberg, "Leon Adams, Wine Expert and Writer, 90," *The New York Times*, September 16, 1995.

293. He also highlighted the few older wineries then operating in the commonwealth, including John June Lewis' Woburn Winery and Mac Sands' Richard's Wine Cellar in Petersburg. By then, Virginia offered a full array of modern wineries to highlight, including Farfelu, Barboursville, Meredyth, La Abra, Rapidan, and more. Leon D. Adams, *The Wines of America* (Boston: Houghton Mifflin, 1973), 55–59; Leon D. Adams, *The Wines of America* 3rded. (New York: McGraw-Hill, 1985), 67–70; Morton, *Winegrowing in Eastern America*, 46–49.

294. Goldberg, "Leon Adams, Wine Expert and Writer, 90," *The New York Times*.

295. A cadre of dedicated columnists recorded the early history of the state's wine rebirth industry, including James Conway, John Harris, and Thomas W. Lippman at *The Washington Post*; Cathy Jett at the *Free Lance–Star*; Beth Crittenden at the *Roanoke Times*; and Jim Raper at the *Virginian-Pilot*. In 1976, Cattell and McKee had purchased the rights to publish Howard Miller's *The Pennsylvania Grape Letter*, which had begun publication in 1974, and renamed it *The Pennsylvania Grape Letter and Wine News*. Beginning in 1983, Archie Smith III began a series critiquing varietals beginning in 1983 for *Wine East*. The series reviewed eastern North American varietals after having tasted a series of same-varietal wines and interviewed the winemakers and growers. Jacques Recht began his series in 1984. *Boar's Head Virginia Grapevine* 35 (Summer 1988); *Boar's Head Virginia Grapevine* 38 (Spring 1989); Virginia Wine Growers Advisory Board, *Status of the Virginia Wine Industry*, 12.

296. The wineries included Barboursville, Montdomaine, Oakencroft, Rapidan River, Shenandoah, Oasis, Meredyth, Piedmont, and Ingleside. Hudson Cattell and Lee Miller, *Wine East of the Rockies* (Lancaster, PA: L & H Photojournalism, 1982), 80–81; Goldenson, *Vintage Places: A Connoisseur's Guide to North American Wineries and Vineyards*, 73–74, 86–95.

297. The book provided a short history of American winemaking, the post-Prohibition pioneering efforts of Philip Wagner and Dr. Konstantin Frank, and climatic information, as well as information on site selection and growing techniques. Morton, *Winegrowing in Eastern America*.

298. Ensrud noted the contributions of Elizabeth Furness, the Smith family at Meredyth, Lucie Morton, Jacques Recht, and, most of all, Felicia Warburg Rogan. Twenty Virginia wineries were selected by Jon Palmer for inclusion in his *Wineries of Mid-Atlantic*, also published in 1988, which included a brief history of Virginia winemaking, as well as a map and directory of all Virginia wineries. Thomas K. Hardy, *Pictorial Atlas of North American Wines* (San Francisco: Grape Vision, 1988), 363–367; Ensrud, *American Vineyards*, 60–72; *Boar's Head Virginia Grapevine* 34 (Spring 1988).

299. The book was republished as an expanded second edition in 1989. The VWGA sought input from consumers, libraries, agricultural experts, and historical societies. R. de Treville Lawrence III, ed. *Jefferson and Wine: A Model of Moderation* (Vinifera Wine Growers Association: The Plains, Virginia 1989); *VWGJ* 2, no. 1 (Spring 1976): 43.

300. Jett, "Future Rosy for Virginia's Wineries," *FLS*; *VWGJ* 15, no. 1 (Spring 1988): 63.

301. The recipes were created by Hilde and were intended to accompany *Virginia Wine Country Revisited*.

302. *VWGJ* 11, no. 4 (Winter 1984): 264; Virginia Wine Growers Advisory Board, *Status of the Virginia Wine Industry*, 12.

303. Weems, *Virginia Wineries: Your Complete Tour Guide*, 74–75; Hilda Gabriel Lee and Allan E. Lee, *Serve with Virginia Wine* (Charlottesville, Va.: Hildesigns Press, 1994), 8–9; Lee and Lee, *Virginia Wine Country III*, 180–181; *VWGJ* 11, no. 2 (Summer 1985): 126; Ann Heidig, "Grape Supply and Demand in Virginia: About Equal for 1987," *Vineyard & Winery Management* (May/June 1987): 48; *VWGJ* 15, no. 2 (Summer 1988): 127; *VWGJ* 16, no. 4 (Winter 1989): 252; Blue, *American Wine: A Comprehensive Guide*, 479; *VWGJ* 18, no. 3 (Fall 1991): 173; Virginia Wine Growers Advisory Board,

*Status of the Virginia Wine Industry*, 12.

304. Virginia Wine Growers Advisory Board, *Status of the Virginia Wine Industry*, 14.

305. Meredyth Vineyards edged out 17 other wineries to win the Governor's Cup for the festival's best wine for its 1983 Chardonnay.

306. Virginia Wine Growers Advisory Board, *Status of the Virginia Wine Industry*, 13, 22.

307. Meredyth Vineyards was the only Virginia winery to sell significant amounts outside the commonwealth, but others were beginning to follow. Elizabeth Hubbard Worrall, president of nearby Piedmont Vineyards, for example, went to Chicago in 1985 with hopes of opening up that market.

308. Virginia Wine Growers Advisory Board, *Status of the Virginia Wine Industry*, 13, 17.

# Chapter 4 Notes

1.  That consuming wine could lead to better health was nothing new; the beverage had long been termed "man's oldest medicine," and the first medical journal reports linking wine to good health had appeared in the late 1970s. The *60 Minutes* report, though, was altogether different, and it electrified the wine industry. The term was coined by Boston University School of Medicine Professor Dr. Curtis Ellison. While he believed white wine, beer, and liquor provided some added protection, they did not provide the same level as red wine. The report noted that the chances of a middle-aged American dying of a heart attack were 300 percent more likely than a Frenchman despite the fact that the average French smoke more, exercise less, and their diet contains 30 percent more fat. "We don't know exactly how," Dr. Ellison later said, "but antioxidants and tannins, especially in red wine, protect the heart, and appear to play a role in thwarting other diseases—cancer, diabetes, osteoporosis, dementia." Laura Boswell, "Winemaking Assumes Festive Air in Region; Tours, Tastings abound in Virginia, Maryland," *The Washington Times*, September 18, 2003.

2.  Over the next two decades, America's demand for wine would grow so strong that by 2010 the United States consumed more wine than France. The *Lancet*, in 1979, tracked the studies of Professor A. S. St. Leger and his associates, which evaluated World Health Organization data and found low levels of heart disease in France's red wine–producing regions. St. Leger suggested that red wine should be examined for its constituents and for ingredients that affected blood lipids and platelet aggregation. Undoubtedly, Virginia's nascent industry benefited from the increasingly publicized health benefits of moderate alcohol consumption. Many Virginia vineyards also started shifting their mixtures to make them more in tune with market desires—especially in light of recent reports that tied red French-American wines to reduced risk of heart disease. Though Americans in 1991 consumed 75 percent white wine and 25 percent red, Virginia wineries began decreasing outputs of whites while increasing reds (particularly Merlot, a Virginia favorite). Given the climate and soil conditions in Virginia, this proved more lucrative for winemakers as red grapes are more temperamental to grow and ferment, but on average, Virginia reds like Cabernet and Bordeaux sold for $11, while Chardonnay and Sauvignon Blanc sold for $7. The phenomenon's publicity through *60 Minutes* led to an explosion in American wine sales—particularly in California—as wine was sold as a remedy for cardiovascular health. Some claims were made that, by January 1992, red wine alcohol sales had increased by 50 percent. *Lancet*, May 12, 1979.

3.  Paul Dellinger, "State of Wine," *Roanoke Times*, December 2, 2001.

4.  Jim Raper, "From Pets to Polo Matches," *VA Business*, September 28, 2009.

5.  Wineries offering yoga included Hiddencroft Vineyards, Lost Creek Winery, Hillsborough Vineyards, Keswick Vineyards, Potomac Point Winery, and The Barns at Hamilton Station. Jim Raper, "From Pets to Polo Matches," *VA Business*, September 28, 2009; Dave McIntyre, "In Grape Shape: Loudon County Cultivates a Fast-Growing Wine Industry," *The Washington Post*, October 14, 2009. Blue Ridge Bridal Shows, which is produced by Encore Event Partners, LLC and hosts five wedding expositions annually focusing on marketing the Shenandoah Valley as an international wedding destination region, announced in April 2010 that it would focus on marketing Virginia wineries in the Blue Ridge region as wedding venues. The first show in the series was held at Prince William's Winery at La Grange, and featured the winery's winemaker and managing partner, Chris Pearmund, as speaker. Lacking, however, were cooler temperatures. Higher temperatures can "boil away" some characteristics of wine grapes. Raper, "From Pets to Polo Matches."

6.  Conaway's position was echoed by Linden Vineyards' Jim Law: "Ten years ago most residents viewed wineries and vineyards as a welcome, benign neighbor. Not only were vineyards romantic, but they enhanced property values. This euphoric period is history now...." James Conway, "General Assembly Matters Pique Readers' Interest," *Richmond Times-Dispatch*, February 4, 2006; Graeme Zielinski, "Neighbors Seek Peace, Owners Seek Growth; Winery Conflict Sours Some in Va." *The Washington Post*, April 30, 2000; Jim Law, "Achieving Balance in Wine Country," *Flavor Magazine*, April/May 2010, p. 83.

7.  Other localities imposed restrictions as well, resulting in a patchwork of regulations that limited the

number of large events at wineries, imposed noise levels, and even limited the number of cases of wine that could be produced. "I remember, we were sitting in the conservatory in the afternoon, and this helicopter came flying very low over the hills," recalled Oasis neighbor Lindy Hart. "We thought there maybe was an accident. (Graeme Zielinski, "Neighbors Seek Peace, Owners Seek Growth; Winery Conflict Sours Some in Va." *The Washington Post*, April 30, 2000). The General Assembly also directed the Secretary of Agriculture and Forestry to conduct a yearlong study of regulations on the economic viability and land use compatibility of the state's farm wineries. The Secretary's efforts mirrored those of a comprehensive 2006 study conducted by the U.S. Department of Agriculture entitled, "The Impact of Wine, Grapes and Grape Products on the American Economy 2007," which estimated that the economic impact of Virginia's wine industry was approximately $290 million. The study also found that the United States was poised to overtake France in wine consumption. See HB 2071, § 15.2-2288.3; HB 1435, 2006 General Assembly Session § 15.2-2288.2; Frederick Kunkle, "No One's Breaking Bread With This Wine," *The Washington Post*, August 31, 2009.

8.    Tarpley Ashworth, "County Planning Commission Work Session Hears Objections From Wine Growers," *Charlottesville Tomorrow*, November 12, 2009. Observers surmised that the idea for the bill came from the owners of Oasis Winery, who had recently lost a case before the Fauquier County Board of Zoning Appeals over fireworks and loud music during an event. (Frederick Kunkle, "No One's Breaking Bread With This Wine," *The Washington Post*, August 31, 2009.) Under former county regulations, special events at wineries were limited to 150 persons, and those with more had to apply for a special permit that could only be granted 12 times per year. King Family Vineyards' owner David King asserted that the proposed regulations would put his winery out of business while others said it was hard to predict the number of attendees at events. (Tarpley Ashworth, "County Planning Commission Work Session Hears Objections From Wine Growers," *Charlottesville Tomorrow*, November 12, 2009.) Music was not permitted to be audible 100 feet away from the winery's property line or inside a neighboring home. Jefferson Vineyards' Chad Zakaib told the Planning Commission, "It is not an easy business, but it will be made less challenging by virtue of the clarity that this ordinance will provide." The Virginia Wine Council's Matt Conrad agreed, testifying that the ordinance "might become a model for the state." Seven months after adoption, Albemarle's Planning Commission held roundtable "feedback" sessions between representatives from wineries and their neighbors. While many neighbors requested stricter noise and event standards, many winery owners wanted clarification on noise levels. In March 2011, the Board of Supervisors adopted an objective decibel standard to measure noise from any event held in a rural setting. "Noise Ordinance Irks Albemarle Wineries," January 17, 2011, NBC29, http://www.nbc29.com/story/13856322/noise-ordinance-irks-albemarle-wineries (viewed May 16, 2015); *Newsplex.Com*, "Supervisors Vote to Change Noise Ordinance to Decibel Standard," March 10, 2011.

9.    The owner of Three Fox Vineyards, John Todhunter, argued that Fauquier's proposed ordinance would stifle the industry. Others asserted their belief that there was no statutory authority for Fauquier's new regulations, said in a Facebook message that the proposed legislation was "so extreme that it will put many wineries out of business." Even with the specter of new regulations pending, Roeder cancelled several outdoor events and cancelled a contract for a roving food cart around his property. Don Del Rosso, "Board Delays Decision on Divisive Winery Proposal," *Fauquier Times-Democrat*, November 2009; "County May Shut Down Wine and Sunsets in Virginia," blogpost by Donna C., November 11th, 2009; Amy Loeffler, "Squash That Vine: Sour Grapes in NoVA Wine Country," *NOVAMAG*, November 12, 2009. The changes, proposed by the staff, after a detailed review beginning in November 2007, were billed by the county's zoning administrator as "a loosening" of the county's ordinances because the current county ordinances did not address winery events. (Amy Loeffler, "Squash That Vine: Sour Grapes in NoVA Wine Country," *NOVAMAG*, November 12, 2009; Don Del Rosso, "Board Delays Decision on Divisive Winery Proposal," *Fauquier Times-Democrat*, November 2009.) Both suits alleged that the new regulations violated the Virginia's Farm Winery Act, which read that the "usual and customary activities and events at farm wineries shall be permitted without local regulation unless there is a substantial impact on the health, safety or welfare of the public." In July

2013, Virginia Attorney General Ken Cuccinelli issued an advisory opinion that some of the county's ordinances violated the state constitution. "A Tale of Two Lawsuits," *Wines & Vines*, February 26, 2013.

10. Jenalia Moreno, "Zoning Law Corks Plans For Winery," *The Washington Post*, March 24, 2005, Prince William Extra. The home was completely restored and refurbished with period furnishings, artwork, and décor, while the exterior gardens were transformed into more-formal English gardens. In January 2012, Pearmund sold his interest in La Grange to a major Chinese firm, Beida Jade Bird. The Chinese company retained Pearmund as managing partner, consultant, and spokesperson until June 2012, when he was fired and barred from future involvement with the winery. The Winery at La Grange was put up for sale in December 2010 for $7 million.

11. Linda Jones McKee, "Washington, D.C., Suburb OKs Winery," *Wines and Vines*, December 26, 2008; Frederick Kunkle, "No One's Breaking Bread With This Wine," *The Washington Post*, August 31, 2009. Hoping to use the venture to keep the land within their family, Kirk learned to grow grapes from winery owner and entrepreneur Chris Pearmund, who also sold grapes to the Wileses while their newly planted vines matured. The Wileses settled on the name "Paradise Springs Winery," to recognize the springs located in nearby Clifton that once provided bottled mineral water in the early twentieth century and were prized for their healing and health powers. Rumor has it that Clifton itself was founded, in part, because of the presence of wild grapes good enough to make wine. Wiles's ancestor, Wansford Arrington, received approximately 1,000 acres, including a portion of the winery property, under a 1716 grant from Lord Fairfax. When an elderly aunt, Esther Podolnick, died in 2006, Jane inherited the estate and pondered ways to preserve the property in the wake of mounting inheritance taxes totaling approximately $750,000. While she considered selling the property to residential developers who would have taken the property out of the family's hands for the first time since 1716, Jane remarked, "I really didn't want to break the chain. I just wanted to really give new life to this place." (Amy Gardner, "Regulations Sour Dream of Winery," *The Washington Post*, December 4, 2008; McKee, "Washington, D.C., Suburb OKs Winery.") The property featured rolling hills, rustic scenery with mature trees, wooden fencing, and an 18th-century log cabin. (Gardner, "Regulations Sour Dream of Winery"; Derek Kravitz, "Paradise Springs Winery Opens in Fairfax after Zoning Battle," *The Washington Post*, January 12, 2010.) "They're trying to blockade this winery," said Chris Pearmund of the county's efforts. "Fairfax is not agricultural. It does not want to be agricultural. If this winery were to open, the county is afraid that more small-parcel wineries would open, and you've got a Pandora's box." (McKee, "Washington, D.C., Suburb OKs Winery"; Gardner, "Regulations Sour Dream of Winery"; William C. Flook, "Fairfax County Sets Aside Zoning Law, Approves Proposed Winery in Clifton," *D.C. Examiner*, December 9, 2008.) Despite the strong showing of support for the winery, the Board of Supervisors rescinded its second vote on learning that it had no ability to either interpret or prohibit enforcement of the zoning ordinance. In February 2009, the Wileses argued their appeal before the Fairfax County Board of Zoning Appeals, which upheld the zoning administrator's opinion. The Wileses immediately appealed to the Fairfax County Circuit Court alleging that the county had overstepped its legal authority to regulate wineries and that its interpretation lacked a sufficient legal basis. *Kirk Wiles, Jane Kincheloe Wiles, and Paradise Springs Winery, LLC* v. *Board of Zoning Appeals for Fairfax County, Virginia*, Case No. CL-2009-0003136 (Fx. Co. Cir. Ct.) (Springfield District).

12. "Growing grapes is not an offensive thing to the environment. But having weddings and parties— that's an unlimited use that could have an impact on the environment," Bonheivert added. Others still expressed concerns that the fertilizer from the grapes would be harmful to the environment. Frederick Kunkle, "No One's Breaking Bread With This Wine," *The Washington Post*, August 31, 2009; Kali Schmumltz, "Neighbors Seeing Red Over New Winery in Fairfax County," *Fairfax Times*, February 23, 2010; Derek Kravitz, "Paradise Springs Winery Opens in Fairfax after Zoning Battle," *The Washington Post*, January 12, 2010.

13. Despite the excitement, reports surfaced of nosy neighbors trespassing onto the winery property to take investigative photos and to harass the winery's employees. Some nearby residents complained that winery representatives had taped "un-invitation" letters to their mailboxes informing them that

their presence was not welcome at the grand opening unless they first met with the winery owners. Kirk Wiles candidly admitted, "We've had to do some things to keep them away…. We've been at this for three years and we're tired of fighting, we're tired of trying to please people."(Layla Wilder, "Fairfax County Lands Its First Winery," *Fairfax Times*, January 12, 2010.) Supervisor Pat Herrity remarked to a reporter that the winery would help preserve Clifton's agricultural heritage: "It's always a great day when we can open a new business that creates real jobs, especially in this tough economy. The winery will be a great addition to Clifton, one of the best-kept secrets of Fairfax County." After the opening weekend, the Wileses agreed to an informal agreement that the winery would not become a large-scale commercial operation. Pamela Barnett, the president of a nearby homeowners' association remarked, "Our concern at this point is not just concern for our area. It's a Fairfax County issue…. We just happen to be the first ones to experience [it]." Complaining about the opening day traffic, Nobel Estates resident Jill Hill remarked, "The traffic was insane; there were people parking everywhere. It was just an ugly, ugly weekend." Responding to traffic complaints, the Wileses subsequently met with Supervisor Pat Herrity and representatives of the Northern Virginia Regional Park Authority to address future parking issues, and the Wileses installed a gravel parking lot on the property. (Kali Schmumltz, "Neighbors Seeing Red Over New Winery in Fairfax County," *Fairfax Times*, February 23, 2010.) The wine is the product of six different cultured yeasts and 100 percent chardonnay grapes procured from Fauquier County's Meriwether Vineyard, owned by entrepreneur and Paradise Springs consultant Chris Pearmund. Meriwether, planted in 1976 and purchased by Pearmund in 1991, is one of the oldest Chardonnay vineyards in the commonwealth. (Dave McIntyre, "Wine: A Virginia Newcomer Wins Big," *The Washington Post*, October 7, 2010.) The winery also fared well in the Governor's Cup red categories, taking home a gold medal for its Norton and Cabernet Franc, as well as a "Best in Category" for its white Sommet Blanc at the Atlantic Seaboard Wine Competition. Paradise Springs has also been a regular feature at the annual Clifton Wine Festival and, in 2011, the winery opened a 10,000-square-foot winemaking building. "Paradise Springs Wins award for Best VA White," *Richmond Times-Dispatch*, October 10, 2010; Frederick Kunkle, "Farm Winery Squeezes by Fairfax Zoning Law," *The Washington Post*, September 4, 2009; *In re* Paradise Springs Winery, LLC, Alcoholic Beverage Control Bd., Appl. #056973,1 (Sept. 3, 2009); Peter Vieth, "Wine Barred: Virginia 'Farm Wineries' Battle Neighbors in D.C. Suburbs," *Virginia Lawyers Weekly*, November 2, 2009.

14. Vieth, "Wine Barred: Virginia 'Farm Wineries' Battle Neighbors in D.C. Suburbs."

15. Virginia Code § 8.01-336(D); Peter Vieth, "Wine Barred: Virginia 'Farm Wineries' Battle Neighbors in D.C. Suburbs," *Virginia Lawyers Weekly*, November 2, 2009. The judge relied on a provision from the HOA's handbook that said that "activities that cause external changes or lead to regular visits by customers are not acceptable." (Alexandra Bogdanovic, "Jury to Decide Whether Tasting Room Can Stay," *Fauquier Times-Democrat*, July 1, 2009.) At trial, the Marterellas' attorney provided evidence that the community's covenants expressly permitted agriculture, and that "farm winery" included retail sales. In addition, he submitted that the Landowner's Council had forfeited its right to prohibit the winery because it had previously approved the smaller winery. He wrote that the Marterellas' "on-site retail sales give rise to both of these occurrences." As to the Marterellas' assertion that the HOA had waived its right to enforce the use restriction, Parker cited other instances in which the prohibition of one use was acceptable even though similar uses had previously been approved. *Bellevue Landowners Council, Inc. v. Charles G. Marterella, et ux,* 79 Va. Cir. 320, 324 (2009); *Marterella v. Bellevue Landowners Council, Inc.*, No. 111625, slip op. at 5 (Va. May 11, 2012); *Fauquier Times-Democrat*, "Marterella Fights On Despite Bankruptcy," August 21, 2013; Philip Carter Strother and Andrew E. Tarne, "Land Use And Zoning Law," *University of Richmond Law Review* 47 (November 2012): 247–254.

16. At least one group, "Virginians for Responsible Wineries," was formed out of a concern for winery marketing activities. Winemaker Jordan Harris, for example, reinvigorated Loudoun County's Tarara Winery—which until recently was better known for its festivals and events rather than the quality of its wine—into a wine-first operation. Graeme Zielinski, "Neighbors Seek Peace, Owners Seek

Growth; Winery Conflict Sours Some in Va.," *The Washington Post*, April 30, 2000.

17. The three-tier system was most likely a reaction to the need to minimize the potential for a criminal element in the legal distribution system. A. C. Grafstrom, "Commerce—Intoxicating Liquors: Wine Lovers Rejoice! Why Vineyards Can Now Ship Directly to Customers and Why Everyone Else Should Care," *North Dakota Law Review* 82 (2005): 557–578; Barbara C. Beliveau and Elizabeth M. Rouse, "Prohibition and Repeal: A Short History of the Wine Industry's Regulation in the United States," *Journal of Wine Economics* 5, No. 1 (2010): 57.

18. Christina Rogers, "Wine Retailers Find Law's Effects Bitter," *Roanoke Times*, December 2, 2006; Rob Johnson, "Bill's Demise is Bitter Fruit," *Roanoke Times*, February 7, 2006; Jacqueline L. Salmon, "Law on Va. Wine Sales Struck Down," *The Washington Post*, March 31, 2002; Portsia Smith, "Wineries Toast Ruling," *The Fredericksburg Free Lance–Star*, May 18, 2005.

19. "Virginia Wine Industry Wants State Laws Changed," *Richmond Times Dispatch*, May 13, 2002; Rob Johnson, "Bill's Demise is Bitter Fruit," *Roanoke Times*, February 7, 2006; James A. Archer, "Wine Solutions Should Help Everyone," *Roanoke Times*, December 28, 2006; Tom Campbell, "Wine-Shipment Law Challenged; Individuals, Wineries are Suing ABC Board," *Richmond Times-Dispatch*, November 18, 1999; Jacqueline L. Salmon, "Law on Va. Wine Sales Struck Down," *The Washington Post*, March 31, 2002.

20. Donald Boudreaux, "Rules on Wine Sales Amount to a Protection Racket," Norfolk *Virginian-Pilot*, July 18, 2002.

21. The three wineries were Hood River Vineyards of Hood River, Oregon, Dry Comal Creek Vineyards of New Braunfels, Texas, and Miura Vineyards of Calistoga, California. (Tom Campbell, "Wine-Shipment Law Challenged; Individuals, Wineries are Suing ABC Board," *Richmond Times-Dispatch*, November 18, 1999; "Free Traders Fight for Wine in Federal Court: Wineries and Consumers Barrel Over Bureaucrats in Virginia Courthouse," Coalition for Free Trade Newsletter, Vol. 4, No. 1, January 22, 2001, http://vintners.net/wawine/misc/cft_012301.pdf [viewed May 16, 2015]). Heatwole's suit was joined by other federal lawsuits in Indiana and Texas, all of which demanded the personal right to order wine directly from wineries outside the state. Judge Williams also found that the ban had "both the purpose and effect of prohibiting an out-of-state entity from participating in direct marketing and shipment of wine and beer to Virginia residents." (Tom Campbell, "Wine-Shipment Law Challenged; Individuals, Wineries are Suing ABC Board," *Richmond Times-Dispatch*, November 18, 1999.) More than a year before the establishment of the Virginia Winery Distribution Company, the Fourth Circuit Court of Appeals ruled in September 2006 that the practice of selling exclusively Virginia wines at the commonwealth's ABC stores was constitutional under the so-called "market participant" exception to the Commerce Clause of the U.S. Constitution. The Federal magistrate was Judge Dennis W. Dohnal. Campbell, "State Alcohol Laws Shaken; Ban on Wine, Beer Shipments Unconstitutional, Judge Rules," *Times-Dispatch*, March 31, 2002; Christopher Dinsmore, "Ruling Could Hit ABC Stores: Judge's Decision on Wine Shipping May Also Threaten Va. Liquor System," Norfolk *Virginian-Pilot*, April 4, 2002.

22. Michael Laris, "Rule Allowing Direct Sale Of Wine in Va. Is Put on Hold," *The Washington Post*, April 2, 2002.

23. Jacqueline L. Salmon, "Law on Va. Wine Sales Struck Down," *The Washington Post*, March 31, 2002.

24. Christopher Dinsmore, "Virginia to Appeal Ruling on Liquor Law," Norfolk *Virginian-Pilot*, April 2, 2002; Chris H. Sieroty, "Virginia Ends Tight Wine Law," United Press International, May 28, 2003. "The new wine shipment law, along with our increased efforts to promote tourism around Virginia's wineries, will allow our wineries to continue to grow and prosper as they put Virginia wines up against wines from around the world," said Governor Warner during the signing ceremony at Albemarle County's Kluge Estate Winery & Vineyard. While Virginia wineries anticipated a boost in sales to out-of-state consumers, wineries found themselves stunted by Virginia's ABC, which proposed a series of post-legislative supplemental reciprocity agreements that delayed shipments and confused Virginia winemakers. "No one is really fully informed as to what the new law…allows us to do," said Krista Jackson-Foster, co-owner of North Mountain Vineyard. "We just tell our prospective customers at this point that we do not ship." Such sentiments were echoed by Gordon W. Murchie,

executive director of the Virginia Wineries Association: "It did not achieve the original goal set for the legislation," Murchie said. "It is more restrictive than anticipated. We are trying to consider how to amend it to make it more acceptable." (Anne Gowen, "Out-of-State Sales of Va. Wines Awash in Legal Confusion," *The Washington Post*, December 22, 2003; Kevin Miller, "Bill Eases Virginia's Wine Trade Rules," *Roanoke Times*, February 1, 2003.) During the interim three-day period between the ruling and the stay, on advice from the Attorney General's office, the ABC department's chief operating officer, W. Curtis Coleburn III, informed store managers to pull Virginia wine from store shelves. Consequently, none was sold. (Tom Campbell, "ABC Ruling on Hold for Appeal," *Richmond Times-Dispatch*, April 2, 2002; Michael Laris, "Rule Allowing Direct Sale Of Wine in Va. Is Put on Hold," *The Washington Post*, April 2, 2002.) Republican Attorney General Kilgore and Democrat Governor Mark R. Warner met that month to discuss the merits of an appeal and potential legislation. When pressed by reporters as to why Warner and Kilgore are "in agreement on the ABC case but not on the equally thorny political and legal issues of [legislative] redistricting," Warner's Press Secretary Ellen Qualls responded, "Booze brings everyone together." (Tom Campbell, "ABC Ruling on Hold for Appeal," *Richmond Times-Dispatch*, April 2, 2002; Campbell, "Liquor Lawsuit Sent Back," *Times-Dispatch*, May 25, 2003.) Under the three-tier system, manufacturers of alcohol must sell their products to wholesalers, who distribute them to retailers. An exception allows state wineries to sell their wines to retailers, as well as to visitors to their businesses.

25. Many Virginia wineries were concerned about not being able to find a distributor or, even if one was found, not having an overcommitted distributor who could sufficiently market their wines. "I can't afford to have a distributor," said J. D. Hartman, then winemaker at Madison County's Christensen Ridge Winery. "It would cost 40 percent right off the top. That's just not feasible for a winery our size." (Associated Press State & Local Wire, "Virginia's Small Vintners Have Little Reason To Toast New Law," July 4, 2006; Brian McNeill, "Bill Seeks to Aid Small Wineries: Reinstation of Self-distribution Sought," *McClatchy-Tribune Business News*, January 3, 2007.) The oldest winery in Loudoun County, Willowcroft Farm Vineyards, sold approximately 60 percent of its 3,000 cases annually at the winery while the rest were sold directly to retailers. (Michael Alison Chandler, "One Case Resolved, Another on the Vine," *The Washington Post*, July 7, 2005; Lois Caliri, "Small Wineries Are Feeling Boxed In," *Roanoke Times*, May 29, 2005.

26. Rob Johnson, "Bill's Demise is Bitter Fruit," *Roanoke Times*, February 7, 2006; Greg Edwards, "Panel to Study Wine-law Revision," *Richmond Times-Dispatch*, January 25, 2006.) Albo's campaign received nearly $50,000 in contributions from distributors in 2006.

27. Associated Press State & Local Wire, "Virginia's Small Vintners Have Little Reason to Toast New Law," July 4, 2006; Greg Edwards, "Wineries' Big Blow," *Richmond Times-Dispatch*, July 8, 2006.

28. "Virginia's Small Vintners Have Little Reason to Toast New Law," Associated Press State & Local Wire, July 4, 2006. Not all Virginia winemakers were dismayed with Albo's legislation, however. Brad McCarthy, then winemaker at Blenheim Vineyards, believed the new law to be an important steppingstone in legitimizing Virginia wines in the eyes of the world. "This will force Virginia wineries to operate in the real world," he says. "Price per quality, that's what distributors look for. This is how wine is sold. And that's the reality that people in Virginia have to address." Bethany Fuller, "New Law Bittersweet for Lynchburg, Va.-area Winery," Lynchburg *News & Advance* September 28, 2006; Brian McNeill, "Bill Seeks to Aid Small Wineries: Reinstation of Self-distribution Sought," *McClatchy-Tribune Business News*, January 3, 2007; Conor Reilly, "Lawmakers, Vintners Push for Bills on Self-distribution," Lynchburg *News & Advance*, January 19, 2007.

29. Some wine retailers found that the markups of wine were anywhere from 15 to 30 percent over the prices previously commanded directly from the winery, which has inflated prices for Virginia wines. See Christina Rogers, "Wine Retailers Find Law's Effects Bitter," *Roanoke Times*, December 2, 2006; Annie Gowen, "Out-of-State Sales Of Va. Wines Awash In Legal Confusion," *The Washington Post*, December 22, 2003.

30. Editorial, "Sour Grapes," *Richmond Times-Dispatch*, July 16, 2006.

31. Jim Vascik, "Free Virginia Grapes From Distributors' Grasp," *Roanoke Times*, November 25, 2006. See also Editorial, "Wine Knot: Red Tape Ties Up Virginia Wineries and Their Customers," *New-*

port-News *Daily Press*, July 27, 2006.

32. Beyond 3,000 cases—which Saxman asserted was the threshold at which most wineries needed to partner with a distributor to grow—the legislation required wineries to use traditional wholesalers. As proposed, the bill would have also allowed self-distribution for roughly half of Virginia's wineries, which produced fewer than 2,800 cases per year. Greg Edwards, "There's Hope for Wineries; Lawmakers Say There is a Chance Shipping Rights Could Return," *Richmond Times-Dispatch*, January 4, 2007; Brian McNeill, "Bill Seeks to Aid Small Wineries: Reinstation of Self-distribution Sought," *McClatchy-Tribune Business News*, January 3, 2007; Larry O'Dell, "Legislation Would Allow Va. Wineries to Bypass Distributors," Associated Press State & Local Wire, January 3, 2007.

33. Administered and funded entirely by the Virginia Department of Agriculture and Consumer Services, VWDC would also share delivery workers, bonded warehouse space, and delivery vehicles. To ease administrative costs, the VWDC system provided electronic purchase orders and invoices, collected and remitted all taxes, and compiled necessary governmental paperwork on behalf of participating wineries. (Michael Felberbaum, "Va. Takes Novel Approach to Wine Distribution," Associated Press State & Local Wire, May 26, 2008.) Structurally, the VWDC is governed by a five-member board consisting of two winery owners, two wholesalers, and the commissioner of the Virginia Department of Agriculture and Consumer Services. "Virginia Department of Agriculture and Consumer Services: Virginia Launches Winery Distribution Company," M2 Press Wire, April 18, 2008; Felberbaum, "Va. Takes Novel Approach to Wine Distribution"; "Virginia Department of Agriculture and Consumer Services: Virginia Launches Winery Distribution Company," M2 Press Wire, April 18, 2008; Greg Edwards, "Distributor for Va. Wineries Launches Today," *Richmond Times-Dispatch*, April 17, 2008; Michael Felberbaum, "Va. Takes Novel Approach to Wine Distribution," Associated Press State & Local Wire, May 26, 2008; Sandhya Somashekhar, "Small Va. Vintners See Hope Amid Marketing Drought," *The Washington Post*, April 18, 2008.

34. Swedenburg, who alleged that New York's laws violated constitutional guarantees of unhindered interstate commerce and the First Amendment's right to free speech, asked for an injunction on enforcement of the laws. Clint Bolick—the party named in *Bolick* v. *Roberts* and one of Swedenburg's customers—filed the lawsuit on Swedenburg's behalf without charge. (Marc Fisher, "Silly Laws Bottle Up Fine Wine," *The Washington Post*, August 1, 2004; Michael Laris, "Rule Allowing Direct Sale Of Wine in Va. Is Put on Hold," *The Washington Post*, April 2, 2002.) The complaint was filed on behalf of the plaintiffs by the Washington, D.C., libertarian public interest group, the Institute for Justice. Calvin R. Trice, "Middleburg Vintner Sues N.Y. Agency," *Richmond Times-Dispatch*, February 4, 2000.

35. Marc Fisher, "Silly Laws Bottle Up Fine Wine," *The Washington Post*, August 1, 2004; Pattie Waldmeir, "Wine Bar Means Limited Choice in Land of Free," *Financial Times* (London), November 29, 2004; Hilde Gabriel Lee and Allan E. Lee, *Virginia Wine Country Revisited* (Charlottesville, Va.: Hildesigns Press, 1993), 57–59; Calvin R. Trice, "Middleburg Vintner Sues N.Y. Agency," *Richmond Times-Dispatch*, February 4, 2000; Indo-Asian News Service, "US Free Trade Receives Blow From Woman Winemaker," September 18, 2006.; Ellen Crosby, "She Vinified, Testified and Changed the Law," *The Washington Post*, June 20, 2007.

36. *Granholm* v. *Heald*, 544 U.S. 460 (2005).

37. Kenneth Starr, the special prosecutor in the Monica Lewinsky case, supported Swedenberg's claims, while Judge Robert Bork, C. Boyden Gray (a counsel to former president George H. W. Bush), and Viet Dinh, an architect of the Patriot Act, joined opposition. Bolick asserted that, despite their conservative principals, reasonable minds could disagree on the wine issue because Bolick's opponents "are there because they have clients who are paying them generously." (Marc Fisher, "Silly Laws Bottle Up Fine Wine," *The Washington Post*, August 1, 2004; Ellen Crosby, "She Vinified, Testified and Changed the Law," *The Washington Post*, June 20, 2007; 544 U.S. 460 at 473.) Kennedy was joined in the majority by Justices Antonin Scalia, David H. Souter, Ruth Bader Ginsburg, and Stephen G. Breyer. Justice Clarence Thomas, writing for the dissent, argued that the majority's ruling would overturn long-established regulations primarily meant to protect minors. See Dissent.

38. Josh Goodman, "Interstate Wine Bottleneck," *Seattle Times*, November 9, 2005; Dave McIntyre, "Bill

in Congress would undo Va. vintner's victory over wine shipping," *The Washington Post*, May 5, 2010; Greg Edwards, "Virginia's Wine Law Largely in Fine Form," *Richmond Times-Dispatch*, May 17, 2005.

39. "An Interview with Felicia Rogan, Virginia Wine Pioneer," *Virginia Wine Gazette*, Summer 1998, p. 8.

40. One 1997 study by the Vinifera Wine Growers Association found that Virginia's wine industry created approximately 4,900 jobs and paid $6.4 million in wages annually. Cathy Jett, "Virginia Vines Couple to Open Winery in Stafford," *The Fredericksburg Free Lance–Star*, April 27, 2006; Brian Braiker, "A Good Year For Virginia Winemakers," *The Washington Post*, August 26, 1999; Kelly Cramer, "Wine is Alive," *Richmond Times-Dispatch*, July 25, 1999; Tom Marquardt and Patrick Darr, "East Coast Wines Get Their Day in the Spotlight," Annapolis *Capital*, June 9, 1999; Lois Caliri, "Small Wineries Are Feeling Boxed In," *Roanoke Times*, May 29, 2005.

41. Lois Caliri, "Wineries in a Squeeze: Not Enough Virginia Grapes—A Growing Concern," *Roanoke Times*, July 19, 1998. Surveys undertaken in the mid-1990s by state viticulturist Tony K. Wolf found that Virginia wineries needed an additional 1,000 tons of grapes annually, and that, at any given time, between 10 and 18 wineries were actively seeking grape purchase contracts from vineyards. The Virginia Winegrowers Advisory Board estimated that Virginia needed to double the commonwealth's grape acreage to 3,000 acres by 2008. Dr. Tony K. Wolf, *Viticulture Notes*, Vol. 16, No. 2, March–April 2001; Tom Marquardt and Patrick Darr, "East Coast Wines Get Their Day in the Spotlight," Annapolis *Capital*, June 9, 1999; Wes Allison, "PSSST! Can You Spare a Grape?" *Richmond Times-Dispatch*, May 10, 1998.

42. While Virginia's wine grape acreage had risen to 2,974 acres by 2013 and, though the commonwealth's wine sales had grown eight percent between 2011 and 2012, there had not been a corresponding increase in vineyard acreage. "Ag Official Urges Vintners to Plant More Grapes," *Richmond Times-Dispatch*, February 3, 2013; Kelly Cramer, "Wine is Alive," *Richmond Times-Dispatch*, July 25, 1999; Dr. Tony K. Wolf, *Viticulture Notes* 14, No. 2, March–April 1999; Kia Shante Breaux, "Grape Production in Virginia at Record Levels," Associated Press State & Local Wire, June 21, 2000. California, Oregon, Washington State, New York, and Pennsylvania.

43. Chris Kissack, "The Components of Wine," Wine Doctor, http://www.thewinedoctor.com/advisory/tastecomponents.shtml (viewed May 16, 2015); Jim Raper, "Ripe For Wine," Norfolk *Virginian-Pilot*, May 25, 2003.

44. "'Commonwealth Quality Alliance' Program Unveiled at Virginia Wineries Association Annual Membership Meeting," *PRWeb*, Nov. 13, 2012, http://www.prweb.com/releases/CQAprogram/VAwine/prweb10124407.htm (viewed May 16, 2015).

45. Jim Raper, "Virginia's Wine Industry Has Matured," *Virginia Business*, October 1, 2008. "Wine competitions serve two purposes: ego stroking and marketing to clueless customers," Linden Vineyards winemaker Jim Law told a reporter in 2003. "I think the winery owners and marketing arms got a bit too much influence…. Winning a medal [at last year's Governor's Cup] had the same impact as getting the envelope from Publisher's Clearing House announcing, 'You are a winner!'" At the 2002 Governor's Cup competition, a record 22 gold and 84 silver medals were awarded. Raper, "Ripe For Wine," Norfolk *Virginian-Pilot*, May 25, 2003.

46. Commonwealth Quality Alliance, http://cqawine.org/approved-va-wines.html (viewed May 16, 2015); The Grape Press, "Commonwealth Quality Alliance," July 2011, pp. 10–12.

47. Oregon, for example, had experienced tremendous success with its Pinot Noir; New York experienced similar excitement over its Reislings, and New Zealand had earned a reputation for producing superior Sauvignon Blancs. "I think we can compete with California and Europe on quality," said Burnley Vineyards owner Lee Reeder. State enologist Bruce Zoecklein agreed: "There's no interest or benefit in trying to out-California California," he told a reporter. "We're attempting to make a product that is a good value and that has some regional uniqueness."

48. Chardonnay was by far the most-planted variety across the commonwealth, followed by White Riesling, Syval, Vidal Blanc, and Cabernet Sauvignon. Only 28 percent was planted in French-Ameri-

cans, and only seven percent was planted with American varieties.

49. Todd Kliman, *The Wild Vine: A Forgotten Grape and the Untold Story of American Wine* (New York: Clarkson Potter, 2010), 192–203; Hilde Gabriel Lee and Allan E. Lee, *Virginia Wine Country III* (Keswick, Va.: Hildesigns Press, 2004), 73, 74. Horton, himself a native of Hermann, Missouri, where the Norton was resurrected in 1965 at Stone Hill Winery, grew up immersed in the region's largely German population, drinking wine, and learning about the formerly dominant Norton grape. There, in his teens, he helped tend vines before studying at the University of Missouri. He enjoyed a brief enlistment in the Air Force before receiving a degree in marketing from the University of Maryland and, thereafter in 1977, moved to the community of Aroda in Madison County. (Ken Ringle, "Virginia's Special Viognier," *The Washington Post*, March 29, 2006.) The Hortons later purchased land in Orange County for a winery and manufactured their grapes into wine at Montdomaine Cellars, which Horton later managed. In 1992, he began construction of a two-story 20,000-square foot English Tudor–inspired winery at the site of his Barboursville vineyard, which opened as Horton Vineyards in 1994. While some industry observers credited Horton for his efforts, others expressed concern over the sheer number of grapes with which he experimented. Horton dismissed such criticism: "Hey, the great Chateauneuf du Pape wines of France can be made of up to 13 varieties. Gives us something to shoot for," he noted to a reporter in 2009. His, for example, was the only Virginia winery to plant Portuguese varietals and the first Virginia winery to release a "port"-style wine since the repeal of Prohibition. ("Horton Vineyards/Montdomaine Explores New Growth," *Charlottesville Business Journal* [March 1993]). Horton's port, a sweet desert wine with five to six percent residual sugar fortified with distilled spirits, was originally made with Norton grapes. The Norton was subsequently succeeded by two Portuguese grapes, Touriga Nacional and Tinta Cão. While Horton specialized in nontraditional "niche" varietals more at home in France's Rhône Valley, its affiliate Montdomaine Cellars, specialized in mainstream varieties, including the house wines at the Inn at Little Washington. (Ann Geracimos, "A growing viniculture: Wineries take root in Virginia and Maryland," *The Washington Times*, September 25, 1997; Faye Chewning Weems, *Virginia Wineries: Your Complete Tour Guide* [Richmond: Auburn Mills, Ltd., 2001], 28, 29; Paul Lukacs, *The Great Wines of America* [New York: W. W. Norton & Company, 2005], 205.) The varietals included Concord, Niagara, and Catawba, as well as Seyval Blanc and Chambourcin grapes, and ultimately Merlot, Cabernet Franc, and Cabernet Sauvignon. (Hilde Gabriel Lee and Allan E. Lee, *Virginia Wine Country Revisited* [Charlottesville: Hildesigns Press, 1993], 93–94; Jerry Shriver, "Virginia Vintner Cultivates Acclaim with Unusual Grapes," *USA Today*, December 30, 1996; Jim Raper, "A Mixed Case," *Virginia Business*, September 28, 2009; *The Wine Exchange*, *VWGA* No. 1 [January 1994]: 17–19.) In 1989, the Hortons leased 55 acres at Berry Hill Farm, located in the corporate limits of the Town of Orange, and the following spring planted 21 acres of Norton, Cabernet Franc, and Vidal. The following year, they added more varieties from the Rhône Valley of France. In 1992, the vineyard expanded by 10 more acres, primarily in Viognier.

50. Reportedly discovered by Richmond physician Dr. Daniel Norborne Norton in the 1820s, the Norton was a richly fragrant and spicy red variety that drifted into obscurity in the wake of Prohibition. The high natural sugar content of the varietal was perfect for bootleg winemakers, who could avoid making bulk purchases of refined sugar, which were monitored by federal agents, and instead water it down and make greater quantities of wine. The Great Depression and World War II had prevented the vineyard from reviving the label after Prohibition ended in 1933. In the 1970s the grapes were replanted improperly and the vines died. Horton was able to obtain cuttings for replanting in Virginia. ("Horton Had a Notion that Norton Should be Revived," *USA Today*, December 30, 1996; *VWGJ* [Summer 1991]: 128. "The Wine Exchange," *VWGA* No. 1 [January 1994]: 17–19.) Horton, however, was not the first post-Prohibition Virginian to grow the varietal. That honor is believed to belong to Mary and A. Keene Byrd who planted a single Norton vine in 1982 at their small vineyard, "The Wistful Vineyard" in Charlottesville. The Byrds purchased their Norton vine from Hermann, Missouri. (*Boar's Head Grape Vine Press* 11 [September–October 1982]; Paul Bradley, "Vintner's Mission: Return Va. Wines to Prominence," *Richmond Times-Dispatch*, April 7, 2002; Weems, *Virginia Wineries*, 28; Jim Raper, "Humble Steward: Try a Virginia Norton on Your Holiday Table," Norfolk

*Virginian-Pilot*, November 19, 2003; Suzanne Hamlin, "Jefferson's Vision Finally Bears Fruit," *The New York Times*, September 15, 1996.) By 2013, some 140 acres of the variety had been planted across the state. Though more than 25 Virginia wineries produced Norton wines by that time, the Norton was not uniformly embraced by all Virginia winemakers. Some, for example, disliked the grape's propensity for sweetness; others loathed its unpredictable acidity and harsh tannins. Today, Horton Vineyards produces only between 2,000 and 3,000 cases per year. Not wanting Virginia's Viognier to taste of vanilla or "a pseudo-Chardonnay," Horton emphatically noted in 2005 that "our style is different than the French or California styles. It's different." Horton often remarked that Viognier was Virginia's "great white hope," and even printed T-shirts for sale with the slogan. Of the multitude of varieties grown in his vineyards, Viognier is the wine he most routinely takes into California competitions. "There is nothing I like better than winning golds in California," Horton says. "When I walk into a store there and see my wine on the shelf, it's great." One winery not enamored with the obscure varietal, Oasis, was not willing to bottle the grape even though the winery had three Viognier acres under cultivation. "I'm still not so sure I'm willing to buy into Viognier as the varietal of the future in Virginia," Oasis winemaker Tareq Salahi said. "I wish the others every success and believe that they deserve a lot of credit, but my concern is that the market just isn't there yet for what is still an obscure varietal." Salahi did, however, find Viognier useful in blends and in enhancing the bouquet of some of Oasis's red wines. ("Horton Vineyards/Montdomaine Explores New Growth," *Charlottesville Business Journal* [March 1993]; Lukacs, *The Great Wines of America*, 208–209.) Horton's foresight had made his winery one of the most-critically acclaimed on the East Coast; he had earned gold medals in national competitions, placements on wine lists in major cities, and 1996 annual sales at $3.2 million that were growing between 35 percent and 40 percent annually. Indeed, perhaps thanks to the obscurity of the grape, Horton has been one of the only varietal that has reached out successfully to California consumers. (Ann Geracimos, "A Growing Viniculture," *The Washington Times*, September 25, 1997; Jerry Shriver, "Virginia Vintner Cultivates Acclaim with Unusual Grapes," *USA Today*, December 30, 1996; Ben Giliberti, "Very Viognier," *The Washington Post*, June 28, 2000.) In the early 2000s, Horton introduced a dry, Brut-style "Sparkling Viognier" made in the *méthod champanoise* style. The wine, apparently referred to as "Dom Virginion," is left in the bottle for four years. (Lee and Lee, *Virginia Wine Country III*, 73, 75.) While experts estimate that only 20 acres were planted in Viognier in Virginia in 1993, demand quickly grew and, by 2007, 180 acres were planted with the varietal. Some have emulated Horton's fruit-forward fashion; others have made wines in the classic Rhoene fashion. Ken Ringle, "Virginia's Special Viognier," *The Washington Post*, March 29, 2006; Giliberti, "Viognier Tries to Find a Foothold in Virginia," Bergen County, N.J., *Record*, July 12, 2000.

51. By the late 2000s, the grape was among the most-broadly planted in the country—in 28 states—and, in 2009, the Austrian glass company, Riedel, developed a unique glass from which to drink Norton wines. "I count myself as an evangelist for the Norton," McCloud told a reporter. "We don't have to cajole it to grow here. It wants to grow here. This is our wine and our style. Let's not be apologetic about it." Literature on Chrysalis's website and at its tasting room exclaims the virtues of the varietal and her business cards include the phrase, "To proudly restore Virginia wines to world renown and celebrate the homecoming of the Norton, the real American grape. (Sarah Hamaker, "Campaigning for Norton's Rightful Heritage—It's the Virginia Grape," *Chrysalis*; Paul Bradley, "Vintner's Mission: Return Va. Wines to Prominence," *Richmond Times-Dispatch*, April 7, 2002; Marie Beaudette, "Grape Escape," *The Washington Times*, June 17, 2002; Lee and Lee, *Virginia Wine Country III*, 177; Laura Boswell, "Winemaking Assumes Festive Air in Region," *The Washington Times*, September 18, 2003. In 1998, the *Virginia Wine Gazette* doubted the fate of the Norton grape.") The consensus seems to be that it can produce a lot of pretty good wine easily, but that probably it is not destined for greatness on its own. No shame there." ("In 2010 Which Wine Will Lead the Nationally-Known Virginia Wine Industry?" *Virginia Wine Gazette* [Harvest 1998]: 1.) McCloud's fascination with the Norton was also the subject of Todd Kliman's 2010 book, *The Wild Vine*, which described the enigmatic history of the Norton grape from Dr. Daniel N. Norton's discovery of the varietal in the 1820s to its rediscovery by Dennis Horton in the 1980s. (Catherine Cheney, "She's Just Wild About Norton," *The Washington Post*, September 9, 2009.) Kliman, dining editor for *Washingtonian Maga-*

*zine*, also prominently featured Jennifer McCloud's personal journey into the winemaking profession. The winery produces Viognier, as well as several wines from Spanish and French grapes, including Albarino, Chardonnay, and Petit Manseng. Lee and Lee, *Virginia Wine Country III*, 177.

52. Richard Leahy, "Petit Verdot: Bordeaux Blender or Ready for Prime Time?" *Vineyard and Winery Management* (July/Aug 1997); "Varietals Are Fine, But a 'Virginia Red' Should Be in the Mix," Norfolk *Virginian-Pilot*, October 10, 2007.

53. "Performance of Alternative Winegrape Varieties in Virginia, by Tony Wolf and Bruce Zoeklein, Vineyard and Winery Management, Sept/Oct 1996, as quoted in Richard Leahy, "Petit Verdot: Bordeaux Blender or Ready for Prime Time?" *Vineyard and Winery Management* (July/Aug 1997).

54. Growth in Petit Verdot acreage was slow, however. Even as late as 2006, Petit Verdot acreage was so small that it went unreported in the state's commercial grape reports. Petit Verdot wines took six of seventeen gold ribbons at the 2007 State Fair wine competition, with one from Breaux Vineyards' making the most impressive showing. In 2010, a Petit Verdot wine from Fauquier County's Barrel Oak Winery won gold out of 260 entries, and Petit Verdot wines garnered five gold medals at that year's annual Governor's Cup competition. Acreage of Petit Verdot increased in Virginia over the prior decade, largely because of global warming, which analysts said allowed the varietal to ripen earlier than Cabernet Sauvignon. (Jack Berninger, "Petit Verdot is Virginia Wine to Try," *Richmond Times-Dispatch*, September 26, 2007; "Varietals Are Fine, But a 'Virginia Red' Should Be in the Mix," Norfolk *Virginian-Pilot*, October 10, 2007.) Wolf oversaw tests of the variety at AREC until 1996, and repeated the tests between 2005 and 2007 at Virginia Tech's Southern Piedmont Agricultural Research and Extension Center ("SPAREC") in Blackstone. The center was established in 1972 on 1,182 acres on Fort Pickett, was intended to provide space for lectures and workshops, and to conduct research on tobacco, small fruits, specialty crops, livestock, and other agricultural commodities important to Southside Virginia. With the closing of Fort Pickett in 1997, the federal government granted Virginia Tech an additional 2,647 acres for educational purposes. Ingleside Vineyards and veteran winemaker Michael Shaps were among the first to produce exclusively Petit Verdot vintages in the early 2000s, and today, several Virginia wineries offer Petit Verdot wines. "Nation's Founding Father Inspires Virginia Wine Makers," PR Newswire, June 17, 2002; Lee and Lee, *Virginia Wine Country III*, 110–111.

55. Unlike traditional grape wines, fruit wines could be produced from less-weather-dependent fruit that could be found year-round. Though they required much of the same equipment needed to produce grape wines, fruit wines were cheaper and quicker to produce, which increased profit margins and allowed vintners to access a greater market.

56. Founded by Mike and Kathy Riddick, Wintergreen was located near the popular Wintergreen Resort and featured a circa-1820 brick manor house, as well as a schoolhouse, a carriage house, and an apple-packing shed. In 1989, with help from state viticulturalist Tony K. Wolf, the Riddicks planted five acres of Seyval and Vidal vines and, later, vinifera varieties. By 1993, the Riddicks had converted the apple-packing shed and carriage house into a winery and by the late 1990s, Wintergreen produced 12 wines, including an award-winning raspberry wine and Chardonnay. In 1999, the winery was purchased by Jeff and Tamara Stone who had relocated from the Atlanta area. By that time, the winery consisted of 14 acres under vine and produced 5,500 cases annually. Fabbioli crafted two appertif pear wines, as well as a popular raspberry merlot and a blackberry wine; Bluemont produced wines from peaches, strawberries, and blackberries; Hiddencroft produced two fruit wines, including one made with Montmorency cherries. (Lee and Lee, *Virginia Wine Country Revisited*, 116–117, 118–119; "Grape Growing, Sense of Community, Both Thriving in Nelson County," *Virginia Wine Gazette* [Summer 1998]: 13.) Owner Doug Fabbioli, a native of New York, spent his youth working in his friend's father's wine cellars before working at Sonoma County's Buena Vista Winery. Fabbioli returned to the East Coast in 1997 as winemaker and vineyard manager at Loudoun County's Tarara Winery. In 2000, he purchased 25 acres close to Tarara on which to plant his own grapes. During this time, Fabbioli also worked for George and Nicki Bazaco on their Windham Winery (later Doukénie), producing approximately 1,000 cases per year. While attending Syracuse University, he studied business management and worked in a friend's father's wine cellars. "I started in the cellars

and just stayed with it, really.... I really loved working out in the vineyard and getting the grapes to grow," he told a reporter. After graduation, Fabbioli headed to California and worked for 10 years at Buena Vista Winery north of Sonoma. While working at Tarara, he lived on the property with his wife, an accountant, and two young sons. Though the winery produced only 8,000 cases per year, Fabbioli learned how to run a winery—assign tasks, give safety lessons, prepare grounds, taste unfinished wines, and organize events for outside groups. Fabbioli attributed the combined position of winemaker and vineyard manager to "be more in touch with the character of the grape and therefore the wine." "I'm able to see the whole picture," he said in 2000. "If I grow good grapes, making the wine is a lot easier." Julie Hyman, "Vintner Sniffs success: New York Transplant Set Roots," *The Washington Times*, September 15, 2000; Laura Boswell, "Winemaking Assumes Festive Air in Region," *The Washington Times*, September 18, 2003.

57.   J. Tobias Beard, "Virginia's So-Called Champagne," *C-Ville Weekly*, October 14, 2008. In 2008, the winery had won high praise for its 2004 Rose Brut from prestigious Effervescents du Monde competition, held in Dijon, France, which pitted 418 sparkling wines from 24 countries.

58.   Thibaut-Jannison's first vintage was made from grapes solely from the Monticello AVA, roughly half of which came from Ivy Creek Vineyard, one of the first commercial vineyards in the state. The older vines produced higher-quality wine, which was then fermented at Veritas Vineyard. A thousand cases of the vintage were released, mostly going to higher-end restaurants and retailers. In 2009, Thibaut received a phone call from the White House staff informing him of the decision to feature his wine during a dinner—at which incidentally Oasis Vineyard's Tareq and Michale Salahi were reportedly uninvited guests. "It feels great to know that some very important people have tasted it, and saw my name on the label," said Thibaut. Unlike the more-traditional Blanc de Chardonnay Brut, "Fizz" is made entirely from chardonnay grapes and boasts modern packaging geared toward a younger urban crowd and a slightly sweeter taste. The thinner Fizz wine bottles require less stacking space than traditional champagne bottles, as well as less fermentation time, giving the wine smaller and less dense bubbles. Thibaut was followed by Charles Genrot at Kluge. "Sparkling Wine from Local Vineyard Featured at Obama's State Dinner," November 27, 2009, http://www.newsplex.com/home/headlines/76419017.html (viewed May 16, 2015); Grace Reynolds, "Claude Thibaut Makes Sparkling Wine in Virginia Using What He Learned Growing up in Champagne and Working His Way up in California," *Flavor Magazine*, December 7, 2009; George W. Stone, "Virginia Sparklers," *DCMag* (September–October 2009); Dave McIntyre, "Drinking Local at the White House Dinner," *The Washington Post*, November 25, 2009.

59.   Governmental agencies also joined the trend. In 2003, the Portsmouth Convention and Visitors Bureau partnered with Hanover County's James River Cellars to bottle its "Portsmouth Lightship Red," which could be found at local farmers markets and used as Christmas gifts for clients of businesses. Shenandoah National Park also partnered with Horton Vineyards to produce a special line of red and white wines offered for sale at park gift shops. Hewit and fourteen other employees hand sorted through two tons of grapes. (Sarah Staples, "Hotels offer special sips with custom wine crushes," *Dallas Morning News*, February 22, 2010; Keswick Hall Website, http://www.keswick.com/ (viewed May 16, 2015).) The first harvest was planned for fall 2011 and visitors could tour the vineyard. See also *VWGJ* 5, No. 1 (Spring 1978): 27. The Williamsburg Winery produced a seventeenth-century-style spiced wine under its "Jamestown Cellars" label, also for sale in Colonial Williamsburg's shops. While the Williamsburg Lodge served 45 Virginia varieties, unlike the private label wines for other Virginia enterprises, grapes for the Williamsburg Inn wine came from California's Napa Valley. Meghan Hoyer, "Personalized Wine Trend Picking Up in the Region," Norfolk *Virginian-Pilot*, November 23, 2003.

60.   The concept of treading lightly on the land had long been endorsed by state enologist Bruce Zoeklein, who counseled winery owners on environmentally-sound practices, including building orientation, insulation, and water recycling. Many of these ideas have been made public through his "Winery Planning and Design," which has been made available on CD http://www.apps.fst.vt.edu/extension/enology/EN/123.html (viewed May 16, 2015).

61.   Environmental sustainability was of personal interest to DuCard's owner, Scott Elliff. "I feel like

our tasting room and our design elements, and day-to-day practices should be in as much harmony as possible," Elliff told a reporter in 2010. Elliff, a Chicago native and retired Northern Virginia business consultant, bought the property, with his wife, Karen, for a second home. After discovering the land had previously been an orchard, and that it wasn't advisable to grow apples, the Elliffs began growing grapes in 2000 as a hobby and sold them to area wineries. After watching some of the wines which used their grapes win awards, the Elliffs began bottling under his own label for friends and family members in 2007. "We were selling wine to friends and at festivals and were getting a lot of positive feedback and we knew we were on to something," Elliff told one reporter. "Everybody raved about our wine and wanted more so we decided to give it a try." Today, DuCard is open to the public, growing ___ varietals on seven acres, with Viognier as its only white grape. Barrel Oak Winery also used natural ventilation and reclaimed wood flooring.

62.  CrossKeys' Mediterranean-inspired winery, which is situated on 125 acres with large rooms for banquets, promotes environmental education to its customers, minimizes the use of pesticides, and donates most of its used corks to local artists for use in projects. The opening of the winery was seen as a coup for regional tourism. "In the past we've sent them to Shenandoah County and down into Augusta County but now we have an opportunity to have them stay right here in Rockingham County, in Harrisonburg, to visit Cross Keys," says Brenda Black, the Harrisonburg tourism manager. At Williamsburg Winery, owners Patrick and Peggy Duffeler planted more than 75 acres of trees, placed 265 acres under conservation easement, populated local tributaries of College Creek with crab, and worked with area landscape companies to compost shredded wood material. Cave Ridge Vineyard and Rappahannock Cellars reused wine barrels and used biodegradable products wherever possible. "Crosskeys Vineyards Joins Green Initiative," July 24, 2015, WHSV (Harrisonburg, Va.).

63.  The pesticide-free winery also used microdrip irrigation to limit water usage, and composted and spread byproducts of the wine production process. "Byrd Cellars Hosts June Events," *Richmond Times-Dispatch*, June 13, 2013; Floor Covering Weekly, "Carpets Plys Brings Cork Recycling to Virginia," December 7, 2009; Floor Daily.net: "Virginia Firm Begins Cork Stopper Recycling, December 7, 2009, http://www.floordaily.net/flooring-news/virginia_firm_begins_cork_stopper_recycling. aspx; http://www.carpetplusonline.com/re-cork-cville/dropbox-locations/ (viewed May 16, 2015); "Customer Service and Promotion Keeps Charlottesville's Carpet Plus On Top," *Focus*, June 2010, pp. 63, 64.

64.  History was particularly important to the Schornbergs and was a major factor in their selection of the property. Edgewood featured a 1911 estate built by a direct descendant of the grantee, Nicholas Meriwether. The property was previously home to a decorated World War I diplomat and later to Art Garfunkel, and historical evidence points to the prior owners' delaying British Colonel Banastre Tarleton's troops in order to prevent their attempted capture of Jefferson and the Virginia General Assembly. While clearing the land for grapes, Al Schornberg discovered Civil War–era artifacts, many of which are on display in a glass case in the tasting room and on a flat-screen television showing the chronology of vineyard construction. Barnard was initially attracted to Virginia because of the challenge it presented and turned down an offer at Beringer because of the potential he saw in the Old Dominion. On the night of June 4, 1781, Jack Jouett rode more than 40 miles from Louisa County to warn Jefferson and the legislature of British troop movement. 9Gordon Kendall, "Keswick Vineyards: Breaking New Ground in Virginia," *Roanoke Times*, July 25, 2007; Lee and Lee, *Virginia Wine Country III*, 80; PR Newswire, "Nation's Founding Father Inspires Virginia Wine Makers," June 17, 2002; Walker Elliot Rowe, *A History of Virginia Wine: From Grapes to Glass* [Charleston, S.C.: The History Press, 2009], 115.) Following Al's sudden passing in 2001, his son, Chris, took over the management of the winery, and served on the Board of Directors of the Virginia Wineries Association and the Virginia Wines and Vines Political Action Committee. (Lee and Lee, *Virginia Wine Country III*, 105–107.) During the so-called "Keswick Consensus," the attendees form teams, and experiment with five varietals to come up with concoctions that are then rated by the full group. Jim Raper, "From Pets to Polo Matches," *VA Business* (September 28, 2009).

65.  Tim serves as winemaker and vineyard manager, having enrolled in horticultural courses at Virginia Tech and received consultations winemaker and entrepreneur Michael Shaps. Paul and Ruth devel-

oped an appreciation for wine while being stationed abroad in Europe and sensed that grapes would thrive on the property. Lee and Lee, *Virginia Wine Country III*, 59–60; Greg Edwards, "Dying on the Vine? Small Wineries Fear Court Ruling Could Force Them to Use Distributors," *Richmond Times-Dispatch*, October 10, 2005.

66. The Todhunters, frequent visitors to Italy, grew a variety of vinifera grapes, and produced Italian-style wines at their winery. The Roeders planted their first vines on the property in 2006 and, by 2010, the winery boasted some 15,000 vines, a large tasting room, and an outdoor patio. Barrel Oak is particularly proud of its affinity for dogs, which play a large role in the winery's branding and overall atmosphere. In a nod to the area's rich history, the Roeders rehabilitated Oak Hill, the circa-1773 estate of the first United States Chief Justice John Marshall, which sits on the winery property. Today, the Roeders use Oak Hill for special events and private tastings. de Vink cultivated several vinifera varieties and constructed a modern concrete and glass winery with an internally-illuminated grain silo. (Rowe, *A History of Virginia Wine*, 104.) The couple was originally persuaded to purchase their property after seeing three foxes during a property-scouting trip. (Lee and Lee, *Virginia Wine Country III*, 228–229; "Delaplane Cellars: Taste the Difference a Decade Makes," *Leesburg Today*, September 6, 2013.) British Wine critic Jancis Robinson wrote that de Vink's "considerable efforts stand a good chance of putting [Virginia] on the world wine map." "Virginia's Climbers," *Financial Times* September 16, 2011; "Wine: First-Growth Virginia? A Fledgling Vintner Wants To Prove It's Possible," *The Washington Post*, March 15, 2011.

67. Bogaty contracted with Chris Pearmund to serve as winemaker and by 2013, the winery was producing wines made from vinifera and French-American grapes. (Lee and Lee, *Virginia Wine Country III*, 212–213, 233–234.) After taking a seminar with state viticulturalist Tony Wolf, the Armors planted a small experimental three-acre vineyard in 1991, which was quickly expanded to six acres of Chardonnay, Cabernet Sauvignon, Cabernet Franc, and Sauvignon Blanc grapes. In 1997, following several years of selling their grapes to other wineries, the Armors constructed a winery with the help of Piedmont Vineyards' former winemaker, Alan Kinne. The Armors converted an old pig barn into a winery building, including a tasting room in the old hay loft on the second floor. The winery, set in this pastoral, if not rustic setting, includes a family cemetery where the farm's original owners, the Yowells, are buried. Sharp Rock Vineyards was opened in 1998. "There are times I just go up to the cemetery and sit there and think, 'Wow, I wonder what life was like for them living here,'" said Kathy East in 2005. "A taste of vintage Virginia," *The New York Times*, May 20, 2005; Weems, *Virginia Wineries*, 48–49; "Hume Vineyards Opens, Features 'Bigger' Wines," *Fauquier Times-Democrat*, Jun. 27, 2011. Like Jim Law, Delmare advocates many of the techniques espoused by Dr. Richard Smart in his *Sunlight into Wine*. By the mid-2000s, the winery produced 5,500 cases per year. Walker Elliot Rowe, *Wandering Through Virginia's Vineyards* (Baltimore: Apprentice House: 2006), 125–137.

68. The county's Department of Economic Development launched a study of the vitality of Loudoun's agricultural sector and to identify new products that could boost the county's agricultural output. The outcome was a study that encouraged farmers to sell finished products, like bottled wine, instead of unfinished traditional commodities like hay, corn, and wheat.

69. Under the passport program, once visitors received five stamps, they were eligible to be entered into a contest for an all-expenses-paid stay at a county bed and breakfast, as well as a $100 credit for dinner at one of the county's destination restaurants. "Loudoun County Wineries Now Served by New Map," *Virginia Wine Gazette* (Holiday/Winter 1998–1999): 32.

70. "LCVA Wins National Destiny Award," convention planit.com September 17, 2009, http://conventionplanit.com/industry_buzz/?p=446 (viewed May 16, 2015).

71. These new commodities may be smaller in scale, but are higher in value—especially when tourists are involved. "What we're seeing is the evolution of a new type of agriculture," said Gary Hornbaker, the county's rural resources coordinator. "It's not silos, it's not dairy farms, but when you put the small-scale operations together, it makes a lot of money." Since 1998, the county's more than 1,400 farms—encompassing approximately 142,000 acres—have seen gross sales more than double since 1998 to over $68 million annually. More than 6,000 visitors visit Loudoun's farms during the county's biannual farm tours, and Loudoun has become a national model for communities looking to preserve

rural lands in the face of tremendous development pressure.

72. The Piedmont Epicurean and Agricultural Center, http://www.epicureancenter.com (viewed May 16, 2015). Hidden Brook featured a winery facility with a large stone fireplace and a log tasting bar constructed from an estimated 1,500 logs that, thanks to friends, was constructed in two weeks. Lee and Lee, *Virginia Wine Country III*, 188–189, 195–196.

73. Consumers also welcomed the new wine regions for, unlike older wineries in Charlottesville and Northern Virginia, wineries in these emerging regions were generally less crowded, and often offered tastings without charge.

74. The slightest change in elevation or slope could also affect how a particular species of grape grows. Northward of 3,000 feet in elevation, any type of grape growing can prove difficult. Mason Adams, "Southwest Virginia Uncorked," *Roanoke Times*, July 16, 2003.

75. Lee and Lee, *Virginia Wine Country III*, 144–146. The award-winning wine, which also took a silver medal at the San Francisco International Wine Competition and a gold medal in an international competition, represented the first time AmRhein attempted a late harvest wine, and the winery procured the recipe for the blend from Brad McCarthy, formerly of White Hall Vineyards, who was then managing partner at Blenheim Vineyards and served as a consultant to AmRhein. McCarthy had previously been honored for his winemaking efforts by receiving the 1997 and 1998 Governor's Cups while working as winemaker at White Hall Vineyards. Grapes for the wine—which were brown and raisin-like (and nearly thrown out)—were produced from the 2001 vintage, one of the best growing seasons in Virginia. Once picked, they were fermented in stainless steel tanks and infused with champagne yeast and a combination of traminette and vidal blanc. (PR Newswire, "Virginia's Newest Wineries Among the Stand Outs In Governor's Cup Competition," June 3, 2003.) The shop, since closed, held wine tastings, and the owners wrote local articles and encouraged consumers to try Virginia wine. (Larry Bly, "Region's Wines Get Serious Attention," *Roanoke Times*, June 13, 2003.) "Central Virginia is still thought of as Virginia wine country, but Roanoke is really emerging," said Michelle Rhudy of the Virginia Wine Marketing Office at the time; Mason Adams, "Southwest Virginia Uncorked," *Roanoke Times*, July 16, 2003; Tom Angleberger, "Winery Employs Vintage Method of Construction Like Fine Wine," *Roanoke Times*, March 1, 1998.

76. MountainRose later hosted a variety of wine-themed events, including dinners, a rose-gardening festival, a grape stomp, and a "Mines to Wines Festival" that showcased ways to reclaim land through vineyards.

77. The facility also provides space for meetings, a farmer's market, agricultural events, and education, as well as agritourism functions and wine-related activities. Chris Bickers, "Southeast Growers Learning Hard Lessons in Wine Grape Production," *Southeast Farm Press*, March 12, 2008; Erica Alini, "Vines Replace the Golden Leaf Across U.S. Tobacco Belt," *Globe and Mail* (Canada), August 20, 2009.

78. Lee and Lee, *Virginia Wine Country III*, 152–153.

79. Richard G. Leahy, *Beyond Jefferson's Vines: The Evolution of Quality Wine in Virginia* (New York: Sterling Epicure, 2012), 57. Holly Grove partnered with the nearby Mid-Atlantic Regional Spaceport ("MARS") and the Virginia Space Flight Academy in 2010 to produce a Bordeaux blend, "Genesis," that commemorated both NASA's decision to locate the MARS facility on the Eastern Shore and Virginia's reentry into the nation's space program. Sales from the wine benefited the Flight Academy, which promoted science, technology, and engineering education for children. Gary Emerling, "Virginia's Vineyards Mature," *The Washington Times*, September 21, 2008.

80. Ada Jacox, ed., *Virginia: First in Wine and History* (White Stone, Va.: River Country Publishing, 2012).

81. Cindi is a lifelong Stafford resident, who spent 17 years as Stafford's emergency services manager; Skip is the president of Spotsylvania County's homebuilders association. Located conveniently off of Route 1 and I-95, the Causeys' winery was founded on a small secluded hill, which stands in marked contrast to the hubbub of nearby Route 1. The property itself was once inhabited by the Patawomeck Indians and Pocahontas is reputedly its most famous member. The Causeys hoped the winery would attract tourists interested in both wine and history. (Cathy Jett, "Virginia Vines Couple to

Open Winery in Stafford," *The Fredericksburg Free Lance–Star*, April 27, 2006.) Before arriving in Stafford, Lasserre had worked vineyards in her native France, as well as Australia, South Africa, and Spain. Not to be dismayed by Virginia's humidity, temperatures, or unique insects and animals, she firmly believed in improving the quality of Virginia's wine by selecting grapes which grew well with the state's climate and soil. "If the wines of Virginia aren't as well known as those of California it's because the wrong varieties were planted in the wrong places," she said. "For example, you still find a lot of Cabernet Sauvignon here which to my mind is a poor fit with the region because it's a late harvest grape which is unable to mature before the temperature drops at the end of the summer," she said. The Causeys partnered with Pearmund Cellars in the Broad Run area of Fauquier County to produce a Norton /cabernet franc blended "Pocahontas Reserve," bottled in commemoration of the 400th anniversary of the founding of Jamestown. The Causeys consulted with members of the Patawomeck tribe in designing the label for the line, which consisted of a deerskin-clad Pocahontas bearing a basket of grapes. Katherine Calos, "Fine Wine, Varied Ways," *Richmond Times-Dispatch*, September 23, 2007; Chris Lefkow, "European Winemakers Tap into Jefferson's Dream," *Agence France Presse*, November 23, 2007.

82. Maison Shaps et Roucher-Sarrazin produces between 800 and 1,000 cases of Chardonnay and Pinot Noir wine annually, which is primarily sold in the mid-Atlantic states, New York, and Boston. At Virginia Wineworks, Shaps assisted other Virginia winemakers and, in 2010, the facility became the first Virginia winery to offer boxed wine in three-liter packaging for retail sale. Despite consumer resistance to nontraditional packaging, Shaps and Stafford promoted their wines in vacuum-sealed bags as providing fresher, longer-lasting, lower-cost wine. Loudoun County's Village Winery and Vineyards followed Virginia Wineworks' lead in 2012, after owner Kent Marrs found boxed wine to be more economical for the winery and the consumer. Rowe, *A History of Virginia Wine*, 110.

83. Rowe, *A History of Virginia Wine*, 106.

84. "Wine Festivals Grow in Dan River Region," *Danville Register Bee*, March 21, 2013.

85. "Live! What: Vintage Virginia Wine Festival," *The Washington Post*, June 1, 2006.

86. Inspired by the popularity of the Virginia Wine Festival, the scaled-down Harborfest tasting featured three wines from Virginia producers, James River Cellars, Rebec Vineyards, and Rockbridge Vineyard. ("Try Virginia Wines at Harborfest Tastings," Norfolk *Virginian-Pilot*, June 7, 2006; Steve Stone, "Harborfest Sails into its 30th Anniversary," *Virginian-Pilot*, June 9, 2006; Stacy Parker, "Neptune Wine Tasting Growing with Venue Move," Norfolk *Virginian-Pilot*, September 15, 2005.) Attendees were to meet winemakers Michael Shaps, Brad McCarthy, Luca Paschina, and Matthew Meyer. Restaurants featured special promotions and price incentives encouraged patrons to sample Virginia wines. Jim Raper, "A Chance to Sample the State of the Grape," Norfolk *Virginian-Pilot*, September 19, 2007; Taste of Bay Tickets on Sale," *Virginian-Pilot* (Norfolk, VA), October 4, 2007; The Return of Pasta E Pani," Norfolk *Virginian-Pilot*, September 2, 2007.

87. The small festival, created to celebrate restoration of the property, offered tastings from five Bedford County wineries. It was repeated again in 2010, and by 2013 the festival had emerged into an annual favorite, attracting 15 wineries, local food vendors, and artisans. (U.S State News, "Blacksburg Fork and Cork Tickets on Sale Now," April 9, 2009; "Roanoke Valley Participates in Wine and Unwind Festival," *WSLS.com*, October 21, 2012; Amanda Codispoti, "Wine Festival Raises More Than Just Spirits," *Roanoke Times*, June 26, 2006; Ron Nixon, "Sampling Out the Vintage," *Roanoke Times*, June 12, 2000.) Jefferson, who commenced work on Poplar Forest in 1806, worked on the house until 1823—three years before his death."Thomas Jefferson's Poplar Forest Retreat Reopens April 1," *Canadian Press*, March 25, 2009.

88. Will Jones, "Festival of the Grape Moves to October to Avoid Summer Heat," *Richmond Times-Dispatch*, August 6, 2006; Cynthia McMullen, "From Afton to Wintergreen, Festival Showcases Virginia Wines," *Times-Dispatch*, April 24, 2008.

89. One event that never occurred: In July 2009, the Charlottesville Omni was supposed to host the three-day "International Food & Wine Experience of Charlottesville," which included wine tastings, food pairing seminars, and an awards dinner. Of the more than 100 wines selected to be featured, approximately 20 were from Virginia. The event was intended to allow patrons to compare the im-

proved quality of Virginia wines against their international counterparts. "It's just like Richmond playing U.Va. or U.Va. playing Southern Cal," said the president of the event's organizing group, Timothy O'Brien. "You only get better when you play against the best teams. Regrettably, because of the high ticket prices and the sluggish economy, the event was never held. "Wine Festival at Monticello 2012," May 7, 2012, available at: http://www.monticello.org/site/press/wine-festival-monticello-2012 (viewed September 17, 2013); Mary Alice Blackwell, "New to Area Wine List: An International Festival," *Clover Herald* (South Carolina), September 4, 2008; Rachana Dixit, "New Wine Festival Planned After Pricey Event Dies," Charlottesville *Daily Progress*, July 22, 2009.

90. During the Allen and Gilmore years, for example, the wine industry often found itself taking a backseat to gubernatorial platforms that included welfare reform and reducing personal property taxes. Leahy, *Beyond Jefferson's Vines*, 165.

91. Warner, who planted the vinifera and Concord vineyard with his wife, Lisa Collis, began experimenting with grapes in 1989. By 2013, Warner was selling his grapes to Ingleside Vineyard's Doug Flemer, who also bottled 40 to 60 cases annually for Warner's personal use. The Associated Press State & Local Wire, "Warner Signs Bills to Help Virginia's Wine Industry," March 19, 2003; Bill Brubaker, "Homes Staying on the Market Longer," *The Washington Post*, January 19, 2006.

92. "2004 Governor's Cup Changes: A Look Ahead," *Virginia Wine Gazette*, Holiday/Winter 1998–1999, p. 5; Jeff Sturgeon, "Festival Shows that Virginia Wine Industry Is Aging Nicely," *Roanoke Times*, June 28, 2004.

93. The plan also proposed a new marketing slogan, "Virginia Wineries: The Next Big Thing." It called as well for using vineyards to help maintain the state's rural character and develop a support-and-supply sector or advertising cooperative within the industry. (Jason Ukman, "Virginia Wine Industry Gets a Boost," *The Washington Post*, June 17, 2004.) In 2011, a new marketing strategic plan was developed to take into account changes in the industry since the original *Vision 2015*, and in July 2013, the Virginia Wine Board, in partnership with the Virginia Vineyards Association, the Virginia Wineries Association, and the Virginia Wine Council, held an industry conference, *Beyond 2015—a Blueprint for Virginia Wine*.

94. During the speech, he called out his recent visit to Blue Ridge Vineyards in Botetourt County: "This beautiful vineyard hosts weddings, attracts tourists, and makes a really good Cabernet. Even better, it employs Virginians." Addressing legislators directly, the governor said with a touch of humor, "I've seen many of you personally and enthusiastically supporting the [wine] industry at legislative receptions." During his speech, McDonnell pledged to introduce beneficial wine industry legislation and to dedicate a portion of the wine liter tax (levied at $3.60 per case of wine) to be deposited in the Virginia Wine Promotion Fun. Cathy Benson, "Bob McDonnell Visits Blue Ridge Vineyard," *Roanoke Times*, August 28, 2009.

95. The group, whose report was issued in 2010, studied local government land use restrictions, ways in which Virginia could become "wine country," signage along highways, and wine tourism models from other states. Policy recommendations included consistent directional signage to Virginia's viticultural areas, tax credits for vineyard establishment and winery expansions, a tourism development fund to accelerate the development of wine-related tourism services (i.e., bed and breakfasts, destination restaurants, etc.), and the attraction of companies to the commonwealth that would provide goods and services needed by wineries. In May 2010, Governor and First Lady McDonnell and Secretary of Agriculture Todd Haymore toured Chatham Vineyards and Winery on a visit to the Eastern Shore, where the governor touted legislative victories during the 2010 General Assembly session passed to help the wine industry. Meeting minutes from the Tourism Subgroup, July 6, 2010, August 12, 2010, Department of Taxation 2011 Fiscal Impact Statement. Haymore was recognized as the wine industry's "Person of the Year" in 2014.

96. As Haymore recalled, Governor Tim Kaine had suggested he closely monitor the wine industry for, as Kaine put it, "Those guys are really on to something." Haymore, chief of agriculture and forestry, is never far from the land. Haymore studied at the University of Richmond, during which he worked for several Southside Virginia lawmakers. Following graduation, he spent worked as a congressional aide for former Democratic Representative L. F. Payne, who represented Virginia's 5th congressional

district (representing much of Southside Virginia). "I think he is a very good listener," Payne told a reporter in 2010. "One of the things that he was always able to do was to go into a situation and really come back understanding how others felt about it. That is a real strength and skill." Following his work for Payne, Haymore received a Master's of Business Administration from Virginia Commonwealth University, worked for Dimon, Inc., a Danville tobacco leaf corporation, and then for Richmond's Universal Corporation, the world's largest buyer and seller of tobacco. "Todd has the public-service experience and an understanding of how that side works," said Virginia's first Secretary of Agriculture, Robert Bloxom. "He has corporate experience, so he understands how that works, and experience in international trade, which is now, and will continue to be, a major part of agriculture. He fits all the niches." Mrs. McDonnell also kicked off the 2010 Virginia Wine Month at Monticello, where she was joined by some 300 wine enthusiasts and representatives from 32 Virginia wineries. She promoted Virginia wine with her husband during a weeklong marketing trip to the Netherlands, the United Kingdom, and Germany in July 2010 as well. The governor's initiative was praised by wineries: "It's important to us because it does tell people how good the natural wines that are coming from the area are. We don't have to go to California and Europe to get great wines," said Robert Longo of Chateau Morrisette. Responding to the governor's call, the Northern Virginia Technology Council, the largest technology trade association in the nation, announced in June 2010 that it would serve only Virginia wines during its functions as a way to promote the Virginia wine industry.

97. While in England, the first couple hosted a reception at the high-end London department store Fortnum and Mason for business executives to showcase Virginia wine. She made no doubts about her preference for red wines—especially once she found out that the natural chemicals included in red wine (resveratrol) help fight heart disease. "What could be better than something that tastes good being good for you?" she asked rhetorically. Joining the governor and first lady were representatives from several Virginia wineries, including New Horizon's promoter Christopher Parker and British wine writer Oz Clarke. The First Lady relied on advice from Barboursville Vineyards' Luca Paschina, vineyard consultant Lucie T. Morton, King Family Vineyards winemaker Mattieu Finot, Veritas Vineyard & Winery's Emily Pelton, and Secretary Haymore. "Wine is Key to Virginia Celebration," *Wines & Vines*, July 5, 2013. Contributing vineyards included Breaux Vineyards, Chatham Vineyards, Barboursville Vineyards, James River Cellars, Silver Creek Vineyards, the Vineyard at Pointe Breeze, and Veritas Vineyard and Winery. The grapes were sent to Barboursville Vineyards where they were combined and fermented for eight months in French oak barrels.

98. "There is a tremendous opportunity to create jobs in the U.S. by doing business in Cuba," said McAuliffe. "Most importantly, we got them to agree to open up the market for Virginia wines. We are going to export Virginia wines to Cuba for the first time ever." He also maintained that the Cubans would hold a Virginia wine exposition at a future date, during which the Cuban government would host Virginia winemakers. Prior to the trip, McAuliffe briefed Governor Bob McDonnell's staff, and met with the head of the Cuban Interests Section in Washington, D.C., Jorge Bolaños, who has a close working relationship with Secretary of Agriculture Todd Haymore. "At Executive Mansion, McAuliffe Puts Out The Welcome Mat," *The Washington Post*, February 5, 2014; "McAuliffe Tries To Woo Lawmakers With Nightly Drinks," *Staunton News Leader*, February 6, 2014.

99. Ruth Intress, "Senate Approves Additional Alcohol in Virginia Wines," *Richmond Times-Dispatch*, February 11, 2000; HB 1230, 2004 General Assembly; *Annual Report For 2011-2012*, Virginia Wine Board, *available at* http://www.vdacs.virginia.gov/about/pdf/winebdannualreport.pdf (viewed May 16, 2015).

100. SB1292, "Virginia's New Corkage Law To Take Effect July 1," *Richmond.com*, June 24, 2011; "Virginia Allows Corkage-But Does Anybody Know That?" *The Washington Post*, February 1, 2012.

101. Sponsored by Delegate Robb Bell, the bill enjoyed the backing of the Virginia Wineries Association. A $25 annual fee would have been collected for each plate, of which $15 would have been credited Virginia Tech's enology research department. "Va. Wine Industry Touting Car Plates," Norfolk *Virginian-Pilot*, April 2, 2007; Michael Hardy and Jeff E. Schapiro, "No Harmony on Marriage Plates," *Richmond Times-Dispatch*, February 1, 2005; Jim Nolan, "Some Special Plates Don't Measure Up this

Year," *Richmond Times-Dispatch*, February 15, 2008.

102. An Appomattox County native, Conrad would later be appointed Deputy Secretary of Agriculture and Deputy Chief of Staff in the McDonnell administration, where he encouraged McDonnell's and Secretary of Agriculture Todd Haymore's advocacy of the wine industry. Alliance's Patrick A. Cushing followed in Conrad's steps beginning in 2010 and, in 2012, Katie Hellebush became the Wine Council's third lobbyist.

103. Jim Raper, "Virginia's Wine Industry has Matured," *Virginia Business*, October 1, 2008. In 2007, Boyd worked with the VWA on a host of other initiatives, including its 2007 media campaign, "Welcome to Virginia—First in Wine: An American Tradition in Winegrowing Since 1607." The campaign—primarily meant to appeal to Virginians—featured a press kit and photo library on CD, which contained overviews of Virginia wine country. The campaign also produced a 12-page color brochure, "Guide to Virginia Wine Country," as well as new website, with facts and figures and links to each winery. "Virginia Wine Industry Launches Design and Media Campaign for Virginians," *Business Wire*, April 23, 2007.

104. Paschina was tapped to represent Virginia's growing wine industry due to his "fierce passion for excellence," which has helped boost Virginia's wine industry, said Tamara Talmadge-Anderson, a spokeswoman for the Virginia Tourism Corporation. VTC also launched its "Find the One You Love" sweepstakes, which offered winners a tour and tasting of the Williamsburg Winery, tickets to Norfolk's Town Point Wine Festival, and a six-night cruise from Norfolk. ("New Virginia Travel Guide Stars Real People with a Passion for Travel," *Virginia is for Lovers*, December 18, 2008, http://www.virginia.org/pressroom/release.asp?id=124 [viewed May 17, 2015]; U.S. States News, "Virginia Launches 20 Getaway Ideas in Celebration of 20th Anniversary of Wine Month," July 23, 2008; Cathy Jett, "State Wine Industry Ripening to Maturity," *The Fredericksburg Free Lance–Star*, October 2, 2008; U.S. States News, "Virginia Launches 'Find the One You Love' Wine Month Sweepstakes," August 1, 2008.) The marketing campaign, which ran from August through October, was adopted by the corporation from an idea created by tourism communication students enrolled in a 14-week class at the Gorge Washington School of Business. Students were divided into teams and given the task of creating an integrated marketing campaign for Virginia wineries. The teams then presented their proposal to marketing executives, including Chris Canfield, vice president of Tourism Education and Development for the Virginia Tourism Corporation. "The response to the class was tremendous," said associate professor Sheryl Elliott. "The students were totally engaged in what they were doing. One even said that the class was a life-changing experience." Catherine Caruso, a member of the winning team, commented, "This project was unlike any I have ever done. It mimicked a real proposal for a marketing campaign. Our judges understood that it was a comprehensive "real-world" work experience." U.S. States News Service, "G.W. School of Business Students Entice Virginia Tourists to 'Find One You Love,'" August 13, 2008.

105. "Save Space in Cellar Next to Bordeaux for Va.'s Old Reds," *Virginian-Pilot*, October 8, 2008; Todd Haymore, "Have a Happy Virginia Grown Thanksgiving," U.S. States News, November 4, 2008.

106. James River Cellars created four wines, each featuring labels designed by Pennsylvania artist Adam Rodriguez and Hanover County resident Sallie Eggleston Xiradis. "Annual Wine Report," *Virginia Wine Board*, available at http://www.vdacs.virginia.gov/about/pdf/winebdannualreport.pdf (viewed May 17, 2015).

107. "We're proud that this event has grown in participation each year as well as in popularity," J. Rock Stephens, then chairman of the Virginia Wine Board, said of the event. "Virginia has some amazing restaurants doing innovative work and Virginia wines are an excellent accompaniment to add that extra touch to a special offering." News Release, "Virginia Wine & Dine Month to Celebrate Love by the Glass," February 21, 2013, Virginia.org; News Release, "Love by the Glass; Virginia Wine & Dine Month to Showcase Local Wines at 500 Restaurants and Wine Shops Statewide This March," February 28, 2012, Virginia.org.

108. Groundwork for the visit was laid with the successful 2007 Virginia Wine Experience in London showing, and the group's itinerary was organized by New Horizon's Christopher Parker and the Vir-

ginia Wine Marketing Office's Annette Boyd. http://www.winewriters.org/ (viewed May 17, 2015).

109. Barbara Ensrud, "Jefferson Would Be Proud," *Wall Street Journal*, August 1, 1997; "Wineries Un-limited Trade Show and Conference to Return to Richmond for Second Year in a Row in 2012," Governor McDonnell News Release, May 13, 2011.

110. The posting of the signs was seen as only the first phase of the program; a new sign was added in recognition of the newly created Middleburg AVA in 2013. "Cross secretariat cooperation is key to the Governor's overall economic development and jobs creation agenda," said Agriculture Secretary Todd Haymore at the unveiling of the program at a ceremony at King Family Vineyards. "This part-nership, along with our on-going work with the Virginia Tourism Corporation, will help spur more growth and opportunities at wineries and their suppliers in rural areas throughout Virginia." "New Sign Program Promotes VA Wine Regions," WRIC.com. Press Release, "Governor McDonnell An-nounces New Virginia Wine Region Signs," April 19, 2012. http://www.ag-forestry.virginia.gov/News/viewrelease.cfm?id=1215 (link worked in 2012).

111. Spurrier also noted that Virginians should view their state's temperature and growing conditions as a strength, and that Virginians should emphasize Viognier as its signature white wine and Petit Verdot as its signature red wine. Spurrier also led a blind tasting of eight Virginia wines and eight interna-tionally recognized wines, which featured panel discussion along with  Anthony Giglio, of *Food & Wine* magazine, and international wine critic Bartholomew Broadbent. As selected by the audience, Virginia wines bested their international counterparts in five of the eight match-ups. "Inaugural Virginia Wine Summit Kicks Off October Wine Month," Press Release, Office of Governor Bob McDonnell, October 5, 2012; "Virginia Vintners Get a Proper Nod," *The Washington Post*, October 15, 2012; "Whole Foods Market Develops a "Crush" on October Virginia Wine Month," *PR Web*, September 27, 2012; "Reston Limousine Bus Selected by Virginia Tourism For Promotion of Vir-ginia Wine Month," *PR Web*, November 1, 2012.

112. Blackstone typically offered warmer temperatures, earlier bud break, a continental climate, and less spring frost damage than at Virginia' Tech's Alson H. Smith Jr. Agricultural Research and Extension Center near Winchester. SPAREC was established in 1972 on 1,182 acres on Fort Pickett, was in-tended to provide space for lectures and workshops, and to conduct research on tobacco, small fruits, specialty crops, livestock, and other agricultural commodities important to Southside Virginia. With the closing of Fort Pickett in 1997, the federal government granted Virginia Tech an additional 2,647 acres for educational purposes. At SPAREC, vines were planted in three-vine plots with 18 vines per varietal, with the goal of monitoring their performance over a 10-to-15 year period. Tonky K. Wolf, "Grape Cultivar Evaluation in the Eastern Piedmont of Virginia (SPAREC)," *Viticulture Notes* 20 No. 5 (September–October 2005); Jim Raper, "Virginia's Wine Industry Has Matured," *Virginia Business*, October 1, 2008.

113. Other institutions participating in the project were North Carolina State University, University of Maryland, The Ohio State University, Pennsylvania State University, Cornell University, and the Connecticut Agricultural Experiment Station. David Nicholson, "Daily Progress," November 16, 2010.

114. Virginia Department of Environmental Quality, "Virginia Green Wineries & Breweries," http://www.deq.state.va.us/Programs/PollutionPrevention/VirginiaGreen/GreenWineriesBreweries.aspx (viewed May 17, 2015). The vines were expected to produce grapes by 2015 and would thereafter be processed into wine by Virginia Tech's Wine/Enology Grape Chemistry Group. Several winemakers worked with Jason Murray, a cooperative extension agent with Loudoun County, to develop a pro-gram to set organic standards. ("Chesterfield Plantation Home to a New Research Vineyard," *Rich-mond Times-Dispatch*, June 5, 2012.) Such organic wine programs were largely modeled on Oregon's "Low Input Viticulture and Enology" program. Walker Elliott Rowe, "Wine Grape Farms Promote Protection of Green Space," *Richmond Times-Dispatch*, June 28, 2004.

115. The program was repeated in 2008 and, in 2009, the program was significantly modified to include tours abroad of French and Italian wineries that mimicked the itinerary designed by Thomas Jef-ferson during his years in Europe. Experts included John Harrington, the director of PBS's 2005 documentary *The Cultivated Life: Jefferson and Wine*. Participants were given a special after-hours

tour of Monticello. They were also given the option of staying on The Lawn or in nearby student dormitories ("America's First Wine Connoisseur," *U.S. States News*, April 19, 2007.) The 2008 tours included tours of White Hall, Oakencroft, Veritas, Afton Mountain, and First Colony. The 2009 program participants visited Lyon, Beaune, Meaursalt, Hermitage and Monforte d'Alba, and explored French-American wine connections with a lecture from Michael Shaps and his former French mentor, with whom Shaps had formed Shaps Roucher-Sarrazin. "America's First Wine Connoisseur," U.S. States News, April 19, 2007.

116. As a part of the course, students reviewed Robert Bolling's 18th-century manuscript, *A Sketch of Vine Culture for Pennsylvania, Maryland, Virginia, and the Carolinas*, and made trips to Bolling's Buckingham County estate, Chellowe. Students also visited Montdomaine Winery. The Darden conference featured national speakers, break-out sessions, panel discussions, and representatives from multiple Virginia wine and beer companies. University of Virginia, Darden School of Business, "Wine & Cuisine Club," http://www.darden.virginia.edu/web/MBA/Student-Life/Organizations/Wine-Cuisine/Wine-and-Cuisine-Club-Food—-Beverage-Conference/ (viewed May 17, 2015).

117. The Reunions Weekend wine tasting built on a similar event offered by Stanford University. The winning wines included wines from Jefferson Vineyards, Sweely, Kluge, and Sugarleaf. "We had been approached by vendors for private label wines, but they were sourcing the wines from California," said Alumni Association President and Chief Executive Officer C. Thomas Faulders. "We felt strongly that the wines should come from our local wineries." To get the project going, Faulders partnered with Jefferson Vineyards' Chad Zakaib and with the Virginia Wine of the Month Club. The 1819 Wine project involved the release of a series of 12 vintages, and the Alumni Association discussed the potential for the inclusion of Virginia grapes into the later releases. Proceeds from the sale of the wine benefited the Rotunda restoration and AccessUVA, and each bottle was packaged with historical commentary by one of the University's architectural professors. University of Virginia Alumni Association, "1819," http://1819wine.com/ (viewed May 17, 2015).

118. It should be noted that PVCC began offering grape-growing and winemaking lectures as early as 1982, led by Dr. Carlo Columbini, a Charlottesville-area vineyard owner, which discussed land-site selection, winemaking, and grape harvesting. One recent Virginia Tech graduate who enrolled in the course and was offered a job at Northrop Grumman touted the success of the program on her life: "I was always interested in wine but thought it unapproachable. I wondered, 'Who makes wine?' And then I realized, 'I can do that!' When I was offered that job, I realized that I would never return to this path if I took a nice little cubicle job." (Leslie Shepherd, "Va's Finest, From Vine to Wine," *The Washington Post*, August 11, 2002.) The program received an award in 2006 for "Excellence in Career and Technical Education" from the Virginia Department of Education. Courses included blending, marketing, crushing, soil preparation, winery design, and more—as weather permits. ("PVCC Wine Internship Program Nets International Award," June 15, 2006.) For the $1,200 course fee, students designed their own labels, bottled wines from French oak barrels, and took home approximately 60 bottles of wine each. "This is the whole shooting match... everything from start to finish, harvesting to bottling," said Greg Rosko, PVCC's viticulture and enology program manager. "PVCC Wine Class Takes Students from Grape to Glass," Media General News Service, October 29, 2008; Patricia Huff, "South Africans Travel to US to Learn New Winemaking Techniques," *Voice of America News*, November 14, 2006.

119. Howard, who first approached the school about the idea for the class, had been engaged in home winemaking as a hobby for some 35 years and had received top awards at the West Virginia State Fair for his entries. The idea for the program came after college representatives toured the Shelton-Badgett North Carolina Center for Viticulture & Enology in Surry County, North Carolina— the East Coast's only licensed and bonded educational winery. The group came away enthusiastic about the possibilities for a similar program in Loudoun. The move led the Town of Purcellville in August 2013 to issue search for land in the town for an experimental vineyard. "Swirl, Sniff and Slurp Away Stress," *Intercom*, June 9, 2006; "Can a Wine Science Training Program Take Loudoun Wines To The Next Level?" *Leesburg Today*, August 14, 2013.

120. Bill Ramsey, "Lone Dave: Say it ain't Solo," *The Hook*, November 14, 2002, http://www.readthehook.

com/92726/dmbeat-lone-dave-say-it-aint-solo (viewed May 17, 2015). A Charlottesville native who met Matthews in the Charlottesville music scene, McCarthy brought with him 17 years of wine industry experience, including work at Montdomaine Cellars and White Hall Vineyards. In an attempt to minimize the impact of the industrial winemaking process on the fruit, McCarthy developed a gravity-fed system to send fruit into juice and vats beneath the property's hillside. He also worked to fashion a planting mix that included weeds from other farms to attract beneficial insects. The winery building is also environmentally-friendly in that it is built into a hillside, and includes a copper roof and recycled wood. (Lee and Lee, *Virginia Wine Country III*, 55; Matt Kull, "Marriage of Music and Wine: Dave Matthews and Brad McCarthy," *Northern Virginia Magazine*, http://www.northernvirginiamag.com/virginia-wine2/ [viewed May 17, 2015].) He began his winemaking career in 1988, working with Shep Rouse at Montdomaine Cellars before heading to White Hall Vineyards in the 1990s, during which he won the Governor's Cup in 1998 and 1999. Lee and Lee, *Virginia Wine Country III*, 54; Kull, "Marriage of Music and Wine."

121. A graduate of Napa Valley College where she studied the science of winemaking, Martin is also a graduate of the University of Bordeaux in France, where she learned to evaluate wine. In classic Bordeaux style, the vines were planted very close together to conserve the grape's flavor. McTaggart, who spent his childhood riding dirt bikes through a friends' family vineyard, spent four years working for a Canadian wine company while training at Brock University's Cool Climate Oenology and Viticulture Institute. (William Glanz, "Cooke Vineyard, Winery to Open in Fauquier," *The Washington Times*, January 14, 2004; Thomas Heath, "Tackling a Legacy: World-Class Vintner," *The Washington Post*, November 19, 2007.) Martin noted to a reporter, "We asked Lucie to plant her dream vineyard, so we gave her the opportunity to plant what she thought was the best possible." Morton opted for a variety of Bordeaux varietals. (William Glanz, "Cooke Vineyard, Winery to Open in Fauquier," *The Washington Times*, January 14, 2004; Monique Beech, "Brock University Grad Enjoying Success in Virginia Wine Country," St. Catharines, Ontario, *Standard*, December 21, 2007; Dave McIntyre, "In Grape Shape," *The Washington Post*, October 14, 2009 Jim Iovino, "An Eno Experience," *NBC4. com*, August 27, 2009.) Boxwood's first vintage was bottled on the property was released in February 2008. "I kept it as a boutique winery so we can be able to control the quality," Martin told reporters. "That's all that really matters for us. It's manageable. We want to be something special. We don't want to be enormous and have to compete with Gallo," said Martin in 2007. See Thomas Heath, "Tackling a Legacy: World-Class Vintner," *The Washington Post*, November 19, 2007; Beech, "Brock University Grad Enjoying Success in Virginia Wine Country") Martin's proposal was similar to one attempted by Loudoun County winegrowers in the late 1990s in order to boost agricultural tourism and help set the county's wineries apart from other regions in Virginia and outside of the state. Potentially called "Northern Piedmont," the idea eventually fell through. Sarah Schager, "Rooting for County-Made Wine," *The Washington Post*, August 26, 1999.

122. In 2005, the Sweelys planted their nearly 40-acre vineyard in Merlot, Cabernet Franc, Cabernet Sauvignon, and Viognier varietals. The same could be true of the Sweelys' other venture, operation of a private equestrian center nearby. Inspired by their oldest daughter, Robin, who is an accomplished internationally ranked equestrian, the couple hired the same designer of the cross-country equestrian track for the 2007 Pan American Games to design a similar tract at Acorn Hill. The Sweelys hoped to combine Virginia's love of horses with its enthusiasm for wine by building a venue for team riding competitions. Ventre, who had previously worked at Jefferson Vineyards, advocated the Bordeaux-inspired "close spacing" method, equating to approximately 1,700 vines per acre. He was insistent upon the cleanliness of the vineyard, consistent pruning of leaves to allow riper grapes. Liz Mitchell, "From the Grape to the Glass," *Culpeper Star-Exponent*, September 20, 2007; L. E. Andrew, "Climbing up on Acorn Hill," *Clover Herald* (South Carolina), September 26, 2007.

123. Dave McIntyre, "Wine: The Cases have Big Plans for Sweely—and Virginia," *The Washington Post*, December 13, 201; Marilyn Cox, "Madison Winery Sold for $10.2 Million to AOL Founder," *Daily Progress*, January 6, 2012. Ventre, who had previously worked at Jefferson Vineyards, advocated the Bordeaux-inspired "close spacing" method, equating to approximately 1,700 vines per acre. He was insistent upon the cleanliness of the vineyard, consistent pruning of leaves to allow riper grapes. Liz

Mitchell, "From the Grape to the Glass," *Culpeper Star-Exponent*, September 20, 2007.

124. Patricia Kluge adored her home: "It is my favorite place in the world," she said in 2009. "It is simply my most perfect spot on earth." The house, completed in 1985, boasted eight bedrooms, 13 bathrooms, theater, library, recreation room, sauna, spa, wine cellar, and card room. It also featured a drawing room reminiscent of an eighteenth-century salon, an Islamic gallery featuring an antique Syrian fountain, as well as a large banquet-size dining room that showcased an antique English rococo mantel, crown molding, and hand-painted wallpaper made in India. Designed by David Easton, he has been prominently featured in *Architectural Digest* and *Town & Country*. John Kluge ranked 35th in the Forbes' 400-richest Americans at the time of his death in 2010. To those in the University of Virginia community, John Kluge was known for donating more than $11.1 million to the University of Virginia as well as a gift of 7,389 acres valued in excess of $45 million. Kluge was a poor German immigrant when his family arrived in the United States when he was seven. Using poker winnings, he obtained a master's degree and built up a radio and television network, Metromedia. Born in Baghdad, Patricia was raised in England where she met John during an exclusive London party in 1976. The two were married five years later at New York's St. Patrick's Cathedral, and Patricia, who was then just 32, began a meteoric rise into high society. Spending her life in the guardianship of older men, she became a belly dancer in seedy clubs. In 1985, she revealed she had once posed nude for a British pornographic magazine, Knave, as well as appeared in a soft-core pornographic film while married to Russell Gay, the magazine's owner in the 1960s. She spent millions attempting to buy her way into high society, including the purchase of a $26 million house near Balmoral, Scotland. The two Kluges were poised to host a benefit for Prince Charles and Princess Diana when the British press revealed her past "expressive" behavior. The benefit was subsequently cancelled in light of the news and Queen Elizabeth reportedly banned any further contact between Patricia and the royal family. Sara Lin, "Billionaire's Ex-Wife Asks $100 Million for Estate," *Wall Street Journal*, October 30, 2009; "Albemarle House for sale in Charlottesville Virginia," Home and Garden TV, August 12, 2010, http://www.youtube.com/watch?v=OSYOimY0jjE (viewed May 17, 2015).

125. David Maurer, "Kluge Celebrates 10th Anniversary," Charlottesville *Daily Progress*, October 11, 2009; Jerry Shriver, "At Thomas Jefferson's Old Stomping Grounds," *USA Today*, July 14, 2006; J. Tobias Beard, "What do Personnel Changes Mean at Kluge Estate?" March 10, 2009.

126. Mondavi, who visited Kluge's estate and tasted her red wine, reputedly stated, "If an amateur can produce this the first time around, you have a brilliant future." Rolland oversaw Kluge's red winemaking while Champs, the owner of premium label Champagne Vilmart, oversaw Kluge's sparkling wine efforts. Thibaut and Gendrot, who hailed from Champagne and Bordeaux respectively, had been classically trained in winemaking in France, and had years of experience under their belts with sparkling wines. (Jim Raper, "For Socialite Turned Vintner, Much is Riding on $58 Bottle," Norfolk *Virginian-Pilot*, May 25, 2003.) Mondavi, for whom Kluge organized a symposium at the University of Virginia in 2002, reportedly told Kluge that, had he been 30 years younger, he would be exploring winemaking in Virginia. "Nation's Founding Father Inspires Virginia Wine Makers," PR Newswire, June 17, 2002; Craig Wilson, "A working Estate: Gardens, Farm, Winery," *USA Today*, April 25, 2003; Lee and Lee, *Virginia Wine Country III*, 85; Nick Kaye, "Vineyard Estates At Kluge Estate Winery," *The New York Times*, April 4, 2008.

127. The Farm Shop offered a full-service kitchen with wines and complimentary foods, and was reminiscent of iconic Jeffersonian architecture but with a complimentary backcountry, rustic feel. Jim Raper, "For Socialite Turned Vintner, Much is Riding on $58 Bottle," Norfolk *Virginian-Pilot*, May 25, 2003.

128. She hoped to turn Fuel Co. concept into a national chain, and the renovated gas station featured a modern canopy over the service bays and purple lights at night. The restaurant opened in 2003, and offered sophisticated gourmet fare, Virginia wines, and posh décor. See Dana Craig, "Filling It Up with Premium," *Richmond Times-Dispatch*, October 12, 2006; Erika Howsare, "Kluge Estate Sued for Unpaid Cleaning Bills," August 7, 2007; Jerry Shriver, "At Thomas Jefferson's Old Stomping Grounds," *USA Today*, July 14, 2006.

129. Jim Raper, "For Socialite Turned Vintner, Much is Riding on $58 Bottle," *Virginian-Pilot* (Norfolk,

VA), May 25, 2003. For example, she boldly charged $58 for her Bordeaux-style red (originally priced at $75), $32 for a sparkling wine, and $26 for fortified chardonnay aperitif. (Tobias Beard, "What do Personnel Changes Mean at Kluge Estate?" March 10, 2009.) Kluge had not only angered nearby residents along Blenheim Road who were concerned over her Vineyard Estates project, but also to the consternation of many, she had previously been appointed to the University of Virginia Board of Visitors despite her having never received a high school diploma. Raper, "For Socialite Turned Vintner, Much is Riding on $58 Bottle."

130. Jerry Shriver, "At Thomas Jefferson's Old Stomping Grounds," *USA Today*, July 14, 2006; David Maurer, "Kluge Celebrates 10th Anniversary," Charlottesville *Daily Progress*, October 11, 2009.

131. Calling her entry into the Virginia wine world a "labor of love," she could frequently be spotted driving around Albemarle County in her black Land Rover, sporting the license plate "1 WINE." Lee and Lee, *Virginia Wine Country III*, 86–87; Craig Wilson, "A Working Estate: Gardens, Farm, Winery," *USA Today*, April 25, 2003; Jerry Shriver, "At Thomas Jefferson's Old Stomping Grounds," *USA Today*, July 14, 2006; David Maurer, "Kluge Celebrates 10th Anniversary," Charlottesville *Daily Progress*, October 11, 2009.

132. J. Tobias Beard, "What do Personnel Changes Mean at Kluge Estate?" March 10, 2009. No one was more surprised to learn of the bistro's abrupt closure than Charlottesville Mayor David Brown who, after having made reservations for dinner with a foreign delegation a few hours before, arrived to find the doors locked and the place shuttered. Kluge's New York public relations representative could only say of the closing that Kluge's pressing commitments with her other projects kept her from devoting enough time and attention to the restaurant. Others, however, questioned such overtures. By one reporter's count, the bistro had gone through five general managers and six chefs in its short life. One of those former managers chided the bistro a "vanity project" for Kluge, claimed it was losing nearly $100,000 per month, and blamed the closing on over-compensated New York consultant chefs who spent too much money on expensive ingredients and too little time at the restaurant. ("Sea Change," *Restaurantarama*, July 10, 2007; "Fuel Co. Future?," *The Dish*, July 26, 2007.) Kluge's silver collection included a high-quality Regency silver dinner service, flatware, mirror plateaus, salt cellars, and a vintage circa 1814 silver-gilt candelabrum. Sotheby's sales materials billed Albemarle House as "one of the most important residences created in the United States since the Golden Age." Kluge dropped the price to $48 million in February 2010 and to $24 million in November 2010. Sara Lin and Juliet Chung, "Billionaire's Ex-Wife Asks $100 Million for Estate," *Wall Street Journal*, October 30, 2009; Erika Howsare, "Kluge Estate Sued for Unpaid Cleaning Bills," August 7, 2007; "Renowned Collections Lead Silver and Objects of Vertu Sale at Christie's," *Artdaily.org*.

133. The sale netted an estimated $15.2 million. Sotheby's printed a 600-page, $65 catalog for prospective purchasers, which included jewelry, sporting guns, decorative fixtures, works of art, books, and more. Kluge's Imperial Chinese clock, with an estimated worth of $1 million, generated "fierce bidding" and was sold to a Chinese collector for $3.8 million. Kluge did not hesitate to place her operation in the same category as some of the world's best-known wineries: "Now that we're in our tenth year we are beginning to feel we are part of the families around the world who are also making wines... Rothschild, Stags' Leap—we're all friends and we all share Michel Rolland [influential French oenologist] in common." (David Maurer, "Kluge Celebrates 10th Anniversary," Charlottesville *Daily Progress*, October 11, 2009.) In September 2010, for example, Kluge and Moses donated $1.2 million to Piedmont Virginia Community College—the largest private donation in the school's history—to fund the construction of a new science building on campus. The couple also donated money to help renovate Charlottesville's historic Paramount Theater, to support a children's medical rehabilitation center at the University of Virginia, and to fund a children's after-school program in Albemarle County. The two worked as well with Virginia Tech and the University of Virginia to develop environmental sustainability programs and even invited students to their property to conduct studies. (Maurer, "Kluge Celebrates 10th Anniversary.") Today, the "Kluge-Moses Science Building" houses modern classrooms and laboratories, as well as space for PVCC's health care professional and science programs. ("PVCC to Hold Groundbreaking Ceremony for Science Building," http://www.pvcc. edu/about-us/history-pvcc/facilities [viewed May 17, 2015].) Kluge and Moses were friends with

the Clintons, and though Kluge originally sent the wines as a wedding gift, the caterer selected them for serving during the rehearsal dinner and reception for the Clintons' daughter, Chelsea. Margaret Brennan, "The Rise And Fall Of Patricia Kluge," *Forbes*, 2011, http://www.forbes.com/2011/03/10/patricia-kluge-lifestyle-billionaire-bankruptcy-estate.html (viewed May 17, 2015)

134. Despite loan payments' being current, the bank demanded full repayment of the outstanding balance based on a loan provision which required certain sales targets for Kluge's wines. The loan, ostensibly advanced in order to turn the Kluge enterprise into an internationally-recognized concern, was followed by two additional loans to the winery in July 2007 and May 2009. (Lisa Provence, "$35 Million Crunch: Credit Lines Force Kluge Winery Foreclosure," The Hook, October 30, 2010, http://www.readthehook.com/66164/35-million-crunch-credit-lines-force-kluge-winery-foreclosure [viewed May 17, 2015].) Kluge and Moses reportedly attempted to engage French, Chinese, and Argentinean interests in financing their business deal. They were reportedly approached by Rothschild Bank in July 2008—prior to the banking collapse—with a plan to raise millions; regrettably those plans fell through.

135. Neither Kluge nor Moses were in attendance at the foreclosure auction. The couple pledged to leave "no stone unturned in attempting to work out a non-contentious refinancing," and that they would "not give up," nor "go quietly into the nite." The bank decided to sell the property in six separate tracts of land, despite concerns that dividing the property would discourage would-be purchasers from carrying on Kluge's wine efforts. The wine facility, Farm Shop, and a majority of the 160-acre vineyard were located on separate tracts. To continue the wine operation, a single purchaser would have had to purchase all three tracts. Some registered bidders felt the price was too high; others were interested in pieces of the property and wanted to see it broken into smaller parcels. Moses wrote in a statement that, at the very moment there was a glimmer of hope in finding a white knight to rescue the venture, "it is disappointing that [the bank has] chosen to take the initial steps towards dismantling the winery as an operating business as well as an auction of the property." The property's trustee with Farm Credit, William Shmidheiser, III, vehemently disagreed: "I've never seen a bank go to this extent to keep it going so the new owner can step into a working concern," he told a reporter. "We're not bottling any wine because the new owner may not want the Kluge label. I don't know why Bill Moses said it's being dismantled, because it's a working winery." Moses later told a reporter that he felt the Farm Credit's foreclosure created a panic which caused the winery's other lenders to follow suit. Lisa Provence, "Kluge Foreclosure: Lots of Interest, Zero Bids," *The Hook*, December 16, 2010, http://www.readthehook.com/65856/kluge-foreclosure-lots-interest-zero-bids (viewed May 17, 2015).

136. Ultimately, the bidding was so low that the bank's trustee halted the process to put a minimum price on the cases. Cases of Kluge's Simply Red went for $2 per case, the 2009 Rose went for $4 per case, and cases of Kluge's 2005 SP Reserve went for $25 per case—all wines that Kluge had previously marketed between $20 and $50 or more per bottle. Lisa Provence, "$35 Million Crunch: Credit Lines Force Kluge Winery Foreclosure," *The Hook*, October 30, 2010, http://www.readthehook.com/66164/35-million-crunch-credit-lines-force-kluge-winery-foreclosure (viewed May 17, 2015).

137. Despite Kluge's attempt to market the property for $24 million, at the time the house and property were assessed at only $16.4 million. Trump was no stranger to Kluge or the Virginia wine industry. In May 1989, he had promoted a nine-day cycling event that featured amateur and Olympic cyclists going from Albany, New York, through New Jersey, Pennsylvania, Maryland, Washington, D.C., and ending at the Rotunda at UVA. They then spent the night in Charlottesville, before heading to Richmond, Arlington, and finishing in Baltimore. Virginia wines were selected to be served at major promotional events for the race, and on Trump's yacht, "The Princess." "Donald Trump Buys Kluge Winery," *The Washington Post*, April 7, 2011.

138. "Trumps Have High Hopes For Vineyard," NBC29.com, October 4, 2011; "Donald Trump Promises 'Something Spectacular' At Former Kluge Winery," *Virginia Business*, October 4, 2011.

139. Gabriele Rausse, who consulted with Kluge in the winery's early years, suggested that there were too many people overseeing the final wine product: "The fact that there were too many chefs involved in the vineyard and all these things is another story." "A Vintner's Vintner," *Virginia Living*, January,

2012.

140. Among the more-notable wine writers were *The Washington Post's* Dave McIntyre, John Deiner, and James Conaway, *Leesburg Today's* Margaret Morton, the *The Free Lance–Star's* Cathy Jett, and the *Richmond Times-Dispatch's* Alan Cooper, Greg Edwards, and Jack Berninger. Edited by Pamela Hess and published by Melissa J. Harris, *Flavor* was published until August 2012 when Harris and Hess began *Foodshed,* a magazine and nonprofit local foods advocacy organization. In June 2011, the *Gazette* restructured its online presence to make it more interactive and lively. The paper hired a longtime contributor, Rappahannock County freelance writer and marketing consultant Mary Ann Dancisin, as Online Editor, and freelance writer/editor and Virginia Wine Experience in London organizer Richard Leahy as Advertising Services Director. The *Virginia Wine Gazette* was one of a handful of publications owned by Recorder Community Newspapers, which included the "New England Wine Gazette" and "Finger Lakes Wine Gazette."

141. Weems, *Virginia Wineries: Your Complete Tour Guide.* Replete with beautiful pictures of vineyards, wineries, and surrounding landscapes, Weems included a short passage reminiscing about the closing of Meredyth Vineyards, which poignantly illustrated the maturation of the Virginia wine industry: "Friends of this venerable winery will miss its singularly beautiful surroundings, its uniquely excellent wines, and its truly imitable winemaker. Its closing surely marks the end of an era in Virginia's modern winemaking history. But just as a portion of the original leaven is to be found in every new loaf of bread, some of the founding spirit of Meredyth Vineyards will be at work in each new winery that opens its doors in what is fast becoming Virginia's golden age of wine." (Weems, *Virginia Wineries,* 128; Beth Crittenden, "News and Notes from the Area's Wine World," *Roanoke Times,* September 25, 1996; Patricia Sullivan, "Diplomat Saw the World, and Then Wrote About It," *The Washington Post,* November 10, 2009; Mary Onderdonk, "Take a Month to Celebrate the Vintages of Virginia," Norfolk *Virginian-Pilot,* October 13, 1996.) In 2002, Washington, D.C., journalist and attorney Elisabeth Frater published an admirable summary of Virginia and Maryland wines in her *Breaking Away to Virginia & Maryland Wineries* (Charlottesville: Howell Press, 2001). Like Weems, Frater covered 60 Virginia wineries, interspersed with short vignettes on topics ranging from the interstate shipment of wines, barrel tastings, and wine grape varietals. In 2004, publishing executive Carlo De Vito authored *East Coast Wineries: A Complete Guide from Maine to Virginia* (New Brunswick, N.J.: Rutgers University Press, 2004), which provided a directory and description of each winery in 13 East Coast states. The book *Barboursville Vineyards: Crafting Great Wines Inspired by Spirits of the Past* (Barboursville: Barboursville Vineyards, 2008), which took Chiles T. A. Larson three years to research and write, recounted the history of the Barboursville property beginning with Jefferson and Governor James Barbour, and Gianni Zonin's twentieth-century quest to acquire and preserve the property. The book was unveiled at a dinner event at the Palladio Restaurant, where chef Melissa Close featured popular wine and food pairings over the past decade. In attendance was Governor Tim Kaine and First Lady Anne Holton, former Governor Gerald Baliles, as well as owner Gianni Zonin and his wife Sylvia. Zonin spoke in Italian, with his son translating his remarks. "It is a serious history in a large format with lavish photographs.... It definitely is a positive addition to Piedmont history, said Carter Nicholas, Barboursville's marketing manager. Jane Norris, "Fresh Off Wine Press," *Clover Herald* (South Carolina), September 9, 2008; Cathy Jett, "Barboursville, Ingleside in Limelight," *The Fredericksburg Free Lance–Star,* September 12, 2008.

142. *The Merlot Murders: A Wine County Mystery* (New York: Scribner, 2006).

143. *The Cultivated Life.* Produced and directed by John Harrington and written by University of Virginia alumnus Alessandro Santarelli, the film included images from the Revolutionary War, scenic views of the Virginia and French countryside, interviews with Monticello staff members, and passages from Jefferson's diary narrated by actor Hal Holbrook. The film discusses differences between colonial and modern wine preferences, Jefferson's plantings at Monticello, his friendship with Italian entrepreneur Philip Mazzei, and Jefferson's wine preferences during his time in the White House and after. The film concludes with an acknowledgment of the fulfillment of Jefferson's dream for a strong American wine industry, both in California and in Virginia. Harrington noted to a reporter that most Americans "have no idea [Jefferson] was often referred to as the founding father of American viticulture.

The pursuit of fine wine and wine culture was second only to his pursuit of liberty." ("A President's Passion," *Wine Spectator*, June 28, 2006; "Of Note," *Magnolia* 20, No. 2 [Fall 2005]: 4; "One More Unalienable Right: Wine," *USA Today*, Nov. 4, 2005.) The film included remarks by wine consultant Chris Hill, King Family Vineyards' David King, Blenheim's Kristy Harmon, Jefferson Vineyards' Chad Zakaib, Veritas, and candid and sometimes humorous commentary from Cardinal Point's Paul Gorman, among others. The film was also prominently featured during the four-day 2010 Virginia Film Festival in Charlottesville, where Charlottesville's Main Street Arena, a 24,000 square-foot versatile multi-purpose ice and venue space, was temporarily converted into a tasting room for Virginia wines. "This film is another example of my desire to showcase and reflect the things that define our region and that matter greatly to people here and throughout Virginia," said festival director Jody Kielbasa to a reporter in 2010.

144. The event helped the Virginia Tourism Corporation garner a "Mercury Award for Niche Marketing" from the U.S. Travel Association for its wine promotional efforts in August 2010. TasteLive works through Twitter, Facebook, and other online social media services to bring together consumers, bloggers, and winemakers to share information about their beverages.

145. Lobbying to bring the conference to Virginia came as the result of hard work by Annette Boyd, who succeeded in selling Virginia as a region with a strong wine community and viticultural and geographic diversity. "Social Media Can Be A Powerful Tool," *Richmond Times-Dispatch*, November 28, 2011.

146. The event was the second one organized by DrinkLocalWine.com, and followed on the heels of a successful 2009 conference in Dallas, Texas, which focused on Texas wines and emphasized the need for America's mainstream wine media to cover the nation's wine industry beyond California, Oregon, and Washington state. Three blogs were represented: "Virginia Wine Dogs," "Schiller Wine," and Northern Virginia Magazine's "Gut Check."

147. Virginia Wine TV was created by Todd Godbout, David Godbout, and Danyelle Ballard. Philip Carter Winery's commercial, which features scenery from the vineyard and a woman in a red dress, included piano music and a voiceover reading from William Butler Yeats's poem, *A Drinking Song*.

148. To prepare the application, Bauer and Collier visited 150 wineries over the course of 150 days, took more than 10,000 photographs, and interviewed hundreds of winemakers and owners. Three applications, "theCompass," "Virginia Winery Finder," and "Virginia Vine Hopper," launched in 2013. "New Virginia Wine App," *Examiner*, March 20, 2011. TheCompass Winery Brewery App, https://play.google.com/store/apps/details?id=com.winecompass (viewed May 17, 2015).

149. Each restaurant prepared foods to go with a wine selected by each winery The event was hosted at Washington, D.C.'s posh Equinox Restaurant. The idea for the series came from Equinox owners Ellen and Todd Gray, who developed the idea following a trip to Napa Valley in early 2003. "There's a symbiotic relationship the wineries have with the restaurants there," said Ellen at the time. "There's a potential for Virginia to be the Napa Valley of the East." Donna DeMarco, "Virginia Wines to Pair with Eateries," *The Washington Times*, March 17, 2003.

150. Then–Virginia Governor Mark Warner also attended and toasted the industry with a quote from 1 Timothy 5:23 from the Holy Bible: "Drink no longer water, but use a little wine for thy stomach's sake and thine often infirmities." "Capitol Hill Luncheon Salutes State's Wines," *Richmond Times-Dispatch*, June 18, 2003; "The New Napa: Virginia Winemakers Show Their Talent for the Vine," PR Newswire, August 26, 2003.

151. In August 2010, sparkling wines from Kluge Estate Winery and Vineyard were served at Chelsea Clinton's wedding in Rhinebeck, New York. "It's cool that Virginia wine, as opposed to the many New York wines [were served] at this New York state wedding, and Kluge were able to get that spotlight," said Kluge spokesperson Kristen Moses Murray. Patricia Kluge and her husband, William Moses, were longtime friends of the Clintons, and the two initially sent several cases of the wines as a wedding gift. The Clinton's caterer then asked if the wines could be served during the reception. ("Clintons serve Kluge's wine at daughter's wedding," *The Hook*, August 12, 2010, http://www.readthehook.com/66977/clintons-serve-kluges-wine-daughters-wedding [viewed May 17, 2015].) Barboursville's winemaker, Luca Paschina was in attendance at the fete but did not have a chance to

meet the new president. "I had no chance to talk to the new president, so much was going on," he said. "It was crazy, a good crazy." The 2006 Cabernet Franc Reserve was served as the red wine for the reception preceding dinner; the Octagon 8th Edition 2005 was selected as the red wine for the formal dinner; and the Brut NV was used during a toast following the formal dinner. (Jack Berninger, "It's Your Turn to Taste Va.," *Richmond Times-Dispatch*, February 11, 2009; Leahy, *Beyond Jefferson's Vines*, 22.) Berninger, "It's Your Turn to Taste Va.," *Richmond Times-Dispatch*, February 11, 2009.

152. Tareq, who received a minority share in the new enterprise, had previously apprenticed with wineries in Australia and Napa Valley, and graduated with a degree in business management and oenology from the University of California at Davis. An entrepreneur hoping to tap into the wealth of Northern Virginia's oenophiles, Tareq also launched his own limousine rental and wine tourism company, "Oasis Enterprises." To pay for some of his company's debts, he reportedly borrowed funds from the winery and, by the 2003, the winery found itself amassing millions of dollars in debt wrought by Tareq's failed tourism ventures, as well as his seemingly endless fighting with Fauquier County zoning officials over Oasis' noisy and crowded events. "Tangled in the Vines," *The Washington Post*, November 5, 2008.

153. "White House Gate Crashers; Tareq and Michaele Salhi Fool Secret Service to Gain Access," *The Washington Post*, November 30, 2009, http://www.washingtonpost.com/wp-dyn/content/discussion/2009/11/29/DI2009112901293.html (viewed May 17, 2015); Giles Whittell, "And Here's Me With the Vice-President After I Gatecrashed the White House," *The Times* (London), November 27, 2009. According to *The Washington Post*, one unnamed source said that the two were admitted entry after appearing insistent on their credentials and given the high number of arrivals on a rainy evening. While it remains unclear as to when they left the fete, photos were posted on Michaela's Facebook page by 9:08 p.m.—perhaps an indication that they knew they were not included on the event's dinner seating plan. Far more disconcerting, however, was that two unauthorized individuals could get so close to so many dignitaries, including the President of the United States. The Secret Service apologized for their failure in admitting the Salahis and that they were embarrassed, they nevertheless asserted that, because every attendee passed through metal detectors, no one was ever in danger. Governor Tim Kaine, who had appointed Tareq to a six-year term on the 15-member Board of Directors of the Virginia Tourism Corporation in 2006, said he was "absolutely not" surprised to learn of the couple's White House antics. As he told one reporter, "If you had said to me, 'Hey, some Virginians crashed the White House party, and there are 7.5 million Virginians. Guess who it might be?' I would have guessed them." (Whittell, "And Here's Me With the Vice-President After I Gatecrashed the White House.") Ultimately, the winery was purchased in May 2013 by an undisclosed buyer for $1.1 million. As of the date of this writing, however, no finality has been reached in the matter as Tareq has vowed "a long, drawn-out legal battle. "Tangled in the Vines," *The Washington Post*, November 5, 2008; Oasis Winery, http://www.oasiswine.com/ (viewed May 17, 2015).

154. The idea for the show was announced in May 2009 and it was to follow similar "Real Housewives" shows that took place in Orange County, Atlanta, New York City, and New Jersey. In the run-up to her selection, she noted in a September interview that "President Obama has made it very accessible for anyone to visit the White House, so that's like a big thing right now." Such suspicions seemed to be confirmed when, in August 2010, the first *Real Housewives* episode was aired with a voiceover from Michaele stating, "I just love to make an entrance." It seemed as though she, among the four other featured well-connected "housewives," was to be the star of the show. Giles Whittell, "And Here's Me With the Vice-President After I Gatecrashed the White House," *The Times* (London), November 27, 2009.

155. Controversy continued to surround the Salahis. Following the White House incident, Tareq resigned from the state tourism board because of, as he wrote to Governor Kaine, the "extraordinary misinformation resulting in the unfortunate negative and tabloid-type media." In May 2010, he and Michaela were stopped in a limousine near the White House by the Secret Service during President Obama's second state dinner. (The two were allegedly headed to a private dinner party). The Salahis divorced in 2012 and in 2013, Tareq fielded an unsuccessful bid to run for governor of Virginia.

156. The success of the cruises prompted Pearmund to offer another cruise in 2010, this time working

through Uniworld to offer a riverboat cruise down the Rhône River in France "We knew a Mediterranean cruise would prove popular with our customers, but the rapid rate at which the cruise has sold has been a very pleasant surprise," commented Pearmund. "Virginia Wineries Take Center Stage in the Mediterranean," PR Newswire, August 6, 2009; "Award-Winning Virginia Wineries to Host Mediterranean Wine Cruises in 2009 with Cruise Holidays of Alexandria," PR Newswire, July 16, 2008; "Wine Aficionados Take Heed," PR Newswire, April 24, 2008.

157. Among the most prominent were Northern Virginia's Virginia Wine Country Tours, Reston Limousine, Choice Limousine, Boomerang Tours, and Chariots for Hire. In Richmond, Love Limousine and James River Transportation shuttled thirsty drinkers to wineries in Charlottesville and Williamsburg. In Charlottesville, Don Rhodes founded Wine Tours of Virginia, while Charlottesville's Albemarle Limousine founded "Blue Ridge Wine Excursions" and worked with wine writer Richard Leahy to devise "Virginia Wine Expert" tour itineraries based on the tastes and preferences of individual clients. In September 2006, Capital Dream Cars—a luxury car rental dealership in Northern Virginia—announced a partnership with Prince Michel Vineyards and Winery which included car rental, overnight accommodations in Prince Michel's VIP suites, breakfast, and a VIP tour of the winery.

158. The hospitality industry followed suit with some of the commonwealth's most-noted hotels, including Landsdowne Resort, Keswick Hall, the Homestead, the Williamsburg Inn, and the Marriot Ranch in Hume, among others, each offering wine vacation packages. Smaller concerns, such as Charlottesville's Arcady Vineyard Bed & Breakfast, featured an on-site vineyard, while Richmond's Maury Place at Monument offered complimentary Virginia wine for its guests. Lee and Lee, *Virginia Wine Country III*, 134–135.

159. A Henrico County native without any formal artistic training, Mize developed an appreciation for fine art while studying at Hampden-Sydney College, and began producing wine-related works in the late 2000s. Using heavy oil paints applied with thick texture known as "impasto," his scenes often depict wine bottles or wine accessories in still-life scenes—many of them featuring Virginia wines. He has produced a coffee table book detailing his work, *The Loaded Brush*, which appeared in 2010. "While I was at Hampden-Sydney I was exposed to art history for the first time and immediately began seeing a future enriched by art and specifically paintings. I saw the Impressionist work of Monet, Sisley and Manet and I said, 'I think I can do that. I want to do that.' I began reproducing paintings from my art books in my dorm room.... I began to not really be interested in anything else but my painting," Mize stated from his Goochland County home, which features a $22,000 state-of-the-art printer. An Atlanta native, Haislip previously painted images of the Greenbrier Resort and later used a variety of mediums, including watercolor, pen and ink, pastels, and acrylics to focus more heavily on wine art. Jack Berninger, "Where Wine Meets Art," *Richmond Times-Dispatch*, February 22, 2009.

160. Savvy insurers found themselves learning the complexities of the wine trade and production processes, such as the origin and value of a particular winery's root stock, the crop damage that could arise from vine diseases or bad weather, and issues associated with pesticide and bacteria contamination. Intellectual property considerations provided the impetus for at least three wineries—Windham Winery (later Doukénie Winery), Waterford Winery (later Village Winery), and Alta Vista Vineyards (later Atillo Vineyards)—to change their names after being sued or threatened with intellectual property infringement or trademark claims. "Hurt Vineyard Celebrates Success as Wine Productions Ramps Up in Virginia," Charlottesville *Daily Progress*, February 17, 2013.

161. Simmers, the last in a line of a German family of farmers, began growing grapes in 1982 as a way to diversify his 400-acre dairy farm. In 1995, he opened Landwirt Winery, followed by Landwirt Bottling a few years later. The demand for Simmers's bottling service eventually forced him to shutter his winery in 2000 to devote his full time and attention to the bottling company. The name "Landwirt" is a German word meaning "farm manager." By the late-1990s, the vineyard had grown to 16 acres of vinifera grapes and by 2000 Landwirt produced 3,500 cases of wine annually. (Lee and Lee, *Virginia Wine Country Revisited*, 190; Weems, *Virginia Wineries*, 106–107; De Vito, *East Coast*, 288; "Landwirt Vineyard: 'Quite Breathtaking,'" *Virginia Wine Gazette* (Summer 1998): 19, 21; John Hagarty, "Piedmont Mobile Bottling Firms Play a Pivotal Role in Virginia Wine Industry," *Hagarty On Wine*,

April 1, 2010, http://www.hagarty-on-wine.com/OnWineBlog/?p=2735 [viewed May 17, 2015].) A fourth company, Cellar Door Services, operated briefly in the mid-2000s. The service was subsequently sold and re-branded "Bottle Boy" in 2003. Lee and Lee, *Virginia Wine Country Revisited*, 47–49; Rowe, *A History of Virginia Wine*, 36.

162. Oakencroft now produces grape juice made from Seyval Blanc, Traminette, and Chambourcin grapes. ("From Wine to Juice: Oakencroft Pioneering Again," Charlottesville *Daily Progress*, January 23, 2013; "Oakencroft Farm: The Juice Vintners," *Garden & Gun* [October/November 2012].) In an effort to introduce the commonwealth's wines to other domestic markets, five fanciful friends with a penchant for Virginia wines in particular formed "Blackslip Wines, Inc." in 2007 to export Virginia wines to Alabama. Blackslip was founded by Rosemary Urban, Deborah Williams, Lynn Leach, Terry Kote, and Kathy O'Reilly. In Huntsville, Alabama, they schemed together over a night in 2006 about a way to bring Old Dominion wines to the Cotton State. Urban, a retired librarian who had a farm in Virginia, had occasionally brought Virginia wine with her to Huntsville, where her four friends both enjoyed the high quality and lamented that such wines weren't available in Alabama. The five committed themselves—mind you, over a bottle of wine—to forming a distribution company. The company, "Black Slip Wines, Inc., focused on Virginia wine and small wineries that were too small to be of interest to distributors. "Before we knew it, we were incorporated and had an importer's license and a wholesaler's license from the ABC Board," said O'Reilly, who was a native Huntsvillian, school administrator, and children's cookbook author. "Our business sets itself apart because we get to visit every winery we represent, meeting the winemaker and tasting the wine," O'Reilly said. Because of this, she said, "we can offer delicious wines that people would not ordinarily be able to enjoy, so we have created a niche." Jana Arnston Payne, "Wine, Women Business," *Huntsville Times*, November 11, 2007.

163. Craig Schulin, "Edwin Wyant is the Owner of the Virginia Wine Experience," March 18, 2009. Sales from the first year totaled $200,000. "And that's pretty darn good," says Carper. "According to our accountants, this is a business that's worth keeping up." The shop received the Virginia Wine Industry Retailer of the Year award in 2003 and 2006, and by 2013, it was carrying wines from more than 50 Virginia wineries. The two, who met one afternoon when Spragins took a plate of cookies to Carper, got the idea to open the store from Carper's husband, who suggested the two contact local wineries to see if they needed help selling their products. Bored with staying at their homes in the nearby Lorton area of Fairfax County, the two began working together as wine representatives and, after visiting Occoquan one day, believed it would be the perfect place for a Virginia wine store. Two days later the two went into business together by putting down a $1,200 deposit on the store; shortly thereafter, they took out a $15,000 business equity line and opened the store one month later. The two spent approximately $12,000 in outfitting the store, often relying on the Salvation Army for décor and supplies. The small 800 square foot store is cozy and features aged bricks, exposed beams, and two comfortable rocking chairs in front of a fireplace. Jack Berninger, "Local Wine Winners," *Richmond Times-Dispatch*, November 1, 2006; "Virginia Wine, All the Time," *The Washington Post*, August 28, 2002; Amy Joyce, "Vintners Seize a Ripe Opportunity," *The Washington Post*, December 13, 2000.

164. Legislation would allow Virginia wineries to bypass distributors. ("VAVino: New Mall Mantra: Go Wine!," *The Hook* July 7, 2005; "Uncorked: Gals Mob VAVino Opening," *The Hook*, August 18, 2005.) Virginia wines served as the central theme of the restaurant, which opened following an enthusiastic public response to a commemorative "Jefferson Dinner" hosted by the Omni two years earlier. "Thomas Jefferson" presided at the ribbon-cutting with local dignitaries and Kalfon standing by. The restaurant's new wine list represented a wide range of wines from around the state, many of them Central Virginia vineyards: Of 52 selections, 34 are from in-state. Foti's Restaurant in Culpeper, for example, offered 20 Virginia wines out of a list of 100. Of the 60 wines offered at Rappahannock County's Blue Rock Inn, 10 were from Virginia. Twelve of the 70 wines offered at Lovettsville's The Restaurant at Patowmack Farm were from Virginia. John Hagarty, "Is Virginia On Your Wine List," Virginia Wine Guide Online, http://vwg-online.com/?p=3308 (viewed May 17, 2015).

165. A resort, named after her nearby 168-acre estate in Fauquier County, featured rooms with private balconies, spa and equestrian facilities, and a wine bar featuring Virginia wines. "Salamander Resort

is going to be one of the most sought-after resorts in the world," Johnson said at a Loudoun County Chamber of Commerce luncheon in 2010. "It will showcase Virginia wineries and produce. My proudest day will come when we open those doors." Todd Gray, chef and owner of the Equinox restaurant in Washington, D.C., was hired as the resorts culinary director. (Erica Garman, "Spa Aims to Turn Cold Shoulder into Warm Embrace," *The Washington Post*, September 28, 2008.) Thomason was a chef educated at the University of Virginia and trained in the prestigious Parisian culinary school Le Cordon Bleu. In May 2006, the restaurant hosted a "Very Virginia Vintage Wine & Cheese Tasting" fund-raiser for the new Five Points Community Farm Market, which offered only Virginia-grown products as a downtown Norfolk community revitalization project. (Debbie Messina, "Farm Market to Open Near MacArthur Mall," Norfolk *Virginian-Pilot*, May 23, 2006; Allison Connolly, "Slow Cooking from Concept to Completion: The Shaping of a Restaurant," Norfolk *Virginian-Pilot*, August 28, 2005; Tammy Jaxtheimer, "Nimble Approach Makes Vintage Fresh," Norfolk *Virginian-Pilot*, April 23, 2006.) The idea for Virginia Wine Factory was featured in *USA Today's* 2010 "Small Business Challenge," which was a six-month newspaper reality series that followed the progress of entrepreneurs nationwide in making their idea a reality. Matthews is a network engineer, while Sawyers is a geotechnical engineer. They began in Matthews's basement and moved to Sawyers's mother's garage when they needed additional space, initially wanting to open the bar in the Gainesville area of Prince William County. "Brambleton March Update: Virginia Wine Factory Coming to BTC," March 20, 2011, http://brambletonview.blogspot.com/2011/03/brambleton-march-update-virginia-wine.html (viewed May 17, 2015).

166. Some, like the General's Wine Trail, offered passports that granted holders special events, discounts, or prizes once a certain number of wineries had been visited. In Northern Virginia, five wineries formed the "Vintage Piedmont" wine trail, which offered participants a rewards card that could be used for discounts at each of the wineries and with participating merchants. In 2002, six Northern Virginia Piedmont wineries formed the "Blue Ridge WineWay" and a related trail, "The Nation's Capital Wine Trail," which offered a two-day self-guided driving four of wineries with a focus on the area's scenery and ambience. Seventeen wineries participated in the "Shenandoah Valley Wine Trail" between Clarke County in the north and Botetourt County to the south and, in Southwest Virginia, seven wineries in close proximity to the Blue Ridge Parkway formed the "Mountain Road Wine Experience." Several more in the far southwestern corner of the commonwealth formed the "Southwest Virginia Highlands Wine Trail" in 2013. Wine trails were local, too. In Nelson County, seven wineries, three breweries, and one cidery formed the "Nelson 151" wine trail, while Bedford County's five wineries formed their own "Bedford County Wine Trail" in 2006. Fauquier County, Botetourt County, Rappahannock County, Loudoun County, and Shenandoah County each boasted their own separate trails.

167. Jack Berninger, "A Mind-altering Tasting," *Richmond Times-Dispatch*, May 23, 2007. Paschina selected Barboursville's 2005 Viognier Reserve, Malvaxia Passito 2003 (a desert wine), as well as the Octagon Fifth Edition, 2001. It was not lost on some observers of history that Barboursville received the honor, given its location between the grand estates of Jefferson and Madison—two avowed antimonarchists. Rather, Barboursville was selected because of winemaker Luca Paschina's consistent quality and because the chef at the five-star Inn at Little Washington recommended Barboursville as a good wine paring with his food. The Octagon, a blend of Merlot, Cabernet Sauvignon, Cabernet Franc, and Petit Verdot that Paschina produces only in exceptional years, had only been produced 11 times since 1990 and was stored in its own barrel-aging room. The Octagon was also reported to be the late West Virginia sentator Robert Byrd's house favorite and received a ringing endorsement from British wine critic Michael Broadbent in the August 2009 issue of Decanter magazine. Maryann Haggerty, "Virginia: Jefferson Sipped Here...And So Can You," *The Washington Post*, June 3, 2007; Jack Berninger, "From Virginia's Piedmont, Wines Were Fit for a Queen," *Richmond Times-Dispatch*, June 20, 2007.

168. The announcement came following a one-day qualifying round at White Hall Vineyards in Albemarle County judged by 10 wine experts. (Jack Berninger, "A Mind-altering Tasting," *Richmond Times-Dispatch*, May 23, 2007; "The Virginia Wine Experience in London Selects 65 Virginia

Wines to Showcase at Historic Wine Tasting," U.S. Newswire, February 21, 2007.) The unveiling of Virginia wines in London during the anniversary celebrations was particularly auspicious given Briton's famous penchant for snobbery and wine's unique history with the crown. Queen Elizabeth I was presented with a sweet spiced wine, Ipocras, at her coronation, while Queen Elizabeth II was presented with Traminac, which had been dubbed "royal wine" since 1710. (Karen Page and Andrew Dornenburg, "Virginia Vintages That Can Hold Their Own," *The Washington Post*, May 9, 2007; "The Virginia Wine Experience in London Selects 65 Virginia Wines to Showcase at Historic Wine Tasting.") The British press, of course, had long criticized New World wines, including those of the Old Dominion, as being too "flabby," "hot" (high in alcohol content), and not complimentary to food. Organizers had hoped that the VWEL tasting event would be analogous to the famous 1976 "Judgement of Paris," which had a revolutionary effect on the international standing of California wine versus its French counterpart. Hoping for a modern-day version of the famous 1976 "Judge-ment of Paris," VWEL selected London because of its serving as the home for several of the world's most-reputable wine critics, including Hugh Johnson, Jancis Robinson, Clive Coates, and Michael Broadbent, who were located there. Further, at approximately 1.6 billion per year, the country is the world's largest importer of wine and the British tended to prefer Virginia's elegant and understated wines as opposed to their sun-drenched, alcoholic, sweet California counterparts."Whereas Califor-nia's wines suffered from a reputation of being too high in alcohol content and sugar, Virginia's hotter, humid climate delivered wines higher in acidity and more moderate in fruity flavors. Mary Jordan, "'Virginia Makes Wines?' Yes, and London Likes Them," *The Washington Post*, May 27, 2009.

169. VWEL's tasting was trumpeted as a success, as Leahy noted at the close of the competition, "We hope that with the acceptance and praise of the top palates of the wine world like Steven Spurrier and Hugh Johnson that the critics, restaurant trade, and the public can realize that Virginia produces wines that can stand with the best from around the world, and give them the respect they deserve." Jack Berninger, "A Mind-altering Tasting," *Richmond Times-Dispatch*, May 23, 2007; Jim Raper, "Wente Winery is Targeting Grocery-Store Shoppers," Norfolk *Virginian-Pilot*.

170. Parker moved to Reston in the 1990s and immediately began following the growth in quality and quantity of Virginia's wine industry. At the program's groundbreaking ceremony held at the presti-gious Institute of Directors building in London, New Horizon offered attendees Virginia wines as well as a live webcast from Breaux Vineyards. (Cathy Harding, "Virginia Wines Have a Champion in England," November 3, 2009.) By summer 2010, thanks to New Horizon's efforts, fifteen Virginia wines were offered at grocery stores across the United Kingdom. (Mary Jordan, "'Virginia Makes Wines?' Yes, and London Likes Them," *The Washington Post*, May 27, 2009.) Following the wine fair, Haymore hosted a reception for England-based alumni from Virginia colleges and universities to promote the state's products and tell them how they could purchase Virginia vintages in London.

171. Evinced today by the State Route 626, named "Korea Road," the area is the only place named "Ko-rea" in the United States. As noted by William Won Hwang, chairman of the Korean-American Association and a wine exporter himself, Virginia's wineries "are more unique than Napa Valley.... This is more customer-based. Hopefully we can have some business with Culpeper County wineries." Reaction from the vineyard owners was equally positive: "I think it's great they want to come try our wines and ship them out," Old House's Allyson Kearney said. "It's awesome." Catherine Amos, "Sisterhood with Koreans Strengthening," *Culpeper Star-Exponent*, September 27, 2008.

172. David M. Dickson, "Heady Hong Kong," *The Washington Times*, June 1, 2009. Tong also met briefly with Governor Robert McDonnell, as well as with Virginia's Secretary of Agriculture, Todd Hay-more, and Secretary of Commerce Jim Cheng.

173. Greg McQuade, "Thank China for Record Breaking Wine Sales," WTVR6.com, August 14, 2013, http://wtvr.com/2013/08/14/thank-china-for-record-breaking-virginia-wine-sales/ (viewed May 17, 2015).

174. Matthew J. Lohr, "The Amazing Rise of Creative New Agribusiness Ventures," Matthew J. Lohr, VDACS, May 17, 2013.

175. Though popular in medieval times, the drink's popularity declined in the 1500s in the wake of the widespread availability of sugar and the rising popularity of beer. Classified by Virginia law as wine,

yet similar in substance to craft beers, many meadmakers produced the beverage in the same fashion as wine, with similar processes of fermentation. Hope Cristol, "Mead in the U.S.A.," *The Washington Post*, April 9, 2003.

176. The Villers obtained at least half of their honey from an ever-expanding apiary on the property, and offered visitors a variety of music and educational events. The Easts relied on their 10 beehives for honey, with long-term plans to expand to more than 100 hives. "Wine Series: Honey, Pass The Mead, Please," *Tri-City Herald*, December 27, 2012; John Crane, "Pittsylvania County Meadery to Debut at Wine Fest Next Month," WSLS.com, Jan. 13, 2012, http://www.wsls.com/story/20846009/pittsylvania-county-meadery-to-debut-at-wine-fest-next-month (viewed May 17, 2015); "A Look at the LoCo Resident Behind the Soon-to-Be-Open, Stonehouse Meadery," *Northern Virginia Magazine*, June 26, 2013; Hope Cristol, "Mead in the U.S.A.," *The Washington Post*, April 9, 2003; Lee and Lee, *Virginia Wine Country III*, 218–219.

177. Lee and Lee, *Virginia Wine Country Revisited*, 111. Using financial assistance from Internet contributors, Cavender used his laboratory to reintroduce the beverage, its unique history, and the wide ranges and styles to common drinkers.

178. Hit hard by the national recession, Parched Group's distillery was auctioned off in June 2013, and was purchased by investors who expressed interest in continuing to use the facility as a distillery. ("Whiskey Startup Goes Down Smooth," *Richmond Bizsense*, August 18, 2010; "Maryland Man Buys Cirrus Distillery At Auction," *Richmond Times-Dispatch*, June 26, 2013.) While Laird's had long produced its "Applejack" beverage, the Bowman distillery was famous for its "Virginia Gentlemen" and "Fairfax County" bourbons. The Bowman Distillery was originally housed in a circa-1892 building on the Bowmans' sprawling Fairfax County dairy farm until they moved the distillery south to Fredericksburg in 1988.

179. Others have emerged as well. In 2013, Jim Taggart and Jeff Fletcher worked to create their Woods Mill Distillery in Nelson County, while former insurance agent and web developer Adam Glick attempted to start a distillery in downtown Charlottesville. Even former Montdomaine Cellars proprietor Michael Bowles tried to open his Montdomaine Distillery in 2013, only to find himself running afoul of ABC liquor laws. After ABC public hearings, he received a license to operate. "Local Business, Catoctin Creek Distilling," Marketwire, October 22, 2009; "The 67-cent Felony: A Veteran Winemaker Runs Afoul of the ABC," *The Hook*, Sep. 5, 2013; "Our Craft Distillery Movement Is Resurging By Leaps And Barrels," *C-Ville Weekly*, September 28, 2012; "Whiskey Town: Can A Craft Distillery Movement Make A Permanent Home In Central Virginia?" *C-Ville Weekly*, January 29, 2013.

180. Part of this came from the quality of Virginia's apples. Though smaller and not as colorful as their West Coast counterparts, Virginia's apples offered more-intense concentrations of sugar, tannins, acid, and aromas—all of which produced high-quality fermentation. Cideries typically feature an orchard, grinders, apple presses, and stainless steel tanks. Weems, *Virginia Wineries*, 94–95; De Vito, *East Coast Wineries*, 304.) Cider, much of which was made from English apples, was certainly the alcoholic beverage of choice for most Virginians. "If you take the consumption of Pepsi Cola and Coca-Cola today, you could equate that with...the consumption per capita for cider at that time," said Tom Burford, nurseryman, orchard designer, and apple historian from Lynchburg. "It was *the* drink." Indeed, Jefferson himself experimented with an estimated 18 different varietals of apples. Jefferson was well-known for creating champagne-like hard cider out of Virginia Hewe's Crab apples. In an 1819 letter about his culinary preferences, Jefferson wrote: "Malt liquors and cider are my table drinks." The Harrises began growing grapes in 1982 and, in 1995, opened a combined winery/cidery in a small stucco building. The grapes were processed and bottled at Hartwood Winery. Edward Ayers, "Fruit Culture in Colonial Virginia," *Colonial Williamsburg Foundation Early American History Research Reports*, April 1973, pp. 129–130; Michel, "Report of the Journey of Francis Louis Michel From Berne, Switzerland, To Virginia, October 2, 1701–December 1, 1702," *Virginia Magazine of History of Biography* 24 (16): 33; Robert Beverley, *History and Present State of Virginia*, ed., with an introduction by Louis B. Wright (Chapel Hill: Published for the Institute of Early American History and Culture at Williamsburg, Va., by the University of North Carolina Press, 1947) 314; Hugh

Jones, *Present State of Virginia* (Chapel Hill, Published for Virginia Historical Society by University of North Carolina Press, 1956), 78, 138.

181. William Whitman, *The Wines of Virginia: A Complete Guide* (Warrenton, Va.: Virginia Heritage Publications, 1997), 81; "Heart of Virginia Winery Tour: History For the Tasting!," *The Fredericksburg Free Lance–Star*, May 16, 2002.

182. The Sheltons purchased the property in 1986, and thereafter planted a variety of apple, pear, peach, and cherry trees. The family created an apple nursery company, Vintage Virginia Apples LLC, in 2000 and today produce an entire line of cider from Winesap, Crab, Pippin, Goldrush, Pink Lady apples, and more. The privately financed cidery project was assisted by the Virginia ABC, the Virginia Wine Marketing Office, and the Virginia Department of Agriculture and Consumer Services. At Potter's Craft Cider, by 2013, the two produced ciders, including their popular flagship beverage, "Farmhouse Dry," made from Albemarle Pippin, Winesap, and Stayman apples. (Brian McNeill, "CiderWorks Aims to Introduce Area to a Whole New Flavor," *Daily Progress*, July 5, 2009; "Governor Kaine Attends Grand Opening of Albemarle Ciderworks," Targeted News Services, July 13, 2009.) To meet rising demand, Bold Rock broke ground on a $4 million cidery in June 2012. "Potters Craft Cider Discovers Its Popularity," *Crozet Gazette*, December 6, 2012.

183. "Blue Bee Cider Adds Artisanal Ciders To The Local Menu," *Richmond Times Dispatch*, July 12, 2013.

184. Cider Week recalled the Old Dominion's wine industry in its younger days and the first "Virginia Farm Winery Week" proclaimed by former Governor Charles S. Robb in 1983. Chiefly organized by the Charlottesville Albemarle County Convention and Visitor's Bureau, the Virginia Wine Board, the Virginia Tourism Corporation, and Nelson County, Cider Week promoted cider tastings, cider-making workshops, and restaurant specials across the commonwealth. VDACS also provided $20,000 grant to nine farmers in May 2013 to help increase the planting of hard-cider varieties across Virginia. The Nelson County study demonstrated the financial profitability of producing cider using similar economic models that had encouraged the development of Virginia farm wineries two decades earlier. In March 2012, sixteen apple growers and cider producers held a roundtable discussion with representatives from VDACS, the Virginia Foundation for Agriculture, Innovation, and Rural Sustainability, and Virginia Tech. The roundtable launched a study of the hard cider industry. (Matthew J. Lohr, "The Amazing Rise of Creative New Agribusiness Ventures," VDACS, May 17, 2013.) Prior to 2011, for example, any cider with alcohol content above seven percent was required to be labeled "wine." (HB1000, Chapter 288 of the 2011 GA Session, § 4.1-213.) The legislation was introduced by Chesterfield senator John Watkins, which permitted cider with 10 percent of alcohol by volume without chaptalization or seven percent regardless of chaptalization." "With 'Strong Heritage' In State, Historic Drink Enjoys Resurgence," Harrisonburg *Daily News Record*, October 24, 2012.

185. The developer of Rockingham County's community "The Glen at Cross Keys" gave buyers a bottle of Virginia wine with each home purchase. The Salem Farm community in northwestern Loudoun County named its internal streets after grapes while marketing materials capitalized on the subdivision's location adjacent to Breaux Vineyards. Such moves reflected a growing international trend begun in the early 2000s to create wine-related leisure-focused master-planned residential communities in renowned winemaking regions, such as California, Italy, and South Africa. The trend was also noticed in states less famous for winemaking, including Colorado, South Carolina, Texas, and New York. (American wine consumption had increased by 25 percent between 2001 and 2006 according to the Wine Institute.)

186. With an idea to produce premium wine using Virginia grapes, the investors were attracted to the site because of what they believed were similarities between the Tidewater region of Virginia and the Bordeaux region of France. The idea also called for the planting of 250 acres of vineyards in nearby Gloucester County; David Ress, "Winery Waiting For An OK," Newport-News *Daily Press*, October 13, 1990; *VWGJ* 13, No. 3 (Fall 1987): 152; Rowe, *A History of Virginia Wine*, 89.

187. Near Interstate 64 and its interchange with Croaker Road, the project, now dubbed "Williamsburg Corporate Campus," would have included a restaurant, 200-room hotel, 400 homes, 446 time-share

units, nearly 350,000 square feet of industrial space, and 116,000 square feet of commercial space, and perhaps as many as 179 acres would have been used for vineyards. The investors received nearly $20 million in taxable bond financing from the Peninsula Ports Authority of Virginia. Like their project in York County, the Williamsburg Corporate Campus project required rezoning approval from the James City County Board of Supervisors as well as approval for the then-property owner to withdraw the land from the county's agricultural district land use program. The program allows landowners to receive substantial tax breaks in return for prohibiting development. In July 1989, over the recommendation of their Planning Commissioners, the James City County Board of Supervisors approved the property owners' request to withdraw. The Board's action cleared the way for approval of a rezoning. (David Lerman, "Group Moving Winery Project to James City," Newport-News *Daily Press*, April 5, 1989; Lerman, "Commercial Project Disallowed," *Daily Press*, June 14, 1989.) The neighbors organized themselves into the "Concerned Citizens of Croaker." (David Ress, "Financing For Winery Gets Go-Ahead," *Daily Press*, October 18, 1990; David Lerman, "Residents Fight Winery Complex With Petition," *Daily Press* June 21, 1989.) An affiliate corporation, Williamsburg Investment Group, Ltd., filed a companion application to approve an 18-hole golf course, an industrial park, and 500 timeshare units adjacent to the winery called the "Williamsburg Corporate Campus." David Ress, "Winery Waiting For An OK," *Daily Press*, October 13, 1990.

188. The York County site also needed rezoning approval, which pitted York and James City counties against one another in an effort to grant the necessary approvals and attract the winery. In December 1991, the winery received rezoning approval from both James City County and York County. In March 1992, York County supervisors agreed to commit $2.7 million to extending water to the York site to "send them a signal" of the county's eagerness to attract the winery development. Mark Steinberg, "JCC Paves Way for Winery," Newport-News *Daily Press*, December 17, 1991; Patrick Lee Plaisance, "York Says Water Will Woo Winery," *Daily Press*, March 31, 1992; Steinberg, "JCC Planners Reject Winery Once More," *Daily Press*, November 13, 1991; Steinberg, "JCC Board Defers Action On Projects," *Daily Press*, November 13, 1991; Plaisance, "Winery Developers Reconsidering York," *Daily Press*, October 23, 1991; Steinberg, "JCC Panel Alters Position, Supports Proposed Winery," *Daily Press*, November 2, 1991.

189. Luxist (Vineyard Estates) Sept 1 2007; Lisa Provence, "Sour Grapes: Neighbors Fermenting Over Kluge Plan," *The Hook*, June 26, 2003; Xiyun Yang, "Fertile Ground for Luxury," *The Washington Post*, August 18, 2007.

190. Cathy Harding, "Kluge's Estate Project Gets 4-star Press," September 25, 2007; Xiyun Yang, "Fertile Ground for Luxury," *The Washington Post*, August 18, 2007; Reed Williams, "Ventures Range from a Winery to Real Estate Development," *Richmond Times-Dispatch*, September 19, 2008.

191. Cathy Harding, "Winery Not Included in Patricia Kluge's $100M Estate Listing," October 30, 2009, C-Ville, http://www.c-ville.com/UPDATE_Winery_not_included_in_Patricia_Kluges_100M_estate_listing/#.VVkOcbkw85s (viewed May 17, 2015); Harding, "Kluge's Estate Project Gets 4-star Press," *C-VILLE Weekly*, September 25, 2007, Charlottesville Tomorrow, http://www.cvilletomorrow.org/news/article/11185-forget-the-6-mi/ (viewed May 17, 2015). Kluge's plans did not sit entirely well with neighboring residents, who voiced concerns over the potential destruction of the natural beauty of the area and the construction of multi-million dollar houses. Kluge dismissed such sentiments: "Like all small communities, whenever you have an idea that's different, people don't like you for it," Kluge said. "But they will get over it and one day will think it's a great idea." Kluge and her husband, Bill Moses, issued a response—derisively chided as the "Dear Peasant" letter by their opponents—asking the surrounding community to reserve judgment. "We're not developers in a vineyard's sheep's clothing," the letter read. "This is a nice transition from large, useless lots to something that promotes agriculture." (Reed Williams, "Ventures Range from a Winery to Real Estate Development," *Richmond Times-Dispatch*, September 19, 2008; Nick Kaye, "Vineyard Estates At Kluge Estate Winery," *The New York Times*, April 4, 2008.) "Albemarle is just getting ridiculous," said neighbor Eddy Booth. "Taxes are shooting up. If they want their wineries, that's fine. Why does everyone else have to pay for it?" Albert Graves, another nearby resident, asserted, "It starts off small, and the next thing you know, there's a shopping center." (Xiyun Yang, "Fertile Ground for Luxury,"

*The Washington Post*, August 18, 2007; Lisa Provence, "Sour Grapes: Neighbors Fermenting Over Kluge Plan," *The Hook*, June 26, 2003.) The project also encountered opposition from Albemarle County officials, who were concerned about the developments impact on a 385-acre portion of the property which was in an agricultural district. Though the county provided a process whereby the Albemarle County Agricultural and Forestal Committee could issue a special permit, the committee declined to grant the approval in April 2003. In response, the Vineyard Estates were reconfigured as a "by-right" subdivision, so as to avoid the necessity of legislative review by the county. (Cathy Harding, "Kluge's Estate Project Gets 4-star Press," September 25, 2007.) The first of the Vineyard Estates' homes, the 6,400-square foot "Glen Love Cottage," was completed in August 2007 and was listed for sale at $7 million. Designed by the same architects who planned Kluge's larger "Albemarle House," the home featured a pool, five bedrooms, and formal outdoor gardens. Deidre Woollard, "Luxist," *Vineyard Estates*, September 1, 2007; Reed Williams, "Ventures Range from a Winery to Real Estate Development," *Richmond Times-Dispatch*, September 19, 2008.

192. The community's developers hired veteran winemaker Tom Payette, who had been named U.S. Winemaker of the Year by *Vineyard & Winery Management* in 1999. "Viniterra Development Experiences Successful Weekend Launch," Marketwire, October 26, 2007.

193. "New Kent Vineyards Will Host the 2009 'A Taste of New Kent' Wine Festival," May 1, 2009; "Viniterra Development Experiences Successful Weekend Launch," Marketwire, October 26, 2007.

194. "Centex Abandons Warrenton Plan," *Culpeper Times*, January 2, 2008. In addition, Centex had difficulty locating on-site wells for water service and needed access to the Town of Warrenton's wastewater treatment plant. Town officials agreed to only if Alwington Farm was annexed into the town's corporate limits; even if the property had been incorporated into the town, however, questions were raised as to whether or not the wastewater treatment plant could handle the new development. "Centex abandons Warrenton plan," *Culpeper Times*, January 2, 2008; Don Del Rosso, "Grapes, Grub & Rooftops," *Fauquier Times-Democrat*, May 22, 2007.

# Index